ENVIRONMENTAL
KNOWING

COMMUNITY DEVELOPMENT SERIES

Series Editor, Richard P. Dober, AIP

Volumes Published

CDS / 23

ENVIRONMENTAL KNOWING
Theories, Research, and Methods

Edited by

Gary T. Moore
University of Wisconsin, Milwaukee

Reginald G. Golledge
The Ohio State University

 Dowden, Hutchinson & Ross, Inc.
STROUDSBURG, PENNSYLVANIA

Copyright © 1976 by **Dowden, Hutchinson & Ross, Inc.**
Community Development Series, Volume 23
Library of Congress Catalog Card Number: 76–4942
ISBN: 0–87933–060–0

78 77 76   5 4 3 2 1
Manufactured in the United States of America.

LIBRARY OF CONGRESS CATALOGING IN PUBLICATION DATA

Main entry under title:
Environmental knowing
  (Community development series/23)
  Bibliography: p. 393
  Includes indexes.
    1. Environmental psychology.   2.   Human ecology.
I. Moore, Gary T., 1945–   II. Golledge, Reginald G., 1937–
BF353.E53   153.7   76–4942
ISBN 0–87933–060–0

FOREWORD

What interchange between people and their environment encourages them to grow into fully realized persons? This book makes some illuminating responses to that question. Cognition is an individual process, but its concepts are social creations. We learn to see as we communicate with other people. The most interesting unit of study for environmental cognition may therefore be small, intimate, social groups who are learning to see together, exchanging their feelings, values, categories, memories, hopes, and observations, as they go about their everyday affairs. The material on social images of the environment is one of the most interesting parts of this collection. It is unfortunate that as yet they are static analyses.

The studies of the development of environmental cognition in children, on the other hand, although still restricted to individuals, are admirable because they portray an unfolding process. Patterns analyzed at one moment fail to tell us where perceptions come from or how they may change. They even fail to convey the flavor of the momentary experience, which is changing into something else. Even more, they prevent us from making a just evaluation, since the quality of a life is not dependent on a single

event, nor even on the finale, but on its form as a realized process. The triumphs of maturity may give meaning to a troubled adolescence, and the wonders of childhood complete a crippled old age.

In place of studying the learning process alone, we could use our studies and methods to help others to learn to see for themselves. This is the most rewarding feature of personal construct theory and method, which tries to surface a person's own way of viewing the world, and to help him or her to clarify and extend personal concepts. (Although as a universal way of thinking, I am less impressed, considering its overpowering emphasis on verbal constructs, distinct categories, and bipolar scales defined by opposites. This is one way of thinking, very logical, very common, very "scientific," culturally much approved. Lord help us if that were the only way that we could make sense of the world!)

Wood and Beck give a clear example of the fusion of research and action in a learning process. When they taught their collaborators a mapping language, they taught them how to see and relate new things. Thinking and communicating are the same, as they say. No wonder that their trained mappers mapped more than the untrained ones. The effect, I should think, was

v

not superficial. Of course, it muddied up the research. Still another example, not reported here, is the work of Philip Herr and Stephen Carr in their Ecologue project in Cambridge (Herr, Carr, Cavelini, and Dowds, Ecologue/Cambridgeport. Unpublished report, Office of Environmental Education, HEW, Washington, D.C., December 1972). They used many of the same familiar research techniques of analyzing environmental cognition, but not to elicit the views of "subjects," for scientific study. The methods were taught to residents to help them understand themselves in relation to their world, and thence to organize to improve that world.

Speaking of mapping, I cannot resist saying something in defense of pictures. Numerous contributors refer to the difficulties in the open-ended mapping techniques once used in *The Image of the City.* Some go further and seem to assume that all graphic techniques lack credit. In that view, since graphic representations are an alien language to most people, to force their use distorts a person's knowledge of the world (thus assuming that thoughts are independent of languages, and are only filtered through them). Wood and Beck show that teen-agers can be taught mapping literacy with ease, and that their maps are then a rich source for understanding more about their images. Of course, their images are changed in the process (I would assume enriched and extended). It would have been interesting to watch their graphic progress while in London. But all images are dependent on some acquired language skill, including the verbal skill we so much take for granted. For example, in applying personal construct theory, Harrison and Sarre must teach their interviewees to improve their use of general verbal concepts and polar opposites. They are helping them to form a view of the world. They could hardly do otherwise.

People will ask a painter what his painting "means," that is, they want it translated into words. But they are not permitted to ask that a scholar draw what his essay pictures. In some instances, such drawings could be made and might reveal difficulties. In other ways, the two languages are incompatible and have different powers. The graphic languages are excellent for communicating multiple relations between things at one glance, in a single complex pattern. That pattern can be clear or ambiguous. Graphic expressions are obviously apt for describing simultaneous relations in space, but also for other tasks.

Any attempt to elicit mental images should use every means and language it can to check interrelated findings and to bring out aspects that are incommunicable in one tongue or another. Our original work used an array of methods—verbal environmental descriptions, imaginary trips in memory, mappings, photo recognition and sorting, interviews while way-finding in the field, requests for directions from passers-by, and so on. There are better techniques today, but I remain convinced that an array of languages must be used, and that the graphic language is just as central as the verbal one. Not just maps, incidentally (however dear those may be to the hearts of geographers, however sacred to imagery), but all kinds of graphic expressions: eye-level sketches, photographs, video tapes, diagrams, models.

I hold a lingering suspicion that many investigators in social science reject graphic means more because of their own difficulties with graphic products, rather than because of difficulties that their interviewees might have. The suspicion darkens as I see how few writers in this volume use maps or pictures to describe their settings. Once you have a drawing, what can you do with it? A map or sketch, however naively drawn, and often just because naively drawn, is eloquent in many ways beyond a mere counting of its named parts (which is a technique imported from verbal analysis). A sketch can be looked at for the sequence in which it was made, its connectivities and gaps, its style, the particular things graphically emphasized and those left out, the evidence of indifference or emotion, the variance in detail, the confidence or timidity with which different parts are drawn, the total structure, and even to some extent for its scale distortions (although the *purposeful* communication of distance and direction in a map is a special skill, which usually requires explicit teaching). Moreover, drawings have that valuable quality of being permanent records, easy to store and to recall, which communicate a great deal beyond their overt content. They are improved, of course, if accompanied by what the person *said* while drawing them or by other evidence. But, in their permanent registration of overtones, they are like those emotional modulations of a voice heard on tape, which are so often lost in written transcriptions.

"Unstructured" drawings (ones structured by the person responding, rather than by the interviewer) have the further advantage, despite all their difficulties, of allowing the person to express something of his own way of viewing the world, just as personal construct methods allow for the appearance of idiosyncratic verbal concepts. Similarities and convergences are then all the more useful and emphatic. To use printed maps, on which the person is asked to indicate what is important to him or where a boundary is, is to lose that quality. You force a conventional view of the world on him, just as when you use a semantic differential test or interrogate by checklist.

In employing any language, it is well to begin by teaching its use, so that your interviewees can use it freely. One may teach the use of a video camera or tape recorder, how to make a map, or how to tell a good story. In the process, one should maintain a record of how the image develops during the teaching, and the language being taught should be as broad and flexible as one can manage. Personal construct categorizing is a very partial language. So is Wood and Beck's Environmental A, not simply because it is a mapping, but because it is a particular kind of mapping. It is the traverse strategy of the surveyor, which is a powerful way of achieving a "true" map, accurate in scale and direction. But there are other ways to draw a city—topological sketches, symbolic diagrams, or illustrative views—that may be appropriate to other concepts. Had there been time, a whole range of techniques could have been taught. Nevertheless, Environmental A is better than being inarticulate, and clearly superior to being dependent on words alone.

Naive "image maps" have been particularly criticized because most people *are* so ill-trained graphically, so befuddled by our verbal civilization that they think that anyone who can draw must have been born with a special genius. If one does not have the time or means to teach good mapping, should one ever ask people to make one? The trained draftsman will tell you more, but the naive one will tell you much, as long as you realize that he knows far more in other languages that he can communicate on his map. A disconnected or distorted map does not indicate a defective mental image. But the very unfamiliarity of the task, like the unexpected question, releases impressions that might otherwise have been suppressed. The elements recorded with difficulty are even more likely to be important ones. See the drawings of children, or the Venezuelan maps collected by Appleyard, some of them made by people who had actually never seen a map before.

We have even asked people to draw eye-level views of places. Perspective sketching is more difficult than mapping, and whereas most Western people will consider a request for a map as within the bounds of reason, they are sure that sketches are only made by artists, or by children who are too young and innocent to recognize their lack of ability. Yet we have found striking information in such drawings made by untrained draftsmen, when we could induce them. Most difficult of all, perhaps, have been the rapid sketches made while driving along a highway, as reported in *The View from the Road* (Appleyard et al., 1964). Even a skilled draftsman cannot do that well. Still, these apparent scribbles tell an interesting, coherent story.

Curiously enough, few investigators are aware of the difficulty that most people have in communicating verbally. People are assumed to be able to talk well. But university students (and professors, alas!) are notoriously poor writers, poor speakers even. Asking someone about their environment often elicits a set of disconnected verbal cliches, until one takes the time to go deeper, or somehow helps the person to communicate verbally. With the advent of photography, and now television, graphic literacy is very possibly rising relative to verbal literacy, although the skill is passive rather than productive.

The diverse ways in which different groups see the same place are important for public policy. Critical for public policy also are the fascinating similarities, arising from features of the environment itself, or from our common biological heritage, or, as the Duncans so nicely illustrate, from similarities in the nature of the social networks within groups that at first glance may seem wildly dissimilar. Similarities of cognition are particularly useful in making city policy. They are essential if people are to communicate and cooperate with one another. Then why not teach each other how to see the world, both to build those social bridges and also to enrich our common experience? Tuan's paper is a shining example of how to enlarge and vivify the perception of the world in that way. Literature (and also painting and photography, of course) is a mine of compelling perceptions of perceiving.

Still another "perspective" could have been added to this book, the perception of design, which has always been concerned with manipulating things to enhance their cognition. The designer's craft is a storehouse of principles and practical examples on how to shape things so that they seize our attention, organize our perception, and convey meaning. True enough, many design principles are contradictory. For the most part, they treat only the object itself, as if that object had some magical, sentient existence all its own. But this traditional knowledge contains important insights. By linking it with cognitive research, we would also help designers themselves to see the process whole.

A number of contributors note the lack of theoretical connections between image and behavior. For the most part, they mean predicted behavior, that is, "think x and you will do y." This is of natural interest for policy, which is always anxious to predict the results of some action. (Incidentally, how about the prediction of a feeling, given a behavior?) But these longed-for predictions continue to separate thought and action. Why not study persons in their environment as they act and feel together? Feelings and ideas are not merely troublesome intervening variables that must be passed through in order to understand visible behavior. Good behavior is by no means a reasonable motive for improving the environment. Feelings and ideas, and the actions and sensations that are part of them, are what it is like to be alive, and the goodness or badness of that experience is the why of policy. Most studies look at behavior *or* cognition, rarely the two together.

This is a book that centers on theory. Theory is a necessity: it links and explains our observations, and tells us what to look for, predict, and test. All too often, theoretical discussions are stupefying to read, despite all their italicizing, capitalizing, and lengthy lists of concepts in hierarchical order. It might be a matter of style, but more often it is because these abstractions are too remote from how people actually experience the world. The theories that keep us awake are those that arise and are tested in the midst of life. Planning action, for its own part, is crippled without theory and reflection, since if action is free of any intellectual framework, then if it fails (or seems to fail, since one has no sure way of knowing) it can only be abandoned, with no one the wiser for it. Theory and action require each other.

In the final essay, Wohlwill notes how often environment disappears in environmental cognition research. Studies seem to be concerned with pure thinking. How infrequently one finds any analysis—even a description—of the setting whose cognition is being investigated, or any thought as to how environmental features might be involved in the process!

Most designers and planners, on the other hand, as they take notice of environmental cognition, simply acquire a new verbal style, add a novel field survey to their repertoire (a survey done, as always, by themselves), and continue to ignore the city as experienced by their inarticulate clients. They are trained to look at place, not at people. Each profession looks along its own nose, and to see perceiver and perceived whole is a difficult business. To link that understanding to public policy is an even more difficult business.

This book is stimulating because it shows, here and there throughout, how the process of environmental cognition can be seen as a developing creative interchange between the person, the intimate social group, and their spatial environment. It is one of those strategic domains where we fuse theoretical research and normative action.

Kevin Lynch
Professor of
Urban Studies
and Planning
M.I.T.

then (and now) in learning theory, proposed that in the course of learning an environment something like a field map—a "cognitive map" as he called it—is established in the brain. This map of routes and environmental relationships determines what behavioral responses rats and men will make. These three authors had much the same notions in mind: that people's behavior in large-scale environments can be explained more completely through recourse to internal, subjective factors than by more traditional external, "objective" factors, and that behavior is mediated by the image of the environment.

Since the late 1950s, there has been a rapidly expanding interest in environmental cognition, spurred on most notably by the appearance in 1956 of Kenneth Boulding's slim but powerful book, *The Image: Knowledge in Life and Society,* by Anselm Strauss's *Images of the American City* in 1961, and, perhaps most influential of all, by Kevin Lynch's stimulating and insightful book, *The Image of the City* in 1960. Boulding's thesis was that humans do not apprehend the nature of reality directly but through a highly learned interpretive process. There are no such things as facts, he argued, only messages filtered through a complex of images— the individual's cognitive impressions of different aspects of the world. Boulding traced the role of these images in various contexts, including biology, politics, history, social concerns, organizations, and finally the theory of knowledge itself. Having an interest particularly in urban phenomena, Strauss argued that it is not possible fully to understand urban social behavior in cities or the processes of development and urbanization without at the same time understanding what people think of their cities. Through literary, observational, and sociological sources he has shed much light on different group conceptions and shared sentiments and symbolism about urban and nonurban environments. Finally, Lynch was interested in what makes different cities and parts of cities more or less imageable and legible. He suggested several categories of urban imagery, which have subsequently become part of our language, and directly inspired a bevy of studies on the images of particular cities and their component parts in a variety of countries and cultures. We shall have

more to say in Chapter 1 about these three books and the ideas and research that they spawned.

Subsequent contributions to knowledge in this area have been made by a wide variety of social scientists and environmental professionals. Some "parent" disciplines have fostered specific new subfields, such as environmental and ecological psychology and behavioral and social geography, whose research directions, journals, and teaching programs are heavily oriented to investigating the interface between experience, behavior, and the environment. These academic subfields complement already established areas such as urban and community sociology, cultural and urban anthropology, human ecology, descriptive urban geography, resource management, and behavioral design and social planning.

Since 1965, the Association of American Geographers (AAG) and, since 1969, the Environmental Design Research Association (EDRA), along with other scientific and professional organizations (most notably the Association for the Study of Man–Environment Relations, the American Psychological Association, the Society for Research in Child Development, the American Institute of Planners, the American Institute of Architects, the Social Psychology Section of the British Psychological Society, and the Institute of British Geographers) and various ad hoc groups in several countries have sponsored forums for researchers and practitioners concerned with environment-behavior relations to share their ideas and research findings. Each year since 1965 a number of scientific reports and special sessions have been presented at these meetings specifically on environmental cognition. The first was a session at the 1965 AAG convention, inspired and organized by Robert Kates, and resulted in the well-known monograph, *Environmental Perception and Behavior,* edited by David Lowenthal. Development of the area has continued through subsequent national and international meetings until the recent publication of David Stea and Roger Downs's special issue of *Environment and Behavior* on "Cognitive Representations of Spatial Environments" and the excellent book by Downs and Stea, *Image and Environment,* published in 1973. We owe a great debt to all these important forerunners, and we hope that this present book may keep alive and advance the spirit of inquiry to which they each contributed.

Purpose of This Book

It was to the dual end of making explicit the theoretical notions implicitly underlying this research, and of challenging various theoretically inclined researchers to articulate testable theories of environmental cognition, that a symposium on conceptual issues in environmental cognition research was convened at the 1972 meeting of the Environmental Design Research Association in Los Angeles. The day-and-a-half symposium was organized and chaired by Gary Moore with the cooperation of David Stea, Roger Downs, and the EDRA conference organizers. A number of position papers were prepared and circulated ahead of time and vigorously discussed. Participants were invited from the fields of psychology, geography, sociology, medicine, anthropology, architecture, landscape architecture, and urban planning.

A year later, at the 1973 EDRA meeting in Blacksburg, Virginia, Reginald Golledge organized a second meeting with assistance from Gary Moore and Steve Kaplan; this focused specifically on some of the latest research being conducted in environmental cognition, much of it by recent Ph.D.'s and doctoral candidates. We were happily surprised to find that many of the papers were empirical outgrowths of the more theoretical and speculative ideas of the previous year. Thus, with the encouragement of several of our colleagues, the idea arose for this book to show the relationships between theory and research in environmental cognition.

This volume, therefore, is based in large part on the formal presentations, commentaries, and discussions of those gatherings. The authors of the 1972 Los Angeles symposium were invited to extend and formalize their theoretical presentations, and new contributors were invited to fill gaps which became apparent during that meeting. The participants at the 1973 Blacksburg meeting were asked to make explicit the connections between their empirical research and the theory or perspective that influenced it or from which it was derived. Finally, commentators have been given the opportunity to revise their thoughts in the light of the revised papers and their subsequent feelings about them.

Organization, Scope, and Audience

The book is divided into three major parts. Part I presents four prominent theories of environmental cognition. Each theory is an attempt to explain a range of empirical phenomena associated with environmental knowing, but each is based on a different set of assumptions about human nature. Most of these theories are derived from, or are extensions to, current psychological theories about intellectual development, but each has been forced to expand in order to account for recent data specifically on cognition of the everyday large-scale environment.

Part II introduces three new perspectives on environmental cognition not derived from psychology; and although theoretical in nature, they do not yet approximate (nor perhaps should they) the hypothetical–deductive model of "scientific" theory. The authors in this part of the book offer a range of possibilities for the construction of theory and the interpretation of data derived from sociology, anthropology, geography, literature, and phenomenology. These new perspectives are already proving to be of great heuristic importance; they open new lines of investigation, suggest new and invigorating questions, and provide a rich array of explanatory concepts. As in the first part of the book, each section is introduced by a major lead-in chapter, followed by one or more empirical case studies that exemplify conceptual points raised in the lead-in chapter, and is concluded by a critical commentary on the ideas and research as a whole.

Part III covers a range of new methodologies for the exploration of the "worlds inside people's heads." Theory, research, data, and method can never be satisfactorily separated, for to attempt to do so leads inevitably to narrow understandings, but in this section we focus particularily on some recent advances in research methodology. In each case, however, the presentation and discussion of research findings are used to elucidate the method under consideration.

The volume begins with a foreword by Kevin Lynch, for which we are most grateful; our introduction follows, in which we compare the theories and perspectives included, along with other possibilities yet to be explored fully, and provide for them all a philosophical, historical, and conceptual context.

In reflecting on this manuscript, we are reminded of a remark by Ferdinand de Saussure, the father of modern structural linguistics, to the effect that there is a crucial difference between a symphony and any particular performance of that symphony. This difference is of course paralleled by the difference between language and speech. Following George Miller, the contemporary linguist, we may extend this distinction to conferences and suggest that there is quite a difference between an actual meeting of scientists and the written results of such a meeting. One of our tasks is to try to reconstruct the symphony to which each of these various players was trying to contribute. The players in this particular orchestra may not have been entirely clear themselves as to what the score was. During the two symposia, as would be hoped and expected, some points and concepts came under considerably greater scrutiny and argument than others, and we may expect the same from this volume—in particular the notions of structure and structural analysis in the social sciences, information surfaces and the information-processing approach to cognition, universals in development, the role of inheritance and genetics in environmental knowing, individual and group differences, and the psychological versus sociocultural determinants of experience, cognition, and behavior. It is interesting that these issues are not unique to the study of environmental knowing or environment–behavior studies in general, but are central concerns of many scientific and humanistic disciplines and, in some cases, of current public debate. A price must be paid for the transfer from symposium to book, but much, hopefully, is also gained. Although undoubtedly much of the informal flavor, the spontaneity, the personalities of the participants and their occasional clashes have been lost, we may hope that more depth and precision of thinking have ensued.

In working on the translation from symposium to book, our main concern has been to present fairly the range of theoretical perspectives currently emerging in environmental cognition, and to show how each is abstracted from or has influenced particular lines of investigation. Time and space, however, prevented us from being able to include all worthwhile contributions. Part I would have been enriched, for example, by the recent work of the psychologist Herbert Pick and his colleagues on cognitive mapping in children, and by the new work of the psychologist-geographer team of Seymour Wapner, Bernard Kaplan, and Saul Cohen, which is derived from the organismic–developmental perspective. Similarly, Part II would have been greatly enriched by the inclusion of a section on the historical perspective on environmental cognition and the study of transcontinental migrations in relation to images over historical time, derived in part from the early writings of J. K. Wright, but now pursued most notably by the historical geographers Martyn Bowden, David Lowenthal, and Hugh Prince. Finally, Part III could have drawn on an ever-increasing volume of work that uses maps, models, verbal constructs, and a myriad of other devices to extract information from people about the environment of the mind.

Although most assume that cognition affects behavior, the work demonstrating this relationship so far is limited, fragmentary, atheoretical, and could not be included. The more applied work specifically dealing with the implications of environmental perception and cognition for design and planning failed to meet our criterion for the same reasons (although there are some very interesting recent beginnings in this line). As partial recompense for these omissions, we have tried in our introductions, as have the commentators in their summaries, to direct the interested reader to the more stimulating source materials on each of these issues. We anticipate that investigations into the design and planning implications of theories of environmental cognition will be an exciting area of future development. Perhaps the next book on environmental cognition will have this search as its explicit theme. We hope the present volume may assist in this development and speed along its realization.

In addition to our concern for representativeness of content, we have also been influenced in the preparation of this book by the audiences to whom we hope it will speak. As the main perceived need at this time in the development of environmental cognition seems to be in the development and testing of theory, our main emphasis has been on the analysis of theory, research, and method. It is thus expected that our main audience will be the wide range of individuals in the social and behavioral sciences and the environmental design and planning professions who are attracted to the problem of relating experience and behavior to the physical and social environment, to systematically describing and theoretically understanding these relationships, and to providing better environmental supports for them.

But we have also been interested in a second reader—the student or would-be researcher or practitioner in these various fields who is becoming interested in environment–behavior relationships, and who wishes to find a firm theoretical base from which to organize and evaluate more concrete readings and real-world observations and on which to found empirical studies and applied design or planning projects. Thus we have been oriented toward providing a book potentially useful as a text in advanced or specialized undergraduate or graduate courses in the variety of behavioral and social science disciplines and architecture and urban planning professions contributing to the study of behavior and environment. The book should also serve a comprehensive set of readings for introductory courses in these fields. We hope that both teachers and general readers will find our introductions and the commentaries at the end of each section helpful for orientation and summary. We have been pleased to hear that already several people have successfully used portions of this manuscript in their classes.

We hope that this book may bring some people to new realizations and open new questions and possibilities for research and application. There are a myriad of questions to be asked about the "worlds inside people's heads," and a bushelful of research studies and projects to be done. We'd love to have your company.

Acknowledgements

We have many, many people to thank for helping us in various ways in the preparation of this book:

somewhat chronologically—David Stea, Roger Hart, and Roger Downs for helping us conceptualize and organize the 1972 Los Angeles Symposium, which provided the original impetus for the book's development; Steve Kaplan, likewise, for the 1973 Blacksburg Symposium; the various commentators at those two meetings who shed new conceptual light on this subject matter; John Archea, Donald Demko, Roger Downs, David Stea, and Robert Kates for encouraging us to think of publishing something based on these meetings; David Seamon, Eli Gerson, Steve Kaplan, Amos Rapoport, and Yi-Fu Tuan for advising on the selection of certain papers and offering constructive criticisms on them; the Ohio State University Press, the New York Academy of Sciences, Aldine Publishing Company, Academic Press, and Goodyear Publishing Company for permitting us to reprint items under their copyrights; our new friend Chuck Hutchinson for his keen interest and warm assistance on all phases of the preparation of the manuscript; the other manuscript reviewers for their helpful comments; N.S.F. Grant GS-37969 to R. G. Golledge for support in preparation of parts of the manuscript; Sarah Bennett and Phyllis Rubin for transcribing and checking tapes; Betty Glasgow, Allison Cahill, and Debbie Mendlowitz for typing various parts of the manuscript; Jeannie Gibbons for preparing the bibliography; Phyllis Rubin, Lauren Leveton, and Ruth Rowles of the Clark University Cartographic Laboratory for preparing several of the illustrations; Tim McGinty of the University of Wisconsin, Milwaukee for his assistance on cover design and graphics; Barbara Zeiders of Service to Publishers for a superb editing and layout job; our various friends and contributors for your patience, understanding, and—for the most part—goodwill in working with us on the preparation of this volume; and, finally, Kevin Lynch for graciously preparing the foreword. To all, we most warmly thank you.

Gary T. Moore
Reginald G. Golledge

CONTENTS

CONTRIBUTORS AND PARTICIPANTS

Participants at the 1972 Los Angeles Symposium

Donald Appleyard, Departments of Landscape Architecture and City and Regional Planning, University of California, Berkeley

James M. Blaut, Graduate School of Geography, Clark University (now with the Department of Geography, University of Illinois, Chicago Circle)

Donald Demko, Department of Geography, Queen's University, Kingston, Ontario

Roger M. Downs, Department of Geography, Pennsylvania State University

Elihu M. Gerson, Department of Sociology, Syracuse University (now with the Langley Porter Neuropsychiatric Institute, University of California, San Francisco)

Reginald G. Golledge, Department of Geography, Ohio State University

Peter R. Gould, Department of Geography, Pennsylvania State University

Basil Honikman, School of Architecture, Kingston Polytechnic Institute, Kingston-upon-Thames, London (now with the School of Design, North Carolina State University)

Mark M. Jones, School of Architecture and Urban Planning, University of California, Los Angeles

Rachel Kaplan, Department of Psychology and School of Natural Resources, University of Michigan

Stephen Kaplan, Departments of Psychology and Computer and Communication Sciences, University of Michigan

Sharon Kaufman-Diamond, School of Architecture and Urban Planning, University of California, Los Angeles

David Lowenthal, American Geographical Society, New York (now with the Department of Geography, University College, London)

Robert A. Lowrey, CONSAD Research Corporation, Pittsburgh

Gary T. Moore, Department of Psychology, Clark University, Organizer and Chairman (now with the School of Architecture and Urban Planning, University of Wisconsin, Milwaukee)

Peter A. Orleans, Department of Sociology and School of Architecture and Urban Planning, University of California, Los Angeles (now with the Department of Architecture, University of Denver)

Mary C. Potter, Departments of Psychology and Urban Studies and Planning, Massachusetts Institute of Technology

George Rand, School of Architecture and Urban Planning, University of California, Los Angeles

Amos Rapoport, School of Architecture, University of Sydney (now with the Departments of Architecture and Anthropology, University of Wisconsin, Milwaukee)

David Seamon, Graduate School of Geography, Clark University

David Stea, School of Architecture and Urban Planning, University of California, Los Angeles

Seymour Wapner, Department of Psychology, Clark University

David Weaver, Department of Geography, Clark University (now with the Office of Coastal Resources Planning, Commonwealth of Massachusetts, Boston)

Participants at the 1973 Blacksburg Symposium

James M. Blaut, Department of Geography, University of Illinois, Chicago

Ronald Briggs, Department of Geography and Population Research Center, University of Texas, Austin

Martin T. Cadwallader, Department of Geography, University of California, Los Angeles (now with the Department of Geography, University of Wisconsin, Madison)

Ann S. Devlin, Department of Psychology, University of Michigan (now with the Department of Psychology, Connecticut College)

Roger M. Downs, Department of Geography, Pennsylvania State University

Harold D. Fishbein, Department of Psychology, University of Cincinnati (not present in person)

David L. George, School of Architecture and Urban Planning, University of California, Los Angeles

Reginald G. Golledge, Department of Geography, Ohio State University, Organizer and Chairman

Stephen Kaplan, Departments of Psychology and Computer and Communication Sciences, University of Michigan

Alcira Kreimer, Department of Landscape Architecture, University of California, Berkeley (not present in person)

Gary T. Moore, Department of Psychology, Clark University, Co-chairman (now with the School of Architecture and Urban Planning, University of Wisconsin, Milwaukee)

Alfred J. Nigl, Department of Psychology, University of Cincinnati

Roger Peters, Department of Psychology, University of Michigan

Amos Rapoport, Departments of Architecture and Anthropology, University of Wisconsin, Milwaukee

Susan Saegert, Environmental Psychology Program, Department of Psychology, Graduate Center, City University of New York

Joachim F. Wohlwill, Division of Man–Environment Relations, Pennsylvania State University

Georgia Zannaras, Department of Geography, Ohio State University (not present in person; now with the Department of Geography, University of Cincinnati)

Other Invited Contributors to This Volume

Linda P. Acredolo, Institute of Child Development, University of Minnesota (now with the Department of Psychology, University of California, Davis)

David Alpaugh, School of Architecture and Urban Planning, University of California, Los Angeles

Robert Beck, Ecole d'Architecture, Université de Montréal

Ian Burton, Department of Geography, University of Toronto

Anne Buttimer, Graduate School of Geography, Clark University

Harold C. Conklin, Department of Anthropology, Yale University

James S. Duncan, Department of Geography, Syracuse University

Nancy G. Duncan, Department of Geography, Syracuse University

M. Sue Gerson, Institute of Urban and Regional Development, University of California, Berkeley

Stephen M. Golant, Department of Geography, University of Washington (now with the Departments of Geography and Behavioral Sciences, University of Chicago)

John Harrison, School of Social Sciences, University of Sussex, Brighton

Frank R. Klett, School of Architecture and Urban Planning, University of California, Los Angeles

W. J. Lloyd, Department of Geography, University of California, Los Angeles

Kevin Lynch, Department of Urban Studies and Planning, Massachusetts Institute of Technology

Herbert L. Pick, Jr., Center for Research in Human Learning, University of Minnesota

Philip Sarre, Faculty of Social Sciences, Open University, Milton Keynes

Myongsup Shin, Department of Geography, University of Minnesota (now with the Korean Central Daily News, Honolulu)

J. Sonnenfeld, Department of Geography, Texas A & M University

Peter Stringer, Department of Psychology, University of Surrey, Guildford

Yi-Fu Tuan, Department of Geography, University of Minnesota

Denis Wood, Department of Landscape Architecture, North Carolina State University, Raleigh

INTRODUCTION

1

ENVIRONMENTAL KNOWING: CONCEPTS AND THEORIES

Gary T. Moore
Department of Psychology
Clark University[1]

Reginald G. Golledge
Department of Geography
Ohio State University

Environmental cognition is the study of the subjective information, images, impressions, and beliefs that people have of the environment, the ways in which these conceptions arise from experience, and the ways in which they affect subsequent behavior with respect to the environment. The terms "information" and "knowledge" have a ring of validity or truth to them; however, this book is concerned with what different individuals and groups *believe* to be true about the sociophysical environment, the condensation or elaborations they put on information, and their *subjective* knowledge, impressions, and beliefs about the environment in which they carry out their everyday lives. We consider the ways in which these images arise, are influenced by direct environmental experience and by external sources like the mass media, and subsequently affect personal and group decisions and behavior with respect to the environment.

For many, the study of environmental knowing or environmental cognition rests on the fascination inherent in finding out what different people's images are of their environment; for a few others the fascination is with a concrete exemplar of the subject–object and mind–body questions. For others, interest in the field rests on the assumption that we can better under-

stand people's actions, needs, and desires with regard to the environment if we know how they conceive of it; for example, what are the images and symbolism that they attach to elements of the built environment, such as different housing styles or different uses of open space, what are their impressions of different natural and recreational environments, and what are their beliefs with respect to natural and man-made hazards, air pollution, depletion of resources, and the myriad other environmental problems that attract our attention? And for some, the study of environmental knowing is a manifestation of their concern for the people-oriented, subjective side of environmental behavior; it is an alternative to the study of urban and regional phenomena from strictly external, "objective," "rational," or "factual" points of view: for example, an alternative to the application to environment–behavior studies of the behaviorist model in psychology, the economic model in geography, or the ecological model in sociology (see the programmatic statements of the newer cognitive points of view in psychology by Lee, 1964; Stea, 1969a; S. Kaplan, 1972; Wapner, Kaplan, and Cohen, 1973; in geography by Burton and Kates, 1964; Cox and Golledge, 1969; Downs, 1970b; in sociology by Firey, 1945; Strauss,

1961; Michelson, 1970; and even in economics by Boulding, 1956). At best the older conceptions of urban life and environmental problems are hand-me-downs from older and distinguished academic traditions; at worst, they blind us to the human realities and experiences of urban and rural life in the mid- and late twentieth century.

The subjective status of the image and its role in behavior has perhaps been expressed most succinctly in Kenneth Boulding's (1956) book, *The Image*:

For any given organism or organization, there are no such things as "facts." There are only messages filtered through a changeable value system . . . . Behavior depends on this image (pp. 6, 14).

Images may be certain or uncertain, clear or vague, global or particular; they may be about probable or improbable events, about the physical environment, or about the undifferentiated totality of the socio-cultural environment. They may be images of "fact" or images of "values." They may be of a specific elements and events or they may be of a symbolic or semiotic character. They may be stable or labile, flexible or rigid. They may be added to in a haphazard manner or in a regular and well-defined way through simple accumulation, or they may be changed and re-organized to incorporate with and respond to new messages. They may arise from real-world experience or through popular literature, the arts, or the media. But one thing is clear: no one person's or group's image of the environment is more "accurate" or true than another's. Each views and reconstructs the world through its own assumptions, values, and life experiences.

Overt behavior depends (at least in part) on images. But images also play an important role in more covert behavior and experience. Commenting on the importance and ubiquity of environmental images, Kevin Lynch (1960) remarked, in his ground breaking *The Image of the City*,

A clear image enables one to move about easily and quickly; to find a friend's house or a policeman or a button store. But an ordered environment can do more than this; it may serve as a broad frame of reference, an organizer of activity or belief or knowledge . . . . [It] plays a social role as well. It can furnish the raw material for the symbols and collective mem-ories of group communication . . . [and] gives its possessor an important sense of emotional security (p. 4).

Whereas the images actually investigated by Lynch were strictly spatial (although his conception of them was much broader), urban imagery can be seen in a much broader framework—one that crosscuts environmental experience and values and enters the entire range of urban and nonurban life. In *Images of the American City*, the sociologist Anselm Strauss (1961, 1968) identified, for example, several varieties of urban symbolism prevalent in literature and common thought: sectionalism versus national concentration, ruralism versus urbanism, cosmopolitanism versus specialization, traditionalism versus modernism. Each of these dichotomies is a basic ambiguity in the ways in which people conceive of urbanization, and each is related to the life style of the different groups holding them.

In a very basic sense, the environment is what we think it is, and as citizens and decision makers we respond to it and deal with it as we conceive it to be. Some years ago, the urban planner Stephen Carr (1967) expressed this view in the following way:

We ask why we should be concerned with the form of the environment and how city form might contribute to the quality of life. To be sure, we lack much relevant knowledge, but worse than that we lack a way of getting beyond our current conceptualizations of city form and its functions. Indeed, the most perplexing problem we face in attempting to improve the relationship of people with their urban environment is the persistence of conventional images and models of conceiving the city in the face of changing urban realities and human purposes.

We may surmise that the same dilemma faces ordinary city dwellers. For in a very real sense, the city is what people think it is. The city that we know personally—the city of the mind—largely determines the world in which we have our life experiences and through which we strive to gain many of our daily satisfactions (p. 199).

Ada Louise Huxtable (1973), the architectural critic, has more recently expressed much the same view in commenting on a New York Metropolitan Museum of Art photography exhibit on Landscape/Cityscape:

Photography as art has had a lot to do with the way we perceive the world and react to it, and to some extent the accepted image of our environment is one that the art of photography has given us . . . . There are as many potential images of the world as there are eyes and minds to frame and interpret them. There is virtually no such thing as uncolored observation, or objective documentation, as long as there is an intelligence behind the camera . . . . They have taught us a way to look at the world, and in turn, we see the world their way.

And that is the rub. The curious thing about images of the environment is that they inevitably structure reality. In both literature and art, the image of the city has always been subject to philosophical and emotional manipulation. . . . Our urban concepts are defined by certain key photographic images . . . . The implications are large, in that we deal with what we see, or think we see, in facing the problems of the environment (p. 26).

DEFINITIONS AND CONCEPTUAL DISTINCTIONS

Formally defined, *environmental cognition* refers to the awareness, images, information, impressions, and beliefs that individuals and groups have about the elemental, structural, functional, and symbolic aspects of real and imagined physical, social, cultural, economic, and political environments.

Let us look at this definition more closely. The general terms "environmental cognition," "environmental knowing," or their brother "environmental perception", refer not only to *information*, with its implication of truth and validity, but also to admittedly subjective *beliefs* based on partial, incomplete, or intentionally misleading information (as in much advertising and propaganda). In addition, these various terms refer to *spatial*-encoded "images" as well as *linguistically* encoded "impressions" about the environment. The referent of environmental cognition is not taken to be conceptually limited to the *physical* environment (although much empirical work has been so focused), but to include the *total life environment*, with its *sociocultural*, *economic*, and *political* aspects. Thus we may as easily talk about people's impressions of the politics of their city (certainly a part of their relevant environment, moreso to the degree that they are affected by local politics, as in increased property taxation of older people on a fixed income) as we may talk about their beliefs about the characters of different parts of the city (boundaries are not so much physical things as they are the dividing lines between two different subconceptions of the city, such

as between "safe" and "unsafe" areas or "good" and "bad" areas, all in quotation marks because we are not speaking of crime or other external, "objective" statistics, but of "the city of the mind").

Environmental cognition, as a term and as a field of study, refers not only to one's image or impression of the *elements* of the environment, but also to *events* (like street fairs or shopping sales or stoop sitting), to *dynamic, functional,* and *cyclic* happenings (like climate, the working of the public and private transportation systems, and the natural and social ecology of the area), to *patterns* and *conceptual similarities* (most citizens tend to make distinctions among the politics, economics, housing patterns, and street layouts of a city; yet with increased information and contact with these systems or assumed conceptual units of a city, they are seen to be parts of a larger structure), and to the *sentiment, personal meaning,* and *collective symbolism* that people give to various parts of their environment (like an old childhood play area, the various homes in which one previously lived, a favorite corner store or park, a scene of romance, a veterans of foreign war monument, or the old upper-class or literary-elite areas). All these are aspects of persons' conceptions of their environment, and all influence their subsequent behavior.

As defined by Downs and Stea (1973b), the more specific term *cognitive mapping* refers to the process by which people acquire, code, store, recall, and decode information about the relative locations and attributes of phenomena in the everyday spatial environment (p. 9). Downs and Stea go on to clarify misconceptions that prevail among the concepts of perception, cognition, representation, attitude, preference, and spatial behavior, and we refer the reader to their excellent treatment (1973b, Chap. 1).

We would, however, like to add a few words about the distinction between perception and cognition, as we see it, and about the concept of representation.

Perception and Cognition: From Stimulus Dependency to Inference

As Downs and Stea have pointed out in *Image and Environment*, the terms "perception" and "cognition" have been applied in a confusing variety of contexts by different psychologists and other behavioral and social scientists. For example, to many experimental and physiological psychologists, perception refers to the reception of external stimuli through the physiological excitation of peripheral sensory receptors; to many social and personality psychologists, it refers to both the sensory awareness of people as social objects and more broadly to the overall impressions that persons form of other persons. To many behavioral and social geographers, sociologists, and political scientists, it has become an all-encompassing term referring to perceptions, images, memories, preferences, and attitudes, that is, to all the psychological factors assumed to affect large-scale spatial behavior. We find the last use of the term too general and not precise enough for further advancement of research on all these different (although interlocking) influences on behavior.

Although the distinctions between perception and cognition fall short of forming a clear dichotomy, but rather fade into differences of degree and focus, certain relative distinctions can be made. The standard criteria for *perception* are immediacy and stimulus dependency (Epstein, 1967). *Immediacy* implies that the behavioral response, whether overt or covert, immediately follows or accompanies energistic impingements on the sense organs; *stimulus dependency* implies that a great proportion of the response variance of what will be called "perception" can be accounted for by the physical properties of the stimulus. Clearly, however, there are a range of behavioral responses that do not accompany or immediately follow stimulation and are not dependent on the stimulus; these behavioral responses we may take to be a function of other than perceptual mechanisms, that is cognitive and other intraorganismic mechanisms. But, furthermore, most perceptual tasks require an interval between stimulus presentation and response, if for no more than the comparison of the task and a standard in the most simple of perceptual situations; it thus may be questioned if anything like pure perception ever occurs without cognition, inasmuch as nonimmediacy and the possibility of mediation by judgmental processes, memory, and assumptions about the stimulus situation obtain.

In its most general sense, then, *cognition* refers to the various means of awareness or knowing that intervene between external energy impingements in the present and the past and the entire gamut of human behavioral responses, present and future. Cognition thus subsumes the more specific concepts and substages of sensation, perception, imagery, retention and recall, reasoning and problem solving, and judgment and evaluation. As such, it includes the various processes by which visual, linguistic, semantic, and behavioral information is selected, encoded, reduced and elaborated, stored, retrieved, decoded, and used (without implying that this is necessarily a linear process or that these activities are as discrete as these terms might suggest, although some argue that both are the case).

Many (not all) contemporary theorists treat perception as a subset and as a function of cognition (e.g., Allport, 1955; Bruner, 1957a; Brunswick, 1956; Gibson, 1950; Ittelson, 1960, Neisser, 1967; Piaget, 1969; Pick and Pick, 1970; Vernon, 1962; Wapner and Werner, 1957; Wohlwill, 1960; see also the review in Wohlwill, 1962). Bruner (1957a), for example, regards perception as basically an inferential process in which the person plays a maximal and idiosyncratic role in interpreting, categorizing, and transforming the stimulus input. Ittelson (1960) emphasizes the hypothesized central role in perception of the person's assumptions about the stimulus situation. Piaget (1969) has made an important distinction between two types of knowing: one is essentially *figurative* and related to the percepts or images of successive states or *momentary configurations* of the world by direct and immediate contact; the second is essentially *operative* and related to the *operations* that intervene between successive states and by which the person transforms parts of the world into recognizable schemata and structures. Visual perception is only one form of figurative knowing, whereas intelligence or cognition is based on the operative mode in Piaget's system. In this view perception still depends on conceptual preinferences and organismic activity. Another view, that of Wapner and Werner (1957), treats perception as a subsystem of cognition, where knowledge about the world may be constructed by many means, perceptual judgments being only one. As development proceeds, perception becomes subordinated to higher mental processes. The organism's available cognitive structures influence perceptual selectivity, which leads to a reconstruction of the world through selected fields of attention. Perception is thus in several of these theories both a *subsystem* of cognition and a *function* of cognition.

Many experiments and examples may be cited in support of the notion of the subordination of perception to cognition. The Gestalt psychologist Koffka (1922), for example, demonstrated that "a structure by which we react to a given stimulus complex remains in the memory of the individual" by showing the figure-ground effects of the edges of ambiguously patterned tablecloths or wallpaper and the perceptual interpretation given them by different individuals depending on mental set. Another Gestaltist, Duncker (1945), was the first of a long line to show the effects of induced movement on perception; although no actual movement is present, the smaller of two lighted objects in a dark room is seen to move, the larger being *assumed* by the person to be stationary. This is similar to the transactionalists' demonstrations (e.g., Slack, 1956) on the effects of familiar or assumed size as a cue to distance; half-sized playing cards at the same distance as normal-sized cards are "seen" or, more precisely, *judged* to be twice as far.

If it is impossible for an observer to see the position, orientation, or distance of an object (and even in many cases when one can), he or she will often fall back on knowledge or assumptions about the object. Vernon (1962) has shown the effects of classification and naming of objects on several aspects of children's perception of these objects, as Carmichael, Hogan, and Walter (1932) earlier showed the effects of naming and the ideas we associate with simple drawings on our subsequent perception, memory, and drawing reproduction of them. Bruner and Postman (1949) showed that general expectancies and already established schemata severely restrict recognition of "wrongly" colored playing cards (e.g., red clubs or black hearts), a phenomena we are all familiar with, sometimes under the fancy label of "intellectual myopia"). A number of other demonstrations and examples of a variety of similar functional relations between perception and cognition could be cited, especially from the transactionalist, the "new look" directive-state, and the sensory-tonic schools of perception (see Allport, 1955; Vernon, 1962). All these arguments, studies, and common experience seem to suggest that when we "perceive" we actually classify objects according to the ideas, impression, and beliefs that he have previously come to associate with them.[2]

There are some important differences in the chapters that follow, but for most of the authors, as far as environmental cognition generally is concerned, a central assertion is that seeing, hearing, and remembering are all acts of *construction* which may make more or less use of stimulus information depending on circumstances. In the constructive process, there are frequently two stages that can be identified: the first of these is fast, crude, holistic, and parallel; the second is diverse, detailed, and sequential (Neisser, 1967).

The Concept of Representation: A Hypothetical Construct

Another term that appears prominently in environmental cognition and in this book, and about which there is some confusion is "representation." In different areas of discourse, this term has been used in a number of conceptually dissimilar ways. In this book, it is used in the sense of a hypothetical construct to refer to hypothesized, not directly observable subjective knowledge of the environment.[3]

Elsewhere, the term has been used in two general senses. In one sense, the more usual one, *representation* refers to the symbolic evocation of absent realities, that is, the re-presentation of something absent from the perceptual field through some other means that stands for or symbolizes the absent thing (e.g., Werner and Kaplan, 1963). Thus, we may speak of a painting representing a landscape, a lawyer representing a client, a random sample representing the population from which it was drawn, and so on (see Bernheimer, 1961). In the second sense, the term is used to refer to *knowledge* or *thought* itself (e.g., Piaget, 1950, 1951). It is this latter meaning of representation that seems to be implied when various writers have spoken of the "images" people have of their environment (e.g., Lynch, 1960; Strauss, 1961, 1968), of the "personal constructs" by which one organizes knowledge of the environment (e.g., Harrison and Sarre, 1971), or of the ways in which one "construes" the environment (e.g., Wapner et al., 1973). It is in this sense that the term is used in the present book.

Piaget (1951, pp. 67-72) has acknowledged the dual use of the term "representation" and has suggested that, to make the distinction clear between the two usages, representation in the sense of knowledge be termed "conceptual representation" or "cognitive representation," while representation in the sense of the re-presentation of absent realities be termed "symbolic representation" or simply "symbolization."

Symbolic representations, although they stand for something else, are directly observable and *external*. On the other hand, cognitive representations, inasmuch as they refer to knowledge and are not directly observable, may be termed *internal* representations. It is clear then that internal representations must be inferred from one or more external, symbolic representations (e.g., sketch maps of a city, poems, or linguistic categories) or from other forms of observable behavior (e.g., search behavior in locating a specified but previously unknown place in the city).

But this raises another issue: if cognitive representations are not observable, what then is their logical status? What do we mean when we say that someone has a "cognitive representation of the environment"? There appears to be three possible responses to this question; representation may be given the status of an intervening variable, a hypothetical construct, or a metaphor.

In the present case, representation is treated as a *hypothetical construct* (see MacCorquodale and Meehl, 1953), that is, as a proposition about hypothetical entities, processes, or events which are not directly observable, which extend beyond, but are used to make sense of, observed behavioral data. As hypothetical constructs, cognitive representations have an allegedly real status; they refer to hypothesized underlying entities or processes that there is reason to believe *do* exist, which are *in principle* observable (i.e., cognitive representations have correlates in other behavioral domains, e.g., physiological processes which could be measured under some ideal circumstances), but which can only be hypothesized

at the present time. The existence of the hypothesized constructs, therefore, is tested empirically by making logical deductions from them. The substantiation of the deductions, although not a sufficient condition for the truth of the hypothesized constructs, is a necessary condition and does provide corroboration for their existence. Thus, as a hypothetical construct, the term *cognitive representation* and its approximate synonyms refers to covert, nonobserved processes and organizations of elements of knowledge. It is a convenient shorthand notation for a set of entities and processes beyond the practical reach or immediate interest of the investigator, but which, nevertheless, there is reason to believe do exist (in the sense that there is some identifiable substrate for them), and which, furthermore, are useful in accounting for other observable spatial behaviors.

It is in this sense of representation as a hypothetical construct that Piaget (1950, 1951) seems to speak when he refers to a "schema" or a "structure," and in which S. Kaplan (1970, 1973a), Stea and Downs (1970b), Downs and Stea (1973b) seem to speak when they refer to humans' "cognitive maps" of the environment. Kaplan uses "cognitive map" as a hypothetical construct to explain how individuals know their environment, and assumes that there is a "correspondence" between known features of the world and an underlying physiological structure. In all these cases, and in the present case, these various substitutions for the term "representation" are convenient shorthand notations for the organization of elements of knowledge and for other uninvestigated processes (e.g., underlying neurophysiological structures and processes, perhaps like Hebbian cell assemblies and phase sequences).[4]

This status of the term is in distinction to the other two possible statuses, as an intervening variable and as a metaphor. As an *intervening variable*, the term representation would simply be a note attached to an economical grouping of measured variables in a statement of functional relationship between other measured variables (MacCorquodale and Meehl, 1953). The merit of an intervening variable is of a purely summarizing character; the relations among all the variables in the functional relationship can be discovered empirically, and it is assumed that nothing is added in the process of labeling some of them as intervening variables. That is, no constructs are hypothesized which have *not been directly measured.*

At the other extreme, as a *metaphor*, representation would have a decidedly "as if" quality to it and would be used to suggest the essentials of what may be going on in a process under consideration, but which it is not presumed characterizes or is a shorthand for other hypothesized entities or processes. Indeed, in the metaphorical use of representation, statements are made in a manifestly unreal way that would seem to imply inner events (the existence of which there is no reason to believe in) or, in other words, statements in which there is an obvious clash between the concrete referent (e.g., cognitive "map") and the possibility of the actual existence of such entities or processes (e.g., a cartographic map-like entity in the brain). Although it has been suggested that most of Tolman's terms are intervening variables (MacCorquodale and Meehl, 1953), it would seem that his suggestion that something like a "cognitive map" exists in rats and men could be better considered as an example of the metaphorical use of the term "representation":

We believe that in the course of learning a maze something like a field-map of the environment gets established in the rat's brain . . . . The central office itself is far more like a map control room than it is like an old-fashioned telephone exchange . . . . The incoming pulses are usually worked over and elaborated in the central control room into a tentative, cognitive-like map of the environment (Tolman, 1948, p. 192).

Although the metaphorical use of representation has an intuitive appeal and may be potentially useful in the creative process of beginning to understand a phenomena, it is also potentially misleading in scientific discussion. Some investigators have uncritically borrowed Tolman's use of the term "cognitive map" without asking about its logical status. Thus, for example, in the study of environmental cognition, the commonly used (and often misused) terms "mental map," "cognitive map," and "cognitive mapping" have sometimes been used to imply map-like representations of geographic or other large-scale environments. But it has been argued before (Stea, 1969a; Downs and Stea, 1973b; Hart and Moore, 1973) that it begs the question to suggest that spatial relations are necessarily represented in a cartographic form. Some individuals have even equated the term "mental map" with preferences and subjective-evaluative responses to the environment, thus implying (incorrectly we believe) that it is necessary for people to have a "mental map" of the relative spatial layout of a region or area in order to have consistent spatial preferences.

In discussing the relation between peripheral and central processors, and between various notions of the cognition of the visual attributes of the world, Gregory (1966) cautions,

We do have "mental" pictures, but this should not suggest that there are corresponding electrical pictures in the brain. It is possible to represent things in symbols but symbols will generally be very different from the things represented. The notion of brain pictures is conceptually dangerous. It is apt to suggest that these supposed pictures are themselves seen with a kind of inner eye—involving another picture, and another eye, . . . and so on.

In any case, it is not possible to suppose that sounds and smells and colors are represented by pictures in the brain— they must be coded in some other form. There is every reason to believe that retinal patterns are represented by coded combinations of cell activity . . . . What the eyes do is feed the brain with information coded into neural activity—chains of electrical impulses—which by their code and the patterns of brain activity represent objects (pp. 7, 69-71).

Treating the concept "cognitive representation" as a hypothetical construct standing for this as yet unmeasured neural cell activity and patterns (unmeasured at least in *environmental* cognitive research) raises a thorny methodological problem of how to ascertain the relationship between *external representations* and the *internal cognitive representations* that are really our interest and which are presumably manifested on various external representations (sketch maps, models, verbal descriptions, scales, etc.); this issue will be pursued later in this chapter and is dealt with in various ways in the following chapters, especially in those of Part III.

Some Fundamental Assumptions and Principles

One basic assumption underlying interest in environmental knowing is that it is a dynamic process whereby information from the external environment is constantly being received, selected, organized, and used to help individuals operate on a day-to-day basis (see especially Chapter 2).

Another fundamental principle is that subjective conceptions of the environment are of quite different natures and are used quite differently across different individuals and groups (see Sections 5 and 6). This may be because of the varying degrees to which past experience can be used in assimilating information from an environment, and because of sociocultural differences in the groups to which different humans belong (see Chapters 9 and 19). Related to this is the notion, expressed by certain theorists, that the needs and value systems of individuals are important in determining the extent of their awareness or knowledge about the environment (see Wapner et al., 1973; see also Chapters 12, 17, and 21). Specifically, it is recognized that, when individual differences are manifested in human behavior and are not assignable to structural (internal or external) causes, the question arises as to what extent those differences are assignable to cultural values, the nature of social interaction, and/or individual needs, values, and personality? In the studies of individual and group differences to date in environmental cognition, a variety of variables has been investigated: different functional user groups, different environmental professionals, artists versus scientists, natives versus nonnatives to a city, sex differences, socioeconomic differences, ethnic differences, group values, national origins, differences in plans for the future, age differences, and developmental differences not necessarily related to age.

A third tenet of environmental cognition is that information extracted from large-scale external environments exists in some type of psychological space. This is the space in which configurations, characteristics, and meanings about the world are held as mental images or cognitive representations. This psychological space need not have the metrics of any recognizable physical space. However, since we argue that training and experience help structure cognition, it seems reasonable to assume that any mental image will reflect at least some of the metric features of an identifiable physical space. This in itself presents the first of a series of problems related to attempts to understand the extent of awareness that any given

individual has about an external environment. Distances, locations, and other geometrical properties of the psychological space need not bear a one-to-one correspondence with their counterpart in physical space. For example, the distance between any two points A and B may be longer, shorter, or equal to the distance from B to A in psychological space (i.e., the symmetry and reflexivity axioms of Euclidean metrics need not hold). Similarly, directions may not be as easily specified in psychological space; they may vary according to the familiarity of the perceived object, its social or cultural significance, whether direction is from or to a major orientation node in space, and so on. In fact, in psychological space it may be possible to specify characteristics such as a direction, but it may be impossible to tie the specified direction into any comprehensible coordinate system. That is why, although we generally impute to the features dealt with in geometry and trigonometry the attributes of a physical space, we may be unable to perform the same tasks or make the same assumption in psychological space. The overwhelming conclusions that can be drawn about psychological space is that the representation of objects in this space need not be a mere one-to-one relation with the same objects in physical space (i.e., psychological space need not be a direct copy of physical space) but, rather, any correspondence that does exist may involve only topological relations or ordinal relations, or indeed may embody only some of the objectively determined metric properties of physical space. What appears to be an essential tenet of environmental cognition, however, is that the information that is held in the mind exists in some form of configuration. Attempts to extract information about external environments then are related to trying to determine the nature of the configuration that individuals use for the storage of their various images, impressions, and beliefs.

In general, therefore, we must recognize that cognitive structures can be defined as nonspecific but organized representations of prior experiences, and when we speak of environmental cognition we are referring to the nonspecific but organized representation of prior experiences with given external environments. We also recognize that the existence of cognitive structures facilitates recall of specific information extracted from environments; it allows us to estimate the degree of awareness and knowledge that people have of environments by determining through visual or linguistic recall tasks the extent of this knowledge or by observing peoples' use of environments. We must also recognize that time and space are extremely important aspects of cognition; since each environment exists in a time-space context, so too will cognitions of those environments. This context may be peculiar to the individual, but it must also have elements in common with the cognitions of other people so that the host of individuals that operate on a day-to-day basis in external environments can coordinate their activities with each other.

Methodological Issues

A fundamental question that can be raised at this stage is how do we become aware of the fact that an individual knows about and of an external environment? For the most part, we have assumed that individuals must know about external environments so that they can exist in them. For example, we each can find our way to our residence, place of work, the stores that we patronize, or the groups with which we fraternize. Furthermore, it seems reasonable to expect that people in general will know the difference between a street and a stream, a traffic light and a roadside light or neon sign, a mass transit vehicle and an individually owned car, and so on. Cognitions such as these appear to be fundamental and necessary to our everday existence. Consequently, we assume that such cognitions exist within the minds of all people.

However, we may also be quite aware of the fact that the nature and extent of these cognitions differ across individuals and groups. When one walks along the street and asks random passersby how to get to a certain destination, it is not unusual to be given a series of quite disparate answers. Nevertheless, each answer may be quite adequate in terms of allowing you to achieve your goal of reaching the given destination. What is of fundamental concern to the researcher in environmental cognition, therefore, is to discover the extent of the awareness or knowledge that individuals have of any given external environment. For the most part, the answer to this question

has involved requiring some form of external representation of the internal reflections and thoughts of individuals about an environment.

At this stage, it seems pertinent to distinguish between environmental cognitions per se, which are the internalized reflections and representations of external phenomena, and the external representations of this information. External representations have taken a tremendously varied form, ranging from written, verbal, and pictorial reports to second- and third-stage inferences about cognition made as a result of observing behavior of humans in the process of analyzing responses to some specific set of tasks. Much past and current work in this area of environmental cognition has been concerned with developing ways and means of externally representing what is within people's minds. Different theoretical points of view and different perspectives have produced a considerable variety of methods for extracting environmental information from individuals and for externally representing it in such a fashion that it can be viewed and analyzed by other people. This book, in fact, is concerned with a number of different theories, perspectives, and methods that have been developed to illustrate the extent of the environmental knowledge of individuals and groups; Part III, including the introductory Chapter 28, treats these methodological issues in detail.

EPISTEMOLOGICAL BASES OF ENVIRONMENTAL COGNITION

Although this book is concerned with the ways in which people know or image their environment, this question may be seen in the more general context of how knowledge in general is attained, that is, how a subject comes to know an object. Inasmuch as the positions taken with regard to this more general epistemological question are similar to positions adopted at various places in this volume, it will be instructive to broaden our sights for a moment and look at the traditional epistemological positions taken with regard to the subject–object question.

In the history of philosophy, psychology, and the other behavioral sciences, there have been a variety of positions advanced on the subject–object question.

Nevertheless, without distorting any particular theory too greatly, it is possible to discern three fundamentally different ways in which the relationship between environment and behavior has been conceptualized—*empiricism* and *environmental determinism, rationalism* and *nativism*, and *interactionalism* and *constructivism* (see Bochenski, 1966). Each class of theories rests on different assumptions about the organism, what factors influence behavior, the nature of reality, and for those which include treatments of knowledge, the way in which knowledge is attained. Each has subsequently led to different formulations of specific questions, research methodologies, and modes of interpretation and explanation of findings.

These three fundamental positions may be thought of as existing on a continuum stretching from, at one extreme, those theories in which experience and behavior are treated as entirely determined by external environmental forces, and, at the other extreme, those theories in which experience and behavior are treated as entirely determined by internal hereditary and biological forces. Not all environmental deterministic and nativistic theories, however, assume or invoke the concept of "representation." Of those which do, there is a shorter subcontinuum from realism to idealism, that is, from those theories which treat knowledge as given entirely through experience to those which treat knowledge as existing prior to experience. By way of contrast for the position taken here, these extreme positions will be looked at in more detail.

The philosophy of *empiricism* (first articulated by the early eighteenth century British philosophers Locke, Berkeley, and Hume) starts from the contention that behavior in general, and knowledge in particular, are strictly under the control of the environment. Reality, in this view, can only be contained in sensation; knowledge of reality is built up from successions of sensations impressed on a *tabula rasa*, a blank slate. Sensory data, however, do not in themselves combine into a composite picture of the environment; relations among the data from various senses are established through habit, custom, and the laws of association.

Positivism and *neopositivism*, as espoused by the nineteenth- and twentieth-century philosophers Comte, Mill, Carnap, Wittgenstein, Reichenbach, and others (see Bochenski, 1966), echoes empiricism and continues the argument that there is but one source of knowledge—sensation—and that through sensation one can only grasp singular and material events. But, whereas the earlier empiricism held that laws were a posteriori, consisting of generalizations from observed singular facts, neopositivism takes the position that laws are a priori, that is, independent of experience; but at the same time they are purely tautological, expressing nothing. They are nothing but "grammatical rules" by which the data of the senses are rendered more manageable. Mind, therefore, and any "content" of mind, such as the representation of the environment, is seen as nothing but an epiphenomena, a copy or reflection of matter. Although knowledge is based on sense data, some neopositivists do acknowledge the role of thought in the organization of these experential data.

Thus, from the viewpoint of *environmental determinism* in twentieth-century science, behavior is defined as consisting of patterns of responses and is assumed to be determined by the environment impinging on a passive organism and selecting and reinforcing particular responses; in short, the world acts on people, and we are the products of forces outside ourselves. The environment is treated as *real*; that is, it is taken to have a real, objective existence independent of the observer. With regard to *representation* and *knowing*, there are three major subclasses of theories: strict *stimulus–response (S–R) theories, mediational S–R theories,* and *cognitive behaviorist theories.* In extreme versions of environmental determinism, such as the S–R theories of classical Pavlovian conditioning and Skinnerian operant conditioning, behavior is treated as determined directly by the environment, and no form of representational activitiy is assumed. In more moderate versions, such as Osgood's (1953, pp. 392–412) mediational S–R theory and Tolman's (1948) cognitive behaviorist theory, respectively, some form of covert representation—"mediational reactions," "expectancies," or "cognitive maps"—is assumed to mediate between stimuli and overt behavioral responses. These mediating responses are said to "represent" the object or situation.

For Osgood, however, the meaning of the term

representation was limited, as he said, "to the objective fact that an organism behaves in such a way as to 'take account of' subsequent events" (1953, p. 394); for Tolman, representation seemed to have additional meaning and refer to abstract ideational processes. Both, however, assume that representational mediating responses or cognitions are built up through sensation arising from experience, and that they are learned and strengthened, or weakened and eliminated, according to the principles of learning and reinforcement. Thus, in both of the classes of environmental deterministic theories that do assume and treat representation, the world is still taken to have a real existence independent of the observer, behavior is assumed to be mediated by covert representations, and representations are treated as formed through sensation and reinforcement.[5]

The opposite viewpoint, the *rationalism* (of the seventeenth-century Continental philosophers Descartes, Spinoza, and Leibniz), starts from the opposite nativist contention that knowledge is given immediately, as an innate idea, before experience; it is a basic act of pure thought that opens all reality to us. Sensation, in this view, gives us nothing but images of individual, particular things; that which is designated by them is given not by sensation but by innate ideas arising from our inherent powers of intellect. Although an external reality is admitted, the form and meaning of reality in general, and the environment in particular, are given a priori; innate concepts precede and determine sense data.

The basic *idealist* thesis, as represented by Brunschwicg and Croce, (see Bochenski, 1966), echoes the rationalist view that knowledge "gives birth to a world which for us is the only world . . . beyond that there is nothing; if there were anything beyond knowledge, its definition would be in terms of the inaccessible and the indeterminable, which would amount to nothing for us" (Brunschwicg, 1897; quoted in Bochenski, 1966, p. 84). Thus, for the strict idealists, the world cannot be reduced to sensation and, in addition, nothing *exists* apart from mind.

Thus, from the point of view of *nativism* in twentieth-century science, behavior is assumed to be determined primarily by genetic and biological factors. Humans are assumed to be born with predispositions to react to the world in predeter-

mined ways. Behavior is treated as the expression or projection of inherited factors in the context of particular environments. Although not all nativistic theories invoke the concept of knowledge (e.g., the ethologists), for those that do, the environment is treated as *ideal*; that is, the existence of an external reality is admitted, but knowledge of the form of reality is taken to be given by the mind in the form of innate ideas before experience (see Chomsky, 1965). In short, the person acts on the world, and the "world" is formed and structured through human consciousness existing before the world. Innate ideas thus precede and determine the form of sense data, and experience in the environment simply allows for the manifestation of these innate ideas in particular instances (e.g., the manifestation of archetypes; see Jung, 1953).[6]

In sum, whereas the environmental determinist position treats behavior as a function primarily of the environment and treats knowledge either as an epiphenomena or, in mediational and cognitive theories, as built up through sensation and reinforcement from the environment, the nativist position treats behavior as basically determined by heredity and biological factors and treats knowledge as innately given before experience.

Although it is certainly not appropriate in the context of this introductory chapter to survey all epistemological and environment-behavior positions, a third major class of postions deserves attention, that of interactionalism, transactionalism, and constructivism initiated by the nineteenth-century German philosopher Immanuel Kant and subsequent neo-Kantians (see Hendle's introduction to Cassirer, 1953, Vol. 1; Bochenski, 1966; B. Kaplan, 1967). This position may be seen as an attempt to bridge the gap or synthesize the above two polarized views on the subject–object question.

Kant argued a position quite different from either empiricism or rationalism. He started with a fundamental distinction between the *matter* or content of knowledge (i.e., that which corresponds to sensation) and the *form* of knowledge (i.e., that which causes the matter to be arranged in a certain order). Reminiscent of empiricism, the *matter* of knowledge is given through experience, but, reminiscent of rationalism, the *form* of knowledge is given a priori.

Knowledge of the world is thus the result of a synthesis that the subject "constructs out of the formless stuff of experience" (Bochenski, 1966, p. 4). The form of knowledge is, therefore, not influenced by the environment; it is constant and universal. For Kant, there were only two pure forms of intuition—space for the outer senses and time for the inner. All other contents of reality are experienced in the context of space and time.

Kant's theory of knowledge is in several ways similar to both the empiricist and rationalist philosophies, but, as both of those schools had one crucial assumption in common that was not held by Kant, it would not be appropriate to see Kant's position (or that of the neo-Kantian philosophers and psychologists who followed him) as *midway* between the two. Whereas both empiricism and rationalism, and subsequently neopositivism and idealism, assume that one can understand the ultimate nature of reality, Kant argued that, since there is no way for us to apprehend the nature of "reality" except through man, it is impossible to completely separate the process of knowing from the resultant knowledge. He argued that there can be no complete understanding of truth in either sense or reason; thus, instead of knowledge ever representing exactly what is real, what we take to be real is a product of the act of knowing—that is, a *construction of thought.*

Kant did allow two means of knowing. Reality might be explored, he said, by scientific method (e.g., physics) or one might explore the processes by which reality is formed by the mind (e.g., genetic epistemology). The two main branches of nineteenth-century philosophy were extensions of these possibilities. Thus, the realists, materialists, positivists, and neopositivists extended the empiricist position to formulate exact principles of mathematical logic and scientific method based on the assumption that reality could be known directly, while the idealists, neo-Kantians, and some phenomenologists worked out systems in an attempt to describe reality solely as the product of intellectual operations. The first school led to an entire denial of mind and the second to the primacy of mind but a denial of knowledge through empirical methods (Bochenski, 1966).

Nevertheless, the *neo-Kantian* theories of knowledge of such philsophers as Bauch, Cornelius, and Cassirer (1944, 1953–1957), and psychologists like Claparède (1943), Werner (1948), Werner and Kaplan (1963), Wapner (1969), and Piaget (1950, 1952, 1954) moved to the more interactive position; all rested on the contention that, far from being strictly a function of the mind, an empirical reality does exist independent of mind, but this reality can only be grasped through the effort of particular minds. Knowledge of "reality" in general, and the environment in particular, is thus seen not as the *grasp* but as the active *construction* of objects. In this view, the subject actively enters into a creative interaction with the environment, the result being a construction or construal of the object by the subject.

This constructivist position on epistemology is related to the more general interactional and transactional positions on environment–behavior relations. In these views, experience and behavior are assumed to be influenced by intraorganismic and extraorganismic factors operating in the context of ongoing transactions of the organism-in-environment. Transactions between the organism and the environment are viewed as mediated by knowledge or cognitive representations of the environment; but these representations are treated as constructed by an active organism through an interaction between inner organismic factors and external situational factors in the context of particular organism-in-environment transactions.

The position is taken that behavior can only be fully understood in the context of the total organism-in-environment situation (see Lewin, 1964) and as a function of the particular ongoing transaction between the two (Mead, 1934; Ittelson, 1960). This transaction includes the organism's construal of past events and future expectations, as well as of particular organismic and situational factors. Far from being passive recipients of external forces moving them to conform to the demands of the external stimulus situation, and far from being driven simply by biological factors and inherited patterns of response, in this view persons are conceived of as active organisms adapting to the world in response to both internal and external demands. It is theorized, therefore, that behavior is more than simply a function either of biological factors or of environmental factors and more than a summation of these two; rather, behavior is an interaction of biological, personality sociocultural, and environmental factors, each in the context of the other and in the context of their mutual interactions.

The position is taken, therefore, that knowledge, or cognitive representations, as a particular form of behavior, far from being simply given through sensation and reinforcement leading to covert responses and far from being given by innate ideas before experience, are formed through an active construction of thought influenced by both the person and the environment and by the transaction between the two. It is assumed in this position, following Kant and contemporary investigators (e.g., Von Uexküll, 1957, in zoology and Whorf, 1956b, in linguistics, to give just two examples), that as it is impossible to separate what is "reality" for an organism from the nature of that organism and its sociocultural context, it is consequently impossible to define "reality" independently of the perceiving-cognizing individual.

Perceiving is that part of the process of living by which each one of us, from his own particular point of view, creates for himself the world in which he has his life experiences . . . . Without taking any metaphysical position regarding the existence of a real world, independent of experience, we can nevertheless assert that the world-as-experienced has no meaning and cannot be defined independent of the experience. The world *as we experience it* is the product of perception, not the cause of it (Ittelson and Cantril, 1960; italics theirs).

Interactionalism, transactionalism, and constructivism are thus attempts to synthesize the two traditionally polarized positions of environmental determinism and nativism. Far from being given simply through sensation and reinforcement on a passive organism, and far from being given by innate ideas before experience, in contemporary constructivist theories, knowledge is treated as constructed through intentional acts by an active organism from the interaction of sensation and reason.[7]

In some respects this position is similar to the mediational and cognitive S-R theories, and may even seem similar to the nativist position. The main similarity with the mediational and cognitive theories is the dual assumption that some form of representation mediates transactions between the organism and the environment and that these mediating representations are important determinants of overt behavior. But, in contrast to these other theories, in the interactional, transactional, and constructivist positions it is assumed, first, that there is a difference between *reacting to* and *knowing about* an object; that is, representational activity in the sense of knowledge is different from other overt behavioral responses (Werner and Kaplan, 1963); second, rather than being formed through the reinforcement of partial responses to stimulation, knowledge is constructed through an intentional act by the organism in response to a full range of inner organismic factors and external situational demands. This position also shares one common assumption with nativism: there is no way to apprehend the nature of reality except through the actions of organisms; but unlike nativism, the interactional, transactional, and constructivist position does not assume that knowledge is innate and simply unfolds with biological maturation, but that it is formed and reformed over the life span.

An important consequence of the transactional-constructivist position, and one which further differentiates it especially from the mediational S-R and cognitive behaviorist views, is that one does not start with a dualistic split between the organism and the environment; rather, what is taken to be the environment is not a reality defined independently of the observer, but a world established or constructed by persons in the context of ongoing transactions in environments.[8]

It seems useful to consider these epistemological positions and the behavioral and social science theories that they have spawned as sets of basic presuppositions about human nature which underlie (explicitly or implicitly) the different current theories on environmental cognition presented in this volume. Until very recently, little attention has been given in most empirical work on environmental cognition (or, for that matter, most work in environment-behavior relations in general) to underlying assumptions about the nature of knowledge, the nature of human beings, the nature of the organism-environment relation, and the implicit models of "man" on which we base our specific ideas and investigations (see Popper, 1965). But whether or not acknowledged outright, assumptions on these issues are implied in *all* research on the human condition. The 1972 Los Angeles symposium on which this book is based was convened to examine these assumptions and the differences among various theoretical systems as they apply particularly to describing and understanding environmental cognition, and this book is dedicated to their continuing critical examination.

HISTORICAL ORIGINS AND DEVELOPMENT OF ENVIRONMENTAL COGNITION

The modern period of interest in environmental cognition originated from the three landmark papers of the sociologist Firey (1945), the geographer Wright (1947), and the psychologist Tolman (1948), and received its major boosts from the groundbreaking books of Kenneth Boulding (1956), Kevin Lynch (1960), and Anselm Strauss (1961). But, since the turn of the century, evidence of interest in various aspects of people's knowledge of the large-scale environment has appeared in the psychological and geographical literature. With the benefits of hindsight, we can even discern the beginnings of an interest in and attempt to understand human beings' knowledge of the environment as far back as the mid-eighteenth century. The earliest report we have been able to find was recorded in 1724 by a French missionary to the Iroquois, P. Lafitau (cited in Claparède, 1943). Lafitau was greatly impressed and recorded detailed observations and thoughts about the ability of the Iroquois and their children to orient themselves and to find their way about in dense regions where the route was unmarked (at least to the French!). The first systematic experiment on human knowledge of the large-scale environment appears to have been conducted by the American scientist Trowbridge (1913), who investigated people's methods of orientation and "imaginary maps." He found what he considered to be two fundamental methods of orientation: a domocentric method in relation to the home, and orientation in terms of the cardinal directions. The first report on aspects of environ-

mental cognition in children seems to have been an observational study by a geographer appropriately named Gulliver (1908). He found that beginning school-aged children could not use the cardinal directions for orientation, but rather consistently relied on their own body position and orientation. Many other early reports concerned memory for places, orientation systems, and disorientation in animal and humans, including ethnographic studies, and the mental working out of spatial relations from routes traveled. A wealth of introspective, ethnographic, observational, and experimental data exists in this literature; it has been underconsidered and underanalyzed (see partial reviews in Claparède, 1943; Hallowell, 1955; Lynch, 1960, Appendix A; Howard and Templeton, 1966, Chapter 10; and Moore, 1973a, Appendix A).

The Current Period: From 1960 On

It has only been since the late 1950s and early 1960s that a concentration of interest in environmental cognition has been noticeable. Although there were several interesting studies during the early part of the century, these studies were for the most part efforts that did not lead to sustained research. Firey, Wright, Tolman, Boulding, Lynch, and Strauss advanced propositions, suggested lines of research, and generally set the stage for the work to follow, but it took a number of years, and in some cases the influence of other writers, before the current period of research was fully launched.

This current period arose from different lines of research conducted in five different disciplines: urban planning, geography, anthropology, sociology, and psychology. During the 1960s these lines of research were, with a few exceptions, quite independent. One can look at most of the writings during this time in any of these fields and see few references to work in the other fields and little evidence of consciously shared theories and methods. For example, in reviewing the literature on the development of environmental cognition, Hart and Moore (1973) found two subbodies of work, both addressing the same issue. One was primarily the work of developmental psychologists concerned with understanding the development of basic spatial concepts, and the other was work from a wide array of geographers, urban planners, and others concerned with knowledge of large-scale environments; for the most part the latter have paid little attention to relevant work in psychology.

In this section, then, we shall briefly look at work on environmental cognition in each of these five disciplines and attempt to show the similarities and differences in the types of issues addressed and the types of methods used.

Urban planning. Kevin Lynch's *Image of the City*. (1960) was perhaps the single most important influence of environmental cognition. Lynch was interested in the *imageability* or *legibility* of different cities, that is, how well different cities and different parts of cities stand out and can be recognized and organized into a coherent pattern in people's minds. He interviewed residents in three major cities—Boston, Jersey City, and Los Angeles. From the residents' sketch maps and answers to particular questions, Lynch integrated the responses into composite maps of the *public image* of each of the cities. Among other things, he suggested that spatial images are comprised of five types of elements: paths, nodes, landmarks, edges, and districts. Lynch's stimulating book has spawned many subsequent studies, especially in urban planning and geography. Urban planning researchers who followed Lynch have been intent mainly to uncover the public images of other cities and parts of cities, for example, cities in the Netherlands (de Jonge, 1962), in Lebanon (Gulick, 1963), parts of Boston (Steinitz, 1968), highways in major American cities (Appleyard, Lynch, and Myer, 1964; Carr and Schissler, 1969), and buildings in Venezuela (Appleyard, 1969b). Recent work by planners has addressed the issues of individual differences in urban imagery (Appleyard, 1969a, 1970b, in press) and alterations of city form to make cities more "imageable" (Lynch, 1960; Carr, 1965; Steinitz, 1968; Appleyard, in press).

Geography. Of the five fields, work on environmental cognition has been most extensive within geography. Interest was first kindled by the lectures and writings of J. K. Wright. Despite his call for investigation of the content of mind, another geographer, Lowenthal (1967), writing 20 years later, noted that the geography of the mid-1960s was still

fairly content to explore the nature of the environment as if this exploration could be divorced from those experiencing and structuring that environment. Lowenthal went on to state:

> We respond to and effect the environment not directly, but through the medium of a personally apprehended milieu. This milieu differs for each of us according to his personal history; and for each of us it varies also with mood, with purpose, and with attentiveness (p. 1).

In geography, interest in man's knowledge of his environment is seen as a subtopic of behavioral geography (Cox and Golledge, 1969; Golledge, Brown, and Williamson, 1972); research on environmental cognition in geography has thus had to wait for the general awakening of interest in subjective aspects of individual behavior in geographic space (i.e., both behavioral and social geography), in distinction to the older traditions of studying the nature of the environment per se (e.g., physical geography and climatography) and the nature of the environment as related to external "objective" measures of group spatial behavior (e.g., urban geography). But in addition to the widening of behavioral and social geography, four particular forces seem to us to have been responsible for the current work: Lynch's book, the massive research program of Gilbert White, Robert Kates, and Ian Burton on the "perception" of natural hazards (White, 1945; Kates, 1962, 1963, 1967; Burton and Kates, 1964), the world of David Lowenthal and Hugh Prince on the "perception" of landscapes (Lowenthal and Prince, 1964, 1965; Lowenthal, 1968), and a variety of approaches to decision making, search behavior, and spatial choice (Wolpert, 1963; Gould, 1963; Golledge, 1967; Golledge and Brown, 1967).

For example, consider briefly the work of White, Kates, Burton, and their colleagues. For over a decade, they have been investigating the relation between people's beliefs about natural hazards and their subsequent behavior. White was interested in why people return to volcano sites and floodplains. It was found that adjustment to possible future hazards, like floods, coastal storms, droughts, and earthquakes, was often suboptimal; that is, the people potentially affected by the hazards took fewer and weaker steps than actually required to minimize or even eliminate the effects. These investigators asked the empirical question as to whether people's responses could be better predicted from their thoughts and interpretations of the situation and of past experiences with hazards than from scientific and technical specifications of actual probabilities of hazards occurring. Such studies were contrasted with the then prevalent U.S. Army Corps of Engineers' cost–benefit analyses and engineering solutions to flood problems. Kates' study of Tennessee floodplains (reported in 1962) was the first study on the perception of hazards. In his inimitable way, he asked how one person's "flood" can be another person's "only high water"?

In another study, Kates (1967) interviewed 371 residents, seasonal home owners, and commercial managers in diverse regional locations along the Atlantic coast from North Carolina to New Hampshire, including people in urban areas with a coastal orientation, in small settlements and fishing ports, and in seasonal recreation areas. He found three main ways in which the threat of severe coastal storms were conceived: (1) 46 percent of the respondents conceived of storms as repetitive events of which they had a reasonable understanding and which apparently they thought that they could not avoid; half of these people expected definite future damage, and most of the other half were uncertain about damage; (2) only 4 percent denied knowledge of the storms and hazards; and (3) perhaps most interestingly, 50 percent conceived of the storms as repetitive events but had some form of mythical or aphoristic explanation which reduced perceived threat for the person, for example: "We get storms once in 90 years; we're not due for another"; or claiming that the storm would not affect them, as "It didn't the last time around"; or, as some elderly couples claimed, that storms are spaced far enough apart to assure security (Kates, 1967, p. 67).

Stimulated by Kates, Lowenthal, Wright, and others, there have been four main lines of geographical research on environmental cognition: studies of contemporary conceptions of aspects of the spatial environment, studies of conceptions of the environment over historical time, studies of cognition of the environment across different cultures, and studies of cognition of various social groups. The largest body

of work has addressed the issue of *contemporary conceptions* of and *attitudes* toward different environments, such as landscapes (e.g., Lowenthal and Prince, 1964, 1965), outdoor recreation areas (e.g., Shafer, 1969), wilderness areas (e.g., Lucas, 1963), cities (Zannaras, 1974; Golledge, Rivizzigno, and Spector, 1975a, b), and larger geographic regions (e.g., Kates, 1962, 1967). In a recent review of this work, Downs (1970b) has suggested that three approaches can be distinguished within this line of work: *structural, evaluative,* and *preferential* approaches. In the structural approach, the question is what environmental information is selected and stored in people's minds and how is it organized (e.g., Lucas, 1963 on people's conceptions of the wilderness, and Golledge et al., 1975, on the cognitive configuration of cities). The evaluative approach focuses on the issue of what factors people consider important about their environment and how they employ them in making spatial decisions (e.g., Kates, 1967). Finally, in the preferential approach, the question is how people assess a set of spatially differentiated objects in relation to a specified behavioral objective (e.g., Gould, 1970b, on people's preferences for various states in the United States).

A second line or research on environmental cognition in geography concerns changing conceptions of the environment as seen over historical time, the *geosophy* research of which Wright and Lowenthal have written. For example, Bowden (1971), using literary sources, studied the various conceptions of the western American interior held by the American public during the nineteenth century, and the relation between changes in these images and phases of migration during this same period. Among other things, he found two conflicting images—one of a vast and arid "Great American Desert" held by the Eastern elite, and one of a rich grazing land, the "Plains," a potential "Garden of the World" held by common people everywhere and by the Western elite. The pressures for expansion of the country westward and the subsequent pushing of the frontier ever further west led to a westward retreat of the desert image in the minds of the Eastern elite and ultimately to its dissolution. However, as Bowden claims, a corollary legend arose just prior to the American Civil

War, that of a renewed Great American Desert, but this time in the minds of the common person influenced by bold stories told by returning adventurers (see also Bowden, 1969, 1973, 1975; Heathcote, 1969; Allen, 1971, 1972; Jackson, 1970).

A third line of research is *ethnogeography*, the overall world view of people of different cultures with emphasis on their "understanding of . . . environmental processes and patterns, the spatial organization they mentally . . . impose on the landscape, their repertoire of resource managing techniques, and their rationale for applying techniques to different portions of the environment" (Knight, 1971). Thus, for example, Blaut, Harman, and Moerman (1959) studied cultural determinants of soil erosion and conservation in Jamaica and found that the chief hindrance to soil conservation in the mountains of Jamaica is lack of awareness on the part of farmers that serious erosion exists or, alternatively, that anything can be done about it.

Finally, there is discernable at least one other major stream of thought on the phenomena now called environmental cognition. Martyn Bowden has suggested (personal communication) that there is a stream which he calls "ecological relativism" emanating from the French sociologist, Vidal de la Blanche (see Buttimer, 1971) through the American scholar and writer on landscapes, J. B. Jackson (1970), which has influenced, among others, the Lowenthal and Prince work already mentioned and, most especially, Buttimer's recent work (e.g., 1968, 1969, 1971, 1972). Each of these writers is interested in people's feelings of connectedness with and appreciation of the sociophysical environment about them.

Before leaving this discussion of the geographical study of environmental cognition, two bifurcations should be noted. There is a mild separation between those who would focus on the *individual*, where group images are assumed to be a sum of individual images (e.g., Kates, 1967) and those who would focus on the *social unit*, assuming that individual conceptions are not independent from each other but rather are derived from the prevailing group conception (e.g., Buttimer, 1972). There is a sharper separation between two essentially different methods of conducting research, between those whose work is based on interviews, questionnaires, scales, and other *quantitatively* scored survey research measures (e.g., Kates, 1967; Lucas, 1963; Shafer, 1969), and those whose work is based on *qualitative* analyses of literature and other written and introspective documents (e.g., Lowenthal, 1961; Lowenthal and Prince, 1964, 1965; Bowden, 1971; Seamon, 1972; Tuan, 1974). Both methods may be used, but the disagreement seems to be between those who are concerned that survey research methods, although "objectively" quantifiable, may prevent the investigator from appreciating the richness and multiple interconnectedness of phenomena, versus those who are concerned that content analyses, while rich, may be overfashioned by the eyes and biases of the investigator and may, therefore, be nonreliable and nonrepeatable. Looked at in total, the vast majority of the work conducted in geography has focused on conceptions of different specific geographic environments. Almost no attention has been given to systematizations of individual differences or to the question of the development of conceptions of different environments; exceptions include the work of Blaut, Stea, and their colleagues on the development of place perception (see Blaut and Stea, 1969; see also Chapter 9) and the work of Golledge and his colleagues on learning about cities and on individual differences in structuring cognized environments (Golledge et al., 1975; Rivizzigno, 1975).

Anthropology. Quite closely related to ethnogeography is the study of cognitive anthropology, the "cross-cultural comparisons of different cognitive systems" (see Romney and D'Androde, 1964; Tyler, 1969). A prime example of cognitive anthropology applied to the study of environmental systems is the study of *ethnosemantics*, which, in the words of one anthropologist, "seeks through interview, observation, and, when possible, experiment, to discover some part of the system of meanings by which people organize the world . . . since the major realization of this cognition is in the words people speak, semantics is considered an integral part of ethnography" (Kay, 1970, p. 19; see also Knight, 1971). Thus, certain students of ethnosemantics have focused on the relation of language to conceptions of the environment. For example, Conklin (1967a; see also Chapter 20) has studied the conceptual components of the indigenous system of agriculture of the Ifugao in the Philippines as these components are seen by the people of the culture themselves. Among other things, Conklin found that the Ifugao conceive of their land in terms of eight different types of land cover formations, each of which has a characteristic pattern of use and change.

Although the work on cognitive anthropology is in many respects different from the mainstream of current environmental cognition work in industrialized Western culture, the issue addressed is essentially the same; the methods and findings of the "new ethnographers" are potentially of great value to the environment–behavior researcher interested in studies of environmental cognitive representations in any culture or subculture.[9]

Sociology. Although predated by Firey's (1945) studies of city symbolism, Anselm Strauss's *Images of the American City* (1961) certainly coalesced ideas and gave direction to subsequent work from a sociological perspective on the question of what people "think and have thought of their cities." However, as Strauss (1968) has shown, sociological interest in what people think about the cities in which they live has roots that go back at least as far as Horace Greeley's lectures of 1850, "Coming to the City," or rather, staying away from the city, which was already thought of as "overcrowded and full of misery" (Greeley, 1850; reprinted in Strauss, 1968, p. 166). Strauss has worked from the premise that it is not possible to fully understand social behavior in cities or the process of urbanization without at the same time understanding what people think of their cities. He and subsequent sociologists are interested in the total, holistic fabric of the structure, function, and meaning of urban and nonurban environments. As with the methodological bifurcation in geography, some sociologists prefer literary sources (e.g., Strauss, 1961, 1968), and others survey research methods (e.g., Orleans, 1973; Orleans and Schmidt, 1972).

Psychology. Finally, we come to psychology, which, of the five disciplines here considered, has so far contributed the least to our knowledge of people's conceptions specifically of the large-scale environment, although this book is replete with new work by

psychologists. Most of the work in the other fields has been addressed to questions of the content of specific conceptions of the environment or even of specified environments. Psychology has been more concerned with the construction of overall, general, *explanatory theories* than any of these other fields; this may well account for the lesser degree of interest in the nature of cognition specifically of the large-scale environment. However, as Kaplan (1973b) has argued, "the structure underlying the spatial map of the world . . . is not different from the structure that underlies *all* cognitive processes" (see also Chapter 2). Attempts have been made to show that certain current major theories of psychology (e.g., the general developmental theory of Piaget and the constructive alternativism of Kelly) fit certain portions of the available data on environmental cognition (Moore, 1972b; see also Chapters 6 and 12).

Some psychogeographic work has appeared recently on the development of children's knowledge of the spatial layout of neighborhoods (Rand, 1969; Moore, 1975a), of cities (Blaut and Stea, 1971; Stea and Blaut, 1973a, 1973b; Moore, 1973a, 1973b; see also Chapters 4, 9, 10, 12, 13, 14), and of the development of children's understanding of the multiple levels of meaning in houses (Rand, 1972).

A number of other psychological studies on the representation of the large-scale environment have been conducted by the British environmental psychologist Lee (1964, 1968, 1970) on the representation of the "living space" of urban neighborhoods and of conceptual distances, by Follini (1966) on microgenetic developmental shifts in the organization of representations of an unfamiliar environment, and by Gittins (1969) on aesthetic versus scientific modes of representing an unfamiliar city. Other recent psychological studies include the following: ethnic differences (Maurer and Baxter, 1972), native versus nonnative differences (Francescato and Mebane, 1973), cognitive mapping and spatial thinking (Bycroft, 1974; Moore, 1975a), the construction of urban spatial images and rule elaboration (Pailhouse, 1970, 1971, 1972), the work of Pick and his students on children's knowledge of spatial layout (Pick, 1972; Pick et al., 1973; Kosslyn et al., 1973; see also Chapter 13), and the recent work of Wapner and his colleagues on age and value differences in the construal of various large-scale environments (Kaplan, Wapner, and Cohen, 1975).

These five somewhat independent lines of investigation from the behavioral and social sciences have only recently begun to come together as researchers from each of the disciplines have seen communalities among their various interests, conceptualizations, and methods, and have begun actively to share approaches and findings. There are still large differences in such things as the emphasis on building and testing general theory versus accumulating data, the focus on environmental differences versus individual and group differences, on qualitative versus quantitative methods, and so on, but there has recently appeared to be concerted efforts from many quarters to understand the variations in approach across disciplines and to look for synthesis in both theory and method (see Chapter 18).

THE FUTURE OF ENVIRONMENTAL COGNITION THEORY AND RESEARCH

The first steps in imposing order onto individual and disciplinary research efforts on environmental knowing is the development of mutual understanding; to achieve this, it is necessary to assume there are common elements of interest and similar underlying assumptions, principles, and hypotheses, and the results of testing hypotheses can be integrated into a broad schema to define aims for future integrative research. Once an embryonic formalistic or psuedo-formalistic structure emerges, concepts and content can be more rigidly specified and more uniformly accepted, and the shape of this multidisciplinary field of interest may take form. Although research work on the cognition of large-scale environments has grown rapidly in each of the disciplines mentioned above, there has been to date only scattered attention paid to possible theoretical bases for researchers interested in these phenomena (e.g., the 1972 Los Angeles symposium). We have shown that this "void" is not really as empty as is generally imagined; the articulation of a series of theories in Part I and theoretical approaches in Part II of this book indicates that a surprisingly high level of development of

theory is emerging for this area of interest. What is of concern, however, is that, in spite of the theory that is available, relatively little has yet been used by most researchers in environmental knowing. What we see as one of the current pitfalls, then, is a certain degree of reluctance to use theories that may be relevant to help us understand environmental cognition. We hope that the efforts summarized in this book will help to circumvent this particular problem.

A second and very obvious stumbling block to continued development of environmental cognition relates to the fundamental methodological problem of trying to determine what people know about environments. There are no universally accepted methods and techniques for extracting environmental cognitions at this point in time, although many of the methods discussed in Part III are becoming more widely accepted. In fact, this is an area in which there is potential for tremendous growth and improvement, that is, experimentation with new and innovative methods for extracting environmental information and for representing it in a constructive, useful, and understandable form.

Perhaps the greatest stumbling block of all, however, is simply the lack of data. When we deal with cognitions of large-scale external environments, we must of necessity deal with individuals. There is no census to which we can turn for information, no directory that we can use to guide our selection of subjects or of environmental information, and no large data banks of environmental cognitions in existence; we cannot use many of our highly developed technical skills for recording the world of objective reality to find out what is in the minds of people. Consequently, most research activity in this area has had to and will have to depend on survey-research-type methods in which responses are elicited from individuals and groups. When one realizes this problem, one automatically realizes a following problem: in attempting to extract information from individuals, the type and nature of the information we extract will depend very much on the method that we use to obtain this information.

In Part III Briggs and Cadwallader show how using different extraction procedures and different analytical methods on the same set of data produces different results. Quite obviously, those interested in environmental cognition research have a tremendous task in front of them in trying to determine which of the many and varied results they get are legitimate, interpretable, useful, and meaningful. It seems, therefore, that environmental cognition research is in for an extended period of search-type analyses in which varied experimental designs, external representational procedures, and analytical methods will be tried and tested again and again until a consensus on what experimental designs are useful and meaningful and on what methods are acceptable has been produced.

The next question that concerns us is the question of what is on the theoretical, conceptual, and methodological horizons for research in this area—where are the leading edges? Quite obviously, we have a number of embryonic theories relating to cognition of large-scale external environments that can provide good building blocks for future investigation and interpretation. What is even more important is that cognitive psychological theory generally is progressing, and there should be considerable spillover from this progress onto the area of environmental cognition. It further seems that as more and more representatives of different disciplines become interested in this area of knowledge they will bring to bear a greater range of background theories and fundamental knowledge about human nature, the environment, and the interface between the two.

It would be only reasonable to suggest that part of the fairly rapid development of theory in this area of environmental cognition is due to the widespread nature of interdisciplinary contact and the free and rapid exchange of ideas among researchers from different disciplines interested in the area. This exchange has facilitated the development of theoretical constructs that are comprehensive rather than discipline bound, general rather than specific; they encourage individuals to think rigorously in specified channels rather than randomly in wide screens, clarify the inferential procedures needed to advance knowledge and understandings in this area, and at the same time help to specify the degree of reliability and objectivity that the accumulating knowledge in the area can achieve. Since the field is still relatively embryonic, however, it is quite possible that we will see

an abundance of rich *conceptualizations* related to different aspects of environmental cognition in the immediate future. These conceptualizations may take the form of heuristic models, which, in turn, may guide research for several years to come. As each conceptualization or heuristic is further examined, refined, and modified, it should take on more and more of the characteristics of theory. Associated with the probable growth of conceptualizations, there should be increased varieties of methods used both in the process of extracting environmental information and in terms of representing and analyzing it. We are confident that there are in existence a sufficient range of methodologies to allow the continued pursuit of knowledge in this area for some time to come, but we also recognize the fact that new methodologies may of necessity be spawned and developed as the rate of knowledge in the field increases.

Finally, what may result from continued research activity in the area of environmental cognition and environmental knowing? First, continued activity in this area will contribute to the fundamental stock of knowledge of humankind. A considerable amount of basic research is going on in this area and will continue to be necessary for the development of the field and the ordering of its knowledge. This basic research will primarily be oriented to the organization of knowledge and theories and the development of methodologies that will help refine and reformulate such theories. Of equally great importance, we hope that the explosion of knowledge in this area will increase our general level of understanding of the relationship between people and their environment. In particular, we recognize the need to gain a greater comprehension of how people use their environments, and Robert Kates's question haunts us: What more do we know about environmental experience, behavior, and use from the decade or so of studies on environmental knowing? Various papers in this book concentrate on different external environments that are available to us—for example, the urban social environments of large cities, the environment of small towns, rural environments, wilderness environments, small-scale local areas, large-scale regions, and so on. Fundamentally, we accept the principle that peoples' cognitions of an environment are determined to a large extent by what is there to be cognized, but that it is the cognition itself rather than the actual physical presences in external environments that determine how people behave. If we can more completely understand how people behave through determining how they cognize external environments, we may have made a significant step toward being able to more satisfactorily interpret, use, and plan natural and built environments.

In short, the long-run aim of research in this area is to use the knowledge that we acquire to give us an increased ability to manipulate external environments for the betterment of humankind. If this aim is achieved in even a very slight respect, the massive effort that is being directed into this area of research will be justified.

NOTES

1. Now also at the School of Architecture and Urban Planning, University of Wisconsin, Milwaukee.

2. There is now a sizable body of research specifically on how and what people visually perceive in the physical environment. Some of the work spawned by Lynch has looked at visual perception and memory of urban spaces, roadways, and buildings (e.g., Lynch and Rivlin, 1959; Appleyard et al., 1964; Appleyard, 1969a; Carr and Schissler, 1969). More experimental work on environmental perception includes Jones (1972), Barnett (1974), Hesselgren (1971), Garling (1969a, 1969b, 1970a, 1970b), Harrison (1971), and Hayward and Franklin (1974).

3. At times in this book, other terms have been used to refer to these internal cognitive processes, but as best we can tell the following terms are all meant to be roughly synonymous: knowledge, cognition, cognitive representation, impression, image, place perspective, and constructs.

4. The neurophysiologist Hebb (1949) addresses the issue of underlying processes in spatial cognition in discussing the similarity between how a rat learns a maze and how people learn the spatial layout of a city (pp. 134–139). He argues that in neither case is it necessary to have an "accurate picture" of the environment, only that a "goal-concept" dominate

and direct a neurological "phase-sequence," and that each part of the route being traversed in the environment reliably evoke the next phase sequence. He states that on first entering a new area one is likely to have a confused "image of the total situation." This primitive neurological phase sequence seems to be similar to Piaget's sensorimotor schema (see Chapter 12). Something like more complex phase sequences may underlie higher-order cognitive representations (see Chapter 2).

5. Considerable research in the study of environment-behavior relations has followed implicitly or explicitly from the environmental determinist position (see, e.g., Barker, 1968; much of the work reviewed in Craik, 1970a; and much of the work in the collected readings of Proshansky et al., 1970, Gutman, 1972, and Wohlwill and Carson, 1972; see also Chapter 35). This position follows from "behaviorism" in psychology and sociology and from "environmentalism" in geography and anthropology. In environment-behavior studies, it has led to questions on such subjects as the stimulus properties of the environment, human responses to different environments, and the impact of different environments on human behavior. The most extreme version of this view seems to be that advanced by the behaviorist designer Studer (1967, 1969), who advocates the manipulation of behavior by designed changes in the environment. Some attention has been addressed to environmental cognition from this viewpoint, the most explicit of which is perhaps that of Golledge and his students, who have investigated, for example, how a "learned model of a city" is built up through "perception of those elements that have a high probability of occurrence in the immediate environment" (Golledge and Zannaras, 1973, pp. 112–113; Golledge et al., 1969; Golledge et al., 1975; see also Chapters 29, 30, and 31).

6. In environment-behavior relations, there is only a small body of work emanating from the nativist position. In fact, from this perspective, the study of the relation between people and their environment is of limited interest, for it is assumed that behavior is not in any important ways affected by the environment. The only questions that might be

asked concern the spatial distribution of behavior over an essentially "frictionless" environment, what limits, if any, the environment places on behavior, and how people alter the environment to conform to behavior. The only strong proponents of this position in environment–behavior relations seem to be a few ethologists writing on human territoriality (e.g., Ardrey, 1966; Lorenz, 1966) who see spatial behavior as a clear expression of inherited animal instincts "characteristic of our species as a whole, to be shaped but not determined by environment and experience, and to be a consequence not of human choice but of evolutionary inheritance" (Ardrey, 1966, p. ix). Most investigators of human territoriality, however, treat it as a mixture of physiochemical inheritance, socialization, and particular situational factors (see reviews by Altman, 1970; Soja, 1971; Alexander and Tinkle, 1968; and Griffin, 1969). A quasi-nativist view is advanced by Alexander and Poyner (1970) who argue that the design of the environment should fit what they call "natural human tendencies," and who suggest ethological-like observation methods to discover the expression of these tendencies in different environmental contexts. Other than some early geographers who believed that the sense of direction was vestigial (see Howard and Templeton, 1966, Chapter 10), there do not appear to be any strict nativists among investigators of environmental cognition.

7. The interactional and transactional approaches to environment–behavior relations are the most recent of the three epistemological positions discussed here. For an excellent and readable philosophic treatment of transactionalism in environment–behavior relations, see Tibbetts (1971, 1972). Little empirical work has yet emanated from this perspective, although several theoretical papers have recently appeared that have indicated lines of empirical investigation (e.g., Ittelson 1970, 1973; Ittelson et al., 1975; Rand 1972; Wapner et al., 1973; Kaplan et al., 1975; Moore, 1975a; see also Chapter 12). A considerably greater body of work, including much of the research on environmental cognition has *implicitly* followed from variations on the interactional and constructivist notions.

It should be pointed out that interactional, transactional, and constructivist notions do not necessarily follow hand in hand; it is entirely possible to have, for example, a nonconstructivist interactional position (e.g., Wohlwill, 1962, who suggests the possibility of accounting for perceptual constancy in terms of "the role of stimulus variables such as amount of surplus cues, or redundant information, in interaction with organismic variables such as age," p. 89).

8. A more extreme position on the empiricist–nativist dimension underlying these comparisons is the phenomenological view, which in a nutshell, holds that "persons are immersed in the world which is simultaneously immersed in persons." Rejecting a strictly cognitive or personality-emotive model of human behavior, the phenomenological position aims at the uncovering and accurate description of the "holistic happening of experiencer-experiencing-thing as it manifests itself in experiential fashion, public or private" (David Seamon, personal communication, 1975). For the phenomenological perspective on environment–behavior–experience relations, see especially, Relph (1970), Tuan (1971, 1974), Buttimer (1974), and Chapters 18, 23, and 26.

9. It should be noted here that the inclusion of ethnosemantics within this review of environmental cognition is not due to this similarity being acknowledged in the anthropological literature (for the most part, students of ethnosemantics seem unaware of similar work being conducted under the label of environmental cognition). However, from our reading of these various literatures, the questions being raised are essentially the same. The assumptions and methods vary greatly for a variety of reasons, most often related to the cultural background of the field and the training of its students. It is interesting, however, that at least one of the best known ethnosemanticists, Harold Conklin does acknowledge the conceptual similarity between his work and that of the urban planner Lynch and of the psychologist Piaget (personal communication), lending support to the contention that these five subfields are essentially approaching the same intellectual problem.

PART I

THEORIES AND
EMPIRICAL RESEARCH

In many disciplines the continuing development of knowledge has had, as its principal concern, the binding together of hypothesis and laws into systems of theories. As Bergmann (1958) put it,

As a science develops, a store of laws and concepts accumulates together with an awareness of some connections, deductive among the laws, definitional among the concepts . . . . At a certain point in the development it pays to arrange this material into theory (p. 35).

A well-validated theory systematizes or logically interconnects isolated knowledge through a system of hypotheses, gives an explanation or account of these hypotheses, and serves as an integrating mechanism for existing knowledge in its domain. Many social and behavioral "theories" are not well validated; rather, they are embryonic in nature and look more like sets of loosely connected hypotheses—some of which may be only partially tested. Many of these "theories" will not progress beyond this point, an argument discussed in more detail in Chapter 6. Like the well-formed theories of physical science, however, these "theories" aim at guiding the search for new knowledge by drawing attention to what has been overlooked in the past, discovering past errors, ambiguities, and gaps, and helping to ensure that the

occurrence of these in the future is minimized. Despite recent pressure (on many sides) for academics to become more interested in the "empirical problems of the real world," there is no doubt in our minds that meaningful research must rely either on a sound existing theoretical base (at least as sound a base as a discipline can provide) or on an integrated and legitimate sequence of hypotheses that require testing in well-defined experimental designs to produce meaningful results.

To support this position, let us discuss briefly some of the ways that theories contribute to research and understanding. As Mario Bunge (1967) has suggested,

The childhood of every science is characterized by its concentration on the search for singular data, classifications, relevant variables, and isolated hypotheses establishing relationships among these variables, as well as accounting for those data. As long as a science remains in this semi-empirical stage it lacks logical unity: a formula in one department is a self-contained idea that cannot be logically related to formulas in other departments of a science (p. 380–381).

Theories organize and systematize bodies of knowledge by carefully itemizing the relationships between bits of knowledge, whether these be statements of fact or law like statements. Once the basic theorized relationships are made clear, further knowledge accumulates by unpacking sets of *interrelationships* among the bits of knowledge and examining their meaning and use. This procedure is generally known as hypothetico-deductive reasoning. If a theory about a given area of knowledge exists, it serves as a datum to which are referred new facts and new sets of relationships. Thus, research findings can be examined for meaning and significance by relating them to existing theory.

The problems faced in theory construction and model building for research in the area of environmental knowing are similar to those facing social scientists generally. Two of the most fundamental are defining the *domain* of a theory and identifying its *universe of discourse* (or the time independence of its relations). Other common problems include *operationalizing concepts* used in the theory and models derived from it, and formalizing the *direction and nature* of the *logical deductive nets* included in the theory.

Problems peculiar to researchers attempting to search for theory related to environmental cognition arise from the fact that they must be interested not only in the external sociophysical environment and the internalizing of human actions, but also with the interface between the two. This raises the problems of how to comprehend and how to represent cognitive and physical worlds. This book is concerned with these problems, and Part I focuses specifically on a selection of theoretical approaches that are relevant to their solution.

Since Part I presents a number of theoretical positions and supporting empirical evidence, let us concentrate for a moment on the interface between theories and empirical evidence. A fundamental dilemma arises when examining this interface:

> The use of theoretical terms in science gives rise to a perplexing problem: Why should science resort to the assumption of hypothetical entities when it is interested in establishing predictive and explanatory connections among observables? (Hempel, 1965, p. 179).

The solution to this dilemma appears to lie in the fact that, to make a meaningful transition from observable data to prediction in terms of observables, there needs to be systematic connections effected by statements making reference to nonobservables. In physics, connections are made between, say, the volume and weight of solids and liquids by referring to the hypothetical entity of "specific gravity." Environmental cognition researchers make at least as much use of nonobservable relations as do physicists; to think about theoretical connections, however, they make a detour through a domain of not directly observable things, events, and characteristics, all of which make it harder to specify the nature of the connection between observables and prediction. Hempel (1965) warns us that a "deductive system can function as a theory in empirical science only if it has been given an *interpretation* by reference to empirical phenomena" (p. 184; italics his). Thus, we find ourselves caught between, on the one hand, a need to examine the interface between empirical evidence and theory, and, on the other hand, a limitation in our attempts to construct theory by not yet being able to clearly define the systematic connections between observables and nonobservables.

To summarize our arguments at this stage, then, we suggest that the stuff from which things such as environmental cognitions, human relations, and social structures are made is not as intuitively evident as are the parameters and variables (such as length, time, and force) available to the physical scientist. Consequently, efforts must be made to distill or abstract this stuff from innumerable events; the selection of events used to comprehend cognitive phenomena depends to a large extent on one's experiences, cultural background, and biases. Despite these limitations, attempts are made to select *fundamental entities* within the field of interest, but the process of selection is frequently so involved, laborious and difficult that it constitutes the bulk of a research effort. It is not surprising, therefore, that researchers may hardly ever get round to stating postulates, let along formalizing a theory in the strict philosophical sense of the word. Much time is spent relating vocabulary terms to some type of referent, which must in turn be abstracted from a rich variety of events, generalizations, and relations. By the time some of these referents have been abstracted and named, there is already a bulky system in existence, which makes onerous the task of seeking out laws and combining these into theories. In some disciplines the task is hardly ever begun. It seems to us to be very much a state of the art of environmental cognition research that many researchers are still "searching for referrents" and trying to distill from an immense amount of data some critical concepts, terms, and elements. Consequently, the bulk of research in this area has been empirical, and comparatively little has focused on theory. This conclusion is somewhat pessimistic, but let us stress that, while only a comparatively small *volume* of work has concentrated on theory, extraordinarily rich results have already been achieved, as the theoretical essays of Part I illustrate.

Four leading theories of environmental cognition are presented along with supporting research. Each theory is derived primarily from psychological theories of cognition and intelligence, although two are based as much on current notions from evolutionary theory and information theory.

Section 1 concentrates on an information-processing approach to environmental cognition. The position paper, written by Stephen Kaplan, is based on current notions of evolutionary theory combined with information-processing theory. Kaplan's paper is one of a series (Kaplan, 1970, 1972, 1973b), each of which builds both theoretically and practically on the results and constructs of his prior theorizing. His paper presented at the 1972 EDRA symposium in Los Angeles formalized the basic structure of Chapter 2, and consequent discussions of reformulated ideas at the 1973 Blacksburg symposium helped to produce the highly articulated and coordinated theoretical position presented here. Empirical research tied directly into Kaplan's theory of adaptation, structure, and knowing is exemplified by the work of his colleagues, Rachel Kaplan and Ann Devlin. In Chapter 3, Rachel Kaplan comments on an extensive ongoing research project associated with the comprehension of natural areas. Individual reactions toward adapting to and learning about natural environmental systems are carefully studied and analyzed. In Chapter 4, theoretical concepts related to the nature of environmental learning are tested by Ann Devlin in the context of migrants new to urban areas.

The papers in Section 1 are of considerable interest in that they all concentrate on the acquisition of en-

vironmental knowledge by adult humans. In other words, their subject populations and the level at which the theories are written concern individuals who have the ability to think in abstract relational terms and to quickly and successfully cope with the business of learning about new environments. In each case, the author has shown that individuals do learn quickly about new environments, and, despite the fact that this learning takes place in the presence of many mixed emotions, they are capable of adapting to existence in their environment in a relatively short period of time. Apparently, the exigencies of everyday living force us to learn quickly to operate in and adapt to both external physical environments and the multitude of sociocultural and economic environments in which we find ourselves. Slowness in assimilating information or adapting to environments is branded as a form of individual deficiency and is seen by societies as something that needs remedying.

In Section 2 the potential usefulness of personal construct theory in environmental cognition is examined. The methodological techniques associated with this theory have attracted considerable attention by active researchers in Europe and North America alike. The researchers come from a variety of fields, as is evidenced by the contributors to this section—a geographer, an architect, and a psychologist. In the position paper, Roger Downs describes the personal construct approach as a well-developed *Theory*. In fact, he takes considerable pains to distinguish between the status of this *Theory* and other less well developed *theories* used in research in this area. In his discussion in Chapter 7 of the use of personal construct theory in two different experimental situations, Basil Honikman reemphasizes the importance of the theory, its essential propositions, and a number of its principal corollaries. He also stresses (as does Downs) the significance of the fact that the theory has a well-developed methodology associated with it, allowing for exhaustive testing of the assumptions underlying the theory and the logical connections made between concepts and theory.

Section 3 relates specifically to learning about large-scale spatial environments. In the position paper David Stea emphasizes the spatial components in the learning process and, in turn, insists that learning about large-scale environments is a process that is distinguished from other classical learning theories in terms of both the spacio-temporal scale over which learning takes place and the complexity of variables that are integrated into understanding and using information obtained from large-scale environments. Like Chapter 2, Stea's paper is the result of a number of years of intense experimental work and the constant reassessment of his central ideas in the light of interdisciplinary contacts (e.g., Stea, 1967, 1969c, 1969d; Stea and Blaut, 1973a, 1973b; Blaut and Stea, 1971). Much of his own experience in disciplines such as psychology, engineering, architecture, geography, and planning are well illustrated in the breadth with which his position is argued and presented. The significance of the departure from classical psychological learning theories as evidenced in Stea's approach is exemplified in the empirical research complementing his paper.

Frank Klett and David Alpaugh provide a case study of learning in a large-scale environment; as they point out it is extremely difficult to try to confine their interpretation of the learning experience to any of the existing psychological learning theories or to describe it in terms of any of the existing mathematical models of learning. While each author agrees that the learning process is evident and is fundamental in allowing people to exist in environments, it is obvious that their theory is developed in complex real-world situations rather than under controlled laboratory conditions. This concern with the richness of detail and complexity in large-scale environments is typical of a great volume of work related to environmental knowing, and is a substantial departure from the more controlled microscale experiments usually associated with the development of classical psychological learning theories.

Finally, in Section 4, Gary Moore continues his attempt to construct a cognitive-developmental theory of how children and adults come to know the sociophysical environment. His theoretical and empirical work has been based in large part on deductions from the major developmental theories of Piaget and Werner, although a number of other concepts have come from constructivism in philosophy, transactionalism in psychology, and from neighboring disciplines. He describes some of the main presuppositions of such a theory as applied to knowing large-scale environments, and discusses a range of recently completed research to illustrate certain of the concepts and hypotheses. Supporting evidence is presented in the empirical case studies by Linda Acredolo (Chapter 13) and by Robert Beck and Denis Wood (Chapter 14).

Linda Acredolo has done careful experiments on the smaller-scale environments of rooms to test the proposition that there are three principal developmental stages in coming to know large-scale physical environments. Robert Beck and Denis Wood, on the other hand, have investigated in great detail the changes in cognitive structures as American teen-agers come to know cities in Europe like London, Paris, and Rome. Both chapters are based on recently completed Ph.D. dissertations, and represent only part of the extensive data each team of investigators has collected, analyzed, and interpreted.

Finally, in Chapter 15, Herbert Pick, Jr., who has himself undertaken considerable research on cognitive mapping using a constructivist–transactional viewpoint, summarizes the papers in this section and comments on the efficacy of current approaches to the development of a general theory of environmental knowing.

2

ADAPTATION, STRUCTURE, AND KNOWLEDGE[1]

Stephen Kaplan

Departments of Psychology and
   Computer and Communication Sciences
University of Michigan

AN INTRODUCTION FOR READERS NOT PLANNING TO READ THIS PAPER

Some years ago there was a newspaper report of a student who decided to travel the several hundred miles between his college and home by bicycle. Upon reaching his destination he announced with some surprise that the country was covered with tiny crossroad towns consisting of one filling station and one grocery store. Clearly, a former expressway habitué had undergone a change in his cognitive map. But he also experienced a change in his beliefs. One might even say that he corrected a prejudice.

The point is that cognitive maps, beliefs, even prejudices are not clearly separable portions of the cognitive apparatus. Rather, they are all cases in which an individual possesses an internal model of a portion of his environment. This internal model presumably arose out of experience (either direct or vicarious). It serves as a basis for imagination and thought. It can be manipulated by the individual in whose head it resides and thus provides a basis for decision and action.

Given this very general description, one might rightly suspect that internal models are rather per-

vasive. A few examples might underscore both their diversity and their influence in determining behavior:

1. The imperialist who believes that natives must be treated like children.
2. The farmer who believes that natural hazards are God's will and not subject to human intervention.
3. The industrialist who believes that people dislike work and thus must be forced and coerced into doing it.
4. The traffic engineer who believes that people want to get from one point to another as rapidly as possible (and could care less what they see along the way).

Note that even the reaction of an individual to a behavior setting must be based on an internal model. People with no prior experience in the particular setting may not know how to act (since they lack an internal model); people with prior experience can describe appropriate behavior in that setting without even being there. Those who argue that the "environment is not in the head" should not be too hasty. Certainly they are correct on technical grounds; nonetheless, an internal model of the environment does reside in the head. It can play a central role in the interpretation of real environments and thus in the resulting behavior.

ON FUNCTIONAL REQUIREMENTS
AND THE ROLE OF MECHANISM

The concept of cognitive maps is a fascinating one and shows signs of taking hold in a variety of fields: anthropology (Fischer, 1971), planning (Greenbie, 1974), education (Reif, 1974), and sociology (Suttles, 1972), as well as psychology and geography (Downs and Stea, 1973a; Gould and White, 1974). But at present the idea that people have a map in their heads remains essentially a metaphor. It is not yet entirely clear in what ways this knowledge of the environment is like a map or, indeed, whether it has enough in common with a map to merit the name. Yet the idea is sufficiently attractive that it is hard to resist the challenge to take the next step, to move from metaphor to mechanism. "Mechanism" is used here in the sense of the machinery that underlies the observed phenomena, in other words, the specification of how it is constructed and how it works. This paper is a continuation of a search for a mechanism that began in "Cognitive Maps in Perception and Thought" (Kaplan, 1973b). The approach I have taken focuses on information processing viewed in its broadest sense of comprehending the environment, evaluating it, planning about it, and deciding on appropriate actions to carry out in it.

A point of view that considers mechanisms in terms of the functions they perform is properly considered a functionalism. Indeed, functionalism in psychology has a long and noble history. It arose as a consequence of Darwin's theory of evolution and had among its early proponents such eminent psychologists as Angell, Carr, and Dewey. William James (1892), functionalism's most articulate spokesman, analyzed the processes and tendencies of the organism in terms of their usefulness (i.e., function) in aiding the organism in making its way through the environment. Such an approach follows from the functionalist assumption that the mechanisms underlying behavior arose not merely by accident, but because of their importance to the survival of the

organism. In this context, the corresponding assumption would be that the capacity and propensity to build cognitive maps arose through evolution. The cognitive map would then be viewed as a response to selection pressures favoring those of our ancestors' generation who were more adroit at processing information.

Thus, the basic strategy followed here is to look for mechanisms that meet the requirements of adaptive functioning. From this perspective it is important to consider information-processing capacities that would have been necessary for survival of the human species. The discussion of these issues, undertaken in the next section, is based on the assumption that the evolutionary environment was uncertain and dangerous. Survival in such an environment requires the capacity of object recognition, the anticipation of future events, abstraction and generalization, and responsible innovation. In discussing why these capacities were essential, the next section outlines some requirements that must be met by an adequate theory of human information processing. In the subsequent section a set of interrelated mechanisms intended to fulfill these requirements is described. The paper concludes with an application of the proposed mechanisms to the problem of way-finding.

ON INFORMATION AND THE MANAGEMENT
OF UNCERTAINTY

Why the emphasis on information in the relationship between people and the environment? In a functional perspective, this question can be viewed in terms of the role information plays in getting along in the environment and, more specifically, its role in survival during the time when humans evolved. At least a beginning of an answer to this question can be made in terms of the three interrelated issues of strategy, speed, and scarcity.

Strategy. When the anthropoid ancestors of humans descended from the trees quite some time ago, they did not find the ground uninhabited. Numerous other species got there first. For the most part the good niches were taken. Survival based on leftovers, on taking advantage of opportunities that happened to be overlooked, requires a strategy that is highly information dependent. There are at least two reasons for this. First, an opportunistic organism must be well informed, and well informed about a great many things, to compete with already well established competitors. Furthermore, since any single food source was necessarily uncertain, a large spatial area would have to be covered to increase the likelihood of obtaining something edible (Peters and Mech, 1975). Considerable spatial information was required to know what to look for, where to find it (e.g., Flannery, 1955), and how to get home again. Humans are home-based communal animals; the capacity to return home was a survival necessity.

Speed. The transition from the trees to the ground had another important influence as well. The ground is a dangerous place. Lacking dazzling speed or exceptional protection in the way of fang and claw or hard shell, the early human was dependent on anticipating events before they got out of hand. This adaptation was facilitated by the good vision developed in the arboreal environment. Likewise, upright posture allowed a better view of unfolding events. The intimate relationship between seeing something at a distance and anticipating it is expressed in the word "foresight." But vision and uprightness themselves are insufficient. To survive ill-equipped in a dangerous environment required that this information-handling capability be used with great speed. Speed, of course, is bought at the price of accuracy. The maintenance of reasonable behavior in the absence of high accuracy is one of the great accomplishments of the information-processing system under discussion. How this is achieved must await the more detailed discussion of cognitive maps and cognitive structure that follows.

Scarcity. Information plays a vital role in the organism's commerce with the environment; it is, in effect, the currency of this relationship. Economists argue that the value of something is a function of its scarcity; given the value placed on information in the human design, one must conclude that it was scarce. This may seem somewhat odd; after all, one central problem of the earth environment is that its inhabitants are inundated with information. But the pressure of speed makes a difference here, as does the

kind of information. Anticipation of danger, or of opportunity for that matter, requires *salient* information. The remaining information is considered merely background if it is innocuous or noise if it is potentially distracting. And there is a scarcity of information if it must be salient and if it must be now.

Thus, pursuing a strategy based on information is made difficult both because of the importance of speed and the scarcity of salient information. Stated another way, the environment that confronted our ancestors was, in informational terms, highly complex and uncertain. They could not know how the weather would turn out. Plentiful deer this year could mean even more next year, or it could mean an oversupply leading to a marked decline next year. That dim figure approaching camp at dusk may be a member of the group or he may not. (It should be noted that the environment of modern man is not markedly different in such respects. Weather and even natural hazards still exist. Resources have been known to become suddenly scarce. And the dim figure approaching can still be friend or foe, even in our times.)

SOME REQUIRED INFORMATION-HANDLING CAPACITIES

The most basic of the required capacities is *object recognition*. Unfortunately, this is a relatively technical and involved issue, which would require a lengthy paper all to itself. Since most students of environmental cognition are more interested in the comprehension of space and of objects in space than in objects per se, for present purposes it will simply be assumed that recognizing objects requires dealing with a great deal of uncertainty. (Readers who find this counterintuitive might find it helpful to consult my previous paper; Kaplan, 1973a.)

Once the problem of object recognition has been identified, several additional mechanisms are immediately called for. The organism must be able to *anticipate* future events. Recognizing a given object (or a configuration of objects that might conveniently be referred to as a "situation"), the organism must be able to anticipate a likely next object (or situation). This capacity to anticipate or predict possible consequences is essential to making intelligent choices. Often, in fact, a single-step prediction is insufficient and a whole network of future possibilities must be explored in order to make a suitable choice. Samuel (1963) develops this argument effectively in discussing his famous checker-playing program. He emphasizes the necessity of "lookahead," the consideration of possible future board configurations necessary for evaluating the next move. The importance of lookahead is not, of course, restricted to games. As I have argued previously, it may be a vital issue in comprehending contemporary environmental trends (S. Kaplan, 1972).

A second requirement is the capacity to *abstract* and *generalize*. Experiences are particular and nonrecurring. Learning is futile if what one has learned can never be applied because that precise circumstance never occurs again. Anticipation, likewise, cannot be of a particular subsequent state but rather of a class of such states. Thus, the capacity to abstract and generalize from experiences is not merely desirable but essential for adaptive behavior.

A third requirement is closely related to the second. There are times when there is no "similar" precedent to go on, when abstraction and generalization provide an insufficient basis for behavior. This depends, of course, upon the novelty of the situation. A circumstance too unlike the past experience of the organism requires innovation. Such innovation must not, however, be random. It must be commensurate with whatever abilities and past experience the organism can bring to bear. Thus, this capacity might most appropriately be referred to as *responsible innovation.* In the traditional psychological literature, the process of generating responsible innovations is often referred to as "problem solving."

Thus, to the basic requirement of object recognition must be added three further requirements for which object recognition is a necessary but not a sufficient condition. Anticipation concerns the prediction of future objects and situations; abstraction and generalization involve going beyond the precise appearance of particular objects and situations in order to be able to treat certain other objects and

situations as "similar" to what one already knows. And finally, responsible innovation is required when similarity fails but some reaction is called for nonetheless.

SOME PROPOSED MECHANISMS

In this section we attempt to provide mechanisms that meet the proposed set of requirements. Just as space limitations precluded spelling out the requirements for object recognition, the detailed development of the mechanism must also go unspecified. At the same time, an acquaintance with this mechanism is necessary, since it serves as a basic building block with respect to the other mechanisms. An abbreviated sketch of what an object-recognition mechanism might look like is provided as background.

Recognizing Objects

The solution proposed for the object-recognition problem is, in simplest terms, an internal model of the object. This permits recognition despite uncertainty and incomplete information. It gradually arises in a person's head through repeated experience with the object.

For those inclined to take their rules of learning and perception seriously, it is perhaps more accurate to say that this mental entity gradually arises through the association of various cues or features[2] which the organism extracts from the object. The rule of association here is *contiguity*; contiguity in turn is assured by the fact that examination of any object leads to the experiencing of a contiguous sequence of cues from that object. Admittedly, the order of cues will be highly variable. But this will tend to promote many cross associations, creating the very order free network required for an entity, rather than a string or list or tree of cues. (For a more complete discussion of the genesis and possibilities of the network structure, the reader is referred to the groundbreaking and deeply insightful work of Hebb, 1949, 1963.)

This discussion of cues and association may cause some to suspect a hidden neoassociationist at work. Although the proposed model *is* elementaristic and associationistic, this is not in contrast to a gestalt or wholistic or organismic approach. Indeed, what we are considering is a *whole* (i.e., entity) that gradually emerges out of a vague, global, relatively undifferentiated state. In other words, what is assumed to occur here is differentiation (à la Gibson and Gibson, 1955) through association (à la Postman, 1955).

To understand how this occurs, it is necessary to descend into the murky depths of the molecular level and look at the basic properties of the system. A system is characteristically made up of elements and relations. The operation of the system is based on the initial condition and the rules of change. Here the elements are neurons and relations are associations or connections among them (which can vary in strength between +1, through zero, to –1. The initial condition is a state of widespread, weak, positive connections among the elements. The rule of change, here the learning rule, is in fact rather complicated Two key properties are as follows: (1) any neuron that helps fire some other neuron will tend to become more strongly associated with it, and (2) the total strength of association of any given neuron with all other neurons shall remain constant. One implication of the second assumption is that, as a neuron comes to be more strongly associated with a particular neuron, it will tend to become less strongly associated with other neurons. Thus, at the same time that the strength of connections among salient elements is gradually becoming stronger, the association with other (i.e., irrelevant) elements is correspondingly weakening. In this way the internal model of an object gradually emerges out of an undifferentiated background of random connections.

This internal model is conceptualized as a network of elements corresponding to cues characterizing the object. It incorporates cues in proportion to their importance, it has the capacity to search for cues that are missing, and it can fill in any remaining incompleteness once substantial evidence concerning the presence of the object has been gathered. The capacity to fill in means that the network of elements will tend to act as a whole, as an entity rather than as a mere collection of elements.

The entity or thing-like property of the network allows it to serve as an element in thought as well as in perception. By the rules of learning that gave rise to it, it *corresponds* to an object in the environment. It is the particular internal model whose activity signals the presence of that object in the environment. When the object is not present but only thought about, this same network, by a lower level of activity, is capable of standing for or representing the object in the thought process. It thus is often referred to as the internal *representation* of the object. Clearly, a representation is an abstraction; it is incomplete, schematic, and partial, which allows it to "fit" a wide range of differing circumstances while being experienced as a "thing" and not as an idea.

Information-Processing Mechanisms and the Importance of Space

The object is a physical entity. The cognitive map implies space. These physical–spatial emphases are by no means accidental; nor are they intended to be restrictive. I have assumed throughout this discussion that the problem of dealing with the physical–spatial environment was a central and challenging feature of human evolution (see Peters and Mech, 1975). Accordingly, human information-processing patterns might be expected to reflect this influence in a profound way. Mechanisms that evolved under pressures of dealing with the physical–spatial environment may now be handling other kinds of information as well. There does indeed appear to be a pervasive use of physical–spatial referents and analogies in the human comprehension of the nonphysical world. Concepts of proximity, order, and distance, for instance, play an important role in a wide variety of nonspatial matters. The domain of human relationships provides numerous examples. People are said to be "close" or "distant," some are thought to be "higher" than others (on the pecking "order"), and so on. The future is often thought of in spatial terms. Thus, one speaks of "distant" goals or of the difficulty in "seeing where one is going." Comparably, issues of value may revolve around the true "path" from which one might be tempted to stray. Indeed, one of the best known deviations is referred to as the "primrose path."

The mechanism concerned with anticipation, that of *sequence*, is at the same time clearly spatial and not spatial at all. In the context of the cognition of space, sequences refer to routes. Yet the paradigm of sequences may actually be temporal; spatial sequences may be coded because they are experienced temporally. (This would be consistent with the rule of learning assumed throughout this paper, that is, contiguity, which states that events which happen close together in time will come to be associated with each other.) Even the comprehension of the ordering (i.e., sequences) of digits in a number and of letters in a word has been shown to depend on a spatial ability (Kinsbourne, 1971).

Abstraction, the next process to be discussed, is obviously pertinent to nonspatial domains; indeed the vast majority of abstractions we deal with are not obviously spatial. But "region" is a spatial abstraction, and "state" (as in "the United States") also fits this description (see Shepard and Chipman, 1970).

Responsible innovation, the final of the processes requiring a suitable mechanism, is usually thought of as essentially nonspatial since most problems requiring an innovative solution are not obviously spatial. But the literature on problem solving frequently characterizes the process as finding a path between start and goal. Thus, way finding can be viewed not only as an interesting problem in the cognition of space but also as a paradigm for problem solving in general.

Anticipation: The Coding of Sequences

Although objects are of undeniable importance in comprehending and reacting to the environment, their recognition per se provides little help in knowing what to do. Selecting an appropriate action requires prediction, that is, an assessment of what might happen next. Knowledge of "what follows what" is essentially a problem of storing sequential information. There are, of course, innumerable reasonably realiable sequences that are frequently encountered in the environment. There are in fact so many that an economical means of coding them is essential. Although the problem of storing sequences has long been recognized in psychology, the solutions proposed characteristically fall short of the necessary economy. Thus, associative chains have been a popular candidate, but the necessity of having a new chain for every new circumstance readily becomes a burden. More recently, tree structures have become popular (e.g., Hunt, 1962). There is a gain of economy here, but even though the flexibility of handling any given problem is enhanced, a new tree is still required for each new problem.

From the point of view of functional require-

ments—ignoring for a moment the issue of structure—the problem is straightforward. A representation should be associated with representations of events likely to follow it. Thus, a sequence is coded as a series of paths connecting representations. Economy in this arrangement is gained through overlap. All sequences having a particular representation in common pass through that representation. Such a highly overlapping structure constitutes a network. But note that, since the nodes of this network are representations and thus themselves lower-order networks, this network is necessarily on a larger scale. It is, in effect, a network of networks. Such a condensation of various spatial experiences into a simplified node and path structure is called a *cognitive map.*[3] In other words, a cognitive map in this framework is a network of representations coding both places and the sequential relations among them.

The proposed mechanism for the cognitive map achieves the economy of storage that eludes the chain and tree structures. The network coding of overlapping and intersecting sequences requires far less structure for the same quantity of information than would more independent forms of organization. Overlap is an advantage not only in terms of storage. It is also responsible for a parallel economy of experience. Since experience with a given object calls up the representation of that object, information about that object will tend to be stored together, despite considerable variance in circumstances, motives, and so on. Likewise, many different experiences that have in common a particular sequence will contribute to the development of the mental representation of that sequence. Thus, one may traverse a given neighborhood from various starting points, for various purposes, and at various times of day. All such information will contribute to the development of the same section of the cognitive map; it will be available for unanticipated as well as familiar purposes and circumstances.

Another kind of economy derives from the fact that the proposed cognitive map structure is not continuous. Rather, it is a discrete approximation to a continuous environment. But such incompleteness, although highly desirable, could also constitute a serious handicap. To be workable, any discrete, incomplete approximation must meet two requirements. It must be connected and it must be susceptible to an increase in completeness if circumstances warrant. Meeting the first requirement is rather straightforward, since a network is by definition a connected structure. Meeting the second requirement can also be achieved readily by making the assumption that the processes which generated the network in the first place continue to operate in its refinement.

Abstraction and the Concept of Layers

The discussion so far has concerned the way consistencies in sensory information can be utilized to build a model of the environment. A useful model must be one that can be applied to many circumstances, not merely to the particular circumstances that gave rise to it. To be more generalizable, experience must be coded in a fashion that introduces abstraction, that somehow ignores or rises above the many particulars which differentiate otherwise similar situations. Of the many ways that organisms achieve this, two are of particular interest here. One involves a simple restatement of assumptions already made; the other, concerning the matter of scale, requires an additional mechanism.

The first mechanism of abstraction is built into the way the recognition of objects is assumed to take place. Only features that are frequently detected when the object is present become part of the object representation. This guarantees substantial information loss; the particulars of any one instance will not become part of the network. (This schematic character of the representation in turn imposes itself on perception. When one identifies an object, one often fails to see or, more precisely, to represent internally aspects of the object that were not contained in the representation.)

A related facet of this "built-in" abstractive tendency is the capacity of the representation to be activated despite missing information. In this way, further generalization occurs; that is, a wider range of circumstances becomes capable of evoking the same internal reaction.

The second mechanism for reducing detail, or increasing abstraction, involves the capacity to shift scale, in other words, to view something as if from a longer perspective.

Certainly, cognitive maps range widely, from that of a neighborhood or even a room at one end to the entire globe at the other. And the capacity to shift scale, to treat a differentiated area as a single region or point on the "map" or to zoom in on a small section of a city, is an essential flexibility in the thought process. A similar problem exists for individual objects. We have concepts for classes of objects and even for classes of classes of objects. The issue in the case of both cognitive maps and representations of objects appears to be a matter of how many levels the concept is removed from sensory experience. A concept of a "street corner" is closer to sensory experience than a concept of a "city." The concept of "dog" is closer to sensory experience than is the concept of "animal."

A possible mechanism to deal with this distinction takes the "distance from sensory experience" metaphor quite literally. Imagine the brain as a series of layers. The first layer would receive feature information from the sensory analyzers. This layer would presumably come to contain a model of the environment closely tied to sensory experience. Since a major source of sensory regularities in the environment is the result of those packages of stimulation known as objects, I have argued that objects should dominate this layer. Sequential information relating objects to each other would also be present in this layer.

The next layer presumably would receive inputs from the prior layer. It thus will come to contain a model of a model of the environment. In this way, it should be possible to develop internal representations of classes of objects and of regions of maps. Higher and higher layers would be less and less closely bound to sensory events. They would also tend to develop later and to be less strongly organized than lower layers. Thus, a philosophy of life, while at the highest and most integrative level, may also tend to be somewhat vague and even to border on the nonexistent on bad days.

Before leaving the concept of layers, one other matter should be mentioned. A system that builds models of models readily evokes the image of something that gets more and more compact as it gets higher, ultimately ending, one must assume, in a point! But the hidden assumption here is that there is a single higher-level organization of the lower-level material. Consider the concept "tree." Although it is recognizable on the basis of many different stimulus patterns and thus can be seen as a point of convergence of many inputs, a "tree" also participates in a variety of higher-level concepts and can thus be seen as spreading out the connection pattern once again. A "tree" participates in such concepts as "living thing," "source of fuel," "landscape amenity," and perhaps "abstract mathematical concept."

Note that these more abstract concepts are also representations. Although the emphasis in the discussion has been on representations of objects, that is, essentially the first-layer representations, the rules for the formation of representations apply at higher layers as well. Higher-layer representations will tend to develop somewhat later, since their input is largely from lower-layer representations rather than from feature analyzers. There is considerable power in this orderly means of generating different levels of abstraction from the same information base.

The existence of layers coupled with the failure of the cognitive system to become increasingly compact as it gets higher yields a structure that is somewhat difficult to classify mathematically. Although at one time the possibility that it might be a semilattice (Kaplan, 1973a, following Alexander, 1965) seemed attractive, this is ruled out by the absence of "least upper bound." A semilattice requires that any two elements have a least upper bound and "that there is a unique *maximal* element which is the upper bound of all elements" (Friedell, 1967, p. 47). In other words, there is again the demand that the system come to a point! On the other hand, the system as a whole is not simply a random network, since this would fail to incorporate the layering concept and the possibility for hierarchies that goes with it. Thus, the structure is tentatively characterized as a "partially ordered network" in the fond hope that the mathematics of such structures will one day be worked out.

The "partially ordered network" designation applies not only to cognitive structure as a whole. At a smaller scale, it is the structure underlying the cognitive map; at a still smaller scale, it is the basis for the representation. The "partial order" at the scale of the cognitive map is the correspondence between spatial properties of the environment and the structure of the network. In other words, at each layer of the system, distance is a meaningful concept. The "partial order" at the scale of the representation has not yet been explored; it presumably relates to the spatial groupings of features in a typical object.

One way to view these various interrelated scales of cognitive structure is to consider the makeup and relationships of the typical representation (see Figure 1):

1. The representation is made up of elements.
2. It receives input from feature analyzers. (This is less the case the higher the layer to which the particular representation belongs.)
3. It is connected with representations in prior layers of cognitive structure. (This is more and more the case the higher the layer to which the particular representation belongs.) It serves as a more inclusive, higher-order concept relative to these lower representations.
4. It is connected with representations at the same layer that it has preceded or followed in frequent sequences. It is these lateral relationships that form the structure of the cognitive map.
5. It is connected with representations in higher layers, with respect to which it may be an instance or example.

Responsible Innovation and the Search Mechanism

The purpose of the final of the three representation-based mechanisms is to deal with the problem of novel circumstances. It is sometimes necessary to act when there is no clear precedent, no prior experience that provides a solution. It must be remembered that choosing any act at random could be perilous indeed. The "responsible" modifier points to the importance of choosing an act that is as appropriate to the setting and to the capacities of the organism as is possible, given the limitations created by the novelty. There is, in fact, a clear parallel to object recognition, where environmental uncertainty requires some astute "filling in." In both cases a tie to the past experience of the organism can serve as a partial compensation for the lack of guidance provided by the environment.

The parallel to recognizing objects is, in fact, far from superficial. To identify an object it is necessary to "find" a suitable representation of that object. To innovate responsibly it is also necessary to "find" something, in this case something that will

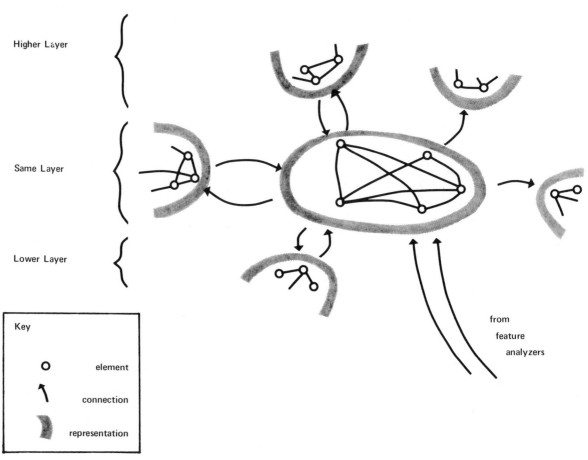

FIGURE 1
Possible connection pattern of a typical representation.

guide subsequent behavior. Before pursuing this parallel further, it is necessary to examine what it is that must be "found" and how this is achieved.

Responsible innovation is usually referred to in the psychological literature as "problem solving." Problem solving can be thought of as figuring out what to do when that is far from obvious. It can also be thought of as a circumstance in which one desires to move from the current state of affairs to a different, preferred state. This, in turn, readily translates into finding a path that takes one from "Start" (the present state) to "Goal" (the desired state). If one can represent both Start and Goal in one's cognitive

system, problem solving becomes a process of searching the cognitive map for a path connecting these two representations.

The existence of a problem requires that the link between where one is and where one wants to be is not direct or obvious; if one had gone from this Start to this Goal many times in the past, there would be a clear path and, accordingly, no problem. Given the lack of any direct connection, one must locate a path indirectly, that is, through existing *subgoals*. Consider the problem of getting from Here to There. A solution requires that one think of a subgoal, Elsewhere, such that one knows how to get from Here to

Elsewhere, and from Elsewhere to There. Sometimes a considerable elaboration of subgoals is required to solve a problem. One may start by identifying a major subgoal, and then still have to identify intervening subgoals between the initial subgoal and Start or between the initial subgoal and Goal.

Thus, it becomes clear that responsible innovation involves facilitating one or more representations, just as was the case for object recognition. The innovation is "responsible" because it is not random but based on the past experience of the organism as represented by its cognitive map. The process is nonetheless innovative, because it involves tracing a new path that was never (or rarely) traced before.

An important difference between object recognition and responsible innovation is the extent of reliance on internal influences and the multiplicity of influences involved. In recognizing an object, the major source of influence is the external object from which certain features are extracted. In problem solving, the goal is not generally present in the environment. Thus, the influence of the goal in the search for a path must be generated by an internal representation. Although Start is in principle the stimulating environment itself, as James (1892) has pointed out, it can be seen in many different ways; how it is seen is often crucial in whether a path can be found or not. Finally, there are the circumstances or constraints that so often influence the process. One is Here and wants to get to There and spend very little money doing it. Or the bridge is out and one is fearful of alligators. The examples need not be spatial. When a poet tries to think of a suitable word to finish a line of verse, semantics, rhythm, rhyme scheme, and numerous other factors constrain his choice.[4]

The approach taken here centers on the consequence of a multiplicity of influences in the search for a solution. This approach was stimulated by and is a greatly simplified version of the "broadcast language" developed by Holland (1974) for dealing with a broad class of problems of this kind. For an intuitive feeling for the operation of the broadcast concept, imagine a system made up of a large number of interconnected points. If any point is active, it will send (or broadcast) a message along all its output lines. If we assume that elements are relatively difficult to activate (i.e., have high thresholds), a *convergence*

of inputs from many broadcasting points is necessary for any next point to become active. In this way the system carries out a sophisticated search, that is, one in which the chosen representation is influenced by a wide variety of criteria.

The sort of structure we have been considering is ideally suited to a broadcast approach. Each element (i.e., representation) has many connections to other elements; furthermore, these connections vary in strength. Thus, the possibility but not the necessity of convergence is built into the pattern of connections. The search process makes possible subtle and varied problem solution; at the same time, there is no guarantee that a solution will in fact be found for any given problem.

ON MAKING ONE'S WAY: AN APPLICATION AND A PERSPECTIVE

Making one's way, that is, traversing a path in space from Start to Goal, requires first that one can recognize critical loci where choices must be made. Given one is at such a point of choice, there must then be some basis for making decisions. One way is to have a specific rule that applies only to that locus. "Turn right at the stoplight" may be part of a recently received set of instructions or a long-practiced ritual. It matters not; if this is all the information one can bring to bear at that point, one is safe only if one is error free and lives in an unchanging environment. Otherwise, having a network of information, a larger picture, is far more adaptive than a rote solution. Such a solution is, after all, a single sequence and not a cognitive map in any sense that distinguishes it from alternative conceptions of cognitive structure. In the ensuing discussion, the focus will be on the components of a network of information, on the points of choice and direction,[5] as the most general and most useful means of making one's way in a spatial environment.

On Landmarks and Regions

Landmarks play a central role in the identification of both points of choice and direction. The more distinctive a place, the more readily it serves as a locus for decision making and a change of direction. Whereas proximal landmarks are thus vital in identifying points of choice, distant ones, in aiding looka-head, are a great help in maintaining direction. When the only available landmarks are close, decisions tend to be forced back onto rote operations ("a left turn just beyond the church").[6]

Regions, like landmarks, are important to both points of choice and direction. Regions can, in fact, be viewed as "oversized landmarks." They are distinctive places, but of considerably greater extent than is the case for landmarks. In identifying points of choice, a region can function as a low-precision landmark. One might take a turn "where the single-family houses start" or "in the general area of the pine woods." A region can also serve in conjunction with a landmark. One might look for the "clearing in the woods" or the "red-roofed house in the wealthy residential area." A region can play an important role in direction as well. One can proceed "through" or "along" or "away from" a given region. As with landmarks, the more readily a region can be seen from a distance, the more useful it can be in guiding direction.

It appears then that making one's way in a spatial environment depends importantly on landmarks and regions. In the discussion so far, landmarks and regions have been considered quite concrete and specific. They are representations for particular places or particular areas. But, fortunately for the flexibility and efficiency of the organism, not all knowledge is of the particular. Rather, knowledge can be viewed on a continuum ranging from the specific on one end to the completely generic on the other. Most practical cases will fall somewhere in between, but the distinction is a useful one. Generic knowledge provides a basis for comprehending new environments based on prior experience with reasonably similar environments. The existence of this kind of knowledge is helpful for understanding the different behavior of the novice and the experienced individual. Even though two individuals have never been in a particular environment before, the one who is thoroughly familiar with that *class* of environments will be more comfortable and acquire helpful information more rapidly than the novice. In the discussion that follows, an attempt will be made to demonstrate that the advantage held by the experienced individual is based on the facilitation provided by generic knowledge in the crucial task of identifying regions and landmarks.

Representations and Kinds of Landmarks

To analyze landmarks and regions in theoretical terms, it is necessary to return to the concept of representation, the central element of the cognitive map within the proposed theory. The representation is distinctly perceptual in origin; it not only provides a basis for perception, it is itself constructed out of perceptual experience. The representation is, at the same time, the basic cognitive element, since in the thought process it can stand for an object or place even in its absence.

A landmark is a known place, a place for which the individual has a well-formed representation. To understand what places are likely to become landmarks, it is necessary to consider those factors that enhance perceptual experience and perceptual learning. Certainly, the frequency with which one has commerce with a particular portion of the environment should play a role in learning. The distinctiveness of the place should also be an important factor, since the more numerous and the stronger the available features, the more readily the representation can be learned. Where blunt sensory contrast is not present, it may be necessary to fall back on a more refined sensitivity to the character of the surrounding area. These factors all play a role in the categorization of landmarks offered here. Although they can be used in a rough-and-ready sense to sort landmarks into different "kinds" of categories, it should be remembered that these are matters of degree; the typical landmark is not exclusively dependent on any single factor.

The first type of distinctiveness is *visual distinctiveness*, as emphasized by Lynch (1960). Visual forms that tower above the landscape are a good example of this property. Visual distinctiveness is sensory in nature; it depends upon factors that can immediately be discriminated from the surrounding environment.

Many landmarks that appear to be visually distinctive can be seen upon more careful examination to reflect instead a second factor, that of *inferred distinctiveness*. This factor depends upon background or regional information; it is thus more cognitive and more experience dependent. An oak tree, for example, can serve as a landmark to the individual who knows that all the other trees in the area are maples. Comparably, a building might stand out for an individual who knows that brown brick is the exception in that part of town. Such inferred distinctiveness can occur at all levels of knowledge. The newcomer to the city may only require half an hour of hapless wandering to discover that the lunch counter that seemed so ordinary is in fact the only one in a 10-block radius. On the other hand, the unusual handling of trim on an elderly building among other elderly buildings may serve as a landmark only for the architect.

Note here the importance of the region as an equivalence class. The inference of distinctiveness is based on being able to treat a spatially unified set of entities as essentially equivalent. Generic knowledge can play a vital role here. When one knows what a pine woods in general contains, it is easier to form a concept about a particular pine woods. Comparably, a concept of the "well kept, small house, older working-class neighborhood" in general allows one to grasp the flavor of a particular such neighborhood with little difficulty. Knowing what stands out is necessarily the complement of knowing what is ordinary or usual.

The third factor in landmark formation has a compensatory relation to the other two. Even if there is nothing particularly distinctive to characterize a point of choice, eventually a concept of that place will develop out of frequency or repetition. Note, however, that the frequency factor does not refer merely to an uncomplicated "number of times experienced." The frequency that matters is the frequency of activation of central processes, or representations, or of "representations-to-be." For the representation of the place in question to achieve this sort of frequency, it is necessary that it serve some function for the individual. Landmarks that are learned primarily on the basis of *functional distinctiveness* will be referred to as *functional landmarks.*

For a place not merely to be passed by with some frequency, but to be frequently thought about, it must have the status of a goal or subgoal. Consider, for example, an individual new to a community and interested in buying groceries. To get to the nearest grocery store, one goes down the road a way and turns right at an intersection (that looks like all the others in the area). Here the intersection is technically a subgoal rather than a goal, but the distinction is of little consequence. Until one finds it, the subgoal can take on all the importance of a goal. Conversely, a goal can serve as an intermediate point of a longer trip, thus becoming a subgoal in that context. In any event, the goal or subgoal status is what converts a behavioral frequency into a cognitive frequency. In route selection, as in other kinds of problem solving, it is necessary to activate the representation of a goal to determine how to reach it. Thus, the more an individual utilizes a particular place, the more commerce, both behavioral and cognitive, he is likely to have with it.

The learning of regions follows essentially the same rules as for landmarks. Here, too, visual distinctiveness has the priority, inferred distinctiveness is next, and the functional basis by itself is slowest and hardest to learn. Identification of a region allows one to call on both specific knowledge (e.g., of the path structure of that area) and generic knowledge (e.g., characteristics of areas of that general type). Regions also, as indicated previously, have a role in the identification of landmarks by providing a background against which one can infer distinctiveness.

Regions, Generic Knowledge, and the Role of Experience: An Introduction to Some Empirical Studies

Regions have a special relationship to generic knowledge. Regional information is necessarily abstractive; it summarizes a range of specific information. Since other regions in other places could have the same properties, regional information is well on its way to being generic. At the same time, both regional and generic information take time to acquire. The "double novice" (both to a particular area and to the class of areas to which it belongs) necessarily labors under a substantial handicap. An environment with visually distinctive landmarks at key points of choice and with a readily comprehensible structure should be manageable even by the double novice. The sort of environment one is more likely to encounter, by contrast, could be formidable indeed.

The illustrative studies in this section deal with very different facets of these basic issues. Rachel Kaplan explores the experience of the double novice in a natural area. Given the redundancy characteristic of nature, visually distinctive landmarks are often lacking and certainly were in the area under study. This throws the individual back on information ordinarily acquired through extended experience. The research program described in Chapter 3 constitutes an effort to explore ways to foreshorten the experience required through the use of simulation.

In Chapter 4, Ann Devlin looks at individuals unfamiliar with the town in question but unusually experienced at adapting to new urban environments. Thus, one would expect generic knowledge to play a substantial role. The town in question was, as is not infrequently the case, deficient in visually distinctive landmarks, thus increasing the likelihood of being able to observe the other types of landmarks in use.

A Perspective

As with the cognitive-map concept itself, the issues raised here are spatial but need not be. The ideas of regional information, generic knowledge, and functional landmarks apply with equal force to an individual attempting to understand the bureaucratic structure that surrounds him and to his efforts to comprehend his spatial world. Indeed, certain issues are perhaps particularly pressing in the nonspatial domain. For example, it has been proposed that a network of points of choice and directions constitutes the necessary information for traversing an environment. The individual with points of choice and some rote operation to be carried out at each has what is in general a poor substitute for a cognitive map. The individual with such information is robbed of confidence, of flexibility, of competence in any larger sense. Yet this is precisely the sort of information that our increasingly expert oriented society makes available.

Ironically, the knowledge explosion has, for many

people, led not to an expansion of alternatives but to a decline in the sense of direction. In part, this has been the result of overload (e.g., Milgram, 1970). It is also fostered by increasing specialization, and especially by the territorial tendencies of the experts who man the specialties. Experts make it clear that ordinary humans are incapable of grappling with, and perhaps of even comprehending, their vital areas of knowledge. Thus, people are not to make decisions they were presumably capable of making when life was simpler. When experts, further, disagree with each other, the ultimate in organized paralysis is achieved. The undermining of common sense and intuition has made a great many things harder to do than they were when we knew less.

People remain examples of the most powerful information-processing system the world has ever known. They can, however, be reduced to frustrated incompetence, as our factories, cities, and institutions have effectively demonstrated. But, if permitted, people can also be a vital source of ability. A sense of respect for this organism that was evolved in the context of information handling might be a good start. A feeling of horror for what this adroit organism can do when thwarted, frustrated, or manipulated also would not hurt. The opportunity to share problems, to comprehend difficulties, to face challenges (which are, after all, out there anyway) would tap much of what is best and strongest in human nature. It is hopefully not too late to undertake this modest revolution. At this late date, it constitutes less an opportunity than a necessity.

NOTES

1. Rachel Kaplan's insight, feedback, and guidance contributed importantly to the development of this paper. I would also like to thank Gary T. Moore and Bruce A. Whitehead for their thoughtful comments. Work on this paper was sponsored, in part, by the Institute for Environmental Quality, University of Michigan.
2. "Feature" and "cue" are convenient terms to describe the results of sensory analysis, but they may be slightly misleading. As Gibson (1946) has long emphasized, much sensory information is

better described in terms of *gradients* than as cues or features. This implies information that is continuous rather than discrete, that varies gradually over an extended area. As I have earlier suggested (Kaplan, 1970), the "location processing system" may possess texture and other continuous information through special arrangements of discrete neural elements. The use of "feature" and "cue" here is intended to include this kind of information. Likewise, relational information is not excluded . Certain cells in the visual system, for example, detect only moving stimuli. They are thus tuned to relational information. But the results of such coding can nonetheless be treated as a feature as far as further processing is concerned.

Another concern raised by the emphasis on features is that such an approach fails to capture the subtlety and wholeness of experience. It is certainly the case that we experience continuities and wholes rather than discrete cues or features. The solution to this quite justifiable concern has been not to abandon the approach, but to, in effect, take it underground. If the features in question are small enough and numerous enough, considerable subtlety can be achieved. This ingenious strategy was initiated by Hebb (1949), extended by Good (1965), and has achieved considerable formal elegance in the work of Holland (1974). The use of halftone to produce a continuous-appearing image provides a helpful analogy. If the screen is small enough, the fact that the scene is in fact made up of discrete dots is not in the least disturbing to the viewer. In this way the properties of the experience and of the basis for the experience can be separated.

3. This term is justified on the grounds that the structure in question can be conceptualized as a space with a distance metric (the number of nodes on a path). Although not a map in the cartographer's sense, the term provides a meaningful, useful, and not importantly misleading analogy for students of various disciplines and for nontechnical people as well. Those who wish to avoid the extraneous nuances inherent in this rather informal use of the term might wish to substitute "abstract coordinated representation" after Moore (1973a), following Piaget et al. (1960). An interesting implication of this distance metric is that, given two sequences of the same physical distance, the one with more places (i.e., nodes) will be perceived as longer. This is in fact what Briggs (see Chapter 30) has found in his work on cognitive distance.

4. These particular examples may appear to involve *conscious* thought, but there is no assumption here that thought is necessarily either conscious or, for that matter, a process expressible in words. Thus, much of what is described here will be known to the thinker only by its results. It will be experienced, in other words, as intuition.

5. "Direction" as used here is a condensation of the information provided by a cognitive map to an individual at a point of choice. Through a search of representations associated with the point where he is, he can determine which of these is nearest his goal. If he can see the place so represented, his direction is obvious. If he cannot, he must locate a subgoal between where he is and the desired place. When he has identified a visible subgoal, he has determined both the direction of the next segment of his route and the landmark at which a new direction and a new landmark must be determined.

6. Peters (1973, 1974), in his research on the spatial behavior of wolves, has found striking evidence for the importance of landmarks in way-finding in a fellow social carnivore. Perhaps owing to the redundancy of their natural habitat as well as to their relative deemphasis of visual information, wolves characteristically create their own landmarks by scent marking. Although humans at times leave trail marks or other signs, they more typically create landmarks cognitively rather than by overt action on the physical environment.

3

WAY-FINDING IN THE NATURAL ENVIRONMENT[1]

Rachel Kaplan

Department of Psychology and
 School of Natural Resources
 University of Michigan

You may have heard it said that moss grows on the north side of trees; you may also know that that is not always true. And sometimes there is no moss at all.

People who have had extensive exposure to natural environments have gained generic information about such settings that enhances their love for and comfort with the woods, streams, and meadows. Familiarity with a variety of such settings leads to a sense of mastery. Having a feeling for different patterns of trail and undergrowth provides information that enables one to predict what other places will be like. For people thoroughly comfortable in such settings, it is often difficult to comprehend the lack of pleasure and even fear that the uninitiated feel in the same setting. Camp counselors, nature guides, and others in a position to introduce nature to the novice are frequently confronted with these fears, sometimes expressed verbally ("Are there bears?" "Where are the snakes?") and sometimes expressed by the hesitation of feet afraid to explore.

The "fear not, there are no snakes here" approach is often no more credible than other "fear not, I am here to help you" approaches. To the person coming to the Big City for the first time, that environment can be as bewildering as are woods and wide open spaces to the veteran of urban life. The fear of getting lost is profound. The same cognitive structures that we depend on for making our way through the environment permit the anticipation of future environments (S. Kaplan, 1973b). If such a lookahead is not well ordered, the effect is one of pain and discomfort. The effect is now; the anticipated event has not even begun to happen. This is quite adaptive. One need not even *be* lost; the mere anticipation of the possibility is potentially discomforting.

The purposes of the research project discussed here were to understand better the nature of the information that leads to comfort in the natural setting and to provide the novice with some of the information that will enhance his confidence—before he finds himself in that setting. We attempted to develop transition experiences that would reduce the novice's uninformed status and to provide these in a setting where the discomfort is not at issue. Such of course is the purpose of most education—developing knowledge toward future needs, techniques for dealing with new situations, ways to anticipate demands, and confidence in oneself as a consequence of prior successful problem solving. All these issues, of course, depend ultimately on the adequacy of the individual's internal model of the environment, and it, in turn, must depend on experience.

From the perspective of the informational approach to cognitive mapping presented in Chapter 2, such transition experiences have to meet certain criteria. The "future" environment has to be presented in a way that facilitates envisioning it. One could verbally describe such a setting (e.g., hilly, lots of trees), but we felt that an approach that permits a grasp of the spatial aspects in one sweep, as it were, would be preferable. To the extent that the mental map one forms of an environment includes such spatial components, it is important to provide these components so that such a map can take shape. This suggests the presentation of a miniature, a simulation, that permits an overview of an area. By its very nature, a miniature must entail abstraction. It requires reduction in detail. On the other hand, such abstraction need not be at the expense of object constancy. A house must still be recognized as a house, despite loss of detail. There must also be some way to assure sufficient contact with the "future" environment so that a mental map can be developed. Such contact will be more successful if it has fascination or appeal, and this will be related to considering what the person feels he wants to know or needs to know about that environment.

Although these requirements are straightforward, their execution is illusive. In the process of carrying out a series of studies, we have grown increasingly aware of how uncharted this area is. In fact, we have not yet found a way to represent a "future" environment that fully meets our criteria. But that is not to say that progress has not been made. Quite to the contrary, this paper will describe our experiences with respect to different kinds of transition experiences, ways of presenting an as yet unknown environment, and assessments of the effectiveness of the procedures. Four studies will be described in the next few pages; subsequently, the discussion will return to the more general issues of effective transition experiences for natural environments.

Study I: Exploratory Study of Cognitive Mapping

The aim of the initial study was to determine the kinds of maps people will draw of a natural area after a brief hike. The salient features of the environment would presumably be determinable from these maps. To maximize comparability, the participants were taken over a predetermined route (in groups of two or three) in a relatively short time (about half an hour). The route covered a great variety of terrains and features, including a river, a pine grove, a large meadow, and steep hills. The setting was the arboretum, 138 acres of university-owned parkland in the middle of Ann Arbor, Michigan. Each of 32 college students (ages ranged from 18 to 45) who went on these summer outings produced a freely drawn sketch map representing the hike. Despite the fact that all went on the same route, these maps showed vast differences. They could, nonetheless, be grouped into three basic kinds: (1) two were pictorial, showing key features in elevation and obscuring geographical relationships; (2) the majority were linear, showing major landmarks and features strung out in sequence with a line representing the path connecting them; and (3) 12 were regional, showing areas defined by types of flora and topographic variation. It was generally true that the areas with fewest landmarks (e.g., a large meadow) were represented as disproportionately shorter than areas with more salient features. The maps made one vividly aware that they provided an indication of only a fraction of what must be in the person's mind about the hike.

Study II: Use of a Board Game as Prior Experience

Having some knowledge of the salient features of this particular natural setting, we approached the task of representing it visually to people who did not know it. A picture map was prepared to show particular features of the area and to provide a general orientation to the various regions and terrains. By applying an acetate overlay with a grid pattern to this map, we created a board game. The object of the game was to gain points, which could be won both by reaching each of three specific destinations and by landing on certain "surprise" squares. Information about the areas was transmitted by extensive encounter with the map, by attempting to reach certain destinations, by communicating terrain variations through different grid sizes, and through the surprise squares, which were coupled with decks of cards depicting plants and animals likely to be found at those locations.

The participants in this study were junior high school students (ages between 12 and 15) who volunteered to come for a trip to a "wooded area." This is not irrelevant; it seems very likely that those who signed up were more likely to be comfortable in such settings. Certainly the ones who passed the sign-up desk in the schools' hallways with exclamations of "Me? The Woods?" were not among the volunteers. These participants, meeting in groups of two to eight, were randomly assigned to one of three conditions. A control group (n=14) explored a large section of the arboretum for a 30-minute period. A map group (n=23) studied the picture map for a few minutes just prior to setting out on their exploration. A game group (n=24) explored the same part of the arboretum, but they had met to play the board game the previous day.

At the end of their half-hour exploration, the participants returned and completed both a freely drawn sketch map and some open-ended questions. Briefly, the results did not show consistent differences between the three groups. The overall satisfaction with the experience was extremely high and, with only one exception, the students were unanimous in their willingness to do it again. Many of the areas in the arboretum were explored equally often by the different groups. There was no clear indication that the prior experience, either the game or seeing the map, had any effect on the unstructured sketch maps.

There were indications, however, that the game group's transition experience affected their behavior in the field. The boys especially explored more extensively.[2] They did not cover much more total distance on their outings, but they penetrated a greater range of areas. Whereas most of the participants chose the same initial direction for their hike, the boys in the game group showed great diversity in this respect. They showed an equal likelihood of starting in the direction opposite the one that seemed most natural (toward the big meadow). This suggests that the game experience had some bearing on their knowledge of the environment and permitted a greater degree of choice in their exploration.

Several reasons precluded more clear-cut results. Al-though the arboretum is in fact an excellent setting in terms of the variety of regions and interfaces it offers and in terms of mystery and surprise, because surprisingly few people are acquainted with it despite its convenient location, it turns out to be a setting that requires no prior information. The large focal open field edged by wooded regions is immediately inviting and has a drawing power. This is the direction almost all the students chose to start their hikes. Not only is the arboretum unthreatening as a setting, the participants were self-selected; as a group they were clearly comfortable in the natural environment. The game itself and the map rendition presented problems that needed to be corrected in the next study.

Study III: Different Games as Prior Experience and a New Location[3]

The problem of having volunteer participants was solved by working through the school system where we had access to seventh graders in four separate classes in a "school within a school" (n=85). For each class we were permitted two class sessions one week apart, as well as school time for the field trips.

Procedure: maps. For two of the four classes, the games were based on maps of the arboretum; for the other two classes, the games were based on maps of a different park to which *all* the groups would later go. Both maps were drawn by a landscape architect who converted contour lines to cloud-like patterns resembling lacework. Unfortunately, the feeling of different heights, different vegetation, and variation in density were not communicated. Although we knew we had the wrong maps when we did the study, the timetable imposed by weather, the school year, and the commitment to the school system meant we had to use what we had. (Figure 1 shows the map for the park where the students went on the field trip.)

Games. Class periods were used for presenting the "map" material; two different game formats were used. Except for the use of the two different maps, each of the four classes followed the same procedure. A Kim-game format was used the acquaint the students with the form of the map: after 1 minute of concentration on the map, a number of orienting questions were asked (e.g., "did you see any water?"). Subsequent discussion included mention of some of

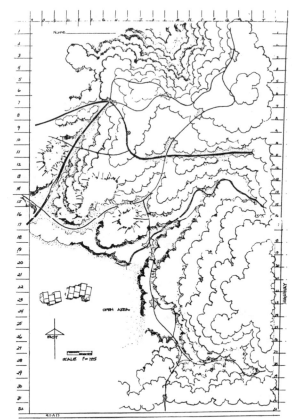

FIGURE 1
"Lacework" rendition of Ann Arbor Arboretum park contour map.

the main features of the map (elevation, boundaries, paths). This was done fairly rapidly and included the whole class (about 20 to 25 students).

A "Battleship" game format was used to transmit information about the path structure of the area. For this the students worked in pairs, each having an identical picture map except that the paths shown on the two maps were complementary. Each partner had to guess the location of the paths missing from his map. At the end of about 30 minutes, the partners would compare maps.

In the second classroom session, the aim was to transfer knowledge about the topography of the area. For this a "20-Question" game format was used with the students again working in pairs, each member having his own map. One member of the pair would "hide" at a particular location on the map and the other would have to determine where his partner was by using the supplied question cards. (See Table 1 for sample questions.)

Setting and field trips. The setting for the field trips this time was a 116-acre park at the edge of the city that has been left relatively wild save for some paths and the encroachment of a housing development at one boundary. It was picked because it is a more difficult natural area in terms of orientation, for getting a feel for the entire place—it is less "legible" in Lynch's (1960) terms. There are more hills and they are steeper. The woods are relatively dense. There are few places from which one can see a vista. In addition, the entrance point is particularly low in drawing power. It is blocked to discourage motorcycles and permits no immediate feeling for what is beyond.

The students were taken in groups of eight in a 12-passenger van to the starting point of the field trip. At the entrance they were given a brief orientation to the park by use of the same base map of the area that had been used for that setting previously. At that point, the groups who had seen this map previously were told that this was in fact the same place; the other groups were told that this area was different than the one they had seen in the map games. They were told they would have to report back to the starting point in 30 minutes; whistles were blown and the van's horn honked to signal them in. The field trips took place in early May (between 7 and 15 days after the second game session), when the trees were just starting to leaf out, and were all in the early morning, even when it was cold and drizzly.

Upon returning from their exploration of the park, the students were asked to draw a map of the park as well as to indicate some particular features on a map that was provided, and to answer a series of questions dealing with how they liked the experience, how confident they felt, and so on.

Results. Although the games were intended to be of some generic value, it was expected that the information gained from playing a game based on the actual area to be visited would be more useful. By and large, the results were opposite to our expecta-

TABLE 1
Examples of "20-Question" Items

Is it flat where you are standing?
Are the trees close to the path where you are standing?
Are you standing on a path?
Can you see a long way down the path from where you are standing?
Are you standing near the beginning of three short paths?
When you look directly up, can you see lots of open sky?
Are you standing east of the stream?
Are you near a 90° curve in the path?
When you look directly up, do you see lots of pine trees?
Does the land near you dip suddenly?

tion. The students who played games based on the *different* setting tended to feel more confident about their knowledge after the field trip than did the students whose games and outing were based on the *same* location ($t = 2.40$, df = 83, $p < .02$, especially true for the boys). The latter group expressed more discrepancy between their expectation and what they found; for the other group there was no basis for such discrepancies. By scoring the structured maps for how far each student ventured on his trip, one has an indication of the willingness to explore. Those whose games were based on the different park scored higher on "adventuresome" than did the other group ($t = 2.00$, df=83, $p < .05$). Not surprisingly, the students whose games were based on the same park as the field trip were more accurate in indicating the location of such features as pine trees and hills on their structured maps ($t = 2.52$, df = 83, $p < .02$).

Discussion. The outcome of this study, although not in the intended direction, permits several conclusions vital to any project of this kind. First, there is clear evidence that prior experience did make a difference. The results leave no doubt that there was a relationship between the transition experience in the classroom and the reactions to the outing in a natural setting. Second, the results make clear that prior cognitive structuring for an unfamiliar outdoor setting must be done well or not at all. This research was premised on presenting information in a way that was readily imageable and easy to understand at first glance. Due to several unfortunate coincidences, it was necessary to go ahead with material the research staff agreed did not fill this criterion. Participants with information they knew to be irrelevant to the

park at hand appeared to have no difficulty ignoring it. By contrast, material that is relevant but misleading has a clearly damaging effect. It is now clear that the resulting cognitive incongruity and confusion can actually detract from an experience in a natural area.

Study IV: Contour Maps and Aerial Photographs

Procedure. The last in this series of studies had many similarities with the one preceding it. We returned to the same junior high school and four new seventh grades classes ($n = 106$). It was October; fall colors were evident, but the leaves were mostly still on the trees. The Kim-game format was again used for orientation; "Battleships" and "20-Questions" were again used, with minimal changes. The field-trip procedure remained largely unchanged. The weather was again unpredictable (ranging from 35° F and dry to 50° F and very muddy in a matter of two days). The questionnaire completed after drawing the maps was improved, based on the results from the spring study.

Once again the park was not identified during the game sessions, but this time all the students had maps of the park where the field trips would take place. The major difference between this study and the preceding one was in the base maps used for the games. Two of the classes had contour maps; while the other two classes had oblique photo-based maps.

The contour maps, identifying elevation differences of 10 feet, showed that the park varied from about 890 to 960 feet. By using halftones, the path system and stream bed were shown against the contour lines;

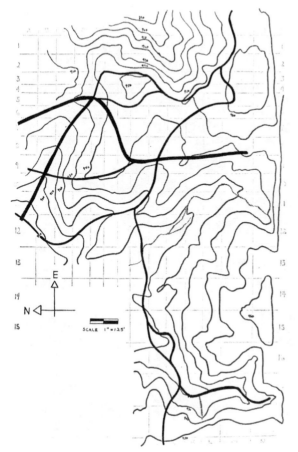

FIGURE 2
Contour map of the arboretum.

the grid system, needed for playing both games, was designated with light gray lines (see Figure 2). Contour maps are highly abstract and not immediately graspable. Before playing the first game, the students using these maps for their games were instructed in "reading" such maps. To play "20-Questions," they had to understand the topography and path system, and so the contour maps were discussed further at the start of the second game session. At this time, a few additional features of the park (e.g., where the pine trees and open field are) were also introduced.

Contour maps and many other maps are based on information "available" from directly above the de-

picted region, a vew that is rarely encountered. A view that would seem to enhance the immediate grasp of an area approximates the view from the window of a low-flying airplane; it is at an oblique angle to the region viewed and at a height that permits a single glance of the region. It was precisely such pictures that we tried to obtain for the photo-based maps. They were taken from the cockpit of a low-flying plane, at an oblique angle, and tried to include the entire park. In fact, given the height the plane had to fly, the pictures included much more than the park, which comprised only a small portion of the photograph, showing little other than the open field and the dense tree cover (although taken in early spring before the trees were leafed out). I think only a bird can actually meet all our height-and-angle criteria! In any event, we "doctored" one of these photographs to show the path system and stream bed, superimposed the grid system, and used it as the "game board" for two of the classes (see Figure 3). Once again, the students were instructed in "reading" the information and in understanding the oblique view. To play "20-Questions," they had to be told about the topography since this is not evident from the "map," but the pine trees and open field were, of course, self-evident.[4]

Results: Group differences. In terms of attitude toward the outing, the students who had played games with the photomap were significantly more positive than those who had used the contour maps ($t = 2.85$, df $= 104$, $p < .005$). This measure entailed a combination of two items, "How did you like going to the park?" and "How much would you like to take another trip like this one, but to another park?", with the mean rating for both map conditions falling between 4 and 5 on a 5-point scale. A third item, "Do you think you might come back to this park?", although uncorrelated with the other two items for the sample as a whole, showed the same pattern: the photomap students indicated a more positive outlook ($p < .01$); the means on this item were closer to the neutral point.

On the other hand, the answers to questions dealing with confidence with respect to way-finding were in the opposite direction: the students who had played games based on contour maps expressed a higher degree of confidence (means 3.0 and 2.7 on a 4-point

FIGURE 3
Aerial "map" of the arboretum.

scale; $t = 2.10$, df $= 104$, $p < .05$). This measure reflects a combination of three questions: "How hard was it to find your way back to the beginning?", "At times, did you feel uncertain of where you were?", and "If you brought a friend here for the first time, do you think he would need somebody to help him find his way?"—scored so that a higher number reflected greater confidence. Using this same measure, the boys showed considerably greater comfort with finding their way around than did the girls (means 3.1 and 2.7; $t = 2.53$, df $= 104$, $p < .01$).

The different map conditions had no bearing on the

students' ratings of the helpfulness of the games in finding their way around the park. Nor did the map conditions affect the students' reply to a question dealing with desired knowledge prior to going to a different place. Over 60 percent of the students in both groups felt it would be useful to know about "where the paths are," "if it was a woods," and "if there was water." They cared least (fewer than 40 percent) to know "what kind of trees grew there" and "what's there" (information often offered before school field trips). Both map formats led to a similar pattern of expectations about the size and number of trees, the size of the park, and the hilliness. The responses to these items indicated that the students generally found these slightly more or bigger than expected.

The variables from the questionnaire, structured map, and sketch map were analyzed using the two different dimensional approaches we have used extensively in other settings (see R. Kaplan, 1972, 1975). Based on these, three dimensions were formed: one dimension dealt with the principal features on the structured map and two separate ones dealt with the sketch map, one reflecting detail information and the other, accuracy and area covered. These three dimensions yielded no differences between the photomap and contour map conditions.

One of the two-dimensional approaches, the ICLUST hierarchical cluster analysis (Kulik, Revelle, and Kulik, 1970), also led to an additional dimension. It included three items from the questionnaire (related to knowing the park well enough to be a friend's guide, the likelihood of coming back to this park, and the expectation that there would be more paths), one item from the structured map (accuracy of indicating compass directions), and one from both map sources (the number of different parts of the park that were visited). High scorers on this dimension also included relatively more nature features than miscellaneous aspects (e.g., presence of people, houses, highway) on their sketch maps. A sense of orientation seemed to be the basis for the grouping of these measures.

Although the dimension is not particularly coherent (alpha coefficient of internal consistency =.45), and the results from it are tentative and only suggestive, we explored the relationship of this orientation dimension to the other variables. We found two things: the contour-map group scored higher on this composite orientation measure than did the photomap group (t=2.09, df=104, p<.05). Among the girls, this result was much more striking than with the boys. Second, the 15 students who indicated that they had made any prior trips to this park scored higher on this measure than did the vast majority (91) who had never been there before (t=2.17, df=.04, p<.05). Prior trips made no difference with respect to any other variables. (Two students from each map

group had made quite a few prior trips to the park; they found the games less helpful, and expressed greater confidence with respect to finding their way about.)

Discussion. The most striking finding of this study is the divergence of the attitude and confidence measures. The photomap condition showed a substantial difference in the predicted direction: these students were more favorable both to the experience and to the thought of future trips. At the same time, the contour-map condition seems to have generated somewhat greater confidence in way-finding ability in the park. Explanations of this unexpected divergence are necessarily after the fact, but they suggest areas of knowledge that should receive further attention in future studies.

The photomap seems to communicate an overall spatial feeling. One can quickly sense from it such information as the rough size of the area, what sorts of things form the boundaries, the balance between open area and dense woods. These seem to provide a nonspecific sense of familiarity for the place as a whole. The role of familiarity or sense of place in environmental preference has been demonstrated in other contexts (S. Kaplan, 1975; Herzog, Kaplan, and Kaplan, 1975). It is not unlikely that the photomap influenced attitude through its effect on familiarity, but this hypothesis has not yet been tested directly.

The contour map, by contrast, focuses specifically on features of the park itself: where the hills are and how steep they are, areas that are relatively flat, and so on. These issues are more directly pertinent to finding one's way in the park, and the greater way-finding confidence on the part of the contour-map group supports this. The interesting aspect of this finding, however, is that the greater confidence was independent of attitude. A sense of confidence and comfort in the natural environment would seem to entail a variety of informational inputs. Generic knowledge, to be sure, involves a great deal more than way-finding or orientation.

Mention should also be made of the problems created by operating on a cooperative basis in a school setting. In our concern to provide the students with a good educational experience, we probably managed to obscure intrinsic differences in the map formats. Both groups were provided with so much additional information that map differences may have been mitigated. The addition of considerable verbal imagery to supplement the visual squiggles of the contour map reduced the possibility of evaluating the "immediacy" of such maps. Likewise, there was no control group in the usual sense; all students had relevant prior information. The outing itself was structured so as to be an enjoyable experience. The students went out in small groups and had the freedom to roam and explore—not usual components of school field trips. The very high overall positive attitude suggests the effectiveness of these factors. That significant results were obtained despite these moderating factors is an indication of their robustness.

Key Areas of Methodological Development

As with any research in a new area, this series of studies has required the development of many tools as well as solution to a number of interrelated problems. In particular, four major areas have required considerable attention. These involve considerations of the natural setting to be studied, the basic representation of that setting (e.g., map rendition), the kind of involvement with the "map" (e.g., games), and the measures used to assess the effectiveness of the procedures.

Choice of natural setting. The ultimate goal of this research is to apply the techniques to more remote, more extensive areas. Places where there is a more realistic consideration of losing one's way are better candidates for needing prior knowledge. When the student knows that he has but half an hour, it is unlikely he will feel overly distraught and uncomfortable. Yet the frequency with which issues pertaining to getting lost were mentioned is astounding. There was hardly a carload heading for the park in which such concerns were not voiced, and upon the students' return to the van after the half-hour's exploration a great many of the comments dealt with this concern. Several people remarked on leaving "trail markers" to help them retrace their steps; some returned to the van well before the whistle blew. In answer to the question, "How is this park different from what you expected?", one student wrote, "I was kind of skair!"

It could be argued that such fears are the province of the young, that we become less fearful as we get older. It is perhaps equally likely that we become increasingly inhibited about expressing these fears! In fact, it is striking how common a worry is the fear of getting lost.

Thus, to be effective for such research, a site must present a challenge. If it is too readily comprehensible, there is little need for prior knowledge. A place that is quite open, providing vistas, permits more orienting cues and would therefore depend less on prior "vicarious" experience. Variations in topography and vegetation and relatively dense woods, as well as intricate path networks or relative lack of paths, probably enhance the usefulness of prior information.

Representation of the setting. This is the single most difficult problem and the most central issue in the area of transition experiences. Most of the difficulties we have encountered in our studies are clearly attributable to this problem. We have searched in vain for maps that give the impression we seek. The closest we have found is the shaded relief map, but it turns out to be extremely costly to create on the scale of a park. It would require indicating single trees and thousands of them. What we are seeking is a map rendition that does not overly distort and yet provides a more intuitive feeling of depth (or height). Its immediacy is of great importance. We want a two-dimensional representation that communicates the "feel" of the place. None of the base "maps" we have used so far has achieved our desired goals.

Involvement with the "map." We have now explored a variety of game formats. The intention in all of them is to require active involvement with the base map and to communicate information about various aspects of the setting. The game-board method we explored in the second study was, in a sense, too much fun. One could play it and win points with minimal regard for the base map. The "Battleships" and "20-Questions" games have both been effective in their aims. The students clearly enjoy playing the games and welcome the experimenters back the second week. Since they are based on familiar games, the rules associated with the games were easily understood and the games proceeded smoothly. The material for the games proved extremely inexpensive and the basic games were flexible enough to be modified to fit any natural area. As such, they hold great promise for use in a classroom setting.

Given a group setting, a game approach holds promise as a means of assuring sufficient involvement with the representation of the environment that is being used in the transition experience. Our studies using games all involved young teen-agers as the participants, but we have had no difficulty in engaging adults in these games as well—although never on a systematic basis. However, such games may not be appropriate in nongroup settings, where prior knowledge may nonetheless be important. We have not explored this area of research, but it would seem that there are a variety of approaches to assure such involvement, provided the base "map" is effective. Relying on a casual perusal of the map is unlikely to do the job. It is striking how much more information one obtains from a painting by using a format such as that Kenneth Clark used in his "Civilization" series, where many views are provided of what turns out to be a single painting. One's attention needs to be guided; without background or generic knowledge, one does not yet know what questions to ask.

Dependent measures. In the end, the knowledge we gain through these studies must come from the dependent variables we use. We are trying to get on paper an approximation of what people have in their minds about material that is not well coded verbally and is complex and diffuse.[5] We have made substantial progress along these lines, but this area still presents some frustrations. Although 12-year-olds are not known for their eagerness to complete questionnaires, this has presented no problems.

The importance of a range of measures cannot be overemphasized. In each study in this series it would have been all too easy to come to erroneous conclusions had only some of the measures been included. The multidimensionality of the effects of different kinds of maps is most strikingly evident in the fourth study, in which way-finding confidence and attitude appear to be barely overlapping domains. The possibility that an informational dimension other than way-finding underlies this attitude effect remains to be studied. It is clear, however, that the knowledge revealed in a map-drawing task taps still different domains.

Questionnaire data, especially if based on choices provided for the participant, are comforting and concrete. Map data are quite the opposite. The unstructured map task seems to be valuable, but it is also fraught with problems. These are not based so much on interrater reliability, which is not difficult to accomplish, as on the inferences one is making. What does a map that utilizes much of the blank page reflect? How can one tell how far the person actually went? How can one interpret the map if the person in fact explored off the paths most of the time?

Intrinsic in the map-drawing task are the very problems that make this area of research so difficult. The map should be an indication of the salient aspects of the environment. What *are* the salient features of a natural environment?

Knowledge and the Natural Environment

Maps of built environments (e.g., street maps) provide extremely abstract material and little general orientation to that environment. They have, however, the inherent advantage that knowledge of street patterns is important and in itself useful. The salient features of many natural environments are not as clearly identified. A map showing only the paths in a natural area the size of a large city is far less effective than the comparable city map, showing only streets. Problems of scale also enter. A method that is appropriate for representing several hundred square miles is less satisfactory for one square mile. Thus, atlases provide useful, readily communicable topographic material for vast areas, and yet these same methods present difficulties when applied on a small scale.

Knowledge of an area is based on much more than the information provided in a map. In the built environment, three kinds of information seem to be particularly salient: (1) the unusual, striking, or distinctly different components—landmarks in the traditional sense; (2) less striking landmarks whose distinctiveness is inferred from a background of regional information (such as "single-family residential" or "relatively new development tract"), against which they "stand out" (see Chapter 2); (3) "functional" landmarks, the collection of distinctive features at those nodes which serve as subgoals along one's path—places where one changes direction, for example. Some of these subgoals assume properties of "personal" landmarks, which are not shared by the public at large, but are just as distinctive and salient in a personal cognitive map (e.g., a friend's house, the place with the great garden, etc.).

What are the analogues in the natural environment, especially for one not well traveled in such bewilderment? The tension between landmark and background can be acute. The awesome, windswept conifer may well be coded as a landmark, a good feature to remember—until, alas, one passes the third or fourth or fifth awesome, windswept conifer. Landmarks have a way of becoming backdrop as elements repeat. With little prior experience, the unique aspects are difficult to discriminate, to code, to recall. Thus, it often turns out to be the nonnatural components in the natural environment that serve as the clearest landmarks. Human artifacts become particularly salient. The characteristic of a region as a whole may be one of the easiest aspects to recognize—forest, a clearing, or tall grasses. If a park can be characterized in terms of separable regions, it should be most easily knowable.[6] The problem of landmarks in the natural environment is thus an integral part of the issue of discriminating unique features against their background. To remember a particular place one has to discriminate it from other similar places.

Paths too can be problematic in natural areas; they are vital but often discouraging. They have a way of disappearing, of parting, or suddenly changing direction. They are demanding. Roots may be protruding; caterpillars may be crossing. The novice nature hiker probably spends more time looking down than does the novice "street walker." Because of the inherent complexities in the path systems of difficult natural areas, the recognition of salient features at points of choice is both vital and frustrating to the novice. It is at these points that the relative inability to distin-

guish among seemingly similar features is particularly painful. Without being able to distinguish features at points of choice, way-finding and route-retracing become problematic. In the built environment such points are often multiply coded. We have learned to distinguish the angle of the intersection, as well as subtleties of buildings, not to mention helpful street signs. To remember that the path intersection had four flowers and some tall grasses against some rocks is quite demanding, especially as one must remember an increasing number of intersections.

We are still a long way from knowing what generic knowledge of natural environments entails. Confident way-finding and orientation in such settings can be enhanced, at least to a limited degree, by prior exposure to relevant information. There are probably limits to the extent that this can be achieved based on specific information alone. A critical component of these skills must be the capacity to identify distinctive aspects of the environment. Landmarks are vital to cognitive map development; their identification is enhanced when one is sufficiently well acquainted with the setting to know what is distinctive.

The fear born of "not feeling at home" in the natural environment is a function not merely of a lack of prior experience with that particular setting, but of a lack of cognitive structure for such settings as a whole. Lee (1972) notes the close ties between such fearfulness and the notion of "sense of place." As he ably indicates, this often expresses itself in a social sense— one feels one "belongs" where social norms are predictable. It is equally true with respect to the physical environment itself. Thus, generic knowledge is required to use experience of the outdoor setting effectively. The importance of a sense of place and the preference for the familiar may well relate to the central role of feeling comfortable with the environment so that the distinctive elements can be differentiated.

NOTES

1. The studies reported here involved quite a few research assistants, graduate students, and others attracted to doing research while enjoying local parks. In particular, Roger Peters, John Merrill, Ann S. Devlin, and Hillorie Applebaum played

key roles in the formulations of the studies, development of games and maps, and the various phases of data collection. Janet Frey is responsible for making sense out of a vast collection of maps that were drawn by the students in the third and fourth studies. Mrs. Toby Butcher's continued eagerness and cooperation made it possible for us to do both the third and fourth studies in her "Small House Project." The helpfulness of the teachers and administrators of the public schools is greatly appreciated. In addition to my gratefulness to all these people, the acknowledgment of the funding for this project is offered with much more personal gratitude than the routine listing of the sponsoring agencies. Between the summer of 1970 and the end of 1973, the Forest Service, U.S. Department of Agriculture, supported this research effort, which was carried out by Stephen Kaplan and myself. In addition to financial support, we felt and welcomed the moral support that went with it.

2. Prior knowledge may actually lead to opposite effects in terms of curiosity. For the boys it seems to have whet the appetite; for the girls, there is the suggestion that it was "as good as seeing it." In addition, across all groups, there were notable sex differences suggesting a speed–accuracy trade-off. The boys tended to go farther, explored more, and saw more different things. The girls were far more accurate in their map renditions and labeled their maps more prodigiously. They proved themselves to be more verbal, offering more answers to the various open-ended questions.

3. Devlin (1973) reported on many aspects of this study, carried out as a doctoral student in environmental psychology under our supervision.

4. Oblique and vertical aerial photographs were also used extensively in environmental learning by the Clark University Place Perception Project. See Muir and Blaut (1969–1970), Blaut et al. (1970), Hart (1971), and Stea and Blaut (1973b) (the editors).

5. The reader is referred to Part III for further proposals on methods for assessing environmental knowledge and education (the editors).

6. The cartographer McCleary and his colleagues have been struggling with exactly these problems recently, especially in the preparation of guide maps for seminatural, semibuilt environments like parks and historic sites. See McCleary and Westbrook (1974) (the editors).

4

Ann S. Devlin
Department of Psychology
Connecticut College

THE "SMALL TOWN" COGNITIVE MAP: ADJUSTING TO A NEW ENVIRONMENT

As a result of the wealth of literature stimulated by Lynch (1960; see Downs and Stea, 1973b), we now have some understanding of the various elements which make up a person's cognitive map; that is, we know something about the maps in peoples' heads of areas larger than they can perceive at a single glance, areas like cities or towns. Theoretical concepts developed around the construct of the cognitive map provide an explanation of how people come to know the environment. As Stephen Kaplan (1973a) has noted,

> The cognitive map is a construct that has been proposed to explain how individuals know their environment. It assumes that people store information about their environment in simplified form and in relation to other information they already have. It further assumes that this information is coded in a structure which people carry around in their heads and that this structure corresponds, at least to a reasonable degree, to the environment it represents. It is as if an individual carried around a map or model of the environment in his head. The map is far from a cartographer's map, however. It is schematic, sketchy, incomplete, distorted and otherwise simplified and idiosyncratic. It is, after all, a product of experience, not of precise measurement (pp. 275–276).

Within the framework of the urban environment, Lynch has identified paths, edges, districts, nodes, and landmarks as the kinds of elements that constitute a person's cognitive map. There are also data on the types of varyingly schematic mental maps that inhabitants have drawn of their cities (Appleyard, 1970b; Moore, 1973b). In the Appleyard study, approximately 75 percent of the maps drawn were coded as sequentially dominant, which in Lynch's categorization means that paths and nodes predominated. With regard to this, Appleyard states, "The dominance of sequential maps confirms the importance of the path system as a structural organizer of the city" (p. 109). We are also becoming aware of the kinds of layouts that make orientation in the city a reasonable task for the newcomer and enable the inhabitant to broaden his base of knowledge more easily (De Jonge, 1962). Within all this work, however, there has been little emphasis on the actual processes by which such cognitive maps are formed in adults. One theoretical thrust has been based on a structural-developmental approach (Moore, 1973b, 1975a; see also Chapter 12). Moore hypothesizes a three-stage developmental sequence moving from (1) undifferentiated egocentric, to (2) differentiated and partially coordinated, and finally to (3) abstractly coordinated and hierarchically integrated. Another possible learning sequence is suggested in the following discussion by Lynch (1960):

For most people interviewed, paths were the predominant city elements, although their importance varied according to the degree of familiarity with the city. People with least knowledge of Boston tended to think of the city in terms of topography, large regions, generalized characteristics, and broad directional relationships. Subjects who knew the city better had usually mastered part of the path structure; these people thought more in terms of specific paths and their interrrelationships. A tendency also appeared for the people who knew the city best to rely more upon small landmarks and less upon either regions or paths (p. 49).

Further along in the book, Lynch also states,

There seemed to be a tendency for those more familiar with a city to rely increasingly on systems of landmarks for their guides—to enjoy uniqueness and specialization, in place of the continuities used earlier (p. 78).

It may be that paths serve as the groundwork, or the initial superstructure, and are punctuated by landmarks at various intersections and nodes. Once the structure is tightly secured in one's head, one is able to "chunk," using Miller's (1956) terminology, and perhaps use a landmark to "stand for" a whole surrounding area or territory. Landmarks may help to tie down or root major arteries, and certainly should make the learning of intersections with landmarks faster and more accurate than those intersections which lack them. In other words, landmarks, because of their visual distinctiveness, provide an important factor in the formation of a cognitive map. As Kaplan theorizes, internal representations, the central elements of the cognitive map, are constructed of perceptual experiences; landmarks are presumably critical perceptual experiences in the formation of a cognitive map.

If perception as hypothesized is critical to the learning of cognitive map elements, the factors that influence perceptual learning should likewise be the critical ones. Visual distinctiveness is one such factor, but there are undoubtedly others, too. Frequency is perhaps the most central of these; the more times an individual experiences a place, the more readily its representation should be learned. Another factor is the role of a place as a goal or subgoal. In route selection, as in other kinds of problem solving, it is

necessary to activate a representation of a goal in order to determine how to reach it (see Chapter 2). There is a meaningful sense in which one's home serves as the "goal" of many treks, thus combining the frequency factor with the special status of the goal.

Another category of influence involves the generic or potentially functional. Thus, when new to a town one might take note of the location of major but infrequently called upon services, such as hospitals. One might expect individuals who have lived in a variety of places to be especially sensitive to such resources. They may also have acquired a special sensitivity as to the likely location of some of these potentially needed functions. It does not take extensive travel, for example, to have a sense for the kinds of shops to be found along Main Street, USA. One may expect the courthouse or police station to have a particular form and to be near certain other kinds of functions.

Thus, there are a variety of different factors in coming to know places, among which are the role of landmarks and the importance of generic information. The more such factors are operative with respect to a given place, the more likely it is that it will be known. To learn more about the role of these factors and the speed with which places become known, an exploratory study was carried out with people who were new to a particular town. In addition, my husband and I later drew daily maps of a different area, when we moved to Connecticut, and these also provide interesting insight into the process of the development of cognitive maps.

Method

Participants. The people involved in the study, wives of navy officers moving to a new duty station in Idaho Falls, Idaho, presented a particularly good group to look at as they had no prior knowledge of that town. Military personnel provide an interesting category of participants for cognitive map work as they so frequently change residences. A total of 26 navy wives volunteered to participate in this study; 13 of them arrived in September (fall group) and 13 in December (winter group) of 1972. The participants ranged in age between 21 and 27, with a mean of 23.8 for the fall and 24.5 for the winter group. For all these women, the stay in Idaho Falls was for a mere six months; it was also the third home in less than a year for all the participants.

Setting. Idaho Falls is a town of about 40,000 inhabitants set in a flat plain; mountains can be seen at the city's edge to the northeast and west. The town is fairly rural in character; the first shoppping center was opened in the early 1970s and the fall of 1972 marked the opening of the first McDonald's. Although no longer completely dominated by the railroad, the tracks still define the main artery of town, and the stockyards still function not far from the town center.

The railroad tracks essentially divide the town into a residential district on one side, identified by a sequence of numbered streets, and the downtown and industrial areas located on the other side of the tracks, identified by a sequence of lettered streets (see Figure 1).

Along the tracks, cars filled with potatoes and sugar beets wait to be moved out by freight trains. (Schoolchildren in Idaho Falls are annually dismissed in the fall to help with the harvest of both these crops.) Idaho Falls has no high-rise structure of any kind, but the town has more hardware stores than most large

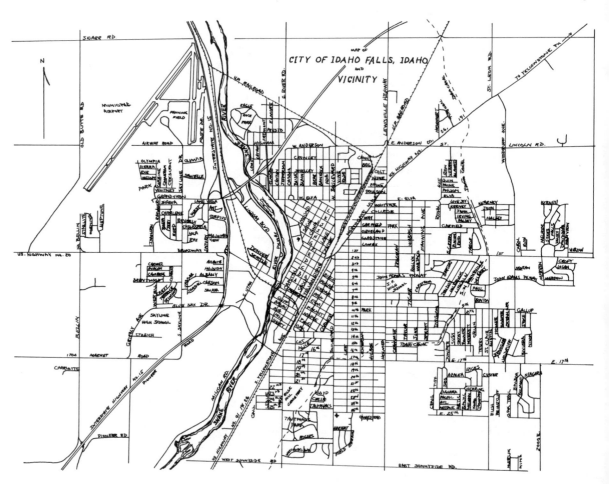

U.S. cities and certainly more snowmobile dealerships. Snow-related activities, such as skiing and snowmobiling, figure prominently in the lives of most Idahoans as the snow usually begins to fall in November and continues to accumulate into the spring. The emphasis on the outdoors, which centers on camping and backpacking in the summer months, continues unabated through the winter season. The most prominent physical and perceptual landmarks are the falls, after which the town is named, on the Snake River running through the center of town, and the Latter-Day Saints[1] temple and hospital not far from the falls.

Design of the study. The fall participants were approached at the conclusion of an orientation meeting held by the navy about two-and-a-half weeks after they had arrived in town. The 13 fall wives who volunteered for the study at the meeting were asked at that time to draw a map of Idaho Falls as best they could on a blank 8½- by 11-inch sheet of paper. No. roads or places were provided; the task was completely unstructured. In addition, the participants were asked to include on the maps their names, arrival date in Idaho Falls, and the number of times a reference map had been used to navigate in the area. The winter group, also consisting of 13 volunteers, completed their initial maps two to three weeks after arriving. The setting for them was a coffee, sponsored for them by the fall navy wives. At this same occasion, about 3 months after the initial orientation meeting, the fall wives were asked to draw their second maps. Again, the maps were drawn on blank 8½- by 11-inch sheets of paper. As no event was scheduled at the proper time, the second maps were mailed to the winter group a few months after their initial meeting.

Results

This exploratory study can be viewed as one that expands the role of the landmark in cognitive map formation and reveals knowledge of the speed with which the cognitive map forms, the types of elements that dominate the map, and the developments that occur—in terms of structure, detail, and accuracy—over a three-month period of time.

Initial maps. What is most striking when looking at the initial drawings is that cognitive maps form very rapidly. After only two and a half weeks in Idaho Falls, these women were able to communicate a great deal of information about the city. The initial maps were heavily dominated by streets (paths); an average of 20.3 streets were drawn and identified by the 26 participants (see Figure 2 for typical maps). The major arteries dividing the town into districts were mentioned by most of the participants. At the same time, it was evident from the maps that each person knew best the particular path structure of her home territory.

There was a clear emphasis on home place in these initial maps. In the vast majority of cases (all but three of the maps), the street on which the participant resided was drawn in and labeled, and generally the maps depicted the region in which the participant resided in much greater detail than other parts of the town. In fact, a few of the women represented *only* that part of town in which they lived; five actually drew a circle around and labeled their "home."

The path structures indicated on the maps showed less variability than did the landmarks. Although paths are imposed on us as a means of moving from one point to another, the things one notices along these routes are necessarily a more individual matter. Thus, the total number of different landmarks included on all the maps was quite high, 30 in all; of these only nine were mentioned by at least 10 percent of the participants. Three of these landmarks can be described as "physically and perceptually prominent." They include the Falls and the Latter-Day Saints' temple and hospital (mentioned by three, four, and six people, respectively). As none of the participants was a Mormon, they used the other medical facilities and religious facilities in town. The Latter-Day Saints' structures were, therefore, true landmarks in the sense of being physically and perceptually prominent.

The majority of the places noted on the maps could be regarded as "functional landmarks." The functional label has been ascertained by the author's knowledge of the use of these facilities and places by the participants. For example, as six of the participants were pregnant during the Idaho Falls stay and two gave birth during their residence in Idaho Falls, Sacred Heart Hospital served a number of functions for the participants: periodic checkups, delivery, and visitation of mother and child. The functional landmarks could be further divided into three categories: the "functional and perceptually prominent" places included those landmarks which qualify in Lynch's sense of being visually distinctive but also having functional meaning for the participants. Such landmarks as the Sacred Heart Hospital, the golf course, and the County Club Shopping Mall fall into this category. Other places lacked visual prominence, but were of functional importance to several of the participants. Albertson's 1st Street Supermarket was cited on four maps. The post office, a popular restaurant, and the Navy Administrative Unit would also qualify for this category. The third category is different from the second only in being more personal; it is still noteworthy because of its functional significance, but the particular place is idiosyncratic, reflecting each person's different encounters. Leading the list of such "personal functional landmarks" is the place called "home," necessarily a different place for each person. Particular restaurants, the car wash, the bus stop, and so on, may be salient places for a given person and would not be expected to be included on many of the maps.

Of all these landmarks, the one that appeared most frequently on the maps (seven instances), the Country Club Shopping Mall, was not depicted on the reference map to which the participants had access. The Chamber of Commerce map (see Figure 1) had been given to all arriving navy families to aid in securing housing. The map included the river, airport, railroad, parks, cemetery, high schools, and hospitals in addition to the street layout of Idaho Falls. The two hospitals, Latter-Day Saints and Sacred Heart, were not represented in name, but were indicated on the reference map with a cross (the American Red Cross symbol). However, only two participants represented the hospitals with such a designation, and on the follow-up maps they both switched to writing out the hospital names. There was no significant correlation between the number of times a participant said she used a reference map and the accuracy of her map. The role of the reference map in learning the area or forming the cognitive map is perhaps helpful, but not sufficient. Experience seems to be the best teacher in cognitive map formation. Structures that appear on the maps, such as hospitals, the library, or high schools, were usually written out and then enclosed by a square or circle, certainly not the way they were seen on the reference map, which merely gave the name of the facility, such as "municipal airport."

In addition to the paths and the various kinds of landmarks, two items that appeared with some regularity on the maps could be considered edges, in Lynch's terms. The Snake River was included on about one third of the maps and the railroad appeared on about one fourth. Both of these are, of course, prominent perceptual units forming boundaries and regions.

The kinds of errors made by the participants seem to be peculiar to the layout of Idaho Falls itself. The majority of the errors were made in such areas as reversal of street sequences, streets branching off Yellowstone Highway at the wrong angle, streets intersecting one another at the wrong place, and the lack of proper orientation of the lettered streets, A to L, in the downtown area to the numbered streets, 1st to 25th, in the residential area. The layout of downtown and residential areas around the main artery (Yellowstone Highway) appeared to be the major stumbling block for the women, as the lettered streets run perpendicularly into Yellowstone, whereas the numbered streets run at, but do not intersect, it at about a $30°$ angle. A "cone" of streets perpendicular to Yellowstone lie between it and the numbered streets (see Figure 1).

Follow-up maps. Three months later, the maps show a striking increase in amount of information; they are more filled in, include many more street names, additional landmarks, and a few additional areas. The home territory was not so much reduced in scope per se as relatively less important as so many other features had become incorporated. The home street remained labeled in almost every instance, but as the emphasis on the streets became fairly evenly spread over the area depicted, the home territory became less obvious. Looking at the follow-up maps, it was no longer clear where the home street was, whereas in the initial map that identification was easily made, as usually only one or two very minor residential arteries were shown.

In the follow-up maps, a total of 117 different streets (38 more than on the initial maps) were drawn in. The total number of streets included in all the

TABLE 1
Landmarks

Landmark Category	Initial Map	Follow-up Map
Physical-perceptual		
Falls	3	4
LDS temple	4	4
LDS hospital	6	5
Functional		
Functional-perceptual		
Country Club Shopping Mall	7	12
Golf course	4	8
Tautphaus Park	3	8
Sacred Heart Hospital	2	5
Idaho Falls High School	1	3
Library	2	3
Functional (shared)		
Albertson's 1st Street Supermarket	4	5
Yellowstone Highway underpass	3	4
Personal functional		
Home	5	3
Other (number of different places indicated)	10	16

follow-up maps (802) represented almost a doubling of the number included initially (471). The relative proportion of streets and various landmarks did not change in the course of three months; rather, both aspects mushroomed, leading to what seems like a doubling of knowledge of the area which consisted of filling in the originally set framework (see Figure 3). The downtown area was better represented on many (10) of the maps, which suggests that in the first two weeks this area may not yet have been explored.

A total of 40 different landmarks, that designation having been given to any structure or point reference on the maps, encircled or not, appeared on the follow-up maps, 10 more than appeared on the initial maps. Across all the maps the number of landmarks rose from 75 to 102. As would be expected, the landmarks showing the greatest increases were the functional ones that were also perceptually prominent. Thus, the Country Club Shopping Mall was indicated on almost half the follow-up maps; the golf course, Tautphaus Park, and the Sacred Heart Hospital all showed noticeable increases. The personal-functional landmarks showed the most instability; a convenient restaurant in the first few weeks may not have been frequented since then. New places were added, still reflecting each person's individual encounters with the environment.

Table 1 summarizes the changes in the frequencies with which the various landmarks were shown. Only instances for which at least 10 per cent of the participants included a particular landmark on at least one of the two maps are included. The entries in the table represent the number of times a place was included; for personal landmarks, however, the entry reflects the number of different places that could be categorized in this way.

Although the increase in the amount of information shown in the follow-up maps was significantly greater for both groups of women, the winter group showed relatively greater increases. For example, the fall group averaged an increase of 8.6 streets, whereas the women in the winter group indicated, on the average, 20.1 more streets in the follow-up maps. (Both these differences are significant; $t=2.60$ and 4.67, df$=12$, $p<.05$ and $.001$, respectively.) Since the initial maps for the two groups were no different in terms of number of streets, landmarks, or labeled items, the relative differences between the groups at the time of the second map drawing are noteworthy. Any explanation of such differences is necessarily after the fact

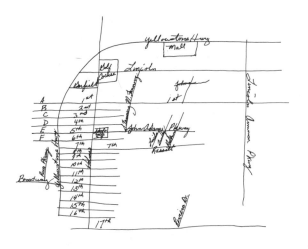

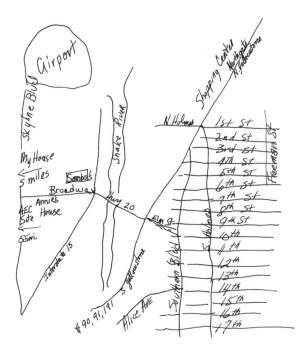

FIGURE 2
Typical adult initial sketch maps of the town.

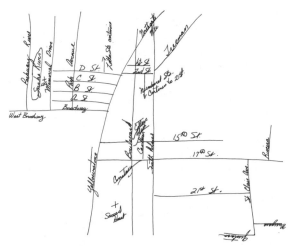

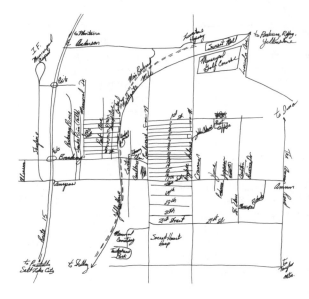

FIGURE 3
Initial and follow-up sketch maps, respectively, from the same participant.

and must be regarded as speculative. However, it is interesting to consider some explanations. It may be, for example, that the amount of initial knowledge one needs to make one's way in a new environment is not so much a function of external factors. To get the basic structure of the town is essential for any navigation through it. However, the patterns of subsequent exploration may show a greater relation to external conditions. Thus, for example, the severe winter climate may have placed a greater restriction on the fall group. For the winter group, there were no striking differences from fall to winter; it was winter throughout their stay.

With regard to map errors, most of the women were able to correct their street reversals and orientation problems although the correct spatial relation of the numbered streets to Yellowstone appeared to elude a few. The layout of this particular portion of Idaho Falls, then, proved to be a continuing problem and emphasizes the importance of a town's layout in the ease or difficulty of forming a coherent cognitive map.

Although the three-month lapse of time between the initial and the follow-up maps produced changes in the filling in of detail, one striking finding was the lack of dramatic structural or cognitive change. When comparing the initial maps with subsequent ones, it is evident that the latter are an elaboration of the basic node and path structure rather than a structural change as a whole. They show a more intricate network, more knowledge within the initial framework (see Figure 3).

Discussion

Three issues in particular call for further comment. First, there is the question of the rate of cognitive map formation and the pattern that this learning process takes. Second, this study suggests the importance of generic knowledge about cities in the reaction to any particular locality. Finally, there is the matter of landmarks. Although visual prominence is traditionally ascribed to landmarks, in this study functionally salient landmarks appeared to achieve greater importance for the participants in terms of the number of times these landmarks appeared on participants' maps.

Rate and pattern of cognitive map formation. In this study, the basic node and path structure of the town was learned very quickly. Not only was the formation of this groundwork strikingly rapid, it also showed remarkable persistence. This suggests that, as one becomes increasingly familiar with one's environment, one does not tend to alter the basic structural pattern. Rather, it becomes more complete, elaborated, extended, and sharpened. It may be that individuals forced to establish new roots so frequently develop certain skills in cognitive map development which others, living in one or perhaps two locations in a lifetime, do not possess. Career military personnel frequently have moved as many as 20 times in a 20-year span of service. Certainly, when you move frequently and do not expect to stay long, the "landmarks" you pinpoint initially may not be the perceptually prominent ones studied in large cities. Rather, the notion of a "functional landmark," the supermarket or shopping mall, for example, may better fit the kinds of structures which these navy wives would first locate.

It may be that structural changes in our cognitive maps do occur during the map formation, but in the very first encounters with a new environment, the first hours and days. To get a better feeling for the very early phases of the formation of a cognitive map in a new environment, my husband and I drew daily maps for a while when we moved to Connecticut from Idaho Falls. The first maps we drew were global in nature. The maps were "area" maps, containing roughly a 15-square-mile area and within that area the towns of New London, Groton, Gales Ferry, and Mystic. These maps were globally spatial, as if we had colored in large areas on a piece of paper in different shades; they were in the correct relationships spatially but with little detail. As the maps were so global in nature, the appearance of detail itself is surprising. Yet the first map for each of us did contain the major artery going through Groton and connecting it and New London, as well as the motel ("home") in which we stayed the first night. These first maps also included the location in Gales Ferry of the apartment we rented the first full day there, the locations of the submarine base in Groton and of Electric Boat, where the submarines are constructed, along the Thames River on the Groton side.

The next maps worked with the same overall spatial framework, but narrowed in on the Groton side in great detail. Shopping centers, restaurants, gas stations, and minor arteries began to appear. What is striking from this experience is how much one is able to bring together in terms of spatial relationships despite little direct interaction with that space. It was our experience in the New London–Groton area, too, that the filling-in process seems to be the dominant one. The successive maps became more detailed within the initially defined structure.

Drawing these maps also made us aware of the interaction between the structure of a particular place and its "knowability." Even after a year in the New London area, my husband and I feel that we could draw a more accurate map of Idaho Falls than of our present area. Size and complexity have an obvious influence on the ease with which cognitive maps are formed. Lynch has shown that differences in the physical layout of Boston, Jersey City, and Los Angeles in part account for the varieties of cognitive maps that residents of these places develop. Clearly the layout of a town is important to its legibility. Some aspects of physical layout may be unique to a place, and it may even be detrimental to anticipate too much general similarity as one goes from one place to another.

Generic issues. The rapidity of cognitive map formation suggests that these participants had prior knowledge of cities in general which they were able to call on in coming to understand this particular town. Certainly, the importance of paths (or roads) is the outcome of a number of converging factors. On theoretical grounds, paths have a vital role; there is nothing one could call a cognitive map without a path-type element. This is paralleled in the emphasis on the streets of a city as a means of organizing or even coordinating space. It is not an accident that a city map is a street map.

In addition to the familiarity of the participants with roads as a means of structuring space, other sorts of generic knowledge concerning roads are available to them. In particular, roads reveal extensive although relatively subtle information about the likely location of various functions. A street named "Main" communicates many messages. Streets at a nonperpendicular angle to a major grid pattern suggest divisions, much as the railroad tracks and the river do. Comparably, the predominance of streets in the drawn maps of the participants in the Idaho Falls study represents more information than just their location. It is implicit in a map-drawing task of the built environment that one indicate the street structure.

Generic urban information also leads to expectations of the locations of certain functions and their groupings. Restaurants are likely in the vicinity of hotels and motels, grocery stores are likely near residential areas, and so on. (Jackson, 1970, in his sensitive essay "The Stranger's Path," traces a variety of environmental regularities of this kind.) A person new to an environment, whether on an overnight stay or at the beginning of a period as a resident, has certain functional requirements that determine some of the spatial encounters. Our maps of the New London–Groton area showed not only that such functional needs are pervasive, but that they play an important role in what one "notices." When the gas tank approaches the empty mark, one is struck that one "incidentally" has noticed the location of several gas stations, possibly including the brands of some of them.

On landmarks. The majority of places indicated on the Idaho Falls maps were places of functional significance. Although paths are necessary as routes, the functional demands in a sense guide where one is going. These places then come to serve a vital role in the mental map of a place. They serve many of the purposes of a landmark. They are initially goals of an outing, but in time they help structure the region and become subgoals (see Chapter 2) with important way-finding implications. It is not unusual to go from one place to another by a route that is not optimal in terms of distance; rather, it includes a sequence of approximations in the right direction that is guided by these known subgoals.

One difficulty with this explanation is the emphasis given to the traditional (i.e., singular and visually prominent) landmark (Lynch, 1960). The interaction of environmental and methodological factors may be the basis for the discrepancy. Idaho Falls is small enough to considerably simplify the way-finding problem relative to the large cities more traditionally studied. It also is lacking in the number of monumental landmarks that are more often found and needed in large cities. The fact that visually prominent and singular landmarks are more likely to be present and to be used in large cities may not be the only reason for their appearance in traditional cognitive map studies. Their great frequency and high agreement may have tended to obscure any role the functional landmark may have played in these studies. Thus, not surprisingly, it required a study of quite a different sort of urban environment to identify the role of this cognitive element.

5

Roger M. Downs

Department of Geography
  Pennsylvania State University

COGNITIVE MAPPING AND INFORMATION PROCESSING: A COMMENTARY

In a time when the quick look at "relevant" problems is a popular style of research, it is refreshing and rewarding to read the integrated writings of a group of researchers engaged in the long-term pursuit of a set of ideas. The preceding three papers are but one outgrowth of an exciting research team that Stephen and Rachel Kaplan have organized and inspired at the University of Michigan. As such, the papers reflect a stage in an ongoing development of ideas, and it is in this context that I shall discuss them.

These chapters enjoy a style of presentation that is articulate, imaginative, provocative, and, above all, persuasive. They reflect a view of environmental psychology that I applaud, a view which argues that the environment is not simply that vast unknown which can be seen through the confines of the laboratory window. We are witnessing instead a true marriage of environmental concerns and the concepts and methods of psychology, which results in a product comprising far more than the sum of its disciplinary parts. This marriage is shown to its advantage in the paper by Rachel Kaplan, which draws on a wide range of tools (maps, games, field trips), places them in a sound methodological and research design context, and addresses a set of exciting questions that have

wide implications. Perhaps the greatest message of these papers lies in the demonstration that a long-term approach to cross-disciplinary problems can succeed. At the risk of hyperbole and overstatement, I would argue that the cornfield which has been flattened by the passage of the quick-look bandwagon can be harvested by a team of careful workers.

A measure of the success of this work can be found in the central issues which these papers identify and discuss. Of these central issues, four are important to the future development of the field of cognitive mapping. These are the questions of the meaning of cognitive maps and cognitive mapping, the role of way-finding, the idea of generating expectations and spatial predictions, and the spillover effects of the capacity for cognitive mapping.

Stephen Kaplan reminds us that the idea that we have a map in the head remains a convenient and intuitively plausible metaphor but that we need to go beyond this appealing metaphor to search for possible mechanisms. This timely reminder is particularly appropriate for two reasons. That the map idea remains only an analogy suggests that we have still not advanced much beyond Tolman's (1948) original use of the map-room analogy to account for the spatial behavior of rats in his classic maze experiment. And we are still susceptible to the criticism leveled at the image idea, which was also developed to account for rat behavior: how is the image used by the rat to generate behavior? Is our rat (or man) still lost in thought in the contemplation of his cognitive map, to paraphrase Guthrie's famous criticism? Kaplan's reminder is also appropriate for those of us who come to this field with a geographic background. It is so easy to allow the cartographic map to dominate our thinking about the form and function of the cognitive map. The analogy can be deceptive and misleading, and Kaplan's paper forces us to confront the purpose of the analogy.

Despite the timeliness of this reminder, I take exception to some parts of all three papers because I see a curious tension and ambivalence surrounding the use of the terms "cognitive map" and "cognitive mapping." I must confess, however, that after several rereadings I am not sure if my disagreement is warranted or not, and so I simply offer it as something for the reader to consider. I see a tension between product (map) and process (mapping). The process–product dilemma is a universal problem for which there is no "right" and definitive answer. However, in using the idea of a cognitive map (or internal model or cognitive structure), it is easy to slip into the belief that a map is something that people *have* stored away somewhere in the head. We get dangerously close to treating spatial knowledge as a form of massive but mysterious cognitive atlas. Along with Kaplan, I am perfectly willing to accept the idea that the environment *is* in the head. That such a position is helpful in understanding human spatial behavior is clear from Rachel Kaplan's paper. But in what way is the environment in the head? It is at this point that I part company with these papers. I believe that we should answer this question by stressing the *process* of cognitive mapping and not the cognitive maps themselves. In this way, we can skirt around a series of problems. For example, we know that people can generate a variety of representations of the same place. We can demand a cartographic map, a pictorial sketch, a verbal description, a scale model, or a series of directions specifying how to get somewhere. People are flexible in their ability to generate cog-

nitive maps: this suggests that we should ask questions about the process of cognitive mapping which allow the person to generate a range of alternative but complementary maps. (It also throws doubt on the value of the analysis of the "errors" in sketch maps in Ann Devlin's paper.) We can also avoid the thorny problem of accounting for these static objects that people have, a problem that centers on the question of storage.

Although I find Stephen Kaplan's model interesting and credible, I would prefer an approach that explicitly concentrates on the process of information *processing* and which, in turn, views cognitive mapping as one particular class of information processing. Cognitive maps are generated to serve a specific purpose and do not necessarily "exist" as a given structural form. What does exist are sets of information and sets of rules (or heuristics) for generating maps. Of course, this position can rightly be faulted, because we still have to specify how and in what form this information and these rules exist. Even though I acknowledge this severe fault, I do believe that we must emphasize mapping rather than maps, and I see in these papers a blurring of this distinction. Both process and product approaches are intermingled, and I think that the reader should consider the value of maintaining the distinction in assessing these papers.

Rachel Kaplan's paper raises another fundamental question about the role of maps, and it is one which has not received the attention that it deserves. In the third study that she reports, a map was prepared to communicate certain spatial characteristics of a wild park area. Unfortunately, the form of the map itself was not successful as a communication device. Despite the totem-like status of the cartographic map in geography, we do not know very much about map reading as a process. We do know that certain shading schemes can be perceptually distinguished and that people can detect the differences among a certain scaling of graduated circles. But how is this abstracted information synthesized by the average map reader to form a holistic internal spatial representation? The many empirical studies of cognitive mapping have taught us that the form of the map requested obviously constrains the information content and organization of the cognitive map. We are flexible in our cognitive mapping abilities, with the capacity to switch (or translate) from one form to another. How does the complementary process work? How do we communicate information or the "feel" of a place to another person? What flexibilities does the map reader possess? How should we make use of these flexibilities in constructing maps? As Rachel Kaplan discovered, there are few answers to these rather obvious questions.

One final observation on cognitive maps and mapping stems from Devlin's paper. She rightly argues that we have placed little emphasis on the actual processes by which cognitive maps are formed (or generated for that matter). In this respect, one of her findings contradicts the conventional wisdom about the process of learning a new environment. A general belief suggests that people initially develop a cognitive structure which consists of a scattering of routes that focus on a very few destination nodes. Such a structure is gradually replaced by a qualitatively different structure, which integrates very many different nodes and routes. Devlin's data suggest that the path and node structure is formed very early in one's exposure to a new environment and that the basic pattern may not change over time. Although such a finding may reflect the peculiar nature of her sample of subjects, it reminds us that we should treat much of the conventional wisdom of cognitive mapping with a healthy degree of scepticism, since it lacks supporting data of other than a personal, introspective nature. It is especially true that we lack solid evidence as to the unfolding of the cognitive mapping process in a temporal context.

A second major issue that is central to all three chapters is the question of spatial way-finding. Way-finding is one basic starting point for understanding the development of cognitive mapping. As Stephen Kaplan's evolutionary argument suggests, the major function of cognitive mapping is in allowing man to solve complex spatial problems on a large-scale, two-dimensional surface. Ironically, our understanding of the process of human way-finding is far less developed than that of creatures lower down the phylogenic scale. Apart from the obvious literature on bird navigation, we could cite the studies of bees by von Frisch (1967), digger wasps by Tinbergen

(1932), and chimpanzees by Menzel (1973) as evidence of attempts to understand way-finding. In comparison, the human literature is both sparse and scattered. Much of this literature is derived from anthropological descriptions and lacks extensive empirical support. In this respect, the paper by Rachel Kaplan (especially the games in study III) is provocative and instructive. This last statement is an appropriate summary of all the work that has been produced by this group at the University of Michigan. It has the timely knack of identifying key issues and providing a sound, provocative introduction to them.

We find additional evidence of this talent in a third common feature of the three chapters in their emphasis on generating expectations and making spatial predictions. They all view cognitive mapping as a "lookahead" or predictive capacity that enables a person to generalize on the basis of past experiences and to use these generalizations (or generic information) in other spatial contexts. Thus, Devlin discusses the idea of the likely locations of various facilities in urban areas, and I believe that this approach has tremendous potential for understanding how people make use of cognitive mapping in everyday life. Whatever we call this process of going beyond the information given (to borrow Bruner's phrase), it is central to our ability to operate in the large-scale spatial environment. It is also central in a developmental sense, since we are discussing people's ability to become intuitive geographers and to extract some of the underlying principles of the spatial organization of society. [An excellent example of this process in operation is given in Bruner's (1959) description of children engaged in a geography lesson.] This intuitive spatial sense is a fundamental part of the generative capacity of cognitive mapping, which is stressed in Stephen Kaplan's paper.

From the very first studies of cognitive mapping, it has been obvious that the ability being discussed is not limited in its application to solving only problems of spatial navigation. We are dealing with an ability that allows us to fantasize, to imagine places not visited, to store and recall nonspatial information, and to engage in creative thinking. There are vast "spillover" functions of cognitive mapping and these are gradually being discussed in the literature. Stephen Kaplan's paper offers some wide-ranging suggestions as to the breadth of these spillover effects. The spatial thinking inherent in cognitive mapping has major connections with thinking and problem solving in general.

Luria (1968) has documented one amazing use of spatial thinking as a mnemonic system, although Bower's (1970) paper demonstrates that the spatial character of the mnemonic system is not a necessary attribute. Huttenlocher (1968) has shown how some verbal syllogisms can be solved by the use of spatial imagery, and this obviously leads to the fascinating literature that discusses the use of visual, and especially spatial, imagery in creative thinking. The two examples that immediately spring to mind are those of the discovery of the spatial form of the benzene and DNA molecules. The connection between chess and spatial thinking is evidenced in the work of Simon and his associates (see especially the 1973 paper by Moran on the spatial structuring of information) and the imaginative discussion by Steimen (1974) of the workings of the mind of a chess player. Although some of these speculations may prove to be wildly overdrawn and mistaken, we should try to incorporate cognitive mapping into the literature of problem solving. Nowhere is this point made more clearly than in the series of papers that Stephen and Rachel Kaplan have either written or inspired.

To produce any overall assessment of these chapters is, I think, impossible at present. They are not final statements but progress reports from an ongoing research program. Nevertheless, certain observations are appropriate. The outstanding feature of this work is its imaginative, catholic approach. We can see this in the context of research design (Rachel Kaplan), in language and expression (Stephen Kaplan), and in wide-ranging thinking (all three). Lest this commentary appear too euphoric and uncritical, there are ideas and approaches that I do not agree with and which disturb me. Although one might like Stephen Kaplan to a master chef in his capacity to mix "solid" ideas with speculation, sometimes the dish is indigestible. As an example, consider the section entitled "On Information and the Management of Uncertainty." I accept the basic position that he is trying to develop, but I find that his argument is seriously flawed in several places. For instance, it is one thing to talk about man taking advantages of opportunities, but it is stretching language to then describe him as opportunistic, with all the connotations of that term. We are also told that "speed, of course, is bought at the price of accuracy." Although I may be accused of quibbling over specific words, I cannot agree with such a statement. Speed is not necessarily bought at the price of accuracy since accuracy presumably means success in terms of adaptive behavior. The measure of accuracy is not faithfulness of representation of the environment but effectiveness in terms of spatial behavior. There are many other statements in this one section that I feel are either unwarranted or unsupported. On a more major level, I do feel that the map–mapping point raised earlier is an important one that these papers do not clarify. In spite of these objections, one cannot help being impressed with the scholarship that is displayed in these chapters. I cannot see that we can expect more of research in terms of provoking us to consider the importance and ramifications of the concept of cognitive mapping.

PERSONAL CONSTRUCT THEORY

6

PERSONAL CONSTRUCTIONS OF PERSONAL CONSTRUCT THEORY

Roger M. Downs

Department of Geography
Pennsylvania State University

Whenever I am forced to talk about or, worse still, write about theory, I become anxious and apprehensive. Such feelings emerge whether I am confronted with Central Place Theory, a teething ring for all "modern" geographers, or with Piagetian Theory, which now commands my attention as a student of environmental cognition. I realize that to admit anxiety about such a fundamental scientific concept as a theory risks both derision and sympathy; in fact, I am so unsure that I worried about using the word "concept" to describe a theory!

George Kelly (1955, p. 495) defined anxiety as the recognition that the events with which one is confronted lie mostly outside the range of convenience of one's construct system. Although you may not be certain as to the precise meaning of some of the words in this definition, you may be able to appreciate why I am anxious. I had agreed somewhat unthinkingly to show how Kelly's Person Construct Theory (PCT) might aid in understanding the processes of environmental cognition. However, the painful gestation of this paper has led to the acknowledgment that I am not sure that I would recognize a theory if I saw one. I "know" what the philosophers of science tell me about the role of theory, but I am not sure if this lies within my range of understanding (or construing). Anxiety stems from an awareness of the lack of a structure for coping with events. How can I tell the differences among a theory, a model, a conceptual framework, and a common or garden idea?

I am conscious of some significant differences in the everyday, scientific usage of the word theory. Sometimes theory has a big "T" as in the Theory of Relativity or Probability Theory. We also recognize a small "t" version, as in learning theory or location theory. Big "T" theories are coherent, explicit, clearly stated, and, above all else, are *used.* Little "t" theories are diffuse, implicit, uncertain, and referred to, but they are *not* useful. As Reginald Golledge wrote of an earlier draft of this paper: "Learning theory and location theories are *used* but may not be very *useful* in understanding things in any but a strict normative sense."

Little "t" theories do not fare well outside of the confines of the campus laboratory or beyond the isotropic plain with its Potemkin-style villages. Little "t" theories are like Procrustes's bed; the real world will not fit into them without suffering some incredible deformations. In contrast, big "T" theories are capable of organizing and making sense of our real-world experience, of providing insights into how the world works, of generating expectations of what might happen. Of all the characteristics that are encompassed by the word "theory," the idea of utility stands out for me. Either a theory helps me to understand the world (the big "T" version, hereafter given a capital T) or I invoke it when I feel the urge to be scientific (the little "t" version, given a lowercase t).

How should I view Kelly's theory of personal constructs? Is it a big "T" theory which helps my understanding or is it a small "t" pseudoscientific invocation? What follows is a personal attempt to answer this question. One attractive feature of Personal Construct Theory is the abandonment of the familiar researcher–subject distinction. Kelly's Theory is reflexive in that it is based on the idea that, whatever the "scientist" does in his "professional" work, his "subjects" are also doing in their everyday lives. He is trying to understand them in much the same way as they are trying to understand the world around them. The scientist's white coat is like the emperor's new clothes. Consequently, I will not try to hide behind the third person passive: this chapter is a very personal, active exploration of the utility of Kelly's Personal Construct Theory in environmental cognition research.

PERSONAL CONSTRUCT THEORY
AS A METHODOLOGY

My introduction to PCT came several years ago when Bob Horsfall, a psychologist, suggested that we consider PCT as a possible solution to some nagging methodological problems in a proposed study of urban cognition (see Downs and Horsfall, 1971). Having recently graduated, both literally by a Ph.D. dissertation and metaphorically through frustration, from the use of the semantic differential technique, I seized upon PCT as the panacea for all my methodological ills. The theoretical component of PCT played a negligible role in this decision. I made the choice from a pragmatic viewpoint only. I "read" the theoretical parts of Kelly's work, but, with the exception of the "man-the-scientist" analogy, they did not register. What did register were the techniques he described, particularly the repertory grid method

which was so convincingly elaborated in Bannister and Mair's (1968) discussion of PCT. I am not alone in my discovery of and choice of PCT and the repertory grid method. Although the number of applications of grid methods has not yet reached crisis proportions, elements such as rooms, houses, shopping centers, neighborhoods, cities, and states have all been run through the mill of the grid method. Given the current time lag for journal publication, we can expect at least as many grid method studies as there were semantic differential studies in the last five years.

Why is the methodology so popular? This is a reasonable question when we consider some of the characteristics of the theoretical parent of the methodological offspring. First, PCT is an also-ran in the "mainstream" of American psychology. For obvious reasons, I do not believe that the respected mainstream is always right, nor do I believe that the truth is bounded by the Pacific and Atlantic oceans. However, Kelly's work is not prominent and does not receive more than an obligatory few pages in most of the standard texts. Such relative obscurity is not the fate of PCT in Britain. The missionary work of Donald Bannister and his group of disciples has had a significant impact on psychology, as evidenced by numerous journal articles and by a collection of theoretical papers (Bannister, 1970a). This proliferation has sparked sympathetic responses among some geographers and architects. Nevertheless, we are not talking about the sort of ideas that you would necessarily expect even a well-read psychology graduate student to know.

Second, such obscurity is accentuated by the genesis and development of PCT. Its origins and major uses lie within psychotherapy and clinical psychology. For obvious reasons, these areas have never been happy hunting grounds for those of us who came to environmental cognition from geography, architecture, or planning. The third characteristic of PCT is perhaps a blessing in disguise. From the viewpoint of mainstream psychology, PCT is unconventional, almost iconoclastic and irreverent, since it abandons such "traditional" concepts as learning, development, and motivation. For a nonpsychologist, the loss of such organizational landmarks and the wholesale slaughter of sacred cows is a cause for celebration in itself.

Conversely, it does make PCT difficult to read and comprehend because it does not fit into any existing theoretical framework. We like to pigeonhole and classify ideas, and PCT's rejection of conventional labels does not lend itself to such a process. Hence the literature discussing PCT is replete with debates over what type of theory it "really is." It is normal to comment on academic pedigree and to trace out a genealogy. Undoubtedly, people will say that PCT is like X and Y: there is no point in this process. The key questions are: Is it set up so that I can use it? Does it help me in understanding the world in general and environmental cognition in particular?

Despite these characteristics which mitigate against the adoption of PCT, several reasons account for the popularity of its attendant repertory grid methodology (see Bannister and Mair, 1968; Harrison and Sarre, 1971; see also Chapters 7 and 34). Grid methods do seem to be a "natural" step in any graduation from semantic differential studies, even if these studies do contain ". . . the unrecognizable mutants which are found in most of the studies claiming to use it" (Stringer, 1972, p. 317). It is too easy to attack the practical failings of the semantic differential studies while overlooking their vital role in introducing the area of environmental cognition to many nonpsychologists. Much as psychologists may find geographic work in environmental cognition to be naive from a psychological viewpoint, geographers find some psychological work to be geographically naive. The environment is not just another variable to be thrown into a multiple regression model; it is the *raison d'etre* of a whole class of behavior, that is devoted to solving spatial problems. We are growing out of the semantic differential, but, like last year's fashions, it was very useful when we needed it.

As an indication of the "natural" growth process, Bannister and Mair (1968, p. 134) argue that

> The semantic differential should not be regarded as a rather simple, quick equivalent of grid method. Grid method can be cast in such a form as to give all the information that might be derived from the semantic differential, plus additional information which is not obtainable from the normal use of the semantic differential method.

An advantage of the grid method is that it has the virtue of combining "personal" detail with the production of "quantifiable" data. It imposes the least number of constraints on the person as he or she tries to communicate his or her understanding of some part of the world. It avoids the "Did-you-beat-your-wife-today?" structure that bedevils so many of the available data-generating procedures. Grid methods allow us to have the better parts of both worlds: we can be humanistic, relevant, and soft while maintaining an objective, scientific, and hard nosed stance.

Another "plus" of repertory grid methods is that they offer a complete package deal in terms of research design. They provide a clearly specified set of alternative data-collection procedures and a series of analytic options. There is even a set of concepts that can be used to structure and interpret the results! The whole package is couched in very simple terms. However, the simplicity can be deceptive, not because of hidden complexity but because of an unappreciated, latent potential for expansion. Grid methods are not a "test," as the idea is understood in intelligence or personality testing. They are flexible techniques that are continually being developed and extended, although Bannister and Bott (1973, p. 168) argue that this process is far from complete:

> However, professional use of grids to date seems not to have fully explored the implications of the idea that the grid is a method, a strategy, a language system, a variable format for data, a set of principles for formalizing information and judgments—it is anything but a test.

All these desirable characteristics made repertory grids a natural prey for the foraging of what are either intrepid pioneers or lucusts, depending upon your perspective. Borrowing has become a hallmark of innovative thinking in behavioral geography and is inevitable in the area of environmental cognition. Ironically, a comment from Kelly (1955, p. 23) might give us pause here:

> It might now be a good plan to start abstracting the scientific principles which are beginning to emerge from our experiences as well as others', instead of poking about in the neighbors' backyards for methodological windfalls.

I believe that Kelly would excuse our trespasses if he were alive to see the state of our backyard.

Although these reasons for the popularity of grid methods as a useful methodology are understandable, are we justified in adopting them from a purely pragmatic point of view? Are we boarding the latest fashionable bandwagon or, to use Kaplan's (1964, p. 28) memorable "law of the instrument," is this another case of a small boy with a new hammer who is finding that everything needs hammering? Unfortunately, this pragmatic approach to grid methods is a true case of putting the cart before the horse. It is *impossible* to separate the *theory* of personal constructs from its operational procedures (i.e., its methodology). One of the many remarkable features of PCT is that it is the product of the integrated thinking of one man, a true brainchild. It grew out of Kelly's teaching and psychotherapeutic practice over a long period of time, and was crystalized in his two volume work, *The Psychology of Personal Constructs* (1955). Although Kelly would have rejected any assertion that this 1955 version of PCT is immutable, it did represent an integrated, coherent statement that linked theory *and* methodology. We cannot accept one without the other; the pragmatic approach will not work. Bannister and Mair (1968, p. 139) make this clear:

The fact that grid technique is so closely related to construct theory presents an interesting problem for users of the grid who approach it without a construct theory orientation. A personal construct theorist, using repertory technique, sees himself as measuring aspects of personal construct systems, as elaborately defined within the theory. A psychologist using the technique purely in an empirical manner, or within another framework, is faced with the problem of deciding what he is measuring. He may decide he is measuring some aspect of "meaning," or "concept formation," or "attitude," and so forth. He must ask himself why he felt it necessary to follow construct-theory-dictated assumptions in his construction of the grid, while feeling free to ignore them in his interpretation of the data generated by it. An infinite number of contradictions can be foreseen.

I recognize, after my early pragmatic applications of PCT methodology, the import of Bannister and Mair's position. To appreciate the value of PCT, we must consider the theory in its own right, and not just as an optional appendix to a desirable methodology. Using my own criterion of utility to distinguish between little "t" and big "T" theories, I cannot avoid looking at the theoretical horse before deciding whether to explore the area of environmental cognition with PCT.

PERSONAL CONSTRUCT THEORY AS A THEORY

The simplest way to begin our assessment of PCT is to ask whether we need any help in understanding the world of environmental cognition. The answer, as far as I am concerned, is obvious: there is a total lack of coherent theory in the area of environmental cognition. I will try to support this outrageous statement and indicate some of the consequences that follow from the lack of theory.

I did *not* say that there is no theory but rather that there is no *coherent* theory. If anything, we have too many little "t" theories. I suspect that many people might secretly agree with Bannister and Fransella (1971, p. 13):

In every scientific discipline bar psychology, workers seem to accept the idea that their science will advance in terms of the building, the testing and elaborating of theories. In psychology, many of us behave as if "theory" were like heaven—a fine place to go when the practical business of living is all over, but not a matter of much concern here and now. We manifest our contempt for theory by using the word indiscriminately.

There are many implications to be drawn from this statement, and none of them are pleasant or desirable. For example, many geographers and architects would have to be classed as agnostics or even atheists with no place to go after the practical business is all over.

Perhaps more central to my concern is the indiscriminate use of the word "theory." The wealth of *theories* makes life very difficult. Innumerable competing and unrelated theories have been adopted on an ad hoc basis from psychology. None of the following comments is intended as personal criticism, but what are the connections between the work on environmental complexity and preference of Kaplan and Wendt (1972) and Wohlwill (1968)? How do the physiological models of Kaplan (Chapter 2), Pribram (1971), and Bogen et al. (1972) fit together? What is the status of the adaptation of Piagetian theory to the development of environmental cognition? In reading this last-named work, I am reminded, perhaps unfairly, of the line from the song that asked, "Where have all the children gone?"

We are currently confronted with a confused mass of *theories* that do not help us to understand environmental cognition. There is no common language for structuring ideas and results, for making predictions and generating expectations. The resultant confusion has hounded the study of environmental cognition since its outset. We still do not have agreement as to the connection between perception and cognition and between image and cognitive map. And where do attitudes fit into the previous set of terms? Paradoxically, this confusion makes the consideration of PCT a simpler task, because there are few orthodoxies to confront, pay homage to, or avoid. We are not yet suffering from what Kelly refers to as "hardening of the categories."

Our existing *t*heories cannot help us to resolve the inconsistencies that plague our data and prevent the accumulation of results. I am still uncertain as to the relationship between the finding of the Place Perception Project (see Blaut and Stea, 1971) and Piagetian Theory as interpreted by Hart and Moore (1973). Similar problems abound in the area of cognitive distance functions, one of the most extensively studied areas of environmental cognition. Distance estimates appear to depend upon who you ask, how you ask him, and which way he is facing! Although some people may conceive of a theory as an unnecessary straitjacket, I view it as a highly desirable life-jacket to support me in a sea of confusing facts.

Another consequence of our lack of coherent theory is the problem that we face in generating interesting and productive research questions. We rely on two strategies. The first, divide and conquer, might be sound geopolitics but it is not notably successful in studies of environmental cognition. We cannot perform the apparently simple arithmetic of adding the pieces together in any form of cumulative structure. (We shall see in a moment the constructive alternativism, the underlying philosophical position of PCT, rejects this piecemeal accumulation of "facts" as being doomed to failure in the first place.)

Our second strategy relies upon a mixture of intuitively supported common sense and negatively inspired attempts to replace unsatisfactory ideas from other accepted approaches. Common sense can only go so far: what is the Hazard Perception Group going to do now that it has studied every conceivable meteorological and geophysical hazard? The replacement

strategy is no better. Do we have to continue the overkill of economic man? It is all too easy for behavioral geographers to blame the failings of location theory on economic man. But we have gone too far; we do *need* him to kick around because he is extremely *useful* in certain normative contexts. Conversely, do we have to treat human spatial behavior as sand in the works of normative theory, as a disturbance factor that affects our predictions and must therefore be controlled away? We desperately need a *positive* framework within which we can generate research problems. In explaining his choice of the man-the-scientist analogy, Kelly (1970, p. 8) argues that

This is not a question of whether or not men do, in fact, live by the canons of science? That, except to an accumulative fragmentalist, is not even an appropriate question. We are not in search of such a neat conclusion, but of a strategic advantage in a long-term quest for understanding. No theory can offer us more than that.

It is just such a strategic advantage that we are currently seeking.

How can PCT provide remedies for all these complaints and match up to my utility criterion? To make my case, many of the following arguments will be deliberately *overstated* and I shall try to redress the balance in the conclusion. By nature, PCT is designed so that it encourages the extension and stretching which will expand its range of convenience. It is one of the few Theories that I do not feel guilty and apprehensive about applying and elaborating. There is no body of purists waiting in the wings to chastise anyone who dares to tamper with the original conception of "the" theory. It is not a fragile creation supported by overly narrow definitions and bounded by a hedge of caveats. Following from the original integration between theory and methodology, it is neither scalpel nor butcher's cleaver. It is a well-equipped hospital operating room, capable of helping a wide range of patients. I believe that environmental cognition should be admitted as soon as possible before terminal diseases take hold.

What is PCT and what does it look like? Rather than attempting to present a potted version of the theory, I have included Table 1, which contains a detailed summary of the basic terms and their definitions. This table is taken from Bannister and Mair

TABLE 1[a]

A. Formal Content of Personal Construct Theory

Fundamental Postulate. A person's processes are psychologically channelized by the ways in which he anticipates events.

Construction Corollary. A person anticipates events by construing their replications.

Individuality Corollary. Persons differ from each other in their constructions of events.

Organization Corollary. Each person characteristically evolves, for his convenience in anticipating events, a construction system embracing ordinal relationships between constructs.

Dichotomy Corollary. A person's construction system is composed of a finite number of dichotomous constructs.

Choice Corollary. A person chooses for himself that alternative in a dichotomized construct through which he anticipates the greater possibility for the elaboration of his system.

Range Corollary. A construct is convenient for the anticipation of a finite range of events only.

Experience Corollary. A person's construction system varies as he successively construes the replications of events.

Modulation Corollary. The variation in a person's construction system is limited by the permeability of the constructs within whose ranges of convenience the variants lie.

Fragmentation Corollary. A person may successively employ a variety of construction subsystems which are inferentially incompatible with each other.

Commonality Corollary. To the extent that one person employs a construction of experience which is similar to that employed by another, his processes are psychologically similar to those of the other person.

Sociality Corollary. To the extent that one person construes the construction processes of another he may play a role in a social process involving the other person.

B. Formal Aspects of Constructs

Range of Convenience. A construct's range of convenience comprises all those things to which the user would find its application useful.

Focus of Convenience. A construct's focus of convenience comprises those particular things to which the user would find its application maximally useful. These are the elements upon which the construct is likely to have been formed originally.

Elements. The things or events which are abstracted by a person's use of a construct are called elements. In some systems these are called objects.

[a]Reprinted from D. Bannister and J. M. M. Mair, *The Evaluation of Personal Constructs.* London: Academic Press, 1968, with the permission of the publisher and the authors. Copyright © by the Academic Press Inc. (London) Limited, 1968.

Context. The context of a construct comprises those elements among which the user ordinarily discriminates by means of the construct. It is somewhat more restricted than the range of convenience, since it refers to the circumstances in which the construct emerges for practical use, and not necessarily to all the circumstances in which a person might eventually use the construct. It is somewhat more extensive than the focus of convenience, since the construct may often appear in circumstances where its application is not optimal.

Pole. Each construct discriminates between two poles, one at each end of its dichotomy. The elements abstracted are like each other at each pole with respect to the construct and are unlike the elements at the other pole.

Contrast. The relationship between the two poles of a construct is one of contrast.

Likeness End. When referring specifically to elements at one pole of a construct, one may use the term "likeness end" to designate that pole.

Contrast End. When referring specifically to elements at one pole of a construct, one may use the term "contrast end" to designate the opposite pole.

Constriction. Constriction occurs when a person narrows his perceptual field in order to minimize apparent incompatibilities.

Comprehensive Constructs. A comprehensive construct is one which subsumes a wide variety of events.

Incidental Constructs. An incidental construct is one which subsumes a narrow variety of events.

Superordinate Constructs. A superordinate construct is one which includes another as one of the elements in its context.

Subordinate Constructs. A subordinate construct is one which is included as an element in the context of another.

Regnant Constructs. A regnant construct is a kind of superordinate construct which assigns each of its elements to a category on an all-or-none basis, as in classical logic. It tends to be nonabstractive.

Core Constructs. A core construct is one which governs the client's maintenance processes.

Peripheral Constructs. A peripheral construct is one which can be altered without serious modification of the core structure.

Tight Constructs. A tight construct is one which leads to unvarying predictions.

Emergence. The emergent pole of a construct is that one which embraces most of the immediately perceived context.

Implicitness. The implicit pole of a construct is that one which embraces contrasting context. It contrasts with the emergent pole. Frequently the person has no available symbol or name for it; it is symbolized only implicitly by the emergent term.

Symbol. An element in the context of a construct which

(continued)

TABLE 1 *(continued)*

represents not only itself but also the construct by which it is abstracted by the user is called the construct's symbol.

Permeability. A construct is permeable if it admits newly perceived elements to its context. It is impermeable if it rejects elements on the basis of their newness.

C. Constructs Classified According to the Nature of Their Control Over Their Elements

Preemptive Construct. A construct which preempts its elements for membership in its own realm exclusively is called a preemptive construct. This is the "nothing but" type of construction—"If this is a ball it is nothing but a ball."

Constellatory Construct. A construct which fixes the other realm membership of its elements is called a constellatory construct. This is stereotyped or typological thinking.

Propositional Construct. A construct which carries no implications regarding the other realm membership of its elements is a propositional construct. This is uncontaminated construction.

D. General Diagnostic Constructs

Preverbal Constructs. A preverbal construct is one which continues to be used, even though it has no consistent word symbol. It may or may not have been devised before the client had command of speech symbolism.

Submergence. The submerged pole of a construct is the one which is less available for application to events.

Suspension. A suspended element is one which is omitted from the context of a construct as a result of revision of the client's construct system.

Level of Cognitive Awareness. The level of cognitive awareness ranges from high to low. A high-level construct is one

which is readily expressed in socially effective symbols; whose alternatives are both readily accessible; which falls well within the range of convenience of the client's major constructions; and which is not suspended by its superordinating constructs.

Dilation. Dilation occurs when a person broadens his perceptual field in order to reorganize it on a more comprehensive level. It does not, in itself, include the comprehensive reconstruction of those elements.

Loose Constructs. A loose construct is one leading to varying predictions, but which retains its identity.

E. Constructs Relating to Transition

Threat. Threat is the awareness of an imminent comprehensive change in one's core structures.

Fear. Fear is the awareness of an imminent incidental change in one's core structures.

Anxiety. Anxiety is the awareness that the events with which one is confronted lie mostly outside the range of convenience of his construct system.

Guilt. Guilt is the awareness of dislodgment of the self from one's core role structure.

Aggressiveness. Aggressiveness is the active elaboration of one's perceptual field.

Hostility. Hostility is the continued effort to extort validational evidence in favor of a type of social prediction which has already been recognized as a failure.

C–P–C Cycle. The C–P–C cycle is a sequence of construction involving, in succession, circumspection, preemption, and control, and leading to a choice precipitating the person into a particular situation.

Creativity Cycle. The creativity cycle is one which starts with loosened construction and terminates with tightened and validated construction.

(1968, pp. 219–221), who are far better qualified than I am to encapsulate PCT. The core of PCT is expressed in Table 1A. Unlike many theories, the basic structure of PCT is carefully stated. It is erected on a fundamental postulate whose ramifications are elaborated in a sequence of eleven corollaries. How many other theories can be expressed so succinctly and explicitly? Certainly not Piagetian theory, which has needed a host of interpreters, nor Barker's (1968) Ecological theory which is trivial and uninterpretable.

Tables 1B and 1C elaborate on the idea of a construct; between them, these two sections present a formal terminology for discussing the nature of a construct and provide a classification of links between constructs and elements of the real world. Table 1D provides a set of diagnostic constructs for describing sets of constructs and the interrelationships between them. Table 1E contains a language for expressing the change in constructs and construct systems. With the possible exception of some of the ideas expressed in this final section, PCT is deliberately written in as content-free a style as possible. This high level of abstraction allows the user to supply a content area that can be structured within the flexible framework of PCT. Although the original focus of convenience of PCT was psychotherapy, I can see nothing within its formulation that prevents an extension of the range of convenience to include environmental cognition.

The opposite is true: PCT positively lends itself to offering an understanding of environmental cognition.

The obvious starting point for this extension is PCT's conception of the role of people in the environment. In this sense, it offers yet another alternative in the endless debate over models of "man." Such an alternative is especially welcome for those of us working in the context of behavioral geography. The behavioral approach has championed the role of the individual over the mass as being the fundamental analytic unit for the development of spatial theory. However, we have a total lack of a necessary theoretical stance with respect to the characteristics of the individual since we have discarded economic man, found Simon's (1957) "satisficing" man to be wanting, and have never felt comfortable with psychoanalytic man. Instead, we have adopted *"plastic man,"* who, chameleon-like, changes his characteristics according to the demands of the research problem in which he is placed. Such obliging malleability has led to the conflicting and confusing results discussed earlier.

There are two long-term research strategies open to us if we accept the need for a replacement for *plastic man.* One centers upon a lengthy and difficult inductive process involving the empirical probing of individual behavior and its determinants in a variety of space–time contexts in order to build up a picture of the individual. We are currently pursuing this strategy by default, since the use of *plastic man* in, for example, the hazard perception studies is beginning to delimit our ability to calculate and assess the likelihood of occurrence of environmental phenomena.

The second strategy is to postulate some characteristics and then empirically test their deductive consequences in a variety of space–time contexts. If we are prepared to adopt this latter, more economical strategy, Kelly's formulation of *man-the-scientist* can serve as an appropriate starting point. Man-the-scientist draws an analogy between the everyday activities of people and scientists. They are both trying to understand the workings of the world around them, to generate expectations and make predictions. They mull over the consequences of behavior based on these predictions and make revisions to their thinking wherever necessary. There is something reassuring in an approach that allows us to avoid the normal problem of the scientist's inhumanity to a lay person, his *subject*. But we should not pursue the analogy too far and overextend it. A person and a scientist are not identical in their pursuit of knowledge. The understanding of a person may not be conscious: it may not be communicable to others, as a scientist's understanding should be. The evidence acceptable to a lay person may not be acceptable to the scientist. How useful is the analogy? We can find the answer to this question and to the little "t" or big "T" status of PCT by considering the following characteristics of PCT:

1. The underlying philosophical assumption: constructive alternativism.
2. The central role of anticipation.
3. The nature of constructs.
4. Systems of constructs.
5. The role of time.
6. The *personal* nature of constructs.

Constructive Alternativism

In establishing PCT, Kelly (1955) developed a philosophical position that he called *constructive alternativism* and which he distinguishes from the prevalent epistemological position of *accumulative fragmentalism.* Accumulative fragmentalism is based on the idea that there is a single truth underlying the world. This hidden truth is revealed only gradually by the patient collecting of bits of knowledge and understanding. Facts are assembled into an enormous multidimensional jigsaw puzzle, although no one expects the puzzle ever to be finished.

This belief in immutable facts is rejected by constructive alternativism. Kelly does not believe that we can come into direct contact with a fact-filled world. Instead, we make assumptions that lead to interpretations, and we then proceed to find out how *useful* these assumptions are. The world around us is open to as many varied *constructions* (or *interpretations*) as we are able to generate. There is no one *right* interpretation to be sought out; there is no holy grail. On the other hand, all alternative constructions are not of equal value. The measure of value is usefulness: do the predictions that constructions generate lead to the sorts of behavioral outcomes that we desire? Our constructions are open to sweeping *re*construction; an obvious historical example is the switch from believing that the universe revolves around the Earth to the alternative Copernican viewpoint.

Truth is not measured by the size of the collection of facts. Kelly argues that the larger the accumulation, the greater the invitation to generate a reconstruction that will reduce the facts to a mass of useless trivialities. Kelly (1970, p. 2) suggests why constructive alternativism may not be popular:

A person who spends a great deal of his time hoarding facts is not likely to be happy at the prospect of seeing them converted into rubbish. He is more likely to want them bound and preserved, a memorial to his personal achievement. A scientist, for example, who thinks this way, and especially a psychologist who does so, depends upon his facts to furnish the ultimate proof of his propositions. With these shining nuggets of truth in his grasp it seems unnecessary for him to take responsibility for the conclusions he claims they thrust upon him. To suggest to him at this point that further human reconstruction can completely alter the appearance of the precious fragments he has accumulated, as well as the direction of their arguments, is to threaten his scientific conclusions, his philosophical position, and even his moral security. No wonder, then, that, in the eyes of such a conservatively minded person, our assumption that all facts are subject—are wholly subject—to alternative constructions looms up as culpably subjective and dangerously subversive to the scientific establishment.

Unless we are very careful, there is a real danger that we shall allow the accumulative fragmentalist position to creep into our explanations of environmental cognition. Learning *t*heory, when used unthinkingly, suggests that knowledge about the world is gradually cumulated through experience. Thus, length of time in an environment becomes the crucial variable that determines one's progress toward the unattainable asymptote of perfect knowledge. Yet, at least on intuitive grounds, we have good reason to believe that urban cognition does not follow such a process. Initially, a person structures knowledge on the basis of a few unconnected, frequently traveled paths through the city. These paths link such basic destinations as work, school, and shopping center with home. Destinations are not interconnected with each other. However, through a process that we do not understand yet (although see Moore, 1972b, and also Chapter 12 for a possible explanation), these

paths become woven together to form an interconnected network. A totally different structure is generated from the original knowledge, a structure that is far more than the sum of the original paths. It is flexible and permits the person to generate plans for making trips over previously untraveled routes (Moore, 1973b). To accommodate and understand such a reconstruction, we need to think along the lines of Kelly's constructive alternativism. We need a theoretical framework which explicitly recognizes that environmental cognition is a *constructive process which generates alternatives.* Knowledge of the environment is not based on the progressive accumulation of the jigsaw-like pieces of a cartographic map.

Although I have detailed the argument with respect to urban cognition, it is obvious that this wholesale reconstruction of environmental knowledge occurs in many other contexts. The stages of development of spatial cognition in young children outlined by Hart and Moore (1973; see also Chapter 12) contain periods during which the child's cognitive structure is radically reshaped. The successive attainment of topological, projective, and Euclidean relationships between locations represents three such reconstructions. The cognitive approach to intraurban migration suggests that families gradually restructure their knowledge and· evaluation of neighborhoods within the city. It is on the basis of these *re*structurings that migration decisions are made. The tourist advertising industry is geared to the deliberate reconstruction of our images of specific places. Highly selective graphics are designed to "put somewhere on the map" or to make one believe that New York is really a safe and pleasant place to visit.

Not only does the basic philosophical position of PCT appeal to me, but I can see how it will allow me to understand the processes of environmental cognition as I construe them at present. The avoidance of accumulative fragmentalism is more than just a minor philosophical concern; it will have a major effect on the future development of the whole field.

The Central Role of Anticipation

Personal Construct Theory allows us to grapple with one of geography's old skeletons—the role of determinism as a means of accounting for spatial behavior. This issue is significant far beyond its historic context. I have the suspicion that there is a real danger of unconsciously falling into a form of neo-determinism in current approaches to environmental cognition. Several factors underlie this suspicion. First, stimulus–response psychology inevitably leads to a determinist position. As soon as we try to argue that this part of a person's knowledge depends upon the form of the spatial environment while that part depends upon the person's constructive ability, we also slide toward determinism. Second, determinism always seems to lurk in the wings of architecture. It would be so convenient for environmental designers if they could ascribe control of human behavior to the physical nature of the environment. Their life would be much simpler.

I am *not* rejecting determinism as such out of hand; rather, I am arguing that we should accept it explicitly *if* (and where) it is appropriate. The philosophical position of *constructive alternativism* provides a way of rephrasing the question:

This approach has clear implications for the great *free will* versus *determinism* debate. One of them is that *free-determined* is a construction we place on acts and it is useful only to the extent that it *discriminates* between acts. To say that man is entirely determined is as meaningless as to say that he is entirely free. The construction (like all our interpretations) is useful only as a distinction and even then the distinction must have a specific range of convenience. A person is free *with respect to* something just as he is determined *with respect to* something else. In this way construct theory avoids the determinist argument that puts the arguer in the paradoxical position of being a puppet *deciding* that he is a puppet . . . . Equally, construct theory avoids the doctrine of unlimited free will which suggests a mankind that cannot be understood because it has no "cause and effect" aspects (Bannister and Fransella, 1971, pp. 18–19).

That the choice between determinism and free will can and should be made is one of the important implications of PCT. The possibility of this choice is contained within the *fundamental postulate* of PCT (see Table 1A), which states that *a person's processes are psychologically channelized by the ways in which he anticipates events.* In Kelly's thinking, people are not inert objects waiting to be impelled into action by forces exogenous to them. They are actively construing their world and are trying to anticipate events so that they can make decisions about appropriate

behavior. Life is a *process* of construing and *re*construing the world in which we live.

Given my own interest in environmental cognition and its relation to spatial problem solving, an activity to which Tolman's term "cognitive mapping" has been applied (Downs and Stea, 1973a), I find this process of anticipation appealing. It answers one of the difficulties inherent in some of the early research on environmental cognition: What were the images *for*? How did people use them in their everyday spatial behavior? These questions occurred because of the essentially static conception of an image as something that people *had*. Kelly's fundamental postulate disposes of these questions by focusing attention on the role of knowledge in anticipating events and the role of knowledge in selecting (or channelizing) appropriate solutions in the form of spatial behavior.

For those of you who still want to know where the theory fits, who are disturbed by the exaggerated claims that I have made, perhaps some of Kelly's (1955, pp. 49–50) own hyperbole may help:

We now have a statement of a fundamental postulate for which we have high hopes. Perhaps there can spring from it a theory of personality with movement as the phenomenon rather than the epiphenomenon, with the psychological processes of the layman making the same sense as those of the scientist, a dynamic psychology without the trappings of animism, a perceptual psychology without passivity, a behaviorism in which the behaving person is credited with having some sense, a learning theory in which learning is considered so universal that it appears in the postulate rather than as a special class of phenomena, a motivational theory in which man is neither pricked into action by the sharp points of stimuli nor dyed with the deep tones of hedonism, and a view of personality which permits psychotherapy to appear both lawful and plausible.

You may not agree with all these goals, but it is certainly true that they reflect many of the issues that confront us in our attempts to explain environmental cognition.

The Nature of Constructs

The basic building block of PCT is the *construct*. A construct is more than simply a way of labeling a part of the world around us. It is designed to help us to understand how the world works so that we can anticipate what is likely to happen; as Kelly (1955, p. 321) emphasizes, "A meaningful construct is one which is designed to embrace the future rather than merely catalogue the past." Kelly (1970, p. 13) points to the source of constructs:

Neither our constructs nor our construing systems come to us from nature, except, of course, from our own nature .... We cannot say that constructs are essences distilled by the mind out of available reality. They are imposed *upon* events, not abstracted *from* them. There is only one place they come from; that is from the person who is to use them.

Constructs are interpretations that are placed on events, ways of *making* sense out of the world. They are commonly referred to as spectacles or goggles for viewing the world. Since the structure of these spectacles is so essential to the potential use of PCT in the area of environmental cognition, I shall try to spell out my understanding of a construct.

In making sense out of our spatial environment, we focus on the replicability of events and places. For something to be considered replicable does not mean that it is identical to something else. Replications are derived from the ability to construe important similarities: hence, the *construction corollary* of PCT argues that *we anticipate events by construing their replications* (see TAble 1A). The profound observation that once you've seen one slum, you've seen them all may be objectionable on humanitarian grounds, but it is understandable on human grounds. The ability to construe replications carries with it the capacity to anticipate and predict. To forestall an obvious comment, the idea of replicability is also at the heart of those existing theories which explain concept formation. However, there are significant differences between the idea of a construct and a concept, as we shall see in a moment.

A construct is organized around the idea of a discrimination that groups the replicative aspects of some parts of the world and contrasts them with the replicative aspects of another part. To establish a construct, you need a minimum of three elements which can be discriminated so that two are alike or similar and the third one is different. In Kelly's original formulation of PCT, he stressed that a construct is a bipolar discrimination which is the fundamental way of viewing the world. Similarity implies difference; they are inseparable. To talk about the city, you have

to have something that it is different from, say the country. However, constructs are *not* intended to be used to discriminate between all possible elements. To me, suburbs are neither city nor country. They are beyond the range of convenience of my construct city–country. In other words, in addition to the idea of similarity and contrast being implicit to a construct, so is the idea of irrelevancy. What is more, constructs have a focus of convenience, sets of elements whose replicability the construct is particularly well suited to handling. What do I do with Los Angeles? It is not country; it is a form of city yet it does not quite fit my essentially European idea of what a city ought to be like. Obviously, my city–country construct is not very permeable. It will not admit some of the elements that I have come into contact with. The language of PCT is rich in its ability to handle my own way of viewing the world. I realize that this is not the best of grounds on which to advocate the acceptance of a theory, but it does answer my criterion of utility.

In using the verbal labels of city and country to try to illustrate one of my own personal constructs, I may do an injustice to Kelly's original formulation of a construct and mislead you as to its nature. A construct is *not* a container that is bounded by two words and into which elements of the real world can be dropped. A construct is not defined by its verbal labels; it does not even need to be capable of verbal expression. A construct is defined and revealed through the pattern of choices and discriminations that a person makes among elements in his or her environment. It is identified by the pattern of objects that are grouped together as being similar, all the places that I choose to call "cities," and by the grouping of places which I call "country." To obtain a feel for this construct, you would have to know the pattern of places that it allowed me to differentiate and understand. This view of the nature of a construct obviously distinguishes it from a semantic differential scale, which is an absolute, verbally anchored yardstick that does not allow for an expression of irrelevancy.

Constructs also differ from the traditional idea of a concept in two important ways. First, concepts are expressions of the is–is not structure. Constructs are more limited in their extent: as the *range corollary* states, *a construct is convenient for the anticipation of a finite range of events only* (Table 1A). A construct does not have to express replications on such a universal scale as a concept. Second, concepts are conventionally expressions of logical opposites; thus, the pure form becomes black–not black, the impure form black–white. Constructs are not restricted to such logical opposites. I have a psychological construct, blue–brown, that I find very useful in understanding my world. It is a personal, *psycho*logical structure that may not be logical, but it works.

Although a construct forms the fundamental building block of PCT, we must not lose sight of the woods for the trees. Constructs do not exist in isolation, and Kelly provides corollaries for understanding the complexity of relationships between constructs.

Systems of Constructs

Constructive alternativism is based on the idea that sense is made, not given, We develop ways of looking at the world which allow us to generate expectations that can guide our behavior. We revise our expectations and predictions as evidence confirms or contradicts them. Although sense is constructed, we do not generate constructs "at will" as the occasion demands. Kelly's dichotomy corollary specifies both the nature and number of constructs: a person's construction system is composed of a finite number of dichotomous constructs. Given this finite number of constructs, the organization corollary expresses the structural relationships that exist between constructs. Each person characteristically evolves for his own convenience in anticipating events a construction system embracing ordinal relationships between constructs. There are many important ramifications which we can derive from these two corollaries that can help us to understand the structure of environmental knowledge.

The idea of a construct system follows directly from the ideas of range, convenience, and a finite number of constructs:

In construct theory it is accepted that any construct has a limited range of convenience and that whole clusters of constructs are designed to deal with particular areas, e.g.,

chemistry, theology, music, politics and so forth. A subsystem can be defined as a cluster of constructs within which high interrelationships exist while there are relatively few linkages between this and other subsystems of constructs (Bannister and Fransella, 1971, p. 162).

There are two important questions that we must ask about construct subsystems:

1. What is the nature of the relationships among constructs within a subsystem?
2. What are the structural relationships among a series of subsystems?

One major concern in studies of environmental cognition has been the construing of specific spatial areas (i.e., a particular city or urban neighborhood) or types of places (i.e., urban shopping centers or recreation areas). Implicitly, we have assumed that construct subsystems exist. However, we have never been certain about their boundaries or their internal structure. Such uncertainty is reflected in semantic differential studies. How do you choose the scales? How do you decide what is relevant and what is not? In the original context, Osgood claimed that a three-dimensional structure emerged from studies of the interrelationships among individual scales. Based on the connotative meaning of words, he labeled this structure the evaluative, activity, and potency dimensions (Osgood et al., 1957). However, for obvious reasons, this structure did not emerge in studies of either specific areas or types of places. The emergent structure was purely a consequence of statistical manipulations on correlations among scales. Although there is nothing inherently wrong with such a procedure, it is unsatisfactory. We cannot answer the objection that a different set of scales or a different analytic procedure might lead to a different structure. We also had the problem of discussing this derived structure. Did we mean to imply that the person really "had" an understanding of this structure, that they "looked" at the world in this way? Although PCT is *not* immune to some aspects of these criticisms, it does offer an alternative way of viewing higher-order structure.

Personal Construct Theory that provides a trip of concepts that are designed to classify the types of relationships which exist between the constructs in a subsystem. Kelly argues that constructs can be differentiated by the way in which they exercise control over the elements of the real world that they are designed to construe. The three types of control are *preemptive, constellatory, and propositional*; all three are defined in Table 1C.

As an illustration of the fertility of PCT in structuring our thinking about environmental cognition, I shall look at constellatory constructs in detail. A *constellatory construct* is one that fixes the other realm membership of its elements; thus, it reflects a form of stereotyped or typological thinking. For example, if this place is a suburb, it must also be middle-class, sterile, manicured, and wholesome. In my thinking, if a place is a small town in Mississippi, it is also backward, segregated, and not to be visited. You may well question the veracity and wisdom of my stereotypical thinking; as Bannister and Fransella (1971), p. 32) argue, it represents a kind of intellectual package deal. Nevertheless, it is not a type of thinking that is restricted to me. Constellatory constructs are prominent in our everyday thinking about and communication about specific areas; consider the litany of Philadelphia "jokes" or the image of California as a "place where . . . ." Each of us could fill in the blanks, probably using similar constructs. Filling in the blanks involves calling upon a set of constructs that always appear together.

We also share collections of constructs that spell out the "typical" characteristics of a slum or ghetto. Much of our knowledge of urban areas is organized around spatial stereotypes of types of places; we speak of the wrong side of the tracks, skidrow, downtown, Little Italy, the suburbs, and, of course, everything beyond the city is in the boondocks. Each stereotype has a collection of expectations (constructs) associated with it. It is a convenient and readily appreciated shorthand symbol of expressing our understanding of the world. Although we may object to the injustice of such stereotypes, they are at the same time valuable and unavoidable. The search for characteristics of similarity and difference is a coping strategy. (I shall consider the possibility of change in these stereotypes in the next section.)

How does PCT handle the structural relationships among a series of construct subsystems? Kelly (1955,

pp. 57–58) views these relationships in terms of order of importance in dealing with a particular part of the real world:

Within a construction system there may be many levels of ordinal relationships, with some constructs subsuming others and those, in turn, subsuming still others. When one construct subsumes another its ordinal relationship may be termed *superordinal* and the ordinal relationship of the other becomes *subordinal*. Moreover, the ordinal relationship between constructs may reverse itself from time to time. For example, "intelligent" may embrace all things "good" together with all things "evaluative," and "stupid" would be the term for "bad" and "descriptive" things; or, if the other kind of subsuming is involved, "intelligent" might embrace the construct *evaluative vs. descriptive* while "stupid" would be the term for the *good vs. bad* dichotomy. Thus man systematizes his constructs by concretely arranging them in hierarchies and by abstracting them further. But whether he pyramids his ideas or penetrates them with insights, he builds a system embracing ordinal relationships between constructs for his personal convenience in anticipating events.

Obviously, the task of disentangling the web of ordinal relations is complex; originally, Kelly's methodology could only disentangle through statistical manipulations and inferences. However, Hinkle (1965) has developed two procedures that allow the person to spell out the network of ordinal connections for the listener. Neither the *implications grid* nor the *laddering technique* (see Chapter 7) is short in duration, but their uses are obvious. For example, we are concerned with the processes of spatial decision-making in intraurban migration. It appears that people use two construct systems, one centering on situation within the city and the other on site and house characteristics. Which comes first, which one is superordinate? We now have a means of answering this question, and we can also determine the relations between the constructs *within* a construct system.

The fragmentation corollary claims that a person may successively employ a variety of construction subsystems which are inferentially incompatible with each other. The impact of economic man is such that we forget that rationality is not a necessary characteristic of human thinking. Inconsistency is possible through the idea of subordinancy and superordinancy of construct systems. For example, many "liberals" have a set of constructs that encapsulate their thinking about the constraining nature of "the" ghetto, and they acknowledge the need for better housing and better welfare services. They may even be prepared to finance these needs through increased taxation. However, the question of the location of this new housing runs up against the superordinate construct system of "neighborhood quality" with its constellation of constructs involving house value, "desirable" neighbors, and so on. The resolution comes from the structure of the psychological system, not from "objective" logic. Many of the coping mechanisms identified in the studies of hazard perception resort to superordinate constructs of religion or fate, which are used to "explain away" the evidence of experts.

This discussion of construct systems is not exhaustive, although it may seem exhausting. As much as possible, I have tried to show that I find PCT to be very useful in handling some of the prevalent ideas in environmental cognition. The structure of PCT is flexible enough to encompass many of my interests. It is also able to accommodate one of my own problem areas, that of understanding the role of "learning" and its effects on spatial knowledge.

The Role of Time

In PCT, life is a process of construing and reconstruing. Since a person's processes are psychologically channelized by the way in which he anticipates events, it follows that the *feedback* from behavior is also of importance. Constructs are testable hypotheses, not immutable yardsticks. Consequently, Kelly argues in the *experience corollary* that *a person's construction system varies as he successively construes the replications of events* (Table 1A). To what extent do environmental construct systems change over time?

At present, the lack of an answer to this question reflects one of the most significant weaknesses in studies of environmental cognition. Applications of classic learning theory have been few and we possess few data collected on a time series basis (but see Chapter 14). Thus, our answer to the question of stability has to be extremely speculative. Bannister and Mair (1968, p. 170) report a study in which part of the task involved construing a set of 15 physical objects twice, at six-week intervals.

In terms of this experiment, it can be tentatively argued that people (as assessed in terms of the stability of their conceptual structure in two subsystems) are more confident as physicists than they are as psychologists—they have more stable systems through which to view objects than those through which to view people.

But are places and areas more like people or objects? We talk about the personality or character of a place in more than a loosely analogous sense (see Chapter 16). Even the most cursory introspection reveals the changes that occur in our way of construing places. Absence makes the heart grow fonder; you can't go home again; a string of profound platitudes springs to mind. In a sense, this dynamic character of PCT is both a strength and a weakness. It forces us to consider issues that we are not well equipped to handle.

Another aspect of change is expressed in the *modulation corollary: the variation in a person's construction system is limited by the permeability of the constructs within whose ranges of convenience the variants lie.* A good example of the shifts attendant on permeability of the construct is settled land-wilderness, which has been prominent in U.S. environmental thought. Nash (1967) documents the subtle changes in this construct as it encompassed varied environmental conditions in the westward spread of settlement. It is not difficult to see the construct within Turner's famous frontier hypothesis. Similarly, the construct "city-suburb" became overstretched in the face of very recent urban development patterns. It was not permeable enough to accommodate them; hence the development of "suburb-sprawl."

From my perspective, PCT forces me to confront issues that cause me anxiety. I know that environmental knowledge develops and changes as a function of experience; PCT provides a language for discussing some of these changes. But it also requires a type of research design that I do not feel equipped to tackle, nor do I see many others in the field paying more than lip service to these requirements.

The Personal Nature of Constructs

At first glance, both the emphasis on the personal nature of constructs and the individuality corollary, which states that persons differ from each other in their constructions of events, might mitigate against the adoption of PCT. It would appear that we are dealing with an idiosyncratic approach, which would therefore not be in conformity with the accepted canons of "science."

Why is there a reluctance to study the individual person for his own sake? Why is the aggregate more scientific? Briggs (1963, p. 59) provides a revealing perspective on this issue:

It was a Leeds clergyman of the 1840s, who with great percipience warned his readers of the dangerous lure of the word "masses." "Our judgments," he stated, "are distorted by the phrase. We unconsciously glide into a prejudice. We have gained a total without thinking of the parts. It is a heap, but it has strangely become indivisible."

Given the current status of work on environmental cognition, I see absolutely no objection to beginning with an intensive study of the spatial knowledge of a few individuals, a task that the methodology of PCT is well-designed to tackle. No one has seriously faulted Piaget for making generalizations from the intensive study of a very few small children. A large sample size does not confer scientific respectability on a piece of research.

Such statements may seem like the release of a swarm of bees from my bonnet. Even if this is the case, I would argue that they are important bees. Some of my own insights into environmental cognition have come from novelists such as D. H. Lawrence, Theodore Dreiser, and Mark Twain (see Section 7). We do need to return to the very *personal* nature of environmental knowledge before embarking on massive, standardized, data-collecting forays. The flexibility of PCT is ideal for this purpose.

However, lest I mislead someone, PCT is *not* restricted to idiographic studies. Kelly himself objected to the preemptive, "nothing but" type of thinking that placed ideas into restrictive pigeonholes. The commonality corollary argues that, to the extent that one person employs a construction of experience which is similar to that employed by another, his processes are psychologically similar to those of the other person. However, we must be careful how we measure similarity. Similar verbal labels attached to a construct do not necessarily imply construct similarity. Similarity comes from similar patterns of construction or discrimination between a set of objects or places. We can begin to develop a set of constructs that are used by most people in dealing with a certain range of places. Consequently, we can use PCT (and its attendant methodology) to operate at a nomothetic level. Alternative constructions are open to us in handling the same data.

CONCLUSIONS

It should be obvious by now that I consider personal construct theory to qualify as a big "T" theory. I find it useful since it provides me with an integrated terminology within which I can develop problems that interest me. The loss of such familiar terms as "cognition" and "learning" is more than compensated for by the richness and flexibility of the language of the theory. It is a comfortable, intuitively satisfying theory. Although many people may take objection to such vague, subjective criteria of acceptance, are they so different from the mathematician's criterion of elegance?

It is important that we can interpret our concerns within the framework of the theory's structure, since this enables us to use the theory to generate research topics. Again, I feel that PCT is helpful to me. Although I have not dwelt on the methodological techniques of the theory, the advantage of a unified theory and methodology cannot be overemphasized. We do not have to indulge in statistical convolutions to analyze the data from repertory grid methods. The person responding to the test does not have to make judgments which are based on tasks that are alien to everyday thinking. The methodology does not rely on deception; to use a concept that Kelly had little brief for, the test has considerable face validity.

By this time, it would appear that I am advocating that everybody should drop everything and start thinking in PCT terms. Although there might be some advantages to this procedure, I am not suggesting such a course of action; PCT is not without its faults! So far my discussion has been euphorically positive. I do not know whether it is a function of the type of proponents of the theory or circumstances in which they work, but I find that a certain orthodoxy surrounds their writing. The evangelist approach is effective up to a certain point, but then actions should speak louder than exhortations. In this respect, Mair (1970, p. 166) offers a sobering assessment of the potential usefulness of PCT:

The word "potential" has to be insisted upon here because, to date, the theory has excited many people but left most baffled as to *how* to make real use of it. Although this is potentially a revolutionary theory, most research using its ideas or the methods associated with them still looks remarkably like much traditional research in many respects. The experimenter still tends to remain outside most studies in grand omnipotence and isolation. True he more often affirms his common humanity with his subjects in the opening paragraphs of his research reports, but somehow he manages, none the less, to remain in the end aloof from the common herd.

There are echoes of such aloofness in the certain attempts to justify studies of environmental cognition as helping "us" to design better environments for "them." There is a tone of aloofness in this paper in that "I" am exhorting "you" to consider PCT.

I am excited by PCT and I am baffled by it. I can also detect some serious flaws in the structure of the theory. If you look at Table I, you may agree that some of the basic concepts appear trivial, redundant, and an overstatement of the obvious. Yet, given the choice, I prefer too much explicit structure to too little. Perhaps of greater importance are the problems that the theory does not come to grips with. The origin and development of a construct is still a mystery to me. In opposition to the earlier quote from Kelly as to the origin of constructs, Sechrest (1963, p. 211) argues that

He is nowhere quite explicit as to the origin of the constructs by which people attempt to make sense out of their universe. Kelly typically writes as if they had some existence apart from the experiences with which they deal and seems to imply that they are imposed upon events. On the other hand, the term *abstract* is frequently used in its verb form to refer to the process from which constructs arise, and the verb abstract ordinarily refers to the development of ideas *out of* experience.

I find the two cycles of transition, which are supposed to link constructs and experience, to be superficial and confusing. Thus, the circumspection-preemption-control cycle seems an unnecessarily complex statement of the obvious. Moreover, it does little to throw light on the ever-present problem of the link between cognition and behavior. The important choice corollary causes me serious problems. What does it mean to say that a person chooses for himself that alternative in a dichotomized construct system through which he anticipates the greater possibility for the elaboration of his system? I can see the application of this corollary in psychotherapy but not in the area of environmental cognition. I can conceive of the choice of an intraurban migrant in selecting a particular suburb as providing a new life for his family. Presumably this reflects elaboration; but how can I *predict* this choice? Without such prediction, this corollary is as useless as the "satisficing" criterion of decision making. We can only *post*dict the "satisficing" criterion by studying the choice actually made.

There are methodological objections to PCT and grid methods. No converging operational procedures exist that can be used as a check on the results of grid methods. However, from a pragmatic viewpoint, I am not sure how much credence I place on this objection since grid methods work in practice. One structural characteristic, cognitive complexity, presents problems. Although it was not originally developed as part of PCT, it has been used to interpret the internal structure of a construct system. The consequences have been confusing, largely owing to the many operational definitions of this intuitively simple idea.

Despite this brief scattering of criticisms, I am still willing to grant PCT the status of a big "T" theory. Although my discussion has been superficial, I hope that it has given a personal sense of why I find PCT attractive and intriguing. I am convinced that it has as much potential as anything else that has been suggested to me and, what is more, I can understand it. For this reason alone I would be willing to use it. I believe that my other reasons for using it carry more weight. As a final comment, Bannister (1970b, p. vii) wrote, "The quality of psychological theory which George Kelly most esteemed was fertility . . . . He meant . . . the capacity of a theory to inspire people, to move them to new ventures, to puzzle them into asking new questions." Since I am inspired, moved, and puzzled, for me PCT is a fertile Theory.

7

PERSONAL CONSTRUCT THEORY AND ENVIRONMENTAL MEANING: APPLICATIONS TO URBAN DESIGN

Basil Honikman
School of Architecture and Urban Design
   University of Kansas[1]

As an architect involved in environmental research, I have always been predominantly interested in finding out the meanings that buildings have for people. This is one of those fundamental and "beautiful" objectives shared by many, yet seldom achieved.

When first I understood the scope of personal construct theory and its location within the overall body of psychology, I enjoyed an almost "eureka"-like experience. A whole series of mental switches clicked into phase. I could see structures of communication between people and buildings being identified in a way that I as an architect could use as a guide. My dissatisfaction with other research findings was suddenly less important, because the possibilities of construct theory seemed to be able to avoid or compensate for most of the inadequacies.

For example, I was not particularly interested in the perception of color on its own, for color is just an integrated part of an environment. Its meaning depends upon its relationship to all the other parts. The person using the environment interacts with it as a whole, and the way in which color contributes to that interaction may or may not be obvious or conscious. In the course of interaction with an environment, a person's evaluation may be totally uninfluenced by color. On the other hand, it may be the most superordinate factor in his appreciation or reaction. Certainly, it seems that studies of color perception do not address themselves to the problem of total environmental meaning; yet the architect really needs insight into how such component parts of the environment contribute to the formation of its total meaning in the minds of the people.

Construct theory offered the chance to see how people looked at a whole environment: how their values and patterns of anticipation matched what they encountered; how they adjusted to or resisted aspects of the environment, and above all how their hierarchies of ideas, prejudices, and beliefs with respect to a particular physical environment and its function were composed.

In other words, I saw a way to trace the effects of simple physical architectural factors and devices on the superordinate meaning structure of the person. I could do this in a molar way without dissecting the environment into small analyzable pieces, which, due to their separation from the whole, lost their influence upon it.

In two earlier papers (Honikman, 1972, 1973) I described a basic methodology and presented some experimentation which showed that the "promise" of this kind of research stood a good chance of fulfillment.

The purpose of this paper is to explain how a construct-theory approach may be used in studies of "architectural meaning." To do this I shall begin by describing three criteria that such a study should fulfill. The criteria result from understanding what a designer needs to know about how people interpret the built environment. Next, a series of techniques will be defined. A report of my work on the constructing of living rooms will serve to illustrate the deployment of the techniques. Other examples of construct-theory research are summarized. The results of these studies suggest directions for further research at both the building and urban scales.

Design-Relevant Research—Problems and Criteria

During the late 1960s, there seemed to be large gaps and inadequacies in the writing on how people understood and gave meaning to the environment. This was particularly true with regard to psychological studies and their relevance to architects and urban designers. Most published studies dealt with the use of either the semantic differential or sketch maps. On both sides of the Atlantic, people were looking for a standard measuring device that could be applied in the evaluation or rating of any environment by any person. Research seemed almost obsessed with "how to measure" without first understanding "what should be measured." As a result of many reactions of this kind, I began to formulate criteria for evaluating studies of environmental meaning. The criteria relate to the extent that the results of a study are applicable, either theoretically or practically, to the problems of the designer.

The first criterion is that the study should relate the physical or tangible characteristics of the environment to the intangible or cognitive or mental characteristics of the way it is thought about, interpreted, and evaluated. This criterion was established because designers' skills are expressed through the physical

spaces that they create. It therefore seemed reasonable to assume that, if a designer could know how the "ingredients" of his design stimulated its overall interpretation and evaluation, he would have valuable feedback. The important aspects of the design would be identified. He or she would have guidance as to how design form and content should be adjusted and how to develop strategies for approaching future environmental design problems.

The second criterion is called the "whole environmental criterion." So many studies seemed to rely on traditional forms of analysis. This meant that environments were being dissected into specific parts, and the fact that people encountered them as total, whole experiences seemed to be overlooked. Any study that focused on, for example, the materials in an environment, was drawing artificial attention to particular parts of it. Materials could well have been very important to one person's experiencing of the environment and totally irrelevant to another's. Studies of this kind failed to recognize either differences in personal interpretation or the fact that people interact with environments as whole experiences.

The third criterion arose out of the second. It requires that the study recognize the individuality or personal nature with which events are experienced. The same argument that was used for the second criterion was used to question the selection of verbal rating scales for general use in environmental evaluation. The student of construct theory knows Kelly's (1955) arguments about how people approach events with their own personal sets of "images" or constructs for understanding them (see also Chapter 6). The meaning of an environment depends very much upon the previous experiences and the "anticipation set" of the person experiencing it. If this is so, it seems unreasonable to expect a respondent to be able to convey to a researcher the meaning an environment has for him if he is unable to use his own personal constructs. It was this criterion that called into question most of the semantic differential and rating scale studies which were published under the banner of "architectural psychology" (see contributions in Canter, 1970; Honikman, 1970; Sanoff and Cohn, 1969; Archea and Eastman, 1970).

A review of the literature over the past 10 years tends to be discouraging to someone looking for guidance in making decisions about what Gropius (1955) called "total architecture" and for designer-oriented research in general.

The meaning and value of things depends on our cognition of them. Until something registers with us it has no meaning. Once we see it, the meaning depends upon what we think it is and the way that assessment fits with what we expect or require it to be. Too few studies face the challenge of environmental meaning. For instance, studies mapping the number of times housewives go to shopping centers yield information about their patterns of use. We can begin to predict from these patterns where the next shopping center should be built, but the more difficult and challenging problem is still not being met: How do the housewives see the shopping centers? What do they mean to them? What kind of qualities should the next center have if it is to make a positive contribution to the environment? The research described in the remainder of this paper is aimed at these issues.

Definitions and Procedures

Construct eliciting. Construct eliciting is the process whereby the informant nominates the particular words he uses to identify the pattern of ideas, qualities, and evaluation that he forms about an environmental event. The words he uses are really "labels" for the constructs, but for the sake of convenience they will be referred to as *constructs*. The *elements* are the environments or events being construed (see definitions of terms in Table 1 of Chapter 6).

Kelly (1955) discussed constructs and their eliciting at length. In the environmental studies with which I have been associated, eliciting has usually been carried out by the triad method. This involved confronting the informant with three events and asking him to state why two of them are similar and different from the third. This usually results in the identification of a *bipolar construct*. For instance, in the case of the living room study that I carried out, two living room environments were considered similar because they were "formal" and the third dissimilar because it was

"informal"; the bipolar construct was therefore formal–informal. This process continues with triads made up of different elements until the informant is no longer able to name any new constructs (see also Harrison and Sarre, 1971, for additional information on this and related procedures).

Laddering. *Laddering* (Hinkle, 1955) may be used to elicit either superordinate or subordinate constructs. If a superordinate construct is to be elicited then questions like "Why . . .?" and "What are the advantages of . . .?" may be used. If a subordinate construct is required, other questions, such as "What evidence do you have for . . .?" or "What makes you feel that . . .?", are used. In either case the constructs are only superordinate or subordinate to the previous construct although the laddering process can, step by step, identify a hierarchy from maximum subordinancy to maximum superordinancy.

Repertory grid. The *repertory grid* is based on Kelly's (1955) "Rep Test." In the living room study (to be described later) a 10 by 10 grid was used with the elements forming the columns and the constructs the rows. The poles of each bipolar construct form the extremes of a 7-point rating scale that runs from +3 to −3. The 10 elements are thus rated in terms of each of 10 constructs. Larger grids may be used.

The grid can be analyzed using the "Ingrid" principal components analysis program (Slater, 1969a, 1972), which can accommodate grids as large as 40 by 40. This program provides the researcher with a variety of information and is designed for many different applications of repertory grids. The following information was used in the living room and housing studies covered in this paper: (1) the loadings of elements and constructs on each principal component; (2) the amount of variance included in each of the first three principal components; (3) the degree of similarity with which the elements were construed; and (4) the degree of similarity with which the constructs were construed.

Resistance to change and implication grids. The *resistance-to-change grid* assists in the verification of hierarchical relationships between constructs. If a construct resists a change to another, it is more important. In a few cases superordinate constructs may be only identified late in the laddering process, and without the resistance-to-change grid it is impossible to know their level of ordinancy.

Implication grids provide a means of finding implied links between constructs. These may not be as strong as more direct links, but in the complex construing of a whole environment they add important facets to the total meaning (see Bannister and Mair, 1968).

Links, linear link diagrams, and implication networks. One reason for adopting the construct-theory approach is that it offers an opportunity to understand the whole meaning structure of an environment for a person encountering it. The *meaning structure* is made up of the various constructs related in ordinal patterns to each other within their principal components and implying each other between principal components. The different ways in which these relationships take place have to be identified in order to depict a formalized representation of the meaning structure. These relationships are called *links*; there are five different kinds, as follows:

1. *Link by component loading.* Here the strength of the link depends on the degree to which the construct is loaded to each principal component. Clearly, the principal component on which it is most highly loaded is the one that represents the *area of meaning* in which the person most usually applies the construct. Elements are loaded to principal components in the same way, and the relationship between a construct and an element can be traced by identifying the principal component to which both are most highly loaded.
2. *Link by eliciting.* An element may be associated with a construct if, during the eliciting process, it was seen to be similar to another element because of that construct. In other words, when an element is directly effective in the eliciting of a construct, the two are linked.
3. *Link by laddering.* When the laddering process is applied to a construct, the resultant subordinate (or superordinate) constructs are related to it in a linear (laddered) pattern. A chain of related or linked constructs results.
4. *Link by parallel implication.* These links are established by the implication grid process; in this case

the first mentioned construct is superordinate to the second, because the first implies the second, whereas the second does not imply the first.
5. *Link by reciprocal implication.* Here each construct implies the other and either may be superordinate or subordinate.

Figure 1 is a generalized diagram of five links. It demonstrates the principle of relating an environment (element) through a major area of meaning (principal component) to the parts of that area of meaning (constructs). Many of the subordinate constructs elicited in the living room study represented physical characteristics, and by following the link lines it is possible to see how these characteristics fit into the informants entire pattern of understanding the whole environment under study. Link types 1, 2, and 3 in Figure 1 all occur within the same principal component, and the constructs are organized in hierarchical chains or lines. For this reason this part of the diagram is called the "linear link diagram." The network of link types 4 and 5 is called the "implication network."

Plotting elements in the construct space. The bipolar constructs used in the repertory grid are dimensions for measuring elements. In the case of the living room study, there were 10 constructs in the repertory grid; the elements could therefore be considered to have been construed in a 10-dimensional construct space. In the same way, the principal components may be thought of as the principal dimensions of the space, the principal areas of meaning in the informants' construing or evaluative process.

In the living room study, analysis reduced the ten initial constructs of each informant to three principal components. Using these as dimensions, the construct space was reduced from ten dimensions to a more intelligible three-dimensional space.

In Figure 2, the first two principal components, because of the large majority of variance they include, form the major areas of the graphical representation of the construct space. The third principal component may also form one axis in a graph relating it to either the first or second components. If, as in the case of the living room study, the third principal component includes only a small percentage of variance

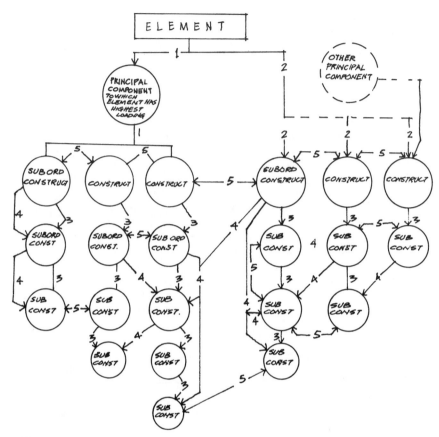

FIGURE 1
Generalized linear link diagram, demonstrating the linking of elements through principal components to constructs.

(in some cases insufficient for it to be significant), it may be convenient to include it on the diagram as an axis that is separate but easily relatable to the two main axes. Each element and each construct is then plotted in the "construct space" by using its loading factors on the principal components (forming the axes) as coordinates. Elements are indicated by numbers in heavy type and constructs by numbers in light type. The resultant diagram provides a visual representation of how elements and constructs relate to each other and how the trends of meaning become evident.

Design Research Applications

The projects included in this section have been selected to demonstrate some of the variety of architectural and planning applications to which the construct-theory approach and its attendant repertory grid methods lend themselves.

Kingston living room study. The first project was begun in England in 1968. The purpose was to see if I could explain the meaning that an environment had for a person in terms of its physical characteristics. In other words, if someone felt that a

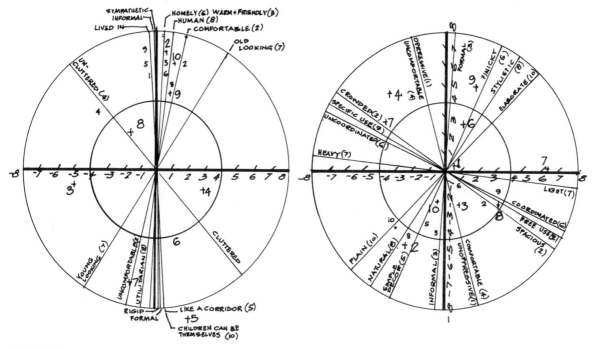

FIGURE 2

Construct-space diagrams for elements in the construct space: left, informant 6; right, informant 29. The heavy axis lines represent the principal components and are divided into scales of eight units. The vertical heavy line in both diagrams is the first principal component; the horizontal heavy line is the second component. For reasons of clarity, the third and least important component is excluded (the original construct-space working diagrams were much larger). The light lines are the construct lines representing dimensions running between the opposite poles of each construct; thus +9 is the location in the construct space of element 9.

particular environment was warm and liveable but unfriendly, how could the architect know which aspects of his design, its materials and arrangements, contributed to this feeling. More important, however, was the need to see the kind of information that a construct-theory approach would yield and whether it related to the needs, as I saw them, of environmental designers. The "environments" used were 17 color photographs of different living rooms and the informants were 40 middle-income, professional people living in the residential areas surrounding Kingston-upon-Thames in London.

Each informant was taken through an interview sequence of construct eliciting, preference identifica-tion, laddering, repertory grid scoring, resistance to change, and implication grid scoring.

The repertory grids were analyzed by Patrick Slater using his Ingrid principal components analysis program (Slater, 1972). The other grids were analyzed by "hand." In order to see how meaning related to physical characteristics, I was looking for links between superordinate constructs representing major areas of meaning or evaluation (such as "very nice," "friendly," or "homely") and subordinate constructs representing physical characteristics (such as "clean lines," "rough bricks," or "earthy colors"). The important feature of the links thus established was that they were all made without requiring the informant

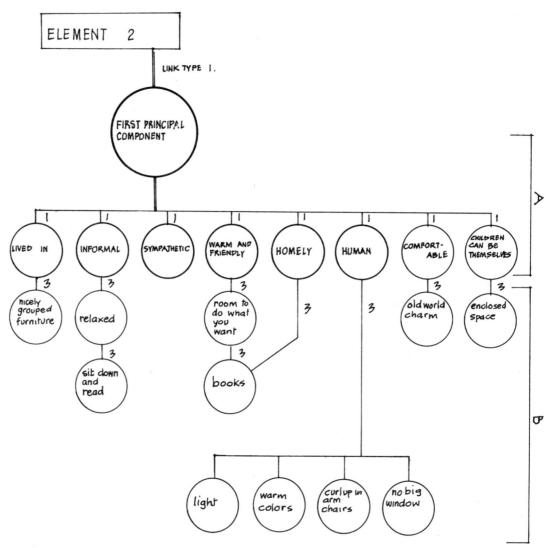

FIGURE 3

Linear link diagram showing the hierarchical structure of constructs within a principal component, informant 6. The numbers indicate the link types. The principal component most highly loaded to element 2 is shown with the heavy connecting line. The other principal components would be shown only if constructs loaded to them are also linked to element 2 by eliciting (link type 2).

to deal with only part of the environment at a time. All constructs were part of the construing of the living rooms as total whole environments.

As the study was aimed at understanding the construing of one particular living room, the results were presented in the following ways (see Honikman, 1972, for complete details). First, a construct-space diagram was prepared; this graphically demonstrated how the superordinate constructs and elements related to the three principal components established by the Ingrid program (Figure 2). Second, link diagrams were drawn showing how, by using links 1, 2, and 3, the hierarchical structure of constructs within a principal component were formed (Figure 3). These diagrams

94

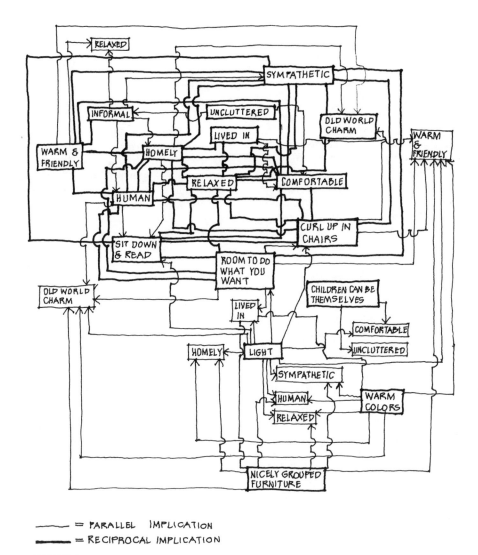

= PARALLEL IMPLICATION
= RECIPROCAL IMPLICATION

FIGURE 4
Implication network showing the relationship between constructs across the "boundaries"
of principal components, informant 6.

related both the elements and the constructs to the principal component so that one could ascertain which particular part of the informant's construct system for looking at living rooms in general applied to this particular living room. Third, implication networks were prepared showing how relationships between constructs were formed across the "boundaries" of the principal components (Figure 4). These procedures were carried out for each of the informants

so that I could identify the different ways that the physical characteristics of this living room influenced each person's construing. Two levels of information were available. First, eliciting and laddering revealed those constructs which registered with the informant. Second, the construct space and implication grids indicated how the informant used the constructs.

Figures 2, 4, and 5 provide an example of how one informant used physical characteristics in his construal of one living room. Begin with Figure 2, which represents the construct space in which all elements, constructs, and relationships of this informant's construing of elements occur. With the exception of "cluttered–uncluttered" and "old looking–young looking," all the constructs are highly loaded on the first principal component. This indicates that the informant evaluates in terms of one major dimension, that represented by the superordinate constructs in the first principal component. The heavy type numbers in the construct space indicate the positions of the 10 elements used in the repertory grid. For instance in this informant's construct space, this living room is shown with a loading of +6.5 on component 1. It is very close to constructs 2, 3, 6, 1, 5, 8, and 9. The only construct in the first principal component that is really far from element 2 is construct 10, "children can be themselves," which indicates that this is the only aspect of the informant's major area of meaning on which element 2 gains a low evaluation.

In Figure 4, the superordinate constructs in the top row of circles ("lived in," "informal," "sympathetic," etc.) indicate the nature of this informant's major component for evaluating the room. The second and lower rows represent constructs of decreasing importance. Some of these are obviously physical characteristics ("books," "warm colors") and others are evaluative ("room to do what you want," "relaxed"). Still others are partly evaluative and partly physical ("nicely grouped furniture," "enclosed space"). By reading up the "link lines," one can see that the "books" (physical characteristic) which the informant saw in the photograph of the living room related within the construct system to two superordinate constructs. "Books" relates to "warm and friendly" through "room to do what you want" and directly to "homely."

Figure 4 is an implication network for the same informant. Here we can see other links and relationships among the constructs. Using the same example, we can see links between "informal" and "warm and friendly," "uncluttered," "homely," "human," and so on.

From this analysis, the architect knows, first, that a living room design for this person has only one major area of meaning to satisfy. He can conclude, second,

that when designing a living room for this person it should reflect the qualities suggested by the superordinate constructs "lived in," "informal," and so on. Furthermore, the designer availed of this information does not need to rely entirely on his own interpretation of what, for example, "informal" or "human" means. Clearly, for this informant, "informal" has to do with being "relaxed," and the physical construct that suggests "relaxed" in this room is "sit down and read." Another part of the principal component is "human," suggested by the physical constructs "light," "warm colors," "curl up in arm chairs," and "no big windows," through which the designer can readily see just what "sit down and read" means to this informant.

Figure 3 shows the construct space for a different informant on the same living room. Here the constructs are more evenly distributed in the construct space, indicating that more than one principal component is important. In this case, the architect has to be sensitive to the informant attaching meaning in at least two areas. The first area (dimension) includes "social–not social," "warm–cold," and "liveable–impersonal." The second includes "organized–random," "characterful–characterless," and "basic–luxurious." The link diagrams and implication networks for this informant would indicate how the subordinate physical characteristic constructs of this informant relate to these superordinate areas of meaning.

In their introductory remarks at the 1973 Blacksburg EDRA Conference session on environmental cognition, Golledge and Moore (1973) drew attention to the need for further research to look at how the characteristics of the environment influence the structure of images. The techniques outlined in the living room study were aimed precisely at this goal. The examination of the diagrams suggests how, for example, the arrangement of furniture and warm colors contribute to the "informality" and general "human liveability" part of informants' images. The diagrams also provide clues as to the different "internal" constructs to which a construct label can relate. "Comfortable" may be used by different people to describe both physical and mental states; in a few instances the same construct label may relate to different meanings in different principal components within one person's image structure.

Kansas housing studies. The methods and techniques of the living room study are being used in two other unpublished studies in the human environment program at the University of Kansas.

Kent Rawson responded to the fact that nearly 40 million Americans change their homes each year and that, although mobile homes account for nearly one third of the nation's single-family homes, their residents are not highly mobile. Rawson argued that because mobile homes are inhabited by blue-collar workers and not by the more highly educated white-collar workers, mobile homes do not appeal to mobile people. Only between 7 and 10 percent of mobile homes ever leave their original sites. Rawson chose to test the argument that the broadening experience caused by mobility affects the cognitive processes by which the concept of "a suitable living environment" is formed and retained. Rawson's preliminary findings indicate that (1) people who move frequently tend to be less satisfied with their residences than those who spend prolonged periods in one house; (2) people who have remained in one place for some time develop a greater number of housing preferences; and (3) preferences vary—low mobility people prefer visual and spatial factors, moderate mobility people prefer more functional considerations, and high mobility people prefer perceptual factors.

In the second study, Robert Chisholm made a comparative analysis of the responses of two socioeconomic groups to a residential environment. He was sensitive to the fact that architects and designers of large-scale housing projects seldom have the opportunity to meet or understand the people who are going to use their buildings. In these cases, architects frequently proceed on the basis of their own value systems and make design decisions that may be totally insensitive to actual user needs or aspirations. Chisholm used the construct-theory approach to try to understand the way in which people from two different social classes construed a total home environment. His intention was to demonstrate how requirements differed between middle- and low-income groups by identifying differences in both the kinds of constructs used and the priorities (or hierarchies) with which the constructs were formed into construct systems. Chisholm found that in thinking about their home environment the middle-income group used more neighborhood, structural, functional, and atmospheric constructs; the low-income group used more spatial, safety, maintenance, and visual constructs.

Additional Research Directions

The previous section has dealt with environmental meaning at an architectural scale. Construct theory can also be used in a similar way at the larger urban design scale. Here the interactions between people and their environments are often less intense than they are within the home. Nonetheless, the meaning of immediate and often-used neighborhoods plays a crucial role in the overall level of environmental satisfaction. The analysis and study of the external spaces of cities has been largely based on observational methods and visual or sensory standards. There is little if any evidence of an examination of the cognition and meaning of cities prior to the publication of the work of Lynch (1960). I would suggest that one of the most fruitful directions for further research lies in a combination of cognitive inquiry with observational techniques, such as Barker's *Ecological Psychology* (1968). The data collection process in Barker's behavior-setting work is almost entirely observational. It embraces an understanding of the nature of a total environment, including people and their physical settings. It does not deal with the way people interpret their surroundings in terms of their emotional needs, expectations, or levels of awareness. These issues of course fall within the realm of cognitive enquiry. All the aspects covered by both the behavior-setting and cognitive approaches are vital to an understanding of a total environment. They include crucial information for the architect; consequently, it seems that a composite research strategy embracing both cognitive and behavior-setting characteristics should be explored.

The need to understand the cognition of architects is an important avenue for construct-theory research. An important part of the whole design process is the way in which an architect integrates physical, technical, cost, and human information into one design solution. Consequently, environmental meaning and socioeconomic data should be presented in a manner sensitive to the architects own system of interpretation and evaluation. In the fall of 1973 a pilot study was conducted to begin to look at the cognition of architectural students with respect to the way designing takes place. The supposition was that, if design takes place with major objectives or goals as important considerations, the principal dimensions of retrospective evaluation should be similar to the predesign objectives. The results did not indicate that this was entirely valid. In some cases, the major goals comprised one principal dimension accounting for large portions of the variance, in others only some of the goals were important, and in still others none were important at all. The implications of such differences among the cognitive processes of designers relate to both the nature and usefulness of design methods. Further research in this direction could influence the teaching of design.

The liveability or quality of life in cities is one of the urgent issues of our times. The City Development Department of Kansas City, Missouri, commissioned a study to define these qualities in relation to that city. The scope of the commission was to produce a research design, but it included an investigation of ways of implementing the definition of liveability and its performance factors within the city's model for managing urban change. In other words, they wished to use "liveability" as one of the factors in their decision-making process. The research design will probably suggest the use of a composite of mapping, construct theory, and survey techniques in order to try to understand what quality of life means to the people of Kansas City. A review of the planning literature reveals over 70 complex and sometimes jargonistic terms, all of which have something to do with quality of life. In spite of this, no comprehensive definition of liveability seems to exist, and certainly there seems very little with which a "man in the street" or nonprofessional planner can identify. So the challenge is to try to identify how the ordinary citizen sees his city in terms of liveability and how he decides for himself just what it really means in terms of the actual and manipulable fabric of the city.

Concluding Thoughts

The question of quality of life is of particular importance. I believe that the major (and perhaps only) justification for the profession of architecture is that it should contribute to the quality of life by improving the quality of the physical environment. Without understanding the meanings people give to environments, it is very difficult to know what constitutes "improvement" or "quality." It was once said that if, at worst, architecture and planning did nothing to reduce the existing standards of environmental quality, a considerable measure of achievement could be claimed.

Information which explains how people construe their environments can add valuable guidance to increasing the scope of that achievement. We need an increase in the kind of research described in this book and a committed, vigorous effort to ensure the strategic implementation of the findings. The ecology of human life in today's urban concentrations requires exacting responses from the whole built environment industry. Without urgent action, even the maintenance of present environmental standards will become uneconomic and impossible.

NOTE

1. Now at the School of Design, North Carolina State University, Raleigh.

8

THE DEMANDS
OF PERSONAL
CONSTRUCT THEORY:
A COMMENTARY

Peter Stringer
Department of Psychology
  University of Surrey, England

Why should one imagine that personal construct theory (PCT) has any relevance for the student of environmental cognition? Surely there are other idiographic techniques than the repertory grid that would give the architect or planner insight into how his clients view the built environment. Probably, there are techniques that would provide data more conformable to the architect's normal method of working. Why does the human geographer need a theory which assumes idealistically that people are forward-looking, active, and individualistic creatures? There are other models of man that concern the geographer more closely, one would have thought.

Social scientists have often alighted on the repertory grid technique out of dissatisfaction with the semantic differential (or a bastard version of it). The idiographic emphasis is attractive, There are comforting overtones of humanism and phenomenology, without any need to sacrifice the goals of obsessive quantification. But the main difference between Kelly's and Osgood's instruments lies in the strength of the theory that backs them. How might one use the grid so as to conform to the assumptions of personal construct theory, which makes much greater demands of the geographer, architect, or planner than

is often recognized? My principal reaction to the contributions of Roger Downs and Basil Honikman is disappointment that they do not appear to appreciate the demands nor wish to take up the challenges offered by PCT.

Spatial Choices—Universities and Shops

Two studies begun in the University of Bristol Department of Geography at about the same time as Harrison and Sarre's (1971) better-known work provide useful illustrations of the way in which many of the suggestions made by Downs and other geographers might be given substance.

Rowles (1972) set out to see whether one could usefully examine spatial choice situations from within individual cognitive systems rather than in terms of the traditional, external, economic and sociocultural variables. He related the choices of university made by applicants for university entrance to their construing of the chosen universities and of their "ideal university." Thirty universities were construed in a repertory grid form, six of which subjects had actually applied to for admission. Their ideal university was also construed. The Euclidean distance between the

99

ideal and the six chosen universities was derived from each grid and was found to correspond at a statistically very significant level with the rank order of preference that subjects were committed to in their application forms. It appeared that the grid was capable of explaining independently observed choice behavior.

It is significant that Rowles did not merely look at the way in which potential students construed a set of universities. He related their construing to real-life decisions to which individuals were highly committed. There is probably a good deal of difference between the way in which individuals construe elements to which they are committed in some way and those to which they are not. Similarly, the process of construing, of completing a grid, should be something that involves the individual beyond the occasion on which it happens. It should have implications for him beyond the experimental–investigative period. As an experience for the individual, if the grid is an encapsulated event, it is unlikely to be rich in content. The clinical origins of PCT and much of Kelly's "philosophy" require that a proper use of the repertory grid and other PCT techniques should permit the subject to construe them as an appropriate and integrated part of life's events. Kelly's viewpoint acknowledges man as the controller of his destiny. Rowles studied locational decision making in a context in which most of his subjects were trying hard to control their destiny. Environmental uses of the grid to date rarely have this flavor.

Rowles' thesis was explicitly interested in the phenomenological stance of PCT, and this is nicely reflected in his interpretation of results. A dictum of Kelly's was that if subjects do not behave in accordance with your hypothesis it might be as well to ask them why. When the information in the university applicants' grids did not match their expressed choices of university, Rowles was often able to explain why from detailed examination of the grids and from supplementary interviews. For example, several subjects told him that they had only applied to Oxford and Cambridge under pressure; their grids revealed that they did not wish to go there. Others revealed a preference for these prestigious universities in their grids, but had not applied to them. In interview they reported that they had been put off by the possibility of strong competition.

The second of the Bristol geography studies is interesting in that it went further in looking at temporal aspects of construing. It also made use of behavioral criteria external to the grid itself. Hudson (1974a, 1974b) was interested in the way in which people adjust to new environments and, more specifically, in how consumers construe the shopping facilities in an area into which they have just moved. The individuals in Hudson's study kept a food-shopping diary for 10 weeks. They then completed a repertory grid in which the elements were the food shops they most commonly visited and a "preferred shop." Hudson hypothesized that there would be a relation between the position of any shop relative to the preferred shop in an individual's cognitive space, as defined by his grid, and the frequency with which he visited it. The expected probability of visiting a shop was expressed in terms of the ratio of its "distance" in the cognitive space from the preferred shop to the sum of distances for all shops in the grid. Expected probabilities were related to the actual probabilities recorded in shopping diaries. There was evidence of a positive relation between the expected and the actual probabilities. It seemed that the way in which individuals construed a set of food shops was related to their shopping behavior in the preceding 10-week period.

It is particularly interesting that Hudson found this relation to be more marked when the actual probabilities were calculated for each of the 10 weeks separately than when the pattern of shopping visits was averaged over the whole 10-week period. One might have expected that averaging shopping visits over the period would have smoothed out irregularities and produced a closer fit. The grids in this study seem to have measured more than the "average image" of shops in an individual's construct system. Grid images were apparently dependent on specific food-shopping behavior and related to actual week-by-week choices.

Hudson himself has pointed out a number of shortcomings in his study. The shop images in the grid are an inadequate expression of the choice processes in which he was basically interested. Detailed aspects of construing and choosing over time might have been explored, in particular, fluctuations in shopping needs and the evolution of construct systems. The decision model implausibly assumed that shop choices were independent. The use of a Euclidean geometry might be questioned; the construct systems of different individuals might be appropriately expressed in terms of different geometries. Environmental grid studies to date are generally pervaded by far less sophisticated shortcomings than these. But these are just the kind of points that need to be taken up.

Participating in Urban Planning

Personal construct theory is particularly suitable as a framework within which to explore situations involving change and the anticipation of alternative futures, and where there is an interaction between an expert and a nonexpert, initiated by the latter. The recent demand for public participation in urban planning is beginning to alter the relationship between planner and public in such a way that planning and PCT are compatible fields of study (see Stringer 1972, 1974b).

The move toward participation insists that people should be regarded as forward-looking, active individuals. Procedurally, participation in planning involves construing alternative futures, that is, alternative planning proposals. Ideologically, it assumes that people should be able to determine for themselves how their environment is developed and should be given opportunities to make an active contribution. Philosophically, it proposes particular advantages for the individual member of society who is allowed to exercise his individuality in the government of society's affairs.

Participation in planning is also self-reflexive from the planner's viewpoint. He has to consider the sense in which everyone is a planner; just as Kelly suggested that everyone could be considered as a psychologist or a scientist. Planners have to integrate their roles as experts and as fellow citizens and must rework their relationships with the public for whom they are planning.

Elsewhere I have described a piece of my own research on planning participation, which set out to stress some of the areas of fit between PCT and the new politics of the planner's professional role (see Stringer 1974a, 1974c, 1975). The research only partially fulfilled my objectives. It was fairly successful in demonstrating how much rich information is gained when repertory grids are considered in a wider system. Background variables, such as age, education, and social class, and variables describing people's relation to the environment that was to be redeveloped and which they were construing, were found to bear a complex relation to what was in the grids. The latter variables included such aspects as the distance at which people lived from the redevelopment area, the frequency and purpose of their visits to it, and their previous knowledge of the planning proposals. People were construing planning proposals with which they were personally deeply involved. A committed construing of imminent change should be an integral feature of PCT studies.

The study demonstrated the value of interpreting relative preferences for planning proposals in relation to a set of personal constructs, rather than as "bare votes," as is often done in participation exercises. An analysis of the content of the 3,000 constructs elicited also proved worthwhile. The way in which constructs were elicited—in this case, variations were introduced in the format of the planning maps that served as grid elements—was found to have an effect on the actual constructs emerging and the way in which they were used.

Although a great deal of information emerged, the study was entirely unsuccessful in two important respects. It entailed nothing in the way of a *sharing* of construct systems between the public that was interviewed and the planners, nor between the public and myself, as a mediating expert. Relationally the exercise was cold. The conversation was too much in one direction, from the public to the planners and myself. We revealed little or nothing explicitly about those aspects of our construct systems about which the public might have justifiably been curious.

One of Kelly's most interesting messages is that psychologists and nonpsychologists, experts and nonexperts are part of the same world. Psychology (and architecture and planning) involves a dialogue and conjoint enquiry by expert and nonexpert into matters of mutual interest. My background in traditional academic psychology, and perhaps my own personality, made it very difficult for me to put this into practice.

Personal-Construct-Theory Approach to Architecture

It seems to be even more difficult to follow up Kelly's message in the context of architectural design, despite the existing base for dialogue in the architect-client relationship. Elsewhere (Stringer, 1970) I have suggested that one PCT approach to architecture would be to consider the sense in which architect and client could be construed as playing the same game:

The client, in his role as man-the-scientist faced with his built environment, construes the replication of events in that environment. These events may be his own thoughts, feelings or behaviour in relation to the environment, or they may be those of other people—his employees, students, children, patients, and so on. What most interests the client is to be given the means of evolving a better construct system for anticipating environmental events; for interpreting, understanding and finding meaning in them. The architect has traditionally been interested in improving the environment in such a way that the client, either an individual or a social group, may find some way of construing a more humane and orderly existence within it. The architect who really wishes to be involved with his client must attempt to construe the client's construct system; if he does not he cannot hope to offer the client a possibility, in built form, of reconstruing events, of looking in a new and possibly more efficient and enjoyable way at events in the environment. The client in turn will realize that it is up to him to construe the architect's construct system if he is fully to understand the organization and meaning which the architect's system has proposed in the new building (p. 8).

Personal construct theory demands that the architect's approach to his client's construct system be much more dynamic than conducting some sort of opinion poll with a repertory grid, and then providing him with what seems to be an appropriate reflection of the grid in the form of a room or building. The grid can be a highly misleading instrument if it is used to pin down the client and as a substitute for dialogue.

There seems to be no great value in arriving at a formulation of man's processes which is based on the past and only attempts to predict and control in a mechanistic way the familiar bits of behaviour which have been pinned down. The architect can represent in built form the relationships he has observed between particular men and their environment. But surely it is much more impressive that he can reconstrue the relationship in such a way as to refresh man's potential experience of the environment. Refreshment and reconstruction do not follow from the petrifaction of the past. Instead of merely designing so as to preserve the particularities of men he has observed, he can design so that they reconstrue the world, change and become new men (p. 9).

If the architect and client are to strive toward a fully elaborated relationship in the professional context, it cannot be done on a hit-and-run basis. Like the therapeutic relationships for which PCT was intended, the architect's and client's construing of one another's construct systems will take a long time. Taking PCT seriously means taking this relationship seriously.

Too often the architect designs what he has to design and delivers it. If the client cannot use it, so much the worse for the client. But is it the architect's job simply to see that a building is erected according to a certain brief, or does he have a responsibility to see that the client modifies and restructures his behaviour in a way that may be more effective and harmonious? If he wants the client to change his attitudes to the environment and his behaviour in relation to it, he must understand the client's conflicts, worries, and predilections, he must understand the system which is the client's approach to anticipating events in the world, where some of the events are his relationships with his environment. A good architect plays an effective role in the light of the personal conceptual system of his client and must do this to accomplish his goals. He does not want to dump his client in a building and leave him to it, but he attempts to move the client toward a reconstruction of his environment and himself which will help him to understand and use it (pp. 10–11).

I do not know of any examples of PCT being applied to architectural design activities along the lines I suggest. However, an appraisal study by Canter (1972) of a new children's hospital in Glasgow, Scotland, comes nearer in spirit than the studies described here by Honikman.

If grids are to be used by architects, planners, and geographers, there must be a practical or a theoretical payoff. On the practical side, we have had no demonstration yet that doing a grid with a client actually does help the process of design, rather than, say, legitimate what the designer produces. "Architectural grids" do not seem to be derived from a clearly worked out idea of what designing implies. It would be interesting, for example, to be able to compare designs produced with and without the backing of the client's grid, to compare designs done with the knowledge of construct systems, but derived in different ways—both within the context of PCT and from a quite different theoretical viewpoint. From an architectural viewpoint it would be interesting to see how far architects with apparently similar and apparently dissimilar approaches to architecture respond similarly or dissimilarly to a given client.

For the psychologist and the theoretician, there is little of interest in being shown *tout court* that people can construe pictures of living rooms, or that "linear linkage diagrams" can be derived from the grids. Something more *pointed* should come from the intermeshing of PCT with a particular field of application. Is PCT a peculiarly effective way of describing and helping forward the relationships between individuals and their construct systems, as these occur in the briefing, designing, and occupying phases of producing a building? Can the examination of these relationships between experts and nonexperts, revolving as the relationships do around a universal feature of daily life (the practicalities of providing living space) and around concrete nonverbal manifestations of construct systems, elucidate and help forward PCT, psychology, and environment–behavior relations?

Kelly's theory makes great demands on those who choose to work with it. Human geographers are prepared to be the borrowers par excellence of the academic world. But borrowing PCT is not like borrowing other theories. Although Kelly would understand the trespasses of geographers, he would not sympathize with them. His theory, if it is taken seriously, insists that it be developed and superceded. To use the theory, we must go beyond it. If you borrow Kelly's suit of clothes, he will be upset if you do not remodel them. It might be better if you were to use them to stuff a pillow!

In short, if one is to work with PCT in environmental cognition, two things are necessary. First, there should be a set of problems within the field that PCT seems particularly fit to help one solve. Second, the working out of the solutions, the play of the theory in one's particular field, should make a positive contribution to the theory. It is a matter of establishing a relationship between two worlds of ideas. Both must profit from the meeting.

ENVIRONMENTAL LEARNING THEORY

9

PROGRAM NOTES ON A SPATIAL FUGUE[1]

David Stea

School of Architecture and Urban Planning
University of California, Los Angeles

Originally, this was to have been a quite traditional introduction to a quite traditional chapter on theory. But it seemed that a more unique beginning was called for. Ideally, it should have gone beyond the mere paying of homage to the recounting of the events that generate theory. For published theory is as much a product of events as of ideas. As I write this, long lines of cars waiting to be fueled have narrowed nearly every highway and altered every city driver's cognitive map. The metaphorical nation has tightened its metaphorical purse strings and metaphorically pulled its belt in a few notches. The supply of lined yellow pads on which I have depended for so long is dwindling, the result, I am told, of a paper shortage. And so I wonder: in an economy of scarcity, will these lines on the cognition of geographical-scale environments ever be transmuted into print?

This is to be my last article on cognitive mapping per se. As such, it ought to have been a neat package; tidy endings are still the rule. But environmental cognition is hardly tidy, and its theoretical underpinnings far from the neatly laboratory-based hypothetico-deductive system which characterizes the explanation and prediction of highly controlled phenomena. More than anything, environmental cognitive theory is amalgamated theory, often a compromise among pieces to best fit the holes in the jigsaw puzzle. It is not the product of one mind, but of many. As a student of Gordon Bower, a grand-student of Neal Miller, and a great-grand-student of Clark Hull, I learned quite early, quite at second hand, and quite impersonally about the theoretical disputes that characterized the history of research in the psychology of learning. But my much later acquisition of environmental theory (acquisiton may be the only word to use) was very personal, and acquired very much at first hand.

It is a short history, but a colorful one, begun while I was a graduate student surviving on monkey food from Karl Pribram's lab, with rat pellets for dessert. Some of my associations with other theoreticians were long term; Jim Blaut, Dan Carson, and Roger Downs, and a number of students were sources of many integrative ideas. Other shorter-term acquaintanceships were also fruitful; late-night rap sessions in Dallas, Pittsburgh, and Baltimore hotels produced many other ideas. I learned about Steve Kaplan's work in this way, and my understanding of Gordon Hewes's ideas was a product of a pleasant evening in the living room of his Boulder home.

As the pieces were acquired, they had to be assembled into what, with luck, might later resemble a coherent whole. One's office is a remarkably bad place to try to effect such an assembly. In mine, interruptions occur at an average (median) of one every 11 minutes, and paper work piles up continuously. This is hardly conducive to connected thought. There are much better places to think. In my case, much integration was achieved in small fishing boats in Massachusetts lakes and on the Sea of Cortes, in the dome car of the Rock Mountain Zephyr, in a mountain cabin in rural Quebec, and in the basement of my parents' home in Brooklyn.

As with place, so with process. Thus, the distinction between work and play has, with time, become blurred. A "working" theory is produced by "playing" with ideas. Musicians play, and so must theoreticians. That's one concept behind the title.

Another is the notion of "fugue." The spatial theme recurs again and again in the works of theorists writing on a variety of subjects; the theme is taken up by a different part of the orchestra each time, so to speak. The complete composition has yet to be played in its entirety; it has been rehearsed only in part, and the results, presented here, are more like program notes than either encyclopedic commentary or a complete score.

As with the music of John Cage, it is possible to permute, to recombine, the movements, and even to alter the structure *within* movements. Read this piece, then, as you will: as written, back to front, or whatever. If the tone fails to suit you, change the dynamics: my *fortissimo* is unlikely to be your *pianissimo* but it may be your *mezzo forte*. Finally, make marginal notes as the need strikes you; most of the ideas that follow began life on the backs of envelopes, restaurant placemats, or railway dining car napkins. As the field began, so shall it prosper and grow.

This composition is divided into five movements:

1. The evolutionary record
2. Neurophysiological underpinnings
   a. Networks
   b. Holograms
   c. The dual-hemisphere theory: two modes of cognition
3. Place learning and early development
4. Learning the way
5. Metricization: the quantitative dimension.

Each movement answers a fundamental question. Given that environmental cognition *does* exist and given that the exercise of such cognition, perhaps more than any other "skill," shapes the way in which we cope with the world around us, we ask: Why? How? When? The theme of the first movement is "Why," of the second "How," of the third "When". The fourth movement is directed at change, and the fifth at quantification of the cognized space to which we refer.

We cannot even attempt to answer *any* of these questions, however, until we have made clear what it is that we mean by *cognitive map*. It is a term with tremendous surplus meaning; a description requires many pages (see Downs and Stea, 1973a, Chapter 1), but a brief definition can be offered instead:

Cognitive mapping is a process composed of a series of psychological transformations by which an individual acquires, codes, stores, recalls, and decodes information about the relative locations and attributes of phenomena in his [or her] everyday spatial environment (Downs and Stea, 1973a, p. 9, modified to avoid sexist pronouns).

A cognitive map, then, is a network of representations of the spatial relations among elements of the "real-world" environment. The meaning of the term "network" will presently be made clear; the precise meaning of "real world" involves heady philosophic hair splitting in which I choose not to become involved.

THE EVOLUTIONARY RECORD

The first fundamental postulate is both simple and clear: cognitive mapping is evolutionarily adaptive. It seems likely that higher mammals, especially free-ranging mammals, require a "sense of place" for survival; they must find places for food, avoid places of predators, and return to the "home" reliably enough to ensure the survival of their young. What distinguishes the primates from other higher mammals is the absence of a strongly developed olfactory sense, which makes them exceeding poor "trail sniffers." If subprimates are cognitive mappers, then olfactorily deficient primates must be even more so, demanding awareness of extended-range "maps." It seems that the most parsimonious cognitive maps should represent the animal's world as it would be if viewed from above. This is undoubtedly less of a problem for arboreal primates than for earthbound man.

Anthropologist Gordon Hewes[2] has expressed the evolutionary view rather well:

As long as our primate ancestors occupied mainly arboreal habitats, consisting of relatively small tracts of forest or woodland, their cognitive maps of their environments did not have to be very complicated. They were (even though olfactorily feeble) probably assisted by olfactory cues from trees and other vegetation in the construction of these mental maps, as well as by sound (e.g., of noisy streams). Their social groups were such that individuals rarely strayed far from the main band, rarely beyond hearing-distance of calls. They fed in groups, as monkeys and apes do still. With terrestrial expansion, some primates still did not make a very drastic shift. Baboon troops still tend to stick close together, and their ranges are still strikingly small compared, say, to the enormous territories of predators like wolves.

But the advent of hunting and/or scavenging, even as a partial supplement to a vegetarian diet, must have transformed the territorial basis for early hominid existence (as has been suggested by a number of anthropologists). Effective early hominid hunters may have roamed over territories approximating the dimensions of those utilized by hunting dogs and wolves. Unlike them, they could not depend on an acute sense of smell to follow game, or to find their way home after pursuing prey. If, as most of us think, the advent of hunting behavior among early hominids was accompanied by a separation from females and young, and the males did most or all of the bigger game tracking, this trail-following ability would have been crucial for survival. Landmarks previously ignored by terrestrial monkeys, to say nothing of forest-bound apes and tree-bound other primates, would become essential features of the environment for effective ventures out after game (or predator-kill scavenging), existence in semi-arid grasslands or savannahs in the dry seasons, when waterholes are widely scattered, and so on . . . .

A greatly improved control and processing of environmental information must have accompanied hominization, up until the relatively recent period when our ancestors become relatively sedentary once again, with the rise of agriculture, or inshore or river fishing. We must suppose that a critical dependence on "geographic awareness" of territories approximating the size of our larger counties in the United States was part of the hominid biogram. For the effective utilization of larger territories, early hominids must have been able, in some fashion, to coordinate their movements and rendezvous activities . . . .

NEUROPHYSIOLOGICAL UNDERPINNINGS

Networks

Kaplan's neurophysiological model (1973a; see also Chapter 2), based on a view of human development as ecological adaptation, provides a logical bridge from evolution to neurophysiology. He suggests four major *types* of knowledge required for survival:

1. Where one is (perception and representation).
2. What is likely to happen next (prediction).
3. Whether it will be good or bad (evaluation).
4. Some possible next steps (action).

Kaplan sets as his task:

To specify the structure required to handle information in an adaptive fashion. This structure turns out to be a cognitive map. There is thus no need to begin by postulating a cognitive map; it *emerges* out of other (and more basic) considerations (p. 66).

Determining "where one is" requires efficient perception, and Kaplan's view is based upon the *neural net* hypotheses of Hebb (1949). Neural elements said to *correspond* with features in the organism's environment assume two states: "on" when the feature is present and "off" when it is absent. In this conceptual system, collections of elements are *defined* by environmental objects to which they correspond:

The collection of associated elements [or *network of associations*] that in general correspond to an object" is a rather clumsy way to refer to what may well be the basic component of thinking and perceiving . . . . Perception will tend to be generic. Generic perception can be viewed as a categorization process (Bruner, 1957a), as the placing of stimulus patterns into appropriate classifications. This process is often viewed as one that tidies up the organism's view of the world, translating the vagaries of fleeting stimulus patterns into orderly equivalence classes (Kaplan, 1973a, pp. 69–70).

This process is also that which produces *representations*. But the organism must do more than simply to represent; it must also *predict* across a wide range of situations. To do this, according to Kaplan, generic information processing requires an *associational network structure* resembling what is termed, in mathematical graph theory, a nonplanar semilattice. Such a nonplanar structure facilitates another important prolegomenon to environmental decision making: *evaluation*. What outcomes are good and which bad, which produce pleasurable and which painful consequences? Such evaluation of potential occurrences is referred to as *motivational coding*. These three concepts, generic perception, associational network, and motivational coding, allow the prediction and evaluation of "next situations," and are represented in the central nervous system by the "network-like" structures mentioned above. In such networks, consisting of points and connecting paths, *distance, direction, and region* become meaningful.

This system for storing many possible situations and the relations among them is the literal *cognitive map*. The structural system has certain properties, defined by Kaplan as follows:

1. *Generality*. The structure underlying the spatial map of the world that people carry around in their heads is not different from the structure that underlies *all* cognitive processes.
2. *Additional properties*. The cognitive map (spatial or otherwise) will consist of generic representations that are motivationally coded and that are *not* related to each other in a simple hierarchical fashion.
3. *Emergent functions*. The same framework that is necessary for short-run, moment-by-moment decision making is also suitable for long-range planning and what might be called contemplative thought (pp. 74–75).

Taken together, these three points have great surplus meaning. Spatial cognitive maps become special cases of general networks of cognitive representations (temporal and other). The network, then, as Kaplan conceives it, is a *necessary* structure for adaptive processing of information. Generic information processing often leads to generic outputs; detail is less important than overall "usability," which accounts for the apparent "sloppiness" in maps drawn by people of their home towns. No tree-like hierarchical structure could produce such results, and none would be capable of "lookahead," "hindsight," or "Remorse"; all these require *representations* and networks of associations between representations. The more sensorily vivid and image-like the representations, the more probable is genuinely future-oriented behavior and the incorporation of a strong temporal dimension in the spatial decision-making process:

Man could not be born with the maps he needs; likewise, he could not afford to wait for an emergency before he begins to develop them. Rather man must be born with a tremendous propensity to make and extend maps; that is, to explore and to learn. Man would have to be a curious, restless animal, not, as some theories have suggested, an animal that lies down and goes to sleep when his primary needs are satisfied.

Man must also have a bias toward action, toward making up his mind quickly and getting on with it . . . . The very possibilities for elaborate and extensive representation of present and future circumstances require a strong bias against too much internal rumination (Kaplan, 1973a, p. 77).

Holograms

It appears that cognitive mapping abilities are pervasive, evolutionarily adaptive, and by no means unique to man, or even to the higher primates. The question implicitly posed by Kaplan (1973a) is, How spatial events *ought* to be represented in the brain to make possible the behavior that we actually observe? He has provided a partial answer (see Chapter 2). Another part of that answer is suggested by other mental activities in which some of us engage.

Consider one possibility, elaborated as follows. It seems that what distinguishes an architect, for example, from many other people is his apparent ability to construct a "building in his head," a piece of mental architecture, if you will, which he can mentally rotate, looking at it alternately from above and from the side. The sculptor does similar things with the sculpture he intends to produce; so may the chemist (recall Kukele's famous dream of the benzene molecule as a ring of snakes, attached mouth to tail), the mathematician, and others. What all these hypothesized mental processes have in common is their remarkable resemblance to a now well recognized but not yet well understood process in optical physics: holography. It is known that a beam of ultra high energy light, a laser, may be split in such a way that part of the light is directed to a photographic plate and the other part reflected from an object to the plate. The result of combining the two beams is an interference pattern on the plate. If another laser beam (a reconstruction beam) is then directed against the plate, the result, at a distance somewhat removed from the plate, is a fully three dimensional image, a hologram.

It has since been suggested by the neurophysiologist Pribram (1971) that this hologram, which seems to so closely mirror the kinds of mental gymnastics that scientists, and especially people in environmentally related disciplines, must almost inevitably go through, may provide a *general* model for brain functions. Thus, the nature of mental representation may be a *neurophysiological* hologram; this represents an *active* model of what may transpire in the interaction between the central nervous system and the external spatial environment, as well. Since there is no other parsimonious model for the neurophysiological basis of environmental cognition (attempts to build computers to engage even in so elementary a task as recognition of rotated patterns are not, even yet, completely successful), this may be the closest that we have come to an understanding of the "great ravelled knot" in our heads.

Holograms . . . possess the property of associative recall. We have all experienced the phenomenon of revisiting an old neighborhood after many years and suddenly remembering shops and doorways and even placements of furniture in the apartment we lived in. Had we been asked to recall these memories without the input from the "reference" objects, the streets and buildings of the neighborhood, we would have been unable to do so . . . .

The image from a hologram has true three-dimensional perspective. By moving his head, a viewer can look around and behind objects in the picture, just as if he were looking at a real scene from different positions . . . .

Experiments by Fergus Campbell and his associates at Cambridge University have provided some direct support for a neural holographic process . . . .

Campbell's experimental result accounts for the fact that a child who has learned to identify the letters of the alphabet by sight can recognize them no matter what size they are. The child readily identifies a 20 foot letter "A" on a billboard even if all the "A"'s he has seen before then have been a quarter of an inch in height . . . . (Pribram, 1971, pp. 89–90).

The search for a neurological analogue to the cognitive map led to the consideration of the hologram as a model (Blaut and Stea, 1971) or a metaphor at almost the same time as Pribram's ideas were going to press. Why did the hologram so intrigue quite independent groups of investigators at precisely the same time?

Holograms have become familiar to the general public through "tricks," such as creating enlarged three-dimensional images of chess boards with each piece the size of a man, so that chess tournaments can be watched by crowds much as they now watch such spectator sports as football. But the importance of the hologram is much more general. If we are dealing with very small objects, such as chessmen, we can enlarge them and see the consequences of manipulating these objects in three dimensions very readily with holograms. Conversely, it appears that it ought to be possible to reduce the imaged sizes of very large objects to make them more amenable to convenient investigation.

Extending this to spatial conceptualization, we might speak of a "psychological hologram" as a conceptual three-dimensional projection of a three-dimensional object. It is a representation, presumably structurally or functionally somewhere in the central nervous system, and the availability of such a representation enables one to walk around such a cognitive model, or to rotate it, or to imagine the consequences of rotation, expansion, or compassion. It is therefore a form of "model thinking," in the sense that it is a "thought-up model."

What sorts of representations are then possible? A sculpture is three-dimensional and often representational, but it differs from a hologram in that the sculpture does not change when the object represented changes. A hologram, however, is a dynamic representation; inserting changes occurring over time, real or psychological, makes it four-dimensional in scope. A three-dimensional man can thus engage in four-dimensional thinking.

Kaplan has set up the requisites for a neurophysiological representation, which he terms a literal cognitive map. Working quite independently, Pribram has produced what is in my opinion a logical complement to Kaplan's idea. Kaplan has specified the elements, the properties; Pribram conjectures *how they work*, how it is that we are able to "play with" our representations in so imaginative a way, presently as well as planfully. The next question that naturally arises concerns possible differences between *spatial* and *nonspatial* representations.

The Dual-Hemisphere Theory: Two Modes of Cognition

One of a number of studies (Bogen et al., 1972), drawing upon work currently underway at the University of California at Los Angeles, the Langley Porter Neuropsychiatric Institute in San Francisco, and elsewhere, indicates that the two hemispheres of the brain have rather different functions. Specifically, the left hemisphere appears to control language, writing, and other linear or nondimensional processes; the right hemisphere controls perception, fantasy, spatial knowledge, and other *gestalt* or dimensional processes. Bogen et al. refer to the left-hemisphere functions as *propositional* and to the right-hemisphere functions as *appositional*.[3] In our society the left-hemisphere functions tend to be the ones strengthened by formal schooling. Somewhat less obvious is another contention made by Bogen and his associates, that *dominant* groups, those with easiest access to the "goodies" of Western society, tend to cognize the world *propositionally*, whereas *nondominant* groups (ethnic minorities and, in many cases, women) are somewhat more likely to cognize *appositionally*; these tendencies are associated with acquired dominance of one brain hemisphere or the other.[4]

Most cognitive mapping abilities appear to be acquired and not to be part of the genetic endowment of the human being; the person must *learn* to represent environments at the geographical scale. I would like to hypothesize, then, that spatial and environmental cognition tends to be *appositional* in early life, and that the effect of formal schooling is to cause a certain shift in mode to *propositional* cognition. I am suggesting, based upon fairly voluminous research (e.g., Blaut and Stea, 1971) that young children understand the world around them in a *gestalt* manner, that they do *not* merely memorize paths from some point of origin to desired goals but understand, in a fundamentally spatial way, the relations among these paths. What results, in adulthood, is much more difficult to specify. Since two-factor theories are popular in psychology, it would be comforting to be able to point to two classes of change that seem to occur and to affect environmental cognition, but there appear to be at least three. The successfully developing child gets "educated" (the relation to learning, as the latter term is used in psychology, remains unspecified), learns to get about in the world, and perhaps most important learns his social role in society. Thus, in my recent work, I have found it necessary to invoke a three-factor theory,

with all three factors related to the appositional–propositional ratio: (1) social role, (2) formal education, and (3) environmental experience.

Social role is usually indexed by sex, ethnic group membership, and socioeconomic status, *formal education* by years of schooling, and *environmental experience* by where and how often one travels, and by what mode (some, such as auto and bicycle, are considered "active"; others, such as bus and train, are "passive" with reference to the person's involvement in controlling his movement). From the foregoing, one reasonable hypothesis, for example, would be that on an *appositional* test of spatial relations, female members of ethnic minorities with a fair degree of environmental experience but less formal education would perform as well as somewhat "better educated" male members of the dominant grouping. Early data (Stea and Taphanel, 1975) indicate preliminary support for this hypothesis.

It becomes increasingly clear that we need to know as much as possible about different conceptions of environments by different kinds of people, having different age-group memberships, ethnic-group identities, and so on.[5] In their search for universals, both architects and psychologists often commit the same error of treating people as though all were the same, omitting consideration of the less than "fully-developed" (smaller and younger) members of the society and of differences in styles, tastes, and environmental understanding among its more "fully-developed" members.

PLACE LEARNING AND EARLY DEVELOPMENT

If spatial abilities play so pervasive a role in *phylogenetic* development, we ought not be surprised to find them playing a central role in *ontogenetic* development as well. In other words, spatial learning *should* occur in quite young children, even though such learning has been largely ignored by psychologists (with the exception of Piaget and Inhelder, 1956; Piaget, Inhelder, and Szeminska, 1960).

But the laws governing the cognition of large- and small-scale spaces *may* be qualitatively as well as quantitatively different. The popular belief (some hold it to be "obvious") is that development of perception or cognition at the same scale must precede such development at the larger scale. But arguments presented elsewhere (Gibson, 1970; Downs and Stea, 1973a, pp. 223–224; Stea, 1974) indicate that we ought not to be surprised by the two developing simultaneously or even by the *reverse* of the "obvious" occurring in the case of many aspects of spatial cognition.[6]

Thus, evolutionarily adaptive large-scale environmental cognition seems to appear at a very early stage in the development of the human organism. Specifically, our data (Blaut and Stea, 1971; Stea, 1973; Stea and Blaut, 1973a, 1973b) indicate that such cognitive abilities are well developed (and also well learned) prior to the usual age of entering school in Western societies. The nature of formal education in such schools, oriented largely to the nonspatial representation of information, is such as to contribute much less to the enhancement of spatial cognition than to other forms. We believe that the basic elements of such cognitive ability are not only well developed before the child enters school, but they are largely *complete* prior to that event (although later *elaboration* is possible and almost invariably occurs).

It is difficult to evaluate the development of environmental cognition using large-scale environments themselves. *Vertical aerial photography* represents one reasonable surrogate; it is the closest genuinely inexpensive simulation of the experience of viewing the world from an airplane; it is an iconic, nonlinguistic *map.* The ability to fully comprehend a symbolic cartographic map clearly involves the ability to establish a correspondence between the map and the land area it represents, or, in the terms of our discussion, fairly sophisticated cognitive mapping abilities. The reading of aerial photographs involves the same abilities and the same basic cognitive transformations: (1) *reduction in scale,* (2) *rotation of perspective* from a viewing position previously experienced to another, unfamiliar, overhead perspective, and (3) *abstraction* from the three-dimensional polychromatic world of reality to the two-dimensional monochromatic world of the black-and-white photograph. What results—the process and product of coordinating these cognitive transformations—is termed *place learning.*

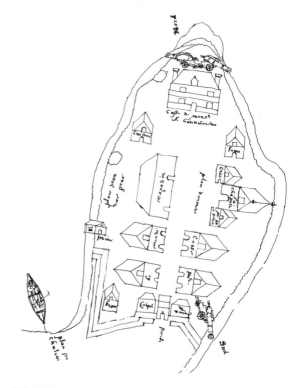

FIGURE 1
"Child-like" map, drawn by an adult: an old map of Montreal.

Place learning is a special case of learning in general. One breakdown of the variables involved in all learning is as follows:

1. A stimulus or complex of stimuli that set the stage for learning or make it possible for learning to occur.
2. An organism, in this case a human child, who is to learn to make a response to the stimuli.
3. An inferred cognitive process within the central nervous system that encodes and stores the experience and recombines its elements in line with previous experience already in storage, a process hinted at by such words as "memory," "thinking," and so on.
4. A response that is to be learned or to be attached to the stimuli.

5. A reward or reinforcement for the behavior (that makes the learning "satisfying" in some way).

6. A relation between the internal state of the organism that makes the reward potentially effective (motivation).

7. Some criterion of "learning"; that is, when can we say that learning has in fact occurred?

"Place," in a psychological sense, is a special case of the stimulus situation. It has two defining attributes: (1) its scale is large relative to the learning organism, and in general too large to be perceived as a whole at one time, and (2) its level of complexity extends to all forms of perceivable objects or events in a given space, and not simply to one category of object or event or person.

Between the external, "objectively observable" world of the child and his manipulation of, or responses to, this world—his environmental behavior—is a nebulous intervening entity. This has its locus, presumably, somewhere in the "black box" of the central nervous system. It acts to integrate what he presently perceives with his environmental memory and current plans. Such a *cognitive map* enables a child to *predict* the environment that is too large to be perceived at once, to establish a matrix of environmental experience into which a new experience can be integrated.

We cannot tap such cognitive maps directly; we can only infer that they *must* exist from certain actions of the child. Earlier studies have shown that he can draw a map of the route from home to school or even his neighborhood, that he can use toys to model his community or a reasonable facsimile thereof, that he can tell the locations of objects he cannot see from

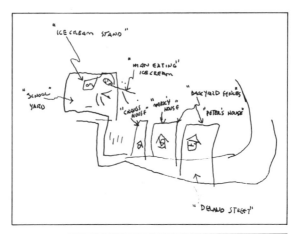

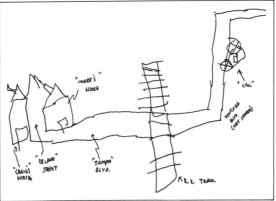

FIGURE 2

Several "adult-like" maps, drawn by the same child:

(a) In response to the question "where would you go to buy ice cream?"

(b) A description of how to drive home from the freeway.

(c) Child's own street with model homes and friend's house. The child's own house is shown with a dirt lawn and a "hard hat area" sign above.

In 2a and 2b, the child's age is 3 years, 7 months; labels have been added by his father. In 2c, the child is 3 years, 8 months.

those he can, although never having traversed a straight-line path between them, and that he can immediately "pick out" new routes from home to a goal on the basis of old routes once traveled (see summaries of these studies in Blaut and Stea, 1971). Theories of learning based upon simple stimulus-response connections fail to account for such integrative human behavior.

There seems to be a conflict or tension between the experimental psychologist's tendency to view learning (especially in the rat) as a value-free process (except for positive or negative values attached to reinforcements and to stimuli that become secondary reinforcers) and the opposite tendency on the part of many educational psychologists to view learning as principally a matter of socialization and, thus, of valence. Place learning lies somewhere between the two. No doubt every higher organism attaches valences to environmental features; hence, a capacity for taking account of values must be built into the model. At the same time, what is being dealt with is not social learning per se.

Another very fundamental property of the place-learning model is postulated as follows: a significantly high proportion of place-learning experiences makes use of small-scale surrogates or simulations of the environmental situation (e.g., pictorial imagery, as in television, aerial photographs, etc.). The assumed rationale is the difficulty a child faces in perceiving and manipulating events at what we have called "a geographical scale" and his or her need to deal with these events in a surrogate, simulated, or small-scale form (it may even be true that this form of simulation is the earliest use of "model thinking" and therefore true scientific reasoning in the child).

The reward for place learning is based in the phylogenesis of the human species: to survive, the human organism and its prehominid ancestors have had to learn how to deal with, and more about, a spatial environment; this learning is certainly repeated ontogenetically in the development of every child. The reinforcements for environmental learning are to some extent rather different from those for social learning and small-object learning: stubbing one's toe is often sufficiently punishing for stepping in the wrong place or in a wrong way; in larger-scale movements, getting lost can be an even worse punishment for not knowing where one is going.

LEARNING THE WAY

The developing child learns its first proximate environment very early in life, and then comes to learn, through a variety of experiences, about environments in general. For that individual, rare in

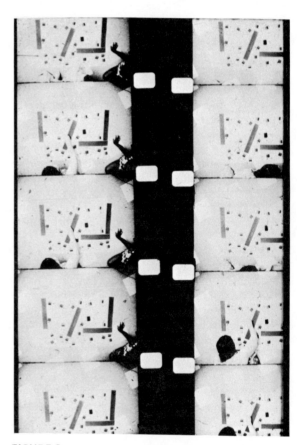

FIGURE 3
Child's construction of a generalized town using an "environmental modeling kit." This illustration is a portion of a 3-second, time-lapse, motion-picture record.

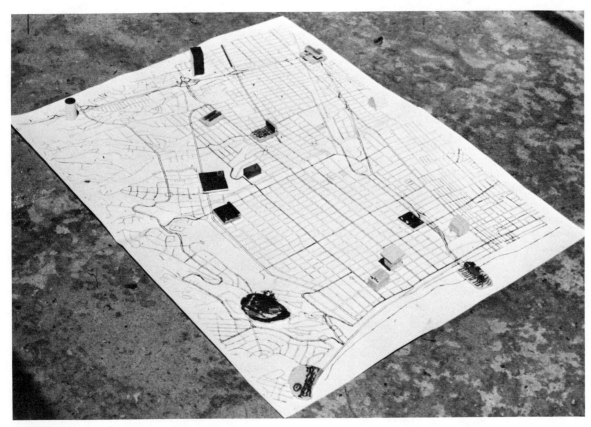

FIGURE 4
Adult's construction of a specific town on an outline base map.

industrialized societies, who spends the remainder of his life in the place of his birth, problems of environmental adjustment may be more temporal than spatial; time changes even the most traditional of places, and new buildings, and freeways must somehow be incorporated into old cognitive maps. But the majority of us will change locations during our lives, some, many times. Not all environmental learning tasks are solved in early childhood; a *framework* for the future learning of spatial environments is established, to be sure, but just how each is to be learned remains undetermined. Surely, one major task faced by each of us is that of learning one's way about a new place. *What is learned* may depend, first, upon the *way* of learning, upon how we *move* through the environment.

The work of Held and Rekosh (1963) indicates the importance of *motor* experience and of *sensor motor interaction* to the development of normal perception. Such experiments indicate that subjects exposed to equivalent sensory stimulation, but different opportunities to interact with an experienced environment, show different degrees of perceptual attainment. Specifically, it appears that the less the motor-environment interaction available to a subject, the less veridical his perception becomes. In terms of environmental learning, these findings seem to have implications for the selection of transportation modes for environmental learning purposes. Passive systems (e.g., buses) may lead to less environmental knowledge than active systems (walking, cycling, driving). Put somewhat differently, one's cognitive map may be both less veridical, in real-world terms, and relatively impoverished when only passive forms of movement are available.

Finding one's way about a new town is essentially a problem in the judicious utilization of paths, junctions, and other environmental cues. A path finder adopts a certain directional bearing, then changes bearing by making a turn, and so on. The result is a *route* from an origin to a goal; a complex of such routes for a given area constitutes a *schema*. Two fundamentally different types of *schemata* appear to be formed, depending upon the coordinate system and mode of imagery utilized, but the two do not appear equally well suited to all places. The distinction should be clear to anyone who has ever taken directions (or given them) over the telephone. One way to give directions is to specify an origin, an initial direction (street name or number), a cue at which one turns right or left, a succeeding cue at which one does something else, and so on, to the goal. This can be mapped or "imaged," but can simply be listed, as well; not even the vaguest graphic image is absolutely necessary. The second way of giving directions is to minimize the emphasis upon specific cues and to give information in terms of compass coordinates and general characteristics of a place. Imagewise, this second strategy allows for the choice of alternative routes within a general framework (Moore, 1973b, 1975a); the former method does not, in the sense that "if you miss a cue (point of choice), you're lost." If images (in their most generic sense) are built up, however, those based upon one of the above systems of route following will be very different from those based upon the other. One will be a conglomerate of independent routes, what Shemyakin (1962) has termed a *route map*. The other, a truly two-dimensional matrix of relationships, he called a *survey map*.

Which is better? That, of course, depends on the situation. A survey map has more general use *within*

a location, and, when relabeled, can be "carried" to new locations with similar morphologies. But a route map is, for many, initially easier to learn, and where channels of communication and transportation are irregular, as is some New England towns, it may work very much better. Exceedingly irregular morphologies often completely defy the survey mapper; no spatial rule can be formulated upon which to base one's plans.

Moore (1973d; see also Chapter 12) suggests that route maps may indeed be developmentally subsumed within survey maps. Put somewhat differently, his findings indicate that representations based upon fixed reference elements (either routes or landmarks) and organized in clusters or subgroups of elements spread over the landscape are subsumed within representations based on a more abstract organizing principle independent of any particular reference elements and organized in a coordinated manner. This real-time developmental progression appears to be related to environmental experience, as indexed by degree of familiarity with the urban area and its subordinate neighborhoods.

The astute reader with a smattering of background in experimental psychology will detect a parallel between the route map–survey map dichotomy drawn above and the response learning–place learning controversy in the psychology of the 1940s and early 1950s. This controversy lined up the followers of Hull (response learners; see Hull, 1952) on one side and the followers of Tolman[7] (place learners; see Tolman, 1948, 1951, 1958) on the other. The response learners held that the subjects of learning experiments (laboratory rats) learned by establishing chain-like associations of responses with stimuli; they learned, in short, the appropriate *responses* to make in the presence of certain stimuli. The place learners held that animals were capable of forming *cognitive maps* (Tolman's usage) and learned what *places* to go to. Ironically, although nearly all the "critical" experiments performed to resolve this controversy were spatial in form (utilizing mazes, runways, etc.), the argument was never conceived in spatial terms. That learning could be *either* response or place, or even *both*, was not explicitly admitted by most (although perhaps implicitly suspected; we know now what role was played by the publication policies of the professional journals).

METRICIZATION:
THE QUANTITATIVE DIMENSION

The cognitive maps of which we have been speaking, conceptions of some part of the physical world, are assumed to be modified by value judgments, motivational factors, and so on. They are often *action spaces* in the sense that they are generated by a person in the process of imagining himself or herself moving through them. Such spaces contain objects and are somehow bounded; that is, the individual knows that there are "things" within the space and he has some conception of its extent. Thus, we may ask a person simply to list all the "points" he recalls in the center of city X. The list gives us the objects in his conceptual space; the distribution of these objects gives us an idea of the extent of this psychological subworld. Moreover, relationships exist among the objects. If we ask the person making the list to place the points of the city center in the order in which he would encounter them in the process of taking a given trip through the city, we obtain one kind of relationship among objects: a one-dimensional, linear ordering. If we ask the person to locate the objects on an outline map of the city center, or to draw such a map, we obtain a two-dimensional ordering.

Characteristics of spaces. I would hypothesize that large, geographical-scale cognitive spaces have the following "quantifiable" characteristics:

1. Each space consists of a series of *points* (not points in the mathematical sense, because our points may have dimension) arranged in a one-, two-, or three-dimensional way.
2. There may be several possible *hierarchical arrangements* among these points in terms of size, importance, and so on. In fact, several hierarchical arrangements may coexist, or may exist at different times within the life of an individual. In a child's drawing of a visit to a zoo, the largest animal drawn is usually the most important to him—often a monkey; similarly, in drawing his home, mother is often drawn much larger than father.
3. If it is possible to get from one given point in the imaged space to another by *any* means of transportation, we say that they are *connected*. If it is possible to get from one point to another by *some* means of transportation, they are *semiconnected*. In either case, there exists a *path* between the points. If the two points are semiconnected, there exists a *barrier* between them. However, the converse is not necessarily true; the existence of a barrier does not necessarily imply that there exists a means of transportation by which it is impossible to get from one point to another. The barrier may simply make certain forms of transportation more difficult.
4. Barriers differ in their *permanence, permeability,* and *quality* (natural or artificial). A construction project in the middle of a superhighway decreases permeability and is impermanent; a flood, also impermanent, reduces permeability to zero. The frontier between Mexico and the United States is temporarily quite impermeable when rumors are received that a shipment of marijuana is expected; all travellers attempting then to cross the border experience difficulty.
5. Barriers may be *symmetrical* (the same when approached from one member of a pair of points as from the other) or *nonsymmetrical*. The city of Providence, Rhode Island, for example, was a nonsymmetrical barrier for most travelers between Boston and New York prior to the completion of the interstate highway; that is, the north–south and south–north routes through the city were different, and it was considerably more difficult to traverse the city in one direction than in the other.

In summary, the space of which we are speaking is bounded (one-, two-, or three-dimensional), and consists of a probably finite (given the limitations of the human organism) collection of points of anywhere from zero to three dimensions, of paths between them, and of interposed barriers.

Topological correspondence. It is hypothesized that when maps are drawn or descriptions given the product is not an exact description of the real world, but that, under specifiable conditions, the order in which these objects appear, and such other ordinal characteristics as relative size, relative path length, and so on, are conserved. The depiction of the "cognitive map" will thus be an *order-preserving transform* when the following conditions hold:

1. The difference in magnitude between the lengths of two paths, the sizes of two subspaces, and so on, is demonstrably recognized (demonstrable in the sense that we have another, independent measure of recognition).
2. The elements involved (points, paths, spaces, etc.) are equal in importance, cogency, and valence (in terms of their relative attractiveness, or goal value), and are equally well known to the subject.
3. Differences in importance, valence, or cogency are in the direction of objective differences in magnitude.

Distance and boundedness.   As indicated at the beginning of this section, different sets of instructions to a person produce cognitive maps of different levels of dimensionality. But even stronger relationships may be elicited, either verbally or graphically. One such relationship is a measure of the spatial separation between objects. We call this *distance*, and assert that we can measure its conception in traditional distance units, such as feet, miles, or kilometers, or in untraditional units, such as time, money, or effort variables. A model for cognitive distance may be specified, based upon mathematically defined metric space.

Suppose that we have three points in space, cities, for instance, which we denote as *a, b,* and *c.* What is meant by "distance separating two points" is generally understood. If we denote such a distance by *d,* and the distance between *a* and *b,* with *a* as the starting point, by $d(b, a)$, then, perhaps we can say something about a few topological characteristics of the space consisting of *a, b,* and *c* and an arbitrary number of other points. If the space is metric, for example, the following relations (or conditions) hold:

1. $d(a, b) > 0$.
2. $d(a, b) = 0$ if, and only if, $a = b$.
3. $d(a, b) = d(b, a)$.
4. $d(a, c) < d(a, b) + d(b, c)$.

Attention is directed to condition 3, the *commuta-*

tivity condition. Specifically, we have hypothesized that $d(a, b) \neq d(b, a)$ when *a* and *b* differ markedly in valence, or desirability, or when the barriers separating *a* and *b* are themselves noncommutative. Existing data (Stea, 1968, 1969a) tend to support this hypothesis.

Another relationship defines the boundaries of the space. The relationship that calls certain points or objects "outermost" and enables us to construct a line by connecting these outermost points also allows us to speak of the *envelope* of a space. A consideration of several possible envelopes conveys to us where the conceptual space ends, or abuts, other spaces. Such envelopes can be drawn, of course, rather than simply inferred from the location of objects. We may ask a subject, for example, to indicate the boundaries of his neighborhood on either an outline or a free-image map. The boundaries may be clear or indistinct; they may be in the form of lines or other imaged areas. A neighborhood may be bounded by a street or another neighborhood. Furthermore, there may be boundaries within the boundaries; as an individual images a city, he may image neighborhoods within the city as bounded entities.

Metricization: looking backward.   The preceding is but a preliminary step, a mere first stab at a quantitative framework for the otherwise qualitative descriptions appearing earlier in the paper. It is no more than a portion of such a framework; others (e.g., Briggs, 1973a; Cadwallader, 1973b; Lowrey, 1973; Lundberg, 1973; see also Chapters 28, 29, and 30) have quite recently investigated various aspects of it in considerably more detail. But the framework *does* point the way to dealing with such quantified or quantifiable concepts as distance, direction, extensity, shape, and boundedness, as they exist in the cognitive realm.

CODA

Descriptions of real-world experiences, illustrative of theoretical positions, are always at least somewhat in order. Since the author of the foregoing piece has oft been described as a "train buff," the following two third-hand anecdotes may be illustrative of some of the cognitive mapping problems with which he

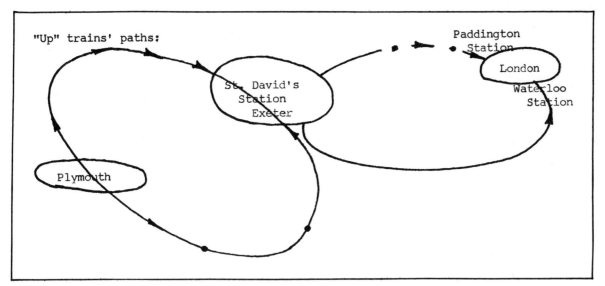

FIGURE 5
"Trainspotter's" cognitive map.

feels most in tune. One refers to the suburbs of Pittsburgh, Pennsylvania, the city in which the author spent his undergraduate years, the other to a part of England with which he is deucedly unfamiliar:

"When I was in Wilkinsburg, Pa.," a psychologist writes, "the trolleys for the eastern suburbs ran north through the town, but the east-bound trains ran south through the town. I arrived on the train and, of course, took the trolley going the wrong way to get to the west. My frame of reference was in conflict all that summer" (quoted in Griffin, 1948, p. 383).

My summer holidays when I was 10 (1957) were spent near Exeter, Devonshire, in the west of England. I remember "trainspotting" at Exeter St. David's railway station, and I learnt something about different orientation with different scales while doing it. The trains from London to Plymouth all passed through Exeter. Look at the pregrouping British Railways atlas. Southern Region trains (ex., L.S.W.R.) came into the station from the north if they were "up" (i.e., going to London). Western Region (ex., G.W.R.) trains coming into the station from the north were "down" (i.e., coming from London). I had to learn that summer to abstract myself to a broader scale (than the end of the station platform where I was always standing) in order to understand this [see Figure 5].

Also, it could be done by noting the number of the locomotive engine: If it was four-figure (ex., 4037, 4929) it was Western Region. If it was five-figure beginning with "3"

(ex., 30719, 34061) it was Southern Region, and headed in the opposite eventual direction though presently in the same local direction.[8]

The reader who is unmoved by the pathos of either of these tales of woe is encouraged to make up his own. Russell Baker did (Baker, 1972) and here are a few excerpts:

Washington, Feb. 24—Intercepted Memo.
From: White House Gazetteer Editor.
To: All holders of "The Official Classified White House Gazetteer: Richard Nixon Edition, 1969."
Subject: Amendments of geography ordered in maps and texts of the aforementioned Gazetteer in consequence of recent changes in the shape of the world.
Classification rating: Medium Hush.
1. Effective immediately, the following amendments are to be made in your copy of "The Official Classified White House Gazetteer: Richard Nixon Edition, 1969," in order to preserve its accuracy as a reference authority on world geography:
A. On pages 30–31, ink out the words "nameless space" which are overprinted in the large white empty area located generally east and southeast of the U.S.S.R. Underneath the inked-out words, write in the word "China." Color it red.
B. (1) With scissors, remove the word "China" from the island shown in map on page 34. (2) Using pale ink, write

the word "Taiwan" in the blue area indicating water around the island. (3) With scissors, remove the island from the map and place it in your wallet; it is now your official credential of admission to all future meetings of the Young Americans for Freedom (Y.A.F.), at which it must be worn pinned underneath the lapel of a pinstripe suit, or, in the case of ladies, inside the brim of a flowered hat.

. . .

F. From your nearby General Services Administration stationery branch obtain an official classified U.S.-approved rubber stamp (6 inches by 2 inches) bearing the word "SHAME." After wetting rubber stamp on a well-inked pad, (1) turn to the map on page 137 and press the "SHAME" stamp heavily over the country shown there until the overprinted name ("Sweden") is no longer legible; (2) turn to the map on page 281 ("Massachusetts") and repeat the above-described process, wetting the stamp on the ink pad as frequently as necessary to obliterate the map.

NOTES

1. Many of the ideas presented here were developed in collaboration with Jim Blaut, who was unable to contribute to the writing of this Chapter. Any misinterpretations of our jointly developed ideas are, therefore, entirely my own responsibility. Much of the material is excerpted from writings which originally appeared elsewhere (*Annals of the Association of American Geographers*, the *Student Publications of the School of Design*, North Carolina State University; the *Proceedings* of the Sociedad Interamericana de Psicologia, Montevideo, 1969, and Sao Paulo, 1973; Bi-National Conference on Geography, Jerusalem, 1969; Second Conference on the Family in the Caribbean, Aruba, N.W.I., 1969, and in several books: *Behavioral Problems in Geography*, edited by Cox and Golledge; *Designing for Human Behavior*, edited by Lang et al.; *Psychology and the Built Environment*, edited by Canter and Lee; and *Image and Environment: Cognitive Mapping and Spatial Behavior*, edited by Downs and myself.

2. G. Hewes, Personal communication to J. M. Blaut, 1971.

3. The choice of the terms "propositional" and "appositional" was not mine, and is perhaps unfortunate. It is patently *not* the intention of this paper to imply that there are people who think exclusively propositionally and others who think exclusively appositionally, that "propositional thinking" is the ability to think "logically" (in propositions), while appositional thinking implies the absence of that ability. Rather, it is proposed that differences in cognitive styles exist, and that one dimension on which such styles may be differentiated (one currently with the greatest neurophysiological support) is that designated "propositional–appositional." "Spatial-aspatial," however, might be a better designator, for current purposes.

4. Gazzaniga (1972) refers to this as the "double-mind view." Others, however, such as MacKay (1966), have questioned the idea of a "double consciousness," the idea that "mind left is poet-like and mind right is the painter in us" (Gazzaniga, 1972, p. 312).

5. See Section 5 for some beginning theoretical and empirical investigations of the social dimensions of environmental knowing (the editors).

6. The (developmentally) earliest directional statement we have recorded was produced by Jed Sadalla, 23-month-old son of the psychologist Edward Sadalla, in late May, 1974. The two were driving out of a parking lot between one half and three quarters of a mile from home. Sadalla was heading for another store, but the child did not know this. As the driver turned left down the street, the child pointed in the opposite direction (which would have been quite correct were they in fact homeward-bound), and said "No, that way— home!" We are assured that young Jed was quite adamant.

7. Tolman was always careful to acknowledge his intellectual indebtedness to both earlier and contemporary theoreticians and researchers, notably Lewin (1936).

8. Personal communication from J. Western, 1973.

10

ENVIRONMENTAL LEARNING AND LARGE-SCALE ENVIRONMENTS[1]

Frank R. Klett and David Alpaugh
School of Architecture and Urban Planning
University of California, Los Angeles

The notion of cognitive representations of the environment, variously called cognitive maps (Tolman, 1948; Kaplan 1973b; Downs and Stea, 1973a; see also Chapters 2 and 9), mental maps (Gould and White, 1968), schema (Griffin, 1948; Piaget, 1951; Lee, 1968), images (Boulding, 1956; Lynch, 1960), imaginary maps (Trowbridge, 1913), or topographic representations (Piaget et al., 1960; Mark, 1972; Hart and Moore, 1973) appears across a wide spectrum of intellectual thought. The way in which such cognitive representations come to be formed and used has been difficult to specify completely, but a few points pertinent to environmental learning do seem clear.

Environmental learning is a process of developing an understanding of an environment through the interaction of an individual with the environment. The ability to understand, navigate, and use an environment depends upon this cognitive representation. This process of learning about the environment (and the options it presents) begins early in the life of the child, and is a process whereby each new representation is a closer approximation to the "real" environment.

As Stea points out in Chapter 9, many different analogies are used to describe this cognitive representation. The analogy used tends to depend upon the disciplinary orientation of the researcher and the aspect of the environment being studied. Because here we are primarily interested in spatial aspects of the environment, we shall refer to only one aspect of cognitive representations—*cognitive* (or mental) *maps* (see Downs and Stea, 1973a, Chapter 1).

Findings by Blaut and Stea (1971) show that children are able to engage in the fundamental processes of map making and map reading, such as rotation from horizontal to vertical views, reduction in scale, and abstraction to semi-iconic signs long before they are exposed to traditional maps. The fundamental processes of map making and map drawing are thought to be closely related to the processes of making cognitive maps. That children can use maps to solve simulated navigation problems (Hart, 1971) is an indication of environmental learning. Although much of the spatial information incorporated into cognitive maps appears to come from moving through the environment, Stea and Blaut (1973a) have theorized that another source may be through the manipulation and observation of surrogates, such as toys.

One major problem in trying to understand the

process of cognitive mapping, especially in the early years of childhood, is that of communication. Young preliterate children have only limited vocabularies and only limited graphic skills with which to communicate their environmental images (Mark, 1972). At more advanced ages this is not as difficult a problem, as there have been successes with interpreting sketch maps. Ladd (1970), for example, used a map-drawing exercise to examine the environmental images and awareness of neighborhood of black, teen-aged boys in a Boston ghetto. Mark (1972) and Moore (1973b, 1975a) have also had success using sketch maps with teen-agers.[2] In spite of the caveats against testing very young children through graphic communication, we decided to risk the problems involved with their graphic abilities in order to investigate their conceptions of their environment.

A few years ago, Blaut and Stea (Blaut, 1969; Blaut, McCleary, and Blaut, 1970; Stea and Taphanel, 1975) proposed two hypotheses about the development of cognitive mapping abilities in young children. They suggested a set of three cognitive transformations that one makes in "building" a cognitive representation of the environment—*scale, perspective,* and *abstraction*—and that these transformations are related to the fundamental processes of mapping. Blaut et al. (1970) hypothesized (1) that the abilities required to make each transformation are all associated so that they are approximately the same at any given point in a child's developmental sequence, but (2) in the early years one would expect the developmentally "primitive" transformations of scale and perspective to develop earlier than the "evolved" transformation of abstraction.

Study I: The San Fernando Valley

In order to test the hypotheses, a relatively simple technique was employed. Three elementary school classes (first, third, and fourth grades) in a predominately upper-middle-class parochial school located in Encino in the San Fernando Valley were selected for study. The first and third grades each had 27 students and the fourth grade had 33; the approximate average ages were 6.5, 9.4, and 10.4 years.

These children were instructed by their teachers simply to "draw the San Fernando Valley." The assignsignment was given in class with a minimum of additional instruction so that each child had to reach his own conclusion as to what response was appropriate. The assignment was carried out during one class session of approximately 40 minues; the drawings were executed on standard 8½- by 11- inch paper.

The resulting drawings were evaluated by a jury on each of three rating scales based on the cognitive transformations discussed above. Points on the rating scale were ordered in terms of increasing development. For example, the perspective rating was concerned with the cognitive vantage point a child takes as he draws his picture; such a vantage point can be inferred by the appearance of elements and their relative positions within the maps (drawings). The *perspective* rating measured, in five parts, what we considered might be the developmental sequence of a child's cognitive viewpoint: it begins with a "primitive" *ground-level* view, proceeds to a *mixed* mode, then to a "more developed" *downward oblique* view, then *partially overhead,* and ends with the more highly "evolved" map-like *mainly overhead* view.

The other two ratings were also divided into five parts. The *scale* rating begins with a "primitive" *subfocal* world view, proceeds to *focal,* then to a "more developed" *local* scale, then valliudinal, and ends with the more highly "evolved" *macro* scale. All these terms are suggestive of the size and scope of the environment represented: the term "valliudinal" was coined to describe a drawing that displayed important concepts of the general shape of the valley as a whole. The *abstraction* rating begins with a "primitive" *realistic* style, proceeds to a "more developed" *schematic* style, and ends with a more highly "evolved" *symbolic* style. Intermediate to "realistic" and "schematic" is a rating having elements of both which was labeled A. Intermediate to "schematic" and "symbolic" is a mixed rating labeled B. The three evaluative rating scales are shown in Table 1.

Each jurist independently reviewed each drawing (the only understanding each jurist had of the evaluative rating was through his own interpretation of Table 1) and recorded an evaluation for each of the three transformations. If there was a majority opinion as to the rating, a drawing was assigned that rating.

TABLE 1

Five-Point Rating Scales of Developmental Transformations of Scale, Perspective, and Abstraction

I. Scale
   i. Subfocal: own immediate personal space (point-like)
   ii. Focal: what an individual could see about him
   iii. Local: area experienced over time (not all elements could be seen at once)
   iv. Valliudinal: displays concept of valley as whole (surrounded by mountains, valley lower than surroundings, shape)
   v. Macro: valley represented as part of some larger system

II. Perspective
   i. Ground level: view as seen from ground (line of sight parallel to ground)
   ii. Mixed: some elements viewed as from ground, some viewed as from a point above ground
   iii. Downward oblique: view is consistently from a point above the ground (line of sight at acute angle with ground)
   iv. Partially overhead: some elements viewed from overhead and some viewed in downward oblique mode
   v. Mainly overhead: almost all elements viewed from overhead (line of sight perpendicular to ground plane)

III. Abstraction
   i. Realistic: attention paid to detail (much effort made to make things look like they are); for example, windows in buildings are put in regular rows
   ii. A: intermediate class between realism and abstraction (combination of both)
   iii. Schematic: still some attention to detail but things are more represented; for example, buildings still look like buildings but windows are randomly distributed
   iv. B: intermediate between schematic and symbolic
   v. Symbolic: very little attention to detail, things are highly represented; for example, buildings are just squares with no windows

This procedure was similar to the one used in Ladd's (1970) analysis of drawings of ghetto teen-agers. Approximately 69 to 85 percent of the drawings (depending on the group being evaluated and the transformation being considered) were successfully rated at this stage. The percentage of agreement varied by class group but averaged approximately 78 percent.

In cases where no initial majority opinion emerged, the drawings were discussed by the group until a majority opinion was achieved. Only in about 6 percent of the cases was no majority opinion reached. These drawings were assigned the model rating of the jury. Some possible limitations might be found in this evaluation procedure, but the number of conflicts was small; those occurring rarely had a very wide spread on a particular rating.

After the evaluation process, each drawing had a triad of numbers from 1 to 5 representing the drawing's relative developmental position on each of the rating scales.

Using these scores, it was possible to test Blaut and Stea's two hypotheses. The first hypothesis—that the ability to make each of the transformations is about the same at any given point in a child's developmental sequence—can be restated more mathematically: there should be a high degree of correlation among the various scores so that, for any particular individual, a high score on one rating should be positively related to high scores on the remaining ratings.

The second hypothesis—that in the early years one would expect the developmentally "primitive" transformation to develop earlier than the "evolved" transformations—can be restated: for the first grade group more of the students will be rated higher on the scale and perspective ratings than on the abstraction rating; for later grades all the ratings will be more closely associated.

Results. Kendell's coefficient of concordance is the appropriate nonparametric[3] statistic for testing simultaneous association among observations on three ordinally ranked ratings. It yields a measure of the degree of association among several sets of rankings. A high degree of association among the cognitive transformations would be reflected in a high value for the calculated coefficient W.

As shown in Table 2, a high degree of association was indeed the case for all grade levels; the null hypothesis of no association could be rejected above the $\alpha = .01$ level; that is, it is highly unlikely (1 in 100) that the observed degree of association would occur if the transformations were not associated.

These results also seemed to show some support for the second hypothesis because the degree of association is least in the first grade, implying differential development of the transformations.

However, upon examining the data in more detail, a

TABLE 2
Kendell Coefficient of Concordance for the Three
Transformations of Abstraction, Perspective, and Scale,
Initial Study

Grade	N	W	X^2	p Level
1	27	.55	43.0	$p < .002$
3	27	.72	56.2	$p < .001$
4	33	.75	71.8	$p < .001$

surprising result emerges. Cumulative frequency distributions for each grade and for each cognitive transformation are shown in Figures 1, 2, and 3. Frequency is defined as the percentage of students *at or above* the given transformation level.

For the third and fourth grades, these figures show graphically the high degree of concordance among the transformations as found above. However, for the first grade, while there is a difference for the various trans-

formations, it is exactly opposite to that which one would expect. There is a greater portion of the class in the upper categories for abstraction than for the supposedly developmentally "primitive" transformations of scale and perspective. The graphs also suggest a rather surprising result: there appears to be a greater portion of third graders than fourth graders in the upper categories of all the transformations, a result that seems to contradict most classical theory, which postulates a monotonic increase in cognitive skills with increased age (at least in the earlier stages of the life cycle). An initial statistical test tended to support this observation in that the null hypothesis of no difference could be rejected above the $\alpha \leqslant .05$ level for both transformations of abstraction and perspective. However, for the transformation of scale, the hypothesis of no difference in performance could not be rejected. One possible explanation is that this transformation develops and *stabilizes* relatively early.

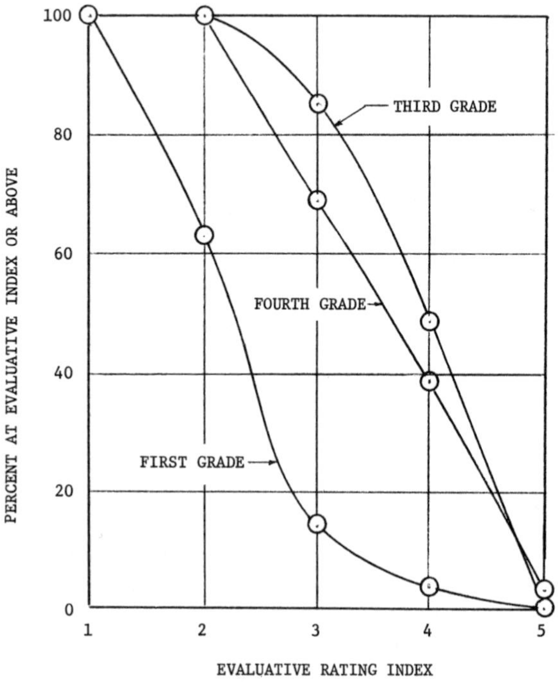

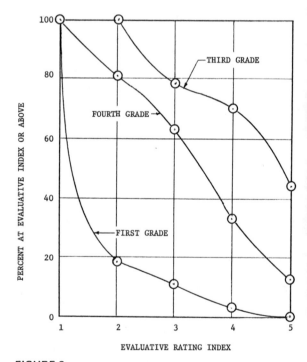

FIGURE 1
Cumulative percentage of the class at or above a given level for the transformation of scale.

FIGURE 2
Cumulative percentage of the class at or above a given level for the transformation of perspective.

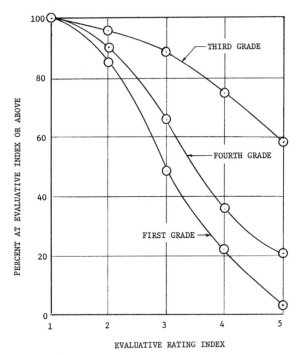

FIGURE 3
Cumulative percentage of the class at or above a given level for the transformation of abstraction.

In a mobile society (especially upper-middle-class Californians) with an emphasis on travel, even a young child is exposed to a wide range of places. This could be a unique opportunity for enhancing a sense of scale.

Study II: San Fernando Follow-up

The results of our first visit to the classroom, in particular, the results showing the relative superiority of the third graders over the fourth graders, were so contrary to expectation that we were anxious to study these children further. There were so many other factors that could have potentially operated on the differences between the third and fourth grade groups, such as intrinsic differences in intelligence or graphic expression, that major advantages were seen in returning to study precisely the same children about one year later.

Accordingly, we used basically the same procedure

we had used on the first iteration. Again a third and fourth grade class were asked by their teacher to draw the San Fernando Valley. This time there was the added advantage of having a set of matched pairs, as some of the children in the fourth grade group in this second study had been part of the sample in the third grade group in the initial study. We felt that by using a matched sample comparison, we could eliminate some of the effects of extraneous intervening variables. The working hypotheses this time, however, were revised to reflect the direction of the findings in the first study. First, we wanted to see if we could replicate our empirical validation of the notion (expressed by Blaut and described above) that the three transformations of scale, perspective, and abstraction are associated at each level of their development. Second, we wished to test the decline in map-drawing abilities, as measured by the three transformation scales, between the third and fourth grade groups.

Results. With the new set of drawings we repeated the jury evaluation process outlined above. While our primary concern was a more meaningful test of the possibility of a regression between the third and fourth grades, the new drawings also provided an opportunity to further substantiate the hypothesis about concordance in the transformations. The results are shown in Table 3. Again, in both the third and fourth grade classes, the null hypothesis of no association could be rejected at or above the $\alpha = .01$ level, thus replicating the results of the first study.

The Wilcoxon Matched Pairs Signed Rank test allows one to assess the significance of difference in performance, on a before/after basis, when the performance measurement is only an ordinal scale. By using individual scores on each of the transformation ratings for both "tests" (third graders = before; fourth graders = after), we were able to test the

TABLE 3
Kendell Coefficient of Concordance for the Three Transformations of Abstraction, Perspective, and Scale, Follow-up Study

Grade	N	W	x^2	p Level
1	—	—	—	—
3	28	.61	49.4	< .01
4	27	.69	53.7	< .01

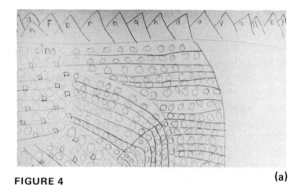

FIGURE 4 (a)

(a) Drawing of San Fernando Valley by Sue, third grade.
(b) Drawing of San Fernando Valley by Sue, fourth grade.

(b)

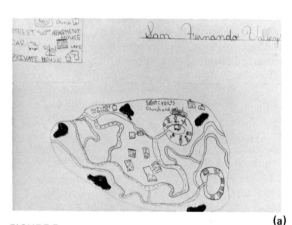

FIGURE 5 (a)

(a) Drawing of San Fernando Valley by Ann, third grade.
(b) Drawing of San Fernando Valley by Ann, fourth grade.

(b)

hypothesis of a decline in performance from the third to the fourth grade. The Wilcoxon statistic was calculated for each transformation and the results are presented in Table 4.[4]

The null hypothesis of no difference could be rejected for both abstraction and perspective, but not for scale, at or above the $\alpha = .05$ level. For at least these first two transformations, then, there is evidence for believing that there is a decline in these cognitive transformations. Because of the small sample size, we feel reluctant to make any decision about the results.

TABLE 4
Wilcoxon Matched Paris Signed Rank Test for Three Transformations of Abstraction, Perspective, and Scale

n	k[a]	Transformation	T	p (one tail)
16	8	Abstraction	5.0	< .01
16	9	Perspective	22.0	< .05
16	4	Scale	5.5	> .30 (N.S.)

[a]Number of cases out of the sample of 16 where differences were observed.

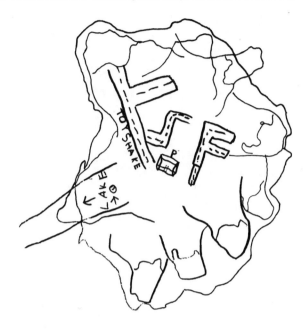

FIGURE 6
(a) Drawing of San Fernando Valley by Bob, third grade.
(b) Drawing of San Fernando Valley by Bob, fourth grade.

General Discussion

The theoretical significance of these findings is difficult to assess at this point. In a study of map-*reading* abilities of some children in Puerto Rico, Stea and Blaut (1973b) found tentative indications of a similar decline between the equivalents of third and fourth grade children. Although no clear conclusions could be drawn from their results (the findings lacked statistical significance), the suggestion exists that the observed "regression" in Encino is not an isolated phenomenon but could apply elsewhere and maybe even cross-culturally.

FIGURE 7
Drawing by first grade student (scale: focal; perspective: ground level; abstraction: A).

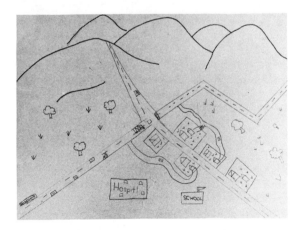

FIGURE 8
Drawing by fourth grade student (scale: local; perspective: partially overhead; abstraction: schematic).

FIGURE 9
Drawing by third grade student (scale: valliudinal; perspective: mainly overhead; abstraction: symbolic).

FIGURE 10
Drawing by fourth grade student (scale: local; perspective: ground level; abstraction: A).

There are two avenues along which we might proceed in an attempt to explain these rather surprising findings: in terms of existent theory and, alternatively, in terms of rival hypotheses based on methodological considerations and circumstances affecting the studies.

An explanation in terms of classical cognitive-developmental theory is convoluted and problematic. Both Werner (1948) and Piaget and Inhelder (1956) speak of the ontogenetic stages in development. In both theories (see Hart and Moore's 1973 review), the first stages are *perceptual* and *action-oriented*; later stages are *conceptual* and *symbolically oriented* and are characteristic of adolescent and adult behavior. In the Encino project, the measures used to evaluate the drawings, and thus the children's cognitive mapping development, progressed from essentially egocentric, perceptual modes to more abstract. conceptual modes (i.e., "perspective" ranged from horizontal to overhead, "scale" from focal to macro, and "abstraction" from realistic to symbolic). Our hypothesis, in accordance with both Werner and Piaget, was that as a child got older his drawings would tend to be evaluated toward the upper end of each scale. That our findings did not *strictly* follow such a monotonically increasing developmental function, but rather were an inverted U curve, with the third graders more advanced on all three measures than either the first or fourth graders, might be accounted for on either of four grounds; the first two pertain to the educational system, the third to media skills, and the fourth to the nature of the development of symbolic functions in the child.

First, the schools could be discouraging the child's ability to represent his environment by providing less and less emphasis on spatial visualization as he or she gets older, revealing an attitude that such activities are "child's play" and not the serious stuff of education. Or, more subtly, the task in visual representation presented to the child in school could generally involve "small" things, weighted more toward description of perceptual space than toward understanding conceptual space. If the latter is true, fourth grade children (approximately 9 years old, about the age when Piaget has found that symbolic thought abilities reach equilibrium) might be at a disadvantage relative to the third grade children in this cognitive-mapping exercise. Although either line of explanation might account for the regression found in the present study between the third and fourth grades, both fail to account for the progression from the first to third grades.

A third possible explanation lies in the child's media skills. In their review of research on spatial cognition, Hart and Moore (1973) warned against the use of children's drawings as a research tool for measuring environmental cognition; they reasoned that drawing abilities tend to lag behind image representation, particularly when dealing with complex wholes. Whether this is a phenomenon of development or the result of a deficiency in schooling is an open question. However, this argument cannot apply to the suggestion of a decline in map-*reading* abilities observed by Stea and Blaut (1973b) in Puerto Rico and would indicate that more is operating here than a question of media skills.

The fourth line of possible explanation derives from Rusch's (1970) theorizing on cognitive development. Rusch has concerned himself directly with the difference between perceptual and conceptual thinking; he defines *perception* as external awareness and *conception* as internal awareness comprised of memory and reflection components. *Reflection*, he says, is mental representation, a "stepping back" from events or perceptual stimuli, a process similar to Werner's contemplative stage of development. Rusch ascribes four levels of meaning to experience and reflection, which correspond to Piaget's and Werner's stages of ontogenetic development. The first two, emotional and kinesthetic experience, deal most directly with experience and sensory information in something close to a direct stimulus–response relationship. As one progresses up the developmental scale, the succeeding levels of imaginal and formal thought become more interpretive mechanisms of sensory experience than modes of dealing directly with experience, and thus effect a detachment of awareness from perceptual reality. Rusch calls this detachment "cognitive distance"; as one attains the ability to think at formal levels of meaning one is as likely to recall experience from memory as to directly interpret sensory data. In this sense there is some distortion of reality with age or level of development, as experience is recollected from other levels of meaning and as this accretion of information is mixed in memory. In formal thought, then, any one conception of experience is not necessarily a response to direct sensory information regarding it. The manipulation and conception of the experience are modeled from preformed symbolic awareness of similar past events, and experience may well be molded to fit the preconception rather than the other way around.

Werner (1948) also considers behavior, perception and cognition to operate on many levels simulta-

neously. Cognitive development, he argues, proceeds from a stage in which behavior and perception are largely egocentric to a stage of more highly differentiated contemplative states (see Chapter 12). Space is understood by the young child primarily as a personal "space-of-action" in which places are oriented and receive their dimensions through the action of the child. At about the age of 8 or 9 there is a move away from egocentrism. Werner quotes as evidence Piaget's finding that at about 8 or 9 the child acquires the ability to distinguish the left and right sides of other persons and thus begins to see things from other than his own vantage point. If the shift at 8 or 9 is a shift from dynamic, concrete, and personal perception of space relationship to one that is more static, abstract, and impersonal, or if, as Werner states, "a child's conceptions are based on egocentrism and concrete modes of experience and they tend to develop steadily toward universal schema," then the increasing importance of symbolic relationships becomes apparent.

In the light of these considerations, it seems reasonable to state that, with regard to the Encino drawings, children with more of an "action" (enactive, sensorimotor, kinesthetic, to loosely generalize these terms) orientation might reproduce functional relationships, but that children with an emerging interest in other less concrete aspects might concentrate more on the symbolic meaning of elements in the environment. This does not necessarily mean that their drawings would be generalized in the sense that we originally anticipated (i.e., demonstrate rotational or metric relationships in the expected style of an adult's formal thinking). It could be that the older child's "symbols" are recollections of past physical experience and that the manifestations of these symbol representations would be difficult to differentiate from the younger child's direct representations of experience. In other words, the physical drawings of each child could be quite similar, but the actual meanings of similar configurations on paper could be completely different in the minds of children in different stages of development.

On the other hand, and perhaps more to the point, many other factors intervened between the two test groups, and these methodological considerations might well account for our findings. Intrinsic group differences in the first study, for which no tests were

11

AN EPIGENETIC APPROACH TO ENVIRONMENTAL LEARNING THEORY: A COMMENTARY[1]

Harold D. Fishbein
Department of Psychology
University of Cincinnati

What I am going to try to do in this commentary is to provide an evolutionary and developmental approach to understanding how children acquire cognitive maps (internal cognitive representations) of the environment. Stea, in Chapter 9, defines cognitive mapping as "a process composed of a series of psychological transformations by which an individual acquires, codes, stores, recalls, and decodes information about the relative locations and attributes of phenomena in his (or her) everyday spatial environment." Both he and Frank Klett and David Alpaugh in Chapter 10, refer to three basic psychological transformations which individuals must use both to build up their own cognitive maps and to interpret, construct, and use external representations of the environment (e.g., "real" maps, drawings, and photographs). These processes are reducing the scale of one's perceptions, rotating the perspective from the horizontal to the vertical, and abstracting one's perceptions to semiiconic signs or to symbols.

Stea and Klett and Alpaugh part company at this juncture. Based upon his own and other's research on children's interpretation of aerial photographs, Stea argues that the development of the ability to perform these psychological transformations is largely complete prior to the time children enter school. Klett and Alpaugh, on the other hand, in their research dealing with children's ability to construct a drawing of the San Fernando Valley, find that, with the exception of abstracting one's perceptions, the other two psychological abilities are far from completely developed by age 10. In discussing their results, Klett and Alpaugh indicate that children's "drawing abilities" may lag behind "image representation" and, hence, imply that the ability of these children to perform the three psychological transformations may have been further developed than was indicated by their drawings.

Looking back at Stea's definition of cognitive mapping, and at the experiments performed by Klett and Alpaugh, one is struck by the absence of any discussion bearing on what seems to be central to the definition—that cognitive mapping in great part deals with information about the *relative locations* of objects in the spatial environment. The three psychological transformations are to a large extent transformations of this information; thus, one natural starting point in environmental learning theory is the study of the nature of the ability of children of different ages to acquire and code this information.

Stea takes an evolutionary and developmental approach to understanding environmental learning and cognition. Within this framework, he states, "Most cognitive mapping abilities appear to be *acquired*, not part of the genetic endowment of the human animal; the person must *learn* to represent environments at the geographical scale" (italics his). As I shall shortly discuss, it is precisely because cognitive mapping abilities *are* part of the genetic endowment of humans that they are acquired. Klett and Alpaugh discuss the relation between perception and conception, "perception" being a direct dealing with sensory information and "conception" being a "stepping back" from perception. My own views are very similar to both of these.

Waddington (1960, 1968) refers to the relationships among the genotype, phenotype, and environment as an *epigenetic system*. The genotype sets the potentials for phenotypic development, and the particular way the phenotype develops, *including how and what the individual learns*, is a function of an individual's genotype and the particular sequence of environments in which the development occurs. Thus, any genotype would lead to different phenotypes in different environments. In some environments, the individual might not reach the stage of being born; in others, he might survive childhood, but no more; and in still others he might reach a ripe old age and produce many children. Hence, the epigenetic system should be viewed as an adaptive system that attempts to maintain a balance or equilibrium among the genetic instructions, phenotypic development, and environment stresses.

Evolutionary processes operate on the epigenetic systems of members of a population. Rensch (1959) has referred to this as an "experiment" in design, and Lorenz (1969), as a "trial-and-success" experiment. Basically, what they mean is that each individual epigenetic system is a trial run or test of a particular design. The design is coded in the genotype, and as the phenotype carries out the genetic code (the instructions for development) in a given sequence of environments an experiment is run. If the experiment

is successful, the epigenetic system is viable; the individual not only survives, but has high Darwinian fitness, thus transmitting his genes (his design) to the next generation. If the experiment is unsuccessful, the individual has low Darwinian fitness. If the offspring of the parents with successful designs develop in a sequence of environments similar to that which their parents experienced, it is highly probable that their designs will also be successful. What happens if the offspring find themselves in a sequence of environments different from that for which they were designed? In all likelihood their Darwinian fitness will be low. If the sequence of environments of all offspring is much different from that experienced by their parents, the species as a whole may become extinct. The evolutionary record, in fact, indicates that there are far more extinct than living species (Newell, 1963).

A number of theorists have argued (Lorenz, 1969; Piaget, 1971; Waddington, 1960) that life processes in general, and evolutionary processes in particular, can be construed as being fundamentally involved with the acquisition of information or knowledge about the environment. In general, the greater the *knowledge* an individual member of any species has of the environment, the greater are the chances that the individual will survive and reproduce in that environment. For an epigenetic system to be viable, the genetic code must contain information (knowledge) of the environments in which the individual is to develop. That is, the set of instructions contained in the genotype is designed for interactions in a particular sequence of environments—the environments to which the parents were adapted. This is why Darwinian fitness decreases when the environments of the offspring are different from those of the parents; the knowledge contained in the genotype becomes incorrect or, at least, inadequate.

In higher animals, the vertebrates, evolutionary processes have produced two basic sets of mechanisms for the acquisition and transmission of knowledge. The first is the hereditary mechanisms obtained in the genotype. The second set of mechanisms is ultimately dependent on the first, but to some extent develops a life of its own. These are the learning mechanisms. It is the genotype which determines the development of the particular structures and functions that enable learning to occur; species vary considerably in the extent to which they are equipped with these mechanisms. Species also vary in the extent to which the learning of one individual can be transmitted to others in the following generations. This phenomenon, transgenerational or cultural learning, has been one of the key features in human evolution and is no doubt linked with the tremendous memory capacities of people.

From a reading of the works of Waddington, Lorenz, and Piaget, it becomes clear that the primary short-range function of the acquisition of knowledge, whether in the genotype or through phenotypic acquisiton, is to enable the organism to act effectively in the environment. For Piaget, all phenotypically acquired knowledge starts with action and is always translatable into action. The long-range function of the acquisition of knowledge is the survival of the species, which also involves effective action in the environment.

This discussion of evolution as a knowledge process has been relatively abstract. A concrete example given by Lorenz (1969) may bring things into sharper focus. This deals with the phobic response of protozoa to noxious stimulation. When these animals are moving in either a neutral or continuously "improving" environment, they keep moving in the same direction. However, when they enter a "deteriorating" environment or encounter a noxious stimulus, the animals stop, move backward a certain distance, and then move forward again after they have performed a turning response. The usual outcome of the turn is to alter the subsequent direction of movement away from the noxious stimulation. However, sometimes the animals turn 360° and proceed to move again into the noxious stimulation, setting the whole pattern in motion again. This whole knowledge process is completely encoded in the genotype—which stimulation is noxious, which is neutral or positive, and the phobic response to noxious stimulation.

As indicated, evolutionary processes act on the epigenetic system, which is essentially a system of development. Thus, any changes produced in the average genotype of a species will of necessity change the ways in which members of the species develop.

Importantly, the epigenetic system is constructed in such a way that only certain types of changes are possible; that is, only certain types of genetic changes have the potential for being adaptive in any environment. You can't directly change a fish into an elephant; but, in fact, elephants do come from fish, with an extremely large number of intervening evolutionary steps. At each step, however, the epigenetic system has to be adaptive in order for the step to be taken.

The primary reason for the conservatism seen in evolution and development must be found, then, in the nature of the epigenetic system itself. The genotype of this system was described as containing a set of instructions for the potential interactions of the phenotype with the environment. This implies that the genotype in some sense contains an image, template, or target of what the phenotype should be like at each point in development. There is some plasticity in the exact way the phenotype will attain the target, but the extent of this plasticity is severely limited. If the target is missed by too much, the individual will either not survive or not reproduce. In other words, as in jazz improvization, some variations work, and others don't. The ones that work in jazz must operate within the constraints set by the rhythm, melody, harmonic structure, and tempo of the tune. The variations in epigenesis that "work" must operate within the constraints of the genotype as a whole, the particular state of development of the individual, and the particular state of the environment when a given set of genetic instructions is set in motion.

There is another aspect of plasticity in the epigenetic system, which Waddington (1960, 1962) has called "canalization." Canalization involves a set of genetic processes which ensures that development will proceed in normal ways, that the phenotypic targets will be attained despite the presence of minor abnormal genetic or environmental conditions. Canalization processes operate at each point in development to correct minor deflections from the sought-for phenotypic targets. Presumably, canalization processes ensure that important phenotypic constancies will occur in all members of a species (e.g., in humans, the presence of two eyes, one nose, two hands, language, spatial understanding, bipedal locomotion). Canalization is a "collusion" of genes to keep the developing organism in balance. Not all characteristics of an individual are canalized, and those which are are not equally canalized. Concerning this last point, Fraser has shown, for example, (summarized in Waddington, 1962) that, when a major gene controlling hair follicle growth in mice is replaced by a mutant gene, the primary facial whiskers are heavily canalized (i.e., are strongly resistant to change), the secondary facial whiskers are moderately canalized, and the hair coat is either weakly canalized or not canalized at all.

It is assumed that canalization processes operate to bring about behavioral constancies throughout the entire lifetime of individuals, and not just the anatomical constancies found during the prenatal stages of development (no canalization research has ever been carried out with humans or with behavior). In other words, it is assumed that not only reflex behavior, but how we learn and what we learn, is canalized. This assumption has also previously been derived by Lorenz (1969), Piaget (1971), and Waddington (1960).

This last point brings us to a definition of learning. In the traditional view of learning, such as Stea's in Chapter 9, emphasis is placed on response modification in relation to some environmental stimulation. Stea also emphasizes motivational and reinforcement components, whereas others do not. Most writers, in addition, wish to rule out maturational factors, native response tendencies, and fatigue (e.g., Hilgard and Bower, 1966). In the present epigenetic approach, *learning* is defined as a set of functions or processes that progressively organizes the individual's future sensory experiences or motor activities or both. These functions are set into motion when the individual interacts with his environment; their long-range effect is to enable the individual to better coordinate his behavior with the environment. Learning is not just reactive to experience, but rather the individual imposes an organization on his experience, the nature of this imposition being a function of his previous learning history and level of maturation. Piaget (1970) refers to this imposition on experience as "assimilation" and the consequent sensory or motor

reorganization produced by the learning functions as "accommodation."[2]

Consider a concrete example. A child has "learned" that all the buildings in his neighborhood are permanent. Every time that he walks a familiar route, even if weeks have elapsed since the last time he took this route, he notes that all the buildings are just where they were the last time. One day he discovers that one of the buildings is gone, producing a reorganization or accommodation of his building-permanence conception. This is typically a disturbing occurrence for a young child, and he wonders whether his own home will be removed. This reorganization has the effect of modifying the child's behavior with respect to all "permanent" objects in his environment; buildings, for example, are generally permanent, and can generally be depended upon as landmarks for finding one's way.[3]

Unlike most traditional definitions of learning, our definition does not rule out native response tendencies and maturational factors. The view is taken that human evolution has produced a species with great plasticity but also a species in which certain kinds of learning will almost inevitably occur (e.g., language, motor skills, spatial understanding). This channeling or these "native response tendencies" have been crucial to our success as a species. In regard to the question of maturational factors, in the child, at least, learning and maturation are intimately connected and cannot be separated. A child does not mature in the absence of encounters with the environment, and successive encounters with the environment occur at different maturational levels. What must be understood is how learning and maturation are keyed to and interact with one another.

Our discussion now brings us to *environmental learning* or the *development of spatial understanding*. As was indicated before, the most fundamental aspect of spatial understanding is that of the relationships between objects in the environment. I believe that the acquisition of this ability is canalized and proceeds through two and perhaps three partially overlapping stages. In the first, the child develops the ability to accurately perceive his immediate environment and to form an internal representation of his perceptions. In the second, he develops the ability to form accurate conceptions of his immediate environment. In the third (if this is indeed a distinct stage), the child develops the ability to accurately conceive of distant environments.

The basic differences between perception and conception lie in the nature of the imagery or internal representations produced (both ultimately are based on *action* and can be translated into action). During the act of *perception*, one builds up an image of objects that is tied to sensory stimulation. Piaget and Inhelder (1969) refer to this image as a "reproductive" or "copy" image. "Anticipatory" images are linked to the child's *conceptions* of the environment, and allow the child to anticipate or predict the appearance of objects after they have been transformed in some way, as well as to reconstruct their appearance when they are out of the field of view. As children mature, their reproductive images become more complete and anticipatory imagery emerges; that is, their perceptual schemes become increasingly differentiated and they develop new conceptual schemes. Although in theory the development of copy images and anticipatory images can be separated, in practice, it is frequently not possible to separate them owing to the fact that the assessment of a child's conception usually involves a perceptual task.

Is there evidence to support the view that the acquisition of spatial understanding is canalized and, moreover, that perceptual understanding of object relationships precedes conceptual understanding? As I indicated before, no canalization research has ever been performed on behavior; therefore, evidence must be indirect and highly inferential. Following Piaget, the assumption is made that observed developmental regularities in behavior provide indirect evidence for canalization. Regarding the second part of our question, I shall briefly summarize the results of one study with which I am most familiar (Nigl and Fishbein, 1973, 1974).

Two experiments modeled after the coordination of perspectives task of Piaget and Inhelder (1956) were performed. In these experiments, a child is seated at a table facing an array of from three to seven three-dimensional geometrical shapes. In the first experiment, the objects were all placed on the same rectangular surface; in the second experiment, a two-tiered platform was constructed and at least one object was placed on each surface. In both experiments four photographs were used. They were constructed in such a way as to uncover the confusions that children may have about left–right, back–front, and up–down projective relationships. In experiment I, one photograph accurately depicted what the experimenter saw, one depicted a reversal of the left and right halves of the object array, one depicted a reversal of the back and front halves of the array, and one reversed both left and right and back and front, which is equivalent to a 180° rotation of the array. The middle two are impossible views of the array, in that no rotation will produce them. In Experiment II, the 180° photograph was replaced by an up-down reversal (i.e., the objects which were on the top tier were shown on the bottom and vice versa). To perform correctly, then, a child had to be able to perceive and conceive of left–right relationships, back–front relationships, and up–down relationships. For example, if a child chose a left–right photograph as often as the correct one, it is assumed that he could not utilize that projective relationship.

On each trial the experimenter either sat next to the child (called the front position), to the child's left, across from the child, or to the child's right, and asked the child to point to the picture that looked like what he (the experimenter) could see from where he was sitting. When the experimenter is seated at the front position, the child's task is essentially a perceptual one; when the experimenter is seated at nonfrontal positions, the child's task is essentially a conceptual one. In the first experiment the subjects were groups of children having average ages of 4, 6½, 8½, and 10½; in the second experiment their average ages were 6, 8, 10, and 12.

The major results were as follows. In experiment I, for the front view, the 4-year-olds performed at about chance level, the 6½-year-olds were correct about 65 percent of the time, the 8½-year-olds were about 85 percent correct, and the 10½-year-olds about 95 percent correct. At the nonfrontal views, the 4-year-olds performed at chance, the 6½- and 8½-

year-olds were correct about 35 percent of the time, and the 10½-year-olds, about 60 percent of the time. Children at all age groups for frontal and nonfrontal positions made left–right confusions most frequently, followed by back–front, and then 180° confusions. In experiment II, for the front view, all age groups performed above a chance level of response, ranging from 50 percent correct for the 6-year-olds to about 90 percent correct for the 12-year-olds. On the nonfrontal views, the 6-year-olds were correct about 30 percent of the time (25 percent is chance responding), the 8- and 10-year-olds were correct about 35 percent of the time, and the 12-year-olds about 55 percent of the time. As in experiment I, left–confusions were most frequent, followed by back–front, and then top–down confusions, which were rare.

What can we conclude from these results? First, regarding canalization, a nearly identical pattern of results was obtained in both experiments I and II, despite the fact that the children in experiment II showed approximately a 1½-year lag behind those of experiment I. Canalization does not require an identical *rate* of behavioral or anatomical development, but, rather, an identical *sequence*. Hence, the results are highly consistent with a canalization interpretation. Second, the results of both experiments strongly support the views that the onset of the state of perceptual understanding of spatial relations between objects precedes that of conceptual understanding, that the two stages overlap, and that perceptual understanding is completely developed prior to conceptual understanding: Due to the existence of a conceptual performance jump at about the time when perceptual understanding is nearing completion, it appears that conceptual understanding is built on perceptual understanding.

What can we say about the "large-scale environment" concerns of Stea and Klett and Alpaugh? Basically, that analyses similar to the above should be carried out in large-scale environments with a variety of children of different ages. This should tell us something about the possible existence of a third stage in the development of spatial understanding and, perhaps more importantly, tell us whether our laboratory analogies have much generality into the "real world." I think they do.

NOTES

1. These comments have been adapted in part from my book, *Evolution, Development, and Children's Learning*, with the permission of Goodyear Publishing Company.
2. In his discussion about the relationship between learning and development, Piaget (1970) makes the following points: (1) learning is subordinate to the child's stage of development; (2) learning involves *invention*, as opposed to being a *copy* of the environment; (3) learning results from *interactions* between the individual and the environment, which are "richer" than what the environment can provide by itself; and (4) learning primarily depends on the fundamental developmental mechanisms of assimilation and accommodation.
3. Probably the least researched area of environmental learning is the "whenness" aspect of the location of objects. Virtually all researchers have studied static arrays, which captures only a portion of what we learn about the environment. See, however, the theoretical considerations along this line in Chapter 16.

DEVELOPMENTAL THEORY

12

THEORY AND RESEARCH ON THE DEVELOPMENT OF ENVIRONMENTAL KNOWING

Gary T. Moore

Department of Psychology[1]
 Clark University

This paper has three major aims: first, to outline the basic postulates of a cognitive-developmental approach to understanding one aspect of person–environment relations; second, to discuss the nature of structures, operations, and transformations in coming to know the everyday large-scale environment; and, third, to review some recent literature, criticism, and neglected lines of investigation bearing on this approach.

There are two reasons for studying development. The study of changes in experience and behavior over the life span is of course a topic of fascination in itself. But as organisms and systems are always undergoing change, we may say that the only thing which is constant is change itself. The study of change and development thus also becomes a basic cornerstone in the understanding of mature forms of experience and behavior.

The theoretical approach presented in this chapter derives mainly from the cognitive-developmental theories of Piaget, Werner, and their colleagues, although the general orientation and some specific notions also derive from other related views on knowledge in contemporary philosophy, psychology, and neurology. It is difficult to pin a simple label on this approach

there are several assumptions about human nature that distinguish it sharply from the dominant contemporary American psychology and, although much less sharply, from some of the other positions on environmental cognition advanced in this volume. I will try to state the position as clearly as possible in terms of six postulates: (1) construction, (2) interaction, (3) action and transaction, (4) mediation, (5) structure, and (6) genesis and transformation.

While treading through this rather rarified realm of abstract concepts and theoretical postulates, we must —both writer and reader—try to keep in touch with the mystery of development. It is entirely remarkable that the infant who has no notion of objects as continuing to exist when out of sight nor any notion of basic spatial concepts, like the difference between parallel and perpendicular lines, somehow, miraculously, comes to have well-articulated knowledge not only of these fundamental spatial concepts but also of everyday large-scale environments like neighborhoods and cities and their complex layouts, functions, and meanings. How does this happen? How does the child, initially sensory oriented but perceptually and conceptually very limited, develop awareness of a multitude of factors about the natural and built environment? How does he or she come to have images of cities, to have perspectives on places, and to have cognitive maps of urban areas? These are some of our guiding questions.

BASIC POSTULATES

The investigation of environmental knowing implicitly bears upon and can be derived from more general epistemological questions about the nature, validity, and origins of knowledge. There are three basic questions to be asked: (1) How does knowledge in general, and knowledge of the environment in particular, come to be; that is, is knowledge real or ideal, or does it follow some other law? (2) To explain intelligence, must we choose between ungenerated structures and structureless genesis, that is, between intelligence as an awakening to a priori "essenses" or "forms" and intelligence as the gradual accumulation of bits of information without organization, or is there another possibility? (3) What is the relation between thought and behavior, both in terms of how knowledge arises from behavior and how knowledge influences subsequent behavior? We may ask these questions as readily about environmental information, images, and beliefs as we may about any other domain of epistemology. It is certainly not possible for me to provide answers to these age-old questions. What I shall attempt to do is to show a consistent, and I feel highly plausible position with regard to them, and show how the research to be discussed later derives from this theoretical position.

The Construction of Environmental Knowledge, Images, and Beliefs

For Piaget, Werner and Kaplan, and other cognitive-developmental theorists, the problem of knowledge is the problem of the relation between subject and object—how the subject comes to know the object and whether there is any justification for assuming that one's impression of the world is "accurate." As Piaget and Inhelder (1956) have stated,

The study of the concept of space, or, rather, of the innumerable ideas involved in the concept of space, is for many reasons an indispensable part of child psychology.

To begin with, it is clear that if the development of various aspects of child thought can tell us anything about the mechanism of intelligence and the nature of human thought in general, then the problem of space must surely rank as of the highest importance.

Philosophers and psychologists have argued about the nature of space for centuries. They have debated whether it is an empirical concept derived from perception or from images, whether it is innate to thought and consciousness, or whether it is operational in character, and so on. Surely here if anywhere is cause for resorting to to experimental psychology, since only the actual data of mental evolution can reveal the true factors operative in the development of the notion of space (p. vii).

The position that Piaget has taken on this question, and to which he has contributed considerable supporting evidence, can be summarized as follows:

(1) knowledge is neither innate nor does it consist only in copying or imitating reality, [but rather] to *understand* reality it is necessary to *invent* the structures which enable us to assimilate reality, and consequently
(2) the actions performed by the subject on reality do not consist simply in the construction of appropriate images and adequate language, [but rather] the subject's actions, and, later his operations, *transform* reality and modify objects (Piaget, 1967, p. 532, italics his).

In taking the position that reality is *constructed* by an active subject, we are *in part* adopting a neo-Kantian position on epistemology (see Bochenski, 1966). Kant (1902; original edition, 1787) argued that our representation of the world does not pattern itself after the world "as it is," but rather that the world, as an appearance, conforms to our ways of knowing and representing it. Kant made a distinction between the "form" of knowledge, given as an a priori before experience, and the "matter" of knowledge, given through experience as dictated by the already existing "forms." There were for Kant only two pure forms of a priori knowledge or "intuition"—space for the outer senses and time for the inner.

Later philosophers of mind and empirical epistemologists across a wide spectrum of thought have been able to reject the notion that certain of our conceptions of reality are innate, while retaining, extending, and empirically demonstrating that both the content of knowing and indeed even space, time, and other "forms" of knowing are developmentally constructed by an inherently active knower.[2]

Mead (1934, 1938), for example, treated "mind"

not as a place in the brain but as an *act*, the act of employing and interpreting signs and symbols and of knowing objects and events by the mediation of significant symbols. He argued that each of four major stages in the act of knowing—impulse, perception, manipulation, and consummation—directly parallels and is in a dynamic indivisible whole with qualities which might be said to "make up the object" (e.g., respectively, qualities that are global, perceptual from a distance, perceptual through contact or manipulation, and emotional). For Mead, the qualities that are said to make up the object are actually relative to and are defined by the corresponding stages in the act of knowing.

Dewey and Bentley (1949) argued that the popular three-way dichotomy between persons, things, and intervening variables derives from our naively accepting popular phrasings about life as if such phrasings were valid apart from inquiry into their factual basis. On the contrary, they argued, all knowing activity, like language and symbolic representation, is "persons in action dealing with things," that is, one common durational event. *Knowings*, therefore, are always and everywhere inseparable from the *knower*; they are twin aspects of a common fact. And because knowings are arrived at by inquiry, it is also impossible to separate in existence the *objects known* from the *process of knowing*.

Empirical support for the constructivist position comes from many quarters. Piaget's books (1929, 1954) on the child's conception of the world and the child's construction of reality show how, from an initial undifferentiated state, the construction of reality proceeds along two complementary paths: externalization by accommodation to the object, and internalization by assimilation to the subject. At various stages in this developmental process what the child takes to be real varies with the structures of knowing presently constructed. It seems that "neither a fixed external environment imposed on a passive organism, nor a preformed intellect creating an external reality, but rather the complementary action of accommodating to the object world and assimilating to the subject's schemas accounts for the mental equilibrium of development" (Zinn, 1969).

Two well-known neurological studies indicate the constructive function of the central and peripheral nervous systems. Lettvin, Maturana, McCulloch, and Pitts (1959) have reported that the retinal fibers in the frog's eye select and transmit to the frog's brain only three particular classes of information: sharply defined boundaries between objects, changes in the distribution of light, and general dimming of light. Similarly, Hubel and Wiesel (1962) reported that the cells in the visual cortex of the cat's brain respond to and encode only information about objects at certain angles and movements in certain directions. Different cells fire in response to different angles, while cells deeper in the brain respond to more generalized characteristics of light. Other cells respond only to movement and then only to movement in a single direction. But not all angles and directions are responded to and the subtleties of light to which we are accustomed do not exist in the cat's world.

Von Uexküll (1957) provides many other interesting examples of the construction of reality for other lower animals. He has reviewed work which shows, for example, that all animals possessing three semicircular canals in the middle ear also have a three-dimensional operational space which permits finding their way home even in the absence of visual cues.

Directly in line with human conceptions of the environment is Whorf's (1956a) hypothesis that language acts as a frame of reference through which we view the world.

We dissect nature along lines laid down by our native languages. The categories and types that we isolate from the world of phenomena we do not find there because they stare every observer in the face; on the contrary, the world is presented in a kaleidoscopic flux of impressions which has to be organized by our minds—and this means largely by the linguistic systems of our minds. We cut nature up, organize it into concepts, and ascribe significances as we do, largely because we are parties to an agreement to organize it in this way—an agreement that holds throughout our speech community and is codified in the patterns of our language. The agreement is, of course, an implicit and unstated one, *but its terms are absolutely obligatory*; we cannot talk at all except by subscribing to the organization and classification of the data which the agreement decrees.

This fact is very significant for modern science, for it means that no individual is free to describe nature with absolute impartiality but is constrained to certain modes of interpretation even when he thinks himself most free. We are thus led to a new principle of relativity, which holds that all observers are not led by the same physical evidence to the same picture of the universe, unless their linguistic backgrounds are similar, or can in some way be calibrated (pp. 213-214, italics his).

Such a view on the nature of thought is not limited to the philosophic and scientific communities. Artists realize that the way they paint the world and even the way they "see" the world is heavily influenced by a host of subjective factors serving to organize the universe in a personal manner. In a recent review of a photography exhibition on natural and urban landscapes, Huxtable (1973) remarked,

Photography as art has had a lot to do with the way we perceive the world and react to it, and to some extent the accepted image of our environment is one that the art of photography has given us . . . . There are as many potential images of the world as there are eyes and minds to frame and interpret them. There is virtually no such thing as uncolored observation, or objective documentation, as long as there is an intelligence behind the camera . . . . They have taught us a way to look at the world, and in turn, we see the world their way.

And that is the rub. The curious thing about images of the environment is that they inevitably structure reality. In both literature and art, the image of the city has always been subject of philosophical and emotional manipulation . . . . Our urban concepts are defined by certain key photographic images . . . . The implications are large, in that we deal with what we see, or think we see, in facing the problems of the environment (p. 26).

In adopting this constructivist position, we are taking the position that as there is no way to apprehend the nature of what we take to be "the environment" except through the minds and actions of persons, and as there is no way to separate the nature of "reality" from the knower, from the stages in the act of coming to know this reality, and from the cultural and linguistic community, it is impossible to separate the process of knowing from the resultant knowledge. There can be no complete understanding of the environment in either sense or reason. Instead of assuming that knowledge can ever copy what is real, we are led to the view that to understand reality is to invent reality, to assimilate and transform it. Thus, what we take to be real is the product of an active, intentional act of knowing.

But this is not to suggest that our knowledge of the environment is independent of experience. All knowledge is of course influenced by experience, but the point is that knowledge does not arise out of raw experience. Knowledge is the product of the active process of human understanding applied to sense experience. This understanding selects and organizes the contents of sense experience according to its own "forms"—its own categories and rules, cognitive structures and operations—but the forms of knowing are neither arbitrary, a priori impositions upon sense experience, nor do they originate in raw experience; like the content of mind, the categories and rules of mind are also constructed.

This position also does not imply that knowledge is strictly an individual matter, nor that our constructed worlds are conceptually separate or unique; that is, the position does not reduce to an absolute subjectivism. The degree to which similar individuals have similar experiences and to the degree to which knowledge and impressions about the environment are communicated among individuals is the degree to which knowledge will be held in common among various social and cultural groups. Reciprocally, there is no doubt that communication and coming to have shared impressions of the world influences how each one of us structures our own individual world.

Arguing that such basic ideas as space and time are neither innate nor strictly determined by experience still leaves open the very central questions of the precise ways in which reason and experience interact, in which categories and content interact, and in which environmental knowing is constructed by the young child in the course of daily transactions with the environment. Do cognitive structures stand in the way of experience? Is it possible to experience oneself-in-environment without reflective abstraction? Do existing cognitive structures and levels of consciousness put a limit on what can be experienced? To what degree do action, perception, and reflection operate in the development of environmental knowing? How much are children influenced at different stages of development by environmental images and beliefs communicated by significant others, by adults and peers, and by the mass media? Some beginning work has been done on these questions, to which we shall turn in a later section (see also Chapter 9), but more extensive studies of these processes are needed.

The Interaction of Biology, Culture, and Environmental Experience

The development of environmental cognition is a complex function of many variables. Certain biological givens of the brain and peripheral nervous system have been mentioned (see also Chapter 2), along with sociocultural factors like membership in a particular linguistic community (see also Chapters 19 and 20). It is clear that a host of other factors affect the development of environmental cognition. Some of the more prominent possibilities include (1) the child's specific history of environmental behavior, activity patterns, and experience; (2) his or her future goals and expectations; (3) needs and values; (4) personality structure; (5) the structure of the prevailing sociocultural and physical environment (see Chapters 4, 29, 30 and 31 on the effects of physical structure); (6) population changes; (7) changes in technology; (8) prevailing public attitudes and values toward the environment; (9) economic and class structure; (10) life style; (11) social group membership and reference groups (see Chapters 17, 18, and 21); (12) stage in the life cycle, level of general cognitive development, and spatial relations ability; (13) national origins and feelings for the landscape; (14) cultural and religious norms, rules, values, and beliefs (see Chapters 17, 19, and 21); and so on. Most of these factors have received some treatment in the general literature on environmental cognition, and several are pursued in depth elsewhere in this volume. What is needed is a better understanding supported by careful empirical investigations of the *functional* and *dynamic relationships* between each of these factors and the *development* of environmental cognition, in other words, what their role is in affecting environmental cognition and how dynamically they operate in coming to know and ascribe meaning to the environment.

Our list of variables that affect environmental cognition can be analytically collapsed into two major categories; we may say that the development of environmental cognition is a function of *intraorganismic factors* and *external environmental* or *situational demands.*[3] The phrase "external environmental demands" is not meant to be limited to the strictly physical environment, thus omitting the effects of the social and cultural environments, prevailing public attitudes, mass media, and so on. Nothing could be further from that intended, for, although some may make an arbitrary split between the physical and social environments, no such split is intended here. The city is both and simultaneously a social–physical entity.[4]

The point is really quite simple: the development of environmental knowing is the result of a dynamic interaction between what the person brings to the situation (inner organismic factors, including genetic and biological factors, needs, values, personality goals, intentions, social, cultural, and religious belief systems, etc.) and the demands made on the person by the situation (external sociophysical environmental factors). There are many theories which treat "cognition" as a function primarily or entirely of contingencies from the immediate human environment, without ever considering the roles of the physical environment, cultural factors, personality, values, or intentions.

It is one thing, however, to state this theoretical orientation and quite another to work out the details of particular functional interactions. Such has been done for general cognitive development but has yet to be demonstrated to any great extent in the context of the development of environmental knowing (see Kaplan, Wapner, and Cohen, 1975, for one of the first works of this type). Many questions arise: How does the development of the child's value system interact with the development of his sense of the surrounding environment? What environmental cognitive differences are there among children of different socioeconomic classes, and why? How do personality variables like introversion–extraversion or impulsivity–reflexivity affect the development of environmental knowing? What effects do the parents' political attitudes and values have upon children's appreciation of the city in which they live? Do children of different subcultural linguistic groups living in the same sociophysical environment (e.g., native Americans versus European-descended Americans) come to know the environment in different terms and with different feelings and meaning?

Action and Transaction

The third basic postulate is the twin notion of *action* and *transaction*. Essential to Piaget's general theory of cognitive development, and to its extensions to the cognition of large-scale environments, is the argument that the motivation for all biological and psychological development is *adaptation*. Adaptation is more than simply preservation and survival; it also includes development from lower to higher orders of functioning. Intelligence is one form of adaptation. Piaget's findings indicate, in contrast to the behavioristic "learning" theory assumption of the child as a passive recipient of information from a "real" environment, that in adapting to its environment the child *actively* initiates contracts, actively assimilates information and accommodates cognitive structures to this "aliment," and in general actively and spontaneously structures its experience and knowledge (Piaget, 1950, 1952, 1954).

These findings are supported by the work of Crescitelli (1955) and Katz (1961) on the action potentials in central nervous system cell communication, and by the work of Held and his colleagues (e.g., Held and Hein, 1963; Held, 1965) on the role of overt action in perceptual development. In studying visual perceptual development in two higher mammals (cats and humans), Held found that motor activity overcomes the effects of visual deprivation (Held and Hein, 1963), and that movement alone, in the absense of the opportunity for recognition of errors, does not suffice for adaptation; it must be self-produced and error-correcting movement, what he has called *reafference* (Held, 1965). The impetus for moving toward higher levels of development comes from this intrinsic, spontaneous motivation coupled with active, self-produced, and error-correcting movement.

The twin notion of the role of *transactions* in environmental cognition is that spaces and places are imbued with character because of the ongoing transactions in which both persons and places are mutually engaged and through which they are mutually defined (see Chapter 16). Environments are thus defined in connection with and through the constructions given them by organisms, while organisms are taken as integral elements and are defined in part in terms of the environment and organism–environment transaction in which they are engaged. The environment is not treated as something around or outside human activity; it is integral to the activity. Not only do events necessarily take place in environments, but events assume part of their quality through the medium of their environment. In transactional theories, systems of descriptions and naming are employed to deal with aspects or phases of action, without final attribution of presumably detachable or independent "elements" or "entities." Transactions, furthermore, are not to be viewed as existing apart from observations or the process of observing them.[5]

The extreme relativism of this view is witnessed by Einstein (Einstein and Infeld, 1938; see Dewey and Bentley, 1949). Einstein argued that although the Newtonian construction was unexcelled for its efficiency within its sphere of viewing the world as a product of forces between unalterable particles, the "properties of the field alone appear to be essential for the description of phenomena" (p. 138).

This position is also witnessed in more recent work in the philosophy of mind. For example, Brown (1972) has argued that perception and meaning are relative to each other and to the configuration between them. Contrary to dualistic and environmental deterministic positions, neither sense datum nor the material object can account for cases of significant perception. The information that a person gleans through a given perceptual situation is identical with the meaning that the situation holds for him; thus, insofar as perception functions as a source of information, *the object of perception is meaning*. Whenever we say we "recognize" an object, we are actually grasping a meaning. Such meanings do not have to be profound, although the more information a person has of a situation from previous transactions with the objects and processes of that situation, the more meaning it will have; but, always, to perceive or conceive of an object is at some level to grasp a meaning.

It is important to contrast this transactional postulate with our earlier interactional notions (see also Dewey and Bentley, 1949). In primarily interactional theories (including Piaget's), concentration is focused on the reciprocal action of persons and things on each other, events are considered in causal terms, and inquiry lies in locating independent units or variables and then determining their interaction (as, for example, between internal and external variables). Most person–environment models treat organism and situation as independent existentially, distinguishable methodologically, and hence interactive on behavior. In truly transactional theories, on the other hand, concentration would be focused on person-in-environment transactions, and objects, subjects, and mind would be seen in indivisible relationship with these transactions. The way to operationalize such a theory, although extremely difficult, would seem to be (1) to describe and classify the types of organism-in-environment transactions in which persons engage, (2) to articulate the stages in the act of knowing relative to these classes of transactions, and (3) to methodologically isolate internal and external variables relative to both the type of transaction and the stage in the act of knowing being considered.[6]

Such a position raises interesting questions. What are the characteristic types of transactions in which children engage, how do they relate to the major stages of the life cycle, and what types and amounts of environmental knowledge, images, and beliefs are acquired relative to these transactions and stages? Are the four principal stages of general cognitive development articulated by Piaget (e.g., 1950) also the principal stages in the act of knowing the environment, as Hart and Moore (1973) suggested might be the case, or is there an entirely different sequence, as others argue (e.g., Downs and Stea, 1973a, pp. 223–225; Stea and Taphanel, 1975)? In what precise ways do internal and external factors meet and mutually influence each other in different types of transactions and in different stages in the act of knowing?

Mediation: The Influence of Environmental Cognition on Subsequent Behavior

As well as cognitions of place arising out of transactions with the environment, subsequent transactions with the environment are presumed to be mediated by previously constructed conceptions. Far from being passive recipients of external forces moving us to conform to the demands of the external stimulus situation, and far from being driven simply by biological factors and inherited patterns of response, we assume, following modern cognitive mediational theory, that persons are active organisms adapting to the world through the eyes of their knowledge of that world. Environmental cognitive structures and particular environmental images mediate environmental behavior. Or, put differently, behavioral transactions with the environment are mediated in part by the individual's knowledge, or cognitive representations, of the total environment–behavior situation. As Huxtable (1973, p. 26) wrote, "The city is what we think it is, and we respond to it as we conceive it to be."

Structure in the Development of Environmental Knowing

Questions arise in the literature about whether the development of knowledge of the environment is a matter of *quantitative accretion* or of *qualitative changes*? Do all people organize knowledge in basically the same way, and does the same person at different times or in different environments organize knowledge in the same way, such that differences between people or variations within the same person are primarily a matter of the *amount* of knowledge or the *extent* of the city known [e.g., Andrew's (1973) recent study on the amount of Toronto known by children of different ages, or Gould's (1972, 1973) work on the extent of children's knowledge of Sweden), or are there also *qualitative structural differences and changes*?

There is now clear and ample evidence that not only do people differ and change in the amount of their knowledge of the environment at different times, but also that they differ and change in terms of the ways they *organize* what they know; that is, they give different structures to knowledge at different times in development. The organism seeks not only to know the world, but also to *order* this world; persons are continuously directed toward giving order and organization to knowledge (see Piaget, 1970b; Moore, 1973d). There are many examples in the literature of structures of environmental knowing, from the early work of Trowbridge (1913) on egocentric versus democentric reference systems, to the Russian work of Shemyakin (1962) and his colleagues on cognitive route versus survey maps, to the very recent work of Barker (1974) on the different modes by which professional and academic specialist groups organize air-pollution information.

In developmental psycholinguistic research, Slobin (1972) has shown how the current organization of a child's mind influences what he or she attends to in the flux of external environments, and that over-regularized forms of conjugation (an overly active recognition of structure) persist for several years and outweigh the effects of practice and reinforcement. Thus, at one stage in the development of language, the child seeks regularities—seeks structure—and is oblivious to exceptions. Later the exceptions are incorporated into and begin to modify the regularities into more complex and more flexible structures. Piaget (1954) has also shown many examples of how the child's current cognitive structure dictates what information can be assimilated and what will be ignored.

Inasmuch as the child's current cognitive structure not only influences what is attended to or ignored, what is assimilated, and how the structure accommodates to assimilation, but also *precedes, selects,* and *orders* the specific parts of environmental experience and behavior that will be attended to and assimilated, it is reasonable to investigate the organization of environmental knowing and the developmental progressions and operations which perform on knowledge before investigating particular images of particular environments. Some of our own earlier work (e.g., Hart and Moore, 1973; Moore, 1973a, 1973b, 1973d, 1975a) has been aimed at articulating and empirically demonstrating different cognitive structures by which children and adolescents organize cognitive mapping information; details will be reviewed in a later section.

Generally speaking, I think the evidence is clear that in the process of coming to know an environment we go through the reiterating process of accumulating new information, trying to organize it, and changing our current structures in the light of this new information. Piaget refers to this as the *assimilation* of new "aliment" or new "food for thought" to

some already existing structure and the *accommodation* of this rudimentary structure to further experience and information. Assimilation and accommodation are simultaneous processes and cannot be separated. Gathering information and structuring it are simultaneous and cannot be separated. What we know about an environment is not just a matter of what cues are readily visible, but also a matter of the inherent ways in which our mind structures information and the socioculturally influenced categories of knowing. What we know about an environment at a given time is also greatly influenced by both the developmental level of organization we bring to the situation and by our own particular style of organizing knowledge.[7]

Genesis and Transformation: Developmental Analysis

Structures of knowing are indescribable without the complementary description of genesis and transformation, of how structures come to be, where they begin, and how they continue to change and evolve. Both Werner (1948) and Piaget (1970b) have pointed out that only by understanding the development of a phenomenon can we fully understand its mature form; thus, complementary to the discovery of structural patterns is the task of ordering and accounting for the transformations between structures.

There are two ways of looking at development. In the first, and more common way, the term is used to refer to changes through time or in relation to age, and these changes are assumed to entail progress; that which occurs later is somehow considered to be more advanced than that which occurred earlier. But such a time- and age-bound definition has certain problems, chief among them being that there can be no a priori grounds for assuming that all changes necessarily entail progress, that later is necessarily more developed. A second, more formal definition, advanced first by Werner (1948; see also 1957), avoids these problems. We may define *development* as qualitative changes, differences, or variations in the organization of behavior such that what are called more developed stages of behavior are more differentiated and logically include and hierarchically integrate what then come

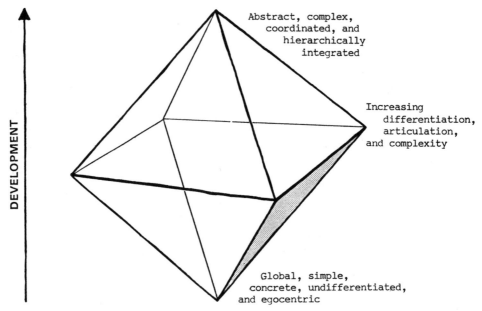

DEVELOPMENT

Abstract, complex,
coordinated, and
hierarchically
integrated

Increasing
differentiation,
articulation,
and complexity

Global, simple,
concrete, undifferentiated,
and egocentric

FIGURE 1
Schematic diagram of the ontogenetic principle of development.

to be called less developed stages and the behaviors associated with them. Because more developed stages are more organized, include more differentiated possibilities of behavior, and include all the behaviors associated with lower levels of development, they theoretically are more flexible than lower stages. Such a definition, stated formally and without reference to age, leaves as *empirical* questions as to whether or not the development of a particular behavior is correlated with age or time, and whether or not higher stages of development are more advanced, more adaptive, or lead to greater degrees of well-being. This general view of development is characterized in Figures 1 and 2.

There are several conceptual domains in which development may be investigated: (1) developmental transformations in individuals or groups over the life cycle, what is called *ontogenesis*; (2) developmental transformations over short periods of time, as in coming to know a new neighborhood, that is, *microgenesis*; (3) *developmental differences* between individuals or groups; and (4) *developmental variations*

within the same individual or group in the context of different organism–environment transactions and in relation to the demands of different environmental situations. Some research, to which we shall turn in a following section, has been done on the structures of environmental knowing within each of these domains.

But first, as we have seen, Piaget argues that the motivation for all development, and thus for the development of environmental knowing, is adaptation, and that adaptation includes development from lower to higher modes of functioning. Such functioning, then, proceeds developmentally from biological and reflexive functioning, to action-oriented and perceptual functioning, to conceptual and symbolic functioning (Werner, 1948; Piaget, 1952; see Figure 2). Although adaptation is intrinsic to all organisms, and adaptation through intelligence is intrinsic to all human beings, intelligence is not believed by these theorists to be inherited. We do inherit, however, a *mode of intellectual functioning* composed of two "functional invariants": *assimilation* (the incorporation of the external world into schemas) and made, have been mentioned briefly above. In the second study, changes had been instituted in the curriculum for the second year that had not been present in the first, thus raising questions about the effects of the total learning environment on a child's performance on any given task. Similarly, the first year's sample was taken shortly after the 1971 Sylmar earthquake at which time maps of the San Fernando Valley were given wide display in the local press. Exposure to this information could explain the heightened awareness of the valley shown by the third grade group relative to their own performance a year later; but the question of their apparent superiority to their fourth grade contemporaries remains unanswered.

In short, the present pair of studies opens more questions than it answers. Before any conclusions can be seriously proposed, the findings of regression in abilities of cognitive representation should be replicated under more controlled conditions. Second, more attention should be paid to the narrative content of the drawings, which has not been analyzed for the present sample. If, for example, an older child's drawing is from a horizontal perspective and at a focal scale (which would have been evaluated at a low level of development in the present study) but has as its subject a factory belching forth smoke and pollution, it is possible that the child is trying to deal with abstract, general systems operating in the environment but is limited to portraying this subject through the visual language learned in his earlier, perceptually oriented stages.

Environmental education. If the findings here can be confirmed, there are some rather broad conclusions that can be made regarding procedures for environmental education among young children. If environmental education is seen as experiential learning, it is clear that young children would benefit most from a range of types of experience with their environment. For older children, the fact of experience is equally important to keep fresh and alive the "external awareness" of details and events in their environment, but strong direction should be given to that experience to give it meaning. The world experienced at random without a careful monitoring of the relationship between perceived events and conceptions of past events apparently becomes confusing and loses meaning with age. Awareness achieved through participation with, and not contemplation of, the complexities of environmental systems would seem to lead to an understanding of the way a young person's world is working around him.

NOTES

1. The authors express thanks to David Healy, Trudy Heinecke, Susan Given-Klett, Jerry Kiley, Pat Kiley, Helene Kornblatt, Clavin Lau, Lee Pasarew, and Leah Reich for generously participating in the jury evaluation process of this study. The authors also wish to express their warm appreciation to David Stea for his encouragement and advice.

2. These classical methods of freely drawn sketch maps, once the only means used to elicit images, have come under considerable recent criticism. See the discussions in Part III (the editors).

3. Nonparametric techniques are the most appropriate in this situation for three reasons: the evaluative ratings are, at most, ordinal in character; such tests do not require any assumptions about the properties of the underlying distribution; and sample sizes are relatively small. See Siegel (1955).

4. Unfortunately, as some children did not sign their drawings and as some were absent, we found only 16 individuals who had produced drawings in both the third grade (initial study) and fourth grade (follow-up study).

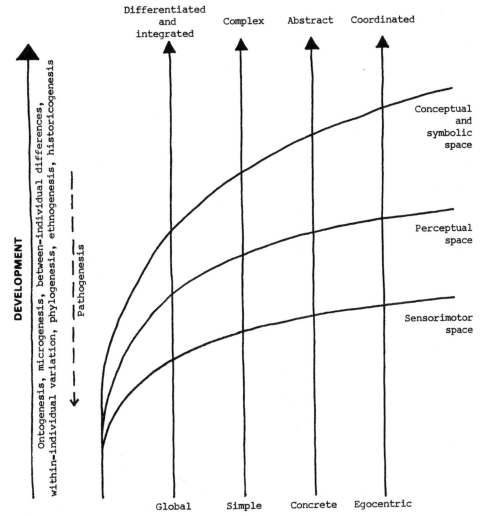

FIGURE 2
Principal dimensions of cognitive development showing also the major types of developmental analysis and the developmental progressions of sensorimotor, perceptual, and conceptual space.

accommodation (the readjustment of schemas to assimilation). Adaptation, then, is the equilibration of assimilation and accommodation. This ever-active functioning assures the construction of environmental knowledge and the ever-continuing transition from any state of temporary structurization to a succeeding one.

Intelligence is *assimilation* to the extent that it incorporates all the given data of experience within its framework . . . that is to say, of structuring through incorporation of external reality into forms due to the subject's activity . . . . Mental life is also *accommodation* to the environment. Assimilation can never be pure because by incorporating new elements into its earlier schemata, intelligence constantly modifies the [schemata] in order to adjust them to new elements. Conversely, things are never known by themselves, since this work of accommodation is only possible as a function of the inverse process of assimilation . . . . In short, intellectual adaptation, like every other kind, consists of putting an assimilatory mechanism and a complementary accommodation into a progressive equilibrium (Piaget, 1952, pp. 6-7; italics his).

But if intelligence in general, and environmental cognition in particular, is neither a form of innate structures nor arises from the bombardment of stimuli on a passive *tabula rasa*, how then does it begin; where is its genesis? Based on his extensive researches, Piaget (1952, 1954) argues that at birth the child is blessed with the above-mentioned mode of intellectual adaptation and with certain rudimentary reflexes, but little else. Evidence from Piaget and his co-workers indicates that building on these rudimentary sensorimotor reflexes, and through a long and involved process, there are six essential developments in the child's construction of the concept of space (see Piaget, 1954; Piaget and Inhelder, 1956; Laurendeau and Pinard, 1970; summarized in Hart and Moore, 1973):

1. The representation of space is preceded by the representation of objects, what is called the *object concept* or *object permanence*—the child's realization, transcending both perceptual and tactile stimuli, that objects continue to exist even if temporarily out of sight.
2. The representation of space arises from the *coordination and internalization of actions*—our understanding and representation of space results from extensive manipulations of objects and from movement in space followed by observing the results of these actions and movements, rather than from any immediate perceptual "reading off" or "copying" of this environment.
3. The representation of space follows from the internalization of the prior *sensorimotor group of spatial displacements.*
4. The genesis of the image of space arises from the *internalization of deferred imitations of actions in space.*
5. There are four general levels, or structures, of spatial knowing—*sensorimotor* (representation through action), *preoperational* (intuitive, un-

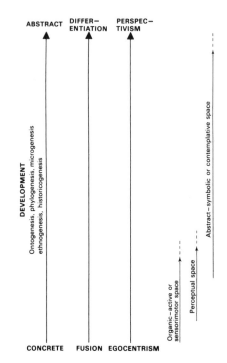

coordinated images of the world based on memories of previously manipulated or perceived objects), *concrete operational* (representation based on real or symbolized objects including systematic, reversible cognitive transformations), and *formal operational* (abstract spatial notions not dependent on real actions, objects, or spaces).
6. There are three sequential classes of spatial relations which are constructed—*topological* (qualitative relations like proximity and separation), *projective* (relations in terms of a particular perspective or point of view like a straight line or triangle), and *Euclidean* or *metric* (relations in a system of axes or coordinates like angles, equal intervals, and metric distance).

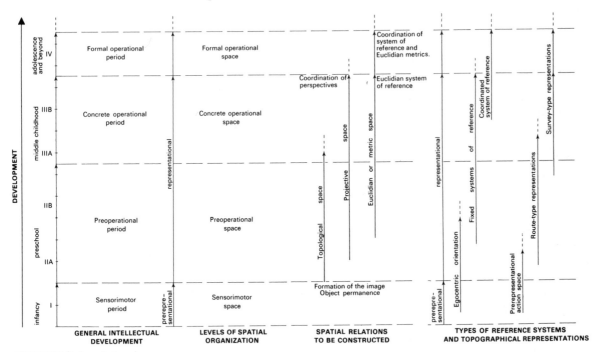

FIGURE 3 (*left and above*)
Graphic summary of findings and hypotheses about the development of the fundamental concept of space and of macrospatial cognition. The left side of the chart shows three of the principal dimensions of development along which environmental cognition may be analyzed. The next three columns summarize the findings of Piaget and others on the development of the fundamental concept of space in relation to general cognitive development. The columns on the far right show some of the hypotheses discussed in the text about coming to know the everyday large-scale environment.

These findings about the child's construction of the fundamental concept of space are summarized graphically in the left center of Figure 3.

STRUCTURES, OPERATIONS, AND TRANSFORMATIONS

Images of the environment have been analyzed in terms of five major components: spatial layout, physical attributes, social–political–economic character, dynamic functioning, and meaning. Although some current work is looking at developmental differences in environmental knowing without artificially assuming these distinctions (Wapner, Kaplan, and Cohen, 1973; Kaplan et al., 1975), most work on the development of environmental cognition has concentrated on the first aspect, the development of the understanding of the spatial layout of urban environments. A further distinction has been made between the fundamental spatial cognition of objects and the macro-spatial cognition of neighborhoods, cities, and other geographical-scaled spaces too large or complex to be apprehended at one time or from one vantage point. Such analytic distinctions do not imply that these two processes necessarily follow different developmental rules, nor (as I think I have been at error on previous occasions for leaving the impression) that there is necessarily a developmental progression from the understanding of layout to the attribution of meaning, or from fundamental to macro-spatial concepts. All three of these are empirical questions that can only be resolved by the results of careful research, although we may make predictions on the basis of the preceding general postulates and the research on spatial cognition.

Structures: Developmental Levels of Spatial Reference Systems

The most extensive body of theory and research on the development of the fundamental concept of space is of course that of Piaget and his associates and followers. In only one case of which I am aware have they extended this work to understanding the organization of children's knowledge of the everyday large-scale environment (Piaget, Inhelder, and Szeminska, 1960, Chapter 1), although several other experiments on model environments conducted by both Piaget and Inhelder (1956) and Laurendeau and Pinard (1970) are also extremely relevant in this regard. On the other hand, there is a large, disparate literature in geography, psychology, and education on various aspects of children's understanding of geographic-scale environments at different ages. A few years ago, Hart and I (Hart and Moore, 1971, 1973) reviewed this literature and tried to show how the general organismic-developmental orientation of Werner, combined with the more specific genetic-structural explanatory system of Piaget, could be useful in the organization and interpretation of these latter macro-spatial data. We advanced an organizing framework (Figure 3) that suggested a number of developmental structures and progressions, some of which were quite literal summaries of the available data (e.g., the central three vertical columns of Figure 3) and some of which were hypothesized on the basis of extrapolations from these data (e.g., the right column of Figure 3).[8] We hypothesized that children's understanding of the spatial layout of the environment falls into three distinct stages of increasingly differentiated and integrated cognitive reference systems, what we have more recently referred to as (1) an *undifferentiated egocentric reference system* organized around the child's own position and actions in space; (2) several different possibilities of *partially coordinated, fixed reference systems* or

ganized in clusters around various fixed concrete elements, landmarks, or places; and (3) an *operationally coordinated and hierarchically integrated* reference system organized in terms of some abstract geometric pattern (see Figure 3, right side; Moore, 1973a, pp. 42–52). It was also hypothesized (Moore, 1972b) that these stages might be systematically related to the principal stages of general intellectual development and to the three stages of the fundamental organization of space and construction of spatial relations (Figure 3, read horizontally). Evidence bearing on these hypotheses will be discussed in a later section.

From a series of experiments by Piaget and his followers on children's understanding of simulated and actual large-scale environments (e.g., Piaget and Inhelder, 1956, Chapter 14; Piaget et al., 1960, Chapter 1), from some of our own work on adolescent's understanding of urban environments (Moore, 1973a, 1973b, 1975a), and from several early experiments and follow-ups to be discussed later, it is now possible to characterize more fully each of these three levels of urban cognition (see Figure 10 later in this chapter for examples of each level).

Level I: Undifferentiated egocentric reference system. The elements included in children's and adults' representations at this level have been found to be limited to those of great personal significance. There is little differentiation among the elements, many are of the same type, and there is no differentiation of the child's point of view from other points of view. When dealing with a route, they think of their own actions first as though these are some kind of absolute, and landmarks are fixed in terms of these actions, rather than vice versa. Children at this level orient themselves in a practical way: up to a point they can anticipate the spatial relations between one landmark and the next as they come to them, but elements and landmarks are not organized in terms of a spatial whole. Positions are located mainly through egocentric, sequential, and topological relations of proximity, order, surrounding, or enclosure, without concern for left–right, before–behind, or distance relations (see also Trowbridge, 1913; Angyal, 1931; Muchow and Muchow, 1935; Claparède, 1943; and Shemyakin, 1962, all of whom also found evidence for this type of representation).

Level II: Differentiated and partially coordinated into subgroups based on fixed references. At this level, the person organizes the environment in terms of clusters or subgroups of elements where the groups are not systematically related one with another, but where the elements are related within the groups. The internal organization of the groupings is often based on functional similarity or topological proximities, on the use of projective relations (especially left–right and before–behind), and occasionally on the basis of relative distance. Each grouping is constructed with a particular, subjectively important vantage point or journey in mind; the partial plans are unrelated because the person is as yet unable to bridge the gaps between clusters or to coordinate one privileged vantage point or journey with the next. No coordinate system is employed to link the groups; in fact, often even the immediately available proximal coordinates of the edges of the paper or model are not used, the result being that a group of objects will be crowded together or run off the edge while other objects are placed with little regard for the position of the first group. At best, the relations between clusters are established in an intuitive or topological way, but these relations do not permit systematic cognitive transformations on the entire representation.

At this intermediate level the various groups seem to be organized in terms of one or more of three different types of fixed references: (1) fixed *point-and-radial* references, like landmarks, an airport, central shopping mall, or traffic intersections, where the area tends to radiate outward like the spokes of a wheel (see Trowbridge, 1913; Lord, 1941; Lee, 1964; Moore, 1975a); (2) fixed *linear-route* references, like major arteries, a river, expressway, or a bicycle path, where the area tends to be tied to and emanate from the route and its end points (see Muchow and Muchow, 1935; Appleyard, 1969a, 1970a; Rand, 1969; Moore, 1975a); and (3) fixed *aerial-spatial* references, like a central business district, a neighborhood, residential area, or a special functional district, where the overall representation tends to be less differentiated and often only consists of zonal or neighborhood units distributed topologically (see Appleyard, 1969a, 1970b; Chapter 2).

In general, representations at this level are charac-

terized by the presence of one or more clusters of subgroups of elements of the city corresponding to different cognized areas or neighborhoods, and by the relative lack of coordination between clusters, such that the result is a sketch map in which the relations among elements within the clusters are at a higher level of organization (i.e., systematic projective and sometimes metric relations) than the relations between clusters (i.e., intuitive and topological relations).

Level III: Operationally coordinated and hierarchically integrated. At this level, an overall coordinated system of reference is constructed through the coordination of left–right and before–behind, different viewpoints, and finally relative distances. Coordination no longer hinges on the subject's own actions; the person can now describe actions and movements in terms of a systematic abstracted reference system, rather than the reference system being described in terms of concrete actions. Partially coordinated plans are incorporated and hierarchically integrated into a larger whole, elements and clusters of knowledge being related to an abstracted geometric-like structure and sometimes (if convenient) to the cardinal directions. When a new subgroup is added to a drawing or model, the person wastes no time in making the different parts agree with each other. The advent of an overall systematic and abstracted structure seems to permit systematic cognitive transformations across the representation.

In general, at this level the person cognitively structures the environment in terms of a single comprehensive and abstracted reference system independent of any personally important or fixed references. Various landmarks and clusters retain some of their own identity, but they are clearly integrated into this larger structure and depend for their placement and part of their character on the larger structure (see also Angyal, 1931; Lord, 1941; Claparède, 1943; Shemyakin, 1962; and Rand, 1969; for evidence for this type of representation). This comprehensive configuration of the interrelations between elements and clusters in the environment permits systematic cognitive operations, particularly the operations of *composition* (all parts are parts of the whole), *identity* (elements retain their identity despite transformations), *associa-*

tivity (reaching in thought any part by a variety of routes), and *reversibility* (imagining a route in the reverse direction).

Transformations: A Possible Genetic-Structural Explanation

Following Piagetian and Wernerian cognitive-developmental theory and the preceding transactional-constructivist postulates, a possible explanation can be given for this three-step developmental sequence (see also Piaget et al., 1960, pp. 21–26).

Through the dual process of assimilation and accommodation, and through what Piaget calls "reciprocal assimilation" of sensory and motor schemata to each other, the infant builds patterns of sensorimotor coordinations, for example, the grasping of a sighted object. These rudimentary perceptual–motor schemata have a ubiquitous tendency toward repetition ("functional assimilation") and are forever incorporating more elements of the environment ("generalizing assimilation") while being altered as they accommodate to newly assimilated experiences. Concurrently, each schema undergoes internal differentiation such that the infant differentiates and articulates into two or more schemata what was formerly one schema. This development is, nevertheless, still at the level of action and sensation; no images or internal representations are yet present. Piaget's research has shown that the genesis of the image lies in the internalization of deferred imitations. He suggests that, once the child has formed images in one domain, this ability is quickly generalized ("generalizing assimilation") to other domains, like space. This important development may be at the root of the genesis of the cognitive representation of environmental space.[9]

The organization of representational space occurs at three levels: intuitive partial operations, reversible concrete operations, and abstract formal operations (see Figure 3). As we have seen, preoperational representations are subject to the limiting conditions of sensorimotor and perceptual activity. Although certain rudimentary and isolated cognitive transformations can be performed, the representation of space is essentially static and egocentric. However, owing to the accommodation of general structures to the

assimilation of experiences in the social and intellectual realms during the early school years, spatial thought becomes decentered from single points of view, and different points of view become differentiated, transformed, and coordinated into logical structures. Thus concrete operational spatial structures come to be formed through the coordination of perspectives from multiple viewpoints. The child has moved from an intuitive understanding and partial organization of space to an operational coordination in which elements and relations are able to be combined, associated in different sequences, and logically reversed in thought. The equilibrium of formal operational space is achieved on the basis of a further reflective abstraction on concrete operational space. With regard to the sequence of stages in the organization of large-scale environmental information and the transitions between stages, the contributing factors are tied in a vicious circle. To represent the environment as a group free from egocentric associations, schemata must comply with an abstract coordinated reference system; but to achieve such a comprehensive system, routes and places must be combined into a coherent group. We witness the transformation from egocentrism to coordination proceeding hand in hand with the transformation from action to logical thought (see Figure 2).

In the stage of egocentric reference systems, landmarks are uncoordinated and changes of position cannot be described. Children at this stage arrange in thought two objects in isolation, but cannot synthesize the links between pairs. Initially, the child's movements are organized as a system of sensorimotor connections between routes and places. Subsequently, construction is intuitive but does not permit of inversion; for example, routes are unidirectional and cannot be reversed in thought. The latter part of this period of egocentric orientation is clearly related to the child's uncoordinated preoperational spatial structure.

As a result of adaptation, transactions in the environment, and the ineraction of internal and external factors, the child assimilates new elements of the environment and decenters from one point of view. The decentering may take one of several forms, for example, first breaking up the sensorimotor experienced route into two end points, one where the child currently is, and the other where he was when at the other end, thus paving the way for reconsideration (on the level of intuitive thought) of the journey itself. Alternatively, as the earlier and subsequent sensorimotor experiences are internalized into primitive images, short links of the route may take on a character of their own. As new experiences are assimilated, as representations accommodate to these assimilations, and as further decentrations continue, the process leads to the first partial groupings of space, that is, the beginnings of the transitional, fixed, partially coordinated system of reference. Journeys themselves may be represented as symmetrical intervals between termini. Egocentric relations have thus given way to relations between objects, and the child sees himself as one object among many in a framework of fixed references. Each subgrouping of elements and relationships expands as a dual function of new assimilation–accommodation interactions and of internal reflections and abstractions from earlier schemata.

Generalizing assimilation assures that the subgroups will begin to overlap or contradict each other. This gives rise to more "aliment" for the structures to incorporate and to accommodate to, which leads in turn to a continuing differentiation of the partial representations. As the overlap and interfusion become pervasive enough, the structures begin to include each other through reciprocal assimilation; a more general structure is constructed, which includes the earlier subgroups as special cases, and the system as a whole becomes fully intercoordinated or equilibrated into the structure of the mathematical group, the structure which underlies the third stage of operational coordination and hierarchic integration.

Generalization to Other Phenomenal Domains

The above formulation, three-stage model, and genetic-structural explanation have so far been limited in their application to the description and possible explanation of ontogenetic developmental progressions on strictly spatial environments. But the findings of a number of studies on children's and adults' environmental cognition, along with general

interpretations of cognitive-developmental and individual-difference theory, have led me to believe that this formulation may be phrased in more general structural terms, and that such a developmental progression may apply not only to ontogenetic developmental changes, but also to microgenetic developmental changes, to developmental differences between individuals, and to developmental variations within the same individual, and may apply, furthermore, not only to the developmental analysis of knowledge of the spatial environment, but also to the equivalent four classes of the developmental analysis of knowledge of the everyday sociocultural environment. In other words, what we may have here is a very general developmental characterization, applicable to the structural-developmental analysis of many aspects of environmental imagery and knowing.

As shown earlier in Figure 2, the developmental analysis of any behavior may be made along four major dimensions: (1) degree of differentiation and integration, (2) degree of complexity, (3) degree of abstraction, and (4) degree of operational coordination. Taken together, these dimensions have led to a formal stage description of the organization of knowledge irrespective of content as detailed in Table 1, and to the derivation of the developmental levels of overall environmental impressions (Moore, 1973a, pp. 59–62) and of urban cognitive mapping, as detailed in Table 2.[10]

Thus, for example, if this general formulation makes any sense, it should be possible not only empirically to order external representations of large-scale spatial environments (like sketch maps, models, and repertory grids) in terms of developmental progressions over the life cycle and over short periods of time, but also to demonstrate empirically the applicability of these three levels to the characterization of differences between individuals in the same environment and variations within individuals in different environments. Inasmuch as the concept of stylistic differences in environmental cognition entails the companion notion of consistency within the individual across situations (Moore, 1973a), it should be possible to show that some of what were formerly thought of as stylistic differences between individuals

TABLE 1
General Schema for the Developmental Ordering of
Cognitive Representations

I. Undifferentiated concrete egocentric
This level includes primitive symbolic representations characterized by:
a. Lack of differentiation, i.e., all information is assimilated to one undifferentiated viewpoint and differences and variability in the subject matter are not recognized.
b. Complete egocentrism, i.e., an exclusive conception of all information from one's own egocentric point of view.
c. Predominance of concrete references, i.e., information is seen in strictly concrete, experiential terms.
d. Lack of overall organization, i.e., systematic relations among the elements of the representation are lacking.

II. Differentiated and partially coordinated into fixed subgroups
This level includes intermediate symbolic representations characterized by:
a. Differentiation without integration, i.e., differences and variability are recognized and aspects of the representation are differentiated from each other but are not integrated into an overall structure.
b. Partial decentering but partially continuing egocentrism, i.e., decentering from own point of view on some but not all aspects and subsequent centering or focusing on some aspects from other points of view.
c. Concrete and abstract references, i.e., some aspects seen in strictly concrete terms while others are seen in abstract terms.

d. Partial coordination into fixed subgroups, i.e., some but not necessarily all information is brought together into partial subgroups, such that the organization of this information within different subgroups is at a higher level than the organization or partial coordination between subgroups.

III. Operationally coordinated and hierarchically integrated
This level includes highly organized representations characterized by:
a. Differentiation and hierarchic integration, i.e., aspects and points of view are clearly differentiated from each other and are integrated into an overall structure.
b. Complete decentering and coordination, i.e., decentering from own point of view on most aspects and subsequent coordination of multiple points of view.
c. Predominance of abstract references, i.e., subject matter information and resultant aspects of the representation are seen in abstract terms.
d. High degree of overall organization, i.e., most information is brought together into subgroups and the subgroups are hierarchically integrated into an abstractly conceived structure wherein the subgroups are subordinated to the total organization of the representation.

are actually developmental differences. It may also be possible to show that this formulation applies to the developmental ordering of verbal representations (free descriptions, simulated editorials, repertory grids, etc.) of the everday sociocultural environment. Evidence bearing on these hypotheses will be examined in the next section.

DEVELOPMENTAL STUDIES OF ENVIRONMENTAL COGNITION

Several studies by Piaget and his colleagues, including one on large-scale environments (see Figures 4 to 7), preceded and greatly influenced the present formulation (see Hart and Moore, 1973). Since that time, a number of studies have followed from or are conceptually related to this general position and the preceding structural-developmental characterization. Each of the four classes of developmental analyses of spatial environmental cognition has now been investigated empirically, and, in addition, some studies have begun to look at the developmental analysis of the everyday sociophysical environment. I will briefly summarize the results of some of these recent studies.

Ontogenetic Developmental Changes in Environmental Cognition

Although most of Piaget's work on the development of spatial understanding has concentrated on fundamental spatial relations, one experiment suggested the ways in which these findings could be ex-

TABLE 2
Developmental Levels of Environmental Representations

Level I. Undifferentiated egocentric

Sketch map or model representations at this level are characterized by being concrete, egocentric, and undifferentiated. The elements of the representation are generally unorganized or organized only topologically in terms of one egocentric point of view or experience in the environment. There is no differentiation of other possible points of view (e.g., a particular concrete experience in the city represented by a string of streets related only topologically).

Level II. Differentiated and partially coordinated into fixed subgroups

Sketch maps or models at this level are characterized by the presence of one or more clusters or subgroups of elements corresponding to different cognized areas of the environment and by the relative independence and lack of coordination between the clusters, such that the result is a sketch map or model in which there are one or more clusters where the relations among the elements within the clusters are at a higher level of organization than the relations between different clusters. Elements within the clusters may be related geometrically, but the relations between clusters may be only topological (e.g., two or more well-articulated clusters corresponding to different areas of the city linked by a single connecting street).

Level III. Operationally coordinated and hierarchically integrated

Sketch maps or models at this level are characterized by an organization based on a coordinated and abstracted reference system to which different elements and clusters of the environment are related and to which they are subordinated. The organization extends across most of the map or model. The elements are related both projectively and geometrically (e.g., a unified, comprehensive map or model organized in terms of a set of major traffic circles and interconnecting major arteries, with angles, shapes, and relative distances taken into account).

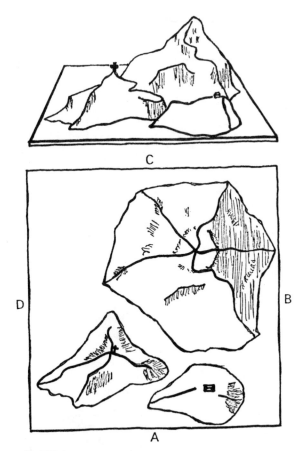

FIGURE 4
Pasteboard model of three mountains used in Piaget and Inhelder's experiment on the coordination of perspectives. The child sits at A, a doll is placed successively at the other positions, and the child is asked to select from a set of sketches what the doll would see (after Piaget and Inhelder, 1956).

tended to predicting developmental shifts in the organization of knowledge of *large-scale* environments. Piaget et al. (1960, Chapter 1) asked children from 4 to 12 years of age to build a model of their school yard and vicinity. After the experimenter rotated the main school building of their model 180°, they were asked to change the rest of the model as necessary (see Figure 7). They found three essential stages in the child's ability both to construct the initial model and to alter it after the change in position. In the first stage (up to about 7 years of age,

corresponding to preoperational thought), the model was thought of only in terms of memories of the child's own actions, landmarks were fixed in terms of actions, elements were not organized in terms of a spatial whole, and reversals were not made when the school building is rotated. In the second stage (from 7 to 9½, the beginnings of concrete operational thought), spatial relations were partially organized in terms of subgroups of landmarks, and parts of the landscape

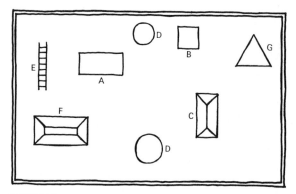

FIGURE 5
Model village used in Piaget and Inhelder's experiment on systems of reference. The child is given a second piece of cardboard and a set of identical objects and is asked to build a second, identical model (after Piaget and Inhelder, 1956).

Supporting evidence comes from Muchow and Muchow's (1935) finding that the life space of the young child is bound together by personal significance and is centered around the child, whereas the life space of adults is bound by more abstract functional and formal relationships. Lee (1964), Rand (1969), and Ladd (1970) all report evidence that children's worlds are divided into what Lee called "local schemata," and that trips and excursions outside the home neighborhood are remembered but not thought of as connected with, or of the same life space, as the home.

A pair of pilot studies were conducted under my direction at Clark University to extend this work on large-scale spatial environments. Cannitello (1970) studied how children develop knowledge of routes in a city. She had children 5 to 11 years of age lead her from their homes to school, and asked them periodically how they knew they were going the right way and at the end to draw a map of the route. She found that younger nonreading children rely on familiar, personally salient cues and have no internal representation of the route from home to school other than by rote memory of houses and other objects along the way. Older children are more flexible, rely on a range of perceptual cues, street signs, and names, and have a

were rotated in terms of these landmarks. Finally, in the third stage (from 8 to 12, the equilibration of concrete operations), spatial relations were quite precise and well organized, landmarks were fully coordinated, the models tended to be constructed either in a network or a radial manner, and reversal of the entire model was easily accomplished.

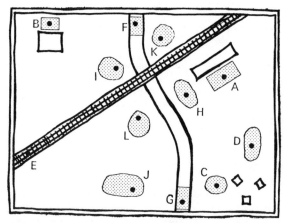

FIGURE 6
Model landscapes used in Laurendeau and Pinard's experiment on the localization of topographic features, comprised of a road, railroad tracks, and five houses of different sizes and colors. On the left are the twelve successive positions at

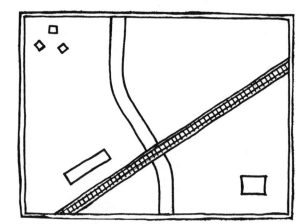

which the child is to place a toy person on the second, reversed model. The shaded areas around each point (not actually shown on the model) indicate the margin of error allowed for each placement (after Laurendeau and Pinard, 1970).

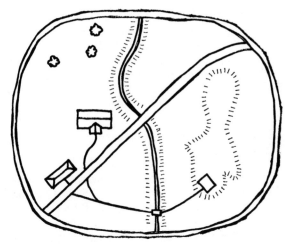

FIGURE 7

Sketch of a sandbox model as constructed by a child of her schoolyard and environs in the experiment of Piaget et al. (1960) on systems of reference in representation of large-scale environments. Having constructed such a model, the child is asked to make any necessary changes to it after the experimenter rotates the main school building through 180°.

rudimentary representation based on the functional and geometric significance of places and connecting links. She interpreted her findings to suggest a three-stage sequence: (1) rote memorization of the route from past actions; (2) general sense of direction of the end point and orientation relative to it; and (3) an organized internal representation based on functional and geometric relations.

Mark and Silverman (1971) were interested in the effects of concrete operations on the cognitive maps of children. Working with 31 elementary school-children from 7 to 12 years of age, they administered standard Piagetian conservation tasks to determine which children had attained the concrete operational level of spatial conceptualization. They then asked each child to make a model of their school and as much of the surrounding area as possible and to conduct them around the model as they would a visitor to the school. They interpreted their findings as tentative support for two hypotheses: (1) that before concrete operations, the child possesses several uncoordinated representations of an area; afterward a

coordinated representation emerges; and (2) that there is a slight time lag, what Piaget would call a "horizontal décalage," between the formation of concrete operations and the formation of a coordinated representation of the large-scale spatial environment. These findings need to be replicated in a more precise way (e.g., no independent judges were used and no tests of significance were performed), for their significance is potentially twofold. First, Hart and Moore (1973) advanced the notion that in understanding cognitive mapping there are two types of development to be considered: the development of the fundamental concept of space and the development of cognitive representation of large-scale spatial environments. We also hypothesized, based on our understandings of Piaget, that the latter macro-spatial relations might grow out of the former fundamental concepts and would therefore appear later. Second, we hypothesized that with the equilibration of concrete operations the child would be able for the first time to coordinate different perspectives of the same large-scale environment, to think of that environment systematically in terms of projective relations and Euclidean metrics, and to construct an abstractly coordinated representation of the environment utilizing these two means (see Figure 3, upper part of the right two columns). An alternative theory proposed by Stea (see Downs and Stea, 1973b, pp. 223-224; Stea and Taphanel, 1975) predicts different relations between fundamental and macro-spatial cognition. There is evidence on both sides of this controversy (see also Chapter 9), so the formulation and conduct of a critical experiment is called for.

Chapter 13 illustrates an ingenious experimental manipulation to test the validity of the developmental stages advanced herein and to see if they also characterize how children organize their understanding of smaller-scale spaces like rooms.

Microgenetic Developmental Changes

Several recent studies have looked at microgenetic changes in coming to know a new environment. For example, in a Clark University master's thesis, Follini (1966) found that, in coming to know a room, there are qualitative shifts in organization over time from global representations of a concrete functional nature to well-articulated and integrated representations of an abstract geometric nature.

Appleyard (1969a, 1970b, in press) conducted a study on "styles and methods of structuring a city," which may, I believe, be interpreted in microgenetic terms. Analyzing sketch maps from 211 residents living in the new city of Ciudad Guayana in Venezuela from under 6 months to just over 5 years, he found two predominant representation types: "sequentially dominant" (the use of roads and rivers as organizing elements) and "spatially dominant" (the use of buildings, landmarks and districts). He suggested that the sequential maps might be more developmentally "primitive" than the spatial maps and, furthermore, that both kinds of maps progressed from topological to positional to Euclidean in terms of structuring. As 75 percent of his maps were of the sequential type, and as the subjects had an average of 1 to 5 years experience in the city, we might wonder if the sequential-topological maps were produced by those with less experience in the city and the spatial-Euclidean maps by longer-term residents, that is, if there might be a real-time microgenetic progression from sequential to spatial representation and from topological to positional to Euclidian structuring. Appleyard's data (1970b, Table 1) support this hypothesis, as there was a relative shift from sequential to spatial structuring with length of residence.

Ann Devlin, in Chapter 4, sheds additional light on this issue, and suggests the interesting notion that generic knowledge about cities in general might play a particularly important role in cognitive adaptation to a new locality.

In Chapter 14, Robert Beck and Denis Wood look at real-time developmental changes in teen-ager's coming to know new cities. In a part of their study not reported here (see Wood, 1973b, pp. 545-588), they analyzed the types and degrees of distortion of sketch maps over time, and found an oscillation from distorted to less distorted to additionally distorted and finally to minimally distorted maps approximating the layout of the city. In transactional–constructivist terms, it would seem that students are equilibrating to one developmental level based on partially coordinated but separated regions organized around fixed references (the findings of Chapter 14). Then as they explore the city more and try to assimilate additional information, this organization breaks down and distortions reappear. More experience subsequently leads to higher and more inclusive levels of organization, and distortions subside again. The current theory suggests the process would continue.

Developmental Differences Between Individuals and Groups

In a recent study, I sought to investigate whether the three developmental levels specified earlier also characterize stable developmental differences between people (Moore, 1973a, 1973b). Worcester high school students between 15 and 19 years of age were asked to draw a sketch map of their city (Figures 8 and 9) and to answer questions about routes and possible detours through selected parts of the city. The first task was designed to assess their level of cognitive structuring of the city and the second to assess the cognitive operations of associativity and reversibility. One month later, the same students were asked to draw a second map of the city. Three judges independently sorted the resulting maps solely on the basis of written criteria into the three levels of spatial representation (see Table 2), and subsequently ordered them from least to most highly organized.

The judges had relatively little difficulty sorting the maps and although working independently, agreed significantly on the classification of maps to levels, thus supporting the hypothesis that these three levels constitute a clear and reliable way to developmentally order sketch map representations of the spatial layout of cities. The classification of subjects remained stable over time; that is, developmental level with regard to the organization of environmental information did not change rapidly.

Examples of sketch maps at each of the three levels are shown in Figure 10. The level I, undifferentiated egocentric representation on the top left is a long serpentine route comprised of personally significant street segments bearing little resemblance to the geographic relations between these streets. The level II, linear-route representation on the upper right is organized around a major commercial thoroughfare,

FIGURE 8
Oblique aerial photography of south Worcester, Massachusetts, centered on Worcester City Hospital and Clark University. Photo credit: Roger Hart.

WORCESTER

FIGURE 9
Standard map of the city of Worcester, highlighting major arteries, lakes, and other features.

a traffic rotary at the left end, and a major intersection at the right. The point-and-radial representation on the lower left is organized in two clusters around focal traffic rotaries, but the clusters are unrelated. In both level II cases, severe projective and Euclidean distortions occurred in parts of the maps, clearly indicating that, although parts of the subjects' representations were well organized in terms of a fixed reference system, other parts were organized at best egocentrically and topologically. Finally, the level III representation on the bottom right is a typical example of an abstractly coordinated representation characterized by the parts being embedded in an overall systematic, geometric-like organization, in this case comprised of two major traffic rotaries and two sets of near-parallel arteries perpendicular to each other.

It was also found in that study that performance on the associativity and reversibility verbal way-finding

tasks was significantly related to level of sketch-map performance on three out of four measures. This is a very important finding owing to the well-known limitations of sketch mapping as a measure of internal, cognitive representation (see Part III). Inasmuch as two independent measures lead to the same indication of the subjects' level of cognitive organization, we can place more confidence in the contention that both measures are reflections of the same underlying construct, that is, the degree of organization of knowledge of the environment. Finally, no evidence was found for significant relations between developmental level of representation and age, sex, or general intelligence, although significant relations were found with grade in school and spatial relations ability (Moore, 1973a, Tables 1 and 2; 1975b; see also Bycroft, 1974).

Developmental Variations Within the Same Individual or Group

In another part of the study (Moore, 1973a, 1975a), developmental analyses were applied to the study of variations within the same students with regard to the organization of their knowledge of different neighborhoods. Subjects were drawn from those determined to be at levels II and III in the first study. These subjects were asked to draw sketch maps of two different areas in the city, a personally familiar area and a less familiar area (measured on a Likert-type scale of degree of subjective familiarity with different parts of the city), and to answer associativity and reversibility way-finding tasks for different areas.

The findings indicated, first, that both techniques were also reliably applied to the smaller neighborhood scale, second, that a significant relation exists between degree of familiarity and developmental level of sketch-map representation, and, third, that a significant relation also exists between familiarity and success versus failure on the way-finding tasks at the neighborhood scale. Thus, these results on variation within individuals indicated that subjects vary developmentally depending on the demands of different environmental situations, and that for the most part subjects represent familiar areas in a level III, operationally coordinated manner, whereas they represent

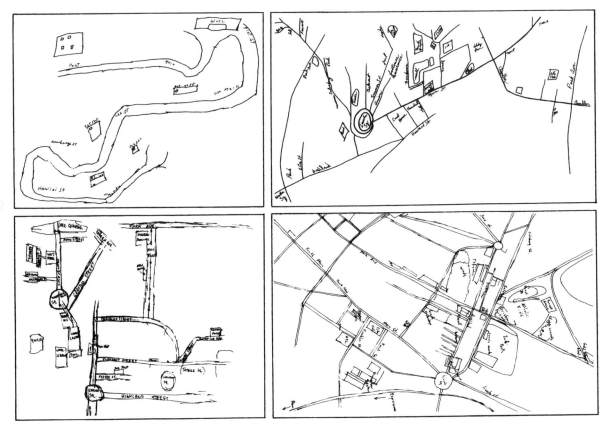

FIGURE 10

Examples of the three essential developmental levels of cognitive mapping. Upper left: level I, undifferentiated egocentric. Upper right: level II, partially coordinated into subgroups in terms of a fixed reference system—linear-route variety. Lower left: level II, partially coordinated—point-and-radial variety. Lower right: level III, operationally coordinated and hierarchically integrated.

less familiar areas in a level II, partially coordinated manner (see Figure 11). These developmental variations within individuals are also manifested on linguistic tasks involving cognitive way-finding transformations.

It is perhaps worthwhile to note, in regard to the earlier allusion to cognitive styles, that the finding of variations within individuals in the use of these types of cognitive representations lends support to the contention that these types are ordered *developmentally* rather than that they constitute different cognitive styles. To be "styles" of representation would mean that they would have to be consistent within the individual and differ in *mode* or *rule* of organization. But we have seen that these ways of representing the environment are not self-consistent across time and situation but vary within the individual in relation to the demands of the situation, and that they are developmentally ordered in terms of both logical inclusion and the cognitive operations that can be performed at the higher level but not at the lower level.

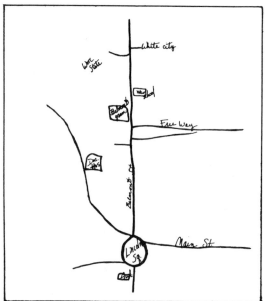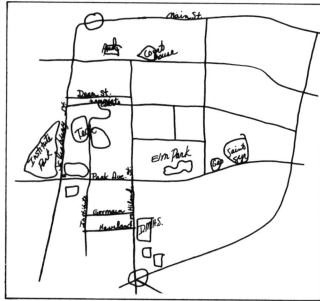

FIGURE 11

Examples of sketch maps by the same person of two different urban neighborhoods. Left (unfamiliar area): level II,
partially coordinated. Right (familiar area): level III, operationally coordinated.

Developmental Studies on Everyday
Sociophysical Environments

The preceding studies have all focused on the
development of cognitive mapping, that is, the development and transformation of the structures of
coming to know the spatial layout of cities and
neighborhoods. But a fascinating area remains to be
explored, that pertaining to the development of
children's and adults' more holistic conceptions of
the sociophysical environment, their beliefs and expectations about how the city works, and the symbolism and meaning they invest in the environment.

A study by Rand (1972) has shown how children
conceive of the interlocking, intimate nature of the
"physical" and "social" environments. Interpreting
drawings from children 5 to 12 years of age, he found
that every step the child takes in deciphering the
functions and principles of the organization of the
house goes hand in hand with a parallel step in understanding the structure and social roles of the family.

Recent work by others at Clark University is looking
at overall impressions of the sociophysical environment, at strategies for schematizing houses and neighborhoods, and at changes in conceptions of the
environment with changes in life goals (see Kaplan
et al., 1975). Quinlan (1972) studied the ways in
which 6- to 8-year-old children and 17- to 22-year-old
university students schematize houses and neighborhoods and the search strategies that they use in
locating a house in a relatively unfamiliar neighborhood. She found that younger children think of
houses in terms of isolated characteristics and adopt a
trial-and-error search strategy based on these isolated
characteristics, whereas older university students
identify houses in terms of a combination of features,
or at least one very distinctive and characteristic feature, and try to create a hierarchy of features and
overall house styles as a clue to planned searching.
Wolfsy, Rierdon, and Wapner (1974) studied the effects of planning to move to a new area on the cognitive
reconstruction of the present environment. Working

with university undergraduates, some with well-articulated plans for the future and some with only vague ideas, they found that the greater the articulation of plans, the greater the projection into the future and the greater the self-world distancing from the current environment. These findings are interesting. They support the notions that with increasing environmental experience children and adults hierarchize the environment, and that people not only conceive of the present environment in terms of their present personal values, goals, and transactions, but also reconstruct past environments in line with current goals and aspirations.

SUMMARY AND CONCLUSION

A number of recent studies have been presented on the development of awareness and representation of the environment that have followed from or otherwise been related to the transactional–constructivist notions presented earlier. In general, these studies have demonstrated empirically a number of things:

1. Children and adults organize their knowledge and images of the environment in line with major cognitive developmental shifts from infancy through adolescence.
2. There is a temporal parallel in the understanding of the order of the spatial environment and of the roles and activities played out therein.
3. There is a conceptual parallel between ontogenetic developmental progressions through childhood, adult short-term microgenetic developmental progressions in coming to know a new environment, developmental differences between individuals of roughly the same age and general intelligence, and developmental variations in the same individual with regard to his or her knowledge of different environments.
4. In each developmental progression, there exist a number of qualitatively different stages, or cognitive structures, by which the world is organized; it is not just a matter of how much is known, but in what ways knowledge is organized.
5. There exist three essential developmental levels in each developmental progression—undifferentiated

egocentric, differentiated and partially coordinated into subgroups around fixed references, and operationally coordinated and hierarchically integrated.

6. To understand how people come to know the environment and how they come to organize their knowledge of the environment, it is necessary to understand the transactions of persons in environments and the interactions between intraorganismic variables, like values, aspirations, and socioeconomic background, and external situational demands, like the cognitive demands of environments of different formal properties.

This chapter has been an attempt to show that it is possible to conceptualize the development of environmental cognition in transactional–constructivist and genetic-structural terms, that it is possible to extend certain propositions from major theories of cognitive development to this new phenomenal domain, and that it is possible to derive from this position certain hypotheses the investigation of which sheds light on the development of coming to know the everyday environment in which we live.

NOTES

1. Now also at the School of Architecture and Urban Planning, University of Wisconsin, Milwaukee.
2. Examples of theoreticians and researchers in other fields who have embraced some form of constructivist position include the following: in philosophy, Dewey and Bentley (1949) and Cassirer (1953–1957); in developmental psychology, Werner (1948), Werner and Kaplan (1963), and Piaget (1950, 1952, 1954, 1970a); in linguistics, Whorf (1956a); in perception, Ittelson (1960, 1962) and Gregory (1966); in psychopathology, Kelly (1955); in sociology, Mead (1934, 1938); in zoology, Von Uexküll (1957); in neurology and biocybernetics, Lettvin et al. (1959), Hubel and Wiesel (1962), McCulloch (1965), and von Foerester (1974); see Papert (1965). In this volume, see especially Chapters 5, 16, and 19.
3. An extremely valid, and personally very helpful, criticism was made by Amos Rapoport at the

1973 Blacksburg symposium to the effect that, in an earlier formulation, I seemed to take the position that development is a product of internal biological and personality factors and external physical environmental factors, thus omitting the crucial role of cultural factors. He argued, furthermore, that any consideration of change in individuals, groups, and cyclic events suffers if one eliminates consideration of similar processes at the cultural and subcultural levels (see also Chapter 19). The crucial role of ethnic and cultural factors in the development of environmental cognition is grossly understudied (but see Ladd, 1970, 1972; Maurer and Baxter, 1972) and is an area of much needed research.

4. It is perhaps an unfortunate accident that most of the work to date on environmental cognition has focused on cognitive mapping of the physical layouts of cities, i.e., has not looked at more holistic environmental imagery, and thus has seemed to imply such a conceptual bifurcation. But see Sections 5, 6, and 7 of this volume (the editors).

5. Transactionalism received its most articulate presentations in the writings of Mead (1934, 1938) and Dewey and Bentley (1949), and was extended most notably into the psychology of perception by Ittelson and others (Ittelson, 1960, 1962; see the review in Moore, 1974b).

6. Additional theoretical suggestions about other aspects of person–environment relations from a transactional point of view are given in Ittelson (1970, 1973), Ittelson et al. (1975), Tibbets (1972), Tibbetts and Esser (1973), Burton et al. (1975), and especially Wapner et al. (1973) and Kaplan et al. (1975).

7. For further discussions and research on cognitive styles of selecting and organizing environmental information, see Appleyard (1969a, 1970b), Gittins (1969), Hart and Moore (1971, pp. 59–62), Moore (1973d), Stea and Taphanel (1975), and Chapter 9.

8. In her commentary at the 1972 Los Angeles symposium, Sharon Kaufman-Diamond of UCLA suggested that this and other structural characterizations might prove to be too static to account for the problem of representation. Referring to Neisser's (1967) work in cognitive psychology, she suggested that "a lot of what we may be talking about when we speak of 'cognitive structures' is ad hoc and constructed just for the purpose, that perhaps we are not storing information in this form or that form, but we have a set of rules, heuristics, and ad hoc ways of doing things which help us to put together information which is stored in an entirely different form, but which is retrieved and organized in a particular manner depending on the purpose of the immediate endeavor . . . . Perhaps the most interesting thing is to get at these rules of construction" (transcribed from tapes of the symposium by the author).

9. Stea and Blaut (1973a; see also Chapter 9) have theorized that the beginnings of the representation of the environment may lie in the child's model building and toy playing, and have begun to explore this direction of research (see also Hart, 1974). No work, however, has followed yet from this present "generalizing assimilation" hypothesis.

10. This is only a brief characterization. The complete criteria and instructions for developmental scoring are contained in Moore (1973a, pp. 53-65 and Appendixes G and H).

13

Linda P. Acredolo
**Institute of Child Development
University of Minnesota**[2]

FRAMES OF REFERENCE USED BY CHILDREN FOR ORIENTATION IN UNFAMILIAR SPACES[1]

To date the majority of studies dealing with children's knowledge of space have looked at performance on "model" spaces, the development of the knowledge of the cardinal directions, or the development of mapping skills. Analysis of the child's knowledge of the spatial layout of the world around him through observation of his behavior *within* that world has largely been neglected.

The two studies to be described here are an attempt to assess the child's knowledge of large-scale spaces by studying his behavior within locomotive environments. More specifically, the goal was to investigate the frames of reference children use to organize the spatial layout of their world. In this context a *frame of reference* is defined as a system or strategy that underlies and, to some extent, controls what an individual uses to code location within an environment. For example, a visitor to a strange city may adopt the cardinal directions as his frame of reference and, therefore, be oblivious to street names or salient landmarks. A second individual, however, may take the opposite tack and rely on more concrete features rather than on the abstract axes provided by a compass.

Based upon Piaget's research of children's abilities to represent space (Piaget and Inhelder, 1956; Piaget, Inhelder, and Szeminska, 1960), the suggestion has been advanced that the development of reference systems within locomotive spaces may proceed through three stages (Hart and Moore, 1973; Moore, 1972b, 1975a; see also Chapter 12). Specifically, the hypothesis is that the child progresses from a coding system based on the relation of objects to his own body (egocentric frame of reference), to a coding system in which landmarks become central features for partial coordination of space (fixed frame of reference), and finally to a coding system based on abstract axes, which facilitate full coordination of space (coordinated frame of reference). The two studies to be discussed were designed to assess the degree to which this hypothesis accurately describes the development within children of the ability to cognitively represent spatial environments.

Experiment I: Maintenance of Orientation in a 10- by 15-Foot Room

Subjects. The subjects in experiment I were 22 three-year-olds and 22 four-year-olds from a middle-class nursery school in Minneapolis. Eight additional preschoolers constituted a control group.

Procedure. Each child was tested individually in a

10- by 15-foot room with a door at one end and a picture window at the other (see Figure 1). The room was bare of furniture except for a small table placed along the side wall to the subject's right as he or she entered, and to which the child was immediately taken by one of two experimenters. The second experimenter remained close to the door. At the table the child was blindfolded and led for a walk around

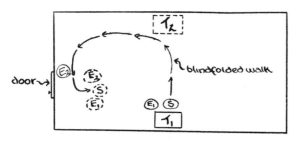

I: Egocentric and Container vs. Object

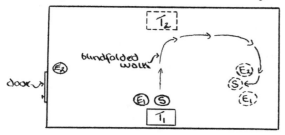

II: Egocentric and Object vs. Container

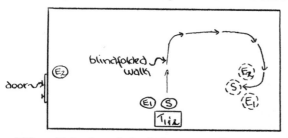

III: Object and Container vs. Egocentric

FIGURE 1

Experimental conditions in experiment I (conditions I and II) and experiment II (conditions I, II, and III). T_1 = original location of table; T_2 = location after walk. Solid circles = original location of individuals; dotted circles = location after walk.

the room during which attention was drawn to the route being followed. During the walk the second experimenter quietly moved the table from one side of the room to the other and then took a position near the point in the room where the walk would be ended. At the end of the walk, the blindfold was removed and the child was asked to return to the spot in the room where the walk had begun. After the child had chosen a spot, a series of five questions was asked to determine if the child was satisfied with his decision. These questions ended with a specific inquiry as to whether or not the table had moved. If at any point the child indicated that the table had moved, he was asked again if he was sure of that decision and was allowed to change his mind.

The movement of the table from one side of the room to the other was motivated by a desire to place a fixed frame of reference based on the only object in the room in conflict with a more coordinated system based on the shell of the room.[3] The child's decision as to his original position in the room was interpreted as an indication of the frame of reference most salient to him. A return to the table in its new location indicated reliance on the object; a return to the wall where the table had originally been located indicated reliance on the container itself.

An egocentric frame of reference defined in terms of the axes of the subject's body was also available. Recall that as they entered the door the children were immediately taken ahead and to their right to the table. Thus, preliminary to the blindfolded walk, they experienced both visually and motorically only one relationship between themselves and the table: the table was ahead and to the right of their bodies. To assess the effects of this limited experience with the table, the blindfolded walk of half the children in each age group was ended close to the door, thereby replicating their original view of the room (condition I). For the remaining children the walk was ended close to the window, thereby reversing their original view of the room (condition II; see Figure 1). In either situation the child's response could be influenced by an egocentric frame of reference, in which case he would be guided by the fact that the table had been seen to the *right* and he had had to move in that direction to reach it. A consequent

salience of each of these relative to one another, three conditions were used, two of which were identical to conditions I and II of experiment I (see Figure 1). Condition III was designed to isolate the egocentric frame of reference and place it in opposition to the other two systems, thereby allowing direct assessment of its influence. As indicated in Figure 1, this was accomplished by leaving the table in its original position throughout the experimental session, thereby keeping the object frame of reference in agreement with the container frame of reference. To place the egocentric frame of reference in opposition to these two, the child's walk was ended at the far end of the room, as in condition II, thereby reversing his original view. Thus, sole reliance on previous experience with the table would lead the child to the blank wall to the right (in the situation illustrated in Figure 1); reliance on either of the other two systems would lead the child to the left, to the table in its new position.

Because the children were each tested under all three conditions, it was necessary to take precautions to minimize transfer of training from trial to trial. First, no child was tested in more than one condition on a given day. Second, the room itself was altered each day so that the container cues were never exactly the same, with the exception of the door. To this end, the curtains covering the two end walls were changed on each trial as was the position of the table. On the first day of testing for each child, the table was to the right as he entered the room; on the second day it was to the left; and on the third day it was once again to the right. Third, the order of presentation of the conditions was counterbalanced across subjects.

Results. In the lower half of Table 1 are the numbers of children in each age group who correctly duplicated their original positions in experiment II. No differences were found between the performances of the 3- and 4-year-olds in any of the conditions. When the data from these two groups were combined and compared to the data from the 10-year-olds, chi square tests using Yates correction revealed a significant difference between the preschoolers and the older children in condition I ($\chi^2 = 5.9$, df = 1, $p < .025$) but not in conditions II or III. In condition I the 10-year-olds were significantly more likely than the preschoolers to correctly duplicate

their original positions. In conditon II this same trend approached but did not reach significance ($\chi^2 = 3.66$, df = 1, $p < .10$). There were no differences between these groups in condition III.

In addition to looking at the performances of the groups within conditions, one can also look at the performances of individual subjects *across* conditions. Table 2 presents the eight patterns of responses possible across the three conditions and the frequency with which each pattern was observed. A plus (+) represents a correct duplication of the subject's original position; a minus (–) indicates an error. The purpose of the with-in-subjects design had been to detect consistency, within a subject, of reliance on a particular reference system. For example, consistent reliance on an egocentric frame of reference would be represented by pattern 7, since that is the only configuration which results from making choices that maintain the relation between the table and one's body which existed at the start of each condition. An egocentric response would successfully duplicate the subject's original position in condition I, but would not do so in either conditions II or III. Likewise, pattern 5 represents reliance on an object frame of reference. Children displaying this pattern were swayed by the location of the table, thus correctly duplicating their original position only when the table was not moved (condition III). Finally, consistent reliance on a container frame of reference is represented by pattern 1 in which correct duplication is achieved in all three conditions.

The most frequently observed pattern within each group was pattern 1, which indicates a tendency at each age to rely on container cues. However, chi square tests revealed that the 10-year-olds were sig-

TABLE 2
Observed Frequencies of Eight Patterns of Successful and Unsuccessful Duplication of Original Position in Experiment III

| | | Patterns | | | | | | | |
| | | 1 | 2 | 3 | 4 | 5 | 6 | 7 | 8 |
N	Age	+++	-++	+-+	++-	--+	-+-	+--	---
18	3	10	1	0	2	5	0	0	0
18	4	8	0	1	3	6	0	0	0
18	10	17	0	1	0	0	0	0	0
		35	1	2	5	11	0	0	0

nificantly more likely to rely consistently on container cues than were either the 3-year-olds ($\chi^2 = 6.0$, df = 1, $p < .025$) or the 4-year-olds ($\chi^2 = 8.4$, df = 1, $p < .005$). Within these latter groups, pattern 5 appeared with relative frequency, indicating consistent dependence on the location of the table by 11 of the 36 preschoolers. Fisher's exact tests revealed that this pattern occurred significantly more frequently among both the 3-year-olds ($p = .02$) and 4-year-olds ($p = .0095$) than it did among the 10-year-olds. No other significant age differences were found in the data from Table 2, and no children displayed consistent reliance on an egocentric frame of reference (pattern 7). In regard to the pattern data, therefore, we can conclude that the 10-year-olds were significantly more likely than the preschoolers to rely consistently on a container frame of reference; the preschoolers, in turn, were significantly more likely than the 10-year-olds to rely on an object frame of reference. No significant sex differences were found.

Finally, sign tests comparing performance on the first and third days revealed no significant increases or decreases in the number of correct responses. Thus, one can conclude that factors other than simple increased familiarity with the room were contributing to the performances of the subjects in experiment III.

Discussion. The results of experiment II provide evidence of consistency in choice of reference system for 46 of the 54 children, but the data do not provide a definitive explanation of the role of the egocentric reference system among preschoolers. Unlike experiment I, the 3- and 4-year-olds in experiment II did not differ from each other in their responses to the experimental manipulations. In each case, a majority of the children consistently relied on container cues, while a subset of the children showed consistent reliance on the object. In contrast, the 10-year-olds showed no tendency to rely on an object frame of reference.

One possible explanation for this difference between the results of experiments I and II may lie in the fact that the space in experiment II was smaller than that used in experiment I. It may be that within the smaller space of experiment II the 3-year-olds were able to retain enough relevant information before they were blindfolded to aid them after the blindfold was removed. In addition, they may have

been better able to "keep up" with the kinesthetic information from their blindfolded walk in experiment II, given its shorter distance. In other words, the 3-year-olds in experiment II may not have been restricted to reliance on their initial movement from the door to the table as the 3-year-olds in experiment I appear to have been. The hypothesis that the space in experiment II was more easily learned is supported by the large percentage of preschoolers who consistently duplicated their original position. Condition II, in which 16 of 22 preschoolers in experiment I chose the table, only elicited 12 such errors among the 36 preschoolers in experiment II. In addition to its smaller size, the slant of the floor in experiment II may have provided the children with a salient container cue not available to the subjects in experiment I.

Although none of the children in experiment II exhibited consistent reliance on an egocentric frame of reference, 11 of the 36 preschoolers did exhibit consistent reliance on an object reference system. Moreover, two sources of evidence indicate that these subjects really did not recognize that the table had been moved. First, the children all persisted in their decisions despite the prompting questions designed to get them to focus on the location of the table. Second, some of these subjects indicated their belief that the table had not been moved by going to the wrong wall to find the door! These children, clearly, were structuring the room around the position of the table rather than vice versa.

Finally, it seems clear that, by age 10, children are capable of using a container frame of reference and, indeed, are inclined to do so to code location within an unfamiliar space. Of course, the role played by size and legibility of environments has yet to be assessed. Ten-year-olds who used container cues in experiment II might revert to an object system, or even an egocentric system, in a different environment. For example, Moore's (1975a) data on adolescents show such within-individual variations in the spatial cognition of a mid-sized city.

Conclusions

The purpose of the two studies discussed here was to test the propositions advanced by Hart and Moore

(1973) and Moore (1972b, 1975a) that the development of frames of reference within large-scale environments proceeds from dependence on an egocentric frame of reference to dependence on a fixed frame of reference to dependence on a coordinated frame of reference. Although the results of the experiments do not provide sufficient information to warrant complete acceptance of this sequence, the studies do provide some supportive data. First, both studies provide evidence that reference systems are not simply the products of armchair psychologists. On the contrary, they represent strategies that impose structure on the child's world and influence what he notices about it and how he behaves in it. In support of the reality of reference systems we can cite the fact that in both experiments the child was simply asked to find the spot in the room where he had been blindfolded. Given these instructions, however, the responses of the subjects all fell into two categories rather than being distributed randomly around the room.

As for specific reference systems, both studies reveal the importance among preschoolers of a fixed frame of reference in which location is coded in terms of landmarks rather than abstract axes. In experiment I the majority of 4-year-olds indicated reliance on the location of the table rather than the cues provided by the shell of the room; in experiment II a subgroup of 3- and 4-year-olds exhibited consistent reliance on the position of the table, even to the extent of going to the wrong wall to find the door. For these children the focus of attention was on the concrete "contained" object features of the environment, not on some abstract conception of the organization of the container itself. In many environments in the child's world such an object-oriented strategy will provide satisfactory guidance. However, not all objects are stationery, and not all environments have objects; eventually, this object system must be replaced by a more dependable objective system based on container cues and abstract axes.

Experiment I also revealed an apparent reliance on an egocentric frame of reference among the 3-year-olds, who seemed to be dependent on the only visually guided experience that they were allowed during the experiment, their initial trip ahead and to their right to the table. The failure of experiment II to replicate

this finding illustrates the important point that the reference system chosen by an individual is closely tied to the specific space in which he or she is located. In this case it seems likely that the 3-year-olds did not exhibit the same degree of egocentrism as those in experiment I because the space used in experiment II was smaller and easier to master. Obviously, additional research is needed to clarify exactly how size exerts such an influence on spatial orientation. In the meantime, the possibility that size may be an important variable should stand as a warning against generalizations about behavior within different sensorimotor spaces, as well as against generalizations from sensorimotor to representational space. In addition, the degree to which visually guided exploration in space affects orientation needs to be systematically studied. These and other interesting questions remain to be answered. However, the studies discussed here, at the very least, demonstrate the value and feasibility of searching for the answers by observing behavior within large-scale sensorimotor environments.

NOTES

1. This research was supported by NICHD Grant No. PO1–HDO5027 from the National Institute of Health to the Institute of Child Development, University of Minnesota, and is based on the author's Ph.D. dissertation. An earlier version of parts of this paper was presented at the Society for Research in Child Development meetings, Philadelphia, March 1973.

2. Now at the Department of Psychology, State University of New York at Buffalo.

3. To facilitate understanding of the experimental manipulations, the terms "fixed frame of reference" and "coordinated frame of reference" used by Hart and Moore will be replaced by terms more specific to the spatial environment under discussion. Within the context of the present experiment, a fixed frame of reference will be called an "object frame of reference" and will refer specifically to use of the *table* as a landmark for coding location within the room. The term "coordinated frame of reference" will be replaced by the term "container frame of reference" and will refer to dependence on the walls of the room for

coding location. Although it is true that the container frame of reference is also based on objects, (the door and window), use of these landmarks in the present situation requires understanding of the axes they represent and the spatial relations between them. Thus, in the present experiment, dependence on "container" cues is taken to be representative of a greater degree of coordination relative to dependence on the table alone and, therefore, representative of Moore's abstract "coordinated frame of reference."

14

Robert Beck
Ecole d'Architecture
  Université de Montréal

Denis Wood
Department of Landscape Architecture
  North Carolina State University

COMPARATIVE DEVELOPMENTAL ANALYSIS OF INDIVIDUAL AND AGGREGATED COGNITIVE MAPS OF LONDON

The principal intention of this chapter is to shed light on the nature of the early cognitive development of urban knowledge as recaptured through an experimentally generated series of sketch maps made by American teen-aged students touring London for the first time.

As in other cognitive mapping studies, we assume that sketch maps embody constructions or projections of internal cognitive schemas and states held with respect to London. Our work differs from previous studies, however, in four important ways. First, the experiences of our respondents were novel ones, thus enabling us to study the early development of urban orientation and knowledge. Previous studies have concentrated on long-term cognitions of environments by residents that only change slowly from year to year. To infer development, such studies require either considerable samples of different age groups or longitudinal studies over the lifetime of individuals. Most studies have used small comparative samples from different age groups. Our own preference was to study development in microgenetic time as evidenced by a series of cognitive maps made by strangers to a city, to whom the city is a novelty. We reasoned that more changes would be happening on the maps in the first few days of knowing a place than after years of being established there. Second, we make no claims that microgenetic development is the same as ontogenetic development, and in fact doubt that the learning process of a tourist visiting the city for a week is the same as that of a native who has different goals, motives, feelings, and attachments toward the city. Third, in most previous studies data have been elicited at one point in time and have been aggregated across subjects according to different sample groups. Aggregated cognitions are important for design and planning purposes in that they represent a consensual view of a place and provide a statistically superior basis on which to draw conclusions. We like individual maps on the other hand because of their uniqueness and the feeling that this is the real thing, whereas aggregated maps are artifactual. As we are interested in both aggregated cognitions and the individual's cognitions, this paper compares results of both these ways of structuring and analyzing data. Finally, cognitive mapping studies have traditionally used sketch maps freely drawn under minimal instructions. In this study the elicited maps were not free sketch maps in the Lynchian tradition, but were assisted by a total mapping curriculum and mapping language (environmental A) that enabled the mappers to build up and re-present their urban knowledge in surfaces and in stages (see Chapter 32).

This report summarizes three major analyses we have performed on a data set of 82 maps made by 31 American teen-agers (23 were female, 8 male) between 15 and 19 years of age (average age was 17.2). They came from the United States east of the Mississippi, from the North and the South, and from cities and small towns. The information is part of a larger study, project Group L, which investigated several dimensions of travel behavior, including personality, interpersonal relations, and the cognitions of Europe before, during, and after a 35-day educational tour in which group L visited London, Rome, and Paris for the first time (Wood, 1973b).

Urban Morphology, Cognitive Development, and Environmental A

The mapping language, environmental A, contains symbols for three basic kinds of urban elements: *points*, or relatively small places like architectural landmarks, intersections (circuses), and so on; *lines*, or routes, streets, paths, and so on; and *areas*, or bounded districts, zones, parks, and the like. Other possible categories of urban elements such as Lynch (1960) has suggested (e.g., edges and nodes) were either adapted to a special case of point–line or point–line–area combination or discarded for the simplicity of the language. Environmental A provides symbols for points, lines, and areas which, when mapped, become representations of the urban milieu. As the language is well learned, a cognitive schema is developed favoring the use of such units as cognitive categories for storing and retrieving urban information. Thus, we may speak of point cognitions, line cognitions, and area cognitions, and, in discussing development, we may refer to changes of organization among these cognitive representations over time.

Our ideas about what constitutes development are integrally related to the morphological categories. For example, we feel that an essential mark of development is the making or unmaking of *connections*. When two regions in maps made on one day are unconnected and on another day are connected, we say

there has been a development. Connections may be manifested through the actual mapping of a *connection route* or the placement of an *area* around two structures, thereby including them in the same category. Or we may infer from proximte *closely huddling points* that they are connected. Another form of development occurs when one large area becomes *differentiated* into smaller areas in subsequent maps. Another indication of development is growth as measured by the relative *frequency* of the three elements. Finally, we hold that urban cognitive development is also indicated by changes in the *veridicality* of points, lines, areas, and regions relative to a cartographic map.

The Three Analyses: Techniques and Results

Four sets of maps were collected in London, the first set (n = 36) on the third day, the second set (n = 27) on the fifth day, the third set (n = 19) on the sixth day, and a few additional maps later. Thanks to the unifying effect of the mapping language, the 82 collected maps were sufficiently comparable to permit a variety of relatively novel analyses while nonetheless preserving the unique configuration of the individual mapper. Among the analytic techniques performed was a derivative of graph theory that permitted a quantitative assessment of the degree of interconnectivity of the skeletal network of each map. Another related the size of the mapped areas with the affective connotations displayed on an attributive overlay. A third examined the degree of consensuality of representation with respect to certain features such as a major street, the Thames, and so on. The fourth and fifth analyses were content analyses performed individually and aggregated. Finally, the sixth analysis allowed the transformation of the underlying skeleton of points and lines to be compared with a veridical map. This report compares only the last three analyses (see Wood, 1973b for complete details of the other parts of the study).

The first analysis to be discussed consisted of an aggregate *content analysis* of the first two sets of maps generated of London. The maps were scrutinized for changes over time in point-line-area elements at regional and local scale. The second analysis compared the information obtained in the aggregate analysis with the content analysis of individual maps and attempted to articulate whether the two map sets were in confirmation or at odds. The third analysis investigated distortions in the overall orientation of the maps. This was a veridicality analysis in which the chief attention was on location rather than content as in the two previous analyses. Through a special technique, the *grid transformation*, we attempted to show distortions of urban form created by mistaken placement of local and regional elements and assemblages of elements.

First Analysis: Aggregate Content Analysis

In the first analysis, urban cognitive development was explored initially through an aggregate analysis of the 82 maps of London. The content of the maps was plotted on a standard cartographic map of London. To start, we delineated regionally organized content on the first map whose point–line–area elements were relatively self-contained, that is, *connected internally* (containing contiguous elements), but which were *disconnected from other clusters* or assemblages of content. These clusters, or as we shall call them, *regions*, were examined in subsequent maps for their pattern changes in the direction of making or breaking connections to other regions, since both are taken as signs of development. This analysis is concerned with the process of *forming a whole out of parts*. The approach is *hierarchic* in that the self-contained regions so isolated are *ranked* in terms of richness of detail and geographic extent. Thus, in London we found a *primary region* superordinate to two other lesser regions. (Secondary and tertiary regions were also found in Rome and seven distinct regions were isolated in Paris.) Since areas are always smaller than regions, changes in the number of areas will prove more useful in the understanding of internal *regional development* as opposed to the construction of the urban mass as a whole. A final aspect of this aggregate analysis was to compare the frequency and balance of points, lines, and areas within and across regions.

Results: regions from the first maps. Using the criteria for regional definition as stated—internal

connectivity and lack of connections to other detailed, extensive assemblages—we were able to discern three regions on the first London maps. Throughout this description the reader is referred to Figure 1, the first aggregated map of London.

A primary region was identified centering around the residence point for group L while in London, Cartwright Gardens located in the extreme northeast portion of the region. The region has two basically rectangular areas hinged at the intersection of Tottenham Court Road and Oxford Street, and two extension routes, Oxford Street and Euston Road, which may or may not connect onto two park areas, Hyde Park and Regent's Park. The latter is less certain to be a part of this region, as we shall see. To the east the boundaries of these regions are ragged, consisting of a few points floating in an area. The northern rectangular subregion is a *university* area; the southern subregion is considered a *commercial* area by the mappers. A unifying axis binding the two subregions together is the Piccadilly Underground Line, which passes through several mapped points in a roughly diagonal direction from King's Cross to Piccadilly Circus.

The secondary region is much smaller than the primary region and consists of a few landmark points hugging the line, the River Thames. It is certainly the commonly known *Westminster* region, with the prominent points being Parliament, Big Ben, Downing Street and Whitehall (which is not however mapped) to Trafalgar Square. We are going to argue that this region is qualitatively different than the primary region. The secondary region was known from two observation points: we crossed the river and viewed Westminster from the South Bank of the Thames as part of our tour of London—this accounts for the river and some landmark points; from within Westminster at Westminster Square one could look up Whitehall and see Nelson's Column in Trafalgar Square as the northernmost point in this region.

The tertiary region we may call the *City* or the *East End*. This region was visited on the afternoon of the first tour day in a separate trip originating at the residence point. In the first maps this region is a weakly imaged area with a few landmark points, most easterly the Tower, most westerly St. Paul's Cathedral.

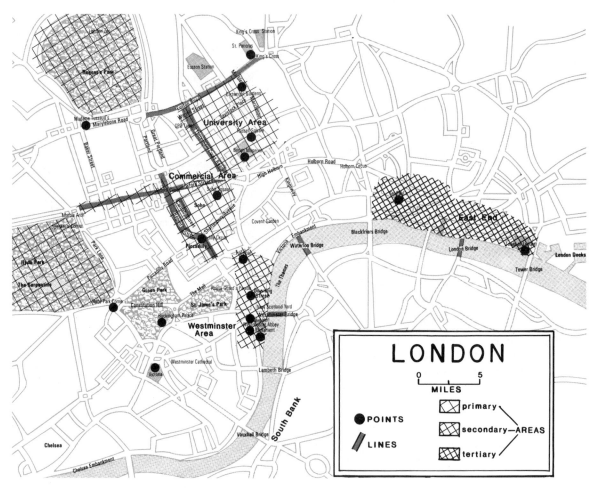

FIGURE 1
Content analysis of the first London maps (*n* = 36).

Regions from the second and third maps. Inspection of the aggregation of the second set of maps (see Figure 2) reveals considerable alteration of the morphology of the primary region by day 5. The maps contain areal redefinitions, route growth, name changes, a tendency for increasing differentiation to importance toward the southern end of the region, ultimately toward *Piccadilly* with *Soho* as a possible geographic center. For the region as a whole there is greater separation from the secondary region in that a possible connecting point (Hyde Park Corner) has

dropped out. It is important to note also that at a more local scale the home area around the dormitory has become more differentiated. In the third set of maps (see Figure 3) there are further transformations of the primary region, which show that group L's cognition of London was far from being stable at that point, the end of the sixth day of touring. Point phenomena, however, became stable in number and although continuing to increase in intensity. Route development takes place to the south and the west, while areal redefinition marks activity in the northern-

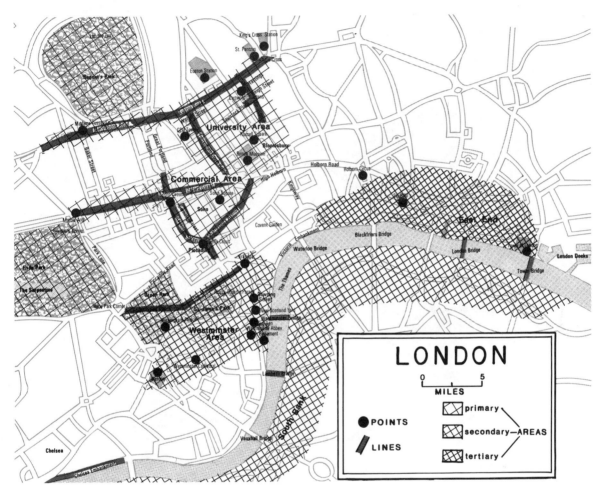

FIGURE 2
Content analysis of the second London maps (*n* = 27).

most subregion. Sophisticated linking of known parallel streets takes place, as seen in the perpendiculars that run down from Marleybone. Moreover, the primary region as a whole is close to an indirect linkage with the secondary region through Buckingham Palace, Green Park, and Trafalgar Square (the northernmost point of the secondary region). Trafalgar seems to be the hinge between the primary and secondary regions.

The secondary region remains stable and small. If St. James and Green Park are included in this region,

we can say that the region acquires its single route, The Mall, connecting Trafalgar Square, Hyde Park Corner through Buckingham Palace. In the second maps (Figure 2) and third maps (Figure 3) the South Bank grows enormously in area, but it is an ambiguous mass seen at a distance that contains no knowledge of points or lines. Its chief role is to contribute to the connecting up of the secondary and tertiary regions along the river. Additional interregional activity is taking place through the addition of bridges between them. The number of bridges increased from three in

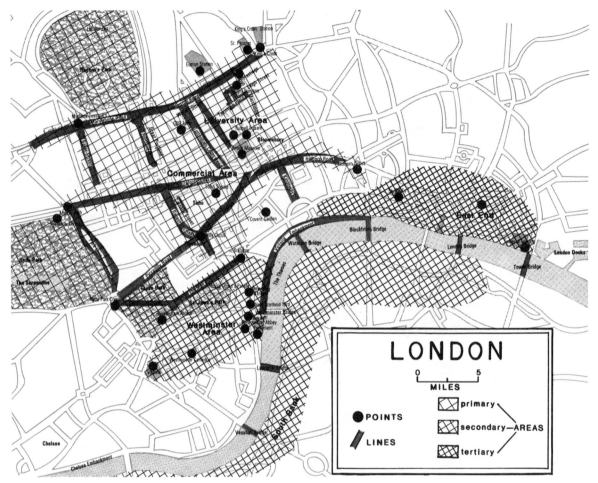

FIGURE 3
Content analysis of the third London maps (*n* = 19).

the first set of maps to four in the second set and six in the third set, all between these two regions. Thus, as a whole the secondary region is stable within itself, but connections have been made (bridging) along the river to the tertiary region. Beside the bridges we may note that the embankment, the walk and drive along the river, had been added by the third maps. In the secondary region, route growth overshadowed point and areal development. We assume that the River Thames strongly influenced this development.

Clearly, it is the river that exerts a strong force in connecting up the secondary and tertiary regions.

In the second and third maps, the tertiary region is largely areally defined with isolated points. There is more change within the region than in the secondary, but far less than in the primary. The region has two subareas in the first aggregation, and this increases to three in subsequent maps. The regions are also cognized by a greater number of mappers from first to second maps. Of course, the same conclusions that we reached with regard to connections developing between the secondary and tertiary regions also apply here. Although we cannot prove it, we intrinsically feel that the secondary region probably grows into the tertiary rather than vice versa. Unfortunately, the individual data do not shed any additional light here.

Summary of the aggregate analyses. Three regions have been isolated, each of which seems to have an individual character with respect to the relative emphasis placed on point, line, and area cognitions and their relations. The regions fall into a natural rank or hierarchy in terms of size, detail, and point–line–area balance. From the first through third maps, the regions grow toward or connect up with each other. What starts as disconnected parts appears to be growing toward a whole. How much longer would it take to grow into a stable whole? Such a question needs data collected over a longer period. We are sure that what we see is only early development for most of the mappers. Recall, however, that at least point cognitions remain stable in number after the first maps. Changes in areas are very slight, but more significant given the small number of areas relative to points. By far the most numerous changes in six days involve line cognitions.

Second Analysis: Individual Content Analysis

The second analysis compares the results of the first aggregate analysis with data drawn from 11 *individual* maps made by four mappers who had a relatively complete set for London (two to four maps each) and who numbered their maps as to the sequence in which they were composed. The objective here was to check whether the regions and their point–line–area components, as defined through the aggregate analysis, in fact exist on the individual maps, or whether it is only when maps are aggregated together that such morphology emerges, that it is only the knowledge of the whole group that is so organized. We also examined variations in detail and point–line–area balance in the individual maps and compared them with the aggregate pictures. An attempt was made to compare maps across individuals in these respects but, given the small number, the results can only be highly tentative.

Results. There is substantial evidence for the existence of the primary region in all maps (see Figure 4). For example, one student, Abrams, mapped only the primary region. Either the primary region was shown as disconnected from either the secondary or the tertiary region, or, as in five maps, the primary and secondary regions were connected by only a single route labeled with a question mark or with the route going through an impossible space. The secondary region, however, was shown as separated from the tertiary in only half the maps, and some maps showed them fused into a common region. It can be seen that the aggregate analysis, by placing all phenomena veridically, masked the possibility (it wasn't "logical") that two of our regions might be initially seen by some mappers as a unity (perhaps to develop apart?). In general, the aggregate maps showed larger and more detailed regions than any one individual can represent. The exception is Abrams, who only included the primary region, but lavished it with detail. The hard-to-make connections on the individual maps support certain conclusions reached on the aggregate maps, particularly that the primary and secondary regions divide somewhere between or at Piccadilly and Trafalgar Square. This is where the confusion is from both aggregate and individual perspectives. The primary region is, as we have said, by far the most extensive and detailed, and this is confirmed in the individual maps. Thus, the majority of our conclusions must be based on the changing morphology of the primary region. All the mappers used numbering to indicate the sequence in which they made their maps. Thus, we were able to learn that the starting point for three mappers took place within the primary region, two at the residence point, and one at the University of London (in Abrams's map, Figure 4 left, a highly academically oriented boy). The other (relatively confused) map originated at Buckingham Palace. The individual maps confirm *in toto* the northern boundary of the primary region as Euston Road-Marleybone Road and King's Cross in the northeast corner. However, the southern pole of the primary region, Piccadilly, is not always shown as connected to the rest of the region.

Moreover, we find Soho Square displaced frequently to the south of Piccadilly Circus, when it

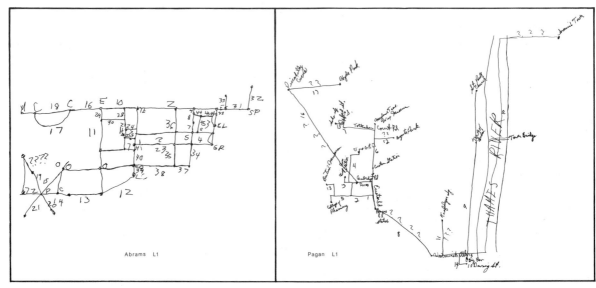

FIGURE 4
Examples of individual skeleton maps: Abrams and Pagan.

should lie north, binding Piccadilly to the University area and immediate dormitory subregion (e.g., Pagan's map, Figure 4 right) stops at Soho Square and can only connect to Piccadilly via the Underground. It may be that this unknown space truly divided the main portion of the primary region from its southern pole. The Piccadilly Underground Line was included in half the maps. If Piccadilly Circus is linked with the primary region, it is probably linked underground. Another important discovery in the individual maps is that the dorm point and immediate street network may be disconnected in the first maps (e.g., Eber) or be connected at the start (e.g., Heller) and break off (see Figure 5). The reason this did not show up in the aggregate areal analysis was that it was not labeled as an area but just left as a locationally proximate group of points and lines. This raises the question that the dorm area may be a genuine region itself but was not always labeled as such. To the northwest of the primary region we had been ambivalent about whether to include Regent's Park. The individual maps appear to favor the conclusion that Regent's Park is not part of the primary region. Eber's maps in particular show it as disconnected from anything else and

differentiate it well internally, showing its extent as far as Camden Town. The aggregate analysis suggested that high-level cognitive development was taking place through the addition of north-south running streets connecting Marleybone, Oxford Street, and Piccadilly. These do not however show up on any of the individual maps examined. They may only be a product of the aggregate maps and therefore a fiction, beyond the reach of any individual mapper. Finally, route growth is the most common type of development in the primary region. This conclusion is based on both aggregate and individual maps. Crossroads, especially Euston-Tottenham Court Road and Tottenham Court Road-Oxford Street, play a role in this region but do not in any other.

Summary of the individual map analysis. This analysis has raised serious doubts about the definition of the individual regions and the relations between regions. The primary region does not look as "together" as it does in the aggregate analysis. The

FIGURE 5 *(right)*
Examples of individual skeleton maps: Heller and Eber L1, L2.

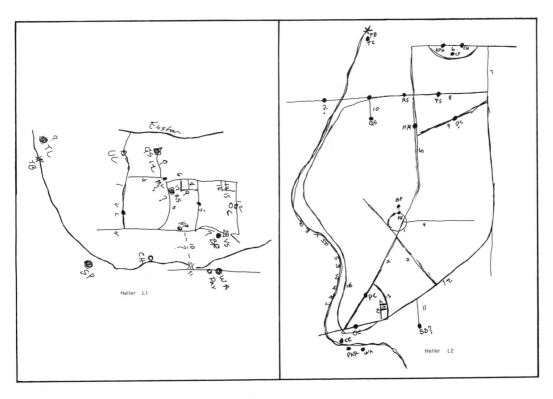

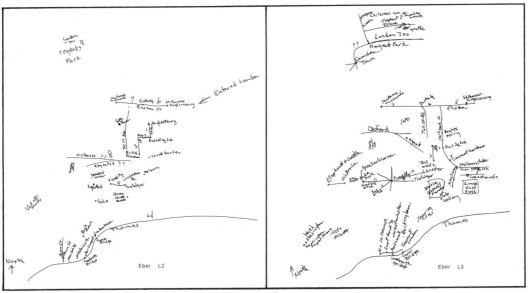

real core of this region is the dorm area and the university area. The best mappers included Piccadilly, but excluded Regent's Park from the primary region. The status of Hyde Park remains ambiguous. At global scale, we are vexed to find instances where the secondary and tertiary regions are located in a common region. Just how frequently this occurs remains to be confirmed in an examination of all the individual maps for London. However, certain conclusions reached by the aggregate analysis have been confirmed in the individual analysis.

Third Analysis: Veridicality Analysis

The third analysis proceeded from a desire to understand the role of locational distortions as found in the individual maps. The aggregate analysis sweeps over this problem, masking distortion by making the data veridical. In this analysis we were able to draw on previous research for techniques to project and measure locational distortions in sketch maps (see Beck, et al., 1973). Basically, the procedure is to transform each individual map onto a regular geometric grid consisting of east–west, horizontal-running "latitude" lines and north–south, vertically running "longitude" lines. Displacements of points and lines from their true positions show up in a wavy grid transformation in which the lines bend to pass through all the points that would be on that line on a standard map. What emerges from the data is an understanding of the way in which the mapper uses scale in his or her mapping strategy and discoveries of systematic distortions in local, regional, and global areas of the city as related to urban entities such as rivers, streets, and districts. Grid transformations also help us isolate the ambiguous interregional spaces and the unknown spaces at or near the borders of the city as mapped.

Results: grid transformation analysis. The grid transformations generally reveal severe distortions in the latitude of the River Thames. The river itself may be drawn in a remarkable number of shapes and lengths. The transformation may appear pinched where longitudinal lines *converge* (e.g., Eber, Figure 6 upper) because Westminster and the Tower of Lon-

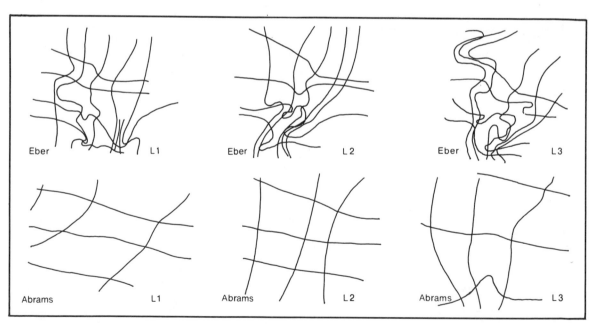

FIGURE 6
Examples of individual grid transformations: Eber and Abrams L1, L2, L3 (read left to right).

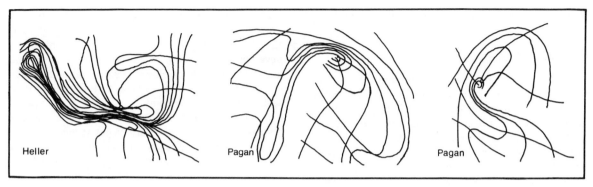

FIGURE 7
Examples of individual grid transformations: Heller (L1) and Pagan (L1, L3).

don have been brought too close together. Or the transformation may show curves that turn back on themselves where the Tower has been placed west of Westminster (e.g., Heller, Figure 7 left). There are also characteristic distortions out toward the *periphery* of the map where grid lines (both horizontal and vertical) *diverge*, especially in the northwest where, as we know, the ambiguity of Regent's Park must be a factor.

Using a larger set of transformations, Wood (1973b) concluded that there is also scale expansion in the university and dorm areas. We have seen that the Thames was was the most significant latitudinal problem, whereas the Piccadilly–Westminster connection proved to be the most significant longitudinal problem. Here Pagan's map is a perfect example (Figure 7 center and right). Her whole primary region has been rotated 180°, with Piccadilly northeast and King's Cross southwest. It has been rotated as an integral unit, which causes severe curvature in the vertical plane of the map. The curves enclose a self-contained unit, which is the primary region. Here is dramatic proof of the boundaries of the primary region and the location of the *disorientation point* at which one region turns into another. Wood (1973b) refers to these effects as "p-cliffs"—perceptual cliffs that mark the boundaries of regions. Lynch (1960) also talks of a fragmented edge where screens are present to block vistas, or where one point may be seen from a number of perspectives. Certainly, Piccadilly is screened from both Soho and Trafalgar Square and can be seen

from a number of perspectives. This evidence pulls us again to the conclusion that Piccadilly is itself a region lying between the university area (containing the dorm area and Bloomsbury) and Westminster. In getting from the university region to Westminster, you must cross two ambiguous regions, Soho and Piccadilly. Thus, there is probably a region between the primary and secondary regions that the aggregate analysis has masked.

Two mappers made gross distortions of placement of local subregions on their maps. However, the regions themselves were correct enough. These mappers seem to have had difficulty in maintaining an overall compass. In fact, their cognition of north, south, east, and west rotates several times during the making of the map; they may well have even worked on the map upside down and sideways. This method of working reveals the *points of choice* at which the map was rotated. The rotation points may be the disjoints between regions. This seems to us a very egocentric way of mapping with respect to compass bearing. Heller's maps suffer from centering London and beginning his map with Buckingham Palace, which is placed in a park, screened by trees, and is a difficult place to find or find your way out of. Heller's maps are also unusual in placing Westminster on the South Bank across from Piccadilly Circus. This may be due to the fact that the tour crossed the river to view Westminster. We have already argued that Westminster was a "perceptual" region, encompassed by the horizon. The displacement of Westminster to the South Bank shows the dangers inherent to the tourist with an egocentric compass.

Summary and Conclusions

Three analyses of a series of experimentally generated maps of London have revealed considerable morphological transformations over time. The transformations reveal a largely shifting pattern of change, sometimes progressive, sometimes degenerative. Different map elements appear, disappear, flare up in intensity (higher percentage of mappers include an element), and die down. Or there may simply be a redefinition (renaming) of the same structure. Some elements like point assemblages remain stable in number if not intensity. Thus, the picture is one of a multidimensional system in which there are some components in steady state, some evolving, and some degenerating all at the same time. We claim that this is simultaneously a picture of the cognitive machinery and a picture of the geographic world of London. We cannot, however, yet determine to what extent environmental A has conventionalized and perhaps simplified the city and introduced some artifacts. Nevertheless in the middle of all this change there seems to be a general growth of the system, for there is an increasing amount of *detail* (*differentiation*) on the maps. The basic subsystems, which we have analyzed as regions, have tended to *integrate*. We also found that the regions tended to form a *hierarchy* of importance in extent and richness of detail. Such findings certainly are anticipated in the organismic-developmental theory of Werner and Kaplan (1963) and more recently of Moore (1975a), who has related and refined some of these ideas to the study of large-scale environmental cognition.

Our results indicate that separate individual and aggregate analyses are necessary to get at the distortions introduced by any aggregate analysis of cognitive mapping. We have found for example, individual mappers who have more areal differentiation than the aggregate maps, and some who have less.

Moreover, we believe it is essential to also undertake a separate veridicality analysis on individual maps, and have found that the grid transformation technique very clearly reveals the compass-directional, spatial distortions that are pulling at the significance system, that is, the content. In this way an analysis of overall orientation complements the analysis of knowledge of individual and grouped places, routes, and areas.

NOTE

1. This chapter is based on analyses carried out in conjunction with the second author's Ph.D. dissertation (Wood, 1973b) submitted to the Graduate School of Geography, Clark University.

15

Herbert L. Pick, Jr.
Institute of Child Development
University of Minnesota

TRANSACTIONAL-CONSTRUCTIVIST APPROACH TO ENVIRONMENTAL KNOWING: A COMMENTARY[1]

Moore has brought together in a promising marriage the transactional and constructivist approaches to the acquisition of knowledge. He has related this union specifically to environmental knowing. Let us examine the two partners in this bond and see what sort of prognosis we might make. One must applaud the effort to bring in the transactional partner since the interaction approach even in its most complex elaboration often seems simplistic. Yet as Moore himself points out, the difficult job will be to make precise the nature of transactions between people and their environments and how these transactions enter into environmental knowing. It would appear that there are two jobs. One is to specify transactions and, at one level, that would appear to be relatively easy. However, the second job is to ensure that at the level specified, the transactions are *meaningful* units to form the basis of environmental knowing. That will be the harder job.

At first blush I would think that the spatial component of environmental knowing would be a poor place to demonstrate the utility of transactions. The argument here is that spatial knowledge is concerned primarily with mobility from one part of the environment to another, and the locations in an environment are more or less equivalent insofar as they represent foci for mobility. Individuals, furthermore, are more or less equivalent insofar as they move from location to location. Therefore, their transactions might be pretty much the same. The conclusion would be that, based on transactions over a period of time, our spatial knowing of the total socio-physical environment, for example, would be pretty much the same as everyone else's and in fact would be quite veridical. In contrast, other aspects of our environmental knowing, the sociophysical, for example, might be more susceptible to the nature of our transactions.

However, on further consideration it is not so clear that this view is correct. Even spatial knowledge may be susceptible to variation dependent on the kinds of transactions we have. The size of a space may seem larger if we engage in expansive activities in it. The distance up a mountain may be perceived as infinitely greater by the young child as compared with the mountaineer. Yet such perception–conception of distance must certainly be modulated by the more direct aspects of one's perception. For example, even for a child the distance up a mountain can be apprehended at a glance from afar, while the same distance over land cannot often be apprehended all at once.

What is probably even more fundamental than the spatial knowledge, however, is the actual process of knowing, or the acquisition of knowledge. The possibility that this depends on transactions is quite exciting. As will become evident in the consideration of reference systems below, the very way we register spatial information may depend on the extent and nature of our transaction with the environment.

The developmental approach as advocated by all three papers in this section may be a particularly sensitive method for demonstrating that transactions do indeed make a difference in our environmental knowing. It may (or may not) be true that the final spatial knowledge of an environment is pretty much the same for mature people who are very familiar with it. However, examination of the spatial knowledge over time, either during ontogenesis or microgenesis, may show the effects of different types of transactions that would not be apparent in the final spatial knowledge. This approach is essentially what Beck and Wood took in getting their teen-agers' maps of London. They found clear developmental trends and some individual differences. Unfortunately, they did not specifically report the kinds of transactions their subjects were having with the environment. The particular developmental trends—increased differentiation within an area, areal redefinition, and increasing interconnection of different regions—may be the result of increased familiarity in almost any form. Nevertheless, the positive results, these developmental changes, suggest the technique is a promising one for studying the effects of transaction in the *development* of spatial knowledge.

The second partner in this union, the constructivist approach, has been courted rather widely by cognitive psychologists. Of course, in perception the classical empiricist approaches of Berkeley, Helmholtz, and more recently Brunswik were constructivistic. They had the observer construct his percepts from the elements of current sensations and associated ideas and images from previous experience. Recently this type of constructivist approach has come under attack from two directions. The first is the recent neurophysiological evidence on property detectors, which I interpret differently from Moore. He regards the evidence of edge detectors, angle detectors, and so on, as support for the constructivist approach. I

rather regard this evidence, if pushed and elaborated to the extreme, as tending to break down constructivism. The suggestion here is that there are specific detectors for almost any aspect of our perceptual experience. That is, perception is made equivalent to sensation, not made up of sensations. The second attack on the classical constructivist position in perception comes from Gibson (1966), who has been arguing for *direct* perception. He suggests the patterns of energy at the receptor surfaces contain information sufficient to specify all our perceptual experience without having to enrich sensations on the basis of past experience. He, in a sense, is arguing that sensation is equivalent to perception.

While the classical constructivist position has been under question in perception, it has come into its own in more traditional cognitive areas. Neisser (1967) was probably the most systematic proponent of this view. More recently the work of Bransford, Barclay, and Franks (1972), Posner (1969), and Rosch (1973) represent dramatic examples of constructivism in cognition. All these investigators have reported work that has a very interesting constructivist property. Subjects are exposed under a variety of tasks to *variations* of a central concept or prototype but not to the prototype itself. However, when subsequently given a recognition, identification, or memory task, they choose the prototype (with which they have never had experience) as much as or more often than and often with more confidence than the variations that they have experienced. An obvious interpretation is that they have generated or constructed the prototype or central concept.

Some colleagues and I (Kosslyn, Pick, and Fariello, 1974; Mohr, Kuczaj, and Pick, 1975) have demonstrated a similar kind of construction with respect to spatial knowledge. In essence, what we did was to teach children to go from a home base X to each of several locations A, B, C, ... They had considerable experience going from X to A, X to B, X to C, and so on, but never from A to B to C. Nevertheless, when tested they were able to generate the spatial relations among A, B, and C with which they had had no direct experience. In one study the space was a locomotive one, that is, one that the children moved around in. In another study the space was a proprioceptive one, that is, one in which the children reached to the different locations. We found that in both tasks children as young as three years old do demonstrate this generative capacity. When does it develop? An intriguing observation was made by Frankel (1972) in a case study of the development of hand-eye coordination in an infant. At two months of age the infant had developed the capacity to get his thumb into his mouth from any position as long as it touched its face. The infant did this by moving both hands toward the mouth and rolling the head so as to bring the mouth toward the thumb. One way to interpret this observation is to say that from a finite set of experiences the infant had generated a spatial mapping of hand–head movements into positions on the face. If such mapping occurs by two months of age, one must begin to believe in Kantian spatial intuitions.

What then does develop with age? Infants, of course, cannot perform the X to A, B, C constructive problem mentioned above. This is at least partially due to lack of motor capacity. However, if the present interpretation of Frankel's observation is correct, they can do something like the X to A, B, C problem at least in coordinating hand movements with skin stimulation. Later, fairly soon perhaps, they can do that sort of generative problem in a reaching space, then in a locomotive space. All these spaces are ones that are perceptually apprehendable in a single act. The problem becomes rather more complex when the spatial relations to be generated involve parts of spaces that cannot be apprehended at once. Then the problem involves integrating spatial information, constructing or generating or inducing spatial relations that are not directly given, storing these in some form of representation, and integrating these stored representations. This is the difficulty in early years faced by the children, studied by Piaget et al. (1960) and cited by Moore, in constructing models of their large-scale environment and the complexity indicated in the work of Beck and Wood, which shows teenagers first integrating spatial relations within a region and then joining the regions.

Thus, what is proposed here is the possibility that even infants and young children have the ability to be generative and constructive in their spatial knowledge in the sense that they can induce spatial relations which are not directly given them but which are implicit in their experience. It is proposed that what

develops is the application of this generative or constructive capacity to larger and larger scale space, eventually to spaces that cannot be apprehended as perceptual wholes, and even to spaces that are not perceived at all but simply conceptualized.

What might account for the application of this capacity to larger-scale spaces? Presumably, Moore's transactions would enter in here, but what is the mechanism by which the development would work? I think it is here where the concept of reference system is most useful. Spatial information must be registered in relation to some particular reference system if it is going to have any meaning. Abstractly, for specifying any given location in two-dimensional space, three values must be known. For example, a position is completely determined if its distance from three landmarks is known. Or a location is completely determined if its distance and direction from one landmark is known. However, direction must be specified in terms of an angle from a direction line and a direction of rotation. Of course, these requirements for a completely determinant reference system might not be met in actual practice or even needed by people in certain sorts of tasks. Young children may operate perfectly well if they can keep in perceptual contact with their parent and simply change the distance from near to far at will. Or in the case of Acredolo's first experiment, a single object in a room may serve as a reference system, and spatial position might simply be encoded in terms of proximity to that object. Her preschool children seemed to use such a reference system more than her 10-year-olds. Acredolo's 10-year-olds respond more in terms of a container reference system but, as Acredolo points out, a container reference system is also specified in terms of particular objects—features of the walls of the room. However, all reference systems are ultimately defined in terms of objects. The geographic coordinate system is specified by the poles, and Greenwich and a celestial coordinate system by stars.

What is true is that reference systems with development may become more and more remote from the sensitive organism. For example, a very proximal reference system would be a body or egocentric reference system such as that used by Frankel's infant determining the position of his thumb. Then there might be an object reference system and a container reference system. Then there might be a municipal reference system specified in terms of prominent landmarks like a river, lakes, hills, and so on, or a street grid system. Then one gets to more remote geographic reference systems like the geographical or celestial. These do not differ in their abstractness so much as they differ in the extent to which they are prominent in the sensient, perceptive world of the person. The parts of one's own body are very perceptually salient, then the parts of one's immediate space or room, then the neighborhood, city, and so on. When one gets to geographic reference systems, the various parts of the reference system are not simultaneously apprehendable; hence, the reference systems, like the cognitive spatial representations referred to earlier, must be kept in mind and mentally manipulated. It is likely that it is in this mortal capacity that important aspects of the development of spatial environmental knowing will go on.

A second likely seat of important development is in the simultaneous use of two or more reference systems. Reference systems obviously differ in their relative efficiency for different tasks. It is ordinarily inefficient to specify the position of a chair in a room in terms of celestial or geographic coordinates. One is interested in the relation of a chair to the other objects of the room, and it is most efficient to specify its position directly in relation to them. On the other hand, it is usually unhelpful to specify the position of a buoy solely in terms of the left or right side of one's body if one is trying to navigate a ship. What is useful is to be able to go back and forth between different reference systems and/or to apprehend simultaneously spatial relations with respect to different reference systems. It is in this ability where important developmental changes may be found. A recent suggestive observation along these lines has been made in some work I have been conducting with Jeffrey Lockman and Nancy Hazen. We have been teaching children to find their way through a configuration of small rooms. After they have learned to find their way, they are asked to construct a model of the "house." In constructing the model, many of the children can get the order of rooms in their route cor-

rect or they can get the overall configuration correct but not both simultaneously. The route seems to be dependent on an egocentric reference system (turn left, right, go straight, etc.), while the configuration seems more dependent on more remote frames of reference. It is the simultaneous coordination of these different reference systems that may cause trouble.

The final point I would like to make in commenting on the papers of Moore, Beck and Wood, and Acredolo concerns the relation between reference systems and cognitive representations. Reference systems are used and relevant in the actual perception of spatial relations and spatial layout. We see where things are in relation to other objects and the shell of the room (Acredolo). But reference systems are also relevant to our cognitive spatial representations. We move our eyes around the front of our house when mentally counting the number of windows, employing an egocentric reference system. We can specify the location of a store to a stranger in our town in terms of a landmark and street coordinate system, or in terms of a geographic reference system, or a combination of both. Thus reference systems seem to be part of our cognitive spatial representations as well as being the organizing foci for our perception.

In summary, I would like to say that the transactional–constructivist part of Moore's approach can be accepted without committing oneself to his particular developmental scheme. I would like to suggest that both cognitive spatial representations and reference systems may develop by incorporation and integration of more and more remote features but do not involve any qualitatively different functions. Qualitative changes may occur in the development of spatial knowing in the degree to which children of different ages coordinate different reference systems in their cognitive representations.

NOTE

1. The research reported in this paper was supported by Program Project Grant 5-801-HD-05027 from the National Institute of Child Health and Human Development to the University of Minnesota and by the Center for Research in Human Learning of the University of Minnesota.

PART **II**

PERSPECTIVES AND CASE STUDIES

EDITORS' INTRODUCTION

Our disagreements with one another as to conclusions are trivial in comparison with our disagreements as to problems; to see the problem another sees, in the same perspective, and at the same angle—that amounts to something.

John Dewey, 1919

Part II focuses on three new and exciting perspectives on environmental knowing. Although there are no hard and fast distinctions between "theories" and "perspectives," there are some relative emphases. Unlike the theoretical approaches in Part I, these perspectives are not cast as rigorously as hypothetico-deductive systems, nor perhaps, as implied in two of the chapters, should they ever be. As is evident in Part I, theories are often more deductively derived (e.g., Chapters 6 and 12, in which theoretical notions are deduced in large part from extant psychological theories), whereas the present perspectives tend to be more inductive and based in large part on abstractions from a variety of conceptual notions *and* real-world observations. This means also that the standard scientific approach to theory building and verification through empirical studies is not as strictly applicable to the evaluation of these different perspectives.

As Wohlwill and Kohn (1975) mentioned in a recent talk, research perspectives, and perhaps even explanatory theories, are not a matter of right or wrong, but a matter of which leads to more interesting questions, more interesting research, which leads to more useful results for application, and which pragmatically is most useful for interpreting data. Thus, the present perspectives illustrate different points of view, draw on a variety of concepts and theoretical notions, emphasize widely different analytic methods, and provide an extraordinarily rich set of concepts to complement the theories of Part I.

Whereas the earlier theories tend to focus on the physical environment, these perspectives are aimed at knowledge, images, and the meaning of the total sociophysical environment. Although both theory and perspective may be looked upon as orienting devices—as heuristics that suggest specific questions and lines of investigation—a theory is also an explanatory system to account for the *whys* of data; the principal function of these perspectives is as a way of looking, a way of orienting us to relevant questions about environmental knowing that we might otherwise overlook. Different disciplines have different ways of conceptualizing the environment and of conceptualizing "environmental knowing"; the ultimate question is what more do we know, or can we know, by looking at environment–behavior relations through these different perspectives, and can we understand each other's perspectives so well that our research and practice can be informed by their summation?

Three perspectives are presented here, drawn from notions, respectively, in sociology, anthropology, and literature. In Chapter 16, Elihu and Sue Gerson, both sociologists, point out the tremendous potential of using sociological frameworks to examine environmental knowing. Their focus is on the order which people give to the world—a perceived, remembered, and expected order about objects, events, and human nature. They see this focus on place perspectives as an aid to better understanding of the interaction of people and places. In contrast to some other positions advanced in this book, they take the position that the place perspectives held by individuals are not individual phenomena, but are the product, as they say, of "interaction among individuals, and thus are simultaneously part of, and set over against, the individual who maintains them." They also take the position, again in contrast to some, that environmental experience is in part a function of the place perspectives held with respect to a place and to other places with which that place is implicitly compared and contrasted. The Gersons then explore in considerable depth four social contexts of place perspectives—the temporal, monetary, sentimental, and ideological order of places. Their position paper is illustrated by a case study of social worlds and "status passages" in Hyderabad, India, by the social geographers James and Nancy Duncan.

We must point out at this stage that there are now a number of other excellent and useful empirical studies in the area of social groups' conceptions and images about environment, and of the influence of socio-ethnic variables on environmental knowing that have been conducted by sociologists themselves or are otherwise strongly influenced by specific sociological concepts or the general sociological orientation (e.g., Firey, 1945; Strauss, 1961, 1968, 1970; Fried and Gleicher, 1961; Rainwater, 1966; Gans, 1962; Young and Willmott, 1962; Buttimer, 1969, 1972; Michelson, 1970; Orleans, 1973; Francescato and Mebane, 1973; and an excellent conceptual and methodologi-

cal critique by Reiser, 1972). For example, in an early landmark paper, Firey (1945) explored the role of city sentiment and symbolism in individual location decisions and in urban planning. This was one of the very first papers to look at the subjective individual and group determinants of social behavior; it contrasted sharply with the strictly economic and "ecological" analyses of that (and we could say the present) time. Firey showed how the symbolic character of Boston's Beacon Hill, the stately and sacred ground of Boston's literary legend, and how the acute awareness and importance of this symbolism in the minds of people living on the hill, served to affect the continuing political decision making and urban planning of that area. The inclusion of the chapters by the Gersons and the Duncans in this volume is a further indication of the tremendous amount of cross-disciplinary fertilization that has appeared when people concern themselves with describing and understanding the social basis of environmental knowing and the characterization of places.

Section 6 emphasizes the importance of cross-cultural perspectives in environmental cognition research and theorizing. The author of the position paper, Amos Rapoport, has written extensively about cultural factors in architecture and planning, and his work is widely read in a range of other disciplines. The volume of evidence that Rapoport presents concerning the value of looking for cross-cultural and subcultural similarities and differences in the meaning ascribed to environment, in subjective definitions of areas and distance, and in orientation and cognitive mapping is overwhelming. Chapter 20, a case study by Harold Conklin, one of the important forerunners of cognitive anthropology, focuses specifically on careful and insightful ethnosemantic analyses of conceptions of landforms as evidenced through structural linguistic methods. He also shows new and important uses of aerial photography and aerial photogrammetry in conjunction and in comparison with traditional and ethnosemantic fieldwork. Chapter 21, a case study by the Duncans related to their Chapter 17, emphasizes the importance of the cross-cultural approach by showing similarities between two rather disparate cultural groups, the old elite of Hyderabad and the working- and middle-class of Boston's old

West End. Although Rapoport emphasizes that both cross-cultural *differences* and *similarities* exist in the awareness and meaning of environmental phenomena, he and Conklin concentrate more on highlighting cross-cultural *differences*; the Duncans concentrate more on showing *similarities* between two groups that one would not normally think of comparing. Adopting this perspective, therefore, allows a true synthesis of knowledge to take place in that considerable additional information and insight are generated by using both aspects of this cross-cultural perspective.

In addition to the two case studies presented here, and in addition to the many referenced in Chapter 19, a number of other cross-cultural studies specifically on aspects of environmental knowing have appeared recently (see, especially, Hallowell, 1955, on space; Spoehr, 1956, on natural resources; Whorf, 1956a, on linguistics; Haugen, 1969, on Icelandic orientation; Blaut, 1953, 1959, and Blaut, Blaut, Harman, and Moerman, 1959 on tropical farming and soil conservation in Singapore and Jamaica; Haddon, 1960, and Saarinen, 1973, on views of foreign lands; Lynch, 1960, Appendix A, on orientation; Segal, Campbell, and Herskovits, 1966, on house and landforms; Dasen, 1972a, 1972b, on space and ecology; Halcomb, 1972, on urban environments; and Stea and Blaut, 1973a, on cognitive mapping).

In a lecture at Clark University in 1970, the cultural geographer James Blaut (Blaut unfortunately is not directly represented in this volume, but see Chapter 9) remarked that, so far in the development of the field of environment–behavior relations, the implicit model followed is that behavior is a function of the person and the setting; thus, the usual way to introduce individual differences is through personality differences between individuals. Contrasted with this are, of course, the cross-cultural and subcultural social group approaches. One context, as Blaut saw it, for anthropological approaches to environment and behavior is to look for or conduct cross-cultural studies that challenge and test the often assumed universal laws of psychology. One of the most important lines of investigation, he argued, as does Rapoport here and as it seems that Conklin also implicitly does, is the embeddedness of cognitive categories in linguistic categories.

In conducting cross-cultural or social group research, there is often an important and difficult trade-off to be considered between the degree of methodological elegance lost and the degree of cultural validity gained. Specific problems include learning the language, values, and important cognitive categories and meanings of other cultures or ethnic–racial groups, phrasing questions in other linguistic categories, interpreting data (in our investigator eyes or their eyes?), and statistical elegance and control. The harder behavioral sciences often criticize the softer for methodological wishy-washiness, whereas the more holistic social sciences often criticize the more atomistic for intellectual myopia. The resolution, hard to come by, may lie in the avenue of successive or cyclic approximations to methodological elegance based on a strongly felt, and strongly experienced, intuited, and observed data base.

The third perspective emphasizes the wealth of information and insights about environmental knowing and experience to be gained from the analysis of literature and phenomenological experience. Yi-Fu Tuan's work is widely known across a range of scientific and humanities disciplines (see especially Tuan, 1968, 1973, 1974). His concern for some time has been to describe and understand human beings' "love for land"; in Chapter 23, he focuses on the sense of environment contained within a range of phenomenological and creative literature—from abstract philosophies to concrete descriptions of particular places and events. He takes the position that literature depicts human experience, and that that experience and its manifestation in literature are a way of knowing, different from the "scientific," but equally valid. Literature, he says, does not aspire to analytic truth; it makes no effort to separate experience from its environmental context, nor makes any special distinction between social and physical environments. He also takes the position that literature is simultaneously a source of evidence for the articulation of experience and images and a creative force in shaping our images. Tuan raises, therefore, the important question of representativeness: to what degree does good creative literature mirror the common person's reality?

The significance of drawing on different viewpoints for examining literary evidence is exemplified in Chapters 24 and 25, two case studies that support the arguments raised in the position paper. Myongsup Shin takes a particular region, the southwestern United States, and illustrates the different points of view expressed in three American novels about a traveler through the region, a native American living in the area, and two French priests who volunteer for extended missionary service there. Whereas Shin reports in detail on a reasonably large region of natural environment, W. J. Lloyd concentrates more on the built environment of the city as expressed in historical novels of Boston at the turn of the century. His paper emphasizes the values and cautions that must be exercised in applying historical analysis to literary works, and shows, contrary to some popular belief, that built environments can be equally as rich and equally as thought provoking as natural environments. Like Tuan, each author points to the importance of an empathic understanding of the literature being analyzed in order to extract from it the greatest amount of comprehension of the "worlds inside peoples' heads." In his commentary, David Seamon raises the question of whether environmental cognition and perception exhaust and accurately reflect the real stuff of human life and experience in a geographical world, and argues in favor of a phenomenological approach, both to literature and to personal experience, in order to illuminate the basic structures of environmental knowing and experience.

Part II of the book is concluded by David Lowenthal, who comments on the nutritive value of the chapters herein.

Our emphasis on the interdisciplinary nature of research on environmental knowing is strongly illustrated in this part of the book. For example, the position paper on the sociological perspective is supported by a case study by two social geographers who interpret their data in terms of concepts suggested in the lead-in paper. The cross-cultural position paper, written by an anthropologist–architect, is illustrated by two studies, one by a leading cognitive anthropologist and one by a pair of geographers. Finally, the section on the literary-phenomenological perspective, although contributed entirely by geographers,

is clear evidence of the strong literary and humanities background of each.

Unfortunately, restrictions of length prevented us from incorporating a number of equally valid and important perspectives. Considerable work has been done from historical perspectives (e.g., Wright, 1947; Kirk, 1951; Spencer and Horvath, 1963; Lowenthal and Prince, 1964, 1965; Lowenthal, 1968; Prince, 1971; Bowden, 1969, 1971, 1973, 1975, in preparation; Bowden and Lowenthal, 1975; Heathcote, 1969; Allen, 1971, 1972; Jackson, 1972; Koroscil, 1973), and a great volume of work has poured out from those employing perspectives derived from the fields of planning and design (e.g., Lynch, 1960; Lynch and Rivkin, 1959; Appleyard, Lynch, and Myer, 1964; Appleyard, 1969a, 1969b, 1970a; de Jonge, 1962; Gulick, 1963; Klein, 1967; Steinitz, 1968; Carr, 1965; Carr and Schissler, 1969; Jones, 1972; Litton, 1972; Barnett, 1974; see Downs and Stea, 1973b, pp. 84–85). Much as we would have liked to have included a sample of these perspectives and new research, and a sample of work applying findings from environmental cognition to environmental design, planning, and management, we found it to be impossible (but see Moore, 1975b). We would urge, therefore, that readers be well aware of the range of other perspectives and complement their reading of this part by extensive readings in these other disciplinary areas.

We feel that the potential contribution of the perspectives presented and alluded to in this part of the book is extremely large and important. As we have said, each perspective is both an orienting device and a heuristic for suggesting new ways of looking at a phenomena and new lines of investigation. For each, one could misunderstand the import by concluding simply that one can study the same questions as before, but in a slightly different way (across groups, across cultures, in literature), or, on the contrary, one could interpret these chapters as a call for asking entirely new questions in entirely new ways—questions and ways that imply a radical shift of emphasis and, perhaps not ironically at all, a new way of looking at and conceptualizing experience and behavior in the world.

SOCIOLOGICAL PERSPECTIVE

16

THE SOCIAL FRAMEWORK OF PLACE PERSPECTIVES[1]

Elihu M. Gerson

Langley Porter Neuropsychiatric Institute
  University of California, San Francisco

M. Sue Gerson

Institute for Urban and Regional Development
  University of California, Berkeley

The term "environmental cognition" (or its brother, "environmental perception") is one simultaneously too broad and too narrow for the sociologist. "Environment" in sociology is a notoriously vague term. As often as not, the term is used to refer to the "social environment" in which people conduct themselves, thereby ignoring the physical arrangements that people make. Often sociologists interested in environment in a larger sense have used "ecosystem" to refer to the broad physical and biological environment of human organization (see Hawley, 1950; O. D. Duncan, 1964), a distinction discussed at length by Alihan (1938). Even in this usage, however, the term has indicated, for the most part, a residual category containing all the variables upon which the analyst is not directly focused. The literature on the subject of environmental cognition, however, if it is clear on nothing else, is clear on the meaning of "environment": the term means *places* and the characteristics of places.

"Cognition," on the other hand, is a term that implicitly separates thinking from other kinds of behavior, and this is a distinction many sociologists are hesitant to make.[2] Since the distinction in any case is not well adhered to by students of environmental cognition working in geographical, psychological, or architectural and city planning traditions of research, we shall not hesitate to substitute the more amenable *perspective*:

An ordered view of one's world—what is taken for granted about the attributes of various objects, events, and human nature. It is an order of things remembered and expected as well as things actually perceived, an organized conception of what is plausible and what is possible; it constitutes the matrix through which one perceives his environment. (Shibutani, 1955, p. 564).

Our paper, therefore, is about *place perspectives.*

The point of studying place perspectives is that we want to understand in greater detail the manner in which places and people interact with one another. From the viewpoint of the sociologist, however, the usual sharp distinction between place and people is easily blurred; for the people at a place are important in giving that place the characteristics it exhibits, and each of these people maintains a perspective upon the place that shapes his conduct toward it. In addition, we are faced with the complicating problem of those who are not at a given place, or who are at it irregularly, but who still maintain some perspective on the place—one which naturally shapes their conduct vis-à-vis the place. And yet, by organizing people's conduct, these perspectives shape the place itself, for in the light of these perspectives a place will attract and repel visitors, residents, government agents, businessmen, artists, pilgrims, and even social scientists, each of whom will act in turn with the others to construct the nature of the place.

This dialectical relationship between people and places may easily seem to confuse an already difficult subject, for many students have relied heavily on a sharp distinction between the "real environment" and the "perceived environment" (see e.g., Brookfield, 1969). For those who have adequate leisure to embrace it, of course, a Kantian perspective on human affairs has always proved of great comfort. Nevertheless, recent events such as the planned destruction of Pruitt-Igoe, one of the first large public housing projects in the United States, suggests that something more than congeniality is needed in the conceptual apparatus we use to define our intellectual and social problems.[3]

One other problem in traditional approaches to the study of environmental cognition must be recast before the work of the sociologist can begin. The perspectives held by individuals are not individual phenomena, as has been commonly assumed; rather, they are the product of interaction among individuals, and thus are simultaneously part of, and set over against, the individuals who maintain them. In one sense, this is merely to restate the dialectical nature of the relationship between people and places; but it is also to emphasize that the relationship is a *social* one on both sides: both places and people are product and producer of "communication and mutual adjustment of behavior."

This approach leads in a fairly direct manner to a series of concrete questions about the way in which people and places interact. There are many possible questions of this sort, and we shall focus upon only some fairly narrow points here. The problem of "the stranger," for example, has been a topic of scholarly concern for many years. The stranger and the place to which he comes are problematic for one another because they are simultaneously both involved and uninvolved with one another; although they have no long-term commitments to one another, their mutual

presence makes it necessary to deal with one another in some fashion. Yet, because of the strangeness between them, they do not know how to deal with one another; their mutual perspectives are inadequate to support reliable interaction (Simmel, 1971a).

Our concern, then, is with the ability of the people at a place to reconstruct the perspectives maintained by others there. The problem of the stranger is, of course, but one extreme situation in a continuum of possibilities whose other end is represented by the long-term native who knows in intimate detail the point of view of almost everyone else. Between these two extremes lies a complex of possibilities.

A person's experience with a place (and, conversely, the experience of others at the place with him) is at least in part a function of his commitments (ideological, temporal, monetary, and sentimental) both to the given place and to other places with which it is implicitly or explicitly compared and contrasted. But this is only part of the story, for any place has characteristics that are essentially independent of the commitments any single individual brings to it. To understand place perspectives as social phenomena, therefore, it is necessary to grasp the characteristics of the place perceived as a series of *contexts* in which perception takes place.

SOCIAL CONTEXTS OF PLACE PERSPECTIVES

For the sociologist, the primary interest in place perspectives lies in the kinds of social order maintained at a place, the tacit assumptions that people make about what happens there (and what happens when these assumptions are violated), and the working arrangements that people have for creating and maintaining viable situations in which they can comfortably conduct themselves (and what happens when this is not possible). This approach implies an enormous range of analytical questions and potential studies; we shall attempt only one of these approaches here by distinguishing several major aspects of the social order at a place, and discussing some of the ways in which variations in social order and variations in place characteristics intertwine to produce variations in place perspectives.

Temporal Order

The first major aspect we shall dsicuss is the *temporal* order of places. Almost every place has both a characteristic pace and a characteristic rhythm. A few studies have described some aspects of the temporal organization of places (Breese, 1949; Foley, 1954; J. S. Duncan, 1972), but little is available in the way of well-established generalizations, and detailed studies are long overdue. Hagerstrand's rather abstract approach (Hagerstrand, 1970; Pred, 1973a) does not permit much in the way of concrete expectations, although it is suggestive of many possibilities. Work by students of urban imagery (e.g., Strauss, 1961; and especially Lynch, 1973) is far more directly concerned with the problems raised here: how are the rhythm and pace of places (along with other temporal characteristics) related to place perspectives? Lynch's work (1973), the only full-length treatment of the subject, is concerned primarily with the esthetic problems of presenting the issue in a suitably evocative fashion. Despite this, a number of useful suggestions may be profitably followed up with serious research.

Each place is geared to a different time scale, pace, and rhythm; the streets of large central business districts are relatively hurried, and conduct along them is measured in terms of minutes, hours at most. Attempts to stretch the time scale of interaction in such places are apt to be interpreted as "loitering," and gentle (or not so gentle) pressure may well be applied by local agents of social control. Lofland (1973) has touched upon this point in her discussion of various tactics of "looking busy" or "respectable" in major public gathering places such as transportation depots. Misperception of (or insensitivity to) the appropriate time scale of conduct often marks out strangers and newcomers in urban centers; certainly New Yorkers routinely assume that those who stroll casually down major streets in Manhattan are "out-of-towners," and therefore to be excused for their lack of manners and avoided as dangerous at the same time. The relatively rapid pace of action on downtown business streets during the day is typically marked by a variety of public clocks, which serve as guides to all who pass.[4]

Other times of the day (and other sorts of places) operate at, and therefore demand, much different rates and scales in their temporal order. Rural imagery typically is filled with "tranquility," "calm," and other terms and images calling to mind slow interaction rates and relatively long time scales[5]; yet the persistent pattern of migration from rural to urban areas suggests that rural temporal order is no more satisfying than urban. Descriptions of rural life in fact often imply that temporal order is most often a fragmented mixture of "too much" and "too little": grinding hard work followed by stupefying boredom. Even the central business district can show radical shifts in pace and temporal scale; it is a favorite device of journalists to show the downtown center of the city very early on a Sunday morning: empty, quiet, slow; the tall buildings echo back footsteps in an eerie fashion; perhaps some fog still drifts among the places of business that makes canyons of the streets. This imagery has been such a favorite in New York for so long that Wall Street at seven in the morning on a Sunday has become something of a tourist attraction.

An important part of the perspective maintained on any place, therefore, will be the assumptions about proper timing in that place. For some, inevitably, the times will be out of joint: elderly people cannot rush across wide downtown streets in the minimal time allowed by many traffic lights; tourists may tend to move more slowly than those who live and work there, and consequently are buffeted by residents rushing to complete work schedules. The vacationer who insists on maintaining an urban pace of activities at a countryside resort may well find himself the object of intense dislike, for many people use such places precisely to escape—temporarily—from a pace that they find too fast, a time scale that they find too short, or a rhythm that they find too jarring, abrupt, and irregular.

Temporal order has implications, not merely for the comfort of those whose personal pace and rhythm may be somewhat discordant with their immediate location, but for other aspects of social organization and place perspectives as well. At larger scales, the pace of activities and variations in their scales imply variation in the rates at which information about places can flow to those who desire it. This fact has many interesting implications, for it is upon information that successful conduct of political and economic order depends. The classic example of the possibilities involved is Andrew Jackson's thumping defeat of the British at New Orleans after the end of the War of 1812, a battle that took place simply because the news of the war's end had not reached the participants. In a recent study, Pred (1973b) has given us a meticulous analysis of the rates of information flow among American cities before the invention of the telegraph. Using the travel times of newspapers among cities as a major indicator, Pred has analyzed the progressive shortening of the time it took news (the raw material from which perspectives are constructed) to reach various parts of the United States over a 50-year period. His figures clearly show that the pace at which place perspectives might have changed increased throughout the period, a fact that must have had major impact on the manner in which individual migrants made decisions about how and where to settle in the United States.

Place perspectives are dependent, then, not only upon the characteristics of the individual and the social world in which he participates, on the one hand, and the social order of the place on the other, but on the larger context in which both place and person conduct themselves as well. To say that the accessibility of information between, say, Washington, D.C., and New York City rose tenfold in the period 1790 to 1840 is another way of saying that people in New York had to take people in Washington into account in their actions far more often in 1840 than in 1790. The perspective of New Yorkers on Washington, therefore, must necessarily have been far more detailed, complex, and rich in 1840 than in 1790—even of those New Yorkers who never went to Washington.

Appropriate questions, then, are the following: What sort of time does this place exhibit? What rates of conduct, what rhythms, what periods are required, permitted, ignored? How do the people in the place negotiate differences between their personal temporal characteristics (or those of the groups and circles to which they belong) and those of the place? When there are conflicting or contrasting temporal orders competing for domination in a place, how are these

conflicts resolved, and with what results? And, perhaps most important, how are the various kinds of social time, work time, sleep time, and ceremonial time related to one another in the perspectives of the people (inhabitants and visitors both) who use the place?

Monetary Order

No less important than the temporal order in forming place perspectives is the *monetary* or financial order. Again, Simmel (1971b) has provided us with the most insightful discussion of the relationship between place perspective and money as a mediator of relations among people:

> The essence of the blasé attitude [of the city dweller] is an indifference toward the distinctions between things . . . . They appear to the blasé person in a homogeneous, flat and gray color with no one of them worthy of being preferred to another. This psychic mood is the correct subjective reflection of a complete money economy to the extent that money takes the place of all the manifoldness of things and expresses all qualitative distinctions between them in the distinction of "how much." (p. 329–330)

Although the character of money as a shaper of social relations has been most extensively analyzed by Marx,[6] little attention has been paid (beyond Simmel's remarks) to the manner in which monetary order shapes place perspectives, and urban place perspectives especially. In contemporary *capitalist* societies, money and monetary order have their impact through the character of places as *real estate*, that is, places as a series of spatially organized property relations in which the governing principle is the right of one person (or a number of people) to exclude others from the use of a particular site. This right is based on the nature of the site as a freely alienable commodity, a way of looking at land that is relatively recent in human history.

Places dominated exclusively by capitalist social organization (i.e., social order in which all sites are seen purely as commodity) have been the exception rather than the rule, and even the most capitalistic of societies (such as the United States and Great Britain) have many places where a purely capitalist perspective is at least contravened by the use of local inhabitants, if not altogether overcome. Conflicts of this sort have been most apparent in recent years in controversies over land-use and zoning policies that permit uses for land which are not profit maximizing in the narrow sense.[7] Perhaps more important for contemporary public issues, the emergence of finance or monopoly capitalism as the dominant form of economic organization in the United States has led to a number of sharp conflicts between the large-scale, long-term land-use patterns of large corporations, and the short-term, smaller-scale competitive uses of traditional merchant and industrial capitalism. Conducted in the language of "humanism" versus that of "rational planning," these conflicting positions have generated considerable excitement in many parts of the country. Generally speaking, the large-scale "rational planners" have had their way with things, first, because of their superior resources and, second, because their merchant and industrial capitalist opposition has often been involved in conflicts among themselves.

Different use by different people has forced considerable variation in perspective as regards monetary order at many sites even in capitalist societies. At one extreme, places confined for the most part to privately owned, single-family dwellings are apt to be focused on other criteria than money in their assessments of themselves as places. At the other extreme, places organized to attract business in virtue of their character as places [tourist attractions, convention centers, "white lights" districts, "locales" in Strauss's (1961) terminology] necessarily are organized around considerations of money, whether the visiting tourist realizes it or not. Tourists are apt to attempt to get "behind" the organization presented to them by the proprietors of a place, since most are perfectly aware that the impression posed for them by proprietors is a front, itself a commodity, dictated by the overwhelmingly money oriented organization of the place. It is possible, however, that there may well be no "backstage," in the sense that the organization of the place around considerations of profit maximization via exploitation of tourists is the only organization at the place. Amusement parks of the penny-arcade type are the most extreme example of this, so extreme in fact that no one really believes that there is a "real life" which goes on privately behind the facades erected by

the proprietors. The proprietors are there simply to make a living; their fronts *are* their backs.

The converse may be true; much of the constant search of tourists for places "off the beaten path" is a search for places that have not yet been "spoiled" by a reorganization around considerations of profit maximization vis-à-vis tourists. Yet it is the very presence of tourists, who demand lodging, food, entertainment, souvenirs, education and a myriad of other services that forces the reorganization of the place. Thus, the typical tourist misperception *early* in the evolution of a place as a tourist attraction is to assume an overly intense organization around money for the place, and therefore to assume that everything (including personal possessions of residents, religious objects, public monuments, and friends and relatives of proprietors) is for sale. Conversely, the typical tourist misperception of places *late* in the process of evolution is to assume that there is something "behind" the "tourist trap" tinsel which is *not* for sale, and to which they may nonetheless have access. Both assumptions can be intensely embarrassing to tourists and proprietors alike.

The important characteristic of places in terms of their monetary order, therefore, is the degree to which the various aspects of the place have become market commodities. Certainly, there are places in which everything has become a commodity, and there are places in which nothing (or almost nothing) is a commodity. The degree to which the market economy has penetrated into the social organization of the place is crucial for understanding the place and forms a central part (correct or mistaken) of everyone's perspective on the place.

Sentimental Order

The most understudied aspect of order at a place is the organization of *sentiments* at the place. The range of emotions that may be legitimately expressed in a place, together with the feelings called out in the people there, constitute the *sentimental order* of the place. Every place is imbued with emotional tone for the people there, and also for many who are not there, but who carry some image of the place with them. Often, as well, particular places or landmarks symbolize strong emotional attachments that people have (monuments serve precisely this function explicitly); thus, places may have emotion-laden meanings for many (inhabitant and noninhabitant) entirely beside what might be expected from superficial examination of the place. It is in the character of places as ceremonial, memorial, monumental and symbolic sites that the intrinsically social nature of any place perspective is most clear.

Some places have *strong* emotional content for a very large number of people, patriotic monuments or religious shrines for example; others have only weak associations for a few. The emotional content of places may be extremely mixed in that some people are affected one way, others in another way, by the place and its symbolic character. There is a variety of place *types* that typically evoke (or are known to intend to evoke) stereotypical emotional reactions from people, whether they are familiar with the particular place represented or not. Thus, bucolic landscapes tend to evoke feelings of calm and peace, no matter which particular bucolic landscape is represented or seen (Schmitt, 1969). Intensely derelict urban slums, on the other hand, evoke feelings of avoidance, distaste, and perhaps pity for those who must live there, again, regardless of which particular slum is at issue. The symbolic meanings of most sorts of places are not so comprehensive. Many working-class neighborhoods, drab, dull, even run-down in appearance as one passes through them, evoke no particular emotion in the *outsider* (or perhaps a feeling of mild distaste); they contain for their inhabitants, on the other hand, a rich complex of feelings for various parts of the place that are associated with important events in local lives (Fried and Gleicher, 1961; Rainwater, 1966).

Just as *nostalgia* for a place can play an important role in shaping the responses of the people who once lived there, the *future* potential of a place can often play an important part in shaping conduct as well. The emotional responses of people to a place can as often be as well motivated by what they see as the future of the place, as by what they see before their eyes. This theme is consistent, for example, in the settlement history of the United States, which has always had a series of future utopias (or at least, bet-

ter places to live) founded somewhere to the west of the current line of settlement. The members of the Massachusetts Bay Colony thought of themselves in these terms, as erecting a "city upon a hill, the eyes of all people . . . upon us." Perry Miller, whose work (1956, 1967) is probably the best on the subject, has underscored the complex nature of the Puritan settlement: first, as a passage into a strange and hostile country, a "howling wilderness"; second, as an inspirational monument to the rest of the world, the future model of righteously conducted social order; third, as intimately entwined with a *natural* moral order. American history is replete with similar examples, and there is no reason to suppose the process is yet at an end.

The emotional tone of a place, the response it calls out in inhabitants and visitors, is thus governed by what has happened at the place and what might happen there. As different participants have different histories and construct different futures for themselves, the sentiments evoked by a place may change; as different people come to the place for different purposes, their emotional responses vary. The bagnio to which gentlemen come for light entertainment and relaxation may be just another sweatshop to the girls that work there, and almost every place can take on a tinge of the exotic, mysterious, and exciting to a stranger. Several years ago, for example, a major airline was selling flights to New York in California by picturing the Brooklyn Bridge in a spectacular aerial photograph with the caption, "Ah, the exotic East." Thus, it is clear that the emotional tone of a place is very much a construct of those using the place.

But this implies that the emotional content of a place is inseparably tied up with the conduct of the place; for if there is an appropriate emotional response to be generated, there must be some inappropriate responses as well that contrast with it, and this implies a social organization of control over emotional displays. There is a variety of very general rules about emotional displays in public; generally speaking, it is considered uncouth to display any emotion strongly, except upon special occasions and in particular places, although "positive" emotions such as joy are more acceptable than "negative" ones such as fear or hatred. "Scenes" involving public displays of intense emotions tend to embarrass others in the area. The scene converts a "path" (e.g., a public street where each person is merely "passing through") into a "place," a public gathering with a focus of attention.[8] The scene thereby converts passers-by into onlookers, and thus into participants. Such a process implies commitments for those involved, sometimes painful—or even dangerous—ones, and are thus to be avoided. Passers-by are therefore reluctant to be drawn in.

Involvement of this sort is dependent upon the loyalties one has to the particular place, how much the site is part of one's own conduct of self. In major business streets, involvements are slight, and people desire them to remain so, for business districts are places where Simmel's "blasé attitude" reigns supreme. Other sorts of places, dominated by other kinds of social organization, have other sentimental orders over them. The behavior that constitutes a "scene" downtown may simply be part of the day in a local residential neighborhood, where the participants and the origins of the scene are known to observers. A burst of inappropriate emotion in some places (e.g., churches) will bring immediate intercession from onlookers, since the inappropriate sentiments are directly and intrinsically disruptive of the conduct of the place.

Sentimental order, then, is composed out of the working arrangements that people have made about the way in which a place is conducted. These arrangements are always subject to disruption, and thus must constantly be renewed. The balance of sentimental order is always a delicate one in that there is no effective way to guarantee beforehand that someone will not choose to disrupt it. This disturbance is of a peculiar kind, given the nature of sentimental order; for someone who throws rocks at stained glass windows thereby disrupts the service taking place, and forcing him to desist does not repair the damage to the sentimental order. Rather, an entire new ceremony must be begun, and the order must be reconstituted from scratch.

Ideological Order

The fourth major aspect that we shall consider of social order at a place is the organization of *ideologies*

about the place. Place ideologies are represented to their publics in a variety of ways—guidebooks, histories of the place, maps, stories, legends, rumors, pictures—that serve to create and recreate images of the place for audiences who may deal with it.[9] These ideologies guide the conduct of all those who use the place; they contain the fundamental assumptions about the place that everyone must have in order to act there at all.

The landscape itself often contains information about itself that can only be interpreted when one is aware of the ideologies of the place; locational information of all sorts is routinely coded in street signs, route maps, and all the other locating devices used by people in a fashion that makes it interpretable only if one has a "larger picture" of the system already available. Mass transit systems are particularly good examples of this, since locational information about routes is invariably expressed in the form of abstract graphics that require a fairly detailed knowledge of the city in order to make effective use of them. The street-grid plans of cities are another very important example. Some cities have street plans that are extremely simple, straightforward, and easy to learn; thus, Chicago's coordinate system enables one to locate anything in the city by simply giving the appropriate corner: "Oh, X is at 1600 west and about 3400 south." Other cities are rather more complex,[10] and no simple system easily applies.

Every city in fact contains a large number of people whose work is in part dependent upon knowledge of the city's plan. Letter carriers, peace officers, truck drivers, and taxicab drivers, for example, are required to have intimate acquaintance with at least some parts of the city. Some of these people (taxicab drivers in particular) routinely deal with a cross section of the general public, and so their images of the city play an important role; especially when dealing with those who are not knowledgeable about the city (and tourists in particular), cab drivers can use their superior knowledge of the city to control the relationship between driver and fare.[11] Real estate brokers are another class of people whose work involves them extensively with detailed knowledge of places, and whose knowledge is important in shaping people's conduct vis-à-vis the city. Palm and Caruso (1974) have studied the manner in which people search for homes and the impact of real estate brokers and their specialized knowledge on the outcome of this search. Their conclusion is that real estate brokers tend to focus the search in areas with which they are familiar, and thus "that an important and dramatic bias is introduced into the search process when the prospective buyer becomes dependent on a realtor for information about the city."

The well-established tradition of research in environmental cognition that focuses on knowledge of the city through the use of map drawing or place-recognition tasks (e.g., Lynch, 1960; Orleans, 1973; Saarinen, 1973a; Francescato and Mebane, 1973) must therefore be expanded to include the interaction among various images of the city, and the degree to which specialized knowledge of places affects various kinds of social situations. Such research has tended to focus simply on the content of individual capacities or skills, or on the distribution of such skills in various populations. Furthermore, the groups studied have tended to be ad hoc in nature, and we have, as yet, no studies showing the distribution of place perspectives in the general population, nor do we have detailed studies of particular groups (such as real estate brokers) whose specialized knowledge makes them of particular interest. Most important, we do not have studies of the *interaction* among differing place perspectives, and the consequences of various kinds and amount of knowledge for various kinds of conduct.

Lack of scope in the studies that have been done has been fostered by the lack of an adequate conceptual scheme to guide and organize research. As long as the images people hold are seen by researchers as being apart from the manner in which people cope with the landscapes surrounding them, research on the subject will be effectively restricted to studying the distribution of images in the population without tying these images to people's conduct. In this sense, the study by Palm and Caruso (1974) represents a considerable step forward, although certainly a wide range of research remains to be done. We must begin to look at the problem from two sides: first, in what ways does the manner in which people conduct themselves act to shape their images of places, and particularly of the places that they routinely use? Second, what are the consequences of different styles, scopes, and amounts of detail in the "mental maps" (Gould

and White, 1968, 1974) held by people for the way in which they interact with one another? The search for a new residence is a natural situation that clearly reveals people's construction of places, and which is important enough to them for whatever resources that they may have to be brought into play. Housing-search processes therefore provide natural research situations in which a large number of variables of interest may be observed.

More than this, some broad analytical categories are needed to stimulate the detailed research that will ultimately construct a fully specified model of place ideologies and imagery. We have yet to consider the impact, for example, of varying *numbers* of ideologies in a place: what happens when everyone has a different picture of the place, and how is their conduct different from situations in which everyone has the same ideology? To what degree, and under what circumstances, do place ideologies become *institutionalized* and begin to carry the force of compulsion in shaping people's conduct? What are the consequences of varying degrees of *consensus* about the characteristics of the place? Are there differences in the *prominence* or importance of landmarks, boundary-defining features, and other landscape phenomena among various people's perspectives, and what impact do these differences have? Such questions can be multiplied indefinitely; the important point is that inquiries into the character of images as constituted by *relations* among people is overdue.

From a sociological standpoint, the interplay between place ideologies and individual skills is at the center of the problem of place perspectives. The ability to master a local place ideology is certainly the basic process involved in constructing a place perspective, and the capacity to transcend the limitations (or take advantage of the opportunities) imposed by a local situation is an important measure of an individual's skill. Without such capacity, a person is effectively crippled at a place, failing in many of his attempts to deal with it and missing many of his opportunities to enjoy it. Future sociological studies of place perspectives and their concomitants, therefore, must be careful to study variation in both individual skill and ideologies in order to understand the organization of perspectives completely. Partial studies of a single group and a single place are of very limited usefulness, and studies that do not vary both place and people are subject to a great deal of mis-interpretation in their results.

SUMMARY AND CONCLUSIONS

With these four aspects of social order at a place and with the characteristics of individuals as they interact with the social order, we have the basic conceptual apparatus to begin posing a variety of questions about the conduct of place perspectives. One important question is the degree to which places interact with one another and how perspectives on one place shape conduct at other places. In a world made up of places that never exchange things, people, or information with one another, the problem of multiple perspectives acting as mutual constraints does not arise. But in fact, of course, almost every place interacts with other places, and hence the orders maintained at each (and the perspectives generated there) act to shape, and are shaped by, the organization of all the places with which it deals, directly and indirectly.

The comparison process among places occurs in many ways, and with many consequences; Boorstin's (1965) discussion of new counties and their seats is about the creation of *new* places and on a *large organizational* scale; Suttles (1972) focuses on *extant* places at a smaller scale. But the comparison goes on at every level of organization, in both old places and new. And if Americans are particularly noted for their "boosting" the advantages (real or imagined) of one place over another in a particularly intensive way, they are not unique; the cathedral-building impulse of the high medieval period was as enthusiastic as the American town foundings of the nineteenth century. Each place constructed must take its place in a network of places within which it must bear constant comparison. Every locational decision made is made on the basis of such a comparison, and the ability of places to "win" new settlers (or firms or governments) clearly plays a crucial part in the evolution of the place. This notion provides us with a second important question about place perspectives: what role do place perspectives play in shaping the locational careers[12] of people and organizations? Conversely, how does the aggregate of careers that

passes through a place affect the organization and history of the place? Strauss (1971) has raised a number of important analytical points to be studied in relating place perspectives to patterns of mobility, both social and geographic. His discussion may be extended to encompass the decisions (and hence the assumptions) of institutions, firms, governments and whole communities, the organizations that shape and structure a place as much as the individuals who live there.

Hughes (1936), in a major paper too long neglected by sociologists and geographers alike, has made a number of points about the way organizations use space; some kinds of organizations divide space into *exclusive* territories (e.g., governments); others *overlap* one another spatially in their operations. In doing so, they may *compete* with one another for clients (or other resources) or *support* one another's work by providing externalities. Similarly, Form (1954) has discussed a number of ways in which organizations shape the use of space. The use made of a place by an organization, however, is dependent upon the organizational place perspective and upon the place perspectives of those who deal with the organization, whether as customers, suppliers, clients, or employees. Tanneries and slaughterhouses have long been excluded from residential areas (or perhaps vice versa) because their operations so impact the responses of people in their vicinity as to make both *that* kind of industrial use and residential activity mutually exclusive. This kind of process, shaping the landscape by shaping perspective on the landscape, can have effects long past the time when the land-use pattern has shifted to other kinds of organizations. Chicago's stockyards, for example, have been inactive for years as slaughterhouses in the strict sense. The noisome slum jungle of "Back-of-the-yards" made famous by Upton Sinclair has become one of the most respectable (not rich—respectable) neighborhoods in the city, inhabited by the mayor, most of the city's senior administrative officials, and all their friends and relatives. But on a damp, warm day, the Chicago metropolitan area—all of it—exudes an effluvium reminiscent of bygone days, when Chicago was hog butcher to the world and not merely its pork belly merchant.

These questions do not exhaust the list of possibilities by any means, nor have we attempted to deal with important issues (such as problems of method) that perhaps should have been raised. In a real sense, the study of place perspectives is in its infancy; and although it exhibits all the enthusiasm (and extremely rapid growth) of the infant, it shows many of the incapacities of an infant as well: uncoordinated, unsophisticated, not terribly strong, and unclear in its self-boundaries. The sociological approach to the subject is perhaps even less mature than those approaches stemming from disciplines, like geography and psychology, that have a natural and intrinsic interest in the matter. Conceiving of places as intrinsically part of conduct, and of place perspectives as an important part of perspectives generally, is not something that comes naturally to the sociologist concerned for the most part with knotty problems of social stratification, political order, and the structure of organizations. Yet just as sociology has much to offer the study of place perspectives (whatever be the defects of *this* attempt), the study of place perspectives has much to offer to sociology as well; for it is only through the study of concrete places and their characteristics that the manifold intellectual problems of sociology can be brought into some relationship with one another. This insight, clearly articulated by Park many years ago (1926), has often slipped from the focus of the sociological eye in recent years; perhaps the development of a strong research tradition in the analysis of place perspectives can bring it back.

NOTES

1. We would like to thank Anselm L. Strauss, James James S. Duncan, Nancy G. Duncan, and David Lowenthal for their very helpful advice and suggestions. Copyright © 1975 by Elihu M. Gerson and M. Sue Gerson.

2. The theoretical approach used in this paper is explained and developed in Rose (1962).
3. Pruitt-Igoe was dynamited by the St. Louis city government in 1972 because the vacancy rate was 70 percent and the project was no longer maintainable. The project is discussed from an architectural point of view in Newman (1972) and from a sociological point of view by Rainwater (1970).
4. For a photographic essay on the subject, see Lynch (1973; pp. 135–162).
5. For an analysis of this imagery, see L. Marx (1964).
6. Especially Marx (1973), but also Marx (1965, vol. 1, pp. 713–774; vol. III, pp. 614–813), and much of Marx (1971, vols. II and III) for the relationship of money and land.
7. For recent summaries of the issues involved, see Whyte (1968), Haar, (1964), and Baldwin and Page (1970).
8. Our use of the terms "place" and "path" in this sense is due to J. S. Duncan (1972).
9. The most extensive discussion of place images is given by Strauss (1961, 1971).
10. The outstanding discussion of American street plans and associated topics is Reps (1965).
11. We are grateful to Edward B. Davis for providing us with this information; an extensive discussion of this will appear in a forthcoming article by him.
12. The term is used here in the sense of Becker and Strauss (1956) and Hughes (1958); a locational career, then, is the sequence of places one lives, together with the accommodations and adjustments one makes at the place.

17

SOCIAL WORLDS,
STATUS PASSAGE,
AND ENVIRONMENTAL
PERSPECTIVES[1]

James S. Duncan and Nancy G. Duncan
Department of Geography
  Syracuse University

Environmental cognition can be examined either from the point of view of an individual (or series of individuals) or as an aspect of social organization. In this paper we focus on some aspects of environmental cognition as a social phenomenon. In Chapter 16, Elihu and Sue Gerson have discussed a number of ways in which social organization both reflects and is reflected by perspectives on a place; our essay is a more detailed discussion and extension of some implications of the work of the symbolic interactionist tradition in sociology.

We shall concentrate on the two concepts of social world and status passage, and show how they may be used to elucidate some of the complex relationships between social structure and individual cognition of the environment. A *social world* is "a culture area, the boundaries of which are set neither by territory nor formal group membership, but by the limits of effective communication. A social world is an orderly arena which serves as a stage on which each participant can carve out a career" (Shibutani, 1962, pp. 136-137). *Status passage*, on the other hand, refers to a transformation of identity, the manner in which a person becomes something other than what he was before (Glaser and Strauss, 1971;

Strauss, 1969; Becker and Strauss, 1956; Hughes, 1958). We shall use and extend these two concepts in order to provide the analytical tools needed to understand some aspects of the way in which change of residence is intimately intertwined with cognition of the environment.

The material presented here is based on a study conducted in Hyderabad, India. The attitudes of two social groups toward their own and each other's residential landscapes were examined. Although we found remarkable consensus among the members of each group concerning the symbolic qualities imputed to the landscapes, we found widely differing and in many respects diametrically opposed cognitions across the boundaries of the two groups. The data were collected over a 4-month period during which we visited the houses of approximately 65 families and conducted long informal interviews, often over an evening meal. The families were members of two elites, one the traditional upper class, which lives in the densely populated old walled city of Hyderabad, and the other a more newly established elite of business and political leaders who live in the new city in residential sections on the outskirts of the urban area. Most members of the old elite have high-ranking jobs

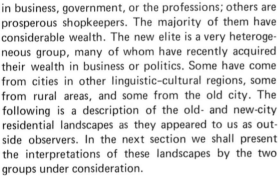

FIGURE 1
New city of Hyderabad, India, showing a typical exterior and a typical living room.

in business, government, or the professions; others are prosperous shopkeepers. The majority of them have considerable wealth. The new elite is a very heterogeneous group, many of whom have recently acquired their wealth in business or politics. Some have come from cities in other linguistic–cultural regions, some from rural areas, and some from the old city. The following is a description of the old- and new-city residential landscapes as they appeared to us as outside observers. In the next section we shall present the interpretations of these landscapes by the two groups under consideration.

The houses of the old elite are large, inwardly oriented structures that appear from the outside as no more than an ill-maintained blank wall with a few shuttered windows (see Figures 1 and 2). For the rich a view of the street is not considered desirable. Because they are surrounded by the landscape of the poor, they take little interest in their exterior surroundings. The construction of their houses therefore reflects their view of the city. To them the old city appears to signify a traditional way of life and a very closely knit social network. In fact, houses and shops that they visit frequently are the only aspects of the landscape to which they attach any more than the most impersonal meaning. Interviews yielded no indication of attachment to the old city as a whole.

The spatial integration of the houses of the rich and poor reflects the historical urban pattern of the interdependence of these two groups. Traditionally, in urban India close spatial association was not stigmatizing except for close proximity to "untouchables," who were segregated. Under the caste system, in which position is fixed by birth, the relative economic status of neighbors is unimportant. In the new city, however, a more "modern" system of social stratification takes precedence, and there appears to be some degree of security gained by living in residential colonies with those of one's own income bracket.

The houses of the new elite are modern and most are smaller than the majority of the old elite's houses. They have large windows and are obviously meant to impress outsiders, for it is clear in some cases that more money has been spent on the outside than on the inside. The view of the road and especially the view of the house from the road is valued. Typically, care is taken to present a well-kept garden and freshly painted exterior.

The interiors of the old- and new-city houses differ greatly as well (see Figures 1 and 2). In the old city the houses are sparsely furnished. However, the most striking feature of the old-city houses to the Western observer is their shabbiness. Paint and plaster are

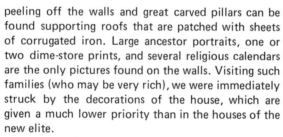

FIGURE 2
Old city of Hyderabad, India, showing a typical exterior and
a typical living room.

peeling off the walls and great carved pillars can be
found supporting roofs that are patched with sheets
of corrugated iron. Large ancestor portraits, one or
two dime-store prints, and several religious calendars
are the only pictures found on the walls. Visiting such
families (who may be very rich), we were immediately
struck by the decorations of the house, which are
given a much lower priority than in the houses of the
new elite.

The attitude of the old elite toward their homes,
while stated in terms of modesty, might be better explained in terms of social networks and patterns of
entertaining. These social networks are tightly closed
and inwardly oriented. Friends are almost exclusively
drawn from within the caste community. Prestige is
derived from hospitality, respect for elders, and contributions to the group; the giving of extremely ex-
pensive weddings is of the highest priority. The decor
of the house conveys the nature of the family history.
The large photographic portraits of the older family
members convey more than simple respect; honor
might better describe it. The fact that the younger
adults are unrepresented symbolizes their lack of
authority in the family decision-making process.

The interiors of the new-city houses are more Western in layout, decoration, and furniture. On the walls
one finds various sorts of framed prints and paintings, and sometimes built-in furniture and glass cases
containing foreign-made plastic toys. There are no
ancestor portraits in the living room. The rooms are
brightly painted and well lit. Refrigerators are often
kept in the dining room for guests to see. Bars are
very popular and are often adorned with humorous
plaques about drinking. A Western orientation, a
nuclear as opposed to joint family, and the openness
of social networks are all reflected in the decoration
of the house.

The emphasis on having an elaborately decorated
and well-maintained house seems to be explained by
the fact that strangers and near strangers are frequently entertained in the house. One's membership
in the new elite is more tenuous than membership in
the old because it is based not on lineage but rather
on money. A visual display, therefore, is used to
affirm membership. A member or potential member
of the new elite uses "louder cues" directed toward a
more public audience, as reflected in the outward appearance of the house.

Perspectives of the Social Worlds

Among the two groups, there is a remarkable lack
of understanding or appreciation of each other's landscapes and the life styles that they believe the land-

scape symbolizes. Both groups explicitly assume that landscape reflects life style and moral and social values. We may illustrate these differences with composite descriptions of one another's landscapes drawn from our interviews conducted in both parts of the city.

The old elite describe the new elite's landscape as "ostentatious display." "The houses with their low walls are showpieces to the public." The houses were clearly seen as reflective of the owner's personality and his group's social attributes. In the same breath in which the houses were criticized, conclusions were expressed about the character of those who inhabited them. The new-city people have "lost their traditional values of modesty and importance of family." The following quotations sum up the old elite's attitude to the new elite:

We do not show off our wealth, nor do we squander it on showpieces . . . . The houses are too small. One must forsake elder members of the family and give up the joint family. . . . They have too much pride and not enough sentiment . . . . The people in the new city are pushy. They are only concerned with advancement . . . . They are superficial. They try to appear better than they are . . . . In the new city you have to drive a long distance to the shops. Then you pay twice as much because the store is well decorated . . . . I would not live in the new city because it is unfriendly and isolated. We have large open courtyards which bring fresh beeezes into the house. The thick walls and high ceilings make the house cool . . . . In the new city the little houses with no courtyards can become unbearably hot . . . . The new city pople go to clubs. They could not have a very good family life.

The new-city residents showed an equal distaste and lack of sympathy for the old-city residents.

They are narrow-minded people who live in narrow houses . . . . The old city is a slum . . . it is dirty, congested and dangerous . . . . I would be afraid to walk down the streets; they are narrow and dirty and full of lower class people and beggars . . . it is medieval and dark. There are no rich in the old city anymore. Maybe they did have money but they have lost it all by now. Why would anyone with money want to live in a slum . . . . They love anything old. They have only small, shuttered windows on the houses. It gets so hot in those houses, it must be stifling . . . . The houses are poorly ventilated and the narrow streets are full of disease. It's not really a city; it is a village organized along caste lines. They are economically and socially backward.[2] They are lazy. The people who live in those big, old run-down houses don't buy air-conditioners or refrigerators and if they do they don't know what to do with them. They have them just for imitation.

We may summarize some of the interesting dichotomies that arose during the course of our interviews as follows: (1) both groups believe the other's area to be *unsafe*, (2) both feel the other's houses to be too *small*, (3) both groups feel that the other group has *less money* and consider each other's spending patterns to be *ostentatious*.[3] Various interesting questions arise when trying to explain this basic lack of agreement. First, there is the question of the differing images conveyed by the same landscape to different groups. The physical appearance and spatial arrangement of buildings thus have very different social meanings. In one case, being separated from friends and neighbors by *open spaces* is considered frightening, whereas being separated from associates by people of *lower status* is frightening to the other group.

The fact that each group believes the other's houses to be small is a case in which the *use* of space influences cognition of the characteristics. Although the old-city houses are larger in terms of square footage, there is less space per person, as the old-city house usually houses a joint family. Space in the old city, however, does not appear to be measured on a *per person* basis but on a *per family* basis. All space is communal space and hierarchically controlled, with the older members of the family having discretion as to its use. The rooms in these houses are large, and private space for each subfamily is not considered necessary.

In the new city, however, even children have their own bedrooms. The house may be smaller, but there are more rooms and individual privacy is possible. In the new city there is far more "visual space" as every house has a view of open areas. To the old-city people, this is useless space and creates unnecessary distance between friends and shops. The old-city people claim to have more money than the new-city people. They say that they own houses in the new city but for investment only. The people who live in the new city, on the other hand, will not believe that "anyone who has money would live in a slum." When spending patterns and priorities differ between groups as radically as between these two, there will undoubtedly be a very significant lack of communication because of misinterpreted presentations of self.

Landscape is a type of communication. It is "read"

and designed to be "read." It is a very complex type of communication in that is usually permits a very broad spectrum of interpretation. People tend to proceed on the unarticulated assumption that others see the world as they do. Much of the lack of understanding between these social worlds is caused by what Suttles (1968, p. 62) refers to as "notational devices." In his study of a lower-class area in Chicago, he suggests that "the differences [between the ethnic groups] . . . are not so much in norms, goals, or general standards, but in the notational devices that each group relies upon to express and encode their adherence to these basic social rules." Members of different social worlds receive bits of data from the landscape and interpret them differently. When confronted with this misunderstanding, both parties are confounded because they see them as pieces of "objective" data that "speak for themselves" to everyone. This perspective explains the striking contrasts in the old- and new-city elites' cognitions of each other's landscapes. This stereotyping of each other and each other's landscapes is inevitable, for it is the only practical course for groups to take. As Suttles remarks, "a personal relation requires a massive exchange of information and cannot be extended beyond the immediate participants. The business of society can hardly wait for such a meticulous examination of an individual's credentials" (p. 26). Thus, the new elite does not see a dilapidated landscape, but rather poor people; and the old elite does not see brightly colored new houses, but rather ostentatious people.

Strauss (1961) has analyzed the simplified, highly stereotyped images that people have of various parts of cities. The following quotation summarizes the situation in Hyderabad well:

The experiences which members have in [any given area] . . . stem from, and in turn affect, their symbolic representations of those areas. Of an area which they never visit, they have no representations unless someone in their circle has visited it and passed along some representation of it. In sum: the various kinds of urban perspectives held by the residents of a city are constructed from spatial representations resulting from membership in particular social worlds (p. 67).

Complete and Incomplete Status Passages

The marked differences between these two elite worlds naturally raises the question, what happens when a person moves from one to the other? More formally, we may ask how such a *status passage* affects environmental cognition. A move from the old to the new city marks a social as well as a physical move. It appears that this move is unidirectional; we did not encounter any cases of families of the new elite moving to the old city. Occasionally, however, women from new-city families will marry into old-city families. Because the home landscape influences the family interaction patterns and life style, a move to another type of landscape marks a significant status passage. Whereas a desire for a more modern way of life undoubtedly precedes the move, the new life style is not adopted in full until the move is made. The formal move is interpreted by relatives as a rejection of traditional values and especially of the joint family. This, as well as the increased physical distance, may strain relations between those who have left and those who have stayed behind. The strained relations are of course accentuated by the fact that the mover is seen not only as rejecting the group that raised him, but as rejecting it for membership in a group that is disdained.

The new-city house is a new presentation of self and as such requires a new self-image if one is not to suffer the embarrassment of believing his landscape speaks unfavorably of him. In the case of a couple, owning a new-city house is perhaps their first opportunity to organize a *joint* presentation of self. We interviewed one young woman who, although originally from the new city, had married into an old-city family. She complained about the traditionalism that the landscape fostered and reflected. She shared the house with her husband's two unmarried brothers and her mother-in-law. She was responsible for running the household yet had no choice as to how it should be run. What appeared to disturb this young woman the most was not being able to decorate the house as she pleased. Here in the old city she felt overpowered by the family image, dominated by the older generations, and that she had lost an important part of her identity. Even after seven years of living in the old city she was unable to change her notion of *individual* status and display to the notion of *group* status and display.

Strauss (1959, p. 37) mentions possessions as presentation of self in connection with status passage, when he says a man's possessions are a fair index of what he is, and it is no accident that men make their symbolic movements, into social classes for instance, by discarding and acquiring clothes, houses, furnishings, friends, even wives. A move to the new city requires a certain redefining process; one must redefine the new landscape as "home," and in so doing one redefines oneself vis-à-vis the landscape. Wirth (1964, p. 94) notes the importance of the location of a man's home to his identity in his classic study of the ghetto. "If you would know what kind of a Jew a man is, ask him where he lives; for no single factor indicates as much about the character of the Jew as the area in which he lives. It is an index not only of his economic status, his occupation, his religion, but his politics and his outlook on life and the stage in the assimilation process that he has reached." Many other students of urban ethnic groups in America have noted the same phenomenon (e.g., Strauss, 1961; Greeley, 1972).

Those who had made the move from the old city appeared to have internalized to a large extent the new elite's interpretation of the symbolic meaning of the two landscapes. To them the old-city landscape symbolized a socially backward community. Conversely, the new-city landscape no longer appeared pretentious and superficial to them. Some of the negative comments by new-city people on the old-city landscape and society quoted earlier were in fact made by former old-city residents. For example, it was a former old-city resident who characterized the old elite as "narrow-minded people who live in narrow houses." Once having lived in the old city, however, a person's cognition of its landscape will never quite match that of the new-city residents. For example, to the majority of new-city dwellers the old-city is a little thought about aspect of Hyderabad. They are familiar with only the external landscape, which is the domain of the poor. Most refuse to believe that there is any wealth in the old city. This ignorance, of course, is not shared by anyone who has lived there or who has close relatives there.

This description is of the *complete* status passage of one who moves from the old to the new city. Some of these passages are undoubtedly more successful than others. One major difficulty is in reconciling one's own self-image with the new presentation of self provided by the modern house and its location. Incomplete status passages, those which are unsuccessful or not yet realized, will be considered because they demonstrate the difficulties inherent in passing from one social world to another. Although the following discussion does not fully capture the complexity of status passages, it does provide a conceptual framework for examining the move from the old to the new city.

The first type of incomplete passage we shall call *nascent* passage. In this group were people who were preparing themselves and their families (who were to remain behind) for an impending passage. In some cases the formal passage, marked by leaving the old city, might be months away, in other cases years. In some cases the passage will never be completed. We interpreted nascent passage as being the adoption of elements of the new-city life style. This type of nascent passage occurred predominantly among the young. The young people who were undergoing nascent passage usually did so *surreptitiously*. Under the joint family system, it is the older members of the family who control the distribution of *cash*. They are therefore in a good position to cut off funds for activities of which they do not approve. They also have *moral* power in that the old elite's life style demands that the young must respect and obey the old.

One of the clearest manifestations of nascent passage is the adoption of new-city ways, which are by and large learned in new-city places. Restaurants, the racetrack, and sometimes social clubs in the new city are popular places where the potential out-migrant goes to eat nonvegetarian food, smoke, drink liquor, talk to girls, and associate with noncaste fellows. It is here that one learns and tries out a new identity. Those who are not so far along in the passage tend to go to the old-city restaurants where they can smoke and talk with friends but not indulge in other activities. These people are not advanced enough in their passage to enjoy or feel comfortable in the new-city restaurants and clubs. They still view these places as foreign and not in line with their self-images. They are unable at this stage to identify fully with the new-city places because these places symbolize a set of values that they have not yet fully accepted.

These are all examples of the relatively *covert* side of nascent status passage. In some cases one also finds more *open* resistance to the old-city perspective. This resistance varies in intensity and depends upon the power of the mover vis-à-vis his family and on the stage of passage in which he finds himself. Strong resistance usually takes place when the mover is well along in the passage. A problem arises as he tries to express and conduct his new self-image, for the funds that would allow him to do so are often withheld. One informant, a successful doctor in his early thirties, said that he was very unhappy living in the joint family because of the control exerted over his affairs by his father. His father would not allow him to purchase the kinds of things that he and his wife wanted, such as a refrigerator and other modern appliances. He also complained that he had no say in the decoration of the house, which he found dreary. He fought with his father constantly over money and planned to establish a household of his own soon. During such a nascent passage the person is shifting reference groups and is conducting the passage by adopting different behavior patterns.

A second type of incomplete status passage can be called an *aborted* passage. An aborted passage occurs when a person moves to the new city and then reverses the passage and moves back to the old city. We encountered three cases of aborted passage and heard of other cases. All had moved back to the old city within one year although they still owned one or more houses in the new city, which they rented out.

These people apparently did not engage in the normal nascent passage. They had not learned the life style of the new elite before formally making the passage. We inferred this from the fact that these people were very critical of the new elite's life style. This lack of adequate preparation for the passage left them with the attitudes and assumptions of the old elite, and yet important aspects of their organization of self linked them to the new elite. When they moved to the new city, they found themselves caught marginally between social worlds (see Park, 1927; Stonequist, 1937). Although they had not entered into the social world of the new elite, they also were no longer an integral part of the old elite, since they had surrounded themselves with another social world's objects. They had not prepared themselves adequately for the passage and therefore found

that, although the physical move had been made, the social passage had not.

The third type of incomplete passage we shall call *partial* passage. Partial passage occurs when the out-migrant still retains many elements of the old city life style. This is different from an aborted passage in that the migrant is content to remain in limbo between social worlds. This state of affairs is not as intolerable as it might appear, for there are a number of these people and apparently they associate with each other. The intermingling of two life styles is very striking among this group. They maintain joint families, and the older members of the family exert strict control over the younger members; but they have largely lost contact with their relatives. These people may be in the process of forming a new social world, located socially between the worlds of the old and new elites. The exteriors of their houses are rather different from most other new-city houses. Two in particular had high compound walls around them and were set back from the road so that they could not be easily seen. They did not have well-maintained grounds. They were dingy white, and the face of one was high with small windows and the same inwardly oriented appearance one finds in old-city houses. The interiors combine elements of both types. The rooms are less open than in most new-city houses. Even though these houses are decorated in Western style, they are much more sparsely furnished than are other new-city homes. These people obviously have maintained the old-city attitude that there is no need to lavish a great deal of money on the decoration of the interior.

Conclusions

Differences in environmental perspectives among social groups may be accounted for in part by differences in their social organization. When we view landscape as a type of conduct, we imply that there is some degree of consensus concerning its meaning, that is, institutionalized perspectives. Belonging to a social group implies sharing a perspective to the extent that there will be no significant barriers to communication. "The important thing, then, about a social world is its network of communication and the shared symbols which give the world some substance and which allow people to 'belong' to 'it'" (Strauss, 1961, p. 67). The objects with which a person surrounds himself *produce* his self in an important sense. But consensus as to meaning need not extend across the boundaries of social worlds. Thus, most people are ignorant of the degree to which various social worlds may attach different meanings to these objects. The constructions of one group may not necessarily coincide with those of the other.

A person's identity is based on membership in one or more social worlds. He then conducts his identity in accordance with the practices of the social worlds of which he is a member. A new identity, as we have shown in our discussion of status passage, carries a new world view, which in turn affects one's perspective on one's everyday environment.

NOTES

1. We would like to thank Elihu M. Gerson, M. Sue Gerson, David E. Sopher, and Anselm L. Strauss for advice, criticism, and suggestions.
2. The members of the old elite that we interviewed were very highly educated. The vast majority of the men and women had Bachelor of Arts degrees and many, including quite a few women, had Master of Arts degrees.
3. For example, we were told by our new-city informants that the old elite spends large sums of money on what our informants consider to be unnecessarily lavish and pretentious weddings, wedding gifts, and funerals.

18

Anne Buttimer
Graduate School of Geography
Clark University

EXPLORING THE SOCIAL DIMENSION OF ENVIRONMENTAL KNOWING: A COMMENTARY

A sociological perspective on the nature of environmental knowing is certainly a welcome one. Pioneers in this field have long sought conceptual means whereby their various partial insights could be related. Our models have tended to anchor themselves either on the individual knower and the dynamics of his perception and cognition of the environment, or else on the environment itself as stimulus for particular perceptual responses. With rare exceptions, we have tended to use either behavioral models of the individual on the one hand or functional models of the physical environment on the other to elucidate patterns of behavior and cognition. We still lack an integrated approach that could accommodate the distinct perspectives implied in these models.

In the foregoing chapters, a new dimension is explored: the social context of behavior and cognition is seen as a pervasively important ingredient in environmental experience. One is left with little doubt that ways of knowing and evaluating places have both a personal and collective dimension. A fresh and critical stance is thus afforded both on individual experience and on the meaning of environments. Places are endowed with social meaning that cannot be read entirely from their physiognomy or functional character; social reference systems within which people conduct behavior mold in considerable measure their organized perspectives on places.

A fundamental corollary to this assertion is that any valid conceptualization of environmental knowing is inadequate if it does not incorporate this collective dimension. The social setting within which people live has a profound influence on what they know, how they learn, and how they use and evaluate space. Insight into this social dimension of the issue could be of value. It is the appropriateness of particular sociological models for the elucidation of environmental knowing that is questionable. Since conventional models in sociology have been designed primarily to investigate behavior rather than cognition, it is hardly justifiable to demand explicit evidence from them on the nature of the cognitive process. The sociological contribution is of a different order: by placing the issue of environmental knowledge within its social context, it unravels layers of influence surrounding both the cognitive processes of the individual and processes and patterns of environmental settings as well. Sociological insight, thus, could provide a necessary, although insufficient, foundation for a more comprehensive and experientially grounded conceptualization of environmental cognition.

From the vast spectrum of conceptual and analytical possibilities that sociology offers for this task, the authors of the two preceding papers have selected two major theoretical stances: (1) the social reference system, and (2) symbolic interaction. Related concepts are also introduced, for example, life style, value orientations, and social organization, each illustrating its distinct, although overlapping significance in the context of place "perspectives." Since the primary *explicanda* of such concepts are behavior (conduct) and perspective, creative adaptations and much empirical experimentation are needed before their relevance to the issue of environmental knowing can be fully explored.

In Chapter 16, the issue is approached from a conceptual vantage point; a great variety of empirical cases are used to illustrate the utility of a key sociological notion. "Organized perspectives" are seen to dictate meanings and values to behavior and the settings in which interactions are conducted. A more specific empirical focus is used in Chapter 17: the contrast of two social worlds and their influence on place perspectives. The nature and salience of people's participation in two distinct social worlds are seen to channel and influence their perspectives and attitudes toward their respective residential environments and also their images of one another. Both papers deal with the interaction of people and places, endeavoring to weave "objective" description of landscapes and behavior with the "subjective" attitudes and disposition of people. In the effort to remain faithful to the spirit of their models, and yet to extend their analytical focus beyond the normal horizons set by these models, the authors inevitably encounter conceptual difficulties. Both of the major frameworks used, symbolic interactionalism and social reference systems, derive from an organismic version of social interaction. They suggest a cross-sectional or ecological perspective on people's relationship to environment. Thus, each "perspective" and each "place" should be described in a metaphor of homeostatic

equilibrium; the models per se do not provide the foundations for a dynamic or developmental version of the interaction between people and place and the modes of knowing associated with such conduct. Yet, in several ways, this is the kind of adaptation that both of these papers suggest. It is the relative success and heuristic import of such adaptations that invite comment and reflection.

Notions such as "social world," "reference group," and "presentation of self," initially designed to elucidate patterns of social conduct and interaction, either assume or suggest forms of knowing one's social environment. Whether such knowledge was previously acquired or learned through the process of interaction was not the explicit concern. What these authors endeavor to do is to make the cognitive aspect of behavior more explicit. The extent to which they achieve this goal is questionable; one could use the terms "perception" and "cognition" almost interchangeably and not lose the essential thread of their arguments. However, there are provocative pointers in this direction. The notion of "organized perspective," for example, so amply illustrated in Chapter 16, sheds light both on the process of learning, on the one hand, and on the processes of social interaction on the other. In exploring some of the cognitive foundations of perspectives, the Gersons have introduced a dynamic quality into the rather homeostatic notion of perspective. They show how places adopt a physiognomy and functional character as a result of particular perspectives, how the interaction of different perspectives influences meanings ascribed to places, and the types of conduct considered appropriate for that place. Clearly, then, they point to avenues of enquiry that could yield more workable guidelines for cross-disciplinary research and also an enrichment of the sociological enterprise itself. In examining the reciprocal relationships between "places" and "perspectives," they extricate a wide range of attendant attributes, for example, types of commitment to places (ideological, monetary, symbolic, and others), motivations and roles (tourists, real estate brokers, businessmen), and the contrasts between residents and nonresidents. But in addition to these myriad ways in which social perspectives interact with space, the Gersons' document how time and the temporal rhythms of behavior are conditioned by social definitions of appropriateness. This is certainly a facet of environmental knowledge that merits further study.

In Chapter 17, the Duncans try to adapt the notion of "status passage" to explicate changing patterns of place perspective. Movement from old to new residential sectors is almost invariably unidirectional, and so is the pattern of status improvement. Yet the "stages" suggested ("partial," "abortive," "nascent," "complete") are not suggestive of any evolutionary sequence: each forms a distinct, discrete type of homeostatic relationship between place and perspective. The typology is provocative, however. Could one not examine the tension between stabilization and change within different components of perspective and life style—family bonds, value systems, economic motivations, and others—to see how knowledge of new social worlds is resisted or acquired? In this way, the role of space and place in the cognitive dimensions of status passage could be explored and the role of status passage in the ascription of social meaning to space.

It is in departing from the conventional "letter" while remaining true to the "spirit" of conventional sociological models, then, that the Duncans arrive at a more dynamic stance on the Hyberabad scene. While explicitly adopting the framework of "social world" to elucidate place perspectives, they actually use the notion of life style, in all its dynamic complexity, to unmask the processes that shape images and attitudes toward place. In fact, social organization represents the stabilizing (conservative) force and life style change the innovative force in shaping perspectives on place. "Social world" is defined as "a field of communication," yet the text does not probe the circulation system within each social world. It is the absence of communication *between* the two social worlds that appears influential in maintaining self-images and attitudes toward the other.

In the progeny of their central concepts, then, both papers share common characteristics. Both attempt to probe the internal frame of reference of action and to interpret behavior and perspective in rational terms. Both validate the thesis that neither "environment"

nor "cognition" can be fully understood until they are seen in their social context. Differences appear in the centrality given to *place* or *social conduct*, and it is here perhaps that the differences in disciplinary background are revealed.

In Chapter 16, *place* is construed almost exclusively in social terms. The physiognomy and functional character of places are seen as the residue of past social perspectives or as the stage for present social conduct. Distinctions between *place* and *space* are never made explicit. How one defines or circumscribes a place is also ambiguous: places can include cities (e.g., New York, San Francisco, Chicago), regions ("rural" versus "urban"), neighborhoods (the North End of Boston), or even monuments. Social perspectives apply to places sometimes in holistic fashion, at other times to particular items (commodities) within a place. To a mind schooled in distinctions between place and spatial relationships (site versus situation), such ambiguity over scale and boundaries may be irritating, just as the sociologist might find the ambiguous use of terms like "life style" and "social group" irritating. Such annoyances are only relevant here insofar as they reveal malaise over the issue of environmental knowing. If one can establish a reasonably sound connection between cognition and "perspective," and if perspectives remain relatively invariable regardless of scale and boundaries of places, the issue need not be examined. Chapter 17, however, provides evidence to the contrary. Old and new elites differ not only in their perspectives on home and immediate environment, but also in the relationship between images of home and those of the city as a whole. In the Hyderabad study, place, too, becomes an active participant in the shaping of social perspective; space itself is seen as a form of communication, a vehicle for the presentation of the social self, and not merely the passive stage on which social interaction is conducted.

The critical issue here, it seems, is the implicit dialectic between place and space: place, conceptualized as formal region, circumscribed morphologically, and space, conceptualized as a continuous surface within which processes operate at varying scales. Places, then, could be seen as *containers* of particular physical and social phenomena, and as *magnets*

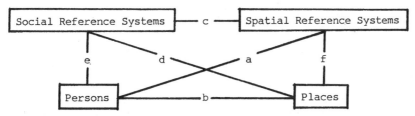

FIGURE 1
Dialectical perspective on environmental knowing: place–space, person–society.

or *points of intersection* for various dynamic spatial processes. In fact, taken together, the papers suggest that a useful analogy might be drawn between an individual person's relationship to social reference systems and an individual place's relationship to spatial reference systems. The evolving character of places could be fruitfully regarded in terms of its ongoing relationship to various kinds of spatial process, for example, changes in circulation systems and media, changes in economic base and market accessibility, migrations and flows of people, and commodities and services. Similarly (as shown in Figure 1), the evolution of an individual's personality—and organized perspective—could be fruitfully examined in terms of his social reference system. To gain a comprehensive grasp of environmental knowing, one needs to be aware of both sets of relationships, although the specific focus of individual research efforts may rest only on a small portion of the whole.

Whether strictly analogous or not, one could use this schematization to reflect on our research efforts to date on environmental cognition, and to get a sense of what we still need in order to construct a more experientially grounded conceptualization of the issue.

Focus has tended to rest on specific types of relationship: (a), (b), (c), or (d) of Figure 1; rarely has the multidimensional character of environmental knowing been explicitly incorporated in an overall approach. Analyses of spatial behavior, action and activity spaces, residential site selection, and shopping behavior have tended to focus on (a), the individual person's relationship to spatial reference systems (Chapin and Hightower, 1966; Peterson, 1967; Cox and Golledge, 1969). The study of proxemic behavior,

territoriality, spatial cognition, and cognitive mapping have tended to focus on (b), the individual person's relationship to place (Lynch, 1960; Altman, 1970; Hall, 1966; Stea and Downs, 1970a). Analyses of time–space horizons (Hägerstrand, 1970), systems of spatial domination (Harvey, 1972; Horvath, 1974), social inequality, and the interlocking of social and spatial processes (Harvey, 1970) have focused on (c) the relationship between social and spatial reference systems. And now we find an example of (d), the impact of social reference systems on meanings ascribed to place, an orientation that has already been pioneered by Webber (1964), Suttles (1968), and Boal (1969). Clearly, in all categories, the relationship between the individual and his social reference system (e) has either been assumed or explicitly investigated through sociological and/or psychological models, as indeed the relationship between places and spatial reference systems (f) has been the focus of much geographic effort. The challenge is somehow to orchestrate the entire research effort on environmental knowing in such a way as to allow all aspects of these relationships to be elucidated eventually.

By setting the issue in this kind of framework, one could specify the unexplored dimensions of environmental knowing and also sense where avenues of cross-disciplinary investigation might be attempted. Consider, for instance, the discordance that people experience in settings where the local spatial and/or temporal rhythm is incongruent with their expectations. Could such conflict be investigated through the use of "cognitive dissonance" models? In other words, could issues raised through sociological investigation not be further explored through the use of psychological techniques? Similarly, conflicts between traditional (or resident) views of "place" and the disrupting effects of spatial systems (e.g., introduction of new roadways, real estate speculation), problems uncovered through geographical analyses, could be further investigated through the sociological methods of perspective change or status passage. In many ways, then, the sociological contribution may be seen as a means whereby the gulf separating psychological study of individuals and the geographical–architectural study of places could be bridged at specific points. But the import of these two chapters goes beyond this. For they have stretched the analytical net of positivist sociology to the point where fundamental questions arise about scientific exploration of "subjective" dispositions and attitudes. Following Weber (1947, pp. 1–30), whose interpretative sociology was designed to elucidate the subjective meaning of actions, they have both employed their models to yield both empathetic and rational interpretations of social conduct. Given the "rational" character of their interpretations, cases are described in the language of typification rather than idiosyncratic experience of the subjects. Throughout Chapter 16, one is constantly tempted to speculate on how all this relates to Schutz's (1970) phenomenological sociology. By changing vocabulary here or there and inserting slightly different concepts, one could envision the essay as part of a collection of "life world" (Schutz, 1967). Obviously, there is a profound philosophical difference between the perspectives nurtured within positive science and those nurtured within phenomenology, but given the thrust of both these essays toward an eluciation of *knowing*, one could well envision a fruitful dialogue of phenomenological and scientific perspectives on place. Each horizon on social conduct revealed in these essays (e.g., presentation of self, social world, and life style), uncovers yet another dimension of a subjective life world within which the processes of knowing the environment have been influenced by these horizons. One should welcome, then, further examples of sociological enquiry into the issue (e.g., on the influence of life style, cultural tradition, family and kinship systems on the meanings ascribed to place).

With these two chapters, one gets a clear taste of the important contribution that sociology can make to the pursuit of present objectives and as a catalyst for a fresh look at the philosophical premises that underlie such objectives. One awaits further creative adaptations of conventional methodologies for widening the analytical net and at the same time laying foundations for a more integrated look at the wondrous complexity of environmental knowing.

position that cognitive processes are concerned with making the world *meaningful* and that there are different ways in which meaning can be given to the world. The view of environmental cognition proposed in this paper is that it is mostly about *giving meaning* to the world rather than *knowing* about it. One consequence is that one needs to take a comparative —cross-cultural at a moment in time and also through time—because the *meanings* that people give to the world are more variable than the ways in which the world is known or even used. I have used this distinction before between the concrete, use, value, and symbolic object (Rapoport and Hawkes, 1970).

The psychological approach, while stressing the mediating function of cognitive representations in the environment–behavior interaction, suggests that these representations result from an interaction of "internal organismic factors" and "external environmental demands" (Moore, 1973b). Introducing the "anthropological" perspective, which is concerned with meanings and the role of meanings, classifications, taxonomies, cognitive splits, and the like, suggests that it is necessary to consider these kinds of cultural cognitive habits (if one might call them that) to understand the way in which the environment is conceived and structured by the individual. People, as active, adaptive, goal-seeking organisms, structure the world as a result of *three* major factors, and I am proposing a *three-element model* or organismic, environmental, and cultural factors that interact to form cognitive representations. Thus, to study differences among such representations (and hence among different aspects of environment–behavior relations) it is necessary to consider the nature and cognitive styles of cultures and subcultures as well as those factors relating to individuals and environments (accepting, at the same time, that these three factors are *themselves* systemically related).

Cognition, unlike perception, generally involves indirect material—information derived from other people, their values, views, interpretations. It is thus, almost by definition, culturally affected. Both in the past, and even more today, indirect means such as media, stories, legends, films, songs, and travel reports provide conceptual categories, names, and values that reflect and shape prevailing assumptions and which

change as culture changes. As culture changes and as values and taxonomies change, these are embodied in images—a symbol mnemonic for affective aspects of environmental experience—and these profoundly affect cognition.

GIVING MEANING TO THE WORLD

Among the various ways in which meaning can be given to the world, a basic one is that signals are turned into messages and hence become part of one's psychomilieu only as they have significance for particular groups; this varies for different groups at different times (Frank, 1966; Davidson, 1972). No generalizations can be made on the basis of one culture at a single moment in time, either about the range of ways of making the world meaningful or about any constant processes or mechanisms underlying a particular way. One can take a cross-cultural approach to environmental cognition from a psychological perspective, but the anthropological orientation is *inherently* cross-cultural.

Taking a broader sample shows that in all cases cognitive representations, classifications, and cognitive maps help organisms use the environment and affect how it is used; thus there may be a relation between the type of environment and the kinds of cognitive representations used. Activity systems, again culturally variable, affect memory, since frequently used areas are known and remembered better; cognitive maps can thus be seen as mnemonic devices (Rapoport, 1972). There is recent evidence that the first symbols used by man may have been mnemonic devices (Marshack, 1971). These concepts also help distinguish between geographic, perceived, used, and other forms of environments, which are all cognitive constructs in this sense (Rapoport, 1970c; Saarinen, 1969).

Looking at environmental cognition in this way raises questions about constancy and variability, about species-specific and culture-specific aspects and their interplay. Whatever the underlying regularities, it is clear that specific cultural differences and variations in the spatial and temporal factors used, how these are organized into spatial worlds, cognitive maps, and orientational systems, and how they relate to taxonomies and affect behavior are most important. Although these questions have received some attention (Hallowell, 1955; Lynch, 1960, Appendix A; Haugen, 1969; Fernandez, 1970), a great deal more is needed, particularly directly related to *environmental* cognition.

The lack of these cultural and anthropological considerations in the study of cognition also affects the discussion about change and progress. Any consideration of change in individuals, groups, and of cyclic events suffers if one eliminates consideration of similar processes at the cultural and subcultural level. For example, it may well be that the cognitive categories and orientational systems (i.e., cognitive schemata and representations) used by Australian Aborigines are as valid and *potentially* useful as ours, and their way of defining place through purely symbolic and conceptual means may be even more useful; at the very least it shows the extreme range of place definition of which people are capable. But this kind of comparison never becomes possible if such factors are ignored. This also leads to a loss of theoretical power so that concepts which could be related tend to be seen in isolation. Thus, for example, "totemistic space" among Australian Aborigines has been described as a unique category (Hart and Moore, 1973). Yet, given the approach here advocated, totemistic space can be seen to form a special part of a larger and more general category of symbolic space. This aboriginal schema thus fits into a larger conceptual model (which is always a useful thing): it becomes clear not only that it is not an early or primitive form but, on the contrary, an extremely sophisticated version of symbolic space defined with physically minimal, but symbolically very sophisticated, means (Rapoport, 1972). In general, then, and in highly simplified terms, the anthropological view is that, in some way, cognition is a taxonomic process: the world is made meaningful by classifying, naming, attaching importance, and generally ordering it by means of a conceptual system. The world is humanized and made habitable, as it were, by having a meaningful structure imposed on it. Given the importance of classification to all science and to the extent that all people act as "scientists" (Kelly, 1955), the stress of

cognitive anthropology on taxonomic processes is most useful.

It is a basic premise of cognitive anthropology that different cultures classify the world differently by the use of different taxonomies, and that this may be linked to the relative importance attached to elements, although there is also some suggestion that all taxonomies may share certain general characteristics as a function of all people being members of one species. Taxonomies, whether of colors, directions, values, or environmental characteristics, are ordering systems that help give meaning to the world; they split space and time. Environmental preference and choice are thus linked to meaning and to conceptual systems. Through classification and ordering, the world is split into various domains and the concrete regions of everyday life may correspond to cognitive domains (Rose, 1968), so that the physical environment as built reflects cognitive regions. Ordering schemas are used to shape the built environment (e.g., ideal cities, ideal landscapes, cosmological schemas) and ordering systems are in turn imposed on environments as experienced.

The built environment, reflecting as it does cognitive organization, involves the organization of space, communication, meaning, and time. These cannot be discussed in any detail (see Rapoport, 1975), but it is clear that insights into these aspects can be obtained by examining how people *conceptually* organize space, time, meaning (i.e., symbols), and communication (i.e., with which classes of individuals does one communicate, when, under what conditions, etc.). These are clearly fundamental cognitive categories and their nature and relationships can best be understood from cross-cultural studies.

Since cognitive domains may correspond to semantic domains (and, in fact, cognitive anthropology has tended to stress the linguistic aspect; see Chapter 20), it would follow that the Sapir–Whorf hypothesis stressing the relation of language to people's view of the physical world may be much more relevant to the built environment and its cognition than it is to perception. Given the fact that differences in perception seem less marked and the evidence less equivocal (although not yet adequately studied), that differences in taxonomies and meanings are much more marked and clear, and that differences in forms and uses of built environment are clearer still, it would seem to follow that the relation of taxonomies to the analysis of both physical form and the order which people impose on the world is a promising line of inquiry (Rapoport, 1973c). In that case, some of the criticisms of the cognitive view in anthropology (Keesing, 1972) do not necessarily weaken its relevance to environmental research, particularly since it has not yet been used in this field to any extent. It is likely that cognitive domains are embodied both in the built environment and the interpretation of the build environment in people's minds. In this view, *the built environment embodies cognitive categories and further ones are imposed on it by the users.* Thus, if we see the environment as encoded information that users decode, environmental cognition plays a role in both the encoding and decoding process; hence the importance of a close relationship between environmental forms.

Such schemata also affect people's thought processes and how and where they travel, and hence possibly link the psychological view of cognition with the view being discussed here. Thus, if people prefer certain domains and avoid others, (as being undesirable, dangerous, "profane"—in a word, *uninhabitable*), they will know them less and this will in turn lead to further avoidance. Domains are either preferred or avoided in terms of certain schemata that are used to interpret environmental cues and thus result in differential preference (Rapoport, 1973c, 1973d, 1975).

It has been suggested that underlying the culturally different ways of organizing the world and giving it meaning there may be certain general principles common to all people. Both the underlying constancy and cultural variability can be revealed by the two major questions posed by cognitive anthropologists (see Tyler, 1969):

1. What material phenomena are significant to people in a culture (and are thus stressed, selected, and used)?
2. Once having selected these phenomena, how are they organized by the people in question?

These two questions seem extremely relevant to environmental cognition because they address the question of which features in the environment are meaningful, either individually or as categories, which are noticed, selected, and used, which are valued highly or little, and how are they are organized into various cognitive representations. These questions have major implications for both design and research. If the mode used, and the distinctions selected, are not related to perceptually meaningful subcultural taxonomies, they may not be significant. One of the most interesting and important questions is precisely *which* features of the environment people subjectively select for organization—what we might call subjective *noticeable differences*. The development of the field of environmental cognition is precisely about substituting subjective reactions and ways of structuring environments for the a priori assumptions of planners or geographers. This substitution relates not only to the question of the selection and organization of features but, more specifically, to a general question about mental maps: are "mental maps" those drawn by geographers of various nonspatial representations that people have about the environment, or should the term be reserved for the spatial representations of the environment and its meaningful features that people themselves hold?

There is a most important question here about the particular cognitive categories (taxonomy) used by different people and their relationship to noticeable differences. It is now widely known that different cultures have large taxonomies of those elements of the environment that are finely discriminated, important, and used, whether it be Arabs and camels, Maoris and greenstone, or Eskimos and wind and snow (Carpenter, 1973). It is possible to list the *potential* noticeable differences in the environment (physical, social, symbolic, etc.), but which will be noticed, which will be understood, and which will elicit "appropriate" (i.e., intended) behavior is culturally variable. In fact, it seems clear from the anthropological literature, at least as I interpret it, that one of the cognitive differences between groups is in terms of these noticeable differences, that is, which features are perceived, selected, and organized. This is also important from a psychological perspective in terms of thresholds and noticeable differences. It follows that one does not know a priori which elements are selected; it is, in fact, one of tasks of cognitive anthropology to discover the categories that are used. Once selected, these elements tend to be ranked in order of high or low, positive or negative, and are organized in various ways. All these processes address one major question: *How do people create order out of chaos?*

The question in this connection is really, How do people discriminate between things and decide whether they are like and unlike? This can be done *either* through *identity categorization* (seeing stimuli as forms of the same thing) or *equivalence categorization* (seeing a set of discriminate stimuli as belonging together). This latter categorization can be done through three broad classes of equivalence categories: affective, functional, or formal (Bruner, Goodnow, and Austin, 1956). In another formulation, it has been suggested that the ways of deciding on like–unlike can be done through enactive, iconic, or symbolic means (Oliver and Horsby, 1970). When applied to environmental matters, it would follow that each of these means emphasizes different features of the environment for establishing likeness and grouping, and these would tend to be organized in different ways. It is a reasonable hypothesis that different cultural and subcultural groups would tend to rely on different criteria of this type. This is, in fact, the topic of ethnoscience in specialized areas such as ethnobotany, ethnomedicine, and ethnogeography. Regarding the environment, a comparable example is the distinction between esthetic and scientific knowing (Gittins, 1969) or the different ways of structuring space conceptually shown by architects and nonarchitects. As noticeable differences in the environment are culturally variable (Rapoport and Hawkes, 1970), this affects the elements noticed, selected, and hence used or designed. Once noticed, elements may be categorized or classified very differently by using different criteria and assigning different relative values to these elements. Given the different conceptual systems operating, they will then be organized into different schemata.

Let us now examine how this cognitive anthropological approach affects some of the major themes in environmental cognition.

SUBJECTIVE DEFINITION OF AREAS AND DISTANCE[2]

It seems possible to identify three major topic areas in environmental cognition: the subjective definition of areas, subjective distance, and mental maps. The first two will be discussed in this section. It is also possible to distinguish between perception, cognition, and evaluation in people's response to the environment. Without elaborating this in any major way, it can be suggested that *perception* refers mainly to the direct experience of the environment through the senses, *cognition* deals with the imposition of order on the environment and all knowledge of it, including that derived indirectly (i.e., not based on direct experience), and *evaluation* or *preference*, although part of the cognitive process, can be seen separately as related to a ranking of elements and qualities along some preference scale. The distinction can also be seen in terms of increasing cultural variability in these three aspects (Rapoport and Hawkes, 1970). Both in the structuring of the environment physically (design, building, organization, shaping) and conceptually (cognitive schemata, mental maps) all three concepts play a role.

Let us briefly examine the subjective definition of areas (see Lee, 1968; Klein, 1967; Golledge and Zannaras, 1973). In this case, the cues selected may vary—they may be physical, social (e.g., homogeneity), social interaction in terms of networks or the house–settlement system, density, and so on. In each case, the definition of these elements is part of the cognitive organization (so that privacy, density, etc., are all culturally variable). For example, a neighborhood defined in terms of homogeneity will depend on definitions of desired interaction (and hence on definitions of privacy as the control of unwanted interaction). This will involve definitions of "wanted," "interaction," and "avoidance," involving both levels and mechanisms of interaction, and definitions of when and with whom one interacts and under what conditions. Also involved will be the specification of mechanisms for the control of interaction—

spatial, physical, social, temporal, or psychological. In fact, the desire for a homogeneous area is a social control mechanism of unwanted interaction. This, in turn, affects definitions of density, the sharing of preferences for particular environmental codes and devices, as well as rules on the use of places (e.g., streets) for particular activities that are extremely variable (Rapoport, 1969, 1973b; Hartman, 1963; Becker, 1973). This definition of an area as suited or unsuited for certain activities is, of course, an example of a cognitive domain.

All of these characteristics and many others play a role in the subjective definition of an area such as a neighborhood or a central business district. The evaluation of such areas as good or bad will then affect the home range and the location and distribution of friends. These, in turn, will affect the knowledge of the city and hence further movement.

Areas are thus also defined subjectively on the basis of attraction, symbolic value, and the like, and there is a large literature on some of these aspects in terms of habitat selection as in the case of intra-urban migration (E. G. Moore, 1972; Stea, 1967; Jonassen, 1961), the evaluation of environments generally as discussed in the literature on migration, the varied landscape preferences of different groups, the changes in landscape preferences over time, and preferences regarding cities or suburbs (White and White, 1962; Glass, 1955; Donaldson, 1969). These can all be understood in terms of cognitive domains such as good-bad, desirable-undesirable, sacred-profane (Eliade, 1961; Littlejohn, 1967). For example, the Australian Aborigine's or African Bushman's love of the desert, the Eskimo's feeling for the arctic, or some residents' positive evaluation of areas regarded as slums (Hartman, 1963; Fried and Gleicher, 1961) can be seen as instances of relative habitability (Fraser, 1968; Rapoport and Watson, 1972).

The concept of sacred-profane typically occurs in primitive societies and is an example of a categorization such as use-avoid with powerful sanctions. This approach enables us conceptually to link the behavior of Eskimos avoiding areas in Alaska because they are dangerous due to spirits, ghosts, monsters, and the like (Burch, 1971) with the behavior of French tour-

ists (or natives) avoiding areas of Manhattan because they are dangerous. The processes are the same and one model fits them; what varies are the criteria and the data used. Preference and the definition of areas in terms of preference, or even common characteristics (stable, upgrading, deteriorating), is also affected by differences in temporal orientation. There are taxonomies of time in terms of past versus future, linearity versus cyclicity that are culturally extremely variable (Doob, 1971; Yaker, Osmond, and Cheek, 1971; Panoff, 1969; Ortiz, 1972). These even vary between the United States and Great Britain and have major implications for the meaning, preference, and ultimately the design and use of the environment; the future orientation of the United States and the past orientation of Britain have led to very different environment evaluations and hence different results, as have the comparable differences between Germany and other European countries (Lowenthal, 1968; Lowenthal and Prince, 1965, pp. 204–208; Holzner, 1970).

We shall see in the next section how these kinds of cognitive schemata may affect behavior and mental maps. At this point, it is interesting to point out that the distinctions proposed are relevant in urban cognition since it appears that there are differences in how the city is perceived, remembered, and valued. Thus, mental imagery is related to value and meaning, which, one might add, plays an important role because of its part in the process of giving meaning to the world. It appears that structural elements are important in how the city is perceived, and social elements are most important in how it is valued; both structural and social elements are important in what is remembered (Rozelle and Baxter, 1972). It would then follow that the subjective definition of areas in terms of perception, evaluation, and memory may be different. Different groups will differ in all three—in what they perceive, what they value, and how they remember things (i.e., the mnemonics used). For example, children have been shown to select apparently minor elements in the city (very different to those expected) and to use these to construct mnemonics (Sieverts, 1969), and children of different cultural background and classes select different elements, attach different importance to them and arrange them differently (Maurer and Baxter, 1972). Australian Aborigines select sets of cues very different from those which we might select; they value different parts of the environment, so that ritual places are more important than economic resources. They construct different forms of mnemonics based on their taxonomies, codified in diagrammatic maps (Rapoport, 1972). There is evidence of cultural differences in the forms of remembering and forgetting, and hence of mnemonics, which will affect this process (Bartlett, 1932).

At this point, there are two potential links with the psychological approach to environmental cognition, which, at least in its recent development, has stressed learning and memory. First, since memory involves the recording of perceptual information, the types of units used (chunks; G. A. Miller, 1956) will tend to vary with culture, since the codes used and how elements are grouped also varies. Since complex environmental information can only be handled through some form of chunking or the use of symbols (Moles, 1966), the variation in the type of units used and their grouping is likely to be important. The form of chunking used is, of course, the result of learning although the process itself is general.

Second, if learning about the environment is hypothesized to be a function of the physical environment, the individual, the group to which he belongs, and the extent and nature of travel, then all are affected by culture. Children, even more than adults, learn conceptual systems through example and enculturation. This learning also occurs through the environment itself. One could further hypothesize that, if the physical environment is congruent with the cognitive schemata of people, the process of learning is aided and the process of forming mental maps is eased and speeded; there would be more sharing of schemata and a clearer definition of areas. Here again cross-cultural studies, particularly of traditional societies, would be useful since in such societies there is a better congruence between physical and conceptual space—the environment is more clearly an expression of cognitive domains and conceptual "places" (Rapoport, 1970c; Rapoport, 1975). Since mental maps consist of places and the distances between

them arranged in a certain specific manner, another major theme of environmental cognition is subjective distance, into which time also enters because distance in many cases is defined in terms of time, as is the case in many primitive and peasant cultures in the United States (Hallowell, 1955; D. L. Thompson, 1969). For example, we find that in one particular culture area, the Anglo-American, there are major differences in one component of subjective distance— its relation to direction. In fact, the results seem to be diametrically opposed. In Britain, Lee (1962, 1970) suggests that distances toward the city center are seen as shorter than those away from the center; Golledge, Briggs, and Demko (1969) suggest that in the United States the exact opposite is true.

The tendency would be to explain such major inconsistencies as being due to methodological or epistemological differences, but the cross-cultural approach being discussed leads to another possibility. The unifying model seems to be one of meaning, so that one can hypothesize that the difference might be due to the meaning attached to urban elements, that is, to preference. In the United States, the center is seen negatively; in Britain it is still seen positively. In any case, this kind of analysis seems more valid and convincing than just the "fact" that subjective distance varies in specific ways. This "attractiveness hypothesis" is supported by studies of the use of Australian beaches (Mercer, 1972) in which preference and relation to downtown are closely linked; given equidistant beaches, those in the direction away from downtown are used more, which I would interpret as being "effectively closer" (although I am only *inferring* this). Similarly, at a larger scale, a number of studies have shown a link between preference and subjective distance (Ekman and Bratfisch, 1965; Bratfisch, 1969), and this also seems to explain subjective distance and time estimates in the case of shops in the United States (D. L. Thompson, 1969). In at least one study in the United States in which this hypothesis was tested, it was not supported (Cadwallader, 1973b), but the weight of the evidence seems to point to the importance of this hypothesis.

The use of a wider sample provides some validity for the hypothesis by contrasting the attraction of the center of the city in Europe (Lamy, 1967; Heinemeyer, 1967) with its well-known negative connotations in the United States, which I would, once again, interpret in terms of the great variability of the value and symbolic aspects of the environment (Rapoport and Hawkes, 1970). There are also cases for which no value, positive or negative, is attached to the center (Stanislawski, 1950); one might suggest that in such cases the effects of direction on subjective distance would be absent or much weaker. More general cross-cultural and historical geographic data tend to support the view that preference is involved (Watson, 1969; Heathcote, 1965, K. Thompson, 1969); this is also supported by major historical cognitive or image shifts (e.g., Nicolson, 1959), all of which can effectively be interpreted in terms of reduction of subjective distance making settlement more attractive. Thus, I would add differential attractiveness (symbolic, associational, social, or schematic) to the five mechanisms proposed as operating in the area of subjective distance—motor response, time and velocity estimates, perception, regular patterns, and symbolic representations such as maps and signs (Briggs, 1973a, p. 187). See also Chapter 30.

All these very diverse examples, and some already discussed previously, take on meaning and become part of a more general model when seen in terms of this broader view of cognition. Places in the environment are classified and named (e.g., center), meaning and value are attached to them (e.g., good or bad), and behavior and use follow in terms of selective attraction or importance, which, in turn, affects the subjective definition of distance. The selective attraction of environments affects people's knowledge of the environment, travel behavior, frequency of use, and in turn their subjective definition of distance and mental maps. Preference for environments affects travel through them, knowledge of them, and then use (see Adams, 1969). This is related to culturally based preferences for environments expressed through selection ("good" areas) and avoidance ("slum" or high-crime areas). Cultural schemata may also affect the sensory worlds in which people live (Wober, 1966; Carpenter, 1973; Hall, 1959, 1966; Eibl-Eibesfeld, 1970) and, hence, the elements they notice and organize in the environment. Environmental preference is also related to arousal levels as a

personality trait. Here, again, there is a link with the anthropological approach, at least to the extent that there is evidence (although not unequivocal) on the relationship of culture, values, norms, and model personality (Le Vine, 1973). Personality is also affected by what individuals learn and expect and by their adaptation levels, and these are certainly affected, at least in part, by cultural mechanisms (within the constraints of man-as-organism). Thus, different cultures have different space–time concepts, different views of reality, and different ways of defining places and giving them meaning.

MENTAL MAPS AND ORIENTATION

The term "mental map" has been used in different ways, which results in some confusion. In my view, for example, preference structures are not mental maps even when these are mapped by researchers. I shall confine the use of the term "mental maps" to subjective spatial representations by people of the environment. Preference structures form part of the broadest class of cognitive constructs (schemata), whereas images can be understood as involving mainly affective and symbolic aspects. In the study of mental maps in the psychological–geographical perspective, a major stress has been on learning and the ways in which mental maps are constructed. In the anthropological perspective, there has been rather little interest in learning, the concern being rather with the nature of orientational systems (and, to a much lesser extent, cognitive maps).

One exception, an introspective study (Wallace, 1965), deals with the selective nature of cues, the relationship to the task and its routinization, the different senses used (all culture related), and the process of first simplifying, then elaborating, then simplifying at a higher level, and so on (related to taxonomic processes and apparently a function of information-processing ability (Moles, 1966). This process raises interesting questions about the stage in this cyclic process at which mental maps are studied. If development is culturally different in sequence and timing, as appears at least possible (Suchman, 1966), it would follow that comparisons might have to be at chronologically different points for various groups to be truly equivalent. The culturally different ways in which areas are selected, classified, named and organized would also have to be considered in any comparison. That cultural differences do affect the system can be seen in situations of culture change. For example, the Fang, in Africa, traditionally used a river-based orientational system, which acted as a framework for cognitive maps. Among younger men, however, this has changed to a *road-based* system; as a result the cognitive schema of village–fields–bush–river has changed to road–town with very different importance, preference, and organization, and probably different mental maps and orientational systems (Fernandez, 1970). Of course, the change is due to the changed relative importance of the two elements, rivers and roads, thus relating to many of the points made above.

A comparison of the construction of mental maps among different groups would reveal differences in framework, sequence, final form, and so on; thus, in addition to the effects of age, sex, class, and travel behavior, cognitive maps may be related to culture. One way of checking this is to study single groups over time so as to be able to relate mental maps to culture change (as well as the more common study of different groups). One way of imposing order on the world is through organizing cues into wholes and using these constructs for movement and behavior, that is, establishing orientational systems. These have been described as codifying and classifying the "whatness and whereness" and their organization into schemata so that people are enabled to navigate (Lee, 1968).

Orientational systems are thus partly related to cognitive domains. Given this, a cross-cultural approach to urban cognition will make its principles more generally relevant—to U.S. cities, to other cities, to cities in the past, or to nomadic societies. The question is how do different cultures and subcultures devise and use orientational systems to impose order on the chaos that is the city or the natural environment; how do they ensure that members of the group share these systems rather than idiosyncratically use the widely varied systems that are theoretically possible, (and have been documented)? Clearly this is done partly through learning and enculturation and partly

through the environment itself (as already suggested). Thus, if, as I have already argued, the order in people's minds as embodied in the built environment and the interpretation of the built environment in people's minds are related, they are also likely to be mutually reinforcing. Once an environment is shaped in a particular way it will be used differently; different organizational–orientational–mapping systems will be used, different directions given, and people will then learn the given spatial system in all these ways.

For example, if we compare Milwaukee, Wisconsin (or any Midwestern city), and Charlotte, North Carolina (which is less typical in the United States) as in Figure 1, we find two very different spatial layouts (reflecting two different cognitive schemata). The contrast is largely one of a block numbering system organized by geographic directions from a point of origin versus named districts, and a grid versus a free road layout. As a result, in Milwaukee directions are to go west down X blocks or miles, then to turn left and go south Y blocks, turn right and go west Z blocks. The address is 1234 W. such a street. In Charlotte, directions are to a *named area*, within that to a landmark (i.e., shopping area), then street intersection and a very *few* blocks. This is taught by the environment (if one uses blocks in Charlotte, one gets lost due to the diverging and curved streets), and one also learns it from people's instructions. It is of interest to note that differences of this type can be found between Western and Japanese cities and in the schemata of the nonelderly and the elderly; thus, it is possible that these are two major modes used by people.

Since orientation is location in space, instructions are meant to enable someone to find a location (address) within a given physical conceptual space using some agreed upon system. The system may vary and instructions may vary in many different ways; these variations have been very well discussed for one American group, taxi drivers (Psathas, 1972), for whom context and familiarity affect directions given. Similarly, directions given vary in Western and Japanese cities as a function of the very different conceptual systems used to organize them.

It would follow from these examples that, for more diverse groups, orientational systems would vary even

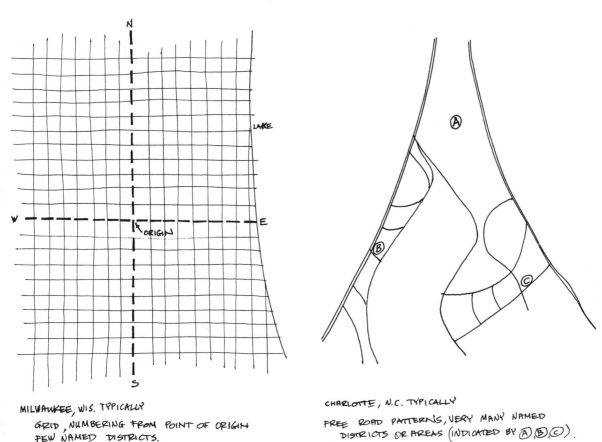

MILWAUKEE, WIS. TYPICALLY
GRID, NUMBERING FROM POINT OF ORIGIN
FEW NAMED DISTRICTS.

CHARLOTTE, N.C. TYPICALLY
FREE ROAD PATTERNS, VERY MANY NAMED
DISTRICTS OR AREAS (INDICATED BY (A),(B),(C)).

FIGURE 1
Schematic layouts of two different U.S. cities (reflecting two different cognitive schemata).

more. At the same time, it is clear that the need for orientation is general and crucial for any motile organism to survive. We can assume that, although this need is universal and there are some general ways of orienting that may be species specific, culturally specific ways of orientation are learned. Thus, even animals, within their specific phylogenetically derived orientational system, have to learn their way about; if the cues used are changed, the organism may lose its way (Eibl-Eibesfeld, 1970, pp. 220, 363–380).

Thus, there is a question of the cues used; that is, what are the noticeable differences in the environment that can be used to construct mental maps and for orientation? Cues are related to culture (e.g., aborigines, Eskimos and many others use cues that are often imperceptible to Europeans), are then organized into various and varying coordinate systems (e.g., subtle sand and vegetation variations or animal tracks are used among aborigines and Bushmen while snow texture, wind, smell, etc., are used by Eskimos who, hence, navigate differently than do Europeans; Carpenter, 1973), and finally different plans are employed to use the system devised. As another example, Trukese and European navigational systems differ profoundly, and this affects both the cues used and the resultant behavior. Europeans start with a rigid plan and the voyage is closely related to it and structured by it. The Trukese begin with a goal and respond to changes *en route*, doing whatever is necessary to reach the objective. The two systems represent two different thought processes and, although the Trukese system cannot be verbalized and thus can only be learned by example, the two are equally effective within their specific contexts (Gladwin, 1964).

As urban environments become larger, more complex, and shared by different cultural groups, orientation becomes increasingly important once again. Orientation thus becomes a crucial element in environmental cognition and takes place through the selection of features and their relation through some system. Thus, any orientational system involves recognition of elements, their mutual interrelationship within a conceptual framework, and the relation of these to the organism. This is then both part of the larger view of cognition being discussed in this paper and a general property of the environment, which can be seen in terms of the relation of things to things, things to people, and people to other people and judgments about these relationships.

If one accepts Lynch's (1960) categories as being valid in themselves, the question still remains of *how* a landmark, node, edge, district, or path is defined, what cues are used, how these are grouped, and how they are then used in orientation. These are all aspects of cognition in the sense in which I have been using it, and require cross-cultural analysis. Thus, the selection of landmarks may well vary, as may the definition of an element as path or edge, so that to a driver a freeway may be a path while to a pedestrian it becomes a barrier; and it will also be classified differently by someone favorably or unfavorably inclined to freeways or cars. This type of context may play a role in orientation, so that a single study of orientation done in (1) Los Angeles, a city of specific character related to the car, with (2) a population that is very car oriented, and given (3) a task that is very car oriented (e.g., Jones, 1972) is not adequate to generalize about urban orientation. The same task given to a different group—not North American, not in Los Angeles, not college students, and in a different city (New Delhi, Paris, or even San Francisco) and

for a different task—may well have elicited a different set of behaviors and cues used. Thus, generalizations about urban orientation can only be done based on a comparative, cross-cultural approach.

As another example, the definition of a district is an instance of the subjective definition of areas discussed earlier, so that the maps produced and the reference points used, as well as the forms of organization, vary with culture as well as with needs and activities. In any study, it would be most interesting to compare the maps themselves and the three levels of organizational development found by Moore (1973b, 1975a) with those in other cultures. For example, in replicating Lynch in a Lebanese city, Gulick (1963) found cultural differences that seemed to suggest a greater stress on social meaning and significance, as opposed to physical characteristics of the environment. This seems to be an important finding, although it has not, to my knowledge, been taken up. In view of some evidence cited above, this raises a most important question (which seems to apply to developmental approaches in psychology generally) about the extent to which developmental changes and stages are culturally variable, either in kind or in terms of sequence and timing.

Certain cues are used to define areas in terms of various criteria whether physical or related to social status, so that people, in fact, judge social status and identity by using environmental cues (Duncan, 1973; see also Chapters 17 and 21; Royse, 1969). These may not only be variable in different cultures but may also be used to judge and evaluate these areas. These judgments affect avoidance, use, movement, and so on, as we have already seen, and, as should be clear from our discussion so far, seem to be a fairly fundamental cognitive act of classifying the world into usable–not usable. This act is also part of the larger choice model, which, I have argued, is fairly central in understanding man-environment interaction (Rapoport, 1973c; 1975).

I has been suggested that a very fundamental division of the world is into edible-nonedible (Simoons, 1961); other dualities have been suggested, such as sacred-profane, clean-dirty, safety–danger, and so on (e.g., Eliade, 1961). The general use of dual classifications seems fairly frequent and affects environmental taxonomies as, for example, in the major distinctions city–county (Davis, 1969) or front–back, which seem very important regarding the environment and affect the communicative value of artifacts and the use of the city. At a more fundamental level front–back may reflect allowed–not allowed, done–not done, public–private, display–nondisplay, and so forth (Fernandez, 1970; Littlejohn, 1967; Austin, 1975; Kamau, 1975; Payatos, 1975). It also seems likely that there is often a middle term involved, so that, for example, between city and wilderness we find the garden—the middle landscape (Marx, 1964).

Since it is generally accepted that mental maps, subjective distance, and definition of areas depend on the environment itself, the paths used, means of travel, frequency of use and familiarity with areas, both the nature of the environment (itself a result of cognitive processes) and avoidance behavior in the environment (as a function of cognitive schemata) will affect mental maps and their metric. For example, in our society the mental maps of housewives with small children and those of their husbands differ (Everett and Cadwallader, 1972; Orleans and Schmidt, 1972). More generally, it can be expected that mental maps of men and women will differ even more in those cultures in which differences in sex role and activity orbits are greater. This is, then, likely to be an important variable in mental map formation.

The preceding has implications for a study of behavioral space in the city as a function of familiarity and level of "development," whether individual or cultural. A useful analogy may be the relationship between the size of home range and age with culture and class. Since it is hypothesized that man–environment interaction is mediated by cognitive representations, it is reasonable to ask whether home-range behavior, mobility, and behavioral space in the city are related to cognitive representations, and to consider whether the very clear differences in such behavior and spaces among children, the elderly, various population subgroups, and whole populations may be related to the developmental level (organismic and cultural) of such groups. It would also be of interest to raise the question of to what extent differences in the nature of movement systems (walking, driving, bicycling, public transport) and direction of travel (all

of which relate to culture and subculture) may be involved in the developmental sequence, which suggests relationships among studies that might otherwise be seen in isolation (Appleyard, 1970b; Appleyard and Okamoto, 1969; Steinitz, 1968; Adams, 1969).

Thus, if we also added to the variables considered the cultural and subcultural cognitive styles, which not only affect the nature of cognitive representations but also the learning process, we might begin to introduce and relate many more of the variables involved in the process of environmental cognition. This would have implications for the design of the physical environment in response to developmental changes (e.g., children or the elderly) but also allow design to respond to culture and subculture, as expressed in cognitive styles (if these can indeed be shown to be significant). If, on the other hand, these were shown not to be significant, they could be eliminated from consideration; but this cannot be done without such a test.

We have seen that the various cognitive processes described affect the use or nonuse of areas, since use depends on attraction or repulsion. As an example, among Australian Aborigines, resources, culture, and myth lead to specific movement patterns, home ranges, and knowledge of the environment (Rapoport, 1972). Similarly, perceived stress, which is related to norms, leads to migration, which in turn leads to use and affects knowledge (Clark and Cadwallader, 1973). Hence, cognition affects home range and use of space. These are also affected by *age*, so that home range, nonexistent for infants, gradually rises to a peak and then declines with old age; by *climate*, so that winter home ranges are more limited than summer ones (Michelson, 1971); by *socioeconomic status*, so that, by and large, high-status individuals tend to have more extensive home ranges than low-status individuals (although this can be reversed in some situations).

In turn, home range and use affect mental maps (which tend to stress *known* areas) and hence affect behavior. It has been shown that in Lima, some population groups, as a function of culture, do not know of the existence of football grounds used by lower-class groups, which form a most important part of their urban systems (Doughty, 1970). This affects the use (or nonuse) of such recreation areas, the evaluation of recreational resources, and also their availability, and hence the evaluation of the adequacy of parts of the urban environment. This evaluation is also affected by the classification of, say, streets and other areas as being available or not for play or other activities, which is a function of shared cognitive rules (Hartman, 1963; Suttles, 1968; Schak, 1972). These rules about use–nonuse are, of course, an important part of the taxonomic, cognitive process and thus affect behavior. There are two things about such rules: they may not be shared and thus generate conflict (which is one reason for the preference for homogeneous residential areas), and they may change with cultural change. In the latter case, behavior, use, and mental maps would change accordingly. For example, in Bali, traditionally, mountains were seen as good and the sea as bad, and settlement and use were principally inland. With colonization and more recently with the growth of tourism (which means beaches), there is a reversal of the traditional categorization. Similarly, different migrant groups have, at various times, categorized environments as habitable or not habitable with major effects on settlement, as has been the case in North America and Australia (Watson, 1969; Heathcote, 1965; K. Thompson, 1969).

Another cognitive process that affects mental maps is time structure. Because the allocation of available time, the rhythms and tempos of activities, and their synchronization will affect how frequently different parts of the city are seen, whether they are seen during the day or at night, during working hours or on weekends (in themselves an example of a cognitive taxonomy!), at leisure or in a hurry, and so on, they will also affect the development of mental maps. In other words, temporal cognitive splits may affect mental maps as much as preference, avoidance, and so on, since how time is used affects which people one meets or misses and hence the evaluation of the social environment.

There is an interesting parallel between this notion of the relation of usable space and mental maps and the notion of the different *unwelten* of animals (von Uexküll, 1957). This notion of *unwelt* seems very important because it suggests, once again, that cog-

nitive representations, orientational systems, mental maps, and the like, are *very basic* and that there is continuity with animals (Peters, 1972; Wynne-Edwards, 1962). There are also some recent attempts to show the importance of mental maps and cognitive constraints for explaining the behavior of people from earliest days (Spoehr, 1956; Glacken, 1966; Davidson, 1972).

CONCLUSIONS

I have suggested that the environment and its design can be seen as the organization of time, meaning, communication, and space. One can also argue, as I have done elsewhere, that the organization of space is the most important and reflects and affects all the others. Hence, I have argued that the process of cognition is involved in both conceptualizing the environment and in designing it.

It is because of this view about the link between cognitive domains and spatial domains that different classifications of space become important. It is also because of this that the view of cognition here proposed is important in (1) comparing environments, (2) studying cognitive maps, and (3) studying effects of environment on behavior. Only through comparative cross-cultural studies can one see in general whether this view is correct and in particular how cognitive domains and spaces are related. What one is looking for is the possible congruence between physical and conceptual space as revealed through semantic domains, codes, schemata, and so on. All these can be understood in terms of the question, *How is the world ordered conceptually and how are conceptual categories expressed both in the physical environment and in people's mental schemata of that environment?*

If one accepts the basic argument that cognition is not so much *knowledge of* the environment as *giving it meaning through imposing an order on it*, it follows that studying what people select and name, how they classify elements, how they organize these through schemata, and hence how they split the world into domains become important. The role of environmental schemata is to help simplify the world and to provide mnemonics so that one can know what to do and where to do it (i.e., how to behave). In this view, mental maps and images are partly simplifying and mnemonic devices that form part of a larger system of simplifying the world. Since memory is important in the use of the environment, mnemonic schemata are important in cognition. This gives us another opportunity to build larger theoretical structures by linking the cognitive processes of, say, Australian Aborigines and American motorists in terms of the mnemonics used (Rapoport, 1972; Carr and Kurilko, 1964).

The view presented here is not exclusive to anthropology. There are related views in psychology (one can interpret aspects of Piaget and Bruner in these terms). There are similarities with the view (Kelly, 1955) that, in the same way that "man the scientist" makes sense of the world, man in the environment makes sense of the environment by giving it meaning through using taxonomies, categories, and schemata. He does that both conceptually and through design, and the two interact. The world is made meaningful through being humanized; one takes possession of it through cultural constructs—whether symbolic or physical—and through attaching meaning. There is also a similarity and overlap here to structural anthropology as well—the cognitive, ethnoscience approach —which is concerned with studying the taxonomic categories of particular groups and generalizing across groups. All have in common this one aspect—that cognition is the process of *ordering* and *giving meaning* rather than *knowledge* and *impression* of the environment.

There are beginnings of parts of this approach in the environmental cognition literature. Thus, when Appleyard (1969a, 1970b) speaks of associational, topological, and positional, structuring in mental mapping, he introduces cultural variability (specially in the associational criteria and partly in the positional). But if we broaden this cross-culturally, we may find other variables in mental mapping, such as the ones we have been discussing (which elements are selected, the taxonomies used, cognitive styles, the categories, schemata, and domains derived, and the symbols and meanings attached). It may then be found that various forms of structuring and giving meaning to the environment exist and are related to

specific cultures and specific forms of the environment. It would be most useful to know the variety of ways of structuring, their range, their limits, their relation to other social and cultural variables, any regularities that exist, and so on.

If environmental cognition is the process of imposing order through the making of places (distinctions), if this process varies and is done in the ways in which I have described it, then urban (and *environmental*) cognition through images and mental maps is a special case of a larger process. It is not merely a way of simplifying the environment and not simply a mnemonic device, but it is a way of establishing *places* in the larger environment. This is a much more fundamental process and has major implications for our understanding of environments that to us, and at first glance, appear chaotic because we do not understand the ordering schemata and the meanings attached to places.

The fact that behavior takes place within the cognized environment and that images and meanings affect behavior relates cognition, as a process of giving meaning, to the communicative function of the environment, and cognition is then involved both in the coding and decoding process. This means that the meaning of features of the environment is a matter of definitions, it is cultural and has to be learned to understand how meaning affects behavior (Brower, 1965; Duncan, 1973). A cross-cultural study of such signs and how they provide cues in behavior settings and affect behavior through rules would be most important. It is even possible that in addition to cultural variability we may also find certain patterns which are common to one species, so that there may be archetypes defined as the most common and likely schemata (McCully, 1971). The suggestion that I made several times about the role of schemata at both ends of the coding-decoding process can be shown diagramatically as in Figure 2 which clarifies the suggestion made above about the importance of congruence between designers' (in the broadest sense) cognitive schemata and users'—and the importance of matching the physical environment to the underlying cognitive schemata. Hence, also the value of studying traditional cultures where this congruence is clear (Rapoport, 1975) and also the difficulty of

FIGURE 2
Diagram of the role of cognitive schemata at both ends ot ehe environmental cognitive coding–decoding process.

the matching process in complex societies because there are many different schemata (Axelrad, 1969), because cues may be unnoticed, not understood, or rejected, and because many groups do not shape their environment.

It follows that it is important to study environments as reflecting ideas and cognitive schemata (Eliade, 1961; Langer, 1953; Kamau, 1975; Austin, 1975; Wheatley, 1971; Rykwert, n.d.; Duncan, 1973), since environments cannot be read, even by scholars, unless the underlying cognitive structure is understood. It also follows that different conceptual approaches and methods should be used in the study of environmental cognition so that the interrelationship between the two major approaches identified here can be studied and all studies can be comparative—cross-culturally *and* through time. This will reveal the full range of cognitive styles, the frequency of various ways of imposing meaning, the relation of cognitive styles to other sociocultural variables, and the relation of cognitive styles to forms of environmental organization.

In conclusion, a general comment may be in order about the cognitive approach as a whole in the context of environment-behavior studies. It is, I believe, most useful, stimulating, and potentially fruitful. It

would be even more so if the broader view of "cognition" were also used and, more generally, if there were more comparative studies. Finally, as for man-environment studies generally, we need to begin to develop larger models and theories comparing many studies not only within environmental cognition work itself but also in different areas of study (Rapoport, 1970b, 1973a, 1973b). What I am really arguing for is that the approach which I have been expounding be, as it were, combined with the types of approaches already being used and illustrated in this book. The final result would greatly enrich the very valuable and most important work that environmental cognition has brought to the study of man-environment relations.

NOTES

1. For a different view about the differences between the psychological and anthropological views of cognition, and the link between them, see Neisser (1968).

2. I shall elaborate on this and other topics in this and the next section in a forthcoming book on urban form.

20

Harold C. Conklin
Department of Anthropology
  Yale University

ETHNOGRAPHIC SEMANTIC ANALYSIS OF IFUGAO LANDFORM CATEGORIES[1]

Ifugao, a subregion of the northwestern Luzon cordillera of the Philippines, exhibits a remarkably high degree of cultural and environmental interdependence. The inhabitants of this mountainous area have long been known for their astonishing feats of engineering in the construction and maintenance of extensive rice terraces, which are visually the most impressive aspect of the intricately patterned landscape (Molano, 1801; see Keesing, 1962; Alarcón, 1965; see Figures 1 and 2). Surprisingly, however, detailed descriptions of this terracing and of related economic activities are conspicuously lacking. Even the rich anthropological accounts of legal, ritual, and social behavior (e.g., Barton, 1919, 1922; Lambrecht, 1932–1951) do not include precise land-use data or other forms of ecological documentation. To some extent, this situation reflects the general unavailability of environmental information on the area, for when I began my research there were no published weather records, reliable hydrologic data, accurate large-scale maps, or cadastral surveys covering any part of Ifugao.

This unevenly chronicled but highly imageable arena of extraordinary hydraulic and agronomic performance thus presents the ecologically oriented field investigator with a considerable challenge. High relief, dispersed settlements, and densely but irregularly clustered agricultural holdings contribute to the observable complexity (Figure 1). Among the hundreds of thousands of terraced fields in central Ifugao, for example, no two fields have the same form or dimensions, except by accident. In surface area, each of these individually controlled inundated plots ranges from as little as 2 or 3 square meters to more than 10,000 square meters (1 hectare).

To describe and evaluate the allocation and utilization of resources in such an uncharted indigenous system of tropical agriculture, it is helpful to consider a number of general questions. How does an ethnographer approach an unfamiliar landscape, determine its conceptual and observable components, and record the changes that may affect these elements and their interrelationships through time? How can meaningful measurements and comparisons be made? How are the often complex data most effectively expressed? Without satisfactory answers to such queries and to their more specific derivatives (see Conklin, 1957; Frake, 1962), one cannot hope to obtain precise or testable evidence of how a particular system has developed and how it is maintained, or to make

FIGURE 1
Ifugao agricultural landscape. A low oblique aerial photograph of a part of Banaue, in north central Ifugao, looking north–northeast, August 12, 1961.

statements about it that have analytic, comparative, or long-term relevance. In a very preliminary fashion, I shall document recent attempts to cope with this type of ethnographic problem in Ifugao.

From July 1961 through 1965, during three short periods and throughout the academic year of 1962-1963, I was able to spend a total of 18 months in the central part of Ifugao, which was then still a sub-province of the Mountain Province. Within a few kilometers of almost any inhabited point in this area, one can observe a wide range of agricultural activities that are obviously related within one larger pattern, but which also reflect local adaptations to

contrasting biotic and physical components of the montane environment. Elevations above sea level range from less than 250 to more than 2,800 meters (from about 800 to more than 9,000 feet), and water resources vary from abundant for all purposes to seasonally deficient.

Based on the first summer's ethnographic and aerial reconnaissance, I chose for regional study and detailed mapping a subarea of approximately 100 square kilometers (about 40 square miles), roughly one tenth of the agriculturally occupied part of Ifugao. In this survey area, which includes the upper reaches of two adjacent valley systems, live approximately 10,000 Ifugao settled in more than 300 dispersed hamlets. Some 25 discrete agriculturally defined districts and several dialect areas are represented.

Within the central northern portion of this subarea I later selected a much smaller sector of about 5 square kilometers for concentrated field study and larger-scaled mapping. Bayninan, one of the 17 hamlets within the agricultural district in this focal area, became the site of our main field base. Checking with practices recorded for test hamlets in four neighboring districts indicates that, at least in outline, the structure of the agricultural system revealed in my study holds also for other central and northern sectors. Wherever Ifugao terminology is cited, however, I use only forms checked in and for Bayninan.

After October 1962, ethnographic work was conducted almost exclusively in the local dialect. Extensive collections, records, and investigations of environmental factors ranging from soils to vegetation were facilitated by cooperation with visiting specialists and by the enthusiastic participation of Ifugao assistants.

Agricultural System

For centuries, with only the simplest of hand tools, the Ifugao have farmed the steep slopes and valleys of their mountainous territory. This firmly established, integral, and continuing agricultural pattern (see Figures 1 to 4) depends on many factors: the availability of water for irrigation and soil transport; suitable earth or stone for construction and repair of embankments; a variety of vegetational habitats as sources of fuel, fencing, and other construction materials; a large number of protected and cultivated plant types including rice, sweet potatoes, legumes, and fruits; domesticated pigs, chickens, and ducks; the presence of mud fish, snails, and other aquatic fauna; sufficient labor to keep up the annual round of repairs, cultivation tasks, and associated rituals; and, most important, the knowledge of how these and many other economic factors are interrelated and how they may be profitably utilized.

The farming system of Ifugao is complex. As in all integral agricultural systems, most of the settings, material components, participants, and routines serve

FIGURE 2
Hamlet site on terraced slope. A closer view of the Banaue hamlet of Panalngan (also visible in Figure 1) showing features of the immediate and distant agricultural landscape, May 18, 1963.

multiple functions. For example, that which the Ifugao call *lūyoq*, the carefully puddled top layer of soil in an inundated field, not only provides a moist, fertile medium in which to grow rice and other wet crops, but this common agricultural artifact is also used for at least 10 other purposes: as a source of clay for coating and lining dikes (Figures 3 and 4); a smooth unobstructed surface across which piles of unwanted or excavated earth can be easily transported on sledge-like drag boards; a substance for vegetable and spice cultivation, which after being mixed with an essential aquatic weed that grows in or just above the *lūyoq* layer is formed into islet-like mounds (Figure 3); a convenient location for preserving hollow-log sluicing troughs used in repairing and filling terraces; a muddy vat for soaking, loosening, and softening bast-fiber plant materials used in tying; a protective and decorative staining agent for carved bowls and other wooden implements; a place in which to set or manipulate a variety of basket traps

FIGURE 3
Stone-walled, irrigated terraces. Contour-terraced, irrigated
pond fields, with vegetable mounds still visible at the right,
February 14, 1963.

for small pond fish; a source of many varieties of
aquatic snails, whose flesh furnishes a continual
supply of everyday food, the shells of some varieties
also being burned to make slaked lime; a seasonal

breeding ground for mole crickets and many other
forms of amphibious or semiaquatic edible fauna; and
a postharvest mud pool for children's sports.

Other parts of the artificial terraces (including the
lower layers of fill, waterworks, borders, and walls)
serve similarly diverse functions. In the local ecosystem, such fields can hardly be treated as simple
farm plots, leveled and watered solely for a single,
seasonal foodcrop. In spite of the strong cultural
bias emphasizing almost every aspect of rice farming,
Ifugao "rice terraces" are in fact multipurpose pond
fields.[2]

To study how these complex pond fields (*payo*) are
constructed and maintained, measured and counted,
assessed and exchanged, how their areas may be compared and the intricate overall land-use pattern made
explicit, it is helpful to begin with some basic cultural
data.

Pond fields. In its most frequent and general sense,
the Ifugao term *payo* means any type of irrigable
farmland that is hydraulically leveled and artifically
bunded. However, differing contexts, which are not
necessarily obvious to the outsider, provide for this
one label a wide range of semantic specificity and
precision. Differences of regional extent, contiguity,
and ownership of single fields or series of fields are
indicated in the word. For example, in terms of economic and legal units, one or more adjoining pond-
field "plots" may comprise a "parcel"; if privately
owned and managed as a unit, one or more parcels
in a district may constitute a "holding." Moreover,
within any clustered parcel, the "main field" (largest
in surface area and least attenuated) is distinguished
from its subsidiary plots. Each of these last four
English glosses translates an optional but determinable and specific sense of the term *payo*. In contrast
with *puquŋ*, meaning a "small insignificant pond
field," *payo* also designates a "well-formed, large
pond field." This distinction is relative only to the
size and shape pattern of fields throughout a particular region. This instance of a common type of
polysemy can be represented as follows:

$$X : a \cdot b / payo_1 \text{ (wider sense)}$$

$$Y : a \cdot b \cdot c / puquŋ \qquad X : a \cdot b \cdot \bar{c} / payo_2 \text{ (narrower sense)}$$

The unmarked term *X* indicates the form of both the generic category "pond field" defined by a combination of semantic features symbolized as *a · b*, as well as of the specific opposite of the marked term *Y*. Neither the added feature of size limitation, *c*, nor any expression of its absence, *c̄*, occurs at the more general level (Jakobson, 1957, p. 5). Subscripts distinguish different senses of the word.

There are many other locally recognized pond-field differences such as soil depth and embankment construction (see Spencer and Hale, 1961). However, these general distinctions illustrate the basic point that in locating, enumerating, and describing *payo* with respect to boundary disputes, inheritance rights, and similar problems, the kind of pond-field unit involved must be specified. Similarly, the relation between such units and other contrasting segments of the agricultural landscape should be established.

Landforms

The Ifugao distinguish hundreds of terrain variations involving forms and combinations of rock, soil, water, vegetation, and the results of agronomic activity. The coverage of this folk classification ranges from broad polysemous concepts such as *lūta* (land, earth) and *bīlid* (mountainous slopeland) to such highly specific particulars as *quduŋo* (limonite) and *qanul* (underground drainage conduits). Like the latter examples, many terms refer to special qualities, aspects, or components of the agricultural environment rather than to contrasting types of land surface in general. However, one intermediate-level contrast set of eight categories, including *payo*, does cover in a mutually exclusive manner all major vegetationally and agriculturally significant land surface types. A brief characterization of each of these locally distinguished landforms, listed in the general order of increasing agricultural involvement, follows:

1. *mapulun* or "grassland" (short, low, open grassland; often also *pulun*). Ridge and slopeland, untilled, covered with herbaceous grasses (*gūlun*, *Imperata* sp., *taŋlag*, *Themeda* sp., and others); public and unmanaged; open, unbounded, minimally valued; a source of outer roof thatch. Without new sources of irrigation water such land is not normally brought under cultivation. The

FIGURE 4
Intercropping of rice and taro. Woman walking along the top of a Bayninan pond-field terrace wall, March 14, 1963.

ridges and slopes of the most distant mountains visible in Figure 4 are largely "grassland."

2. *qinalāhan* or "forest" (public forest, distant forest). Slopeland, undisturbed soil, covered with various types of dense woody vegetation (from lower altitude mid-mountain climax forest to pine forest and mossy cloud forest types), public (for residents in the same general watershed area), and unmanaged; a source of firewood, other natural forest products, and game. See the most distant

slope in upper right of Figure 4.

3. *mabilāu* or "caneland" (cane grassland, high grassland, second growth, *runo* association). Mostly slopeland, unworked soil, covered with various stages of second-growth herbaceous and ligneous vegetation dominated by dense clumps of tall canegrass (*bilāu, Miscanthus* spp.); some protection and management (canegrass much used for construction, fencing, and so forth). See the higher uncleared slopes in Figure 2 and the closest background vegetation in upper right of Figure 4.

4. *pinūgu* or "woodlot" (private forest or grove; regional synonym *muyuŋ*). Slopeland, unturned soil, covered with high tree growth (timber and fruit trees, erect palms, climbing rattans, and so forth), privately owned and managed (undergrowth clearance, selective cutting, and some planting of desired tree, vine, and bamboo types). Boundaries are definite and relatively permanent, although without artificial markers. Such groves are valued for timber and other products, as a nearby source of firewood, and for protection of lower farmland from excessive runoff and erosion. See tree growth areas in vicinity of hamlets in Figures 1 and 2, and the darker rise in background, upper right of Figure 4.

5. *hābal* or "swidden" (slope field, camote field, kaingin; referential synonym *qūma*). Slopeland, cultivated and often contour-ridged (especially for sweet potatoes). Other highland dry-field crops (including taro, yams, manioc, corn, millet, mongo beans, and pigeon peas, but excluding rice except at elevations below 600 to 700 meters [2,000 feet] above sea level) are also cultivated in small stands or in moderately intercropped swiddens. Boundaries remain discrete during a normal cultivation cycle of several years. When fallow, succession is usually to a canegrass association. See the cleared patches on slopes in lower right of Figure 1 and in the background of Figure 2.

6. *lattaŋ* or "house terrace" (settlement, hamlet terrace, residential site; also *latāŋan*). Leveled terrace land whose surface is packed smooth or paved but not tilled; serving primarily as house and granary yards, work space for grain drying, and so forth; discrete, often fenced or walled, and named. See Figures 1 and 4.

7. *qīlid* or "drained field" (drained terrace, ridged terrace; often also *naqīlid*). Leveled terrace land whose surface is tilled and ditch mounded (usually in cross-contour fashion) for cultivation and drainage of dry crops, such as sweet potatoes and legumes. Drained fields, although privately owned, are kept in this temporary state for a minimum number of annual cycles before shifting back to a more permanent form of terrace use.

8. *payo* or "pond field" (bunded terrace, rice terrace, rice field; ritual synonyms: *banāno, daluŋēŋe; lubog, bākah*). Leveled farmland, bunded to retain irrigation water for shallow inundation of artificial soil, and carefully worked for the cultivation of wet-field rice, taro, and other crops; privately owned, discrete units with permanent stone markers; the most valued of all landforms. See Figures 1 to 4, 7, and 8.

From the contrastive properties noted in the first sections of each of these descriptions, one can derive a field-checked set of distinctive and minimal componential definitions for each of the eight landform categories:

Relevant oppositions (with respect to slope, soil, cover, and use):

$L : \bar{L}$	Leveled	:	Not leveled
$T : \bar{T}$	Tilled	:	Not tilled
$W : \bar{W}$	Wooded	:	Not wooded
$M : \bar{M}$	Managed maximally	:	Not managed maximally

Analytic definitions (symbols at the left stand for Ifugao categories but are derived mnemonically from English glosses):

G	Grassland	$\bar{L} \bar{T} \bar{W} \bar{M}$
F	Forest	$\bar{L} \bar{T} W \bar{M}$
C	Caneland	$\bar{L} \bar{T} \bar{W} M$
W	Woodlot	$\bar{L} \bar{T} W M$
S	Swidden	$\bar{L} T$
H	House terrace	$L \bar{T}$

D Drained field $L\,T\,\overline{M}$
P Pond field $L\,T\,M$

Each formulaic transcription accounts for the essential features visually distinguishing one landform from the others in a unique, concise, and nonredundant statement. The use of the term S always refers to a farmed slope ($\overline{L}\,T$), term H to an untilled horizontal surface ($L\,\overline{T}$), and so forth. For ethnographic mapping of cadastral data and for many other recording tasks, these distinctions are crucial, and for most identificational purposes they are sufficient.

These landforms also represent many contrastive patterns of use and change. Each category thus embraces more than can be adequately covered by the synchronic combination of a small number of vegetational, cultural, and edaphic features. Additional parallel attributes and multidimensional contrasts abound. Many implied differences in Ifugao landform classification relate only to past or potential changes in time and space determined by transitional restraints within the agricultural system. To analyze these alternatives and the restrictions governing them, it is helpful not only to focus on precise definition (Malinowski, 1935, pp. 79-87; Conklin, 1962), but also to consider patterns of succession from one differential stage of land usage to another.

Time and Space

After examining many records of changing terrain characteristics through seasonal, annual, and longer cycles of agricultural activity, similarities and connections as well as contrasts and oppositions obtaining among the landform types are easily discerned. They may often be expressed in diagrammatic form. In fact, all essential, ethnographically attested, sequential links interconnecting these eight landform types can be represented in the form of a finite directed graph (see Busacker and Saaty, 1965), as in Figure 5.

Vertices stand for the eight landforms and directed arcs represent possible changes through time (recursive loops indicating "internal" cyclic progressions). Special markings include the shape of the labeled nodes (square versus triangular, for leveled versus slope land); solidity of the node enclosure (broken versus

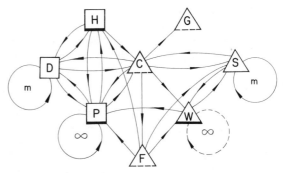

FIGURE 5
Graph of the eight landform types in Ifugao.

solid line, for nondiscrete versus discrete status); thickness of node base (extra thick versus normal line, for preferred terminal versus less preferred or nonterminal status); loop symbols (*m* versus ∞, for desired minimization of cycles [one season for D, drained field; about three years of S, swidden] versus desired perpetuation of normal cycles); and form of feedback arcs (broken versus unbroken line, for indefinite duration versus definite duration of cycles).

A large number of relational inferences are derivable from this network. The vertex C, caneland, for example, is the only articulation point in the network; its removal disconnects the graph and isolates the least involved pendant G, grassland. C is also the only node adjacent to all others. These clearly displayed features of the digraph underscore the non-recursive, unbounded, central but *intermediate* position of this landform, and reflect both its lack of sequential restrictions and its unique status as the normal extended fallow or second-growth association in the area. As abandoned terrace land loses its shape, a former P, pond field, D, drained field, or H, house terrace, may shift rapidly to C, caneland. It is the most generalized, as well as the most frequently encountered, of the agriculturally involved landforms.

A multigraph expanding the partial bilateral symmetry of the network could easily be constructed to show additional paired sets of contrasts linking correspondingly adjacent nodes. Note, for example, the correlation between P and D on one side and W and S on the other in terms of recognized microclimatic and biotic variation, which parallels the already indicated differences of slope and cultural evaluation. One can observe even more directly that such specific, hypothetical, one-step successions as G to W, G to D, P to S, F to G, and F to C are explicitly excluded from this system.

From such observations, it is apparent that for a community of Ifugao farmers an ideal long-term sequence begins in an initial, homogeneous, natural state of F, forest, and develops into an agriculturally dominated environment covered exclusively by P, pond field, W, woodlot, and H, house terraces. One of the easiest ways to assess the relative economic standing of an Ifugao agricultural district is to note the degree to which this target condition has been approached (see Figure 1).

In addition to facilitating the analysis of ideal or potential patterns, however, the general digraph also serves as a base from which actual cases can be represented. In the recording of recurring subcycles (sequences passing through some but not all nodes), successions worked out for individual sites can be expressed as partial subgraphs of the network. To illustrate, the history of a particular pond-field site, first cleared in 1937, follows (with years of duration of each landform in parentheses):

$$F(n) \rightarrow S(4) \rightarrow W(6) \rightarrow P(2) \rightarrow D(2) \rightarrow$$
$$[1937] \quad [1941] \quad [1947] \quad [1949]$$

$$C(6) \rightarrow S(5) \rightarrow W(3) \rightarrow (P(6+)$$
$$[1951] \quad [1957] \quad [1962] \quad [1965]$$

This progression can be represented as in Figure 6.

Such a series of short-term changes in the status of terrace land can be observed only at the periphery of an irrigated sector. At the "center" or the putatively oldest site of every agricultural district (*himpuntonāqan*), one finds a single, named, ritual plot or parcel (*puntonāqan*) that is traditionally the first to be planted, transplanted, and harvested. Owners of land at and near such sites tend to keep walls and fields in excellent condition and in a perpetual P state. The validity of genealogically linked chains-of-title recounted to establish the relative age, size, and ownership of these core fields is easy to assume but difficult to check. In a few instances,

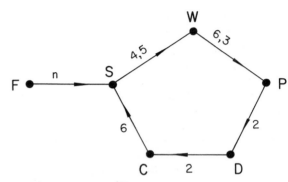

FIGURE 6
Graph of the history of a pond-field site first cleared in 1937.

photographs from the early 1900s have provided useful documentation of the remarkable continuity of pond-field margins and land use in these central areas.

The use of aerial photography. Aerial photographs can provide even better evidence, although the earliest available documentation of this type goes back only to 1945 (when the purpose of such photography was primarily to locate General Yamashita's troops) and is of very uneven coverage and quality. Recent aerial photography of the area, flown for this project (Conklin, 1967b, pp. 111–120; see the figures) meets the necessary standards for photogrammetric mapping. Coupled with detailed ground surveys, these photographs have been of immense help in relating Ifugao classifications and farming practices to locationally precise land units (see Conklin, in press).

To plot distances, areas, and gradients in an area of high relief, carefully compiled terrain maps are a necessity. Their previous unavailability for Ifugao severely limited the planimetric accuracy of even the best sketch maps (e.g., Beyer, 1908; Lambrecht, 1932, pp. 3–5) and village plans (Lambrecht, 1929), and apparently discouraged completely any attempts to chart the irregular boundaries of the terraced pond-field areas. Fortunately, as a result of recent developments in high-resolution aerial photography and machine mapping (Thompson, 1965), it is now possible, with relatively few ground control points, to determine contour differences of less than 2 meters from 1 : 12,000- to 1 : 20,000-scale stereopairs,

21

James S. Duncan and Nancy G. Duncan

Department of Geography
  Syracuse University

HOUSING AS PRESENTATION OF SELF AND THE STRUCTURE OF SOCIAL NETWORKS[1]

In this paper we suggest by means of a cross-cultural comparison that the key to understanding the social meaning of housing and its variable use in presentation of self (Goffman, 1959) lies in the structure of social networks. It is that which underlies whatever explanation has been proposed in terms of ethnic, social class, or cultural differences. Observation of two groups from different classes and cultures provides the material for this study. One group consists of working-class Americans, the other of upper-class Indians.

Much cross-cultural research to date centers on differences in the cognitive structuring of the environment. Rather than focusing on these differences, we consider some interesting similarities which serve to strengthen our hypothesis that differences in the communicative value of housing are due to differences in the structure of networks. We feel that there is a need for work that examines cross-cultural similarities as well as differences in environmental cognition. Cognition, in our view, is a socially constructed and managed phenomenon. Objects or groupings of objects such as home environments have social meanings. In other words, these meanings are developed and maintained or modified by groups; they arise out of the interaction among members of a social world. These social meanings or institutionalized cognitive images give rise to the possibility of communication through the use of objects. Individuals surround themselves with certain objects in order to communicate aspects of their social identity (e.g., socioeconomic status or group membership). Housing in certain cases is of importance in communicating identity (Duncan, 1973). This is especially true within certain types of social networks.

The study of *social networks* is in its infancy and there is not yet a consensus among researchers as to its definition. For the purpose of our study, it can be defined rather simply as a set of linkages among a number of people. These linkages indicate interaction usually among close friends or relatives whom one sees often. Researchers who use the social-network concept are exploring it in a number of different directions. Some are attempting to develop a model of the morphology and dynamics of a network. Others are attempting to discover the behavioral consequences of various types of networks. Our study is an example of the latter attempt. It is not intended to be a contribution to the study of the structural characteristics of social networks; rather, it broadly generalizes about the structure of the networks under consideration in order to show how this is linked to the role of housing in the communication of social status.

The data on the Indian group are drawn from our own field research on the new and old elites in Hyderabad, India. In this paper we will concentrate on the old elite, although referring to the more modern and recently established new elite for the purpose of comparison. The American material is drawn primarily from Herbert Gans's study *The Urban Villagers* (Gans, 1962) and is supplemented by data drawn from other studies of the American working and middle classes.

The methodology employed in our study of the old elite of Hyderabad was unstructured interviewing and observation. No quantitative analysis of the social networks was attempted. Therefore, our description of the structure of the network is impressionistic. Nevertheless, we believe in the accuracy of our observations in reference to the network as a whole. Similarly, because Gans did not use the concept of a social network in *The Urban Villagers*, we have had to rely on qualitative data concerning the predominant friendships and entertaining patterns among the West Enders.

The Old Elite of Hyderabad

The ancestors of today's old elite were well-educated and maintained positions of influence and wealth in the city for well over a century. Today the old elite continue to live in the old walled section of the city. Their attachment to their ancestral homes, although they are located in a physically decaying area of the city, may not be uncommon among old moneyed classes elsewhere, especially those whose fortunes have waned and who are consequently somewhat downwardly mobile. This may be because their locally based prestige is not easily transferable to other places, even newer areas of the same city.

The old elite lives among the poor in contrast to the new, commercial, and professional elite who live in Western-style, class-segregated housing estates. To the passerby the large houses of the old elite appear to be no more than ill-maintained blank walls, indistinguishable from the buildings in which are found the flats of the poor, shops, offices, and small industries.

Inside, the houses are spacious and comfortable, but drab and sparsely decorated. There is no evidence that any but a minimal amount of attention is paid to the decoration of the home. The paint on the walls is usually faded and peeling. Art and furniture are very inexpensive. We were told, for example, that 7 to 20 rupees ($1 to $3) was too much to spend on a print, and therefore calendars distributed free by merchants were hung in the living room. Where one finds any upholstery, it is apt to be quite frayed. The dingy appearance of the house clearly does not stem from a lack of money,[2] but from the relative unimportance of having it well decorated. In fact, many with whom we spoke to were proud of the appearance of their houses. As one informant said, "We do not show off our wealth or squander it on showpieces." Another asked, "Why spend money on the house? It is fine the way it is. It won't fall down."

The low priority assigned to the upkeep and decoration of the house is understandable in light of the following. Membership in the old elite is determined by family and caste background and therefore it is an extremely exclusive group. Although a majority of the members are rich, wealth is not a primary criterion of membership. The social networks of the old city group may be characterized as impermeable and highly connected. We have chosen the term *impermeability* to describe the closed nature of the social network of the old elite. It refers to the fact that new links are rarely if ever added to the network except through birth and marriage. *Connectedness*, as defined by Bott (1971, p. 59), who introduced the term, is "the extent to which people known by a family know and meet one another independently of the family." Most members of the old elite know one another or certainly know of one another. Although there are too many people involved for all to see each other frequently, important news of the various families' events and activities spreads throughout the network.

The old elite can be considered a peer-group society;

they associate primarily with relatives and close friends of the same age and sex. According to one of our informants, at least 90 percent of the guests entertained in an average old elite home are relatives. Although not specific as to percentages, other informants indicated an even higher proportion.

The treatment of outsiders at parties is indicative of the impermeability of the network. A young man held an outdoor birthday party with over a hundred guests, all of whom were relatives, the only exceptions being ourselves and the host's employer and his assistant. These two men were completely isolated from the rest of the party.[3] The women and the young children sat in two large circles chatting among themselves while the men sat in similar circles a few feet away. The two outsiders sat by themselves on chairs that had been placed for them a short distance from the men's circle. The host would spend some time with them and then drift off to talk with his relatives. No attempt was made to incorporate the outsiders.

A member of the old elite need not use his house as a cue to his socioeconomic status because this is well known by those whose opinions he values, and, as one would logically expect of those with impermeable social networks, "outsiders" do not serve as an important reference group. Personal status within the group is determined by age and contribution to and participation in group functions. Although the old elite claims not to spend money on the house because it would be immodest, this explanation is questionable, for huge sums of money are spent on group events such as lavish weddings and funerals. It is interesting that they consider the new elite pretentious and immodest on the basis of the proportion of their income spent on housing, for, ironically, the new elite claims the weddings of the old elite to be much too extravagant to be in good taste.

As an upwardly mobile group whose networks are unbounded and loosely connected, the members of the new elite wish to advertise their social standing publically. Membership in such a group is tenuous and must be continually communicated to strangers. Thus, the physical appearance of the interior and especially the exterior of the house is used as a rela-

tively "loud," outwardly oriented, nonverbal set of cues.[4]

The West Enders of Boston

Herbert Gans's *The Urban Villagers* (1962) is a study of a group of working-class Italian-Americans in an area since designated as a slum and demolished by the city of Boston. To the residents, however, "slum" was a misnomer; they regarded the West End as a pleasant, low-rent area.[5]

The West End, as described by Gans was similar in general landscape type to the old city of Hyderabad. It had crowded, narrow streets. Some of the tenements were vacant and dilapidated and the alleys were filled with garbage. The outside and hallways of many buildings were dirty and in poor condition; the individual apartments were spotlessly clean, but no particular attention was paid to their decoration. The condition of the exterior of the buildings could be accounted for by the fact that they were rented, and the residents were no doubt reluctant to spend money on a structure that they did not own. This did not however, account for the fact that those residents who could afford to spend money on the decoration of the interior of the apartment did not, although the middle-class renter typically did. The explanation for this, we shall argue, lies in the structure of social networks and the entertaining patterns of the West Enders.

The social life of the West Enders revolved around informal, routine peer-group gatherings that took place in the home. The peer group according to Gans (1962) was a relatively unchanging group consisting primarily of relatives.

The group also includes god-parents and friends who may come less regularly . . . . Included among the unrelated individuals are friends of long duration, as well as more recent friends. Though the latter may be newcomers to the group, they are likely to have been known to the group, before, because as already noted, everyone knows everyone else . . . . Recruitment is not deliberate, however, and self-conscious "mixing with people" is explicitly rejected. A mobile woman who had left the West End suggested to the West End relatives one night that women ought to get out of the house and mix with people. But her relatives, discussing it afterwards, thought that this belief was a result of her being childless, for which they pitied her. Similarly a relocation official spoke to a West Ender about the new social experiences he would encounter in a new neighborhood; the West Ender replied angrily: "I don't want to meet any new people" (p. 75).

The social network of the West Enders thus can be described as similar to that of the old elite, that is, *relatively impermeable* and *highly connected*. The network was impermeable in the sense that the individual clusters, i.e., peer groups within the total network, were composed of relatives and friends of long standing; new members were not sought out. Contacts among members of different peer groups did take place, although outside the home, usually in the street. Gans states "everyone knows everyone else," (p. 75) although he is clearly not speaking literally, for elsewhere he states that ". . . everyone might not know everyone else, but as they did know something about everyone, the net effect was the same" (p. 15). Although Gans does not use the term "network," this is clearly what he means when he says "everyone."

Most West Enders took a dim view of the middle class and the "outside world."

West Enders not only keep their distance from the middle class, but they will reject other West Enders who stray too far from the peer group society and adopt middle class ways. Relatives and friends whose tastes for furniture and clothes begin to move in a middle class direction are criticized for having gone "high society," and people who have moved away from the group are described as renegades or deserters. Only those few who can achieve upward mobility in the occupational sphere without becoming "uppity" in their consumption patterns and their choice of friends are likely to be spared from scorn (p. 221).

The West Enders' cognition of their housing also is similar to that of the old elite.

Housing is not the same kind of status symbol for the West Enders that it is for middle class people. They are as concerned about making a good impression on others as anyone else, but the people to be impressed and the ways of impressing them do differ. The people who are entertained in the apartment are intimates. Moreover, they all live in similar circumstances. As a result they evaluate the host not on the basis of his housing, but on his friendliness, his moral qualities, and his ability as a host. Not only are acquaintances and strangers less frequently invited to the home than in the middle class, but they are also less important to the West Enders' way of life, and therefore less significant judges of their status. Thus, West Enders, unlike the middle class, do

not have to put on as impressive a front for such people, and there is no need to have "an address" or a well manicured yard in a carefully zoned neighborhood. Indeed, the people who had to satisfy such status needs through housing could not live in the West End, and had to move. Such a move meant leaving the group, and subjecting themselves to criticism, for it implied that the old neighborhood and the neighbors were no longer good enough (p. 21).

The following quotation illustrates the relationship between type of social network and cognition of housing.

The West Enders themselves took the poor maintenance of the building exteriors, hall and cellars in stride, and paid little attention to them . . . they did not consider these conditions a reflection on their status. Having no interest in the opinions of the outside world, they were not overly concerned about the image the West End had in the eyes of outsiders (p. 315).

Just as the old elite spends a great deal of money on group display, so do the West Enders: "The highest status accrues to the person who makes the most material and non-material contributions to the group, without using these to flaunt or indicate his economic or cultural superiority" (p. 27).

We have undertaken a brief survey of the literature on the working class in the United States to ascertain whether or not the West Enders as described by Gans are typical of the working class as a whole. Miller and Riessman (1961) give the following description of the working-class person:

He is family centered; most of his relationships take place around the large extended, fairly cooperative family. Cooperation and mutual aid are among his most important characteristics. While desiring a good standard of living, he is not attracted to the middle class style of life with its accompanying concern for status and prestige (pp. 90–91).

Berger (1968), Komarofsky (1967), Rainwater (1966), Dotson (1951), Lopata (1971), and Shostak (1969) in their studies of the working class also confirm the fact that socializing is largely restricted to relatives and a few intimates; others are excluded from the home. Another characteristic of the working class that is distinct from the middle class and helps explain why it does not use the house or apartment to communicate social status is the fact that, as Kahl (1967, pp. 141–144) points out, whereas the middle class combine their social life with their business life and hence entertain business contacts and potential contacts in the home, the working class maintain a strict separation between the work and family spheres. Seeley et al. (1963, pp. 48–49) found that among the American middle class the house played a central role in confirming status and aiding in upward mobility. In contrast to this, Berger (1968) finds that working class people ". . . apparently do not think of their homes primarily as status objects" (p. 84). It appears, therefore, that the structure of social networks and the role of housing in presentation of self that were found among the West Enders of Boston is not atypical but extends across the working class in the United States.

The Structure of the Social Networks

It is important at this point to outline the reasoning behind our contention that social networks provide a logical explanation for variations in the communicative value of housing. Housing, in our view, can be an important form of nonverbal communication, especially for those such as the new elite of Hyderabad and the American middle class who have regular contact with strangers and who repeatedly face the problem of having to present their "membership card." Housing can be important for several reasons. First, through it one "speaks" to a larger audience than one could reach verbally. Second, it acts as a check on verbally claimed identity because it indicates a degree of financial commitment to that identity and allows one to demonstrate that he is familiar with the appropriate choice and arrangement of household objects associated with his claimed identity. Third, investing in a house provides a relatively permanent evidence of wealth as opposed to investing in entertaining, which is transitory, at least among those with permeable networks, although, as we shall argue, it is not transitory for the old elite and the West Enders.

Permeability. Our term permeability refers to a property of social networks similar to that described by Barnes (1969) as "boundedness"; however, we prefer the former because it has a less structural connotation. It emphasizes the variable degree of openness to the addition of new links.

Members of groups with permeable social networks such as the American middle class and the new elite of Hyderabad act out their identity before the public in general because the latter includes innumerable potential members of the group. They also have a habit of viewing the public not as a hostile "outside world" but as an audience to be impressed. Just as the social organization of the group is structured to handle strangers who are to become new members, so the individual members of the group develop skills to deal with strangers. Housing is particularly important when communicating with strangers because it is most useful during the initial stages of presentation of self in which one convey's his or her social-group membership. This is because housing can indicate group membership far more effectively than it can reveal personality or other individual characteristics, which usually become of interest only after group membership is established. Furthermore, housing is useful for those who belong to permeable groups because these people must continually show that they satisfy the criteria for membership, which is only minimally necessary for those who are born into an impermeable network. Where wealth is an important qualification for membership, the house and its furnishings provide permanent and tangible evidence of such qualification.

As has been illustrated, the old elite and the West Enders have virtually impermeable social networks; consequently, the house does not play a large role in presentation of self. This of course is not to say that it has no role at all. On the contrary, it must conform rather strictly to the group's norms of what is appropriate.

If members of a social group are to communicate effectively among themselves, they must agree upon a set of priorities to guide them in the allocation of resources to various forms of presentation of self. It is clear that among the old elite and the West Enders a high allocation of resources to the house or apartment would not only serve little purpose, but would be frowned upon as improper.

Connectedness. Links in a social network serve as channels for the transmission of information. Information travels more easily through a highly connected network in which ". . . there are many relationships among the component units" (Bott, 1971, p. 59) than through a less highly connected network in which there are few such relationships. Assuming that people wish to maximize the diffusion of favorable information about themselves, one might ask how this is best accomplished in light of constraints of time and money. This, we claim, depends upon the structure of social networks.

In a highly connected network, participation in group activities and the spending of large sums on important family events is usually an efficient way of acting out one's group membership and gaining prestige. Information about these events travels throughout the network and therefore one can rely on word of mouth as a method for establishing and maintaining one's reputation. One's contributions to the group become well known throughout a highly connected social network, or at least a large section of it, and in this way actions that would be transitory and limited to the original audience become reified by word of mouth.

On the other hand, the networks of the new elite of Hyderabad and the American middle class are loosely connected, unbounded, and the pattern of links surrounding an individual change over time. This type of network is generally inefficient for transmitting information about the individual. Spending on transitory events is less rewarding than spending on a relatively permanent evidence of wealth and social status, such as the home. News of group displays such as parties and wedding receptions does not carry very far through the network.

In a loosely connected network, one must act before a diverse group that is constantly changing and whose members do not know one another. One must be able to repeatedly present oneself to a variety of new audiences without depleting resources; thus, one invests money and time on the home.

Conclusions

There has been a long-standing debate among sociologists as to whether attitudes toward housing could be accounted for by social class, ethnic, or cultural differences. It was not until we examined housing cross-culturally that we were able to discover the correlation between the role of housing in presentation of self and the structure of social networks. This correlation had been previously masked by class and ethnic differences, because there is also a high correlation between the role of housing in presentation of self and both class and ethnicity in the United States. By examining two groups of widely differing income levels, income can be ruled out as an explanation for the similarities between the old elite and the West Enders in the way they view housing. Similarly, by examining groups in two different cultures, culture and ethnicity are ruled out. The important characteristic the two groups share is the impermeability and the connectedness of their social networks. We have argued that, it is quite logical that if one's socioeconomic status is well known throughout the total network of people who serve as one's reference group, one need not spend much money on furnishing and decorating the house or apartment. Conversely, the house will usually be used to communicate social status if one belongs to a permeable and loosely connected social group in which one continually comes into contact with new and potential members who must be informed of one's own claim to membership. One must have a relatively permanent artifactual indicator of social status and group membership through which to communicate directly to each person as one cannot count on one's reputations spreading through a loosely connected network or reaching others who are not yet included in the network. Accordingly, it appears that the structure of social networks is the key to understanding the social meaning of housing and the extent to which it is used in presentation of self.

NOTES

1. We would like to thank Shah Manzur Alam, Justin C. Friberg, Elihu M. Gerson, M. Sue Gerson, Dharmendra Prasad, David J. Robinson, and David E. Sopher for advice, criticism, and suggestions.
2. Many of the members of the old elite were *lakhiaires* (a *lakh* equals 100,000 rupees) and owned houses in the new city for investment purposes.
3. As Western academics who had worked with the old elite for three months, we were a special class

of outsiders who, due to our relative intimacy with certain members of the old elite, were tolerated by some and welcomed by others into the mens' and womens' circles.

4. The appearance of the interiors and exteriors of the houses of both the old and new elite are dis-cussed in Chapter 17. A more detailed examination of the two groups is to be found in Duncan (1974).

5. Gans's findings are supported by other research on the West End, most notably that of Fried and Gleicher (1961) and Fried (1973).

22

J. Sonnenfeld
**Department of Geography
Texas A & M University**

IMPOSING ENVIRONMENTAL MEANING: A COMMENTARY

For most culture groups, the measure of environmental understanding is in the ability to obtain adequate nourishment and shelter from the environment, and to feel (and be) secure within it. The significance of a cross-cultural approach to the study of environmental cognition is in essentially similar terms: it promises understanding of how populations with various sensitivities, experiences, and values come to know their environment, its productive potential, the hazards and risks it contains, and what it requires for remaining productive and predictable over time.

Cognition implies knowledge and understanding of environment, but it has also been conceived more broadly as the source of environmental meaning. Amos Rapoport's paper is in large part an attempt to make a case for an "imposing of meaning" concept of cognition. In doing this, it raises a number of questions that are relevant to what Harold Conklin's and James and Nancy Duncan's papers also contribute. At the least, one is obliged to ask whether the reconceptualization of cognition proposed by Rapoport is an extension of, a substitute for, or simply a semantically altered restatement of the more conventional view of cognition as the means by which people come to know and understand the world.

Cognition as Intended Meaning

If I interpret Rapoport's position correctly, meaning is imposed on the environment not only by the way we order or categorize stimulus elements, but also by the way in which we design our landscapes through manipulating or imposing control over critical elements and events in such a way or to such a degree that the *intention* of the design is unequivocally communicated to others. Whether or not an intention is in fact communicated is a function of the cognitive power of others, who may or may not be able to decipher (decode) the intentional landscape. But is "environmental intention" as used in this sense a cognitive function? I think not. An intention seems postcognitive to the extent that it builds on previous knowledge of environmental potential; and it is precognitive or cognition-manipulating to the extent that it is directed toward communicating with and influencing others' behaviors. The Duncans' paper supports such an inference, as do Rapoport's own references to the encoding activities of designers and planners.

The Duncans' paper inquires into the strategies used for communicating social status. Through cross-cultural analysis, they show ostentatious residential display or its lack to be a function of social relationships that can and do transcend class and culture. In effect, the Duncans' concern is also with how meaning is imposed on the landscape; they imply that *status meaning* is conveyed by encoding social values onto the residential landscape. This is reasonable within the context of a homogeneous social system. To the extent that one deals with a consistently valuing system, status decoding will probably be consistent with the encoder's intentions. But when discrepancies occur in the values of the broader society and the values themselves are in a state of flux, there can be no guarantee that meaning will be communicated or interpreted as intended. It is this latter, variable interpretation of the intentional landscape, rather than the intention to impose meaning on the landscape, that constitutes the critical cultural problem in the cognition of designed environments.

Conklin's paper suggests a different kind of issue; it raises the interesting question of how one decides on criteria for the mapping of culture-specific land-use patterns. Conklin's problem is that of the field researcher who is aware of possible discrepancies between the land-use features the researcher considers critical, and those the land users responsible for creating the patterns consider to be critical.

Clearly, different folk with different land-use systems may have different ways of classifying or evaluating the elements of their environment, and using knowledgeable informants may be the only way of obtaining this information. But that one group may wonder about another's system of classification and attempt to devise an appropriate methodology for probing it is perhaps more revealing of the nature of cognition than the already familiar fact that cultural groups may differ in their sensitivity to and understanding of the environment. Yet Conklin at least treats a cognitive issue in his emphasis on the identification of stimulus elements that although

"visible," may still escape the eyes of the naive observer.

Rapoport's concern with the built environment is quite different. The planner or designer may be said to impose meaning on the landscape in order to communicate his ideas for facilitating the use of space, or for facilitating action, comfort, or control. Granted, as Rapoport claims, there may be discrepancy between the intention of an environmental plan or design and its interpretation by users; the cognitive conflict is not in the intention but rather in the assumption that the plan will communicate what the designers intended, and thus will lead to compatible user behaviors. The planner may seek understanding of the success or failure of his design, the validation of which is also a cognitive function; but here he or she becomes an interpreter of an only partially known world, including not only the designed landscape but also other people whose values, needs, and satisfactions are only partially known.

To summarize, cognition includes many processes that together make it possible for us to know, be aware of, and understand our world. In a sense, meaning *is* imposed on environment when we categorize, classify, or name the elements of our environment. But that imposing of meaning which implies a physical rather than conceptual manipulation of environmental elements, and which uncritically assumes veridical communication, seems to exceed the bounds of cognition.

Intentional and Nonintentional Environments

An additional cognitive problem is raised by this concern with meaning—that of the difference between the intentional and nonintentional environment, between the constructed or built environment and the more natural worlds we also occupy. Information derived from the cultural or designed environment (assumed knowable by those for whom the environment was designed) is likely to be different from that derived from the nondesigned, natural, or unknown environment. For the latter, the achieving, retaining, and transforming functions of cognition apply to nondirective stimuli from nonintentional environmental systems; therefore, environmental behaviors are likely to be more variable and certainly less predictable. Behaviors, however, need not be any more incompatible between populations nor disruptive of environments for having been based on meanings derived (imposed) by users rather than on intentions previously encoded (imposed) by designers. For the designed environment, constraints necessary for sustaining an environmental–behavioral system of relationships can be built into the system and made obvious to users. In the nondesigned environment, by contrast, awareness of system constraints is likely to be less obvious and thus more demanding of the cognitive powers of user populations; implicit is a need for greater sensitivity to feedback from behavioral impacts, and the ability to adapt as necessary to system demands that have other than immediate human welfare at issue.

Congruence Versus Flexibility in Cognition

The question of adaptation potential has special relevance to the congruence issue raised by Rapoport. Given tendencies to increasing complexity of built environmental systems, and the increasing social and geographical mobility of populations, the critical cognitive issue for the planner or designer is not so much the consistency between designer and user cognitions, but rather the adaptability and flexibility of user populations. Rapoport seems to suggest that discrepancies between designers' intentions and users' cognitions can be and ought to be avoided, but this may prove difficult given the potential for environmental and economic constraints on what can be accomplished, and given the uncertainty also of future user populations. The high level of social and geographic mobility is especially critical. This mobility does not permit one to predict who the occupants of a given space will be over the life of a constructed environment.

One might also question the value of accommodating for given cognitive styles that can persist even lacking any special advantage, just as long as these are also lacking in any special disadvantage. Indeed, cognitive styles may simply be products of a specific prior culture–environment relationship, with no special value other than that they satisfy the needs of such a relationship. If this is the case, one can assume that new relationships with different environments will be productive of cognitive styles just as functional as the old. It is perhaps only when new relationships are not sufficiently different from the old that resistance to change occurs, with such resistance being no indication of potential for change to more effective styles should change be in order.

Conclusions

I suggested earlier that cross-cultural study of environmental cognition could be justified in terms of the value of understanding how different populations come to know their environment, its potential, and its limits. Currently, there is competition for limited space and resources leading to culture conflict. Competition and conflict, in turn, imply the need to decide on issues of environmental priority. Planners increasingly will be required to contend with mixed and changing populations; they will have to decide whether to accommodate to the diverse needs of these populations, or, instead, to require user adaptation when demands prove incompatible with the availability of space, resources, and funds.

A model of environmental cognition that focuses on cognitive styles implies diversity and, too often, rigidity of the associated cognitive structures or representations. Together, diversity and rigidity also suggest the potential for conflict. Perhaps what is needed is a cognitive model that emphasizes, instead, the capacity for change, based on flexibility and adaptation potential. Adopting a *conflict model* requires the planner to consider the needs of diverse populations and assumes the ability to provide adequately for these; an *adaptation model* permits one to focus, instead, on the longer-term needs of the man–environment relationship and assumes the ability to adapt.

Those who would suggest accommodation as the solution to the problems of an increasingly diminishing world seem to minimize such adaptation potential. Although requiring adaptation may also mean minimizing the ability of the planner to satisfy the environmental needs of mixed populations, it is clear that satisfying such needs becomes more difficult the greater the diversity that has to be accommodated for within the confines of a limited environment. Past accommodation to diversity has probably been a major source of current levels of diversity. Ironically, the value of diversity is in the options it provides for accommodating the pressures of a changing environment. But this ignores the issue of what happens to those unable to adapt, who generally also do not sur-vive. I would submit that to require adaptation does not in itself eliminate diversity; rather, it provides a new context for development of a diversity more appropriate to the needs for survival in a changed and changing world.

Implicit is a dynamic concept of culture that assumes the likelihood, if not also the desirability, of continued cultural change.

LITERARY AND PHENOMENOLOGICAL PERSPECTIVE

23

LITERATURE, EXPERIENCE, AND ENVIRONMENTAL KNOWING

Yi-Fu Tuan

Department of Geography
University of Minnesota

Literature depicts human experience. Experience may be defined as the sum of means through which we know reality and construct a world. Experience includes sensation, feeling, perception, and conception or cognition. Feeling is a way of knowing. Through the senses of smell and touch, for example, we articulate a world, just as we construct intricate worlds through the use of our eyes, and with the help of language, images, and nonverbal symbols. In scientific literature "cognition" is often treated as explicit knowing, as an activity that is able to express itself with words and diagrams. In imaginative literature "cognition" is a component of experience: its explicit character shades imperceptibly into the more tacit forms of feeling and seeing. Literature depicts human experience in specific contexts, that is, environments. In scientific works "environment" is conceptually separated from the human organism so that their relationship can be analyzed. Literary works do not aspire to analytical truths; hence, they make no effort to separate experience from its environmental context, and make no clear distinction between social and physical environments.

Literature presents "slices of life," actual and imaginary. It tells us what it is like to feel, see, know, and imagine under both commonplace and exceptional circumstances. Literature is of course not life; it is a picture or an articulation of life. Its value to science is that it makes certain basic human experiences visible and public. What does a medieval poet see when he looks at the night sky? What are the different senses in which a farm laborer can be said to *know* his land? How would the coffee shop appear to me if the friend I expect to see is not there? Answers to such questions lie in some form of symbolic articulation, of which literature, coding experience in words, is perhaps the most important.

Literature is a child of its time. Folklores and stories, epics and lyrics, articulate the inchoate feelings and perceptions of a people, but they also guide and direct these feelings and perceptions. From one viewpoint literature is a diagnostic index or evidence of culture; from another it is a creative force directing culture, enabling people to see their world in new ways. To understand the relation between literature and experience, including cognition, requires that we look at literature from both viewpoints.

LITERATURE AS EVIDENCE

Literature powerfully clarifies and unifies experience, yet even as it performs these functions it unveils deeper ambiguities and discontinuities in experience. The paradox results from the fact that literature has multiple levels of meaning. At the surface level, a story is a narration of events and facts: it is like the scientific report of an explorer. A story such as O. E. Rølvaag's *Giants in the Earth* (1927) is based on personal experience. It tells a great deal of what life is like for a pioneer farmer in the northern Great Plains. Walter Prescott Webb, the historian, uses Rølvaag's novel as a source for his scholarly work (1931). Literary art can be exploited in various ways, all rather superficially, for the information it offers. One type of information is the material conditions of livelihood. A novel reveals what one person, a sensitive observer, knows of his society and of the natural world with which it is enmeshed. For lack of more precise and objective reports, the evidence of imaginative literature may be all that we have to reconstruct the past. This use of literature reduces it to the humble status of rather unreliable data.

A better use of literature is for its power to express the intellectual concerns of a people at a particular time and place. The works of Chaucer may be a poor source for reconstructing, objectively, the English landscape and economy of the fourteenth century, but they are invaluable to our understanding of a cleric's world view in the late medieval period; what Chaucer records and does not record are both revealing.

Still better is the use of literature for its power to clarify the nature of experience, for at a deep level literature is the accurate depiction of the ineffable in much of our lives. Most people have difficulty in articulating even simple feelings and thoughts. Writers present a world that we have known (i.e., experienced) and yet know only darkly; explicit knowing requires the illuminating structure of words and images. Literature is cognition at a certain level of synthesis: below it are our turbid feelings and interfused thoughts; above it is the disintegration of synthetic experience into components, the place where science begins.

Finally, literature mirrors, and mediates among, the contradictions of society. Inescapable and timeless human problems are adumbrated in elliptical tales. Such tales display structures that intimate characteristic patterns of human thought. The structures appear without conscious effort. They are not neces-

sarily a part of an artist's deliberate attempt to express the ineffable and so illuminate experience; often they are recognized only in retrospect, that is, in subsequent analysis.

Factual Data

The mining of literature for factual information concerning people and places is rarely done. For the geographer and historian it is the last resort to which one appeals when other sources of information fail. In pictorial art, Gombrich (1962) reminds us how undependable illustrations can be. The Nuremberg Chronicle has woodcuts depicting cities. "What an opportunity such a volume should give the historian to see what the world was like at the time of Columbus! But as we turn the pages of the big folio, we find the same woodcut of a medieval city recurring with different captions as Damascus, Ferrara, Milan, and Mantua" (p. 60). Treated as the source of factual data, literary art suffers a similar handicap; in the writer's imagination the city as symbol can easily override the city as a particular configuration of brick and mortar.

But different kinds of literature exist. Lyrical poems, folktales, myths, legends, and realistic novels vary enormously in their content of facts. From a poem of the T'ang dynasty we may know how Ch'ang-an looked at night or what kinds of trees and animals existed. From French realistic novels of the nineteenth century we gain a rich, sharply etched image of France (see Levin, 1963). Balzac, Zola, and Flaubert claimed to be merely reporting what they saw. Balzac described himself as society's scribe. Zola had a good reporter's curiosity and respect for details. He believed that a great source of poetry is the study of unvarnished nature. As for society, Zola had no fear of its dirty linen. Flaubert's masterpiece, *Madame Bovary*, bears the subtitle "Moeurs de Province," as though it were a sociological treatise. Travel accounts and place descriptions by novelists are rich sources of factual data; one thinks of such works as Lawrence Durrell's *Alexandria Quartet* (1962), Henry Miller's *The Colossus of Maroussi* (1941), and V. S. Naipaul's *An Area of Darkness* (1965). A behavioral scientist imposes his categories of thought on the statistical data that a census bureau has collected for other purposes. Out of the diverse sorts of statistical material he constructs a geography or a sociology of a special kind. What kind of a work would result if a scientist were to choose to build his image of place, not on someone else's statistical data, but on someone else's sensibility, for instance, the 91 works that together make up Balzac's magistral *La Comédie Humaine* (1940)?[1]

Conceptual Frame

Literature is read not for its factual content but for its distinctive viewpoint (conceptual frame), and even more for its articulation of experience. The past is knowable only through the artifacts that remain, and particularly through the most precisely expressive artifact, literature. How did the medieval man view his world? What kinds of evidence do we have other than the literary? Folk views in the Middle Ages can perhaps be inferred from what we know of their work schedules, the material bases of day-to-day living, and from their participation in religious festivals. The medieval philosophers present no special difficulty. They speak for themselves; we know the conceptual frame of a Duns Scotus and a Thomas Aquinas almost as well as we know that of a John Dewey or Ludwig Wittgenstein. Literature at the level of philosophical discourse is explicit; the cards are all on the table, or should be. With poetry, songs, fables, and moral tales, the conceptual frame is only adumbrated. Such loosely built frames, however, are a better index of how people, high and low, order their day-to-day experiences than are the rational schemata of the philosophers.

How did medieval man view his world? From literary evidence dating back to the fourth century (see Lewis, 1964), it would appear that a lettered person, or one who had been subject to the influences of literature, saw his world somewhat as follows. The earth is infinitesimally small by cosmic standards; it is a mathematical point given a central place as a sort of "esthetic convenience" in order that the celestial beings—the stars and planets—can dance around it. The medieval cosmos is vertiginous. Absolute up and down have meaning. The earth is the lowest place; movement to it is downward. Stars are at a great distance in the modern view. To the medieval observer they are at a great height. "To look out on the night sky with modern eyes is like looking out over a sea that fades away into mist, or looking about in a trackless forest—trees forever and no horizon. To look up at the towering medieval universe is much more like looking at a great building" (Lewis, 1964, p. 99). The medieval universe is immense but it has definite limits. The fear of great open spaces (Pascal's "le silence eternel de ces espaces infinis") does not appear in medieval poetry. The principle that objects seem smaller as their distance from the observer increases was well known in the Middle Ages. But the principle was seldom applied to either art or literature. Nature, for Chaucer, is all foreground; we never get a landscape. The medieval imagination focuses on the foreground, where objects and events are vivid as to color and action, but it is careless with scale. The first explicit delineation of perspective appears much later, in Shakespeare's play *King Lear* (see McLuhan and Parker, 1969, p. 14). Scale is carefully noted, and so also the onset of vertigo, the fear of dizzying height and distance:

Edgar:

Come on, sir; here's the place. Stand still. How fearful
And dizzy 'tis to cast one's eyes so low!
The crows and choughs that wing the midway air
Show scarce so gross as beetles. Halfway down
Hangs one that gathers sampire—dreadful trade!
Methinks he seems no bigger than his head.
The fishermen that walk upon the beach
Appear like mice; and yond tall anchoring bark,
Diminish'd to her cock; her cock, a buoy
Almost too small for sight. The murmuring surge
That on th'unnumb'red idle pebble chafes
Cannot be heard so high. I'll look no more,
Lest my brain turn, and the deficient sight
Topple down headlong.

When the medieval man looks at the sky, he does not see it as empty space, for he knows that vacuum is something that nature does not allow. If it is daytime, he sees the air filled with light proceeding from a living sun, rather as his own flesh is filled with blood proceeding from a living heart. If it is nighttime, he does not merely see a plain vault pricked with separate points of light, but a regional, qualitative sky, from which, first, the different sections of the great zodiacal belt and, second, the planets and the moon are raying down their complex influences on the earth, its metals, its plants, its animals, its men and women, including himself (Barfield, 1957, pp. 71-78). The conceptual frame of the Middle Ages is known to us through the literature that has survived. Without doubt some latent frame of knowledge guided the medieval man's behavior and perception, but how and to what extent we do not know. When the poet Jean de Meun looked at nature, did he really see things that we do not see? (de Lorris and de Meun, 1962). Or is "seeing" used fluidly to mean both perception in the narrow optical sense and in the sense of intellectual comprehension? Such questions have no answer when we address them to the past. Even when we direct them to the present, the answers are not readily forthcoming. Thus, we know how the world views of certain nonliterate people differ significantly from our own; we are less sure how these differences in conceptual frame affect the direct experience of phenomena.[2]

The Articulation of Experience

Art articulates experience. Inchoate feelings are transposed into significant forms that can be seen. Art presents images, not models. A particular juxtaposition of paint evokes a landscape and a mood that is the result of certain experiences. Art does not say how the experiences arise in particular settings, nor how brush strokes on canvas can symbolize—evoke powerfully—a real place. It is not a blueprint showing "how things work." Literary art uses words to realize images of experience. Because words are also the traditional means by which we explain, there may be a tendency to confuse description with explanation, particularly since both contribute toward understanding. However, literary works, like other modalities of art, do not explain; what they do is to enable us to recognize, with the immediacy of a revelation, the multivalent character of experience.

Literature presents a body of psychological data. William James (1902) recognized the importance of such data and made ample use of literary sources. Among modern psychologists, Hadley Cantril and Charles Bumstead mined literature for its articula-

tion of complex human feelings and perceptions that find little echo in scientific works. In their book *Reflections on the Human Venture* (1960), Cantril and Bumstead note, "The characteristics and qualities that make human experience what it is must first be recognized before they can be described and then dealt with. It is the sensitive novelist, poet, or prophet who seems so far to have done best in combing such recognition with faithful description" (p. xi). Behavioral scientists have made little use of the sociopsychological data in literature. The nuggets of experience offered by a novelist or poet are not readily subsumed under the abstract categories with which scientific researchers feel at ease. Moreover, the relationship of psychological data in literary works to human action on a large scale seems tenuous; and the detailed information in literature is rarely pertinent to the mapping of behavior of economic importance.

Literature depicts experience, bringing into the middle ground the things that are buried in our subconscious. The housewife's response to a sociological questionnaire is the tip of the iceberg. A novelist's purpose is seldom with the exposed tip; his concern is with the murky depths where light imperfectly penetrates. What are some of the murky perceptual-cognitive experiences that literary works succeed in bringing to light? Here are five examples. They direct our attention to (1) the perception of absence, (2) the physiognomy of places, (3) the world of fleeting noises and light, (4) ambiguity in the interpretation of shared perceptions, and (5) the association of human emotions with events in nature. The possibility for choice of illustrations is limited only by one's familiarity with the literature that successfully portrays the vast range of human experience. The following examples give only a hint of the kind of psychological data, pertaining to man in his physical setting, that literary works provide. Note that the first three cases illustrate, as it were, direct perception, the second pair reflective perception or ratiocinative awareness.

Perception of absence. "Grief fills the room up of my absent child" (Shakespeare, *King John*). Many people know what it is like to step into a familiar room and be struck by a sense of absence—a lack that is almost tangible. Perceiving the absent is described in detail by Jean-Paul Sartre (1966). He uses his literary powers to provide a vivid image. Consider the following hypothetical situation. I have an appointment with Pierre at four o'clock. I arrive at the café a quarter of an hour late. Pierre is always punctual. I look at the room, the patrons, and I say, "He is not here." I could also have said, "I suddenly saw that he was not here: I encountered absence." Yet the café with its patrons, its tables, its smoky atmosphere, and the sound of voices, rattling saucers, and footsteps which fill it—the café is a plenitude of being. I expect to see Pierre, and, as Sartre says, "my expectation has caused the absence of Pierre *to happen* as a real event . . . . I have *discovered* this absence, and it presents itself as a synthetic relation between Pierre and the setting in which I am looking for him. Pierre absent haunts this café and is the condition of its self-nihilating organization as ground" (p. 42). Sartre begins with a phenomenological description of a possible event, using the technique of a novelist. He then analyzes negation philosophically. From the facts themselves, one can proceed to either philosophical or scientific analysis. But first one must be aware of a body of facts.

The physiognomy of places. Knowing a place, like knowing a person, is not normally a matter of making a conscious effort to synthesize discrete perceptions nor is it one of focusing on particular landmarks in the landscape. We know a place through its essential style or physiognomy, made up of many sensory elements that reinforce each other. As Maurice Merleau-Ponty (1962) puts it,

Paris for me is not an object of many facets, a collection of perceptions, nor is it the law governing all these perceptions. Just as a person gives evidence of the same emotional essence in his gestures with his hands, in his way of walking and in the sound of his voice, so each express perception occurring in my journey through Paris—the cafés, people's faces, the poplars along the quays, the bends of the Seine—stands out against the city's whole being, and merely confirms that there is a certain style or a certain significance which Paris possesses. And when I arrived there for the first time, the first roads that I saw as I left the station were, like the first words spoken by a stranger, simply manifestations of a still ambiguous essence, but one already unlike any other. Just as we do not see the eyes of a familiar face, but simply its look and expression, so we perceive hardly any object. There is present a latent significance, diffused throughout the landscape or

city, which we find in something specific and self-evident which we feel no need to define (p. 281).

A world of fleeting noises and light. The human senses of sight, hearing, touch, smell, and taste are extraordinarily refined and responsive. When we do not suppress their messages, the world seems intensely alive; we stand in it transfixed. However, the practical chores of living require that we suppress most of what we sense, and attend—mainly through the eyes—to those cues that enable us to act. Every practical act, from brushing one's teeth to winning a game of golf, has a limited aim and hence makes highly selective use of our senses. The reality that behavioral scientists study tends to be a world of limited aims and purposeful acts. By contrast, a novelist or poet is likely to be concerned with those occasions when people simply wait, daydream, or are aware of the environment without tailoring that awareness to the demands of immediate action. How would the world appear when our eyes do not evaluate it in the interest of action and we are free to attend to different kinds of stimuli? Such a world must seem tremulous, fleeting, and unstructured. Virginia Woolf's novels provide many illustrations. Here is one from *To the Lighthouse* (1927):

And now as if the cleaning and the scrubbing and the scything and mowing had drowned it there rose that half-heard melody, that intermittent music which the ear half catches but lets fall, a bark, a bleat; irregular, intermittent, yet somehow related; the hum of an insect, the tremor of cut grass, dissevered yet somehow belonging; the dor-beetle, the squeak of a wheel, loud, low, but mysteriously related; which the ear strains to bring together never fully harmonized, and at last, in the evening, one after another sound dies out, and the harmony falters, and silence falls. With the sunset sharpness was lost, and like mist rising, quiet rose, quiet spread, the wind settled; loosely the world shook itself down to sleep, darkly here without a light to it, save what came green suffused through leaves, or pale on the white flowers in the bed by the window (pp. 212–213).

Ambiguity in the interpretation of shared perceptions. Literature mirrors the ambiguity, ambivalence, irony, paradox, and misunderstanding that frequently plague real life. When we watch other people from a distance, objectively, they seem to have strong wills and simple minds; they are always doing something, talking to friends, inspecting colored slides, tinkering with the carburetor. They appear rarely at a loss. By contrast, we know ourselves introspectively, with the result that we feel weak-willed although possessed of subtle minds. We recognize our own indecisiveness and ambivalence. In others, the internal debate is invisible; all we see is the commitment to action. Suppose that two persons are looking at the landscape. They agree in what they see; they agree even in the landscape's surface meaning. Need more be said? More can be said and more is likely to be said in a work of imaginative literature, concerned to plumb the psychological depths, then in a scientific report, which needs to simplify data in the interest of comparability. Unvoiced ambivalence in the interpretation of perception is illustrated by the following incident from Paul Bowles's novel, *The Sheltering Sky* (1949):

Kit took Port's hand. They climbed in silence, happy to be together. [They watched the sun set over the desert.]

"Sunset is such a sad hour," she said, presently.

"If I watch the end of a day—any day—I always feel it's the end of a whole epoch. And the autumn! It might as well be the end of everything," he said. "That's why I hate cold countries, and love the warm ones, where there's no winter, and when night comes you feel an opening up of the life there, instead of closing down. Don't you feel that?"

"Yes," said Kit, "but I'm not sure I prefer the warm countries. I don't know. I'm not sure I don't feel that it's wrong to try to escape the night and winter, and that if you do you'll have to pay for it somehow."

"Oh, Kit! You're really crazy." He helped her up the side of a low cliff. The desert was directly below them, much farther down than the plain from which they had just climbed.

She did not answer. It made her sad to realize that in spite of their so often having the same reactions, the same feelings, they never would reach the same conclusions, because their respective aims in life were almost diametrically opposed (pp. 99-100).

Attitudes to nature. Literary works reveal that human beings are capable of a great range of response toward nature. That response is tinged with varying degrees of emotion. Note, however, that just as the most theoretical understanding of nature is rooted in desire—a passon for order—so even tactile feelings are filtered through the cognitive structures of the brain, and hence are a way of comprehending. Scientific works register man's intellectual experience of reality. Poems, essays, and novels record webs of feeling, that is, how feeling and external circumstance parallel each other or interpenetrate, and how circumstance both incites feeling and is yet colored by it. Experiences of nature are almost infinitely varied. The following types are readily recognizable in the imaginative literature of the Western World. As we review them, it is worthwhile asking how many are considered in scientific surveys of environmental perception and cognition.

1. The experience of well-being as when the senses are wakened and stimulated by nature. Pasternak describes it thus in *Dr. Zhivago* (1958):

The earth at the doctor's feet, inside the trench and in the ruts of the forest road, was hard with ground frost and heaped with small dry willow leaves, curled up in little scrolls. The autumn smelled of these brown, bitter leaves and of many other things. Greedily he breathed in the mixed peppery smell of forbidden apples, bitter dry twigs, sweetish damp earth, and the blue September mist that smoked like the fumes of a recently extinguished fire (p. 341).

2. A special quality of delight in nature that can only be expressed as nature delighting in its own existence. The common notion that birds sing out of happiness shows how easily human beings project their own feeling into other kinds of sentient life. Anthropomorphism simultaneously enables man to make sense of the world and extend his sensibility, his emotional range. Even inanimate nature sings in Psalm 65: "The little hills shall rejoice on every side . . . the valleys shall stand so thick with corn that they shall laugh, and sing."

3. Gratitude for God's creation. Whereas people throughout the world praise nature for its provisions, the Judaic-Christian tradition shares with other higher religions the distinction of allowing people to voice gratitude even for the destructive aspects of nature. "For the precious things of heaven, the stars, the sunsets, the clouds, yes, even for the storms, we thank thee Lord" (Deuteronomy 33:13).

4. Oneness with nature. Literature treats this popular theme with varying degrees of immediacy. "My heart leaps up when I behold/A rainbow in the sky" (Wordsworth) states a relationship almost as unreflective as "I shiver when the temperature suddenly

drops." "The force that through the green fuse drives the flower/Drives my green age" (Dylan Thomas) suggests the kinship of all life processes. Less immediate is the recognition of analogies and parallelism between nature and human life. The technique of the simile has been used since the time of Homer: "Even as are the generations of leaves such are those likewise of men" (Iliad).

5. Sermons in stone. The idea that nature is a source of spiritual health and inspiration attained wide popularity in the eighteenth century. It persists today in the sentiment for wilderness, in the characterization of wilderness as "nature's cathedral."

6. The immensity and indifference of the earth. The sense of wild and uncontrollable nature rarely ruffles the prose and poetry of Western Europe: Dicken's Kent and Flaubert's Normandy are cozy and domesticated. By contrast North America and Russia are raw, and writers respond to the rawness with depiction of the "moody tyrannies of the sea in Dana and Melville, the archaic horrors of the ice-world in Poe's *Gordon Pym*, and the image of human nakedness in Tolstoy's *Snowstorm*" (Steiner, 1961, pp. 33-34). In Europe disillusionment with nature began to stir even before the middle of the nineteenth century. Tennyson's works, for example, show no inclination to associate nature with beauty—much less with benevolence and spiritual qualities. In this, Tennyson anticipated the mood of later poets, such as Stevenson and Hardy (see Beach, 1936, pp. 411 ff.).

7. Nausea. Cruel or kind, nature still communicated in romanticism's after-glow. In the writings of Jean-Paul Sartre (e.g., 1938) it no longer does. To the deeply alienated man the pebble on the beach, a tree stump, or at times even one's own hand is gratuitously there, real and grotesque, incapable of melding with the categories of meaning that people need to conduct day-to-day affairs. A reality that is viscid, intransigently present yet meaningless, arouses the feeling of nausea. T. S. Eliot, like Sartre, expresses the modern hollow man's sense of distance from nature. In Eliot's poetry, the evening sky is likened to "a patient etherised upon a table," (1953a, pp. 3-7), and the wind symbolizes nothingness and the moon "has lost her memory. A washed-out small pox cracks her face" (1953b, pp. 14-16).

Literature, Thought, and Society

People can speak fluently, even creatively, without knowing the language's grammar. Likewise, an inspired writer can set out to compose a poem or a novel, and yet be ignorant himself of facets of its hidden meaning and structure. Scientific statements strive for perfect lucidity and explicitness; they eschew hidden meanings. The surface structure of imaginative works, on the other hand, may be a mere scaffolding for the plumbing of hidden significances, most of which can only be hinted at and some of which are unknown to the writers as they labor over the surface expression.

Literature mediates among the contradictions and polarities of human experience; at the most basic level these are life and death, male and female, we and they, sacred and secular. Such dilemmas create enduring tensions in individual lives and in society. Solutions may diverge widely in surface details and yet show common structural traits. The solutions are not final. The perplexities endure and are answered repeatedly in variant forms. Literary themes resist change for they contend with the same fundamental dilemmas; so Orestes reappears as Hamlet, and Job reincarnates as J. B. (see Hartman, 1970, p. 145). Certain mythical motifs transcend culture and survive time. They are elemental ways of ordering experience. A primitive order is created through the making of binary distinctions. The recognition of antinomic pairs seems to be congenial to human thought. In some respects the brain works like a digital computer. Paired oppositions are very prominent in myths. For example, the story of the Garden of Eden begins with the opposition of Heaven and Earth, which is mediated by a fertilizing mist drawn from the dry infertile earth. The distinction life–death is blurred and then repeated; Adam as well as animals are formed from the dead dust of the ground, fertile Eve is created out of the rib of infertile Adam. The opposition Heaven-Earth is paralleled by the later antinomic pairs Man-Garden, Tree of Life-Tree of Death (see Leach, 1967). In the Tsimshiam Indian myth of Asdiwal, which is a world apart from Genesis, Lévi-Strauss (1967) discerns a complex of cosmological and geographical oppositions:

Cosmological (vertical axis)	High-low, heaven-earth
Geographical (horizontal plane)	West-east, water-land, sea hunting-mountain hunting
Cosmological in form (vertical axis, geographical in content)	Peak-valley

Such paired oppositions are not merely a stage toward the abstract classification of people and things. They are rooted in perdurable human puzzles. Their emotive tinge results from human associations: peak-valley is a binary distinction in geography but it also symbolizes male-female dichotomy. Dilemmas are resolved, or blurred, through the introduction of a mediator. Myths tell hermeneutically how this comes about. Mediation occurs as events but events require physical settings for their realization. A landscape can symbolize a moral state. Man is drawn to opposite moral states, to antithetical landscapes. The antinomic settings of city and wilderness, each a pole of attraction and repulsion, are mediated by the garden or "the middle landscape." Occidental literature, from Virgil to Frost, plays variations on this theme of the uneasy search for the ideal place (see Marx, 1968).

In summary, certain types of literary work embody perennial myths. The structures of these myths are indexes to favored patterns of thought, as thought grapples with the problem of reconciling man to nature.

SCIENCE AND ART AS CREATIVE FORCE

Art, like science, radically affects our perceiving and thinking. Together they articulate the world. The world we see, understand, and in which we act is not given to us through naive experience. "Naive experience" is almost a contradiction of terms. We see the world, Foss (1971) says, as our existing conventions (categories, projective rules) enable us to see it. Who are primarily responsible for these concepts and conventions? Answer: the makers of symbolisms, that is, the pioneer scientists, writers, artists, and poets. Symbolization and perception reinforce each other and it is futile to ask which comes first. Being able to conceptualize is seeing (although not necessarily with the eye), and seeing is believing, that is, being able to affirm the world conceptually and emotionally.

Scientific conventions or paradigms affect the perception of scientists. A change in paradigm results in a changed configuration of reality. It is like the shift in gestalt such that what looked like a duck now looks like a rabbit; scientists see new and different things even when they are looking with old instruments in places they have looked before. Thomas Kuhn (1970) provides several well-documented examples from the history of science. I introduce two of them here to provide analogies with paradigmatic shifts in art and literature. For Western astronomers sunspots and a new star emerged in the heavens immediately after Copernicus. Using traditional instruments late sixteenth-century astronomers repeatedly discovered that comets wandered at will through the space that was previously reserved for the immutable planets and stars. It is as though, after Copernicus, scientists saw different things and lived in a different world. Another example from the history of science is the perception of the pendulum. Before Galileo, Aristotelians saw not a pendulum but a swinging body that was constrained by a chain and falling with difficulty. Galileo saw it as a pendulum, that is, a body that almost succeeded in repeating interminably the same motion over and over again.

I raised a question earlier concerning medieval man's perception of nature and heaven. Did man in the Middle Ages really *see* different things or did he see the same things as moden man but *interpreted* them differently? Kuhn raised this question with regard to the scientist's perception following a change of paradigm. Did Aristotle and Galileo really see different things when looking at the same sorts of object? A common view is that the interpretations differed but that the observations were fixed once and for all by the nature of things and of the perceptual apparatus. On this view, Aristotle and Galileo both saw pendulums, but they differed in their interpretations of what they both had seen. This would be true if data were stable. Kuhn argues, however, that data are not unequivocally stable; a pendulum is not a stone falling under constraint. In the absence of stable data the process whereby an individual makes the transition from constrained fall to pendulum is not one that resembles interpretation. The interpretive enterprise can only articulate new categories and conventions, not create them. Creation is an unstructured event like the gestalt switch. Scientists often speak of the "lightning flash" that "inundates" a previously obscure puzzle, enabling its components to be seen in new ways (Kuhn, 1970, pp. 120–122).

An artist might call the "lightning flash" a visitation of the muse. Scales fall from the artist's eyes; he is confronted by a new world which he proceeds to articulate. As Foss (1971, p. 237) puts it, "Norman Rockwell fulfills . . . paradigm-induced expectations; Picasso breaks through the existing and, at his most creative, establishes successor paradigms which, in turn, mobilize new expectations. By the margin that new paradigms mobilize expectations, these become the new forms. What constitutes realism (representational art, accurate description, etc.,) is adjusted accordingly." To a complaint that Picasso's portrait of Gertrude Stein did not look like her, the master is reported to have replied, "Never mind, it will." Landscape painting, when it first appeared in Europe, signified a radically new way of seeing nature; spatial continuum was segmented or framed, and its elements—trees, rock, brook—organized in a special way to conform with the sight lines of an individual viewer. Constable offended his contemporaries; yet we have come to accept his landscapes as the quintessential representations of the English scene (see Clark, 1935). The camera has made most of us slaves to the perceptual conventions of an earlier age. The tourist composes the scene with his camera as would the hack artist of a fossilized academy with his canvas and paint brush. Impressionists shattered the convention of viewing the landscape as an arrangement of solid three-dimensional objects in perspective space; we are directed to focus on light and color. For those who are educated to appreciate impressionist art, sun-drenched lands are shimmering patterns of light and color. Any creative act, however small-scaled, influences perception. Cartoonists affect our images of politicians even though the sketches are abstract and the distortions grotesque. Clever gossip distorts our appraisal of a person even against our will. Goodman (1968) says, "That nature imitates art is too timid a dictum. Nature is a product of art and of discourse" (p. 33).

Literature, like other forms of art, has the power to make vivid images out of our normally confused feelings and perceptions. A page of well-chosen words can crystallize a world that would otherwise escape notice for lack of definition. By providing tantalizing images of possible idyllic worlds, literature can break conventional modes of thought to initiate new lines of thinking, new attitudes, and new enterprise. Marx and Freud have radically altered our perception and interpretation of man. Who are the people who have transformed our esthetic and moral valuations of nature and of man's physical setting? Painters like Cezanne and Picasso and architects of the Bauhaus school have undoubtedly altered modern esthetic sensibility. Poets such as James Thomson and William Wordsworth have modified and expanded the nature consciousness of literate Englishmen. But have writers of imaginative literature influenced the *popular* perception of environment to the degree that places once shunned become foci of attraction?

Paradigmatic revolutions in science and art affect first the scientists and artists. As their influences spread, people at large also learn to see the environment in new ways and alter their behavior in environment to conform with the new perception. Changes that affect the esthetic sensibility of large numbers of people are likely to be slow. The desert does not become a tourist attraction overnight. When such large-scale changes occur, scientific literature, more or less popularized, plays often the leading role because it appeals to practical ends; it draws people's attention to the utilitarian values of neglected places. Philosophers and poets play two complementary roles: by boldly articulating their intuitions they may open venues for the scientific search itself; writers enhance the appeal of places by making places seem desirable in themselves and for their spiritual messages.

Consider the changes in attitudes toward the desert and the mountain. In the middle of the nineteenth century, Anglo-American visitors to the dry lands of the American Southwest were often critical of what they saw. To some the country had a "sickening" and "nauseating" mien. Within a century the image so altered that New Mexico could call itself the Land of Enchantment; it has become a station for discerning tourists and aspiring artists (see Tuan and Everard, 1964). Medical opinion that favored the dry climate was no doubt a major influence in reversing attitudes to the stark landscapes of the Southwest and to dry lands in other parts of the world.[3] However, non-utilitarian influences were also at work. It is a part of the occidental ascetic tradition to see in the desert not only desolation, but an austere beauty. Even Anthony, the pioneer hermit of the Egyptian desert, showed a love for his barren home when he said, "My book, O philosopher, is the nature of created things" (quoted in Chitty, 1966, p. 6). To St. Jerome (1893) "a town is a prison, and the desert loneliness a paradise." A stark scene uncluttered with the riotous demands and distractions of organic life satisfies a longing for purity. The desert's uncompromising lines and mineral hardness assuage a desire for permanence and for an esthetic that is ascetic, not self-indulgent.

Since the eighteenth century European travelers to North Africa and the Near East have often demonstrated a partiality for the simple life of desert peoples in their bare world of sky, stone, and open vistas. The appeal of fertile and accommodating landscapes is easy to understand: green hills, fields of corn, and bubbling brooks symbolize life. The "lifeless" desert is a minority taste, but it has loyal and eloquent partisans. Few natural settings are as well served by literature as the desert, particularly since the latter part of the nineteenth century. Writers such as Charles Doughty, T. E. Lawrence, Norman Douglas, Antoine de Saint-Exupéry, and Albert Camus have tinted the vision of occidental man. The desert is high adventure and glamor. Movies, inspired by the literary perspective, have enhanced the romantic image of the desert. They succeeded in popularizing an environment that is basically antagonistic to life.

Attitudes toward mountains have undergone parallel changes. In the classical period, mountains commanded awe; they were the dwellings of the gods. Through much of European history, however, mountains were viewed with distaste. Epithets in common usage in the 1650s included insolent, surly, uncouth, sky-threatening, and "Earth's Dugs, Risings, Tumors, Blisters, and Warts" (see Nicholson, 1959, p. 35). In the eighteenth century, literature began to depict mountains in a more favorable light. People saw that they could be sublime rather than horrendous. By the nineteenth century, mountains were perceived to be sublime and beautiful. Now mountains are beautiful and picturesque. What brought about this reversal in esthetic judgment? How could the "warts" of yesteryear become the "beauty spots" of current sensibility? There was a change of paradigm, but unlike the paradigmatic shifts in science, which could occur "overnight" and be attributable to a major genius, the change in the esthetic evaluation of mountains was spread over two centuries and cannot be credited to the writings of any one person or to esthetics as such.

The appreciation of mountains was prepared for by their greater accessibility in the eighteenth century; population increased, roads improved, and mountains no longer seemed remote and forbidding. Mountains, moreover, acquired the reputation for health: they rose above the pestilential plains; their pure air exercised a benign effect on patients suffering from lung diseases. A medical literature proliferated to promote the virtue of mountains, helping to change their image. Other forces of a more intellectual and esthetic nature were also at work. In the seventeenth century the image of perfection was still the circle. Mountains and oceans were grotesque departures from the ideal of a perfectly spherical earth. They manifested a fallen world. By the beginning of the eighteenth century, however, philosophers and poets began to challenge the geometrical canon. Harmony, it was perceived, could rise to a higher order than simple form; irregularities had their own grandeur. Nature's God was not just a geometer drawing circles in heaven on earth but delighted in "a gay profusion of luxurious bliss," "unbounded beauty," and "a complex stupendous scheme of things" (Nicholson, 1959, p. 329). Scientists like John Keill, philosophers like the third Earl of Shaftesbury, and poets like James Thomson transformed the cognitive frame of Europeans, enabling them to see nature in a different, more romantic, light.

ON THE QUESTION OF REPRESENTATIVENESS

Literature mirrors human reality. A difficult question to resolve is that of representativeness. Is imaginative writing idiosyncratic or does it express a culture's common and profound values? Any answer must confront two points that have already been raised: (1) literature can be read at different levels, and (2) literature is both the presentation of experience we have had and the forging of new experiences.

Classics of literature can be read at different levels or from different perspectives. The works of William Faulkner express, from one point of view, the genius and limitation of one individual; it is possible to treat them as clinical data that reveal primarily the personality of the author. From another viewpoint the novels of Faulkner contain an enormous amount of objective information concerning a small part of the American South. They direct our attention not to the obsessions and unique history of the author, but to the customs and values of a people. Reading the novels, we learn how Mississippians feel and act in the peculiar context of the South's social institutions and physical environment.

From a third perspective, Faulkner's Yoknapatawpha county is a window to the world. Ambitious artists, no less than scientists, aspire to the universal: the scientist proceeds logically through the route of abstraction; the artist proceeds paradoxically through devotion to the specific and the concrete. Gogol wrote: "The town and its maelstrom of gossip should be portrayed as a chaos depicting the futility of mankind in general." His problem was how "to reduce the universal image of futility in all its forms until it can be embodied in the futility of that town, and how to magnify the latter until it will approximate to an image of planetary futility" (quoted in Pritchett, 1973, p. 181). Implicit in imaginative literature and more or less explicit in existentialist philosophy is the belief that "if one looks closely enough at the details of the world, one will find there, not analogies, but actual visible instances of the structure of reality. One can *read* the world, and, by looking at it in detail, one can understand its meaning" (Warnock, 1970, p. 136).

Literature is simultaneously confession, ethnography, and universal symbol. When successful, it transcends the limitation of mere personal confession, mere fact gathering, and mere engagement in philosophical generalities (e.g., Tillyard and Lewis, 1939).

A question of interest to the social scientist remains: Is the novelist's picture of a region accurate? We can look at the evidence. The accuracy of Faulkner's picture of the South, for example, receives support from the factual data gathered by Frank L. Owsley (see Brooks, 1966, p. 13). It hardly needs saying that on questions of discrete fact the treatise of a historian and the tables of a sociologist carry greater authority than the works of a regional novelist. However, the local gazetteer and the regional novel share one common human defect: both are highly selective and therefore partial records. Which, then, presents a truer picture? Is it the gazetteer because the facts are correct, or is it the novel because it depicts many more facets of an integral reality? Perhaps an analogy would help: the gazetteer is like the defective photograph of a human face showing accurately only the ears, mouth, and hair. The regional novel is like a painted portrait; none of the sitter's individual features are correctly represented and yet he is recognizable. Remove the names of people, towns, and rivers, and it remains possible to recognize the English midlands from a novel by D. H. Lawrence. By contrast, a gazetteer or regional geographical description is likely to be incomprehensible without the explicit labels.

Literature depicts perceptions, attitudes, and values. Do they reflect those of society? The question has two parts: one is whether the fictional characters are good portraits of real people, and the other is whether the concerns of the author—the themes and values he chooses to stress—are also those of society. In pulp literature (e.g., *True Story* and *True Confessions*) the portraits are not good; they cater to the fantasies of their readers. Yet for that very reason they may mirror truly the desires and aspirations of their readers. In a statistical and sociological analysis, Albrecht (1956) finds it to be true that the values expressed in stories written for mass consumption represent those of middle American society. By contrast, in high-class literature (e.g., stories in *Atlantic* and *The New Yorker*), the portraits of people and society are good. The fictional characters appear real and they can do nasty things. This does not mean, of course, that well-educated people take nastiness to be one of their values. Their codes of behavior and ideals of happiness are in fact not so different from those of the middle class. What distinguishes the two groups is that the better educated people are open to a larger world, and they are more willing to contemplate human diversity, including the range of follies, dispassionately. Lower-class literature, in short, reflects the values of their readers but tells little about their world; it is closer to dreams than to ethnography. Upper-class literature is closer to ethnography than to dreams; the broad themes it takes up extend far beyond the personal experiences and ideals of their readers.

Is Homer representative of ancient Greece or Faulkner of Mississippi? The answer is no, for the genius is a superior instrument and unrepresentative by definition. Yet he is representative to the degree that he articulates the more profound experiences of a people. In that sense he is the voice of the people; he is representative man. The claim would be empty if it is not recognized by the people. The ancient bard presumably had his admiring circle of listeners. His epics spoke to their condition and captured their imagination; indeed they speak to the human condition for they continue to stimulate the mind and emotion of many modern readers. Faulkner's world is not a private fantasy; it is a voice of the South and, to his admirers, a microcosm.

Can one measure representativeness by the size of the readership? Yes, if we are concerned with explicit values and desires; more people, by far, read Margaret Mitchell than William Faulkner because she more accurately depicts the people's daydreams and aspirations. The answer is no, if we are concerned with concrete experience and values expressed in behavior. Serious works have fewer followers than romances that appear in women's magazines and adventure stories that cater to male fantasies. Serious literature is less accessible to the general reader for various reasons, but not necessarily because its themes are exotic and esoteric. On the contrary, it often disturbs precisely because it focuses on the commonplace—the pains, irritations, frustrations, the boredom and the ecstasy, the ambivalence and ambiguities in much of even well-ordered lives.

Serious literature tells us what we "know" but would rather forget. Here is the paradox of the second point. Imaginary works enable us to see our own deeper experiences. Readers recognize their own condition, their understanding of life and world, in a poem or story. In this sense the work of art simply holds a mirror to ourselves and offers little that is new; yet the very fact that we can now *see* what once we could only vaguely feel makes the experience seem new. To some people the images offered by literature are so disturbing that they are denied as accurate reflections of real experience; such people will not learn from literature. To others, literature can alter their frame of vision and hence also the direction of their lives.

The question of representativeness now shifts. We no longer ask whether literature reveals common values. We say that literature can impose common values. It does so when it has had the opportunity and time to exercise its power over the minds of a large segment of the population. Literature is a force. Unfortunately, great works of art are only a force, capable of swaying the masses, when their meanings are simplified beyond recognition and taken out of context. The poetic utterance is a voice in the wilderness; prose writers do somewhat better. Blake's *Holy Thursday* made the same social protest as Dickens's *Oliver Twist*—and more succinctly—but Dickens had the influence and aroused the conscience of a nation. In general, literature is a measurable force when it has become propaganda. The effectiveness of words, oral and written, to alter our frames of perception may be overlooked by behavioral scientists, but it is clearly recognized by propagandists of all stripes, from advertisers on Madison Avenue to fundamentalist preachers and politicians.

CONCLUDING REMARKS

Behavioral scientists who wish to understand how people respond to their world have yet to explore systematically the evidence of imaginative literature. The literary perspective has been neglected because the evidence is not in quantitative form, and because the experiences described in literature rarely throw much additional light on the way people pursue rational economic ends. These are not sound reasons for neglecting the literary testimony. The data of literature are not given in quantitative form but some of the phenomena depicted may be quantifiable.

The special value of literature to the behavioral scientist is that it draws his attention to facts and relations in the human world of which he may be ignorant. A scientist's ability to formulate pregnant hypotheses is limited by his personal history and by the scientific schema under which he habitually operates. Literature opens up other intensely human experiences and presents a different perspective on the structure of reality. It can raise questions in the scientist's mind and lead him to formulate hypotheses. He can then collect the kinds of numerical data that he feels comfortable with, and systematize them according to the models of his craft.

Literature often depicts perceptions, attitudes, and values that have no immediate effect on action. This would seem to be another reason for its neglect. The behavioral scientist tends to focus not only on observable behavior—people and things moving over space—but on actions that have economic consequence. A geographer, for instance, may be concerned with the mapping of a businessman's route to work. As an aid to explanation, the businessman's "cognitive map" is also of interest, the schema he uses to go from one place to another. What the behavioral geographer is disposed to overlook are the twenty minutes the businessman spends waiting for the bus to take him home. In those twenty minutes the businessman is not doing anything that can be mapped, nor is he doing anything for the economy. He may feel rage, frustration, or resignation; he may think about last night's council meeting and the new transportation plan, or he may dream of Eden, but none of these feelings and thoughts has an immediate impact on action: when the bus finally arrives he gets on it and goes home. Yet, as literature often reminds us, it is in the period of waiting that people are likely to fantasize and make plans that, when the right time comes, enable them to forego their current routine for another world view and another mode of life. The mental maps of literature are cosmographies and idealized worlds: they help us to understand on the one hand the stable structures of mental life, on the other, the visions that can lead to change.

Finally, behavioral scientists might consider literature as a force, creating new patterns of cognition. Both scientific and imaginative literature have the power to transform the image of the world; in both this power to influence the mass mind is proportional to the degree that literature is simplified and distorted.

NOTES

1. Balzac's massive collection of short stories and novels has a cast of 2,472 named and 566 unnamed persons. Many of these works of fiction can be grouped under the headings of "scenes from private life," "scenes from provincial life," and "scenes from Parisian life." See Hunt (1959, p. 440).
2. For a further treatment of the influence on environmental experience of cross-cultural differences in conceptual frameworks, see Chapter 19 (the editors).
3. See Chapter 24 for the use of the American Southwest landscape as a setting for the moods in novels (the editors).

24

Myongsup Shin
Department of Geography
  University of Minnesota

GEOGRAPHICAL KNOWLEDGE IN THREE SOUTHWESTERN NOVELS

The idea of *fiction* associated with literary art usually discourages us from regarding novels and poetry as valid objects of study in our disciplinary efforts. When compared with the generally observable subject matter of science, the world of feeling tackled by fictional writers is certainly unreal and thus easily neglected by men of scientific profession.

Fictitious as it may seem, the felt experience of literature could provide us with some valuable insights into the workings of the human mind in a way that results of scientific inquiry might not. For literature mirrors reality (see Chapter 23), although not in perfectly lucid and verifiable terms. We remember the message in John K. Wright's (1947, p. 15) address delivered some time ago:

One function of my hypothetical professors of aesthetic geosophy—though God forbid they be called by such an atrocious title—would be to prevent the oncoming generations of geographers from becoming too thickly encrusted in the prosaic and to render the study of geography more powerful than it would now seem to be in firing the artistic and poetic imaginations of students and public.

It is much in the spirit of Wright's foregoing observation that I accommodate his concept of "geosophy" in this study—the study of geographical knowledge from any and all perspectives—with an eye to demonstrating the validity of discerning patterns of emotion-perception relationship from the landscape descriptions of three rather randomly selected novels.

The Scope of This Study

In his essay on topophilia, Yi-Fu Tuan (1961, p. 32; see 1974) suggested that geographers "might take time off from their practical duties and join—at least now and then—the artists and poets in portraying the splendor of the earth." In his article "Use of Simile and Metaphor in Geographical Descriptions," Tuan (1957, p. 11) also pointed out the need for geographers to employ "imagery, and words chosen to give full appreciation to that object of geographical curiosity, the landscape."

This study is an attempt to see the extent to which the "sense of place," as used by Shepard (1967, Chapter 2), permeates the vocabulary of three works of fiction on the American Southwest. The novels considered here are Albert Pike's "The Inroad of The Navajos" in *Prose Sketches and Poems Written in the Western Country* (1967, originally 1834), N. Scott Momaday's *House Made of Dawn* (1967), and Willa

Cather's *Death Comes for the Archbishop* (1927). Relevant passages will be extracted from these works to explicate the main thrust of my endeavor: to ascertain the relationships between landscape perceptions and changes of character mood.

The Setting

It is well known that writers often use landscape description as a technique to create a certain mood or atmosphere in their story. The monotonous and austere heath country portrayed by Emily Brontë to symbolize the stark realities of family conflict, or the exciting variety and minute details of nature described by Thoreau to signify his transcendental philosophy, may serve as examples:

On an afternoon in October, or the beginning of November, a fresh watery afternoon, when the turf and paths were rustling with moist, withered leaves, and the cold, blue sky was half hidden by clouds, dark grey streamers, rapidly mounting from the west, and boding abundant rain (Brontë, 1971, p. 262).
   The sun was setting . . . . It seemed insensibly to grow lighter as the night shut in, and distant and solitary farmhouse was revealed, which before lurked in the shadows of the noon. There was no other house in sight, nor any cultivated field. To the right and left . . . were straggling pine woods with their plumes against the sky, and across the river were rugged hills, covered with shrub oaks, tangled with grape-vines and ivy, with here and there a gray rock jutting out from the maze (Thoreau, 1963, p. 29).

Landscape description in American literature came of age with the rise of local colorism in the late nineteenth century. The local-color fiction, bridging romanticism and realism at a time of increasing industrialization and westward expansion, placed emphasis on natural scenery and the modes of everyday life in frontier settlements (Bredeson, 1968). The American Southwest was one of many native scenes and cultures with which the reading public of that time wanted to be acquainted, and about which a number of surveyors, traders, and novelists wrote.

Pike's *Prose Sketches and Poems Written in the Western Country*

Among those who became interested in the Southwest at an early date was Albert Pike. An Easterner by birth, Pike made a trip to New Mexico at age 22 with a group of hunters and traders (Warfel, 1941). The obvious motive of the trader's party notwithstanding, Pike's real aspirations were to attain literary fame. So, during his journey to Taos over the Santa Fe Trail and his subsequent year-long sojourn in the Taos–Santa Fe area, the former schoolteacher recorded both the minutes of his experiences across the plains and the "human geography" (his words) he encountered in northern New Mexico.

An awkward situation in the East caused Albert Pike to venture west from his native Massachusetts. While still at home, he wanted to obtain an education at Harvard; financial conditions worked contrary to his wish, however, and this same situation also prevented him from marrying a girl he had courted. Nor did his school teaching and poetry writing bring him sufficient reward. By the time he reached St. Louis, where he hoped to join a traders' group headed west, Pike was quite a restless man (Weber, 1967). Therefore, he was interested in the Southwest only as a place from which to draw monetary and literary success. This puts him in the outsider's position in terms of his view of that region.

It is perhaps his status as an outsider that enabled Pike to produce a short fiction, "The Inroad of the Navajos," which is a highly photographic observation of the Taos–Santa Fe area. This story is about a Mexican–Indian hostility set in one of the rocky canyons around Taos. The opening scene could put a modern documentary film maker to shame:

Above, below, and around me, lay the sheeted snow, till, as the eye glanced upward, it was lost among the dark pines which covered the upper part of the mountains, although at the very summit, where the pines were thinnest, it gleamed from among them like a white banner spread between them and heaven. Below me on the left, half open, half frozen, ran the little clear stream, which gave water to the inhabitants of the valley, and along the margin of which, I had been travelling. On the right and left, the ridges which formed the dark and precipitous sides of the cañon, sweeping apart, formed a spacious amphitheatre. Along their sides extended a belt of deep, dull blue mist, above and below which was to be seen the white snow and the deep darkness of the pines (Pike, quoted in Warfel, 1941, pp. 15-16).

This paragraph is not just an imaginary scene in a fiction—it is an actual description of the author's "own arrival at Taos, which he approached from the East through the valley of the Fernando de Taos" (Pike, 1967, originally 1834, p. 147). Having made a general observation of a new environment unfolding before him, the Eastern visitor looks over the townscape lying ahead:

Directly in front of me, with the dull color of its mud buildings, contrasting with dazzling whiteness of the snow, lay the little village, resembling an oriental town, with its low, square, mud-roofed houses and its square church towers, also of mud (Pike, quoted in Warfel, 1941, p. 16).

Something of a value judgment is evident in these remarks. The undignified size of the village and its poor adobe structures as perceived by the stranger as anything but exotic. The appearance of a little Spanish-Mexican settlement, after the rather stimulating experience of the natural grandeur surrounding it, falls far short of the aspiring writer's expectation. The sight of a muddy pueblo may have looked at least picturesque from a distance, but upon entering it the visitor only discovers a few irregular dirt lanes and a cluster of earthen houses. Even the churches are of mud, he notes. Inside the village, all he can find is an assemblage of indistinct huts and Mexicans driving their lean mules. It is a depressing scene for an Eastern intellectual, especially on a wintry morning in northern New Mexico after a long trip through the vast grassland. In the record of his journey back to Nebraska, Pike actually recalls the hardship encountered during his first entry into New Mexico: "starving, and through snow three feet deep" (Weber, 1967, p. 236). His unsympathetic view of the Mexican village may have been unduly distorted because of the cold and hunger that had vexed him through much of his travel to Santa Fe.

The point here is not so much to see how Pike's hunger affected (as it most certainly did) his perception of the environment as to mark the pervasiveness of landscape portrayal in his writings about the Southwest. In spite of his explicit remark that "The west has now become a home to me" (cited in Weber, 1967, p. 223), Pike saw the Southwest strictly from a spectator's standpoint because, nowhere in his work, does he suggest any sense of attachment to the people he met or to the work he accomplished while there.

Momaday's House Made of Dawn

House Made of Dawn is about an Indian named Abel, who had lived with his grandfather in the pueblo of San Ysidro until he was drafted into the U.S. Army. The period covered by this fiction is from 1945 to 1952, during which Abel, the veteran, leads a sadly decadent life, unable to adjust himself to the changed conditions of living back home. The white man's economy now dominates his country, and the Indian instincts in Abel find the imposed life style hard to follow—or perhaps it is his own growth to manhood that is harder for him to accept.

Abel's life is in a way a reflection of the Indians' plight in general, struggling to survive in two different worlds, one inherited from their ancestry, which is fast disintegrating, and the other encroached upon by the enterprising Anglo culture. The novel is rich in vivid images and descriptions of natural environs. What Tuan (1961, p. 32) has called "the full flavor of landscape" may be illustrated by the following passage:

From the top of the drift they could see a good stretch of the river; at the far reaches it gleamed and glittered like crumpled foil, but directly below it was black and invisible, for there was a long thicket of willows and tamarack on the opposite bank. There were narrows upstream, where the river branched around a bar of rocks and reed. And just beyond, where the streams converged, there was the faintest quiver on the moonlit water, a dance of lights against the black hills in the distance (Momaday, 1967, p. 109).

The imagery of motion in tranquillity pictured seems to symbolize the failing struggles and sense of evanescence in life experienced by Abel and his grandfather. The impressive projection of landscape features is the beauty of Momaday's fiction, compensating for the absence, probably intentional, of clear-cut plot lines. His novel, like Cather's, suggests something deeper than the camera-eye effect notable in his landscape portrayal. That is, Momaday's nature descriptions bear a close relation to his hero's mood and the events affecting him. For example, Abel's recollection of his happy boyhood experiences ties in with the romantic autumnal setting projected in flashback:

It was late in the autumn and clear, and the great shining slopes, green and blue, rose out of the shadows on either side, and the sunlit groves of aspen shone bright with clusters of yellow leaves and thin white lines of bark (p. 181).

The enchanting sylvan setting portrayed above is in reference to a memorable bear hunt in which Abel once took part when he was younger. The excitement of the chase, the sensation of plants and other obstacles under foot, the subconscious awareness of the refreshing surroundings—all became an integral part of Abel's early Indian experience. An equally enchanting setting is notable in the following passage that suggests the imagery of a glorious sunrise paralleling a joyous horseback ride, somewhat prior to the bear hunt. Dashing out into the cornfield on his black horse, Abel saw the sun coming up "bright, brighter than water, and the brightness would be made of a hundred colors and the land would almost hurt your eyes" (p. 154).

The splendor of nature throughout Momaday's novel is reserved mainly for the hero's memories of his blessed past, now irrecoverable. The intermittent projection of natural scenery thus symbolizes Abel's mental leap into his earlier days of freedom—a defeatist's tendency in the face of his realities, beset with the onslaught of a foreign culture and the need to fulfill his obligations as an adult. Nature portrayed under these circumstances is mostly overcast, rainy, or cold. The pattern is not always consistent, however, in that natural events as described by Momaday often guide man's mood rather than being guided by it.

If Albert Pike represents the outsider's viewpoint with respect to the Southwest, N. Scott Momaday would represent the perspective of an insider. The same land and people that the nineteenth century writer Pike described in photographic detachment with only selective appreciation were for Momaday the very source of symbolic rejuvenation.

Cather's *Death Comes for the Archbishop*

This novel was written by a renowned, classic American local colorist, Willa Sibert Cather. Of her major works, this is the only novel based on the regional setting and ecclesiastic history of the Southwest. The story spans the 40- or 50-year period prior to the arrival of the railroad in that region.

Born in Virginia, Willa Cather traveled with her par-

ents to Nebraska at the age of ten. Her growth in the prairie country became a vital source of her creative writing. As Cather (cited in Foerster and Falk, 1960, p. 1016) put it, "That love of great spaces, of rolling open country like the sea—It's the grand passion of my life." She occupies a position somewhere between Pike and Momaday in terms of her interest in the Southwest.

Death Comes for the Archbishop is a story of two French priests who volunteer for missionary work among the natives of the north Mexican territory. The center of their activity is also the Taos–Santa Fe area, only wider in scope than Albert Pike's experience.

The two main characters in the novel, Fathers Jean Marie Latour and Joseph Vaillant, meet in France during their training to become Catholic priests. The central figure is the bishop, Fr. Latour. Through his sensitive eyes and extensive travels, a panorama of Southwestern landscape is portrayed amid the unfolding of human affairs.

The opening scene of Book One in this nine-part novel portrays a uniform and barren desert landscape through which the bishop-designate, Fr. Latour, drives north on horseback with a pack mule. An intelligent, aristocratic, and scholarly man, who is particularly sensitive to the shape of things, Latour finds the valley country of Rio Grande "so featureless—crowded with features all alike" (Cather, 1971, pp. 17-18).

To the eyes of this lone traveler first encountering the northern country of Mexico, the landscape appeared "heaped up into monotonous red sandhills, very much the shape of haycocks." The undertone of grievance implicit in this observation indicates the priest's exhaustion after a long seaborne journey from New Orleans to Galveston, followed by the solitary trek over the bleak expanse of land. The platitude of topography in northern New Mexico as first seen by the French priest is reiterated in this phrase: "blunted pyramid repeated so many . . . times upon his retina." The sense of tension and weariness underlying such withdrawn views of surroundings contrasts nicely with the relaxed mood of the same priest at a later date. By the time he has established friendship and familiarity with his new home, the bishop "accepted chance and weather as the country did, with a sort of grave enjoyment" (p. 232). Under such circumstances, the priest "slept anywhere and preserved a countenance open and warm."

The effect of mood on environmental perception is amply suggested in the descriptions of landscape by Cather. For instance, as Latour enters the new land, the small oasis he comes across after some wandering in the desert appears "greener than anything" he had seen before. That a man's physical conditions influence his feelings about space is again apparent in the instance in which the little peasant village around the oasis appeared "rosetinted" as Latour saw it after good food and rest. His obviously exaggerated impressions of the scenery before him indicate his recovery from weariness of the previous day.

Cather's landscape description is also used as a premonitional device, as suggested in the following passage: "Before the hour was done they [Latour and Vaillant] did indeed come upon a wretched adobe house, so poor and mean that they might not have seen it had it not laid close beside the trail" (p. 66).

As part of their usual itinerary, the two missionaries were on their way to Mora from Santa Fe. The foregoing description of a pathetic roadside house, preceded by such seemingly unrelated phrases as "raindrops," "lead-coloured clouds," and "grey daylight," points to an ill incident about to befall the priests. To illustrate the point, the mean-looking adobe belongs to a hobo who robs and murders passersby for money. The two missionaries would surely have met a tragedy had it not been for the danger signal gestured to them by the villain's captive wife. The words "wretched, poor, mean" regarding the appearance of the hobo's house, like those suggesting bad weather, were evidently to forebode the evil man's plot. In this context, a somewhat different episode will be presented below to examine the combined use of premonition and parallelism (i.e., landscape changing as man's mood does) in Cather's scenic portrayal.

One winter evening in Santa Fe, Latour was going through one of his occasional periods of doubt concerning his career as a Catholic priest. As if to symbolize his state of mind, the full moon cast a pale "luminousness over the heavens, and the towers of the church stood up black against this silvery fleece" (p. 212). Being aware of his own occasional lapses into melancholy, the bishop went to the sacristy to recover his peace of mind. But in the dark sanctuary Latour encounters the figure of a woman kneeling. An old Mexican woman, Sada, who he knew to be the house servant of a Protestant family, had managed to get away from her work for a few moments of prayer at his church. The family whom she serves has not allowed her outdoors for 19 years, not even on Sundays. The dreary nocturnal atmosphere and the dark image of the church tower seem to symbolize Sada's ragged countenance and sad life as Latour discovers her. But a deep sense of faith displayed by the indigenous lady, despite her dismal position in life, moved the bishop so much that later he confessed to his friend, Father Vaillant, that never before "had it been permitted him to behold such deep experience of the holy joy of religion as on that pale December night" (p. 217).

The episode with the woman, Sada, marks in a sense the climax in Bishop Latour's spiritual growth in the New World. An awareness of the lofty spirit held by a most miserable lowly human being, such as Sada, reassured him of the true meaning of his work as pioneer missionary and gave him a fresh perspective on life. Latour's appreciation of nature also grows keener in proportion to the degree of his inner maturity and understanding of the native ways of life in the Southwest.

There was so much sky, more than at sea, more than anywhere in the world. The plain was there under one's feet, but what one saw when one looked about was that brilliant blue world of stinging air and moving cloud (p. 233).

Humanized landscapes (Tuan, 1973) are indeed what the pioneer missionary now perceives in his surroundings. Thus, when freed from the duties of his bishopric, Latour spends time tending his orchard and garden, urging his successors to plant trees wherever they go. In retrospect, the aged priest realizes that "the society of learned men, the charm of noble women, the graces of art, could not make up to him for the loss of those light-hearted mornings of the desert" (p. 249).

The desert, which 40 years prior had seemed so

featureless and bleak to Latour, now would not be traded for anything else.

Concluding Remarks: Variations in Landscape Description

The works of three writers spotlighting the Southwest have been sketched in the context of landscape perception in descriptive terms. The visual impressions of topography, climate, and cultural landscape portrayed by Pike, Momaday, and Cather indicate how pervasive the language of geography can be in some works of creative literature. The *sense of place* embedded in the landscape descriptions examined here is closely associated with the turn of events and the mood of the main characters, especially in the novels of Momaday and Cather. As far as our three writers are concerned, variations in the use of landscape description as a technique in creative writing may be classified into four major categories: (1) *pathetic fallacy*, (2) *parallelism*, (3) *premonition*, and (4) *photographic description*.

To elaborate, I noted earlier that Momaday identified himself strongly with the Southwest. His novel is particularly replete with descriptions in which the dominant element is *pathetic fallacy* and a tendency to *romanticize* the natural scenery. In this type of fiction, changes in the appearance of landscape generally reflect changes in the hero's mood, and vice versa.

In Cather's case, landscape portrayal carries the characteristics of *premonition* and *parallelism*. That is, ill weather forebodes danger or unhappiness, and beautiful scenery accompanies or indicates happy events. In her fiction, human affairs are always guided by natural phenomena.

The word to typify Pike's landscape description is probably *photographic* in the sense that the writer or hero is not emotionally involved in his observations. This is understandable in light of the brevity of Pike's stay in the Southwest, and from the fact that he made no deep attachments to anything or anyone while there. Both in his fiction and travelogue, Pike's scenic description has nothing to do with indicating mood or events. Something like paralellism is notable in his observations of the cultural features of northern New Mexico; the seemingly emotional qualities in his descriptions, however, only reflect the degree of his physical comfort (or better yet, discomfort) in traveling.

These categories are of course not unique to the three works introduced here, nor do they exhaust the range of mood-event relationships indentifiable in the literary evocations of landscape. Rather, under the cloak of fiction, they suggest the different ways in which human beings can respond to their physical environment. What we call pathetic fallacy, for example, is not a mere pathology of the literary imagination but a fairly common type of man-environment relationship. Just how common it is has yet to be explored.

Works of fiction enable us to appreciate the complexity of human ways. They show that much of man-environment relationship is *drama*. The dramatic element in human lives is normally absent in scientific studies. By examining patterns underlying the descriptive vocabulary of our three Southwestern novels, we seem somewhat better equipped to understand what John K. Wright meant when he suggested a more esthetic approach to our disciplinary endeavors. At a time when the intangible properties of the human mind such as images and perception have become a legitimate academic subject matter, landscape descriptions in literature merit more than passing attention by students of geography and environmental cognition.

25

W. J. Lloyd
Department of Geography
  University of California, Los Angeles

LANDSCAPE IMAGERY IN THE URBAN NOVEL: A SOURCE OF GEOGRAPHIC EVIDENCE[1]

How can we know the thought of a people concerning urban spatial structure and landscape? Novels of city life are sources of evidence that on the surface appear to offer a plentitude of information on individual, everyday geographic awareness. But can the contribution of novels be focused on intellectually significant and nontrivial aspects of space and landscape? And can novels be studied as evidence for solving larger problems of social science, or can the landscapes of novels be studied only to better understand the novels themselves? Novels, as art forms, are seriously flawed if viewed as conventional sources of geographic evidence. With rules of evidence poorly developed, specific research foci incorporating these tempting but elusive sources cannot be defined. What follows is a consideration of, first, the strengths of novels as sources of evidence for problems in environmental knowing; next, the weaknesses of these sources; and, finally, a review of research strategies able to tap the strengths while avoiding the weaknesses. The specific question from which this inquiry arises concerns the known urban geography of late nineteenth-century Boston, and examples are drawn from 10 novels of Boston life written during the last two decades of that century.[2] The attendant issues to which this paper is addressed, however, extend generally to the derivation of environmental knowledge from fictional literature of any time or place.

Environmental images found in urban novels divide into two general categories: individual character geographies and author's narrative. The former consist of thought, dialogue, and behavior involving space or landscape, and attributed by authors to specific characters or characterizations. The latter, which range from objective description to fantasies of the author's imagination, resemble personal geographical essays or vignettes. In the first instance, the author is doing what he does best—creating characters. In the second, he is doing what the geographer calls his own—understanding and explaining space and landscape. The distinction may be a fine one, especially when author's narrative proves valuable in helping recognize the author's viewpoint as it surfaces in his characters. But the distinction is attractive in that it emphasizes the author's strength at creating geographical experience in his characters and the geographer's strength at discerning broader geographical understanding from that evidence. Indeed, individual character geographies come close to being a unique contribution of novels to environmental knowing. Narrative falls, rather, into a larger class of sources of landscape description, a group not directly of concern here.

Contributions of Character Geographical Evidence

Using evidence from individual character geographies of urban novels raises a variety of pleasant prospects. Evidence at the level of the individual includes place and landscape identification, form elements, and meaning components.[3] The fundamental questions answerable with this data are the following: what kinds of people show knowledge of or contact with what locations or landscapes; what is known of abstract environmental forms; and what cultural, social, and personal meanings, or combinations of these, are attached by individual characters to different parts of their environment.

Individual characters are usually identified by significant social and personal traits. In the 10 Boston novels are found personal data for some 25 wealthy heirs and businessmen, 20 middle-class white-collar and professional people, and 8 representatives of the working class and the poor. Within each group are found different individual patterns of life. For example, in W. D. Howells's *The Rise of Silas Lapham* (1884), the self-made millionaire, Silas Lapham, works daily in the business district, an area seldom visited by the wealthy Beacon Hill aristocrat, Bromfield Corey. And where Silas must drive uncharacteristically slowly in the narrow, crooked streets, Corey walks leisurely through the district, viewing the landscape as a stranger (pp. 17, 148). Along with each bit of character evidence comes a context fitting the observation into the evolving life of the character, helping to make the geographical evidence interpretable. Arlo Bates's cynical artist Arthur Fenton in *The Pagans* (1884) has only to think of the North End to be repelled by it, while a number of wealthy and middle-class ladies actively frequent the area. This difference is clearly understood in the context of an increasing philistinism of the artist and the various charities undertaken by the latter group (Bates, 1884, pp. 161, 267; 1898, p. 24).

Within the worlds of the characters and contexts of the 10 Boston novels, the first category of evidence about the known environment is spatial and land-scape identification. Included here is evidence of character awareness of the spatial organization of their city and of the location and nature of objects in that space. Place identification by the 53 characters shows 19 with some knowledge of Beacon Hill, 15 in some way connected with the Back Bay, 14 with the South End, 12 with the Common and Public Garden, and 10 with the North End (see Figure 1). Landscapes identified by characters, often in connection with specific locations, less frequently as references to general landscape types, include fashionable streets, once-fashionable but now declining areas, boardinghouse districts, middle-class residential areas and suburbs, slums, and parks. Additional geographical evidence identified by characters covers connections between different locations and modes of travel associated with these connections. Walking, horsecars, carriages, hacks, sleighs, and steamboats all receive some attention for the various journeys to play and socialize, less often to work, and least often to shop.

Form elements, comprising the second major category of individual geographical images or awareness, also concern both space and landscape. Spatial form is recognizable in Hamlin Garland's *Jason Edwards* (1891) where newly arrived newspaperman Walter Reeves discovers the West End, North End, and South End, using Washington and Tremont Streets for orientation (p. 8). Spatial form also enters into the housing search of Marcia Hubbard, the pregnant young wife in Howell's *A Modern Instance* (1881). After investigating the South End, Charlestown, and Cambridgeport, she settles on a house in the West End because of its location adjacent to her husband's place of work (p. 245). Form applies equally well to identified landscapes, such as the tall buildings and irregular roofs in the North End described by Arlo Bates's two priests in *The Puritans* (1898, pp. 222, 268), or the rows of red houses, lamplights, and railway tracks seen by Olive Chancellor of *The Bostonians* (James, 1886, pp. 26–27) on a journey from Beacon Hill into the South End.

If identification and form of spatial elements represented the entire contribution of character geographies to environmental knowing, the rewards would barely justify the effort needed to isolate the geographically relevant information. Fortunately, evidence concern-

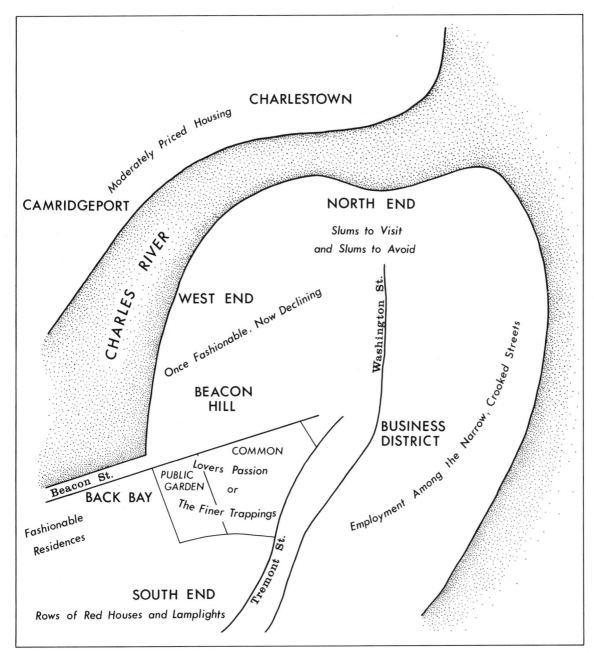

FIGURE 1
Landscape meanings drawn from the urban novels of late nineteenth-century Boston.

ing meaning, the third type available, is so intrinsically powerful that it puts to rest any fears of the effort not being worthwhile. Meaning gets at the heart of major cultural divisions in nineteenth-century Boston, where the business district is a place of familiarity surrounding the daily workplace of the aggressive and climbing Silas Lapham, but it is a place of estrangement to the declining aristocracy of Bromfield Corey (Howells, 1884, pp. 17, 148). Meaning also involves less subtle cultural divisions, with the North End frequently recognized by native Americans as an unwholesome, immigrant residential area, a place clearly apart from the city of proper Bostonians (Bates, 1898, p. 24; Butterworth, 1883, p. 207).

The geographical evidence of urban novel characters also includes meanings of a social nature. The commonplace, rural New England background of the Hubbards in Howells's *A Modern Instance* (1881) keeps them from seeing at first any impropriety in the public display of lovers passion on the Common. But as they gradually enter the mobile middle class of the city, they cease to frequent the Common, coming to prefer the more elegant trappings of the Public Garden for outdoor relaxation. Their initial failure to take offense with the Common is given even finer interpretation from the knowledge that the Hubbard's background before coming to Boston was one of religious liberality and not Puritanism (pp. 27–28, 204). Other meanings may involve social distance, even social distance distorted, as when wealthy Olive Chancellor rides the horsecars to satisfy her intellectual yearnings to be bourgeois and mingle in the common life (James, 1886, p. 26). Still another set of social meanings revolves around family life. Marcia Hubbard's residence change is brought on by the anticipated arrival of her first child, and the eventual choice of accessibility over housing cost is ultimately founded upon her unwillingness to give up serving one o'clock dinner at home to her husband (Howells, 1881, pp. 240, 245).

Personal meanings also have a place in the analysis of known environments as reminders that the whole of individual experience contains much that is apart from the standards of culture and society. One Anglican priest in Arlo Bates's *The Puritans* (1898) regularly visits the North End to play out his fascina-

tion with Roman Catholicism by pursuing absolution in a church of that denomination. To him, the North End means a place where Catholic churches are found and where he can pursue his highly individualistic fantasy (p. 22). A less bizarre personal meaning embraces the wealthy but unfashionable Hallecks of *A Moden Instance*, who hold a deep attachment for their home and garden in the declining West End and refuse to follow society in its flight to the Back Bay (Howells, 1881, pp. 231–234).

Weaknesses of Character: Geographical Evidence

Rather than continue any further into the strengths and pleasant prospects for individual character evidence of environmental knowledge, a number of worrisome pitfalls must be faced. The first set of problems concerns data availability and accessibility. Urban novels of the late nineteenth century exist in sufficient numbers for only a handful of the largest cities. Availability improves somewhat for the twentieth century, but still is likely to be insufficient for any individual city of less than highest rank. The question of defining what constitutes a sufficient quantity of data is perplexing, and experience with the Boston novels indicates quantity is especially difficult to combine with variety of viewpoints and landscapes. The total available characters form an inverted social pyramid, and the more numerous high-status characters also tend to be more fully developed. This leads to an imbalance in evidence availability favoring the residential and recreational landscapes of the wealthy. Characters belonging to the lower strata tend to have minor roles with correspondingly fewer views on their own habitats. Suburban characters and landscapes are similarly few in number. This imbalance refers specifically to Boston novels, but perhaps a more general point is that the researcher wishing to study the environmental knowledge of a broad range of the city's population for all parts of the urban scene is not assured equal access to all the categories of information he might recognize as vital to his research design.

Categorization and measurement of evidence can be managed through the use of content-analysis techniques if frequencies of clearly similar meanings will satisfy research goals. Adherents to this approach stress its objectivity and reproducibility, features that add credence to any interpretation of evidence. However, some doubts about the desirability of total commitment to content analysis of urban novels must be raised. Work with the Boston novels indicates that object places and especially object landscapes about which knowledge or attitudes are held are not easily comparable between novels and require some researcher finesse before initial categories can be established for subsequent content analysis. And whereas content analysis works well when a few major concepts are being critically examined, it is not flexible enough with objects as ill-defined and extensive as knowledge of urban environments. Increasing the number of novels should alleviate some of this problem, but only for the few most frequented places, such as Beacon Street or the Common. The remainder of the city is either ignored or handled in a manner less formal than content analysis.

A further objection to content analysis is that a high degree of objectivity may tend to obscure the highly subjective nature of the sources and give them a false aura of truth. Tied into this objection is the observation that content analysis measures only "the surface meaning of the text. Semantic devices such as irony or hyperbole cannot be taken into account" (Osborne and Reimer, 1973, p. 99). To get full meaning from sources such as novels, the subjectivity of the researcher in his interpretation of a subjective source must be recognized, and the findings presented and argued with this potential for bias clearly in view. If the scientific need for reproducibility is then lost, there arises in its place the need for including, in the body of the researcher's argument, evidence retaining something closer to its original form than a numerical summary. In the case of the urban novels, a forceful argument would require quotation and interpretation of critical passages directed toward the urban environment, including full consideration of the strengths and weaknesses of alternative interpretations.

The last major set of difficulties with urban novels as sources of environmental knowledge involves the central force behind every novel: the author. Most problems surrounding authorship cannot even be identified for certain because of the nonexistence of standards against which to measure the accuracy or truthfulness of the finished novel. With such writers as William Dean Howells or Henry James problems appear minor; they pay considerable attention to landscape description and developing a sense of place, and they earn their readers' respect as novelists who know their city and can draw upon true images of it. But what of less gifted writers? In *Jason Edwards*, author Hamlin Garland (1891) uses landscape as a vital part of his attack on conditions of everyday life in late nineteenth-century America, and his descriptions of working-class environments and of character reaction to them strain the English language to its limit for deprecating modifiers (pp. 24-51, 68-70). But Garland is at no time the cool observer of landscape with the penetrating vision of Howells or James. With all Garland's landscape awareness so sharply pointed by his theme, his landscapes cannot be reduced to objective analysis that ignores the inherently subjective bias of that theme.

Bias from literary creations other than theme can alter landscape views in even more subtle ways. And where notice might be taken of literary bias, the researcher is still essentially powerless to objectify the evidence. He can use some care in selection of authors and become involved in past and current writings of literary criticism. But there can never be an entirely satisfactory control over source quality and accuracy in any traditional historical or scientific sense. Novelists are not reporters, nor even semi-objective social commentators. They are artists whose work should be treated as a special source of subjective evidence.

Alternative Research Strategies

Accepting that urban novels and the geographic evidence of character thought and behavior offer tantalizingly valuable insights, and recognizing that serious difficulties surround the use of novels when compared with more conventional sources, is any reconciliation possible? Careful definition of research aims provides an answer. The concluding paragraphs outline briefly how three somewhat related research orientations satisfactorily accommodate evidence from novel characters.

Geosophy. One major approach to research involving novels is J. K. Wright's "geosophy" or the study of geographic knowledge from any and all points of view (Wright, 1947). As early as 1926, Wright maintained "some novelists have had an even clearer vision for the facts of geography that are of most significance to the average man than do professional writers on geographical subjects" (p. 490). A geosophic emphasis would focus on how cities were viewed or were thought to be viewed as a means toward knowing how cities can be viewed. Thus, the truthfulness of the image of Marcia Hubbard choosing her residence location is secondary to the creation itself as a culturally relevant insight into the geographical ideas of a society not completely committed to the separation of home and workplace.

Humanistic geography. The research focus of humanistic geography provides a second approach to using character evidence for geographical studies. Defined as landscape or environmental appreciation (Parsons, 1969; Meinig, 1971), humanistic geography aims toward balancing certain deficiencies in current social science through a deemphasis of simplification and prediction, coupled with an emergence of concern for alternative human values, be they esthetic, ecological, or otherwise, relating man and landscape. In his brief review of the existing kinds of literature bringing humanistic appreciation to individual localities, Meinig (1971) notes that "the skillful novelist often seems closest of all in capturing the full flavor of the environment" (p. 4). Novelists are not seen as sufficient for the research focus Meinig presents, but that hardly detracts from their contribution as sources of humanistic understanding for the much broader educational and research needs of environmental appreciation.

The focus of research in humanistic geography accepts the subjective involvement of the researcher and the likelihood of more than one valid interpretation of the evidence. The researcher does not objectify the evidence; rather, he openly interprets it in support of his argument. Geographic understanding of a place such as late nineteenth-century Boston is enhanced by an evaluation of the depth of feeling involved in the meaning relationships between characters and their landscapes. The strength of the argument presenting this evidence, including the literary skill of the geographer himself, establishes the basis for determining the worth of the research effort. This worth is not determined positively, but requires a subjective evaluation by readers familiar with the general area of concern.

Phenomenology. J. K. Wright's (1947) awareness of viewpoint and the common man, of human desires and motivations, of intuitive imagining and subjectivity offers an early hint of a third research focus for the study of the environmental images of fictional characters. More recently, these same concerns have reappeared through the introduction of phenomenological concepts into North American geography by Relph (1970), Tuan (1971), and Buttimer (1974). Sidestepping the question of the desirability of total application of phenomenological method(s) in geography, the present discussion is adequately served through recognition of the phenomenological conceptualization of man. This approach emphasizes the unpredictable, information-generating inhabitant of a subjective world, knowable in terms of his consciousness, an approach different from the behaviorist model of a predictable, information-transmitting inhabitant of an objective world, knowable in terms of his behavior (Hitt, 1969, p. 658). The former embraces the creativity and consciousness brought to a novel by its author, whereas the latter runs head on into the problems of insufficient numbers of directly comparable cases and inadequate measurement raised earlier. Emphasis on phenomenological man over behaviorist man leads to research focusing on the intentional structures and attendant meanings of man's everyday experience and away from quasi-mechanistic systems (Buttimer, 1974, pp. 23, 37). Rather than attempt to explain and eventually predict environmental knowledge and behavior, this research studies the subjective and imaginary passages of landscape evidence from novels for the insights they allow about how people are thought to be relating in a personally meaningful way with their environment. Identification of these relationships becomes a starting point for a deeper understanding of the nature of subjective experience.

Conclusions

From a general question of the prospects for knowing the thoughts of city dwellers concerning their urban environments, this paper has proceeded to inquire into the strengths of novels as sources of that thought, their weaknesses, and alternative and supportive research orientations. That the three research orientations themselves have weaknesses is beyond question; indeed their weaknesses are the strengths of positivist social science.[4] The point is rather that evidence unacceptable under a positivist approach need not be ignored. Imaginative literature may be quite unacceptable for the reconstruction of objective man–environment relationships. But the human experience and striving found in the literature of different times and places justify attempts at its use in understanding the subjective world of persons.

NOTES

1. An earlier version of this paper was presented as part of a special session on Landscape in Literature at the Annual Meetings of the Association of American Geographers, Seattle, April 1974. This paper is in part an attempt to answer some searching questions raised by Professors C. L. Salter, Edward Soja, David Stea, James Blaut, Howard Nelson, and Gary Dunbar during the author's 1973 Ph.D. orals.

2. The ten novels are Arlo Bates, *The Pagans* (1884) and *The Puritans* (1898); Clara Louise Burnham, *"No Gentlemen"* (1881); Hezekiah Butterworth, *Up from the Cape* (1883); F. Marion Crawford, *An American Politician* (1885); Hamlin Garland, *Jason Edwards: An Average Man* (1891); William Dean Howells, *A Modern Instance* (1881) and *The Rise of Silas Lapham* (1884); Henry James, *The Bostonians* (1886); and Maria Louise Pool, *Roweny in Boston* (1892).

3. Lynch in *The Image of the City* (1960, pp. 8 ff.) discusses images in terms of identity, structure, and meaning. Harrison and Howard, in "The Role of Meaning in the Urban Image" (1972), use a four-part division—physical appearance, physical location, cultural meaning, cultural association—for identified images.

4. Questions of the propriety of humanistic and phenomenological approaches to geography and of the strengths and weaknesses of a more positivist approach are roundly discussed in the introduction and commentaries to Buttimer (1974) by E. Soja, J. Blaut, T. Hagerstrand, E. Gibson, and Y-F. Tuan, as well as in the main portion of the paper itself.

26

David Seamon
Graduate School of Geography
Clark University

PHENOMENOLOGICAL INVESTIGATION OF IMAGINATIVE LITERATURE: A COMMENTARY

As a unit, the three preceding chapters representing the literary perspective on environmental knowing indicate that humanistic study can usefully complement scientific research. In fact, taken together, these chapters remind one of the phenomenologist's credo of "to the things themselves."[1] Like phenomenology, they suggest that students versed in a scientific approach to man's cognition of the environment might profitably fall back to the basic structures of environmental knowledge and experience and ask themselves if the primary concepts assumed in their theories—for example, image, cognitive map, environmental cognition and perception—exhaustively and accurately reflect the real stuff of human life in a geographical world. As a whole, the chapters point out that, unlike science, imaginative literature does not reduce human experience into simpler, more manipulable units, but searches out universality through an articulation of experience in its manifest richness and concreteness. With proper sifting and interpretation, this richness of experential detail can help the student of environmental knowing to better clarify the premises and notions from which he proceeds to create his theories and interpret his data; it can present him with potentially new perspectives that lead to new questions, new hypotheses, and perhaps eventually new models.

With varying degrees of success, each paper illustrates the multilayered nature of environmental knowledge. As Yi-Fu Tuan explains in Chapter 23, cognition for the social scientist generally deals with explicit intellectual knowledge. It requires an active human agent who consciously manipulates himself or herself and the things in the environment. This agent could be likened somewhat to an efficient switchboard operator who receives messages from the outside world, deciphers them, and then decides how he or she will respond. In contrast, writers of imaginative literature depict cognition as an imprecise part of experience that blends imperceptibly with other, less conscious ways of contacting reality. Like the student of cognition, the creative writer recognizes that at times we are active human agents consciously molding and deciding our life events, but that at other times we can be a storehouse of anger, or a body moving habitually through space, or a container of wonderment that has just seen the first snowflakes of winter.

In literature, knowledge of environment is a subtle and ambiguous coalescence of the conscious and the subconscious, the intellectual and the emotional, the real and the imagined, the spontaneous and the habitual. No doubt this multiplicity of experiential meanings imposes a heavy and awkward burden for the researcher whose prime wish is reduction and simplicity. On the other hand, the imaginative writer *does* articulate the human situation, and *does* bring to light "the murky perceptual-cognitive experiences," as Yi-Fu Tuan labels them. In this sense, then, literary descriptions of experiential complexity serve as a beacon, illuminating underlying dimensions of the person's existential dialogue with the environment. A thorough inventory of literature that highlights particular individuals' dialogues with particular geographical environments should provide a valuable categorization of the multiple and intertwined layers of environmental knowing.

The papers presented here make a helpful start in suggesting the nature of these multiple levels as literature presents them. W. J. Lloyd's study discusses a fairly conventional dimension of environmental knowing—how characters portrayed in ten novels depicting life in late nineteenth-century Boston cognize their environment in terms of identifiable places, their spatial relations, and their personal meaning. This analysis is rather simple and suggests an amplification of the conventional environmental imagery studies conducted by Kevin Lynch (1960) and other researchers (de Jonge, 1962; Gulick, 1963; Francescato and Mebane, 1973). Rather than asking actual residents to construct their mental images of Boston, as Lynch did, Lloyd has used urban novels as a data source, and a considerable portion of his paper advantageously considers the strengths and weaknesses of this particular method. His study, then, highlights imaginative literature as an indicator of individuals' cognitive knowledge about the geographical world in which they find themselves.

In Chapter 24, Myongsup Shin attempts to uncover another dimension of environmental meaning in literature. Although this study is weak because it too arbitrarily relates a particular author with a particular use of landscape description, it is an instructive first attempt at interpreting how environmental description can be used by the writer to imply emotional and symbolic meaning. Shin argues that, in the three novels he considers, the authors use description of landscape to signify different ways of responding to the physical environment—in this case, the southwestern part of the United States.

Because he does not identify with the area, the traveler Pike describes the Southwest in fairly objective fashion; Momaday, strongly attached to the same place, echoes deep emotional involvement in his descriptions. A third variation is Willa Cather's novel, *Death Comes for the Archbishop*, which uses the landscape of the Southwest to foreshadow events. Shin's paper points out, then, that landscape as portrayed in literature can signify emotional and symbolic meanings as well as provide an objective account of landscape. One difficulty here, however, is that Shin seems to confuse the significance of the environment for the novels' characters with the authors' techniques and points of view. For Momaday and Cather the landscape is a metaphorical vehicle for capturing attachment to place or for signaling what is about to happen. The environment does not necessarily have symbolic value for the characters themselves. Thus, Shin's analysis more correctly discusses the figurative use of landscape description rather than a particular dimension of environmental knowing.

Although the symbolic meaning of landscape hinted at here by Shin does not necessarily reveal individual environmental knowledge directly, its study is still an essential part of a literary perspective on people's experiential dialogue with environment because literary symbols and images manifest aspects of this interplay that are perhaps invisible and impregnable to conventional techniques of social science. As Leo Marx (1968) explains, "because imaginative literature remains one of our most delicate and accurate means of joining ideas with emotions, public with private experience, I believe that it can provide insights into the relations between mind and environment which are unavailable elsewhere" (p. 122).

Most of the studies considering the meaning of environmental metaphors and symbols have been written by students of literature (see, for example, Conron, 1973; Marx, 1964, 1968; Watson, 1970; Weimar, 1966; however, also see White and White, 1962, who are both philosophers; and Strauss, 1961, 1968, who is a sociologist). Generally, these literary scholars do not consider the practical implications of their interpretations to real-world environments, and may even discount such a connection (see, for example, Weimar, 1966, pp. 1-6). Marx, however, himself a student of literature, believes that the imaginary landscape interpreted correctly can indicate much about what the real-world landscape is for people, or what it might better be. In his article, "Pastoral Ideals and City Troubles" (1968), he discusses a perennial landscape pattern in American literature: retreat and return—from the city, to the country, to the city again. By means of this geographical sequence, Marx explains, writers can signify a vocabulary of feelings in terms of environmental images. Thus, people seeking a simpler way of life return to nature, relieve their discomfort, and so return to the urban situation refreshed.

Marx concludes by suggesting how this pattern of environmental images in literature may have some relevance to the problems of the actual landscape. For example, the great frequency with which this sequence occurs in American literature signifies that social scientists and planners should consider in more detail "the subjective and in large measure traditional, aesthetic, or symbolic significance that our culture attaches to images of the external landscape—urban, rural, and wild" (p. 139). One concrete measure of this significance, Marx suggests, would be a detailed analytic inventory of the various satisfactions that people have realized, or have claimed to realize, from these various environments.

Marx's study, then, outlines in cogent fashion an approach that social scientists might use if they wish to investigate environmental symbols and images in literature. To be valuable pragmatically, these studies might not only interpret the meaning of geographical mataphors, but also attempt to relate their significance to real, everyday experience of environment. This is a difficult task requiring considerable sensitivity, but, as Marx's study reveals, it can provide striking insight into the more intimate dimensions of man's outlook on his geographical world.

If Lloyd and Shin's papers represent studies that begin to investigate specific cognitive and symbolic meanings related to environmental descriptions in literature, then Yi-Fu Tuan's paper in contrast seeks to sketch in broad strokes the multiple layers of environmental knowledge and experience that literature might reveal through phenomenological analysis. His overview incorporates the cognitive and figurative components of geographical description, and also illumines other significances of man–environment depictions—as a helpful portrait of factual information on the man–land dialogue, as a cogent sketch of particular world views, as a partial reconciler of people and nature, and as a creative force that influences environmental perceptions and attitudes.

In terms of environmental knowing, the dimension discussed by Yi-Fu Tuan that is perhaps most important is the articulation of experience in imaginative literature. Phenomenological analysis of such descriptions may reveal patterns of experience that the social scientists and planners may have ignored before or only considered imprecisely. Yi-Fu Tuan lists five examples of how literature isolates and articulates environmental experience: by concretizing the uncomfortable sense of absense, by characterizing the instantaneous quality of our immersion in the everyday lived world, by portraying the fleeting presence of noise and light, by describing the frequent ambiguity of shared world views, and by contrasting varying human attitudes toward nature.

Each of these themes represents topics and perspectives that conventional work in environmental perception, cognition, and attitude studies has yet to consider, or considers in only partial fashion. For example, in his comments on the physiognomy of place, Yi-Fu Tuan explains that environmental knowledge does not necessarily involve the active synthesis of discrete perceptions of environmental objects and space, but incorporates instead a holistic understanding of place through that place's essential and instantaneous manifestation of itself to us. To exemplify this abstruse point, he quotes an extraordinary passage from the French phenomenologist, Merleau-Ponty (1962), who, although technically not a writer but a philosopher, conveys forceful articulations of experience that compare equally in quality with the best of literature. In the quotation, Merleau-Ponty sheds new light on our knowledge of place: that it requires no conscious effort, but occurs instantaneously, before we can be cognitively aware of it. Thus, Paris, as Merleau-Ponty poignantly discerns it, is not a composite of percepts or a cognitive representation, but a way of being, an ambiguous essence expressing itself in a self-evident way that requires no conscious definition. This view on environmental knowledge is considerably different from the perspective of most cognitive theorists, who usually argue that the individual somehow actively structures the elements of his environment through the use of an intellectual representation, sometimes called a cognitive map (see, for example, Downs and Stea, 1973b). If Merleau-Ponty is right, however, the everyday world is before us before we cognitively know it, changing and shifting indiscernibly as we pass through it. Thus, Yi-Fu Tuan suggests that literature provides an alternative picture of how people know the environment as they find themselves in it. What is needed, then, is a more thorough study of how literature characterizes the "physiognomy of place" and how this characterization compares with the conventional view of environmental cognition and perception.

In a similar way, Yi-Fu Tuan's brief comments on attitudes toward nature also suggest a way of knowing the environment that has not yet been considered analytically to any extent in existing environment–behavior studies. Although we are convinced of the material ecological connections between humans and nature, we are less convinced of the value or even the existence of any spiritual bonds between people and the landscape. Yet, as Yi-Fu Tuan makes clear, imaginative literature often emphasizes the communal link between people and nature—a link that may manifest itself as an experience of well-being, a communion with oneness, or a feeling of religious gratitude. In a time when we need to become more ecologically responsible, social scientists could make a valuable contribution if they considered in greater detail the various ways in which writers (and for that matter, painters, musicians, and other artists) have described the experience of knowing nature, in order to eventually determine if any of these encounters can be experienced by ordinary people through education or other means of sensitization. Such a study would

necessarily require great reverence and sensitivity, and is perhaps a subject beyond the realm of an "objective" social science. However, insight into how the spiritual interaction between people and nature deepends our awareness of our place as one small earth creature in a vast interconnected whole may provide an important key for alleviating in some small measure the ecological plight of our planet today.

As a whole, then, these three chapters indicate that investigation of imaginative literature provides penetrating depictions of our experiential dialogue with the environment. In understanding people's outlook on their geographical world, an analysis of literature reveals the multiplicity of ways in which we may "know" our environment. Such analysis perhaps best provides a phenomenological function, in that it articulates the taken-for-granted patternings of ordinary and extraordinary geographical experience, and so gives them a presence that concerned students can organize and then probe in greater depth.

In other words, a phenomenological investigation of literature provides one way of illuminating more precisely our environmental situation, and so better helps us to attune our modes of knowing the geographical world with our modes of experiencing it. In fact, the articulations of environmental experience alluded to in the preceding chapters suggest that the existing models of environmental perception and cognition are very much out of tune with lived experience. What may be required, then, is a fresh look at environmental experience, using literature and other sources of direct experiential data to return faithfully to its original dimensions, which exist before the abstraction and reduction of conventional psychological models.[2] Such a task is formidable and implies that much of the existing work on environmental cognition and perception is of dubious validity. If our wish as social scientists, however, is to genuinely describe and explain people's experiential dialogue with their environment, then this task is required and must be performed many times afresh by many people. Eventually, we may establish accurate contact with the underlying "realities" of human environmental experience.

We must also not forget that a consideration of

literature as it presents our geographical lived world is a humanistic endeavor that leads to knowledge of self. By uncovering and understanding environmental experience as other, more sensitive and creative individuals have known it, we, as more typical people, may become aware of patterns in our *own* experience that we had not known before. In this way we ourselves become more sensitive to our *own* geographical situation, and so we grow as persons.

NOTES

1. See Spiegelberg (1965, particularly Vol. II, pp. 659–699) for a valuable introduction to the phenomenological method, and Tuan (1971) for an incipient sketch of phenomenology's use in environmental studies.
2. See Merleau-Ponty (1962, 1963) for a difficult but cogent critique of traditional psychological paradigms.

27

HEROES AND HISTORY: A COMMENTARY

David Lowenthal
  Department of Geography
  University College, London

This book resembles a hero sandwich, a long, large roll sliced almost in two and stuffed with a medley of strange goodies. Like a hero, it takes time and effort to digest. The upper and lower halves of the roll, "theories" and "methods," respectively, are of roughly similar compositon: each comprises scientifically testable hypotheses and the application of various methods—personal construct theory, semantic differentials—to particular aspects of environmental understanding and behavior. As with its culinary counterpart, the theoretical top is crustier than the methodological bottom, which has a dense and doughy texture.

It is with the sandwich filling, however, that this commentary mainly deals—that more or less delectable conglomerate of meat and cheese, spices and salads, that provides most of the hero's flavor and nutritive value. These ingredients, in themselves highly disparate, stem from such separate if not conflicting cuisines as anthropology, geography, and literature. Heated up in a melting pot they might emerge as a unified essence, but only at the cost of their distinctive individual qualities. Without blending them into a flavorless pap, let us see what these ingredients have in common.

The case studies presented here share a humanist perspective, an assumption that it is the quality of human life that matters most in environmental experience and a fath that the humanities afford the best insight into this realm of knowledge. To be sure, sociology, geography, and anthropology are also social sciences, relying heavily on deductive reasoning, reproducible results, and statistical sampling and analysis. But the contributors to this section are more committed to modes of inquiry that borrow little from experimental science.

Toward this difference of approach the editors exhibit some ambivalence. Their general introduction states that the perspectives on environmental cognition in Part II "do not *yet* approximate the hypothetical-deductive model of scientific theories" (my italics), implying that more data and greater precision will someday repair the defect. But their foreword flatly asserts that these perspectives, although "valuable in suggesting new lines of investigation and providing explanatory concepts, . . . are not themselves testable in a hypothetical-deductive manner." This section's authors would probably prefer the second characterization. They are not trying to approximate a "hypothetical-deductive model"; without dismissing science as spurious, they choose to eschew scientistic approaches in favor of humanistic ones that enable them to focus on important questions often ignored or trivialized by scientists. And because they take pains to communicate intelligibly, their speculations convey meaning and carry conviction. One is struck by the contrast between the opacity of many of the papers on theory and method and the relative clarity of this section. A devotion to scientific methodology for its own sake often obscures the message of the former; a concern for human understanding makes the latter, with one or two exceptions, essays that are a pleasure to read.

Disciplinary eclecticism is an additional virtue of these contributions. The sociological perspectives are mostly by geographers; the anthropological (cross-cultural) perspective is presented by architects and geographers; the "literary" perspective is entirely in the hands of geographers. Thus, it is geographers, perhaps less confined than other scholars to an exclusive disciplinary approach and to the usual accompanying jargon, who here offer insights into the various worlds of their social science and humanist colleagues.

Different worlds, yes, but essentially one world; and the point is important. For man is not a social animal today, a creative artist tomorrow, and an economic creature next week; he is at one and the same time all of these and many other things. An approach to environmental knowledge that focuses on single perspectives to the exclusion of their indivisible wholeness substitutes a tidy model of reality for the amorphous and shifting complexities of everyday life.

If any overarching perspective, beyond humanism, embraces all these approaches, it is their dependence on historical understanding. All insights about social, cultural, and geographical environment—especially those exemplified in literature and painting—are embedded in the experience of particular people in specific times and places. How people view and articulate their experience is a product both of their own place in history and of that of their successive interpreters. The very words used to describe environmental conditions and responses alter in force, context, and meaning over time.

The way history and historical awareness affect

what we know about the environment and how we interpret it can be briefly illustrated. We view the past both as different from and also as a determinant of the present. Environmental understanding alters over time partly because environmental and human circumstances change, partly because knowledge accretes: we know not only what we experience directly ourselves, but also, indirectly, much of what our forebears and their historical ancestors believed about the environment. Such information is always fallible, its content and perspective changing with each generation of historians; what we believe about the past may be erroneous, what people in an earlier epoch "knew" about the environment may have been mistaken; their knowledge or ignorance may have influenced later developments in ways we misapprehend or fail to understand. To put our own environmental knowledge in a historical context thus helps us to realize that what we know and do is determined not simply by logic or necessity but by what has happened to other men and their environments in times past.

Historical awareness is also crucial to understanding that time lags are inherent in all environmental relationships. Environmental events, human responses to them, and resultant attitudes and policies all take place, endure, and give way at differing times and tempos. Temporal gulfs between environmental conditions, environmental beliefs, and environmental behavior are inevitable. For example, a society that has expanded into virgin lands with abundant resources is apt to develop a confident and profligate attitude toward land and resource utilization. This behavior then becomes embedded in national ideals and stereotypes about environmental relationships. A subsequent change in environmental or human conditions—climatic deterioration, soil erosion, the exhaustion of open land—will vitally affect many but will not soon alter the mental set of most; generations may elapse before national understanding of environment takes account of the changed circumstances, which will by then usually have changed again. And even after people have come to realize that resources are more finite or ecosystems more fragile than their forebears supposed, engrained behavioral habits and institutional constraints will continue to enforce environmental action at variance with that understanding.

The disparities between environmental circumstances and historically inherited beliefs and behavior are universal, but they vary in degree and import. The extent to which people in different cultures and communities are concerned about such disparities and seek to reform institutions or ideals so as to resolve them is itself historically conditioned. To explore how men confront and respond to such dilemmas, and not simply to naively given environmental circumstances, is a task that deserves the joint efforts of all scholars, scientists, and humanists alike.

PART III

METHODOLOGICAL CONSIDERATIONS

EDITORS' INTRODUCTION

A number of new methods for the study of the worlds inside people's heads have been proposed recently. Until a few years ago the usual methodology employed a form of analysis of self-report external representations, such as freely drawn sketch maps and verbal descriptions. Both these approaches have come under considerable criticism, and the result has been the development of a wide range of new, more sophisticated methods for the analysis of environmental knowing (e.g., Craik, 1968, 1970a; Mark, 1972; Lang, Burnette, Moleski, and Vachon, 1974; Michelson, 1975). The principal aim behind the development of these new methodologies has been that of circumventing the pitfalls of the early approaches while drawing on the current expertise of a range of disciplines, such as psychology, geography, sociology, architecture, and planning. In fact, one of the more interesting trends in research related to environmental knowing is the common use of methodologies borrowed from many disciplines. It is not unusual to see a geographer using psychophysical scaling techniques (e.g., Briggs, 1972; Zannaras, 1973; Golledge, Rivizzigno, and Spector, 1975) or a psychologist using the geographer's cartographic devices (e.g., Moore, Chapter 12; Winkel, Malek, and Thiel, 1969) or designers and planners using a mixture of their own, geographical, and psychological techniques (e.g., Appleyard, 1969b; Sanoff, 1968).

Part III consists of a general introductory chapter and three subsections concerned with the use of psychophysical scaling, maps and models, and verbal constructs in environmental cognition research. In Chapter 28, Golledge discusses in categorical terms a range of methods used to elicit or externalize environmental knowledge objectively. This chapter emphasizes the fact that researchers interested in determining the extent, organization, or other characteristics of an individual's knowledge of the environment face a very fundamental problem in trying to *extract* that information from the individual. This extraction process is perhaps the most critical problem associated with empirical work in this area, for the analytical devices subsequently used on extracted information rely very much for their validity on the way that the desired knowledge is obtained and objectively presented for analysis. Accordingly, considerable emphasis is given to a range of methods from different disciplines that *have* been used, or *are* being used, to extract environmental knowledge. Some consideration is then given to the different ways in which this information can be preserved and summarized. This latter discussion focuses on the danger of trying to represent information by calling on skills that are beyond the capabilities of subjects. This particular warning is reinforced in a section discussing methods for analyzing externalized cognitive representations, where it is strongly suggested that particular care be paid to the selection of *analytical* devices (such as parametric and nonparametric statistical tests) to use on cognitive information. The final section of Chapter 28, raises a number of critical but unresolved problems relating to both methodological and theoretical issues in the field of environmental cognition.

Following the introductory chapter, Chapters 29 and 30 illustrate the use of psychophysical scales and multidimensional scaling methods for the analysis of cognitive information. For example, Martin Cadwallader works at a regional scale and attempts to recover a configuration of urban places in the California system based on people's estimates of how far the places are from a selected origin. Realizing that different analytical methods may yield different results (see Lowrey, 1973), Cadwallader carefully examines his data from two different points of view and comments on the significance of the support that each method provides for the other. Ronald Briggs works at a much finer scale, concentrating purely on the measurement of cognitive distance *within* an urban area. He examines a series of distance estimates over routes that vary from straight lines between points to those with multiple turns or bends between origin and destination. Again, careful attention is paid to the type of scaling devices used in the data-collection phase and to the selection of statistical methods used in the analysis of the results. As was mentioned earlier, it is not unusual to see the use of methods attributable to one discipline used by members of another; here, for example, we see both Cadwallader and Briggs, who are geographers, drawing extensively on experimental designs and analytical methods developed in the field of psychology.

Section 8B reflects recent work that utilizes different types of physical models and improvements to sketch mapping techniques, along with other media-oriented methods for eliciting environmental knowledge. For example, Denis Wood and Robert Beck concentrate on developing a cognitive mapping language that allows the subject to record in very graphic form exactly what he or she remembers about the elements, spatial relations, and various qualitative, symbolic, and emotional attributes of different environments. Their paper is an excellent example of current attempts to overcome the deficiencies associated with individual differences in the ability to draw sketches and maps of environments (see also Section 4). Their paper is also innovative in that they allow subjects to incorporate on their maps the *feelings* that they have about segments of their environment.

We should note here that, although the Wood and Beck cognitive mapping language is suitable for graphically symbolizing *cognitions* of external environments, there have been other attempts to develop graphic symbol systems for recording environmental *perceptions*. Examples of these latter methods include Halprin (1963, pp. 193-215, 1965, 1969, pp. 30-43, 92-103), Appleyard, Lynch, and Myer (1964, pp. 21-37), Carr and Schissler (1969), and Thiel (1961, 1971, 1973, 1974). The systems developed by Halprin and by Appleyard, Lynch, and Myer were for recording strictly visual or audial experiences while subjects were walking or driving through complex environments. The Thiel system extends also to graphically recording a sense of place and the emotions associated with places. Each system has the potential for being used in cognitive studies; for example, the notation of one's feelings *in situ* could be used for noting one's image of the character of a place *after* visitation. It is in this latter area that Chapter 32 sheds light.

Georgia Zannaras, on the other hand, presents partial results from a more complete study (Zannaras, 1973), which takes into consideration Craik's (1970) advice to use multiple methods of analysis to examine individuals in their environments. Zannaras's original study used a complex experimental design involving maps, three-dimensional models, slides, and field trips. In the present chapter she concentrates on presenting the results of the analysis with maps and models and shows the differences that can be obtained if one or another of these methods is primarily used. The multiple-method approach adopted by Zannaras is one that appears to offer considerable promise in studies of environmental knowing. For another example, Moore (1973b; see also Chapter 12) used the triangulation of multiple methods to ascertain in two independent ways the cognitive structures underlying adolescent's images of the environment. In his case, both a graphic-structural measure (structural analysis of sketch maps) and a linguistic-operational measure (verbal way-finding tasks) were used and the findings compared (but see the criticism in Bycroft, 1974).

Section 8C illustrates two quite different methods for extracting environmental knowledge based on the analysis of verbal constructs. Whereas the preceding chapters examine concrete and permanent external environments, the research work of Stephen Golant and Ian Burton concentrates on examining more abstract and ephemeral features of the environment. Their subject matter is that of environmental hazards —intermittent occurrences that seem to have vastly different properties in different places and from the point of view of different groups. Golant and Burton note that not everyone agrees that an environmental hazard has occurred at any particular point in time. Various assessments of and reaction to grades of environmental hazards are examined by using semantic differential techniques. This latter methodology has appeared quite frequently in research into environmental hazard perception and in examinations of the significance of cross-cultural differences in the assessment of environmental information (e.g., White, 1945; Kates, 1962; Sonnenfeld, 1966).

Whereas the semantic differential method was developed in a context free of any particular theory, the repetory grid method discussed by John Harrison and Philip Sarre, and earlier in Chapter 7, is tied intimately to Kelly's personal construct theory (Kelly, 1955; see also Chapter 6). Chapter 34 reports on how a repertory grid design can be used successfully to elicit environmental knowledge from relatively large groups of people. The authors suggest how the knowledge that is extracted in this manner can then be used to reconstruct environments from the point of view of sample respondents.

Part III is concluded with a general commentary on research strategy in environmental cognition by Joachim Wohlwill, based in part on his oral comments given at the 1973 Blacksburg symposium. The continued interaction among a wide range of fields interested in environmental cognition problems has prompted a tremendous exchange of methods and analytical devices. The result is that current studies are being more rigorously designed and are capable of objective verification; this is in direct contrast with many of the earlier attempts, which were not only very subjective in nature, but were contained much more within disciplinary boundaries.

Although each of the methodologies presented here varies considerably in terms of the experimental design required and the degree of sophistication of the analytical tools that can be used on its output, each method aims at obtaining and examining the various structures and meanings that people give to large-scale external environments. Having rather briefly summarized a few of the points made in papers in the section, we now turn to allowing the reader a more detailed examination of the papers themselves.

28

Reginald G. Golledge
Department of Geography
Ohio State University

METHODS AND METHODOLOGICAL ISSUES IN ENVIRONMENTAL COGNITION RESEARCH

Cognitive information is by definition peculiar to an individual. Although each individual necessarily has his own unique cognitive transformation of environmental information, there is abundant evidence to indicate that many people are aware of the existence of the same things. Awareness can be generated by any of our senses, and differences of opinion as to what *is* in the environment may occur when different senses are used in the information-extraction process, when physiological qualities of the senses differ among observers, when different transactional modes are used to elicit information, and when sociocultural values of individual observers differ. It is quite critical, therefore, to become aware of the range of methods that utilize different skills to extract information from the environment.

If we are to penetrate the "unique experience" barrier and to discover what environmental features are known by many individuals, what structures they impose on the environment, and what meaning they give to things that they become aware of, we must have satisfactory methodologies for extracting this information. However, as Hart and Moore (1973) have pointed out, to accomplish these aims we must be aware of the type of representational skills avail-

able to individuals at different stages of their physiological and psychological development, and select appropriate methodologies that allow individuals to use these skills to manifest aspects of this knowledge to others. Figure 1 summarizes their views of the representational skills most likely to be in existence at various states of physical and intellectual development. We shall make use of this conceptualization throughout this discussion.

In earlier sections of this book, we have seen theorizing about *how* people extract information from external environments, and we have been presented with a number of different perspectives illustrating how researchers from different disciplines interpret and use the cognitive information thus obtained. In this paper we shall focus on three critical methodological problems related to environmental cognition research and shall discuss some of the general issues raised by attempts to solve these problems. The three general problems to be considered are the following:

1. What methods can we use to *extract* meaningful cognitive information from individuals about large-scale external environments?
2. How can the information thus extracted best be

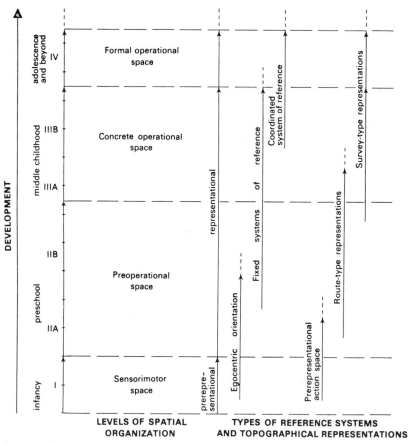

FIGURE 1

Schematic representation of the development of geographical orientation and of types of reference systems that underlie cognitive representations of the everyday large-scale environment, shown in relation to the major periods of cognitive spatial development. [Reprinted from Hart and Moore (1973) with the permission of the authors and publisher.]

manifest so that others can become aware of the extent of an individual's cognitions of such environments?

3. How can we best *analyze* the material that is thus presented?

As each question is dealt with in turn, reference will be made to examples given in this book and to other work in the general field of environmental cognition research.

CLASSIFICATION OF METHODS

There is a tremendous range and variety of methods used to extract cognitive information about large-scale external environments. Most of these can be classified in terms of the following:

1. Their reliance on inferences based on naturalistic as opposed to experimenter-controlled behaviors.
2. Whether inferences are made from behavior that is

directly observable as opposed to making inferences from past histories.

3. The extent to which responses themselves are elicited directly from individuals using self-report procedures or participatory activities, as opposed to making "second-stage" inferences from a variety of indirect judgmental tasks.

Each possible extraction procedure can be used in natural or controlled environments. Earlier in this book, for example, we saw a number of individual experiments that used both natural and partly controlled environments in their experimental design. The results were then used either to construct theory related to environmental knowing (see Chapters 2, 5, 9, and 12) or for some practical or teaching application of the knowledge thus acquired (see Chapters 7 and 14). Let us now examine in detail some of the methodologies used in the extraction process. Brief summaries of a range of techniques, their related procedures, and examples of the use of each method are found in Table 1.

Let us stress at this point that Table 1 is not comprehensive, but merely emphasizes some of the major methods that have been used to elicit environmental information from subject populations. Other summaries are provided in Craik (1970a), Mark (1972), and Downs and Stea (1973a). The format chosen in this table is designed to bring out some of the basic methodological differences mentioned earlier, and to summarize the type of skills that subjects must have to adequately respond to any given method. Popular ways of objectively representing information elicited by each method are also given. Let us now briefly summarize the information contained in each of the major segments of Table 1.

EXTRACTING ENVIRONMENTAL INFORMATION

Experimenter Observation in "Naturalistic" and Controlled Situations

Two different procedures have been chosen to illustrate how inferences about cognitive information can be made from observable behaviors in different "nat-

ural" environments. The first involves tracking people through known and unknown environments and observing their responses to different events, elements, and structures that appear in the environment, and the second involves making inferences from behaviors in various "clinical" type situations. Way-finding tasks are typical of the first of these procedures and have been used by a wide variety of researchers, as can be seen in Table 1. Geographers in particular have spent considerable effort tracking the movement patterns of people in many different environments. For example, Zannaras (1973) conducted a field experiment in which she took people to a particular place in an urban environment and asked them to get to a given destination. The path selected and the cues used to help select a path were then recorded by the experimenter as the individual completed the task.

Other researchers, such as Marble (1967), have suggested attaching miniature transmitters to individuals and vehicles so that their movement patterns around urban areas over specific time periods could be recorded. This form of electronic experimenter observation appears a little more practical than actually following individuals around. The actual tracking of people as they move about environments for the most part has been replaced by questions that elicit responses regarding which parts of their environment are used and how frequently they are used. Reconstruction of movement patterns from both experimenter observation and self-report techniques has become an indispensable tool for many researchers interested in problems related to knowing and using environments.

Four different strategies for observing overt activity under controlled or partly controlled experimental conditions are summarized in Table 1. These are subject-controlled classification procedures, subject role-playing activities, constructive toy play or model building, and animal experimentation.

Subject-controlled classification procedures simply involve *individuals* in sorting environmental occurrences, or constructs related to such occurrences, into classes. Class divisions can be specified by the experimenter or can be left to the discretion of each respondant. In the latter case, it may be much harder to

TABLE 1
Methods for Extracting Environmental Cognition Information

Method	Procedure	Subject Skill	External Representational Form	Example
Experimenter observation in naturalistic or controlled situations	Experimenter observes or tracks movements through actual environments (e.g., crawl patterns, search behavior, overt spatial activity, actual wayfinding, etc.)	Cognitive Concrete Psycho- motoric	Observations Reports Maps Tables	Lynch (1960) Marble (1967) Ladd (1970) Jones (1972) Devlin (1973) Zannaras (1973) R. Kaplan, Chap. 3
	Experimenter infers degrees of cognitive knowledge from behavior in unstructured "clinical" situations	Cognitive Concrete Motoric	Charts Profiles	Werner (1948) Piaget and Inhelder (1956) Hart (1974)
	Subjects reveal environmental knowledge in the process of sorting or grouping elements of actual or simulated environments	Cognitive Abstract Relational	Lists Tables Composite maps	Downs (1970a) Wish (1972) Zannaras (1973) Golledge et al. (1975)
	Subjects adopt roles or perform acts in simulated and/or real environments	Cognitive Abstract Relational	Photographs Tables	Ittelson (1951) Milgram (1970) Saegert (1973) Acredolo, Chap. 13
	Subjects arrange toys or objects representing environmental elements or model environments, and experimenter observes the sequence of acts in positioning elements and/or using the environment	Cognitive Concrete Motoric	Analog models	Piaget et al. (1960) Blaut and Stea (1969) Laurendeau and Pinard (1970) Mark (1972) Hart (1974)

(continued)

TABLE 1 (*continued*)

Method	Procedure	Subject Skill	External Representational Form	Example
	Experimenter deduces cognitive information from nonhuman activities (e.g., animal acts, machine simulation)	Cognitive Psychomotor	Observational schedules Tables	Tolman (1948) Peters (1973)
Historical reconstructions	Experimenter deduces environmental knowledge from written descriptions (novels, poems, etc.) and/or past pictorial representations of environments, usually from horizontal or oblique perspectives	Affective Psychomotor Linguistic	Novels Poems Paintings Philosophies Sketches Diaries Content analysis	Lowenthal and Prince (1964) Heathcote (1965) Gleason (1972) Bowden (1975) Tuan, Chap. 23 Shin, Chap. 24 Lloyd, Chap. 25
Analysis of external representations— participatory activities	Subjects are asked to write descriptions of what they are aware of in environments	Affective Psychomotor Linguistic	Written reports Contact analysis Item analysis	Lynch and Rivkin (1959) Carr and Schissler (1969) Appleyard (1969a) Winkel et al. (1969)
	Subjects are asked to describe orally a given environment	Affective Linguistic	Oral reports Type Transcriptions Interview Protocols	Lynch (1960) Carr and Schissler (1969) Gittins (1969) Craik (1970a) Moore (1973b) Zannaras (1973)
	Subjects draw sketches or sketch maps representing environments	Affective Graphic Relational	Pictorial sketches Sketch maps Quantitative and structural analyses	Lynch (1960) Shemyakin (1962) Stea (1969d) Appleyard (1970b) Ladd (1970) Moore (1973b) Wood (1973a)

Method	Procedure	Subject Skill	External Representational Form	Example
	Subjects arrange toys or make models representing environments	Affective Cognitive Concrete Motoric Relational	Models Arrangements of toys	Piaget et al. (1960) Blaut and Stea (1969) Mark and Silverman (1971) Stea (1973) Hart (1974) Stea, Chap. 9
	Subjects show existence, location, proximity, or other spatial relations of environmental elements; use of symbols to represent such elements	Cognitive Graphic Abstract Relational	Base maps with overlays Notation systems	Lynch (1960) Thiel (1961) Appleyard (1969a) Wood and Beck, Chap. 32
	Subjects asked to identify photographs, models, etc.	Affective Motoric Abstract Relational	Verbal Protocols	Piaget and Inhelder (1956) Laurendeau and Pinard (1970) Stea and Blaut (1973b) Zannaras (1973)
Indirect judgmental tasks	Selection of constructs which reveal environmental information; adjective checklists, semantic differentials, repetory grid test, etc.	Cognitive Abstract Relational	Word lists Tables Graphs Grids	Kelly (1950) Downs (1973) Honikman, Chap. 7 Harrison and Sarre, Chap. 34 Golant and Burton Chap. 33
	Paired proximity judgments and other scaling devices that allow specification of latent structure in environmental information	Cognitive Abstract Relational	Maps Tables	Briggs (1973a) Lowrey (1973) Golledge et al. (1975) Cadwallader (1973) Golant and Burton, Chap. 33
	Projective tests (e.g., T.A.T.)	Affective Abstract Relational	Verbal stories	Burton et al. (1969) Saarinen (1973b)

understand *what* information is contained in the sorting procedure. A critical task is to reveal *what* has been extracted by appropriate representational and analytical procedures and how subjects proceed in the sorting process. Wish (1972) uses this approach to recover cognitive configurations of the world's nations; Rivizzigno and Golledge (1974) have also used this method to discover which of a collection of places in a city are thought to be located near each other.

Experimenter observation of the actions of individuals and groups in manipulating or using different environments is represented in Chapters 3 and 13. Mark (1972) has used an artificial environment to examine children's toy play patterns and then attempted to reconstruct environmental information by observing both the locational patterns (or positional arrangement) of toys and the children's action patterns with respect to these arrangements. Examining children's play patterns has been an effective research tool in psychological research for many years. Only recently, however, has the same method been used by other disciplines to extract information about how people order and use large-scale environments.

Observation of subject role-playing activities has been a standard tool for clinical, transactional, and environmentally oriented psychologists. A great deal of the work on topics such as illusion, perception, and transactions between people and different environments, has relied on this methodology (Proshansky, Ittelson, and Rivlin, 1970). However, there has been little use of these methods outside the field of psychology. The fourth method, that of making inferences about environmental cognitions after observing various forms of animal behavior, has also largely been confined to psychology (e.g., Tolman, 1958; Calhoun, 1962). It is interesting to note, however, that experiments concerning the effect of say crowding and noise on cognitions of environments, studies that had their conceptual origins in animal experimentation, have produced significant findings concerning variations in the richness and complexity of environmental cognitions developed under such circumstances (Milgram, 1970; Saegert, 1973).

Historical Reconstructions

The methods for extracting information from individuals about large-scale environments presented in the previous sections attempt, either through immediate experience with the environment or by recall methods, to determine individual internal reflections about the environment by examining verbal responses to a series of carefully worded questions. An alternative approach is to concentrate on the reports about environment that are *written* by individuals—again, either while they are actually experiencing the environment or based on their memory of that environment.

The papers in Section 7 focus on the literary perspective and illustrate both these situations. Shin, for example, comments on the day-to-day written experiences of travelers in the southwestern part of the United States and analyzes these experiences for impressions of the physical environment. Lloyd concentrates on extracting information from novels concerned with urban experiences at the turn of the century. There appears to be a mixture of direct experience and recall in the novels examined by these researchers, but each study tries to reveal what selected authors knew about the environment that they were discussing. Tuan is much more general in his approach and covers a wide variety of reports on a range of abstract, philosophical, and other written experiences. In each case, however, he focuses on the cognitive structure of the knowledge that writers have about the external environments with which they are concerned.

Much of the research in this area has been done under the label of "environmental perception" rather than environmental cognition. Authors such as Meinig (1962), Bowden (1969, 1971, 1973), Heathcote (1969), Kates (1963), Brookfield, (1969), and Lowenthal and Prince (1964), have tried to reconstruct what people observed in landscapes in the present and in the past. A fundamental aim was to show how perception of, and attitudes toward, different environments influenced the course of history. This approach differs considerably from that of the literary perspectives in Section 7 in that it does not search for the same levels of "awareness" that Tuan, Shin, Lloyd, and Seamon seek.

Mention should be made of the potential usefulness of paintings and other art forms as a source of environmental knowledge. This area is still virtually untapped by social and behavioral scientists; art may well prove equally as fertile as literature as a source of this knowledge.

Analysis of External Representations

In research that involves the analysis of external representations experimenters ask subjects to produce an "external" representation of information contained in their mind about an environment. This involves the subject in producing a "self-report" of such information.

Self-report methods for extracting information about large-scale external environments draw on psychomotor, affective, and cognitive skills. Specific devices include verbal and written reports, sketches, free-flowing conversations, and "map" and model making. Self-report methods are suitable for recording current actual experiences with environments and the memory of those experiences. For example, Carr and Schissler (1969) and Zannaras (1973) both exposed their subjects to real and abstract environments and asked them to record what they observed in those environments. Carr and Schissler developed a head-mounted eye camera system which focused on the precise things in the environment that were noticed by a selection of car drivers and their passengers and in this way allowed for experimenter verification of what was reported. In her study of the influence of urban form on environmental cue selection and way-finding, Zannaras drove with human subjects through three cities and requested that they record what cues were used to decide on the route-selection process. At a more abstract level, Zannaras also presented her subjects with a range of slides of actual physical environments and had them record which features represented on the slides were of use to them in deciding where they might be in an actual city.

As opposed to examining the report of an individual at the time that they are perceiving or expe-

riencing a particular external environment, Lynch (1960) compiled city "images" by searching the responses people made to him when asked a question that relied on their memory of an environment. For example, urban residents of Los Angeles, Boston, and Newark were asked questions concerning how to get to certain places in their city; this forced each respondent to use his or her memory of the location of critical environmental cues along the path to each specified destination. This reliance on memory could have produced a tremendous variability in the content of individual responses, but the environment obviously appeared to be similar enough to a range of respondents that a fundamental set of important features were impressed on the mind of most of the people interviewed. Thus, although specific locations of places might well be clouded in an individual's memory, the fact that they remembered things such as nodes, landmarks, paths, edges, and districts was seen by Lynch and formalized into one of the earlier definitive statements on the nature of information extracted from the environment by individuals. The problem of relying on memory was handled a little more thoroughly by Carr and Schissler (1969), who pretested subjects for their ability to recall information prior to sending them out to compile their self-report statistics. Few studies in environmental cognition research have been as thorough in their methodological approach as this particular study.

In the early stages of environmental cognition research, perhaps the most widely used self-report technique was to require an individual to draw a sketch map of an environment, recording on that sketch map the information he or she considered to be significant (for examples, see Table 1). Individuals were asked to construct these "maps" both in the physical presence of stimuli in the environment and based on their memory of the environment. Lynch's (1960) work is the classic example of the use of this method for extracting environmental knowledge. Anderson and Tindal (1971), for example, requested a sample of young children to draw maps of their neighborhoods and of the paths they took to school. Tilly (1967) and Howell (1969) examined the city sketch maps of a range of children in Toronto and

New York (respectively) and illustrated how an increasing amount of detail appeared on the sketches of older children. Unfortunately, no control was attempted for cartographic knowledge or skills in many of these earlier studies. The resulting analyses were frequently invalidated by investigators trying to compile information from such sketches at a data level that was highly inappropriate in terms of each individual's graphic representational abilities. Asking an individual with limited graphic representational capabilities to construct a map of the environment severely limits his or her ability to show the extent of knowledge, just as it limits the type of inferences that can be drawn from the use of such methods. This problem is not nearly as intense when the subjects are adult humans who have the ability to structure their thoughts in a more abstract fashion and to produce external representations that summarize their cognitions. When Appleyard (1970b) asked residents of Cuidad Guyana to draw maps of their city, he was dealing primarily with a subject population that was capable of performing the task he set them (but see the criticism of Francescato and Mebane, 1973). Again, however, the general problem of variation in cartographic ability was not considered and takes something away from the consequent interpretation of what appeared on the map and the order and form in which those things appeared.

One of the more innovative uses of sketch maps is that by Moore (1973a, 1973b, 1975a). In this study maps were used to help distinguish different levels of representation, a problem that tied in nicely with developmental theories of cognition. In this case, no attempt was made to measure or categorize the exact information contained on the maps other than to determine whether the *drawers* were at undifferentiated egocentric, differentiated and partly coordinated, or abstractly coordinated and hierarchically integrated representational levels. The information on the maps was, therefore, used to draw conclusions about the comparative *internal structurization and representational ability of the subjects* rather than to provide information on *how much* information subjects had about a place. Moore's procedure appears to fill a substantial gap in that it takes "cognitive mapping"

out of the purely empirical phase and makes it a tool for testing relevant theory.

Self-report methods have been used in both a positive and negative manner. For example, the cases cited so far all require individuals to state their knowledge of particular places or to reconstruct representations of that knowledge. It is inferred either that what is not said is not known or that what is not pointed out is of relative insignificance to the individual subject and, consequently, does not warrant appearing on his final representation.

An alternative procedure has been used to find out what individuals do *not* know about external environments. For example, Ley (1972) discovered the nature of the information that a collection of inner-city youths in Philadelphia (both black and white) had about their environment by asking them to define the places that they would *not* venture into. He found that many areas outside a "local turf" had never been physically visited but were areas of high psychological stress or areas of repulsion. In other words, although some segments of Philadelphia had never been experienced by his respondents, they developed strong negative images. In this case, the areas were not positively "known," but entered the awareness space of his subjects through information channels that classed them as being dangerous and repulsive. In further studies of people's reactions to different areas in the city, Ley was able to define a "stress surface" for parts of the inner-city area into which suburban residents vowed they would not enter. Again, the respondents had no specific experience with these areas, but exhibited a general hostile or negative reaction to the areas and places within them. As such, the areas represented substantial "holes" in their awareness space, but the strong negative feeling or high stress produced by considering them was sufficient to warrant inclusion in their cognitive "map."

Thus, in addition to the self-report methods based on *actual* experience and memory, we have a third way of extracting information about the external environment, by tapping knowledge acquired from external secondary information channels. This latter method appears to be particularly important and is perhaps underrepresented in the environmental cognition literature. Although a number of studies (such as those conducted by Zannaras, 1973, and Golledge et al., 1975) illustrate that a subject's *actual* experience is a critical factor in determining the degree of reported familiarity with places or things in urban environments, there is also strong evidence that secondary information sources are extensively used by populations to bring elements of the objective environment into their levels of awareness or knowing (e.g., Kreimer, 1973; Donaldson, 1971). As might be expected, actual personal experience of elements of an environment is fairly critical in determining how familiar they appear to each individual. However, secondary information sources, such as television, newspapers, radio, and friends, all provide input to the total amount of information that people have about their environment. Environmental information can, therefore, be acquired by an individual during actual exposure to environments, by relying on recall of some previous exposure, or by tapping secondary external information sources.

Indirect Judgmental Tasks

Whereas methods in the previous section focus on a subject producing an external representation in direct response to experimenter stimulation, the methods of this section are designed to obtain information in a less direct manner. For example, subjects may be asked to select adjectives that best describe their "feelings" about a place; the experimenter may then deduce *knowledge* of the place from the responses. In other words, as opposed to obtaining the direct external representations of the previous section, these methods aim at uncovering *latent* information about environments. They rely on inferential procedures and "indirect" experimental designs.

For example, an increasingly popular method for extracting environmental knowledge is through the use of various judgmental procedures such as are required by psychophysical scaling procedures and by the repertory grid. In Chapters 29, 30, and 33, various scaling procedures are used to unpack the latent spatial structure of environmental knowledge from judgments made about such environments; in Chap-

ters 7 and 34, the repertory grid methodology is used to elicit from individuals a wide range of constructs related to specific environments. The constructs obtained are then ordered through the use of principal components analysis so as to produce meaningful groups; these groupings are then analyzed to discover the nature of the environmental information contained within them.

As opposed to this direct factoring of responses obtained from individuals, an alternative approach is to use multidimensional scaling techniques to impose a spatial structure on the information obtained by examining paired-comparison judgments made by individuals about places in an environment (see Zeller and Rivizzigno, 1974; Golledge et al., 1975). In this latter methodology, individuals are asked to scale the degree of separation of all possible pairs of places in an environment. The scaled responses are then put into one of a variety of multidimensional scaling algorithms and a configuration of the places is obtained. The derived configuration represents the latent structure implied in the pairwise judgment procedure and is based on a mathematical procedure for maintaining the monotonic relations contained within the original scaled responses. Each place in the configuration represents a feasible location for an element of the environment, given the subject's judgment of how close or how far apart each pair of places is. If judgments can be collected for a sufficiently large number of places, it is a simple matter to develop a mapping procedure that transforms locations in objective reality into the subjective configuration obtained through the multidimensional scaling procedure (or vice versa). Representations of a total environment can then be compiled which maintain the distortions that are specific to each individual. In other words, a series of cognitive configurations are obtained which represent the spatial information that individuals have about elements of an environment. Thus, knowledge of where places are is used to reconstruct disturbed and distorted maps of objective reality.

Unlike the previous examples, which concentrate on observable properties of external spatial environments, Chapter 33 illustrates a methodology for determining the extent of knowledge that individuals have about less concrete and permanent features of the environment. Using the semantic differential scaling technique, the authors attempt to assess how much knowledge individuals have about environmental occurrences such as storms, floods, and other hazards. Their research emphasizes how much individual variability exists in the interpretation of abstract concepts that describe real-world events. For example, many respondents had different views of what constituted "a flood" or of what could be called "serious damage." One critical idea to come out of this research into people's knowledge of hazardous situations is the multidimensional nature of concepts such as "hazard" or "environmental threat." Factors such as the frequency of exposure to the hazard turn out to be extremely important in the individual's assessment of whether or not an environmental occurrence is seen to be a "hazard." For example, Rooney (1967) has shown that in many cities in the northern and western part of the United States, snowfalls of 4 to 6 inches are regarded as everyday occurrences and are not treated as hazardous either by individuals or by city governments. On the other hand, residents of many eastern cities regard a similar type of snowfall as being an extreme hazard, and city governments in those areas spend a considerable part of their budget to overcome what they consider to be hazardous situations.

Issues in the External Representations of Cognitive Information

As mentioned earlier, external representations of cognitive information about large-scale environments have been compiled directly by subjects and indirectly by experimenters. Individual subjects, for example, have provided an impressive array of written and oral descriptions, sketches, pictures, and maps of different environments. They have also been asked to scale, group, or order things in (or constructs relating to) various external environments. Whether directly obtained from subjects or indirectly derived by experimenters, the result is a great variety of ways to *represent* this cognitive information externally. Let us deal first with direct subject representation of environmental knowledge.

When an experimenter asks an individual to compile a sketch or "map" or an area, he or she is asking for an exhibition both of the recall abilities of the individual and of his or her cartographic and graphic representational skills. Since the bulk of the responses obtained in this way does not directly include the individual's idea of how he or she scaled the phenomenon represented, it is difficult to interpret the results and even more difficult to analyze them. Early attempts at representing those elements of the external environment that were important to people relied heavily on pictorial representations. It is interesting, therefore, to see the suggestion in Chapter 32 that pictorial "languages" be developed for representing today's large-scale environments. As Tuan (1974) and Lowenthal and Prince (1965) have pointed out, artistic representations of past environments have been of critical importance in preserving information about such environments. However, with the development of still photographic and movie film technology, the role of artistic representation of environments has declined substantially. This decline has been paralleled by a dramatic change in the variety of techniques used to represent environmental knowledge. Since there are considerable parallels between literary and artistic means of representing environmental knowledge, and given that the procedure required for determining environmental knowledge from literature has been covered earlier (see Section 7), these methods will not be discussed here. Instead, we turn to less time-honored and more indirect ways of representing cognitive information about external environments.

Obviously, if external representations of environments have no observable scaled properties as indicated by the compiler, they can at best be interpreted in terms of nonmetric or topological measures. For example, one can examine sketch maps and produce frequency distributions of the number of times that certain places are mentioned in the environment or the number of times that certain areas, districts, and so on, are produced on the sketch. One may also observe the *sequence* in which things are placed on such sketches. Thus, some type of *ordering* of places based on location may be obtained from such representations. However, rarely are the criteria used to determine their arrangement explicitly determined. This leaves the interpretation of such representations open to considerable abuse and distortion. For example, an individual may compile, sketch, and order things in terms of their perceived importance, their size, of some other distinguishing characteristic. To then interpret the ordering in metric terms and to suggest that the ordering is based on spatial proximity to the individual may be a complete misinterpretation of the information contained in the sketch, unless the individual is clearly in an egocentric phase of reference. This and many other problems associated with sketch "map" production have thrown considerable doubt on the value of trying to extract metric and geometric information from sketched material. What has been quite legitimate, however, has been the compilation of composite "maps" by *experimenters* based on the frequency of the occurrence of elements in individual representations (e.g., Lynch, 1960; Appleyard, 1969a). Problems may appear, however, when researchers attempt to analyze the informational content of such maps; more of this later.

A strict cartographic representation of cognitive information is possible, however, if one can discover the nature of the geometric transformation that is made by an individual when he or she stores environmental knowledge and then reproduces it for an observer. We suspect that most people understand fundamental spatial relations such as proximity, distance, separation, and so on, although each of these is subject to distortion by illusion or by physiological deficiencies in the subject. Experiments that are designed to recover individual judgments about one or more of these spatial relations can search for a meaningful transformation of the individual's cognitive information. Examples of such transformations have been extensively documented in the psychological literature (Ittelson, 1973); specific transformed "maps" have been compiled by Tobler (1975) and Golledge et al. (1975). Good results have been obtained using multidimensional scaling methods to cartographically represent cognitive information. For example, Golledge et al. (1974) used multidimensional scaling procedures to determine a number of map transformations based on subjective estimates of interpoint distances between places in a city. It was also shown how similar configurations could be achieved through the analysis of individual

judgments about the proximity of places. Each case can be termed a true *cartographic* representation because each identifies a scale transformation of reality; this scale transformation can be mathematically determined and made explicit. Considerable metric information can be extracted from such representations of cognitive phenomenon.

When we examine an individual's knowledge about an environment and attempt to represent it in some easily observable form, we must remember that *meaningful* representations of environmental phenomena can be achieved only if one is able to recover the type of transformation made between the transformed phenomena and objective reality. For the most part, therefore, accuracy in representing cognitive information about the environment has been most complete through experimenter-compiled representations. However, in many cases either the specific information given by experimenters to individuals when they are seeking environmental knowledge has been inadequate for detailed interpretation of their representations, or individuals themselves are completely unaware of the type of transformation that they are making; thus, it has been impossible to deduce in satisfactory terms the nature of such transformations. What is obvious, therefore, is that considerable attention must be paid in the future to determining the most appropriate metrics for the representation of cognitive information.

At present, the bulk of representational efforts use two-dimensional Euclidean geometries. Very little experimentation has taken place with the use of Minkowskian and other metrics in the representation of cognitive information. Until exhaustive studies are made as to the nature of the metric that best allows meaningful representation of cognitive information, there can be only moderate satisfaction with the representational efforts that are currently available.

Rather than trying to reconstruct the individual's cognition of the arrangement or pattern of things in an environment, many researchers, particularly those involved with repertory grid analyses, have been concerned with grouping or ordering things in the environment in a nonspatial sense, or defining *groups or classes of constructs* that relate to things or places in the environment. This methodology exists on much firmer ground both as far as a theoretical basis is concerned (Kelly's, 1955, personal construct theory) and as far as operational techniques are concerned (repertory grid and principal components analysis). Given that the data input is a series of scale values associated with pairs of constructs, conventional multivariate analytical techniques such as principal components analysis can form meaningful groups of constructs, groups of symbols, or groups of things in the environment that are represented by the scaled responses. "Meaning" in this case can be defined subjectively by the individual or objectivity by an experimenter. In this type of analysis there is no need for uncovering the type of transformation that an individual makes of the geometry or metric of objective reality. All that is sought is some communality in how he or she interprets the content of the environment.

We have, therefore, two major approaches that produce external representations of large-scale external environments: the first tries to reproduce the *geography* of an external environment using a range of cartographic and pseudocartographic methods; the second is concerned simply with classifying cognitive information about an environment in terms of its *content*. The work associated with ordering the content of the environment and extracting meaning from this ordering has to this date progressed somewhat further and more satisfactorily than attempts to reconstruct the geography of environments. However, it is suggested that, with appropriate experimental designs and the use of methods (such as multidimensional scaling techniques) which determine latent spatial structures, representation of the geography of environments might soon be on a level equal to that of the representation of environmental content.

ANALYSIS OF COGNITIVE REPRESENTATIONS

Although many attempts at analyzing the results of experiments that aim to extract information concerning people's cognitions of environment have been rather abortive, there have been sufficient steps made in the appropriate use of analytical procedures to give us considerable hope that more complete and meaningful analyses will be forthcoming in the future. Previously, we mentioned that the analytical methods that could be used to examine cognitive information about environments would depend very much indeed on the experimental designs used to extract information from individuals about environments. Those designs which produce information at nominal or ordinal data levels quite obviously restrict consequent analytical methodologies to the nonparametric field. Simple analyses, such as the frequency counting of items mentioned in various reporting techniques, and content analysis of verbal and written reports appear to be well suited to this level of information.

Throughout Parts I and II, we were provided with a range of theories and perspectives on environmental cognition research; this variety emphasized the interdisciplinary nature of interest in the topic and illustrated that a melange of research methodologies is appropriate in producing, analyzing, and understanding what people know about external environments. For example, in Part I on theory, R. Kaplan uses gaming simulation procedures, *t* tests, and hierarchical clustering techniques to analyze her data; Klett and Alpaugh use nonparametric tests such as Kendall's coefficient of concordance and the Wilcoxin matched-pairs signed-ranks test to analyze intergroup differences found in their scaled data; Honikman relies on repetory grid methods and principal components analysis; and Moore and Acredolo use standard parametric and nonparametric statistical tests for finding the significance of differences between group performances. In Part II, a range of somewhat different and more subjective methodologies is presented, from the Duncans's focus on comparative social organizations and Rapoport's plea for more critical crosscultural comparisons, to the literary, geosophic, and phenomenonological analyses suggested by Tuan, Shin, Lloyd, and Seamon. With the exception of Chapter 32, the papers in Part III all make use of some form of statistical analysis. Cadwallader and Briggs use psychophysical scaling devices and standard statistical tests; Zannaras uses analysis of variance; Golant and Harrison and Sarre and Burton apply multivariate statistical techniques in their analyses. I have also previously mentioned the use of nonmetric multidimensional scaling methods such as those used by Golledge et al. (1975), Mackay, Olshavsky, and Sentell (1975), and others.

Since the range of appropriate methodologies appears extremely large, no further attempt will be made to list them here; rather, it seems appropriate to sound a warning note. We have already mentioned the inappropriateness of extracting ordered metric information from sketches that have, at best, topological or ranked information on them. Texts such as Siegel (1955) give a reasonable treatment of the range of nonparametric statistical tests that can be used to assess the significance of responses which are represented by data at nominal and ordinal levels.

We urge, at this stage then, that considerable attention and care be paid in the analytical phases of research into environmental cognition. All too often there is a tendency to use analytical methods that are quite inappropriate to the level of data collected.

CURRENT METHODOLOGICAL ISSUES

Some critical issues that have emerged in past and current research into environmental cognition are as follows:

1. Should environmental cognition research be channeled into the formal positivistic hypothesis testing scheme that many of the social and behavioral sciences adopted during the 1960s for analytical purposes?
2. Should investigations into environmental knowledge take the form of a controlled search activity such as can be achieved, for example, through extensive use of repertory grid methods?
3. Should our efforts of acquiring information about the extent of environmental knowing be confined to real-world situations or hypothetical situations?

The problem of determining the extent of individual and group knowledge about environments is of considerable current importance. Methodological issues consequently are of an importance almost equal to the theoretical issues raised in earlier segments of this book. Much of the information that we are collecting (and have collected) is of dubious value because of poorly designed experiments that yield low-value data. Much more critical attention to experimental designs that are capable of yielding meaningful representations of cognitive knowledge appear to be essential if progress is to be achieved in this field. Once progress in this area is made, further input into various formative theories of environmental cognition can proceed apace. In this way, our level of understanding of the external environment will increase, and our level of understanding of how people cognitively represent elements of the external environment and how they use them in their everyday commerce with those environments should also substantially increase.

29

COGNITIVE DISTANCE IN INTRAURBAN SPACE[1]

Martin T. Cadwallader[2]

Department of Geography
  Portland State University

Distance is a fundamental variable in geographical research (Watson, 1955), but the complexity of its role as a factor in spatial decision making has only recently been appreciated. As Malm et al. suggest, distance is "a very complex notion, quantifiable in physical, economical, time and a variety of sociological terms" (p. 9), and it is readily apparent that more meaningful measures of effective distance are required if we are to adequately account for identified patterns of human spatial behavior.[3] It is my thesis that cognitive distance is one such measure. Although the difference between real and cognitive space has long been recognized (Trowbridge, 1913; Lewin, 1936), the implications of this for human spatial behavior have yet to be fully explored.

Cognitive distance is a factor in at least three major types of decisions concerning spatial interaction: (1) it affects the decision to stay or go, (2) it affects the decision of where to go, and (3) it affects the decision of which route to take. As Forbes (1964) has noted, "Accessibility is something which exists only in the mind of the likely traveller" (p. 13).

Having argued that cognitive distance promises to be a useful explanatory variable in the context of spatial behavior, the research reported here attempts to describe and explain the form of the relationship between cognitive and real distance. This is an important step because, if accomplished, it will enable us to transform physical space into the relevant cognitive space, which is the space in which people are making their locational decisions. One has to assume, of course, that there is some consensus among people as to the nature of this space.

It is pertinent at this point in the discussion to say something about the difference between cognitive distance and perceived distance. The notion of perceived distance has attracted the attention of psychologists for a number of years (Blank, 1958; Künnapas, 1960; Roberts and Suppes, 1967; Baird, 1970). However, what I am concerned with here are those physical distances too large to be perceived in one glance (Stea, 1969a). Specifically, I am working at the intermetropolitan scale, and this necessarily assumes that people can think about distances in the abstract, without actually "seeing" them. The term "cognitive distance" is more appropriate for these "unseen" distances. Our cognitions include not only that information gathered from direct experience (as in perceived distance), but also information gathered from various other sources, such as road maps. In this way individuals are able to cognize the distances to places they may never have actually visited.

Previous Research

Research into the relationship between real and cognitive distance is not new, but it has generally suffered from a lack of consistency in the methodological procedures employed. This has made the comparison of results somewhat difficult. For example, the way in which subjects are required to provide distance estimates varies from study to study. Bratfisch (1969) utilized the complete method of *ratio estimation*, which entails asking subjects to compare two distances and then estimate one distance as a percentage of the other. This general methodology was also followed by Golledge, Briggs, and Demko (1969), Lowrey (1970), and Briggs (1973a). Lee (1970), on the other hand, required *direct mileage estimates,* although this was accomplished by a scale on a piece of paper. In the present study, mileage estimates, *travel time* estimates, and the scaling technique known as *direct magnitude estimation* (Torgerson, 1958, p. 104) are all used to allow comparison of results obtained by different methodologies.

Previous research also varies with regard to whether subjects were asked to conceptualize straight-line distances or not. For example, Lee used shortest walking distance, whereas Bratfisch used straight-line distance. This difference appears to be mainly a function of the spatial scale of the studies. Those concerned with intercity distances tend to use straight-line distance; those concerned with intraurban distances tend to use shortest walking distance. In this study straight-line distances are used. This follows from a theoretical assumption made here that individuals tend to work from some kind of cognitive map, rather than retracing in their mind specific trips that they might have taken in the past (Tolman, 1932). Although it is as yet uncertain what actually transpires inside the "black box" of the human brain, most researchers in the area make the assumption that some form of externalized "map" can be drawn from the spatial relations held in the mind (Lynch, 1960; Gould, 1973; Golledge et al., 1975).

Finally, most studies have aggregated the individual

estimates, consequently masking the possibility that a number of different relationships might exist at the individual level. Lowrey's (1970) study was different in that each subject estimated the distance to a different set of self-chosen points in the city, whereas in other studies a common set of points was chosen by the experimenter. In this research both aggregate and individual data are used, thus allowing comparisons to be drawn between the results obtained at different levels of analysis.

Despite this confusing array of methodological procedures, preliminary research has suggested that there are some regularities in the relationship between real and cognitive distance. Evidence as regards the exact nature of the relationship is contradictory, however. Stapf (1968) found a linear relationship, whereas Tobler (1961), Bratfisch (1969), Golledge et al. (1969), and Briggs, (1973a) all conjectured that the psychological distance function is curvilinear. It is also noteworthy that Golledge et al. produced evidence to indicate that the relationship only tends toward nonlinearity as the distances become large, and that the speed with which nonlinearity is approached is influenced by direction (p. 63).

However, as suggested above, these studies all used different methodological tools. Following this, it is difficult to deduce whether the different results are really contradictory, or whether they just reflect the use of different techniques. In this respect the present study is of some value, as it describes how results can change according to methodology and demonstrates the necessity of working at the individual level.

Methodology

Data for this research were collected by questionnaires from 50 subjects in West Los Angeles. These subjects comprised a statistical population, rather than a random sample drawn from such a population. The subjects were not randomly chosen as the aim was to use subjects that all lived within three blocks of each other. In this way they would all be estimating the same real distances. Because we are dealing with a statistical population, rather than a sample, statistical inferences cannot be made regarding the results of the investigation (see Gould, 1970a, p. 442).

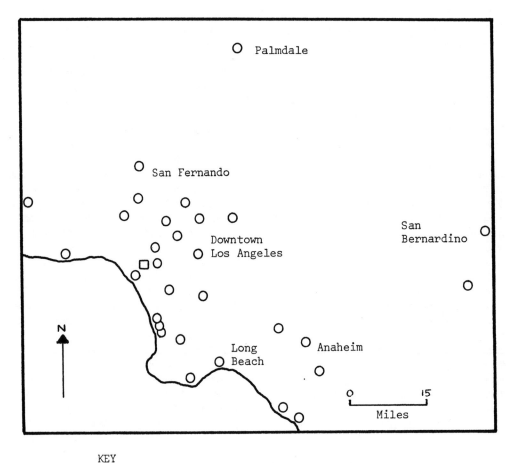

FIGURE 1
Distribution of cities from the Los Angeles Basin involved in the study.

The statistical measures are, therefore, only meaningful in a descriptive sense, and for this reason no tests of significance are reported.

Subjects were asked to estimate the distance from their home to 30 cities in the Los Angeles Basin (Figure 1). Each subject was asked to estimate the same set of 30 distances in three different ways: (1) absolute mileage estimates, (2) travel time estimates, and (3) the method of direct magnitude estimation

was used, which is a technique that has been used by psychologists to measure such sensory magnitudes as loudness (Richardson and Ross, 1930; Ham and Parkinson, 1932; Stevens, 1956). It is utilized to establish a scale of subjective magnitude.

The usual procedure in the method of direct magnitude estimation is one in which the experimenter selects a particular single stimulus on a given physical continuum and assigns a number to its subjective magnitude. The observer is then presented in turn with the members of a set of variable stimuli and is instructed to assign to each variable stimulus a number (whole number, fraction, or decimal) which seems to him to be proportional to its subjective magnitude as compared to the standard. The judgments are expressed in terms of subjective magnitudes, and the psychophysical scale is, therefore, obtained directly (Corso, 1967, p. 257).

In the case of this research, the variable stimuli presented to the subjects were pairs of "points" (e.g., home–Long Beach), which the subject then had to estimate the relative distance between.

An example will make the use of the technique clearer. Assume that there are 100 subjects and 10 real distances $(A, \ldots, J)$ for which estimates are needed. The distance E can be assigned the standard value of 10, and then the subjects are asked to rate the other distances accordingly. If an individual thinks distance I is twice as long as distance E, he or she will assign I the value 20; if he or she thinks I is only half as long as E, he or she will assign I the value 5, and so on, until all the distances have been estimated. Using the mean estimate of each distance, the table below might be constructed. This indicates that, on the average, A is estimated to be half the length of E (the standard), although in reality it is slightly shorter than this. If these two distance scales are then plotted against each other, the relationship between them can be identified.

In the case of the experiments reported here, the standard distance was assigned the value 100, as this is easy to divide into simple ratios; it also enables the subjects to think in terms of percentages if they so desire. The distance selected as the standard varied across questionnaires, as it is inadvisable to describe the form of a psychological magnitude function on the basis of only one standard stimulus (Stevens, 1956). In all, five different standards were used. As suggested by Stevens, the standards were all somewhere in the middle of the range of variable stimuli (real distances). The context effect also needs to be considered when scaling variable stimuli. Does the order in which the stimuli are presented make any difference to the respondents' judgments? Although the evidence on this is inconclusive, the problem can be circumvented by presenting the stimuli in varying orders. In accordance with this, five different lists of cities were compiled, the order of the cities being determined by random-number tables.

Finally, it is appropriate to say something about the overall validity of this scaling technique. What is desired, of course, is a method that allows the subject to make estimates that are truly representative of his own sense of distance. We do not wish the method to influence the results. The quantiative estimation of subjective magnitudes is not easy, however, and because we do not know what an individual's estimate should be, we cannot apply any independent criterion of validity. In this situation, therefore, we have to choose a suitable method largely on the basis of intuitive appeal and common sense.

Results

The data were first analyzed at the aggregate level. That is, the median estimates to each of the 30 cities were obtained and then plotted against real distance. This was done for the scaled estimates (from the method of direct magnitude estimation), the mileage estimates, and the travel time estimates. Medians were used because for every city the distribution of estimates, although displaying marked peakedness, was positively skewed. In the case of the relationship between cognitive time distance and real-time distance, the real-time distances were calculated by using the average operating speed of a car over both surface streets and freeways, during off peak hours. For this purpose, following the guidelines of the Los Angeles

	Stimulus Variable									
	A	B	C	D	E	F	G	H	I	J
Real relative value	4	14	7	9	10	12	14	15	18	16
Estimated relative value	5	12	7	7	10	10	12	12	14	10

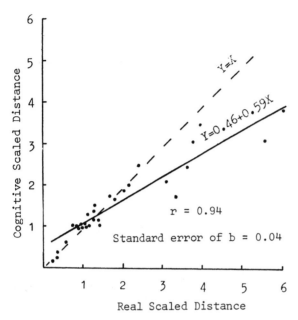

FIGURE 2
Relationship between cognitive scaled distance and real scaled distance.

FIGURE 3
Relationship between cognitive mileage distance and real mileage distance.

Region Transportation Study (1971), the average freeway speed was taken as 55 miles per hour and the average surface street speed was taken as 28 miles per hour.

The relationship, in all three cases, appears to be linear, with Pearson correlation coefficients of .94, .96, and .96 (Figures 2, 3, and 4). However, the slopes of the regression lines vary. When using the scaled estimates, cognitive distance increases with real distance, but at a less than proportional rate. Alternatively, in the case of the mileage estimates, cognitive distance increases at a rate that is slightly more than proportional to real distance. These results, then, illustrate the point that a methodological difference in data collection can influence the rate at which cognitive and real distances covary. It should be noted, however, that the standard errors of the slopes in the regression equations, with the exception of the relationship between real scaled distance and cognitive scaled distance, suggest that the slopes are not far from unity.

The identification of a linear relationship is compatible with the results obtained by Stapf (1968), but is in contrast to the nonlinearity found by Tobler (1961), Bratfisch (1969), Golledge et al. (1969), and Briggs (1973a; see also Chapter 30). One explanation for this lies in the different methodologies employed, as described earlier. However, the relationship was examined further, to see if results obtained at the aggregate level are compatible with those obtained at the individual level.

Correlation coefficients and regression equations were calculated separately for each individual (Tables 1, 2, and 3). As can be seen from this analysis, the correlation coefficients obtained at the aggregate level exaggerated the strength of the linear relationship, although a large number of the coefficients are still in the vicinity of .80 or above. The same is true as regards the *b* values in the regression equations, where the distinction between the cognitive distance measures is less clear than that suggested by the aggregate analysis. Noting that some of the correlation coeffi-

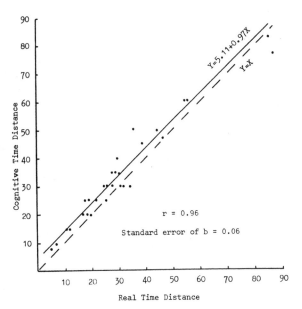

FIGURE 4
Relationship between cognitive time and distance and real-time distance.

cients were .75 or less, and bearing in mind the conflicting results of Tobler, Bratfisch, Golledge et al., and Briggs, a sample of these were investigated more closely to uncover any nonlinearity. Scatter diagrams were plotted for each of the sample individuals, but

TABLE 1
Cognitive Scaled Distance: Pearson correlation coefficients and *b* values for cognitive scaled distance and real scaled distance

Coefficients	Frequency	b values	Frequency
.50 or less	1	.01– .25	4
.51– .55	1	.26– .50	15
.56– .60	3	.51– .75	10
.61– .65	1	.76–1.00	5
.66– .70	2	1.01–1.25	7
.71– .75	8	1.26–1.50	4
.76– .80	7	1.51–1.75	0
.81– .85	8	1.76–2.00	0
.86– .90	8	2.01–2.25	0
.91– .95	7	2.26–2.50	1
.96–1.00	1	Over 2.50	1

TABLE 2
Cognitive Mileage Distance: Pearson correlation coefficients and *b* values for cognitive mileage distance and real mileage distance

Coefficients	Frequency	b values	Frequency
.50 or less	2	.01– .25	1
.51– .55	1	.26– .50	0
.56– .60	2	.51– .75	5
.61– .65	3	.76–1.00	14
.66– .70	2	1.01–1.25	11
.71– .75	6	1.26–1.50	8
.76– .80	3	1.51–1.75	5
.81– .85	6	1.76–2.00	2
.86– .90	9	2.01–2.25	0
.91– .95	13	2.26–2.50	0
.96–1.00	0	Over 2.50	1

TABLE 3
Cognitive Time Distance: Pearson correlation coefficients and *b* values for cognitive time distance and real-time distance

Coefficients	Frequency	b values	Frequency
.50 or less	0	.01– .25	0
.51– .55	1	.26– .50	2
.56– .60	0	.51– .75	10
.61– .65	3	.76–1.00	17
.66– .70	4	1.01–1.25	12
.71– .75	5	1.26–1.50	4
.76– .80	3	1.51–1.75	1
.81– .85	9	1.76–2.00	1
.86– .90	13	2.01–2.25	0
.91– .95	8	2.26–2.50	0
.96–1.00	1	Over 2.50	0

there was little evidence of a curvilinear relationship that would fit the data more closely than the linear model originally chosen.

Although it is not yet possible to conclusively specify the functional relationship between real and cognitive distance, these results suggest that the relationship is *linear*. They also point to two important methodological questions. First, they show that subjects react differently when presented with alternative ways in which to give their distance estimates. Second, they highlight the need to work with individual data.

Deviations Between Real and Cognitive Distance

In addition to specifying the nature of the relationship between real and cognitive distance, it is important to examine why individuals over- or underestimate real distances. That is, we need to explain the deviations between real and cognitive distance. This can best be accomplished through a set of explanatory variables that includes both *attributes of the stimuli (cities)* and *attributes of the subjects.*

Previous researchers have indicated that the cognition of distance is influenced by the *direction* of the stimulus (city) in relation to the subject, although there remain some doubts as to the exact nature of this influence. Lee (1970) compared the cognitive distances involved in journeys toward the center of town and journeys away from the center of town, and found that there was a much greater overestimation of outward journeys. Experiments conducted by Golledge et al. (1969), however, have yielded results that appear to be in direct opposition to these findings. Although finding that cognitive distance does vary with direction, they note that distances away from the central business district tend to be underestimated, while those toward the central business district tend to be overestimated.

Another factor that should be considered is the *relative attractiveness* of the stimuli, as measured by the subjects themselves. At the level of distances that can be "seen," psychologists have shown that individuals distort distances according to their attitudes toward the stimuli (Smith, 1953; Beloff and Beloff, 1961; Beloff and Coupar, 1968).[4] Preliminary investigation at the urban scale also seems to suggest that the valences attached to the stimuli will influence the distance judgments to those stimuli (Lee, 1964). Thompson (1963) also presented evidence for this when he found that, as regards consumer behavior, the nature of the destination influences consumer evaluations of time and distance. Similarly, in a small experiment conducted at Brown University, Buckman (1966) tested the hypothesis that the cognitive distance from a more desirable city to a less desirable city is greater than the conception of the same real distance in the opposite direction. Her results suggest

that those who prefer the starting city do indeed tend to make greater distance estimates than those who prefer the terminal city.

An individual's *familiarity* with a particular stimulus (city) should also influence his or her distance estimate to that stimulus. Here it is hypothesized that the more acquainted a subject is with a given stimulus, the more accurate will be his or her distance estimate to that stimulus. This question of familiarity is closely related to the notion of information space, and it is reasonable to argue that those individuals who possess the most information about the spatial system in question will exhibit the most accurate distance estimates (see Gould, 1973).

Finally, characteristics of the individuals themselves should also be useful in explaining their distance judgments. Golledge et al. (1969) have discussed *length of residence* in this context, and their results suggest that an effective learning process enables established residents to estimate distances more accurately.

Before testing for the influence of direction, attractiveness, familiarity, and length of residence, it was felt advisable to remove the influence of real distance by standardizing the estimation errors, as the estimation errors wil obviously tend to increase with increasing real distances. The estimation errors were standardized by subtracting the real distance from the cognitive distance and then dividing by the real distance. A negative standardized estimation error (SEE) would mean that the distance was underestimated. For each individual there are two measures of his standardized estimation errors: (1) those derived from the scaled estimates (SEE_1), and (2) those derived from the mileage estimates (SEE_2).

To investigate the influence of direction, the mean standardized estimation errors for the cities toward downtown were compared with those for the rest of the cities. A t test was not computed, as in statistical terms the subjects form a population rather than a sample. The results are therefore again descriptive, as opposed to inferential.[5] As can be seen from Table 4, the distances to cities toward the center of the metropolitan area tend to be overestimated relative to the other cities. Although the variances of the

TABLE 4
Relationship Between Standardized Estimation Errors and Direction

	Mean	Variance	Skewness	Kurtosis
SEE_1 toward downtown	.203	.391	1.304	2.873
SEE_1 away from downtown	−.041	.368	1.980	6.669
SEE_2 toward downtown	.957	1.551	5.315	47.125
SEE_2 away from downtown	.544	1.094	5.473	51.056

distributions are fairly large in comparison to the means, the measures of kurtosis and skewness support the contention that the two distributions are from different populations. In all cases the distributions are positively skewed. Also, the measures of kurtosis, which describe the general peakedness of the distributions, indicate that the distributions are more peaked in the middle than the normal curve. These results, then, are in direct contrast to those of Lee (1970), but are compatible with the evidence presented by Golledge et al. (1969). However, more controlled experiments, involving the estimation of equal distances in opposite directions, need to be carried out before we can specify the exact nature of the directional influence.

An attempt was also made to explain the standardized estimation errors in terms of the familiarity and attractiveness of the cities, as measured by the subjects themselves. The measures of subjective familiarity and attractiveness for each of the 30 cities were obtained by again using the method of direct magnitude estimation (Torgerson, 1958; for a different procedure, see Moore, 1975a). The results of the correlation analysis, however, fail to substantiate the hypothesized relationships between estimation errors and familiarity and attractiveness (Table 5). It should be noted that N varies as a result of missing observations in the data set.

It was also hypothesized that length of residence would influence distance estimates, the hypothesis being that long-term residents would exhibit the more accurate estimates. Length of residence was measured in two ways: (1) by how long the subject had been living in the Los Angeles metropolitan area, and (2) by how long he or she had been living at the present address. Again the results are somewhat less than encouraging (Table 6). Although there is a tendency for the relationship between the standardized estimation errors and the length of residence to be negative, meaning that as length of residence increases the estimation errors decrease, the evidence is far from conclusive as the correlation coefficients are very low. Again, it is not meaningful to statistically test if the coefficients are significantly different from zero, as the subjects do not represent a random sample drawn from a larger population.

In general, then, there is some evidence that direc-

TABLE 5
Relationship Between Standardized Estimation Errors and Familiarity and Attractiveness

	r	N
SEE_1 with familiarity	−.0066	1,152
SEE_2 with familiarity	.0167	1,138
SEE_1 with attractiveness	−.0965	1,399
SEE_2 with attractiveness	.0514	1,374

TABLE 6
Relationship Between Standardized Estimation Errors and Length of Residence

	r	N
SEE_1 with length of residence in Los Angeles	−.0460	1,399
SEE_2 with length of residence in Los Angeles	−.0594	1,374
SEE_1 with length of residence at present address	−.0267	1,399
SEE_2 with length of residence at present address	.0354	1,374

tion influences cognitive distance, but the measures of familiarity, attractiveness, and length of residence appear to be unrelated to the standardized estimation errors. This inability to satisfactorily account for deviations between real and cognitive distances might be due to inadequate measurement of the variables. Also, it is obvious that there are other explanatory variables that have not yet been considered. For example, the presence or absence of either physical or social barriers might be of some importance in this context. Similarly, the question of information was not explicitly considered. Another problem concerns the independence of the explanatory variables. If there is excessive interdependence among them, the use of simple correlation analysis will be insufficient to isolate the true explanatory factors. In this respect, future research in the area might focus upon the use of factor analysis as a methodological tool.

NOTES

1. I would like to thank William Clark, Reginald Golledge, and Gary Moore for their comments on an earlier draft of this paper. The use of the U.C.L.A. Campus Computing Network is acknowledged.
2. Now at the Department of Geography, University of Wisconsin, Madison.
3. For discussions of this point, see Deutsch and Isard (1961) and Cadwallader (1973a).
4. For example, Beloff and Beloff (1961) identified a relationship between perceived distance and the positive or negative valency of a set of photographs of human faces.
5. In this particular instance, significance tests would not be valid as, statistically, there is no larger population to which the results can be inferred.

30

METHODOLOGIES FOR THE MEASUREMENT OF COGNITIVE DISTANCE

Ronald Briggs

Department of Geography
University of Texas at Austin

Geographers have become increasingly interested in the spatial behavior of individuals, both in its own right and, more particularly, as an explanatory process for environmental structure (Harvey, 1969; Golledge, 1970). This concern with individual spatial behavior has resulted in a partial abandonment of the concept of "economic man" and its replacement by the concept of "behavioral man." The spatial behavior of "economic man" is derived solely from a set of assumptions, those of utility maximization, perfect knowledge, and complete rationality on the part of such individuals (Abler et al., 1971). By utilizing these assumptions, study of the actual behavior of individuals can be avoided and emphasis placed on the environmental structure, which generally can be observed, measured, and analyzed with greater facility than individual behavior. In contrast, postulates concerning "behavioral man" are realistically based upon an actual analysis of existing behaviors.

A central theme in the analysis of the behavior of individuals has been a differentiation between the objective or "real-world" environment and the cognitive representation of this environment held by individuals (Boulding, 1956; Downs, 1970b).[1] It is held that the behavior of an individual is a reaction to his or her cognitive representation or "image" of the environment rather than to the objective environment per se.[2] Thus, the actual spatial behavior of individuals can only be understood if the nature and form of these cognitive representations is known.

Techniques for the isolation and measurement of cognitive phenomena lie beyond the realm of traditional geographical methodology. This paper discusses the application of some techniques from psychophysical scaling to the measurement of one very specific, and ostensibly relatively simple, phenomena, that is, cognitive distance. Stress is placed upon detailing the methodology, enumerating the problems involved in its application, and emphasizing the complexities involved in the analysis of cognitive structures.

The substantive problem concerns the influence of environmental structure upon the cognition of distance. The basic thesis is that, for equivalent objective distances between points (nodes) within an urban environment, cognized distance varies as a function of the environmental structure at and between these points. Following from a model of the cognition of spatial location (Briggs, 1972, 1973a) and discussions of possible mechanisms for the cognition of distance

(Briggs, 1973b), two specific research hypotheses were derived. The first maintained that, for equivalent objective distances, cognized distance from a common origin point would be greater to locations toward downtown relative to the point than to places away from downtown. The second hypothesis stated that pairs of points of equivalent objective distance apart but linked by routes involving turns or bends will be cognized as farther apart than points linked by a straight route. Thus, both hypotheses relate to situations involving different underlying environmental structures. In the first case it is the marked changes in environmental structure with increasing distance from downtown; in the second, it is the existence of bends or turns in the road network.

The Experiment

The model of spatial cognition together with empirical studies in the literature suggested a whole series of factors, in addition to those under study, likely to influence cognitive distance (Briggs, 1972, 1973b). Adapting Torgerson (1958) we can suggest three possible types of factors:

1. *Subject-centered factors* in which cognized distance may be a function of the characteristics of the individual, such as age or sex.
2. *Stimulus-centered factors* in which cognized distance is a function of the characteristics of the points between which distance estimates are obtained, of the environment in which these places are embedded, or of the routes linking them.
3. *Subject–stimulus-centered factors* in which cognized distance is influenced by *interactions* between the subject and stimuli points; examples here might include the subject's familiarity with and evaluation of the locations or the routes linking them.

Unfortunately, in any real-world, as against a laboratory, situation, many of these factors will be present simultaneously; thus, it is exceedingly difficult to obtain an evaluation of their independent influence. Solution to this problem may be approached either through the careful choice of experimental situations that successively and independently isolate each variable under study, or by the statistical control of these variables by utilizing such techniques as multiple correlation. Similarly, factors that are not the subject of study but could possibly influence the criterion variable must be controlled. Again, this may be approached either through the careful choice of experimental situations so that such variables are constant, or through a randomizing methodology which seeks to select subjects and/or stimuli upon a strictly open and unbiased basis on the premise that the many variables so included will be counteractive such that no individual one will significantly affect the criterion variable.

The more common approach in geography is to manipulate experimental variables through multivariate statistical techniques and control others through randomization. This approach was rejected for the present study because of the relatively large number of stimuli and subjects it would have necessitated and the relatively high levels of noise that would have been present in the data. The latter, particularly, has the potential to obscure relevant information, and the possibility always exists that the absence of any significant results can be attributed to failures in this statistical manipulation and the control mechanisms. In their place, manipulation of the experimental variables and control for likely influences not under study was achieved through the careful choice of the experimental situation. By first utilizing a carefully controlled situation, any existing significant effects are more likely to be uncovered. Given that they have been shown to exist, their influence in the more general situation usually considered in the multivariate statistical approach can then be explored.

Subjects. Some evidence exists suggesting that cognized distance is influenced by familiarity with the end points and routes linking them (Golledge, Briggs, and Demko, 1969; Stea, 1969a). Differences in familiarity are likely to stem from length of residence in the area and the frequency with which particular routes and places are utilized, a function of the individual's activity pattern. Activity patterns themselves are at least a function of place of residence and employment, socioeconomic status, and stage in the life cycle (Chapin and Brail, 1969). Since the research hypotheses were not directed toward examining inter-personal differences in cognition, it was important to first eliminate, as much as possible, any noise resulting from these factors. Thus, a sample was sought that had maximum homogeneity in regard to activity patterns and places of residence and work.

It was assumed that a sample of students would meet the above criteria, in addition to having the advantage of convenience in data collection. Each has the same place of work and many live on, or in the immediate vicinity of, the campus and thus have the "same" place of residence. Furthermore, similar life styles among students should result in similarities in their spatial activity pattern and thus in the frequency with which particular routes are utilized. Similarity in life style along with length of residence was further controlled by only using students enrolled in sophomore courses and whose home town was not Columbus, Ohio, the city used in the study. Thus, the sample consisted of 248 students, and the experiment was conducted in class groups of approximately 45 students each.

Stimuli. Twenty points (locations) within Columbus were chosen such that each could be assigned to one of four groups determined on the basis of two binary variables; "away from downtown" versus "toward downtown," and "along a major north–south artery" (High Street) versus "off this artery." These relations are specified relative to a twenty-first point, the main entrance to the university, which lies on the north–south artery approximately 2½ miles north of downtown. This served as a common origin and the experiment examined the cognition of distance from this point to each of the 20 locations. The range of the objective distances was from 1.0 to 4.5 miles approximately.

The 20 locations were chosen on four criteria, primarily aimed at ensuring that differences in node characteristics did not influence cognized distances: (1) distances measured within any one of the four groups were similar to those in the other groups, (2) the locations were clearly familiar to the subjects, (3) all locations were of the same node type, and (4) nodes should not elicit strong additudinal responses from subjects since this influences cognized distance (Thompson, 1963). Major road intersections, which

should all function as link nodes, were the only locations likely to meet the three criteria and be sufficient in number. However, the street-naming system, which partly utilizes numbers, restricted the locations available since extensive use of numbered streets would provide crucial information on distance relations. Therefore, although the final locations chosen were primarily street intersections, none of which were based on two numbered streets, a few landmarks were included from necessity. The origin point was chosen as the main entrance to the university since it was in close spatial proximity to the homes of the subjects.

Cognized distance measures. Measures of each subject's cognition of the distance from the common origin point (the main entrance to the university) to each of the 20 stimulus points (locations) were obtained from two types of raw data: *direct mileage estimates* and *ratio estimates*. To ensure that results obtained were not a function solely of the method of data collection and analysis, two methods of collecting data were employed. However, it should be noted that there is a significant difference in the phenomena being measured by these two techniques. The first technique is dimensionless and measures the cognition of relative distance itself. The second is a measure of an individual's cognition of the mile measurement scale and is dependent upon the individual possessing some conception of the amount of spatial separation corresponding to a mile unit.

Each of the two types of raw data (mileage estimates and ratio estimates) were analyzed in two ways: one method obtained measures of cognitive distance for each subject (*individual* data); the other obtained a mean measure of cognitive distance over all subjects (*average* data). Thus, the hypotheses could be tested on four types of data: individual mileage estimates, average mileage estimates, individual scale values, and average scale values, the latter being estimates of cognized distance obtained from the ratio estimates type of raw data.

For the mileage estimate data, each subject was given 20 line scales, one for each location. The scales were 50 centimeters in length and divided in 1 mile increments up to 7 miles (the longest objective distance being a little over 4 miles). The subject was instructed, if familiar with a location, to place a mark on each scale to represent the road distance, by the most direct driving route, from the common origin point to the corresponding location. The distances so indicated were interpreted as measures of cognitive distance. These were used either separately for each individual as *individual mileage estimate* data, or the arithmetic mean was taken over all subjects, thus generating one *average mileage estimate* for each location. This methodology follows Lee (1970).

For the ratio estimate data, each subject was presented with 7 sheets of paper of the type shown in Figure 1. Each sheet had one of the 20 locations as a standard, and subjects were instructed to assume that the short line at the top of the sheet represented the road distance to this standard point. Each of the remaining 19 locations corresponded to one of the long lines on the sheet. The subject was instructed to place a mark on each of these long lines such that it indicated the road distance to the corresponding location *relative to the road distance to the standard* (this

being represented by the length of the short line). By dividing the length of the short standard line (7 centimeters in all cases) by the length of the long line up to the mark placed on it by the subject, an estimate is obtained of the ratio of the distance between the common origin point and the standard location, relative to the distance from the same origin point to the location corresponding to the long line. This technique is similar to that used by Lowrey (1973).

In the example shown in Figure 1, the particular location chosen as the standard is Union Railroad Station. The subject is instructed to assume that the length of the short standard line represents the distance from the main entrance of the university (indicated as Long's Bookstore which lies opposite the entrance) to the Union Railroad Station. The mark placed by the subject on the second long line, which corresponds to the intersection of Broad and High streets, is assumed to represent his or her cognition of the distance from Long's Bookstore to this

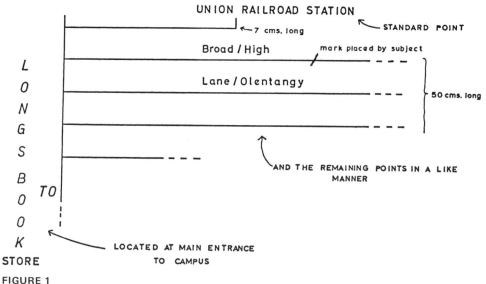

FIGURE 1
Example of data sheet used to obtain ratio estimates.

intersection, using the scale provided by the length of the standard line and its corresponding cognized distance. Thus, a ratio estimate can be obtained:

$$\frac{\text{length of standard line}}{\text{length of long line up to subject's mark}} = \frac{\text{cognized distance to Union Railroad Station}}{\text{cognized distance to Broad and High streets}}$$

$$= \frac{7 \text{ cm}}{10.5 \text{ cm}} = .667 = {}_hx_{ij}$$

= ratio estimate = raw data

If each of the 20 locations is used in turn as the standard, a 20 by 20 raw data matrix, $_hX$, can be assembled for every subject. Let $_hx_{ij}$ represent an element of the hth subject's data matrix. If rows represent the location used as the standard, then each element, $_hx_{ij}$ represents the ratio of the cognized distance to the standard (i) relative to the cognized distance to location j, for the hth individual.

To reduce the large number of estimates necessary from each subject if presented with all 20 locations as standards, each subject used only 7 locations as such. Thus, each location was used as a standard by one third of the sample, which resulted in each of the 20 locations being used by at least 80 subjects. As a consequence, for any one subject, no complete data matrix X could be assembled. At a maximum, X contains 7 completed rows, although even within these, certain elements may be missing since subjects were instructed to avoid making estimates for locations with which they were unfamiliar.

To control for learning and order effcts, which have been shown to be significant (Lowrey, 1973), the order in which individual sheets were presented to subjects was randomized. In addition, the order of locations upon a sheet was separately randomized for each standard, although for a given standard the order of locations was the same for all subjects.

The scale value measures of cognized distance are obtained from the ratio estimate raw data. For each subject there are 19 ratio estimates available relative

to each of seven locations acting as standard. Torgerson (1958, pp. 104–112) has shown that a least-squares estimate of the cognitive distance to the location acting as a standard is given by the geometric mean (or arithmetic mean of the log values) of the 19 ratio estimates available relative to that standard, together with the ratio of the standard distance to itself (assumed to be 1 in this case). Thus, if $_hx_{ij}$ is the ratio estimate for the hth individual of the standard location (i) relative to location j, and $_hv_i$ is the scale value estimate of the cognized distance to the ith location for the hth subject, then

$$_hv_i = 20\sqrt[20]{\prod_{j=1}^{20} {}_hx_{ij}} = \text{anti ln} \frac{1}{20} \sum_{j=1}^{20} \ln\left({}_hx_{ij}\right)$$

$$i = 1, \ldots, 20$$

That is, it is the sum of the logarithms of the ith row of the subject's raw data matrix X, divided by the number of columns of this matrix, where the principal diagonal is assumed to contain 1's.[3] These geometric means ($_hv_i$) are referred to as *individual scale value* estimates of cognized distance.

Because each subject used 7 locations as standards, scale value estimates of cognized distance to 7 locations are potentially available for each subject. However, the number of individual scale value estimates actually available, even for the whole sample of subjects, is quite small. To obtain even one scale value estimate, the subject had to give ratio estimates relative to *all* the other locations. Since subjects were instructed not to give these if they were unfamiliar with the locations, to obtain even one scale value estimate the subject had to be familiar with all locations. Unfortunately, this proved to be a relatively uncommon occurrence; thus, if no more than 2 out of the 20 ratio estimates for any standard were missing, the average ratio estimate for the whole sample was inserted.

Average scale value estimates of cognized distance were also obtained. For each of the 20 locations analyzed, some subset of the sample estimated its distance relative to each of the remaining 19 points. Thus, a total of 380 different ratios was estimated. Although each was presented to a minimum of 80 subjects, the actual number of estimates obtained varied from 32 to 74. For each of the 380 ratios the arithmetic mean was calculated over all subjects who gave an estimate. These averages are contained in the 20 by 20 matrix, $\bar{X}$. Ones are placed in the principal diagonal and the rows relate to the locations acting as standards. The same technique applied to each subject's raw data matrix was applied to the average matrix, $\bar{X}$. Thus, the geometric mean of each row is interpreted as the *average scale value* estimate of cognized distance for the location corresponding to that row.

Measures of objective distance. Objective distance was measured from street plans using driving routes. For the locations lying off High Street, several routes were possible, but, because of the grid-pattern street layout, distances were similar to within one tenth of a mile. In two cases a slightly more direct route was available than that through the general grid pattern of streets, and the average of this route and the grid-pattern route was used. This was legitimate since ratio estimates had been averaged over subjects who were likely to use either route. These map measures were checked against actual driving distances measured on a car's odometer. As a consequence of driving factors such as one-way streets and "no left turn" signs, slight discrepancies existed in some cases. The driving distance rather than the map distance was used in these cases. Finally, to allow direct comparison between these objective measures and the scale value measures of cognitive distance, the same transformation applied to the subjective data was applied to these objective measures; that is, ratios were formed and the geometric mean calculated.

Hypotheses testing. A power function of the form $Y = aX^b$, where Y is cognized and X objective distance, was used to relate objective to cognized distance. The parameters, a and b, were estimated by regression, from the equation $\ln Y = \ln a + b \ln X$, separate fits being obtained for each of the four groups to which the locations could be assigned: (1) locations away from downtown involving straight

routes, (2) locations away from downtown involving routes with bends, (3) locations toward downtown involving straight routes, and (4) locations toward downtown involving routes with bends. The relative positions of the regression lines and the values of the parameters for each group were compared to ascertain whether the underlying environment or route structure influences cognized distance. Hypothesis 1 implies that the b values should be greater and the regression lines lie above in group 3 against group 1, and group 4 against group 2. Hypothesis 2 implies a similar situation for group 2 against group 1, and group 4 against group 3.

Results and Conclusions

With respect to the hypotheses, the relative positions of the regression lines and the size of the b parameters indicated that, as hypothesized, distances to locations toward downtown are overestimated relative to those away from downtown (Figure 2). Tests on both the b parameters (Table 1) and the overall coincidence of the regression lines established statistically significant differences in most cases, except for the average mileage estimate data.

The comparison of straight routes against those involving turns (Table 1) showed higher b values for the latter as hypothesized, but markedly smaller a values; as a consequence, regression lines for the former lie above the latter in apparent contradiction to the hypothesis (Figure 3). Since the a value is a scale factor, this suggests that a different scale is being used by the subjects for routes with bends as against straight routes. It is suggested that this scale is the air line rather than road net distance. Thus, there appears to be an influence of air line distance in addition to that of turns themselves upon the cognition of distance for routes involving bends.

Comparing the four types of distance measures, the results obtained for the hypotheses were generally consistent. However, the use of the average measures does make statistical significance more difficult to establish. Examination of the individual measures shows marked subject variability in distance estimation; thus, relatively large numbers of subjects are re-

TABLE 1
Parameters of Power Functions for Location Groups

	a Value[a]	b Value[a]	Test on b Values — Hypothesis 1	Test on b Values — Hypothesis 2	No. of Observations
Individual mile estimates					
Straight away (group 1)	1.57	.54	$p < .025$	$p < .005$	803
Bends away (group 2)	1.10	.74			889
Straight toward (group 3)	1.49	.67	$p < .05$	$p < .01$	909
Bends toward (group 4)	1.06	.90			884
Individual scale values					
Straight away (group 1)	1.08	.76	$p < .005$	Opposes	196
Bends away (group 2)	.85	.63		hypothesis	194
Straight toward (group 3)	1.11	1.08	$p < .001$	$p < .025$	191
Bends toward (group 4)	.98	1.48			191
Average mile estimates					
Straight away (group 1)	1.92	.47	NS	NS	5
Bends away (group 2)	1.33	.68			5
Straight toward (group 3)	1.89	.56	NS	$p < .10$	5
Bends toward (group 4)	1.32	.85			5
Average scale values					
Straight away (group 1	.86	.66	$p < .025$	Opposes	5
Bends away (group 2)	.71	.49		hypothesis	5
Straight toward (group 3)	.90	1.02	$p < .01$	NS	5
Bends toward (group 4)	.81	1.22			5

[a]For $Y = aX^b$.

quired to achieve reliable results. The scale value measures have an advantage in this respect since the 19 ratio estimates per individual upon which each scale value is based lead to greater stability.

As was pointed out above, whereas the mileage estimate and scale value measures may be considered as different techniques for measuring the same phenomena (e.g., see Chapter 29), they are in fact measuring different attributes. The parameters are quite different and thus considerable care should be taken in comparing exponents found in various experiments when different techniques are utilized. Enquiring as to the more appropriate of the two measurement approaches used here, if decision making is based upon an evaluation of relative distances, as has been suggested by several authors, then the scale value measures would appear to be the more suitable since the ratio estimates from which they are derived

replicate this process. Even though this can be suggested, the best method of obtaining the ratio estimates has not been established. The method used here, that of marking lines upon a sheet of paper, turns a measurement of cognitive phenomena into a perceptual task, an assumption that may not be valid.

In conclusion, we might suggest that the methodological problems in the examination of cognized disance are far from solved. The most appropriate measurement techniques have not been clearly established, yet we do know that they influence the results. Control of variables not under study is another critical and difficult task. For instance, the results obtained here concerning distances toward as against away from downtown may be attributed to the environmental structure itself, or to its influence upon travel times and trip patterns. Some replication in terms of locations, nodes, subjects, and measure-

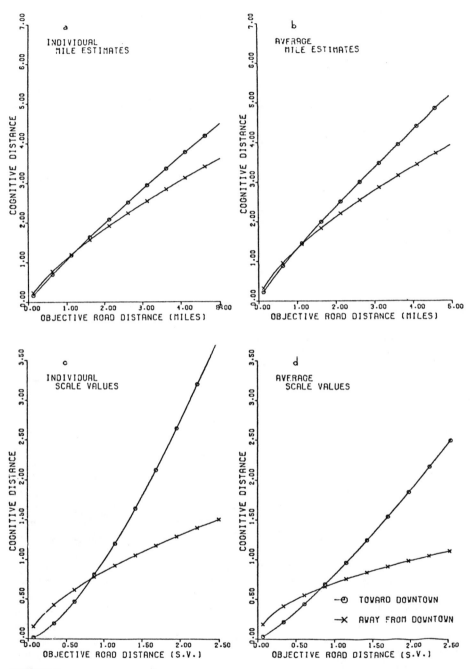

FIGURE 2

Comparison of power functions for locations toward versus away from downtown for each type of data for straight routes left (groups 1 and 3) and routes with bends right (groups 2 and 4).

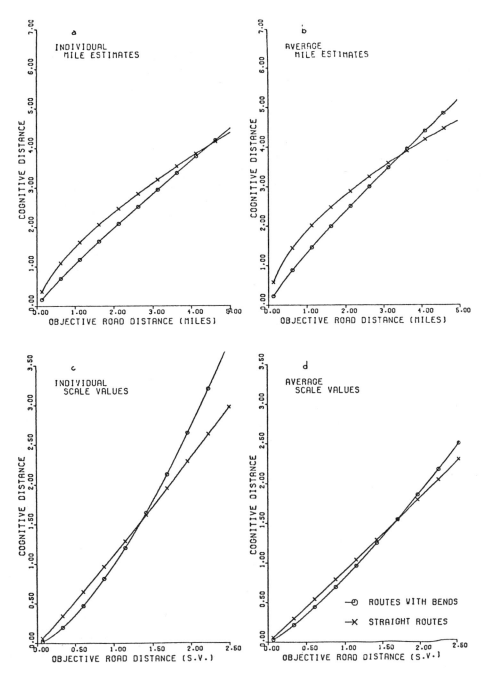

FIGURE 3
Comparison of power functions for straight routes versus those with bends for each type of data for locations away from downtown (groups 1 and 2) and toward downtown (groups 3 and 4).

ment techniques would add greatly to the reliability of our information regarding the cognition of distance.

NOTES

1. The objective environment is differentiated not so much on the basis of its measurability and quantifiability on some objective standard or scale, but more on its externality from, and commonality for all behaving organisms. The cognitive environment is taken to be the representation of the objective environment held by each individual. It is internal to the individual and has the potential of being unique for each.

2. Environmental determinism, as the term is understood by geographers, is not rearing its ugly head. As used here, "environment" is everything external to the individual, and his or her reaction to these externalities is conditioned by internal processes.

3. Since this represents the ratio of two distances to the same point, it can legitimately be assumed to be 1.0

31

Georgia Zannaras

Department of Geography
Ohio State University[2]

THE RELATION BETWEEN COGNITIVE STRUCTURE AND URBAN FORM[1]

Much research has verified the existing relationship between the environment and the cognitive processes of the individual within urban settings in the fashion that "what is seen is dependent upon what is there to be seen" (Carr and Schissler, 1969), but many questions remain. Not all urban places have the same spatial structure. Thus, one might ask if a particular structure (arrangement of urban elements) facilitates or hinders the development of an urban image (Carr, 1965). One might also ask whether differences exist in the importance attached to the same environmental features as potential way-finding clues by observers in various urban structures. The research reported here examines the second question and compares the use of two alternative methodologies.

The studies of Lynch (1960), Carr and Schissler (1969), and Jones (1972) are most relevant for the present work. These studies have mainly focused on small parts of the urban area. In the studies, similar types of features are mentioned by different observers in both areal and linear (sequential) images. This suggests that perception and cognition of the urban environment are related to the actual environment. From this base, we can probe the effect different spatial forms of cities have on the importance

attached to environmental features (cues), which are to be used later as clues in way-finding.

Conceptual Model for Studying the Role of City Structure in Image Development

The underlying basis for this study of urban cognition is a model with four component parts: (A) urban environment (city structure); (B) characteristics of the individual; (C) spatial mobility (behavior); and (D) the image of the city. The interaction (AB) between the environment (A) and characteristics of the individual (B) as evidenced through past spatial mobility (C) produces the image (D), which in turn affects further mobility (C). Figure 1 illustrates the overall relationship of these components. A brief discussion of the components and the way in which they are defined in the present study follows.

City structure refers to the spatial arrangement of the major features common to all cities—land use, buildings, neighborhoods, and street networks. Three common physical models of urban structure based on the arrangement and transition of these features exist in the geographic literature: (1) concentric zonal (hereafter referred to as zonal), (2) sector, and (3)

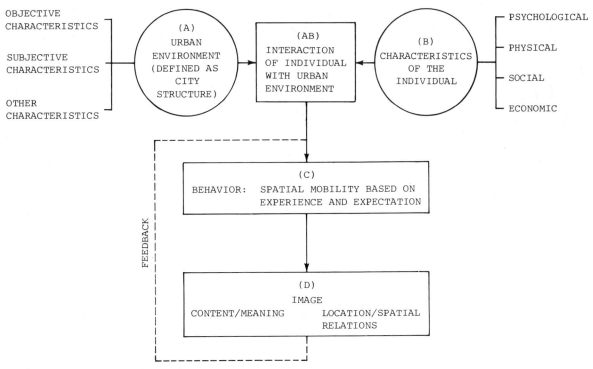

FIGURE 1
Conceptual model relating the components of urban cognition.

multiple nuclei (hereafter referred to as the mixed form) (Thomlinson, 1969). The zonal model has a central core surrounded by a circular arrangement of land uses. In the sector model, the individual land uses originate at the central core and expand outward along the major arterials in a wedge-like fashion; one land use generally dominates the entire sector. The arrangement of land uses in the third model, as it is defined in the present study, constitutes a mixture of the zonal–sectoral patterns[3] (see Figure 2.). Although reality causes distortions in such abstractions, it is possible to find cities whose internal structure approximates the abstract formulations. Three examples used in this study to represent different city structures include the cities of Marion (zonal), Newark (sector), and Columbus (mixed).

Personal characteristics influence what the individual sees or interprets in the environment and what eventually becomes part of his or her image of the city (Carr and Schissler, 1969). Although many different characteristics influence an individual's actions, those characteristics which represent an individual's participation or involvement in the environment are thought to have greater influence in the development of city images (Lee, 1964; Steinitz, 1968; Harrison and Howard, 1972). Examples of such characteristics included in this study are (1) length of residence in a large urban place (operationalized by a three-way classification: 0 years, 0 to 3 years, and more than 3 years); (2) urban experience (defined as the place where the individual spent most of his or her life up to age 18, that is, rural, small city, or

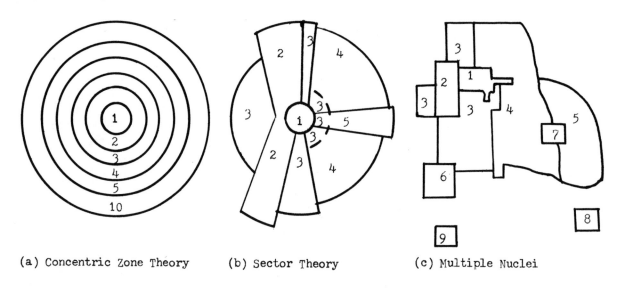

(a) Concentric Zone Theory   (b) Sector Theory   (c) Multiple Nuclei

Key:

1. Central Business District
2. Wholesale Light Manufacturing
3. Low-class Residential
4. Medium-class Residential
5. High-class Residential
6. Heavy Manufacturing
7. Outlying Business District
9. Industrial Suberb
10. Commuter's Zone

FIGURE 2
Internal structure of the city: classic models (after Harris and Ullman, 1945).

urban–suburban environment); (3) downtown shopping propensity (defined as the tendency of the individual to patronize shops in the city center as opposed to those in shopping centers); and (4) navigational experience [operationalized by the agreement expressed to the statement: "I find traveling (driving) in an urban area confusing."] .

Spatial mobility simply refers to the external behavior or movement of the individual from one location to another (e.g., from a point on the periphery of the city to the city center). The individual's actions in urban space are influenced, among other things of course, by past experiences in similar environments and his or her image of the city (Carr

and Schissler, 1969). These images are thought to consist of two parts: (1) location–spatial relations (Moore, 1973d, 1975a) and (2) content–meaning (Harrison and Howard, 1972). Each urban image contains a variety of objects whose meaning may be defined with respect to the object's function, history, general significance, or even its importance as a potential clue in way-finding in the city. Each object has a location in the city and enters into spatial relations occurring between it and the other contents of the urban image. Knowledge of the spatial relations between urban objects can be used in identifying one's location in the city. Comparing the importance attached to similar objects as potential way-finding clues in various city structures and the accuracy with which individuals are able to locate their position within these structures provides valuable information concerning the effect that the various city structures have on the development of spatial images of the city.

Hypotheses

Four hypotheses are examined in this study. The first three concern the effect of city structure on image development. The fourth hypothesis examines the effect of the personal characteristic "length of residence in a large urban place" on image development.

Hypothesis 1. *City structure is significantly related to variations in the mean importance assigned to the environmental features as potential way-finding clues by a sample of respondents.* The basis for hypothesis 1 is found in the reported relationship between the actual and imaged environment (Carr and Schissler, 1969). If the relationship is accepted, it can be said that *city structure* plays a significant role in the exposure and grouping of features both in the actual environment and in the individual's mind. Since city structure summarizes the operationalization of urban space and features, it can be used to succinctly represent the urban environment for use in studying images of different city forms.

Hypothesis 2. *The features of "land use" will be most important in the zonal structure; "traffic" features will be most important in the sector model.* The basis for hypothesis 2 is found in the design of the city structure models. In the *concentric zonal structure*, each zone consists predominantly of one land-use type. As an individual moves from the periphery to the city center, he or she will experience several land use changes along the route. Given that the land uses on the route reflect the zonality of the city as a whole, it is plausible to expect the changes in land-use features to be dominant over all other features. The arterial network forms the basis for the *sectoral structure*. Each sector starts at the core and expands outward. The sector consists theoretically of one type of land use bounded between street or traffic arteries that separate it from adjoining sec-

tors. Since land use is fairly uniform within the sector and presumably along the arterials, the individual experiences no profound land-use changes on the trip to the city center. Therefore, one would expect the traffic features to be more salient in the environment and also in the image of the urban environment.

Hypothesis 3. *City structure has a greater discriminatory power than any of the personal characteristics examined.* Hypothesis 3 has its origins in the conclusions offered by Carr and Schissler (1969). They state that the actual environment largely determines what is seen and remembered. Support by others (Jones, 1972; Appleyard, 1970b); Steinitz, 1968) for this conclusion leads one to believe that this relationship tends to dominate all other relationships reported concerning the influence personal characteristics have on the image formation process. Therefore, it is felt that city structure will account for a greater proportion of the variation in the mean importance measures than will any of the individual characteristics.

Hypothesis 4. *Of the personal characteristics considered, the length of residence in a large urban place will be most meaningful in discriminating between cue importance over all features.* Of the many possible individual characteristics a researcher can select, the *length of residence* is most often chosen for studies of urban images. Appleyard (1970) and Steinitz (1968) cite the factor as meaningful with respect to an individual's knowledge of the existence of features and activities in the city. Golledge, Briggs, and Demko (1969) report its influence in the perception of urban distance. From these studies, it appears that the length of residence is used to represent the individual's "use" of the city. Actual activity information such as the number of visits to shopping centers, parks, the city center, museums, and so on, may give a better insight into the individual's use of the city; but, lacking such detailed information, it appears an approximate picture can be gained by substituting the length of residence. Based on the results of other studies, it is felt that the length of residence in a large urban place[4] will perform better than the other personal factors in distinguishing differences in the importance assigned to different urban features.

Experimental Procedure

In defining the study, the necessity of devising a method of presenting *city structures* to observers that permitted (1) reducing the complexity of reality, (2) uniformity in what is seen by observers, and (3) making conclusions applicable to the real world became evident. With these goals in mind, a model of environmental presentation involving four displays was developed. This model appears in Figure 3.

The first column in the figure shows the types of models that are used in coping with real-world complexity. Iconic models represent properties of the real world at a different scale; analogue models repre-sent one property by another; symbolic models represent properties with symbols (Ackoff et al., 1962). Each model, moving from the iconic to the symbolic, represents an increase in the level of abstraction as well as a decrease in the amount of information conveyed. The third column shows one method of operationalizing some control over the mix of environmental stimuli that interact with the observers at each stage. In this paper, we are immediately concerned with the use of maps and models in the study of urban images; therefore, only their design and use will be discussed. (Detailed descriptions of the design of the four displays and their use appears in Zannaras, 1973.) Prior to discussing the

MODEL OF ENVIRONMENTAL PRESENTATION

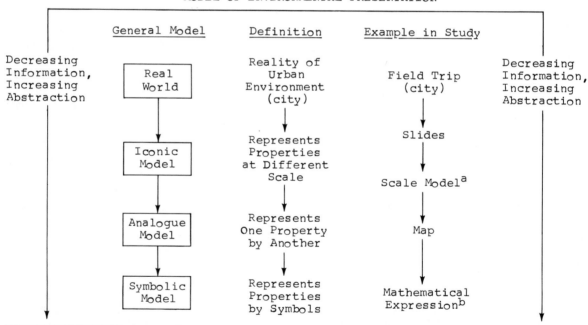

[a] If all properties were represented at a minimum scale, a table model would be an iconic model. The scale model in the study is a combination of the iconic and analogue models.

[b] No example of this type is used in this study.

FIGURE 3
Model of environmental presentation.

map and model displays, it is necessary to briefly describe the method used in selecting the environmental features included in the displays. (Again, for a more detailed discussion, see Zannaras, 1973.)

The selection of environmental features to be included in the displays was determined in two ways: (1) by examining the features mentioned in prior published articles on city images; and (2) by conducting two pilot studies designed to elicit a list of features whose existence in the environment was noticed and reported by passing observers.

Maps and models were fashioned according to the generalized land-use plan of the three above-mentioned Ohio cities, each of whose structure roughly represented one of the three common physical structures. Both displays were simply labeled with a number: I, II, III, with I representing the sector model (Newark), II the concentric-zonal model (Marion), and III a mixed model (Columbus). Black and white maps were designed to portray six different land-use types, traffic lights, railroads, streams, and streets. A sample map for City I (sector, Newark) appears in Figure 4.

The models, built of styrofoam, used both color and vertical exaggeration to differentiate land-use patterns (see Figures 5 to 8). Other environmental features included on the models were traffic lights represented by yellow map tacks, street direction signs painted in white on black streets, railroad crossings, streams, freeways, and a number of specific features, such as churches, banks, named commercial establishments, and so on, printed in black on white thumbtacks. In all, a total of 34 generalized features and a varied number of unique features (i.e., unique to each particular city) appeared on each model. (For analytical purposes, the features on the models were later grouped into 10 cue types.) A removable frame of plywood and clear mylar which stood 2 inches above the base covered each model. This apparatus allowed each participant to work directly above the model.

Data with which to test the hypotheses were provided by a sample of college students. For the maps and models displays, the respondents were asked to select and follow a route of their choice from the periphery of the city to the city center. The respondents marked their choices directly on the maps and on the mylar covering the models. They were then requested to rate the features that appeared along their route on a five-point scale with five verbal anchors: (1) not important, (2) not very important, (3) indifferent, (4) important, and (5) very important,[5] each indicating how important that feature would be if they were trying to relate the route to a stranger who desired to trace their journey. In other words, the respondents rated each feature with respect to its potential as a way-finding clue. All the respondents repeated the procedure three times, once for each city. In an effort to minimize any possible effects owing solely to the order of display presentation, the order was counterbalanced across subjects.

For the analysis of the data, the importance ratings were transformed into an interval scale in which the rating was defined as a proportion of the total importance possible for a feature on the given route. A number of analyses of variance with allowances for unequal cell sizes were performed on the data.[6] The first test involved an analysis of variance on the relationship between city structure and the mean importance for each environmental feature. The second test examined the relationship between the individual characteristics and the mean importance assigned to each environmental feature. Interpretation of the results was accomplished in two ways: (1) examination of the number of significant *F* values observed for the different cue types when grouped by the factors of city structure and personal characteristics, and (2) examination of the observed means for each environmental feature when grouped by the city structure factor.

Results

The findings based on the mean importance of the environmental features (or feature types) as potential clues in way-finding are discussed in terms of the hypotheses above. Detailed information regarding the two displays is given where deemed appropriate or necessary.

Hypothesis 1 suggested that city structure would be significantly related to variations in the mean importance assigned to the environmental features or cues as potential way-finding clues by a sample of respondents. Importance measures were obtained for a total of 19 cues or cue types that appeared on the maps and models. The city types differ significantly for 11 of the 19 possible cue types (see Table 1).

For the map display, the F values indicate that the city types differ significantly with respect to mean importance for five of the nine environmental features (the letters refer to the listing of features in Figure 9): (a) low-density residential land use, (b) high-density residential land use, (f) institutions, (h) railroad crossings, and (i) streams. Of the five features, two are land-use features upon which the display structures are defined. Railroad crossings and streams have an

FIGURE 4 (*below, right, and page 344*)
Work maps of cities I–III: Newark, Marion, and Columbus.

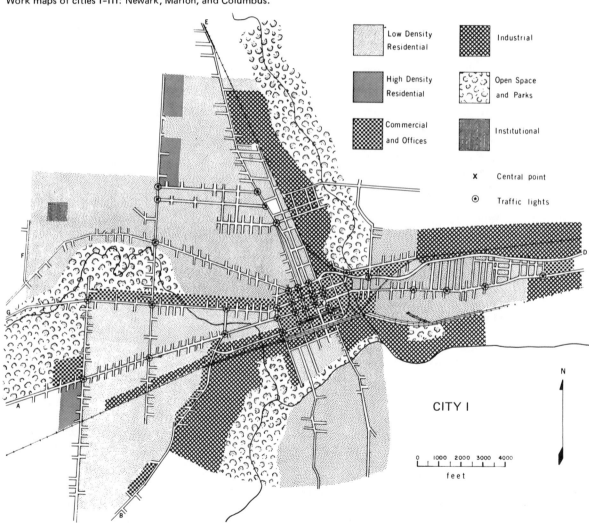

Low Density Residential

Industrial

High Density Residential

Open Space and Parks

Commercial and Offices

Institutional

X   Central point

⊙   Traffic lights

CITY I

N

0   1000 2000 3000 4000
feet

indirect effect on land-use patterns. Institutions are often sprinkled throughout the urban scene, although most are not found in the central core of cities.

The cities do not differ significantly with respect to cue importance for the features (again, the letters refer to the listing in Figure 9): (c) commercial land use, (d) industrial land use, (e) open space, or (g) traffic lights. The cue importance means for these features are quite similar for the three city types (see Figure 9). Visual inspection of the graph suggests that the means for these features are higher than those for the features which are significantly differentiated by city type. Adding the three means for each cue (one for each city) to obtain an average mean produces a ranking in which the means for the four nonsignificant cues are higher than those for the five significant cues.

This result promotes the idea that the four features are thought to be dominant in all city structures by the respondents and are therefore rated highly important, whereas the remaining five features, although not as important, are more apt to serve as distinguishing features along the various routes, which when taken together are reflective of the structure of the city.

The F values for the models indicate city structure differs significantly with respect to six types of environmental cues (the letters refer to the listing of features on Figure 10): (b) traffic, (d) church, (e) bank, (f) stream, (g) park–cemetery, and (h) large buildings. *City structure* does not discriminate between cue importance for four types of cues: (a) schools, (c) land use, (i) shopping centers, or (j) unique

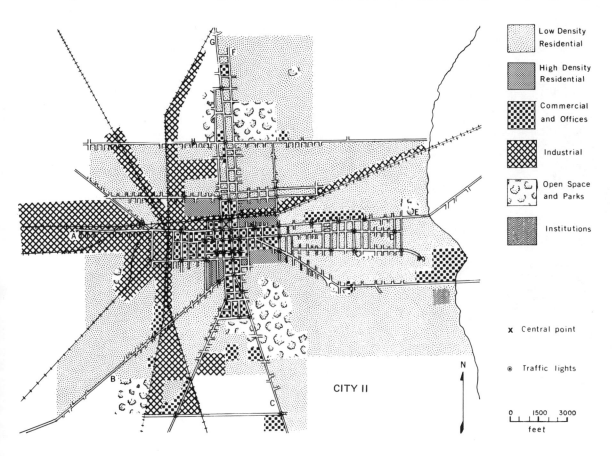

	Low Density Residential
	High Density Residential
	Commercial and Offices
	Industrial
	Open Space and Parks
	Institutions

x   Central point

⊚   Traffic lights

0   1500   3000
feet

CITY II

N

features. Figure 10, the graph of the cue importance means, provides further insight into the similarities and differences between city structures with respect to the importance assigned to the particular cue types. The graph suggests greater similarity in mean cue importance exists between city I (sector) and city III (mixed) for all cue types except churches and shopping centers. For these latter cues, city I and city II (zonal) are more similar with respect to mean cue importance. Both city I and city II had an unusually large number of "churches" along the prominent city-center routes. "Churches" were both fewer in number and less visually dominant along the major routes of

city III. "Shopping centers," which appeared in city III (mixed), often occurred within the built-up area and were, therefore, less visually dominant than those in cities I (sector) and II (zonal). Thus, it may be assumed, the respondents assigned lower importance ratings to these features in city III because they lacked visual dominance and were, thus, less likely to be very useful as clues in way-finding.

In summary, hypothesis 1 suggested that city structure would be significantly related to variations in the mean importance assigned to environmental features as potential way-finding clues. The hypothesis is confirmed for 11 of the 19 environmental features exam-

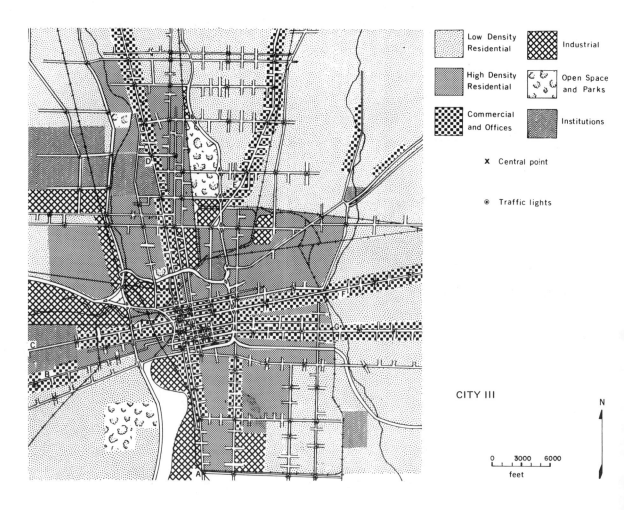

Low Density Residential

High Density Residential

Commercial and Offices

Industrial

Open Space and Parks

Institutions

X   Central point

⊛   Traffic lights

CITY III

N

0   3000   6000
feet

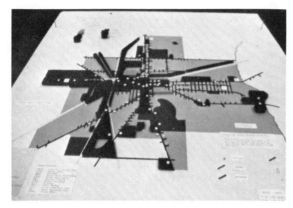

FIGURE 5
Overhead view of model for city II (Marion).

FIGURE 6
Oblique view of model for city II (Marion).

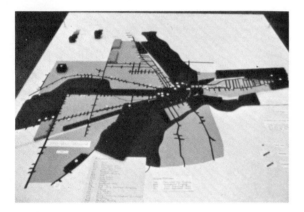

FIGURE 7
Overhead view of model for city I (Newark).

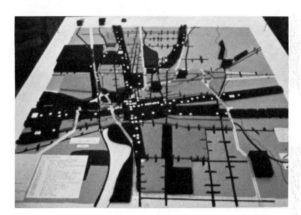

FIGURE 8
Overhead view of model for city III (Columbus).

ined in the map and model displays. In each display, the hypothesis is confirmed for more than half the features included in the particular display (maps: five of nine features; models: six of ten).

It was suggested in hypothesis 2 that the "land-use" cue type might be most meaningful for the concentric zonal structure (city II), whereas the cue type "traffic" might be most important in the sector model (city I). The expected ordering of the means for "land use" is, from most important to least important: city II (zonal), city III (mixed), and city I (sector). To test this hypothesis, it is necessary to form a composite

"land-use" cue type mean by averaging the means for the six individual land uses on the map display. The observed ordering for the cue type "land use" differs with the display: (1) maps: III, II, I, and (2) models: III, I, II. The expected ordering of the means for "traffic" is, from most important to least important: city I (sector), city III (mixed), and city II (zonal). Again, it is necessary to form a composite "traffic" mean for the maps. The observed ordering differs with the display: (1) maps: II, I, III, and (2) models: II, III, I.

The results do not confirm the hypothesis. Given

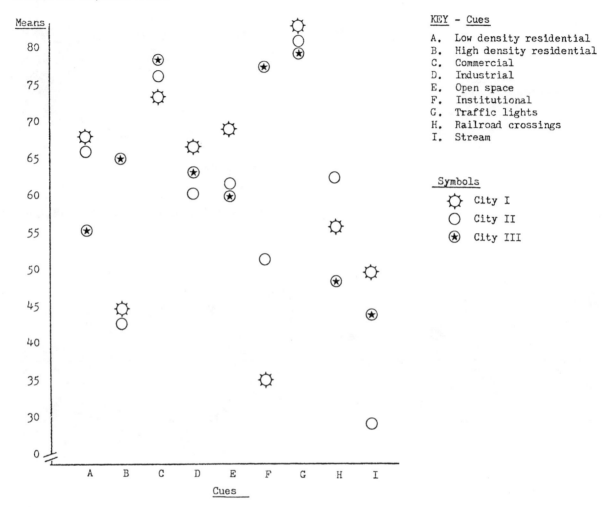

FIGURE 9
Graph of means of cue importance when classified by city structure for map displays.

the differences across displays, the interpretation of the results is somewhat complicated. For these displays, the cue type "land use" is most important for city III, the mixed structure. The reason for this result is not immediately evident; it may be solely a function of the displays used.[7] The cue type "traffic" is consistently most important for the concentric zonal structure, city II, for both displays—a reversal of the hypothesized occurrence.[8] Traffic generation

may offer a possible explanation for the deviations of the observed and expected ordering of the importance means. In zonal structures in which land use changes occur along routes, one expects the land uses to be visually dominant. Often, however, each land use generates a different amount and type of traffic. Therefore, the cue type "traffic" may be more salient than that of "land use" for the individual driver in the zonal structure. In the sector struc-

TABLE 1

Summary of Significant F Values by Display When Importance Measures are Grouped by City Structure

Environmental Cue or Cue Type	Maps	Degrees of Freedom[a]	Models	Degrees of Freedom[a]
Low-density residential	4.166[b]	2,265		
High-density residential	16.891	2,216		
Commercial	NS			
Industrial	NS			
Open space	NS			
Institution	25.901	2,127		
Traffic	NS[c]		8.293	2,327
Railroad crossing	5.921	2,308		
Stream	8.367	2,248	12.263	2,248
Land use			NS	
Schools			NS	
Church			6.357	2,295
Bank			10.672	2,299
Park–cemetery			5.532	2,182
Large buildings			7.252	2,318
Shopping center			NS	
Unique			NS	
Total number of different cues	17			
Total number of cues on display	9		10	Total 19
Total number of significant F values	5		6	16

[a]Degrees of freedom vary due to missing data related to the presence or absence of a feature along selected routes.
[b]Significant at .05 level; all others significant at .01 level.
[c]The cue "traffic" represents "traffic lights" only on the maps; when "traffic lights" and "railroad crossing" are combined, as in the model display, $F = 3.293$, significant at .05 level.

ture, city I, "land use" is fairly constant throughout the sector; thus, one expects traffic generation to be fairly constant as well. This may result in the motorist's attention being diverted to other features in the environment.

Hypothesis 3 suggested that city structure would exhibit a greater discriminatory power than any of the individual characteristics examined. In comparing the discriminatory power of city structure and the selected personal characteristics, we find that a larger proportion of the features exhibit significant F values when discriminated by each city type than when discriminated by any single individual characteristic. From Table 2, we can see first for the map display

that five of the nine cue type features have a significant F value when classified by city type. The number of significant F values observed when the map data are grouped by the personal characteristics ranges from zero to three out of nine possible values. The models display results in six of the ten cue types having significant F values when classified by city type versus from zero to five out of the ten possible values for each of the personal characteristics.

Of the personal characteristics examined, it was suggested that *length of residence in a large urban place* was expected to be the most meaningful personal characteristic in discriminating the cue importance measures over all features. For both displays,

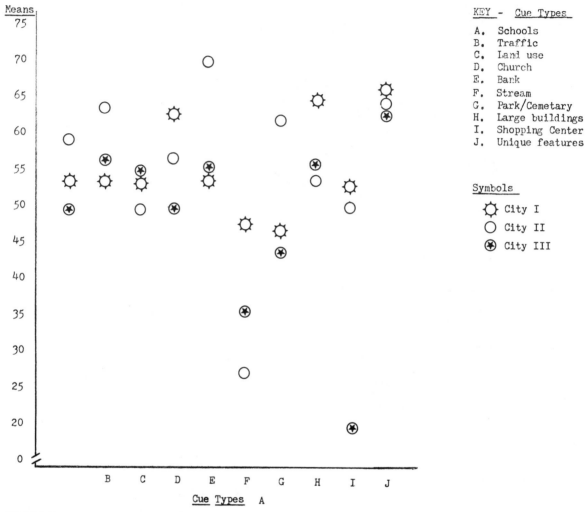

FIGURE 10
Graph of means of cue importance when classified by city structure for model displays.

no significant *F* values occur for the features when classified by this personal characteristic. The most meaningful personal characteristic for the map display is the characteristic "*navigational experience,*" with three significant *F* values. For the models display, the characteristic "*downtown shopping propensity*" is most meaningful, with a total of five significant *F* values. These results suggest that personal characteristics which represent an individual's active commerce with the environment are more important than those which could conceivably represent a passive existence within a given environment. Personal characteristics such as "length of residence" or "urban experience" tell us very little about the nature of an individual's existence in a city—it may be an active or passive existence. These characteristics

TABLE 2
Summary of the Number of Significant *F* Values by Display and Single Basis of Classification

Display	Bases of Classification					
	City Structure	Length of Residence	Urban Experience	Downtown Shopping Propensity	Navigational Experience	Number of Cue Types– Display
1. Map	5	0	2	1	3	9
2. Model	6	0	0	5	1	10
Total significant *F*'s	11	0	2	6	4	
Total possible over two displays						19
Possible *F*'s (%)	52.6	0	10.5	31.5	21.1	100

allow researchers to make certain assumptions about an individual's experience with a city; for example, the longer a person has lived in a city, the more likely it is that he or she has traveled throughout the city and is knowledgeable about the location of its shops and the like. Although the assumptions are not unfounded, it is imperative that we try to isolate characteristics that do tell us about the individual's actual involvement with the urban environment.

Conclusions

The final discussion will briefly summarize the results of the study and comment on the methods of environmental presentation used. The implications the study has for city planning are also considered.

Findings. The results indicate that city structure has an important role in urban images when considering the differences in judged importance of environmental cues as potential way-finding clues. The variations in the arrangement of land uses in cities do influence the importance attached to the features in the cities. For both displays, city structure has a more influential role in distinguishing among the importance measures than does any single personal characteristic tested. Taken together, the personal characteristics show a edge over the importance of city structure with 12 significant *F* values as opposed to 11 values. Finally, of the personal characteristics examined, the active characteristics "downtown shopping propensity" and "navigational experience" are better in discriminating among the importance

measures than are the more traditional characteristics of "urban experience" and "length of residence." The findings concerning the role of the personal characteristics suggest that further research in identifying all meaningful personal characteristics and their role in environmental cognition is necessary.

Two methods of environmental presentation, maps and models, were used in the study. Both methods were abstract representations of urban reality. The comparability between the two displays would have been enhanced if the difference between the displays had been restricted to the level of abstraction. In this study, additional "noise" was introduced by the differences in the number and types of environmental features on the displays. These differences also hampered efforts in isolating the effect of the two displays on the cue importance measures. A few general comments, however, can be made concerning the use and effectiveness of the displays. The sample did not appear to have any problems in working with either the maps or models. Agreement between the maps and models for some hypotheses existed; in fact, agreement with the results from the slide and field trip conditions also existed (Zannaras, 1973). For example, the feature "traffic" was considered to be most important in the zonal structure (city II) on all four displays. The value of the importance mean for the feature "traffic," however, decreased in magnitude as the displays approached reality (field trip). In choosing between the two methods, the author would select the model display for use in another study. This method would permit greater versatility in presenting an authentic urban environment than would a map display; furthermore, it would have great cost advantages (in both currency and time) over an actual field trip condition.

Implications for urban planning. This study has shown that variations in the judged importance of environmental features as potential way-finding clues can be related to city structure. In the study, city structure was defined solely on the basis of the land-use activity patterns found in the commonly accepted physical models of cities. This is somewhat of a crude definition of city structure. It ignores the variety of specific features and the frequency with which these features occur in cities. Planners might be advised to develop general models of the spatial arrangement of specific features and test subject response to these models as a first step in their quest to fully understand the influence of the spatial environment on the observer's image of and behavior within that urban environment. Although this study has shown that variations in the judged importance of features as way-finding clues can be related to city structure, it has not made any statements concerning the ease of way-finding in the different structures. It seems logical that a difference could exist. If this difference can be isolated and related to a particular spatial pattern of city activities, planners may achieve a city design that can reduce the stress and inefficiency of present urban spatial mobility.

NOTES

1. This research is based on the author's Ph.D. dissertation submitted at Ohio State University (Zannaras, 1973), and made possible by grants from the National Science Foundation (RF–3086–A1) and the American Association of University Women. The author would like to thank Richard C. Jones, Reginald G. Golledge, and Gary T. Moore for their helpful comments.

2. Now at the Department of Geography, University of Cincinnati.

3. The multiple-nuclei model is sometimes interpreted as a mixed model with instances of both zonality and sectorality. The model (city III) used in this paper is of this type.

4. "Length of residence in a large urban place" was used rather than the characteristic "length of residence" because some people in the sample at the time of the study did not live in the same city as did the rest of the sample. All the respondents, however, had lived or were living in Columbus, Ohio, and thus had knowledge of the city, which was used as the basis for city III (mixed model).

5. The distance between the anchor terms was assumed to be equal.

6. The analysis of variance performed on the data included both single and cross-classification analyses as well as a form that allowed investigating the effects of repeated measurements on the same observations. The effect of the latter was simply a deflation in the absolute value of some of the observed F values, but not a change in the number of significant F values observed for the various tests. Only the results of the one-way analyses are reported in this paper.

7. The cue type "land use" is most important for city II (zonal) in the slide and field trip displays as well. The expected ordering of the importance means (II, III, I) appears only for the slide display. Since the slides were taken throughout the city areas, this display more nearly represents the actual structure of the real city. Therefore, the observation of the expected order of importance means for the slide display is heartening.

8. The cue type "traffic" is also most important for the concentric-zonal city (city II) on the slide and field trip displays.

32

TALKING WITH ENVIRONMENTAL A, AN EXPERIMENTAL MAPPING LANGUAGE

Denis Wood

School of Design
North Carolina State University

Robert Beck

Ecole d'Architecture
Université de Montréal

The use of sketch maps, generated by cartographically naive mappers, as data in investigating the interaction of persons and the environment has become a familiar method of much environmental psychology, behavioral geography, landscape architecture, urban and regional planning, and other disciplines. A brief survey of the literature up to 1974 uncovers better than 50 such studies of various locations, primarily of cities, employing sketch maps as essential data, and their number is growing rapidly. Although there exists enormous methodological variety among these studies, at their core and heart lies the freely solicited and freely drawn sketch map, whose use was pioneered by Kevin Lynch during the late 1950s, and given great publicity in *The Image of the City* (1960).

The basic idea behind the freely solicited and freely drawn sketch map is to obtain from the sketch mapper a map or sketch of a place that has been minimally defined by the researcher. In fact, the researcher may not even tell the mapper what to map, as when the researcher is looking for boundary descriptions of the entity in question. Fundamentally, the mapper is given a sheet of paper and a writing implement and told to map a given environment. The resultant map is then analysed (ordinarily a content analysis is performed) and conclusions are drawn with respect to the environment sketched, the mapper, or the process of interaction between the mapper and the environment.

In a relatively small number of cases, the approach has varied somewhat. The mapper may be told to sketch a certain portion of the environment with the boundaries specified. In another case he or she may be handed a portion of a map with a blank interior and asked to fill it in. Excluded from our present discussion are tasks wherein the mapper is given a standard map and asked to notate it in some fashion, ordinarily by describing boundaries of a neighborhood or region. For the most part, however, the subject is handed a blank sheet of paper and is left alone once it comes to mapping.

It has seemed questionable to us whether such methods are capable of generating data reflective of anything but the ability of the mapper to cope with the task set. From the point of view of executing the map, the project is formidable. In many cases he or she has never drawn a map before, and in some cases he or she has never even set paper to pencil for drawing purposes. Some mappers suffer from a form of graphophobia. In any of these eventualities, there is distinct evidence of graphomotor inhibition or serious lack of skill and practice. How does a mapper faced with the task for the first time set about creating a graphic vocabulary for the reification of reality? What sort of inhibition is induced by the necessity of transforming a nonplanar world into one that is? How does the naive mapper come to grips with scale, generalization, detail, and symbolization? Or what happens when a mapper is faced with a case of creeping failure of perpendicularity wherein he has inadvertently shaved five degrees off every right angle, so that when he comes to finish there is suddenly no room on the map for a whole neighborhood?

It might be asked why, with these drawbacks, the method has survived and indeed prospered? By sketching a map of a complex environment, the mapper should be able to communicate an enormous amount of information to the researcher and *to specify its spatial interrelatedness.* It is easier to *draw* three dots than to *describe* their relations: "The first one is to the right and below the second but to the right and even with the third only the same distance away and . . . ." This is especially true for 10 or for 100 dots, all of them with the interrelations of distance, direction, inclusion, and so on. This interrelatedness is screened by the distortions introduced by the formidability of making a map from nothing. Have you tried it? We must stand amazed, not at the failure to connect, not at the distortions of scale, not at the ludicrous attempts at freeway underpasses, but at the fact that anything comes through at all. But the mapper could reveal so much to the researcher if only they could communicate. The reason they fail to communicate is because they are not presently speaking the same language.

Almost all students in the United States are taught to "read" maps and generally to practice at copying maps from geography books by the time of junior high school. However, it is possible that we are yet a graphically illiterate people, and that, although not taught as such today, graphics should become one of the four, five, or six R's.

Faced with this question in the design of a research project in the spring of 1971, we answered that it was

not too much to hope that people could be readily taught to communicate with researchers using maps. The only real problem in using maps as a channel of communication was not the design of the language itself, nor even the design of a curriculum to teach the language to sketch mappers, but rather the extent to which the language would *shape* the resultant maps, making them reflect not the environment or the mapper's interaction with it, nor even the mapper's inability to grapple with the problems of mapping, but merely the language as such. That is, the question became, would it be possible to learn anything from the maps that we had not actually put into the language itself? Kevin Lynch,[1] for example, has argued to us as follows:

> I am not convinced yet as to the fallacy of (relatively) instructionless mapping. It produces results of lesser comparability, but not in other ways, and the researcher's ideas are imposed on it to a lesser extent . . . . [Your language] obviously changes the way your mappers see their environment.

The geographer, Hugh Prince,[2] has put it even more strongly:

> Your approach to the techniques of mapping are, it seems to me, heavily authoritarian. It simply is not true to assert that maps are unintelligible unless they obey a set of grammatical rules (like a language) or theorems (as in maths). Pictograms of very idiosyncratic construction may be read by all sorts of people without too much formal teaching . . . . How much of what is represented in the maps is [Wood and Beck] directed, and how much is spontaneously kid-directed? Would the kids in *Lord of the Flies* have set about mapping their island in the way you recommend? Can you say what the kids discovered *for themselves* from their experience?

No, we cannot say what kids discover for themselves, but then, neither can the kids themselves *say* what they discover, not without recourse to a language, which would inevitably impose its categories on the experiences and its syntaxes on the possible ways of ordering them. Communication cannot and does not take place outside of language, silent or spoken, whereby the "reader" can have some clue as to the intentions of the "writer." If you accept Whorf (1956a) and agree that language shapes perception and that language is the medium of communication, then you are in a bind, for it is clearly better to have a literate population drawing sketch maps than an illiterate one. And if this is so, then it is practically mandatory that researchers teach their mappers some mapping language. As with other languages, speakers may turn a mapping language to their own use, modify it, and make it malleable and responsive to their "best" and "truest" understandings possible. Or they may allow the language to strangle them. In the end it is a matter of the presence or absence of a creative skill in communicating that makes all the difference. Finally, a language may in and of itself be restrictive or expansive. This is a function of the particular language. Whether the language we have developed is one or the other speaks to the quality of our attempt at constructing a graphic mapping language, but not, we think, to the question of whether a mapping language is or is not a good thing in and of itself.

Environmental A

Environmental A is a graphic mapping language designed for use by American teen-age students touring Europe for the first time. It was meant for urban environments, the "A" indicating our feeling that it is a first trail to be followed by other, improved urban languages. Our students used the language frequently, mapping the cities of London, Innsbruck, Venice, Rome, and Paris as often as possible. Our objective was to use the maps to generate understanding of the *development* of urban imagery, simultaneously giving practice in the use of the language. (the results on development are described in Chapter 14.)

Environmental A consists of a *vocabulary* of signs, marks, and name labels for points, lines, and areas, as well as a set of *rules* for manipulating these symbols and organizing them into a useful map. The rules of this game—and it was taught as serious fun—comprise the *grammar* of the language. Like other generative grammars, the rules suggest the ways in which point, line, and area symbols can be assembled into structures.

Grammar: rules for the skeletal map. For the first map, each student was encouraged to use point and line symbols to build up a *skeleton* maximizing centrality, proximity, and connectivity. Here is a summary of the instructions (see Wood, 1973b, pp. 80–117 for the complete instructions):

1. In the center of the paper place a small dot. This dot represents the center of whatever you are mapping. In London this may be Trafalgar Square, in Paris the Place de la Concorde, in Rome the Forum. Always remember that this first dot is the center.
2. Stand at this point in your mind. Visualize the way the streets run off from this point. Travel down them in your mind until you come to a second point. This point must not be too far away from the first and at the same time must not be adjacent to it.
3. Before you place this point on the map, visualize in your mind the distance between the two points. Remember that this distance will set the scale for the entire map.
4. Now connect these two points with a simple line.
5. Pick a third point in the same manner that you picked the second point. Connect this third point to either or both preceding points as possible.
6. Proceed in this manner to build up your skeleton. Connect each new point to as many preceding points as possible. Work from the center of the map out to the edges. Don't go jumping all over the page.
7. Label each point. Use abbreviations wherever possible.
8. Number each line segment as you put it on the map.
9. Use question marks to indicate uncertainty of direction and length of line segment.

In practice, of course, this whole approach was not always followed, but the last thing we wanted was for the language to constrict the students' desire and ability to communicate. *The point of the rules was to emphasize connectivity, proximity, and centrality, but when the emphasis on these aspects worked to the detriment of others, the kids were encouraged to break the rules and do their own thing.* Thus, one girl insisted on creating a skeleton that consisted on her first attempt of nothing but points without connections. Had we insisted on the connections, her map would have been greatly impoverished. As it was, she was able to work out increasing numbers of connections on subsequent maps.

Many of the suggestions of Environmental A were stated simply to reemphasize again and again the problems of scale. The insistence on starting with the center of the mapped environment in the center of the paper is basically a scale-related issue, for otherwise disproportionate amounts of paper are given to tangential areas. It also allowed us to monitor notions of urban centrality, despite the broad hints about what we believed the center to be. Interestingly, a number of kids would fix the city center in their minds and work toward it from the edge. Although this operation of centrality was sometimes only mental, it did help control scale distortion. The instruction about numbering lines was included to help us understand the sequence of construction of the skeleton map.

The mappers' use of visualization is strongly stressed in the skeletal stage of map development. The navigational character of maps is strongly visual. Note that the skeletal stage does not include the location or description of areas or the mention of attributes. Areal, descriptive, nonvisual, and attributive aspects of the environment were reserved for overlays put on afterward. The skeleton is concerned exclusively with relative location and connectivity–with the establishment of a spatial framework or net for the city. Thus, the skeleton is concerned with only a part, but a unified organic part, of the mapping process. Since the amount of information to be included on this sheet is circumscribed, it leaves the sheet cleaner, uncluttered, and hence easily susceptible to change by erasure or addition. It is also a lot easier to analyze. We reasoned that teaching location and connectivity would be the most useful to the mappers for actually getting about London. This being the case it would provide the satisfaction for using the skeleton as a base or primary map.

The seventh rule requested that each point on the skeleton map be labeled. Labels were an immense aid in analysis in that we knew *what* various points were

(and could thus correlate the map with the environment in question) but, more basically, we thus knew that the elements mapped were intended to be something at all. It is entirely possible to cover a sheet of paper with connected points and have none of them refer to objects in the world. Encouraging the students to label their points encouraged them to map the real world—that is, to honestly complete the mapping exercise. The labeling advantages from the kids' point of view were entirely different. For some kids, verbal language is more potent than graphic signs in knowing where places are. Labeling was, however, most often done in conjunction with a graphic symbol expressing identity in three ways: place, its name, and its location relative to other places.

In addition we utilized a place-name roster, which contained the names of places in each city grouped according to their point, line, or area categorizations. For example, Piccadilly Circus is a point name, the Strand a line name, and Soho an area name. In practice the mappers were encouraged to work with the roster as a primer, a memory jog, scanning it back and forth, visualizing and remembering places and routes as they worked out from the center of the map. That is, we were not concerned so much with their ability to remember places through names, but more with their ability to locate such names as places in space relative to one another.

Rules for the overlay sheets. A final, tenth rule pertained to the overlay sheets: "Put all additional information on the overlays." These were using multiple sheets of tracing paper. On the first overlay the kids were asked simply to outline and label *areas* of the simplest and broadest sorts: Downtown, East Side, Main South, and so on. For four additional overlays, they were introduced to other more descriptive symbols, which were of four types: point, line, area, and attribute. These symbols enabled the kids to clothe the skeleton. In this manner, their first point could now be identified as a building, rotary, plaza, hotel, school or what have you. All *points* would thus be described on the second overlay. On the third sheet of tracing paper went *line symbols*, allowing the student to discriminate among superhighways, paths, rivers, railroad tracks, and the like. A fourth sheet was reserved for *descriptions of* *areas*, whether consisting of right-angle grids of streets or sinuous suburban tangles, whether industrial, residential, commercial, or park, and so on. Finally, a fifth overlay was left for the *attribute symbols*. These enabled a kid to tell us how he *felt* about any point, line, or area. He could *describe* its character (hot, cold, crowded, empty, etc.), *evaluate* it, and even note the occurrence of "personal" experiences and describe them in similar terms.

A composite map would, in principle, consist of six layers, one on top of the other: (1) the skeleton of points and lines, (2) the outlines and labels of areas, (3) point descriptors, (4) line descriptors, (5) area descriptors, and (6) attribute designations. In practice few kids employed all six layers, and some combined all the descriptors on a single overlay; but few kids violated the sanctity of the skeleton or the basic area overlay. Thus, the typical map consisted of three or four overlays.

The symbol system. Two basic criteria were used in the design of the symbolic language. The first was the ease with which the symbol could be drawn. Symbols that we expected to be used a lot were made more schematic than symbols less likely to be frequently employed. The second was that the symbols be easy to recognize and easy to remember. These two criteria were frequently at odds. The symbols and their meanings were contained in a primer-sized book that the students carried about with them and used when mapping.

To develop symbols easy to recognize and remember, we used *pictographic symbols*. Thus, a bench stood for a bench, a flower for a flower, a crumbling pillar for ruins, and so on (see Figure 1). We also used *pictographic synecdoche*; thus, an olive with a toothpick in it stood for bars, the bank teller's grill for banks, and a table for an outdoor cafe. These symbols made more or less immediate sense to our students and were relevant with respect to the environments being mapped, but were somewhat laborious to draw. Symbols more likely to be frequently employed were *simplified*. Thus, a simple square stood for a single, freestanding private home. This square was manipulated to derive a government building, a hotel, or a skyscraper, and was initialed to form various levels of schools. A similar *series of changes* was hung on an

arrow entering a variety of basic shapes to represent transportation terminals, as a bus station and a dock (Figure 1, bottom). The symbols selected may or may not be the best possible, but what was important was that in our presentation of these symbols to our mappers we *explained* what the symbol was meant to be or how it was meant to function.

Following the same general procedure, we developed *line symbols* (see Figure 2). Some of these were very frequently used and hence simple in the extreme, being essentially variations on a line. Others were more interesting. Wherever possible we encouraged the formation of line symbols out of *rows of point symbols*. Thus, a row of bars (a line of toothpicked olives) or a street lined with showrooms (a series of boxes with "S" inside) were simple repetitions of point symbols. These point aggregations ultimately functioned as environmental attributive symbols. In this manner, if a street gave a sense of being heavy with bars, the bar symbols would march along the street even though the street might actually involve a mix of activities. The kids could express the overall *feeling* of a street rather than describing it exactly. There were also *standard symbols* to represent linear phenomena (Figure 2, bottom).

This type of aggregate symbol was carried over strongly into the *area symbols* (Figure 3). It allowed the kids to speak about an area or part of the city that might have a complex mix of elements. An industrial area contains bars and restaurants and wholesale and retail establishments tucked in here and there. It would be impossible to designate an area as industrial if the kids felt compelled to represent in detail what was actually on the streets in question. Thus the area symbols drew heavily on the point and line symbols in *unspecified mixes*. For example, an industrial area symbol could include the warehouse symbol (a forklift truck), the manufacturing symbol (a hammer), and the factory symbol (a belching smokestack), along with an area street pattern symbol (a checkerboard grid if the street pattern were predominantly right-angle grid, or a mare's nest of curving lines if that were the general impression). In this manner, symbols for entertainment districts, dock areas, commercial centers, areas dominated by offices, parks, and so on were constructed (see

BENCHES - this is a simple drawing of a bench

FLOWERS - this is a flower for flowers

RUINS - this symbol is a crumbing pillar

BAR - this is symbolized by an olive with a toothpick in it

BANK - this is symbolized by the grill at the bank teller's window

OUTDOOR CAFE - this is a simple drawing of a typical cafe table

HOME - the single, freestanding private home is symbolized as a simple empty square. Joined together you have ROW HOUSES.

HOTEL - the basic home symbol (a square) with an X drawn larger than the square over it

SKYSCRAPER - this is a rectangle with a blackened arrow pointing away from the street

SCHOOL - a school is the basic home symbol (the square) with an identifying letter inside the square

ELEMENTARY SCHOOL

HIGH SCHOOL - including Junior High

UNIVERSITY - including colleges

TRANSPORTATION
TERMINAL - the basic symbol is an arrow entering and stopping in a simple geometric shape. The shape depends on the type of transportation.

BUS - a circle

BOAT - a boat shape

TRAIN - a square

SUBWAY - a square

AIR - a triangle

Ⅲ Ⅲ Ⅲ	BANKS
🙶 🙶 🙶 🙶	BARS
🍸 🍸 🍸	OUTDOOR CAFES

┼┼┼┼┼┼	STREETCAR - this is surface rail transportation which is not a railroad. It is for SUBWAY tracks when they surface.
┥ ┥ ┥ ┥	SUBWAY - this is the streetcar symbol broken to indicate that it's underground

FIGURE 2
Examples of linear symbols composed of multiple point symbols.

Figure 3). Following our lead, areas of other mixes of functional activities could also be freely constructed and were so constructed by the mappers.

Attributive symbols followed suit (see Figure 4). These symbols are entirely different from the preceding point, line, and area symbols for two basic reasons: (1) these are not symbols of places themselves, but of feelings one might have about places, in other words, attributes of places, and (2) these symbols were to be used to modify other symbols, and to be used in as many combinations as possible or necessary. Thus a mapper could use one, three, or even ten different symbols to modify just one area, square, or street. Furthermore, the attribute symbols could be used to modify each other as well. Thus, one may use the noise symbol and then modify that to indicate whether one liked the noise or not. Sometimes noise is appreciated; at other times it's a drag. With Environmental A you can say which! Thus, danger, (a skull and crossbones), clean (a broom), dirty (a nasty six-legged creature), litter (an overflowing garbage bin), really love it (cupid's arrow), feeling of sadness (tears from an eye), and others used simple pictograms. Other notations relied heavily on commonly used symbols in less usual contexts:

FIGURE 1 (*left*)
Examples of point symbols in Environmental A.

ancient (÷), modern, up to the minute (X), negative feeling (–), positive feeling (+), upper class (£), run of the mill ($), cheap (¢), and Wow (!). A comma (,) was used to express a pause and was defined in the dictionary as follows: "This place was the pause that refreshed. It might be quiet in a crazy city, the personal touch in a mechanized world; anyway, use a comma to modify other symbols, or put them alone anywhere." Parentheses ( ) referred to "Whenever you have had a personal experience and don't want to explain, just put the place in parentheses. Somebody was nice to you, whistled at you, spit at you. Don't explain, just put it in parentheses." Using these symbols the kids could modify any other. The Ritz Hotel might be symbolized as a dot on the skeleton, a hotel on the point overlay, and decorated with a British pound sign on the attributive overlay to indicate its classy character, the whole enclosed in parentheses, and so on.

The students were encouraged constantly to expand the vocabulary and to modify the rules. There were blank pages left in their dictionary (each student carried a small booklet containing the entire language) in each category for just this purpose. One kid suggested using a miniature Oscar to represent movie theaters; another employed a strip of bacon as symbolic of the London striptease joints. Still another girl wrote the entire history of her experiences in

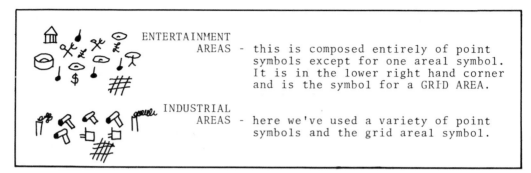

FIGURE 3
Examples of complex areal symbols composed of individual symbols.

Europe using a patois composed of English and Environmental A. The most significant aspect of Environmental A was that it made mapping a full-range communication system. The kids could tell us about not only the shape and directions of the city streets, but whether they were wide, pleasant, dirty, clean, lined with strip joints, showrooms, whether they were crumbly old or marvy modern, and whether they liked the place or not. In this sense, the vocabulary also worked as an incentive to complete the skeletal structure of the metropolis by overlaying it with personal meaning and value. This may be its most significant role.

It is vital to remember that Environmental A is more than a collection of symbols. It is also a set of rules for ordering them on a map surface. Commenting on the rules themselves, Lynch[3] noted that ". . . the technique is exactly that of the surveyor developing ground control: establish a station point, traverse to another, make a loop or network. It is a powerful way of controling spatial data . . . !" The approach was not developed, as it happens, by analogy with surveying, but through a searching examination of our own difficulties in drawing maps, but Lynch is substantially correct: the method definitely (as we shall show) produces sketch maps of high veridicality and detail because it provides a medium for coming to grips with environmental experience. The combination of rule system with vocabulary results in a mapping language that allows the sketcher to communicate

his experience of the world, not his inability to draw a map.

Comparative Analysis of Group L (Environmental A) and Group K (Instructionless) Sketch Maps

Although it is pleasant to be able to assert that a mapping language, and Environmental A in particular, is bound to improve communication between mapper and researcher, it is something else to go about demonstrating this empirically.

Environmental A was taught through the mail to 34 American teen-agers several weeks prior to their departure for Europe. The curriculum was mailed out in two packages, both of which were returned to us prior to actual departure. First the students were encouraged to map their home environment without instructions. The resultant freely drawn sketch map was then analyzed by the student through a set of questions designed to bring as many of the problems of mapping as possible into the foreground (with special emphasis on the issue of scale). Then the student was taught the various stages of the mapping system. This practice led to the creation of at least five maps: one produced without instructions or other aids and four assisted by the language.

On the basis of the returns (see Wood, 1973b, pp. 120–168), we could see that most of our students had made a good start on the language and could assert definitely that it had improved the mapping of their hometown environments.

☠	DANGER -	when you feel hostility in the air, use a skull and crossbones
🖌	CLEAN -	it sparkled it was so clean. Use a broom.
🐀	DIRTY -	the place was so dirty you didn't want to touch anything. Use a rat.
🗑	LITTER -	litter was everywhere. Use an overflowing trash basket.
💘	LOVED IT -	you fell in love with the Plaza San Marcos, all the pigeons and color. Use a smitten heart.
👁	SADNESS -	the scene overwhelms you with a sad feeling in the pit of your stomach. Use a crying eye.

FIGURE 4
Examples of attributive (value) symbols.

These kids were obviously different from other groups of teen-age students touring Europe for the first time. There was, however, a similar sociocultural group of 43 students about to take the identical tour at the same time in another bus. The group familiar with Environmental A was called group L; while the group unacquainted with the language was group K.

On their third day in London the students in group L drew their first map of the city. On their fifth day in London both groups L and K answered a set of questions designed to compare their experiences in the city to that point. Immediately following the administration of this questionnaire, both groups were asked to map London, group L according to the instructions of Environmental A, and group K in the best-approved instructionless mapping style. This process was repeated in an identical fashion in Rome. Group L had, of course, produced another map of London and maps of Innsbruck and Venice in between, but that was the only fundamental difference between the experiences of the two groups prior to their arrival in Rome.

Results. In both London and Rome, groups L and K generated *identical place-name lists* in response to the question, "Where have you been, and what have you done in London?" Better than 12.5 percent of group K mentioned 17 points, 4 lines, and 2 areas, and better than 12.5 percent of group L mentioned 16 points, 4 lines, and 1 area. The similarity was more than quantitative. Nine of these items were mentioned by both groups with the same frequency (Tower of London, Tower Bridge, the Thames, Parliament, Big Ben, Buckingham Palace, Hyde Park, the University of London, and the British Museum); another six items were only one frequency interval apart (12.5 percent; Westminster Abbey, Trafalgar Square, Piccadilly Circus, Oxford Circus, Carnaby Street, and Madame Tussaud's). A few of the items not mentioned in common *were* the result of group-unique experiences, such as the fact that they lived in different (though proximate) dorms. When the results of a content analysis of these lists were plotted as a function of their frequency on a map of London, the resemblance is thoroughly convincing. Even when the total data were taken into account (i.e., those places mentioned by less than 12.5 percent of the populations), the results were startlingly similar, especially when it is remembered that group K was a third again as large as group L. Group L generated 66 different places or things in London (items), listing them a total of 347 times (instances); group K generated 81 items for 562 instances. Thus, when asked to verbally report on their experiences, the two groups responded in a similar fashion. Nor is there anything the least bit astonishing about these lists: they represent the quintessential introductory tourist's London. Both groups took the same tours at the same time.

But this similarity did not extend to the maps sketched by the two groups. To heighten the effect of the comparison, we shall compare the maps drawn by group L on their third day in London with those drawn by group K on their fifth day in the city. That is, the group K maps were created by students with two additional tour days. Both sets of maps were subjected to a content analysis with the following results: group L generated 176 items for 839 instances, while group K generated 128 items for 709 instances. Thus, the group smaller by one third, the group that generated less items and instances verbally, came up with nearly one third again as many items with two days less experience in the city. That's pretty remarkable.

The dissimilarity is even more marked when we look at the breakdown of these items into points, lines, and areas. Group K actually did generate more points than group L, 89 items compared to 84, for 594 instances compared to 455. Group K did not, however, generate more lines, coming up with 29 (86 instances) to group L's 50 (211 instances). And when it comes to areas, the differences are ludicrous. Group K mapped only 10 areas (for 29 instances); Group L mapped 42 areas (for 173 instances).

The qualitative distinctions are perhaps even more astonishing. First, the influence of the place-name roster does not seem to be a factor. Consider the areas mapped by the two groups. Of the 42 areas mapped by group L, 20 were included in the roster, while 22 were not; of the 10 items mapped by group K, which did not have the roster to work with, 9 were included on the list while only 1 was not. That is, group L not only mapped twice as many items not included on the roster as group K did altogether, but it mapped fewer items on the list than off; Group K mapped nine times as many places on the list as off.

When the results of this sketch map content analysis were mapped according to frequency on a standard map of London, another difference became apparent:

the items mapped by group L blanket the whole of London, show a great deal of connectivity, and result in an integrated and detailed map of the city; the items mapped by group K cluster almost exclusively around their dormitory with a mere 8 items scattered fragmentedly elsewhere in the city (as compared with 41 items covering the city for group L). The group K maps failed to reflect their knowledge of London as reported verbally; the group L maps faithfully reflected and expanded upon their knowledge of the city as reported verbally.

We divided the space of London into three envelopes. The smallest envelope included the dorms of the two groups (they were 50 yards apart) and anything visible from them, the street, the ends of the block, a couple of intersections, a few shops, and so on. The next envelope included everything within one third of a mile in any direction. The largest envelope included all London beyond one third of a mile's distance. The space of the inner envelope was visible from the doors of the dorms; the middle envelope was within 5 or 6 minutes' walking distance; the outer envelope got into bus and subway distances. Using these envelopes as a criterion, both groups performed similarly on their place-name lists, but not on their sketch maps. Of the points sketched by group K, 10 percent fell within the smallest envelope, compared with only 5 percent of the points sketched by group L. Of the lines sketched by group K, 10 percent fell within this same inner envelope, compared with only 4 percent for group L. Turning to the next envelope, we discovered that 69 percent of the points and 41 percent of the lines sketched by group K fell within one third of a mile of the dorm, whereas only 23 percent of the points and 20 percent of the lines sketched by group L fell here. When we turned to the outer envelope, everything beyond a one-third-mile radius, we discovered that 77 percent of the points mapped by group L fell outside this radius compared with a meager 31 percent for group K. These results are conclusive: the maps of group K are dormicentric, while the maps of group L are oriented to London as a whole. Of the points group K named on its verbal lists, 65 percent were beyond the one-third-mile radius; of the points group K mapped, only 31 percent are out there. But of the points group L listed, 78 percent were beyond this limit, while 77 percent of those mapped were out there. Group L's maps *did reflect* the state of its verbal knowledge about London, but group K's maps did not.

There was only one real variable at play in the comparison and that was Environmental A. Group L had it, and group K did not. The language allowed group L *to communicate its experience and knowledge in map form.* Lacking instruction in a mapping tongue, group K could only babble.

Graphically illiterate, there is no way for group K or for most subjects in most cognitive mapping studies to communicate what they know, not only of the connective structures of which they must have at some level been aware in order to navigate in the city in question, but of anything more elemental or symbolic at all. Before a sketch mapper may be expected to communicate something to a researcher, he or she must be taught a language that both can understand. Any work investigating reported cognition of large-scale environments employing sketch maps as primary data must take this into account.

And if, in the process of learning this mapping language, the sketch-mapper's outlook on the world is reconstructed, so much the better. We would much sooner converse with a reconstructed outlook than not converse at all.

NOTES

1. Kevin Lynch, personal communication, 1974.
2. Hugh Prince, personal communication, 1973.
3. Kevin Lynch, personal communication, 1974.

LINGUISTIC AND SEMANTIC CONSTRUCTS

33

Stephen Golant
Department of Geography
  University of Washington[2]

Ian Burton
Department of Geography
  University of Toronto

A SEMANTIC DIFFERENTIAL EXPERIMENT IN THE INTERPRETATION AND GROUPING OF ENVIRONMENTAL HAZARDS[1]

Previous research in human response to natural hazards has relied heavily on the use of such common nouns as "floods," "earthquakes," and "droughts," while choosing to disregard the existence of known variations in the individual interpretation of such concepts (Burton and Kates, 1964). Questions and experiments have focused on individual perceptions of a hazard or on specific hazard dimensions such as magnitude and frequency (Burton et al., 1968; Saarinen, 1966), without knowing in what ways and in what degree entire concepts may have different meanings to different respondents. It is recognized that improved understanding and capacity to predict human behavior in hazard situations depends in part on devoting more research effort to exploring the preconceived ideas and feelings held by individuals concerning potential hazards (Golant, 1969). Human beings continually distinguish between, and estimate the degree to which, environmental situations are beneficial or harmless or threatening. The evaluation is a function of the stimuli received from the environment and of the manner in which these stimuli are processed or interpreted. As Lazarus (1966) expresses it:

The appraisal of threat is not a single perception of the elements of the situation, but a judgment, an inference in which the data are assimilated to a constellation of ideas and expectations (p. 44).

By "meaning" of hazard, then, we wish merely to refer to the significance of the hazard to the human organism before he is bombarded with environmental stimuli depicting the hazard. We employ a standard psychometric technique (semantic differential) by which the meaning of twelve hazard situations can be derived for a sample group of subjects. We are not concerned at this time whether this "meaning" has been acquired as a result of actual previous experience with a hazard or merely from contact with television documentaries, books, or any other communications media. We are interested in those preconceived ideas, feelings, or expectations held by the individual with regard to a particular hazard, no matter how they were formed. We wish to focus, therefore, on one aspect of the cognitive process of appraisal, one which the literature suggests to be an important if not the most crucial factor in understanding individual response to hazard situations (Burton et al., 1969;

Drayer, 1957; Hudson, 1954; Lazarus, 1966; Pervin, 1963; Williams, 1957).

The Semantic Differential

The semantic differential is a psychological scaling technique that makes use of linguistic encoding as an index of meaning. It uses a combination of association and scaling procedures in measuring the psychological meaning of concepts—in our study, hazard. Osgood, Suci, and Tannenbaum (1957), the principal innovators of the technique, describe the basic ingredients of the method as follows:

We provide the subject with a concept to be differentiated and a set of bipolar adjectival scales against which to do it, his only task being to indicate, for each item (pairing of a concept to a scale), the direction of his association and its intensity on a seven-step scale. The crux of the method, of course, lies in selecting the sample of descriptive polar terms. Ideally, the sample should be as representative as possible of all the ways in which meaningful judgments can vary, and yet be small enough in size to be efficient in practice (p. 20).[3]

Figure 1 provides an example of our procedure. The subject was asked to place an *X* in one of the seven space locations.

The connotative meanings of concepts, therefore, can be thought of as representing points in what Osgood et al. called "semantic space, a region of some unknown dimensionality and Euclidian in character" (p. 25).

Each semantic scale, defined by a pair of polar (opposite in meaning) adjectives, is assumed to represent a straight line

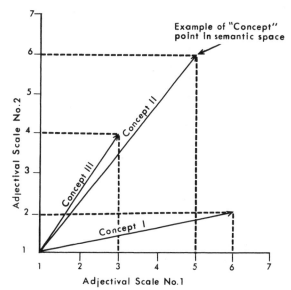

FIGURE 2
Graphical expression of a semantic space.

function that passes through the origin of this space, and a sample of such scales then represents a multidimensional space. The larger or more representative the sample, the better defined is the space as a whole (p. 25)

Figure 2 offers a very simplified graphical expression of a semantic space displaying how three different concepts have been differentiated by two bipolar adjectival scales (two-dimensional space). It is clear, then, that ". . . the larger the number of scales and the more representative the selection of these scales, the more validly does this point in the space represent the operational meaning of the concept. . . . Difference in meaning between two concepts is then merely a function of the differences in their respective allocations within the same space" (Osgood et al., 1957, p. 26).

In the development of the semantic differential technique, Osgood et al. went on and postulated on the basis of empirical experimentation that the semantic space could be efficiently defined by three orthogonal dimensions or axes of the space, which he referred to as the *activity, evaluative,* and *potency* dimensions (pp. 31-75).

TORNADO

FIGURE 1
Example of the semantic differential testing procedure for the cognitive interpretation of "tornado."

TABLE 1
List of Concepts

1. Earthquake
2. Tornado
3. Snowstorm
4. Flood
5. Housefire
6. Building collapse
7. Boat accident
8. Auto accident
9. Air pollution
10. Water pollution
11. Riot
12. Epidemic

TABLE 2
Bipolar Adjectival Scales

1. Passive	Active
2. Orderly	Chaotic
3. Natural	Unnatural
4. Stable	Unstable
5. Widespread	Localized
6. Peaceful	Ferocious
7. Fair	Unfair
8. Dissonant	Harmonious
9. Slow	Fast
10. Strong	Weak
11. Private	Public
12. Important	Unimportant
13. Relaxed	Tense
14. Erratic	Periodic
15. Determinate	Fortuitous
16. Yielding	Tenacious
17. Artificial	Natural
18. Controllable	Uncontrollable
19. Pleasant	Unpleasant
20. Light	Heavy
21. Constrained	Free

Elements of the Semantic Differential Test

Concepts. The 12 concepts used for the test are listed in Table 1. They comprise a heterogeneous group of hazards of varying genesis, scale, frequency, and magnitude of event and consequence.

Scales. In Table 2 are the 21 bipolar adjectival scales that were employed in the analysis representing prominent scales of the evaluative, potency, and activity dimensions as defined by Osgood and his associates. In addition, several other scales were selected that had not been represented highly on any of these three initial dimensions because they appeared to represent appropriately the character of the twelve concepts.

Subjects. The semantic differential test was given during July and August 1968 to 58 subjects, primarily university summer extension students. This sample was treated as a homogeneous group with no attempt made to examine subgroups of subjects based on either psychological or socioeconomic traits.

Treatment of data. Every subject judged each concept against the 21 adjective scales, each scale thereby being responded to 696 times. In the actual test schedule given to each respondent, both the scales and the concepts were randomly arranged so that no apparent order was discernible. Figure 3 gives a schematic presentation of the data analysis. The first stage was concerned with summarizing how each concept was described in terms of the adjectival scales and in examining how the direction and intensity of response varied from one concept to another. The analysis involved the construction of a 21 by 21 matrix of adjectival scale means, which were classified by intensity and direction of polarity. The second stage of the study consisted of a statistical analysis of (1) the interrelationships between the various adjectival scales, and (2) the interrelationships between the 12 concepts. In both instances the overall purpose was to simplify and discern the structure of the interrelationships or more precisely to delineate patterns or dimensions of human meanings toward the concept of the hazard.

Statistical Analysis

Two principal statistical methods were employed to analyze the data. the interrelationships among the concepts and the scales were measured by the coefficient of correlation. Second, factor analysis (principal components solution) was employed to explain these interrelationships in terms of distinct patterns or dimensions. A 12 by 12 and a 21 by 21 correlation matrix were constructed, respectively, for the sets of concepts and scales. If subscripts i and k refer to the scales, j and e to the concepts, and v to the subjects, the correlation matrices were found by computing as follows:

$$\frac{\displaystyle\sum_{j=1}^{12} \sum_{v=1}^{58} (x_{ijv} - \bar{x}_{i\,.\,.}) \cdot (x_{kjv} - \bar{x}_{k\,.\,.})}{\left[\displaystyle\sum_{j=1}^{12} \sum_{v=1}^{58} (x_{ijv} - \bar{x}_{i\,.\,.})^2 \cdot \sum_{j=1}^{12} \sum_{v=1}^{58} (x_{kjv} - \bar{x}_{k\,.\,.})^2 \right]^{\frac{1}{2}}} = [R_{ik}] \; 21 \times 21 \quad \text{for all } i, k$$

and

$$\frac{\displaystyle\sum_{i=1}^{21} \sum_{v=1}^{58} (x_{ijv} - \bar{x}_{.j.}) \cdot (x_{iev} - \bar{x}_{.e.})}{\left[\displaystyle\sum_{i=1}^{21} \sum_{v=1}^{58} (x_{ijv} - \bar{x}_{.j.})^2 \cdot \sum_{i=1}^{21} \sum_{v=1}^{58} (x_{iev} - \bar{x}_{.e.})^2 \right]^{\frac{1}{2}}} = [R_{je}] \; 12 \times 12 \quad \text{for all } j, e$$

The factor analysis technique has been discussed in several sources and will not be reviewed here. For a description and evaluation of the technique, see Cattell (1965a, 1965b), which also list the principal references. Following the computation of the concept and scale factor matrices (derived initially from the two simple correlation matrices), three concept factors and four scale factors, respectively, were orthogonally rotated to a normal varimax position, approximating the notion of "simple structure."[4]

Concept-Scale Polarity Matrix

By totaling the scores given for each scale and each concept for every subject (i.e., summing over the 58 subjects) and dividing each total by the number of subjects, a 21 by 12 matrix of means was constructed.

The means ranged from 1.1 to 6.6 and were analyzed on the basis of the five categories shown below:

The resulting matrix is presented in Table 3. From it, relationships can be discerned about concepts, scales, or concepts and scales. Reading along the rows reveals the various ways to which any particular adjectival scale was responded; reading down the columns, the meanings given to the concepts; and, of course across and down, that is, looking at any one cell, reveals the relationship between the concept and scale.

"Earthquake," for example, can be and was described as active, chaotic, moderately natural, unstable, moderately localized, ferocious, moderately unfair, dissonant, fast, strong, public, important, tense, moderately tenacious, natural, uncontrollable, unpleasant, moderately heavy, and free. In addition, the average respondent has neutral feelings as to whether an earthquake is erratic versus periodic, or determinate versus fortuitous. The word picture of "air pollution" is distinctively different and is de-

General Form		Adjectival Scale Example	
1.0–2.1	Polar (+) or (−)	1.0–2.1	Passive
2.2–3.3	Moderately polar (+) or (−)	2.2–3.3	Moderately passive
3.4–4.6	Neutral	3.4–4.6	Neutral
4.7–5.8	Moderately polar (−) or (+)	4.7–5.8	Moderately active
5.9–7.0	Polar (−) or (+)	5.9–7.0	Active

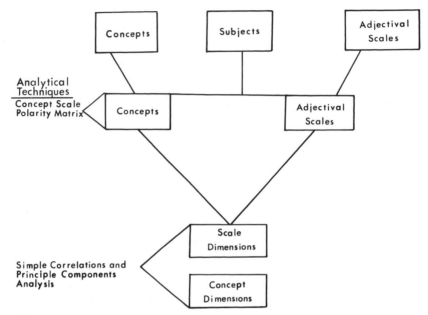

FIGURE 3
Schematic presentation of data analysis.

scribed as moderately active, moderately unnatural, moderately unstable, moderately widespread, moderately ferocious, moderately unfair, moderately dissonant, moderately strong, public, important, moderately tense, moderately determinate, moderately tenacious, artificial, moderately controllable, unpleasant, and moderately heavy. The average subject has neutral feelings as to whether air pollution is orderly versus chaotic, slow versus fast, erratic versus periodic, and constrained versus free.

These two examples provide an illustration of the average "meaning" these hazards have for the subject in terms of the selected adjectival scales. The selection of the scales, of course, as was emphasized earlier is the crucial operation. The "meaning" of a hazard is restricted by the nature of the adjectival scales selected. This is probably the most useful aspect of the semantic differential, for it allows the researcher to "filter out" that "meaning" of the hazard possessed by a group of subjects that has the greatest utility in reference to the particular hazard situation or situations being studied—that is, the

"meaning" which will provide the greatest understanding as to how the group of subjects are likely to appraise a hazard situation in which they find themselves. The next section will examine the adjectival scales used in this study which attempt to discern any similarities in their response pattern that might be useful in determining the selection procedure.

Table 4, describing the intensity of response to each of the hazards, summarizes a major portion of the information presented in the previous matrix. The frequency of polar, moderately polar, and neutral adjectival scales has been recorded and ranked. Of the 21 adjectival scales describing "tornado," 16 were polar in form with only 2 moderately polar and 2 neutral responses. The concept "snowstorm," on the other hand was described by 6 polar adjectival scales, 8 moderately polar, and 7 neutral adjectival scales. "Water pollution" presents yet another pattern of response with 4 polar, 14 moderately polar, and 3 neutral adjectival scales. Table 4, used to identify intensity of meaning, with the concept-scale matrix to supply more detailed information including direc-

TABLE 3
Concept-Scale Polarity Matrix[a]

Scales	Earth-quake	Tornado	Snow-storm	Flood	House-fire	Building Collapse	Boat Acci-dent	Auto Acci-dent	Air Pollu-tion	Water Pollu-tion	Riot	Epi-demic
Passive (PA)–active (AC)	AC	AC	AC	AC	AC	AC	mAC	AC	mAC	mAC	AC	mAC
Orderly (OR)–chaotic (CH)	CH	CH	N	CH	CH	CH	CH	CH	N	mCH	CH	mCH
Natural (NA)–unnatural (UN)	mNA	NA	NA	mNA	mUN	mUN	mUN	mUN	mUN	mUN	mUN	N
Stable (ST)–unstable (US)	US	US	mUS	mUS	mUS	mUS	mUS	mUS	mUS	mUS	US	mUS
Widespread (WI)–localized (LO)	mLO	LO	N	N	LO	mLO	mLO	N	mWI	mWI	mLO	N
Peaceful (PE)–ferocious (FE)	FE	FE	mFE	FE	FE	mFE	mFE	mFE	mFE	mFE	FE	mFE
Fair (FA)–unfair (UF)	mUF	N	mFA	N	mUF	mUF	N	mUF	mUF	mUF	mUF	mUF
Dissonant (DI)–harmonious (HA)	DI	mDI	N	mDI	mDI	mDI	DI	DI	mDI	mDI	DI	mDI
Slow (SL)–fast (FS)	FS	FS	mFS	mFS	FS	FS	mFS	FS	N	N	FS	mFS
Strong (SG)–weak (WE)	SG	SG	mSG	SG	mSG	mSG	mSG	mSG	mSG	mSG	mSG	mSG
Private (PV)–public (PU)	PU	PU	PU	PU	N	mPU	N	mPU	PU	PU	PU	PU
Important (IM)–unimportant (UM)	IM	IM	mIM	IM	IM	IM	IM	IM	IM	IM	IM	IM
Relaxed (RE)–tense (TE)	TE	TE	N	TE	TE	TE	TE	TE	mTE	mTE	TE	TE
Erratic (ER)–periodic (PR)	N	N	mPR	mER	mER	mER	N	N	N	N	mER	N
Determinate (DE)–fortuitous (FO)	N	N	N	N	N	N	N	N	mDE	mDE	mDE	N
Yielding (YI)–tenacious (TN)	mTN	mTN	N	mTN	mTN	N	N	mTN	mTN	mTN	mTN	mTN
Artificial (AR)–natural (NT)	NT	NT	NT	mNT	mAR	N	mAR	mAR	AR	mAR	mAR	mNT
Controllable (CO)–uncontrollable (UC)	UC	UC	UC	N	mCO	N	mCO	mCO	mCO	CO	N	mCO
Pleasant (PL)–unpleasant (UP)	UP	UP	N	UP	UP	UP	UP	UP	UP	UP	UP	UP
Light (LI)–heavy (HE)	mHE	HE	mHE	mHE	mHE	mHE	N	mHE	mHE	mHE	mHE	mHE
Constrained (CS)–free (FR)	FR	FR	FR	FR	N	N	N	N	N	N	N	N

[a]m, moderately; N, neutral.

tion of meaning, together give a very revealing cross-sectional view of the concept. There is obviously considerable similarity in the average meaning given by the subject to several of these concepts. These similarities will be analyzed statistically when "dimensions" are considered.

The Scale Dimensions

The four varimax rotated factors explained only 45.8 percent of the variance of the correlation matrix, but the factor structure that did emerge revealed some distinctive response patterns (see Table 5).

TABLE 4
Analysis of Intensity of "Meaning"

Concept	Frequency of Adjective Response					
	Polar		Moderately Polar		Neutral	
	No.	Rank	No.	Rank	No.	Rank
Tornado	16	1	2	12	3	9
Earthquake	14	2	5	11	2	11.5
Riot	10	3	9	7.5	2	11.5
Flood	9	4	8	9.5	4	6
Housefire	8	5	10	5	3	9
Auto accident	7	6	10	5	4	6
Building collapse	6	7.5	10	5	5	3.5
Snowstorm	6	7.5	8	9.5	7	1.5
Boat accident	5	9	9	7.5	7	1.5
Air pollution	4	11	13	2	4	6
Water pollution	4	11	14	1	3	9
Epidemic	4	11	12	3	5	3.5

It is always difficult to identify "factors," and in this type of analysis there is an even greater difficulty, if not danger of error, because there is the possibility that the researcher will provide a subjectively biased interpretation of what the responses "mean" when identifying factors. Nevertheless, while some may disagree with the labels placed on these factors, it is likely they will agree that there is an internal consistency in each group of adjectival scales that has been defined.

The first factor, explaining the largest variance (18.0 percent), has been identified as *stability* because it contains a predominance of adjectival scales depicting various states of equilibrium or deviations from some "normal" condition. We interpret these scales as representing that part of the "meaning" of the hazard related to its potential impact or effect, describing as they do levels of confusion, activity, discord, and unpleasantness.

Factor II has been identified as *controllability*, including adjectival scales that appear to describe the natural, uncontrollable-unnatural, controllable dichotomy of hazard genesis.

Factor III has been labeled *magnitude* because virtually all its adjectival scales with the exception of "determinate-fortuitous" (which had, however, a rather low factor loading) suggest the meanings of magnitude, strength, or seriousness. In an aspatial sense, for example, are the scales light-heavy, important-unimportant, strong-weak, and yielding-tenacious. The adjectival pairs of widespread-localized and private-public on the other hand suggest magnitude or extent in a spatial sense.

Factor IV has been termed *expectancy* because it appears to suggest a "meaning" depicting the likelihood of a potential hazard occurring or, more correctly, its regularity of occurrence. Perhaps we are reading in too much here; perhaps other adjectival scales would be more appropriate to suggest this aspect of hazard meaning.

Each of these dimensions, it is suggested, describes one aspect of what is meant by "meaning" of a hazard to a subject.[5] There are undoubtedly others, and their formation and application should depend on the kind of information required about the subjects' preconceived ideas and evaluations of the potential hazard.

The Concept Dimensions

Care must be taken in interpreting similarities between concepts as revealed by Table 4. The imposing

TABLE 5
Rotated Factor Analysis of Scales

Scale	Loading	Osgood et al. Dimensions
Factor I: Stability		
Passive–active	–.516	Activity
Orderly–chaotic	+.627	Evaluative
Stable–unstable	+.471	Unassigned
Peaceful–ferocious	–.757	Potency
Dissonant–harmonious	+.543	Evaluative
Slow–Fast	–.629	Activity
Relaxed–tense	–.717	Evaluative
Pleasant–unpleasant	+.489	Evaluative
Factor II: Controllability		
Natural–unnatural	+.832	Unassigned
Fair–unfair	+.520	Evaluative
Artificial–natural	–.805	Unassigned
Controllable–uncontrollable	–.575	Unassigned
Factor III: Magnitude		
Widespread–localized	+.514	Unassigned
Strong–weak	+.460	Potency
Private–public	+.685	Unassigned
Important–unimportant	+.434	Evaluative
Determinate–fortuitous	–.372	Unassigned
Yielding–tenacious	+.442	Potency
Light–heavy	+.518	Potency
Factor IV: Expectancy		
Erratic–periodic	+.436	Unassigned
Free–constrained	+.667	Potency

Summary of Rotated Factor Structure

Factor Number	Identification	Eigen-value	Variance Explained %	No. of Loading Scales
1	Stability	3.79	18.0	8
2	Controllability	2.61	12.4	4
3	Magnitude	1.88	8.9	7
4	Expectancy	1.35	6.5	2
	Totals	9.63	45.8	21

of numerical boundaries defining the "polarity" of adjectival scales can create severe interpretation problems. The most important, perhaps, is that no distinction is made as to where in the frequency interval the response lies. While scores, for example, of 2.1 and 2.2 are placed in different categories, 2.2 and 3.3 are placed in the same category.[6] Statistical analysis employing simple correlation and factor analysis there-fore provides a more rigorous approach for determining concept similarity.

The three rotated factors explained 76.7 percent of the variance of the correlation matrix. Table 6 summarizes the factor structure of the concepts, with Figure 4 displaying the factor loading values of the 12 hazards on the initial two factors.

The first and largest "explaining" factor (34.3 per-

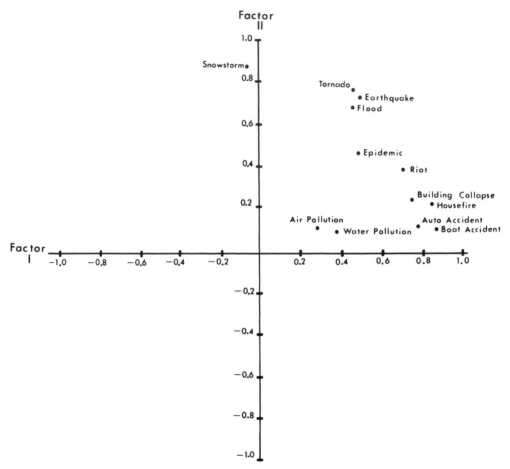

FIGURE 4
Loading values of concepts on two principal factors: man-made hazards and natural hazards.

cent of the variance), termed *man-made hazards*, includes those hazards with the highest frequency of occurrence, and which directly or indirectly originate from some form of human action and that specifically involve physical objects or structures. As a group, they assume a somewhat median position in terms of the intensity of feelings and response they evoke.

Factor II, labeled *natural hazards*, explaining 24.4 percent of the variance included, on the other hand, those hazards originating directly from the natural environment, the genesis of which people influence

little if at all. These hazards are far less frequent in occurrence and of much greater scale and magnitude. With the exception of the snowstorm concept, these hazards generated more extreme and intensive feelings and ranked high in the number of polar adjectival responses received.

Factor III, explaining 18 percent of the variance, included the hazards of air and water pollution. This factor has been labeled *quasi-natural hazards*, including hazards that have originated via an intimate and disrupting association between man and his

TABLE 6
Rotated Factor Analysis of Concepts

Concept	Factor Loading
Factor I: Man-Made Hazards	
Housefire	+.820
Building collapse	+.757
Boat accident	+.847
Auto accident	+.794
Riot	+.676
Epidemic	+.482
Factor II: Natural Hazards	
Earthquake	+.754
Tornado	+.767
Snowstorm	+.862
Flood	+.691
Factor III: Quasi-Natural Hazards	
Air-pollution	+.895
Water pollution	+.862

Summary of Rotated Factor Structure

Factor Number	Identification	Eigen-value	Variance Explained %	No. of Loading Concepts
1	Man-made hazards	4.11	34.3	6
2	Natural hazards	2.93	24.4	4
3	Quasi-natural hazards	2.16	18.0	2
	Totals	9.20	76.7	12

natural environment. These hazards generated few polar or neutral adjective responses, but a large number of "moderate" responses.

The factor analysis has revealed three distinctive groups of hazards defined by our subject sample in reference to a particular set of adjectival semantic scales. The semantic differential thus provides a very sensitive type of classification procedure, one that is based on the significance of the hazard to a subject and focused on a "meaning" of the hazard which is most useful and interpretive to a researcher attempting to understand and predict individual appraisal of a potential hazard.

Conclusions

We have emphasized the importance of the preconceived idea or expectation held by a subject ("meaning") with regard to a potential hazard as being a crucial factor in understanding or predicting human response. We have adopted a psychological technique by which "meaning" can be examined, and applied it to a group of 58 subjects. The results of the experiment suggested that the technique represents a very useful and efficient approach by which the "meaning" of a hazard can be derived. In addition, it was shown to be a very sensitive instrument that could be utilized for the classification of hazards. Subsequent research directions suggested by this study include: (1) additional experimentation with the semantic differential using various hazard types and other adjectival semantic scales; (2) further experimentation using different subgroups of subjects identified either by socioeconomic or psychological traits; (3) attainment of standardization in construction and application of technique; and (4) application of the results of this and similar studies to the larger problem of understanding and predicting human behavior in hazard and disaster situations.

NOTES

1. Reprinted from *Geographical Analysis*, April 1970, *2*, 120-134, with permission of the authors and publisher. Copyright © 1970 by the Ohio State University Press. All rights reserved. The authors with to acknowledge the helpful comments of John Sims of the University of Chicago on a draft of this paper. Mary Barker, then of the University of Toronto, assisted in the design of the S–D test. The research reported here was supported by a grant by the U.S. National Science Foundation.
2. Stephen Golant is now at the Departments of Geography and Behavioral Sciences, University of Chicago.
3. See Kerlinger (1964, Chap. 32) for a more recent discussion.
4. Helpful criticism and suggestions regarding the statistical analysis were provided by Ian Spence, Department of Psychology, and Geoffrey McDonald, Department of Geography, both Ph.D. candidates at the University of Toronto. All computer programming for this study was performed on the 360-65 computer system at the University of Toronto. See Dixon (1967, pp. 169-84) for a description of the factor analysis program.
5. It is noted that the dimensions of this analysis do not concur with the generally persistent evaluative, potency, and, activity dimensions of Osgood and others. There are two possible explanations—the concepts of this study are not mutually exclusive or independent of each other, and, second, as Krech and Crutchfield (1948, pp. 195-196) suggest, scale dimensions are not constant over all types of concepts and subjects.
6. In initially choosing these class intervals, however, we attempted to minimize this problem.

34

John Harrison
Geography Laboratory
  University of Sussex

Philip Sarre
Faculty of Social Sciences
  Open University

PERSONAL CONSTRUCT THEORY, THE REPERTORY GRID, AND ENVIRONMENTAL COGNITION[1]

One of the most unfortunate aspects of the study of environmental cognition to date has been the use of a wide range of ad hoc methods of eliciting environmental images. This essay emphasizes the advantages of using methods derived from explicit theory and tested in practice, and focuses on one such method, the repertory grid. The authors are by training geographers, and therefore write from a geographical perspective, but we believe that the issues raised in the paper are widely relevant to many of the disciplines within the social sciences currently involved in the study of environmental cognition.

Previously, we have argued on theoretical grounds in support of wider use of the repertory grid method, and have outlined the basics of its use (Harrison and Sarre, 1971). In the present paper we concentrate first on empirical results to illustrate, substantiate, and extend our case. These results demonstrate that the grid is a very sensitive method of measuring people's mental images of their environments, that, although it is difficult to establish absolute criteria by which methods may be judged, the repertory grid enjoys significant advantages over other methods of eliciting information about images, and that the data derived from the grid are suited to both interindividual comparison and aggregation over a number of individuals. It is also apparent, however, that the connections between images and behavior are as yet unspecified in real-life situations (although there is some laboratory evidence that *elicited* constructs are more closely related to behavior than are *supplied* constructs; see Stringer, 1973b).

A second extension of our previous argument is the consideration not just of the theory behind the grid method but also of the philosophy behind the theory (see also Section 2). Careful analysis of philosophical assumptions has become particularly pressing since geography, far from being reduced to a conformist monotony by the adoption of quantitative methods, seems to be growing in an unprecedented number of directions (Chorley, 1973). Probably the two most important paradigms of the moment are the "scientific" and "relevance" paradigms. We shall argue that the repertory grid has a role in both, and that personal construct theory may help behavioral geographers to clarify their own philosophical position, as well as throw light on the problems of the people who respond to their interviews.

Methodological Advantages of the Repertory Grid

Individual data. It is axiomatic in personal construct theory (Bannister and Fransella, 1971; see also Chapter 6) that the important ideas which an individual uses in regulating behavior are personal. Thus, the methods of gathering data that are derived from this theory, of which the repertory grid is the best known, are specifically designed to function at the individual level. This applies both in terms of the elements and of the constructs to be used. In a geographic context, elements are usually places, although other possibilities are not ruled out. The set of places to be considered is elicited by asking the respondent to name places to fit the interviewer's definition. These definitions can be general or specific. For example, a study of images of the city of Bath, England (Sarre, 1974) asked subjects to "name fifteen to twenty places in Bath which are important to you in your everyday life"; in another study subjects were asked to supply specific places to fit experimenter-provided definitions like "your local pub," "your children's school," "the best building in town which is threatened by redevelopment," or "the worst eyesore in the city." Although personal construct theory stresses the likelihood that places wil be idiosyncratically defined, practical uses of the grid have not usually differed greatly from more ad hoc approaches in treatment of individual places, except insofar as they elicit places from subjects where in other approaches the experimenter supplies them. Greater differences occur in the repertory grid's treatment of the ideas used to discriminate among places.

Personal construct theory assumes that the ideas used by individuals to discriminate among elements of the environment are idiosyncratic, unless there is firm evidence to believe otherwise. It names the ideas *constructs* to emphasize that ideas are put together by the person rather than existing independent of one another.

The repertory grid elicits constructs by asking the respondent to discriminate among the elements that have been elicited. The usual method is "triad sorting" whereby the respondent is asked to consider three elements at a time and to state an important way in which two are similar and the other different. This results in the definition of a difference in adjectival terms, and the interviewer then works with the respondent to ensure that the adjectives used are truly opposites (but see Chapter 6) and that they enclose a sufficient range of ideas to accommodate the elements under consideration. This may involve some redefinition, but once these criteria are satisfied, the adjective pairs are taken as *verbal definitions of personal constructs*. For example, one subject in the Bath study initially responded by saying that two of the three places were "Georgian" while the other was "modern." These adjectives seemed to be opposite but, bearing in mind that the set of elements used also included a public bath-house dating from the Roman period, they proved not to be sufficiently extreme. Once "Georgian" had been replaced by "old," it seemed more natural to take "new" as the opposite. It is worth noting that one problem of the repertory grid is that personal constructs are not always so clearly logical. Often they seem satisfactory to the respondent but not to the interviewer. As long as the interviewer is satisfied that the criteria of judgment have been made clear, he or she is obliged to accept the respondent's verdict because the intention of the method is to reveal how the *respondent* actually thinks and not to induce him to conform to the interviewer's standards.

Details of the elements and constructs elicited in the Bath study appear elsewhere (Sarre, 1973, 1974; Harrison and Sarre, 1974). Here we are concerned only with the methodological implications of the range of constructs elicited and the low degree of overlap between individuals. In this study, where the range was not limited in advance, the constructs ranged from quasi-objective descriptions of places, through those that described the relationship between person and place or evaluated the place by the person, to those which stated the emotional response of person to place. No other study of urban images appears to have found such a wide range of constructs, because they have used methods which intentionally or unintentionally constrain the type of construct that can be elicited. Although problem-oriented studies of urban images may have to constrain responses to save time in interviewing and analysis, it seems essential for exploratory and basic research

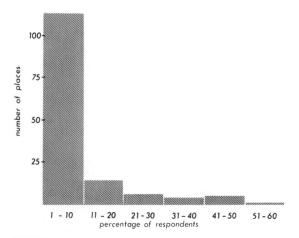

FIGURE 1
Bath; number of places elicited from given proportions of respondents.

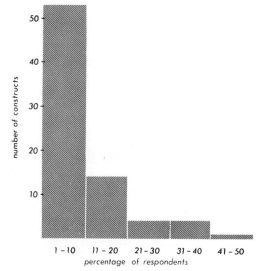

FIGURE 2
Bath: number of constructs elicited from given proportions of respondents.

studies to establish the full range of constructs potentially available so that selection can be enlightened rather than arbitrary.

Histograms showing the numbers of identically named places and constructs elicited from various proportions of the Bath respondents appear in Figures 1 and 2. These show a very low degree of agreement between respondents. The vast majority of both places and constructs were common to no more than one tenth of the sample and only one place was common to more than half the people. The implications of this low agreement have been discussed elsewhere (Sarre, 1974), but the particular feature which concerns us here is the fact that, although the repertory grid is highly sensitive to individual variation, the resultant data can also be aggregated over a group of people while retaining the individual content.

Aggregated data. An example of a method of insensitive aggregation is the practice, introduced by Lynch (1960), of drawing composite maps of city images based on the proportion of respondents mentioning places. The use of Lynch's method on the Bath data produces an image map as presented in Figure 3.[2] This map is both sparse, in the sense that only 29 places are mentioned, and disconnected, because not a single major road is mentioned. It em-

phasizes that lack of agreement among respondents can give the appearance of a very weak urban image, even though the raw data are rich. For example, each respondent referred to more than half the places in Figure 3 and rated substantially more, including places supplied by the interviewer. Of course, with large samples it is necessary to filter out a good deal of the idiosyncratic information, but with small samples, such as those used by Lynch and in the Bath study, this seems unnecessary and undesirable.

The advantages of the repertory grid method are even greater in the case of aggregating constructs. Personal construct theory deemphasizes the verbal labels applied to constructs: different people's constructs should not be assumed to be the same because they carry the same label nor different because they have different labels. The relationship between constructs is best expressed by comparing the scores of a set of elements in terms of the constructs. When elements have been scored in terms of a category scale (e.g., on a semantic differential between the polar opposite adjectives), as was the case in Bath, comparison can be made by calculating product-moment

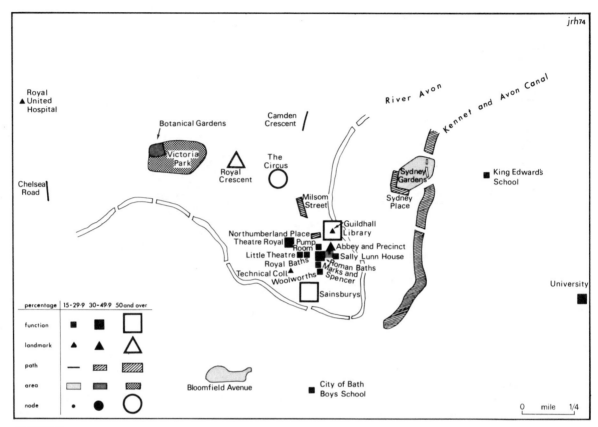

FIGURE 3
Composite group image of Bath.

correlations between constructs. In the case of single individuals, the relationship between constructs can most conveniently be established by a principal components analysis. Problems arise, however, in aggregating the results of groups of individuals.

Similar problems arise in analyzing data from semantic differential studies (Osgood et al., 1957; Snider and Osgood, 1968; see also Chapter 33). The method normally used is to calculate the mean scores given by members of the group to particular elements in terms of particular scales. The matrix of mean scores can then be factor analyzed to establish the main axes of variation in the set of scales in use. Personal construct theory questions the casual use of

mean scores as they ignore all differences between individuals. The data collected in Bath were analyzed both in the style of the semantic differential and using a method devised for use specifically on repertory grids (Slater, 1967; see also the example in Chapter 7). Full details of these analyses are available elsewhere (Sarre, 1973, Harrison and Sarre, 1974), but the briefest summary will demonstrate the advantages of the repertory grid methodology.

Slater's (1967) method requires that all constructs be applied to a standard set of elements. The individual repertory grids can then be added to produce a "supergrid" whose axes are (1) the common set of elements and (2) the set of all constructs, including each person's version of any standard constructs. In the Bath study, the construct supergrid measured 25 places by 334 constructs. Slater's method allows the derivation from this supergrid of latent roots and construct loadings and is thus analogous to principal component analysis. In the present case, three components were significant and interpretable: ugly-functional-used versus beautiful-aesthetic-typical Bath (32 percent of the variance); use-like-feel at home versus feel strange-dislike-move past (11.5 percent); and uninvolved versus involved (7.4 percent). Both the interpretation and the size of these components seemed reasonable in view of the fact that analyses of individual respondent's grids had frequently produced two components (functional-esthetic and identify-not identify) and had a common pattern of variance extraction of 30 to 40 percent on the first component, 10 to 25 percent on the second, and 8 to15 percent on the third. No individual grid had less than three significant components.

Comparison with semantic differential analysis. The Bath data could also be analyzed using the semantic differential since each grid contained a set of 25 standard places and 9 standard constructs in addition to those elicited. Using just these standard places and constructs, the first stage of the semantic differential type of analysis computes a mean score for each place on each construct. The second stage subjects the matrix of mean scores to a principal component analysis, but the solution obtained differed radically from any other analysis of the Bath data in that only one component was significant: it extracted no less than 79 percent of the variance. This unique result is a product of the method aggregation in which the use of *only standard* places and constructs sacrifices much information, and in which the calculation of only mean scores eliminates a majority of the variance present in the original data. It thus seems likely that in semantic differential studies, group solutions can be quite unrepresentative of the structure of meaning held by the individuals who made up the group. In this respect the repertory grid method with Slater's analysis seems superior, in that it retains sensitivity to the individual respondent, while producing data that aggregate satisfactorily.

A further question is whether grid results can be of use in a wider theoretical context. Stea and Downs (1970b) have pointed out that the results of studies of environmental cognition at the individual level have not yet been satisfactorily incorporated into general environmental and behavior theories (see also Harvey, 1969). It seems likely that one of the main reasons for this lack of integration has been the ad hoc nature of many of the techniques used to measure mental images. A further difficulty has been that many different techniques have been used by geographers working in different subfields. A whole range of psychological concepts (motivation, perception, learning theory, attitudes, stimulus-response models, psycholinguistics, sign theory, etc.) and their associated techniques has been incorporated into the geographer's problem-solving tool kit, but there has been little attempt to link these concepts into a framework of "geographical psychology" so that a common body of theory can develop.

The grid test goes some way toward solving this difficulty. The grid is very far from being ad hoc, and is closely linked to and directly derived from a coherent body of psychological theory (see Chapter 6). In addition, the grid test is extremely flexible, and can be used to study any kind of perception (for examples of different uses, see Bannister and Mair, 1968). The hope is then that personal construct theory and its associated interview technique will be able to provide the comprehensive framework for the integrating studies of environmental cognition and behavior so obviously required.

Cognition and Behavior: Personal Construct Alternatives to Economic Man

But what exactly does a grid interview provide in the context of relating cognition to behavior? What are the possibilities of using the output from a grid test to contribute to the development of theories of human spatial behavior? These questions can be resolved in part by considering one specific discipline—geography—and one common concept—economic man.

Geographical theories about the spatial behavior of retailers, and the resultant spatial distribution of shops, have hinged either on a version of the theory of demand (Christaller, 1966; Berry, 1967) or on rent theory (Garner, 1966, 1968). Both these theories rely in turn on the notion of *economic man* as a basic postulate. Economic man knows about all possible alternatives, including the behavior of all his competitors, is able to react instantly to any change in circumstances, and is able to select that strategy which will maximize profits and/or minimize costs. Generally, then, we can safely say that economic man is assumed to possess qualities which clearly are unrealistic when compared with our everyday knowledge of human behavior. Whether this lack of realism is important is a different matter. Some economists, and a number of geographers and planners, believe that it is, and have made various suggestions as to how the concept can be modified (Boulding, 1950; Clarkson, 1963: Parr and Denike, 1970; Pred, 1965, 1969; Webber, 1971). Others, such as Machlup (1967), maintain that economic man is simply a useful heuristic device, a theoretic symbol that need not have direct, observable, concrete meaning, but which can be used to derive prediction about behavior at the aggregate level. We do not wish to discuss the relative merits of these two viewpoints here, but rather to see how the economic man concept *could* be modified using personal construct theory and the repertory grid test. The two questions to be addressed are (1) How would personal construct theory describe an "economic man," such as a retailer? and (2) How far will the output from a grid test enable us to *operationalize* this description? Answers to these questions can be illustrated by the results of a small survey of shopkeepers in Bristol, England (Harrison and Sarre, 1974). We interviewed 41 shopkeepers, including 7 from a newly built out-of-town shopping center, using the grid test on a standard set of 27 elements describing the shop and its environment.

Reverting briefly to the formal content of personal construct theory (see Bannister and Fransella, 1971; Bannister and Mair, 1968; see also Chapter 6), the basic postulate of the theory states that "a person's processes are psychologically channelized by the ways in which he anticipates events." In the context of economic man, therefore, we can say immediately

that our revised economic man will be *anticipatory rather than reactive.* Instead of changing his prices when others change theirs, relocating when competitors relocate, and so on, our retailer will try to anticipate what is going to happen, decide on a strategy, and act accordingly. Interaction between retailers will therefore be much more like a subtle and difficult game than the rather mechanical notion of economic man would have us believe. The game theoretic analyses of decision making put forward by certain geographers (e.g., Gould, 1963; Stevens, 1961) thus become of interest, although the mathematical and conceptual problems involved in generalizing a game framework to include many factors with multiple goals appear to have precluded extensive development of these ideas.[3] However, personal construct theory can tell us a good deal about the way in which information is acquired, stored, and used by the individual retailer.

As pointed out above, the theory emphasizes the *personal* way in which an individual acquires and uses information; the individuality corollary to the theory states quite clearly that "persons differ from each other in their constructions of events." In the context of "revised" economic man, therefore, we should expect different retailers to have different ways of looking at their environments. The personal nature of construct systems is reflected in the verbal labels given to constructs that result from the grid test. in the Bristol retailing study, a total of 270 constructs were elicited during interviews with 41 respondents, and these constructs could be adequately accounted for by 65 construct categories. Of these 65, 25 were used by only one respondent, and were thus completely personal or unique, and only 3 were used by more than 40 percent of the respondents. The *content* of these constructs is also of interest. The three most commonly used constructs were the following: connected with personal service versus unconnected; draws people in versus does not; and contributes to the atmosphere of the shop versus does not. Other constructs used by more than 25 percent of the sample were the following: important for turnover versus unimportant; connected with knowledge of the trade versus unconnected; connected with reaction to market served versus unconnected; concerned with quality versus not concerned; and contributes to good service versus does not contribute.

These constructs give a great deal of information about the way in which retailers think about their shop and its environment. It seems that retailers are not simply "economic" men, but use a large variety of strategies to help them survive in their retail environment. None of the constructs elicited from this group necessarily contradicted the economic man concept, but, taken together, they give a far more detailed and clear picture of the way in which retailers are likely to behave. In a sense, therefore, information about personal constructs could allow us to respecify normative concepts so that the mechanisms by which people adjust to their environment are explicitly taken into account. Instead of postulating that retailers adjust prices to competitive levels, for example, we are able to demonstrate that a large number of "none-price" strategies are utilized—service, creation of a pleasant atmosphere, use of knowledge about the trade, emphasis on quality, and so on. Garner (1967) has already drawn attention to the possibilities of using this type of information to modify the threshold concept of central place theory; Pred (1967) has shown concepually how some knowledge of the information possessed and utilized by individual entrepreneurs could be used to revise location theory.

Problems of aggregation. Although the sensitivity of the grid to individual variations in cognition thus enables better specification of the ways in which people interact with their environment, there are obvious problems in using this information when it is derived from a large number of people. The problem of aggregating idiosyncratic grid results has already been dealt with in the discussion of the use of Slater's (1967) variation of principal components analysis. The question now arises as to whether this technique enables us to describe a "revised economic man" using information taken from a group of people. Put more simply, economic man in his original form is a generalized and highly abstract "average" person. Is it possible to use the improved specification provided by personal constructs to create a *revised* "average"

description that will be applicable in large numbers of different situations? Results from the Bristol retailing study show that, if all the 41 grids obtained are placed end to end and analyzed as one "supergrid," three components derived using Slater's program explain 48.4 percent of the total variance. Moreover, these components are themselves interpretable. Component I structures elements of the retailers image of his environment in terms of both physical position and the personal control that the retailer is able to exert over them. component II refers mainly to the way in which different elements of the image are seen as helping to make the shop profitable. Component III describes the shopping center, that is, the external environment of the shop, differentiating between movement and activity elements on the one hand, and elements relating to the physical position and character of the shopping center on the other. The "average" conception of a group of shopkeepers thus appears to make very good sense, and it would seem possible to use the axes of this "average" image as a basis for describing the way in which retailers generally consider their environment.

As a final contribution to a better understanding of economic behavior, the experience corollary to personal construct theory can be invoked. This corollary states simply that "a person's construction system varies as he successively construes the replications of events." Thus, we might expect retailers with different experiences, of different ages, and so on to construe the environment in different ways, and hence to behave differently. It should be possible to group retailers according to these differences in cognition and behavior, and these groupings may well be different from the grouping according to "goods sold in the shop," which forms the standard basis for normative analyses of the retail system, such as that provided by central place theory. In the Bristol study, for example, it was possible to show that significant differences in cognition occurred among groups of shopkeepers with different experiences of shopkeeping and who were situated in different physical locations. One might expect these groups to behave differently, and to adopt different strategies in their attempts to make their shops pay.

Thus, personal construct theory and its attendant repertory grid methodology appear to provide a meaningful framework for attempts to modify the behavioral postulates of geographical theories. In the light of three of the theory's axioms, it seems possible to modify normative theoretical concepts such as economic man so that individual variations, the complexity of cognition and changes in images over time are all taken into account. Moreover, the grid test provides output that enables these modifications to be specified operationally.

In view of these optimistic conclusions about the methodological value of the grid test, it seems paradoxical that many of the advantages of the method derive from its basis in personal construct theory, yet little effort has been made to use personal construct *theory* to improve general theory in environment-behavior relations. This is not to suggest that personal construct theory is a ready-made theory of behavior; its weaknesses in omitting motivations other than learning and in neglecting decision making make it unsuitable as more than a theory of cognition, if one is thinking in the usual "scientific" categories. However, just as methods are enlightened by theory, so theory is illuminated by the value position upon which it is based. In the case of personal construct theory, the assumptions and values, both explicit and implicit, are considerably wider than those of positivistic research. There seems a clear need to consider the general nature of personal construct theory, not merely to facilitate the introduction of the repertory grid as an empirical method, but as one source that may provide geographers and other social scientists with some insight into the paradigms which may be relevant to understanding human experience and behavior in the context of large-scale sociophysical environments.

Value Implications of Personal Construct Theory

We mentioned previously that one of the main reasons for the adoption of a "behavioral" approach in geography was dissatisfaction with the assumptions about human behavior made by many of the positivistic theories that geography adopted in its search for scientific respectability during, and after, the "quantitative revolution" over the last 15 years. Personal construct theory and its repertory grid test can be used to modify these assumptions and bring them more into line with our knowledge of everyday human behavior. However, the philosophical implications of using personal construct theory do not end here, for the theory is as much a statement of an alternative way of looking at humans as it is a more efficient scientific tool. Furthermore, personal construct theory's alternative view fits in with several of the philosophical developments currently taking place in geography and other social sciences. As such, the theory can be dubbed revolutionary in the sense that it challenges us to review and criticize the way in which we practice social science, and throws a different light on the relationships between social scientists and society.

The philosophical position of personal construct theory is that of *constructive alternativism*. According to this position, no person's mental construction of the world is a permanent or absolute truth; all are subjective to a degree and subject to constant revision. This position can be contrasted with what we might call *accumulative fragmentalism*, whereby truth is collected gradually fact by fact. Personal construct theory recognizes that new contacts can render whole areas of facts redundant and meaningless. Since the theory was developed in a clinical setting, one of the main results of this position was an emphasis on the possibility and desirability of liberating clients from the regressive and stultifying influences of their past behavior, or, as Bannister and Fransella (1972, p. 12) have said, personal construct theory "... takes as its own central concern the liberation of the person." In putting forward such a position, Kelly (1955) and those who followed him sought to dissociate themselves from both the behaviorist tradition of American psychology and the Freudian tradition, and to create a new type of psychological theory that would bring unity and more humanitarian focus to the study of human behavior.

It seems doubtful, however, that Kelly himself was fully aware of the philosophical implications of his proposals. At least one recent author (Holland, 1970, p. 115) has shown convincingly, for example, that Kelly had an unfortunate tendency "to push his imaginary opponents into extreme positions in order to criticize them: personal construct theory is then made to appear so modest and reasonable (as it is in many ways) by comparison with others' theories."

In a sense, therefore, Kelly seemed unable to apply the philosophy of constructive alternativism to his own appreciation of alternative psychological —not a new or unreplicated phenomena! Holland goes on to point out that, despite the obvious parallels between personal construct theory and an existentialist position, Kelly felt unable to identify with a position held by those he regarded as "despairing subjectivists." Kelly thus used what can only be regarded as propaganda techniques to push forward his theory, and, at the same time, fought shy of a confrontation with the possibility of complete subjectivity, or intellectual anarchy, both of which personal construct theory might be construed as holding forth.

Interestingly enough, these two issues, that is, the way in which theories are accepted or rejected in science and the position of scientific investigation vis-à-vis the personal social philosophies of scientists, have much concerned philosophers of science over the past 10 years. This concern has recently overflowed into geography and other social sciences. Kuhn (1970) put forward the view that science proceeds not by a continuous process of rational enquiry, but according to a discontinuous series of paradigms or universally accepted standards. When one paradigm becomes unacceptable, a form of scientific revolution takes place, new standards are set up, and new problems are formulated and attacked. Feyerabend (1970) goes further by pointing out that scientists often indulge in propaganda activities during periods of scientific revolution, and that some of the greatest advances in science have been the results of what he calls counterinduction:

There are circumstances when it is advisable to introduce, elaborate, and defend *ad hoc* hypotheses, or hypotheses which contradict well-established and generally accepted experimental results, or hypotheses whose content is smaller than the content of the existing and empirically adequate alternatives, or self-inconsistent hypotheses, and so on (p. 22).

Whether or not we accept Feyerabend's subsequent plea for an anarchistic approach to knowledge, it seems obvious that an acceptance of the lack of a stable and universal system of standards also involves an acceptance of the position that science is ideological. At any one time, scientists will accept a particular set of standards because they believe it to be correct or want to believe it to be correct, not because it is actually so. As personal construct theory immediately tells us, this belief may well be transitory, but it will still influence the way in which scientists construe their world, their role in society, and so on. Counterinduction provides one method of discovering the "ideological ingredients of our knowledge" (Feyerabend, 1970, p. 52) by setting up, comparing, and challenging alternative constructions of reality.

One of the most important results of the discussion about ideologies and belief systems in science is an emphasis on the nature of observation. If we accept that beliefs and values enter into the *activity* which is science, the notion of "objective" observation becomes a difficult one to support. Many (perhaps all) scientific observations themselves depend on theories of optics, cognition, and the like, and all observation is through the senses, and therefore through the belief system of the observer. From the point of view of the behavioral and social sciences, the most important aspect of observation is that it is interactive. The recurrent discussions of observer effects in psychology experiments (e.g., Rosenthal, 1966) and the attempts to develop noninteractive methods of measurement (Webb et al., 1966) testify to the importance of this problem for the activity of social science. Again, personal construct theory is quite explicit on this point. The theory is reflexive, governing both observer and observed, a fact that some have found disturbing. To quote from Landfield (1971),

The assumption that people do function within different frameworks of meaning, even as they may share common ground, leads to a disconcerting line of enquiry. How frequently do our descriptions of another person, e.g., confused, represent the actual state of that person's thinking, and how often do they represent our own limited ability to understand the social and emotional language within which the other person is functioning? How frequently do our descriptions of another person, e.g., as defensive, point to our own lack of appreciation of the ways in which that person thinks? How often do we assume that our own language is so important that it should communicate adequately if the other person is sufficiently bright? And, most disconcerting of all, how many "objective," "scientific" studies tell more about how we function as investigators—the nature of our values and ways in which we prefer to learn—than what our subjects value most and how they prefer to learn and understand? (pp. 158–159).

At the pragmatic level, Landfield and others (e.g., Hollingshead and Redic, 1958; Hunt, 1951) have shown empirically that success in psychotherapy often depends on the compatibility, in terms of both background and current construing, between patient and therapist.

How do these ideas relate to personal construct theory's use in environmental cognition? Geography, as just one of the disciplines contributing to this field, has been involved recently in a major paradigm shift during the "quantitative revolution" in an attempt to systematize the subject. Now it seems that the subject is changing again, with explicit recognition of the ideological content of the quantitative phase from which we are just emerging and pleas for a more socially aware and problem-oriented form of enquiry (e.g., Harvey, 1973). Personal construct theory is important precisely because, as shown here, it emphasizes the value basis of our "scientific" judgments and puts forward a particular form of social commitment, the emphasis on the value of the individual and the worth of his or her goals and aspirations, as a guideline for the conduct of inquiry.

Moreover, this awareness and commitment have very important practical implications. In the field of planning, for example, Stringer (1973a) has used the grid test to demonstrate that the information which the public derives from published plans varies considerably with such things as coloring and level of schematic representation, etc. Reiser (1972) has pointed out that a class bias has been built into many studies of environmental cognition especially because of a reliance on verbal interview material. These findings are very important, for they demonstrate that attempts to involve the general public in the design and planning process, now mandatory, at least in Britain, are doomed to failure unless adequate methods of tapping individual goals and aspirations are made available to architects and planners. The grid test may provide an important vehicle for interaction between

planners and the public (Sewell and Little, 1973) and may thus help to solve the problems of alienation, frustration, and cynicism which have confronted those who have attempted to mobilize and make articulate community feelings on planning issues (Nicholson and Schreiner, 1973).

Conclusions

We have attempted to assess some of the broader methodological and philosophical implications of adopting personal construct theory as a research paradigm and the repertory grid test as a data-collection method. To date, both authors have been very much involved in the problems of using the grid test in specific situations, and this paper represents something of a broader view of the work we have been doing. As such, it is a tentative statement, and some of the conclusions we reach may be unacceptable to other workers in the field. Nevertheless, we consider it important to raise these issues and to encourage a wider discussion of the social and philosophical implications of the work carried out by social scientists. Personal construct theory seems to be an admirable vehicle for such discussions, since it forces us to rethink our approach to social problems, at the same time providing very concrete and practical guidelines for carrying out research. Above all, the theory reminds us that as behavioral and social scientists, or as architects and planners, we interact with and study people who are "scientific" in their own sense, and who have their own variable and articulate ways of looking at the world.

NOTES

1. Grateful acknowledgment is made to the Trustees of the Frederick Soddy Fund, especially Professor Tom Elkins, for their support and encouragement during the preparation of this paper.
2. The reader will note that the classification of places departs somewhat from that of Lynch. This is because the set of places elicited in Bath did not fit Lynch's scheme. Full details are given in Sarre (1974, p. 36).
3. This is true for game theoretic models, but not for simulation gaming (the editors).

35

Joachim F. Wohlwill

Division of Man-Environment Relations
  Pennsylvania State University

SEARCHING FOR THE ENVIRONMENT IN ENVIRONMENTAL COGNITION RESEARCH: A COMMENTARY ON RESEARCH STRATEGY

There are diverse ways of comparing the set of chapters that make up this section on methodology. They vary, first, in terms of the theoretical frameworks within which they are carried out. Although not all contain explicit statements of theoretical position (as befits the methodological emphasis intended for them), it is apparent that they start from very different sets of theoretical assumptions, from the modified psychophysics represented by Briggs and Cadwallader's studies, to the person-centered approaches of personal construct theory of Harrison and Sarre and Golant and Burton's equally person-centered focus on expectations and meanings.

A second, equally obvious dimension of difference relates to the response modes utilized, that is, the "representational forms" discussed in such comprehensive and thoughtful fashion by Golledge in his admirable review of methodological issues in this area of research. Here again we find Briggs and Cadwallader representing one pole, in a sense, at the "objectivity" end, in their utilization of distance estimates, and Golant and Burton occupying a position a pole apart, that is, at the subjectivity end, in their reliance on semantic-differential ratings on verbally defined scales lacking any objective referent to the object of judgment (e.g., "yielding-tenacious" with reference to air pollution or auto accident).

We may further agree that Harrison and Sarre's "personal constructs," elicited by asking subjects to verbalize bases of difference among triads (i.e., of locales), falls near the subjectivity pole of response, and that Zannaras's importance ratings represent a sort of intermediary zone between these poles, just as the theoretical position implicit in her paper tends to fall between the information-processing framework of Briggs and Cadwallader and the cognitive-structure framework of Harrison and Sarre. It now becomes apparent that there is a virtually perfect relationship between the status of these five studies with respect to these two attributes. This is hardly surprising; one would expect theoretical preferences to determine, or at least strongly influence, the choice of response measures (although this relationship is not always as clear as in the present instance). Nor is it a coincidence to find that the five studies can be arranged in the same way in terms of still a third criterion, that of the conception of environment underlying them, and the extent and mode of manipulation of environmental variables. Since this dimension happens to correspond to this writer's dominant "personal construct" where research on environment and behavior is concerned, it is the one that will be emphasized in the consideration of these five chapters.[1]

The focus on a concrete, objectively defined feature of the geographical environment, which one would expect to find in research by geographers, emerges most clearly and obviously in the twin studies by Briggs and Cadwallader on the cognition of distance, both of which abstract a specific physical variable, that of geographic distance of a set of loci known to the respondents, from the unwieldy mixture of information and noise that makes up our everyday environment. At the other extreme lie the papers by Harrison and Sarre and Golant and Burton, in which any attempt at specifying environmental features or variables in terms of an objective referent is eschewed altogether. As we shall note in more detail shortly, in the case of the personal-construct approach espoused by the former, environments are in general merely sampled at random, to provide a variate for the manifestation of dimensions of individuals' environmental meanings. Similarly, Golant and Burton come no closer to specifying particular environmental characteristics than to present a series of verbal concepts representing generalized classes of events falling into the broad category of environmental hazards. Once again Zannaras's study is intermediate between the two extremes (although probably closer to the former), with its attention to one major and surely important, but not fully elaborated, environmental variable, that of structural features of a city, along with a set of specific environmental cues whose role in the conveying of information required for wayfinding was to be determined.

Let us examine more closely the major features of these three types of studies and the rationales underlying them. Briggs and Cadwallader are interested in very much the same question, that of the shape of the function relating objective to estimated distances, along with the role of certain additional variables, such as the types of judgment made (absolute or relative), and, in Briggs case, the difference between straight-line distances and those based on itineraries that included right-angle bends, as well as that between distances toward and away from downtown.

The common interest in the functions relating ob-

jective to cognized distance marks this pair of studies as an important extension of the experimental psychological research on distance perception (see Vernon, 1970, Chapter 8, and Baird, 1970, for recent reviews of this literature). But, even though some of these studies (e.g., Gibson and Bergman, 1954) did involve the presentation of fairly long distances, up to 500 yards in some cases, they differed in a crucial respect from those of Briggs and Cadwallader: the distances being judged were always directly accessible to the subject's view, which was obviously not the case in the latter two studies. Thus, the judgments could not be based on any perceptual cues, which is of course precisely the feature of this research that qualifies it as cognitive rather than perceptual.

At the same time the question arises, for both of these studies, as to the actual basis on which such judgments of verbally presented distances are made. Probably the two most likely factors implicated in these judgments are *times* of traversing the distances in question and *information* derived from road signs, odometer readings, and road maps. The latter factor, along with information from incidental conversation, and the like, concerning not only actual mileage distances, but location of points relative to one another in geographic space, may have played a major part particularly in Cadwallader's study.

Although these latter sources of knowledge about distance would be difficult to control, and we have no indication as to the ways in which, and the extent to which, they may have in fact been used as a basis for the subject's estimates in either study, the matter is somewhat different as far as the first-mentioned cue, that of time, is concerned. First, the time estimates are more veridically, that is, linearly, related to objective travel time than the distance estimates to objective distance, raising the possibility that the subjects did in fact base these latter judgments on the former, although it obviously does not establish this as a fact. There is, however, further presumptive evidence pointing in the same direction from both studies, in the findings of both Briggs and Cadwallader that distances toward the center of the city were overestimated relative to those away from the center.

Admittedly, hypothesizing time as a mediating cue for distance estimates in these two studies fails to account for the curious contrast between the apparent curvilinearity of Columbusian space and the linearity of Angelinian space. Conceivably, the linearity of Cadwallader's functions is related to the use of specific communities to identify the target distances, as compared to the less readily identifiable points in and around the Columbus area employed by Briggs. Thus, the former may well have provided more of an opportunity for his subjects to utilize veridical information through other sources (such as those suggested above), to supplement and perhaps supplant the reliance on the time cue. In Briggs's study, on the other hand, this cue could well have operated in more unadulterated fashion, which might in fact account for the curvilinear form of the latter's functions, if we assume that time estimates follow the curvilinear relationship typically found in psychophysical judgment (see Stevens, 1956).

These are of course highly speculative guesses, considering our lack of information on the actual sources of information with respect to distance available to the subjects in these studies. They serve to remind us, however, that in the absence of direct perception, judgments of distance must be mediated by experience-based cues of this sort, so that a search for a determinate function relating "cognized" to objective distance may in fact be pointless. An interesting question arises in this connection: suppose that one were to eliminate both the time factor and other extraneous sources of distance information, and force subjects to base their distance estimates purely on knowledge about location in space of the points defining the distances (such as might be gleaned from a perusal of maps lacking mileage indications, or travel experience through an area under conditions of widely varying speeds)? One suspects that in this case the outcome might well reveal a merely topological organization of space, with distances being represented at most in a roughly ordinal sense, that is, preserving a rank-order relationship to actual distances.

But, the uncertainty as to the basis for the judgments in these two studies notwithstanding, they remain interesting attempts, all too rare in this area, to study systematically the relationship between a clearly defined geographical variable and a behavioral index of the cognition of environmental spaces. They are

also notable for subjecting specific attributes of the target stimuli (the distances) to experimental manipulation in such a way as to permit the investigators— praise be—to state particular, theoretically derived hypotheses concerning the effects of these manipulations.

Let us move now to the opposite pole of environmental cognition research, represented by Golant and Burton's study of the semantic space constituted by a set of environmental-hazard concepts, as well as Harrison and Sarre's presentation of the personal construct theory approach. Both deal with eminently central questions of psychology, transcending by far the rather limited focus on the cognition of distances of the previous two studies. They concern such questions as the meanings attached to environmental events and the attributes that individuals abstract from the environmental manifold in making comparisons among different locales. These are not only intuitively appealing questions, but questions that a comprehensive account of environmental cognition must at some point address and come to grips with. One may agree further that, *in principle*, information concerning meanings of environmental concepts may be of value in predicting behavior (e.g., in response to hazards, as suggested, although none too emphatically, by Golant and Burton). Similarly, it is difficult to quarrel with Harrison and Sarre's assessment of personal construct theory as a potentially humanizing counterforce to economic or behaviorist models of environmental behavior. Yet, taken purely as contributions to the methodological repertoire of environmental cognition research, both approaches raise a number of questions that, particularly given their great popularity in this field, deserve closer attention than they have received thus far. Let us consider three such questions in particular; although clearly interrelated, they may usefully be discussed separately.

First, just how appropriate are these methods to this field? Harrison and Sarre note that a "whole range of psychological concepts . . . has been incorporated into the geographer's problem solving toolkit, but there has been little attempt to link these concepts into a framework of 'geographical psychology' . . ."; they proceed to argue that the grid test is at an advantage in this respect, and express "the hope . . . that personal construct theory and its associated interview technique will provide the comprehensive framework for integrating studies of environmental cognition and behavior so obviously required."

The reference, first, to "geographical psychology," and subsequently to "behavioral geography," is worth noting. The authors appear to be using the terms interchangeably, but there is a very important question lurking in the background here: to which discipline is work such as this intended to contribute? As long as the research involves clearly delineated relationships between geographical and behavior variables, as is the case in Chapters 29 and 30 on cognition of distance, the answer to this question is at best a matter of personal preference, and hardly of much moment. But when personal construct theory, and more particularly its main tool, the repertory grid technique, is applied to the environmental cognition area (and the same point applies to use of the semantic-differential technique), this condition ceases to be true: there are, in fact, no clearly defined geographical variables that are placed into relation with behavior. What we have, instead, particularly in the case of the repertory grid, is a set of personal constructs applied to a randomly chosen set of geographical locales. As such, the results of this type of research may be of interest to a personality psychologist. It is difficult to see how such results can be incorporated into the study of geography, as an environmental social science.

In this connection, it is useful to remind ourselves that the semantic differential was designed as a tool for the analysis of verbal meaning; similarly, personal construct theory represents an attempt, on the part of a cognitively minded clinical psychologist, to examine the way in which a particular individual constructs the world of her or his *interpersonal* relationships. Thus, in both cases we are dealing with problem areas concerning conceptual organization, at the level of the individual in Kelly's case, at the level, more typically, of the "group mind" in Osgood's. Neither tool was invented for the purpose of dealing with representations of the physical environment by the individual, and although it may be possible to apply it to this field, it is not at all clear that they are ideally suited to this purpose. Above all, neither approach provides any information whatever on *relationships* between features of the environment and their cognitive representation by a person. They are based on constructivist theories of certain kinds of knowledge (even if this constructivist character remains implicit in Osgood's derivation of the semantic differential from stimulus–response mediation theory); by the same token, they are emphatically *not* theories of perception, which presuppose a referent to specified attributes of a directly experienced stimulus environment. In this sense, one is forced to take exception to Harrison and Sarre's statement that "the grid test . . . can be used to study any kind of perception."

A second, closely related question to be asked of these models concerns their treatment of the environment. What, in fact, is the role of environmental variables or features in this type of research? In the case of the environmental hazards study, the environments are presented at a purely symbolic level through verbally defined concepts referring to specific environmental events. These are presumably abstractions entrusted to the respondents from experience of a predominantly vicarious form; one assumes that not many of the subjects have had occasion to have direct experience with them, except for snowstorms, air pollution, and possibly auto accidents. (An interesting question in this connection might be how a more immediate form of experiencing some of these events, as through the much publicized movies *Earthquake* and *Towering Inferno* might affect responses to these concepts.) In any event, we have little basis for knowing what, concretely, the respondents' frame of reference was in rating a flood or tornado on the various semantic differential scales.

In the case of the repertory grid, if we consider the research on the city of Bath referred to repeatedly in Chapter 34, the environmental referents are at once more determinate and more elusive: more determinate in the sense that specific locations in this community, identifiable on an actual map (see their Figure 3), serve as the elements for the triad comparisons from which the individual constructs are derived, and more elusive in the sense that the defining or determining attributes of these elements are left unspecified and unknown to any except a small minority familiar with this town. In either case, then, the data are more revealing for what they tell us about a particular group's semantic meanings of the idiosyncratic categories of their cognitive world than about an individual or group's mode of processing particular information from an environment. Here again we see that geography has been (happily?) left behind.

We come back to the point that these techniques represent ways of obtaining information about meaning, or personality, which cannot be readily made use of by the environmental psychologist, or the behavioral geographer, until they are in some way placed into relationship with aspects of the actual environment that gave rise to these responses. An interesting, although rather half-hearted and unconvincing attempt to do just that, in the context of personal construct theory, is contained in a recently published study by Hudson (1974b), in which the repertory grid technique is applied to the shops of a city (Bristol, England). After listing the diverse constructs that emerged from this study on the part of his subject sample, Hudson decided to examine two of these that had an objective referent, distance and expensiveness, and related these to objective measures of each of these characteristics. There are, unfortunately some infelicities in the treatment of the data that leave unanswered the question posed by the author concerning the correspondence between objective values and subjective impressions of the shops' prices and distances.[2] More fundamentally, however, the author displays a gingerly and almost apologetic attitude toward this kind of veridicality testing, which is considered to go counter to the philosophical basis of personal construct theory.

Actually, veridicality is far from constituting the most revealing type of question to ask concerning the environment–construct interplay with the data of this kind. For instance, it appears that "location relative to the University" was one of the most frequently used constructs, although for some individuals it was defined in terms of distance, for others in terms of location on or off a bus route to the university. The question arises, what is the functional significance of this construct, in relation (1) to the type of shop in question, (2) the availability of alternative shops of the same type, and (3) other aspects of the shopping environment, such as cost, comfort, and size of shop?

It is information such as this that might allow one to make use of personal constructs in predicting or explaining shopping behavior (a goal explicitly envisaged by Golant and Burton for their future hazard research, although there again a matrix of concrete environmental information would be required to achieve such a goal). But even apart from such a larger frame of reference, a clearer environmental anchoring for this research would help to explicate the meaning and basis for the constructs themselves—as in the case of a construct such as "shop atmosphere," synthesized, it seems, from several individual constructs, such as "pleasant shop environment," "personal atmosphere," and "attractive shop environment." An attempt to specify the particular shops that elicited such constructs and the possible environmental features that related to them would surely add interest to this type of information.

A third question that is again intimately related to the preceding concerns the nature of the information that the methodologies employed by Golant and Burton and by Harrison and Sarre provide. There are two points to be made in this regard. First, the results of a factor analysis of semantic-differential ratings or of a personal construct analysis represent a purely descriptive enterprise. There is no attempt made in any way to explain behavior; more to the point, no hypotheses are stated of any kind. Description is a necessary phase of any infant discipline, but it is not at all clear that the type of information contained in these analyses can be usefully employed as a stepping-stone to a more systematic, theoretically grounded effort. This is particularly true in the case of the repertory grid, since it is explicitly predicted on the utilization of individual response records, which are difficult to generalize.[3] Indeed, the techniques are difficult to apply even to a simple comparative study, comparing two different populations of respondents, for instance, since the outputs of these analyses are not readily translatable from one data matrix to another. Even when they are and the technical difficulties, for example, of factor matching, are resolved, they can still only indicate differences among such attributes of a factor analysis or repertory grid test as the *number* of factors or constructs, or conceivably differences with respect to the apparent meaning of such factors or constructs for different groups. But data of this kind cannot answer questions relating to the mode of processing information in the environment that might account for these organizational structures.

There is a further aspect to both of these methods that needs to be brought into the open. They rely exclusively on verbal responses. The implicit assumption, of course, is that a respondent's use of words will reveal something of the organization of his or her mentality. The validity of this assumption is rarely put to the test, however, and appears particularly dubious when the individual is forced to apply verbal dimensions to verbally defined concepts that have no determinate relationship to the former (as in rating the concept "air pollution" on the dimension "orderly–chaotic"), or to offer open–ended, ex post facto "explanations" for choosing the two members of a triad of again verbally presented elements that the person considers to belong together. It is useful to bear in mind that words are no more than overt responses of a particular sort, and cannot always be accorded a privileged status as revealing directly the form or content of mental image or constructs, at least in the absence of some determination of their reliability and, above all, their external validity. After all, how much faith would we place in the substance of Hamlet's environmental imagery, in his famous interchange with Polonius in which he "perceives" a cloud as a camel, a weasel, and a whale in turn?[4]

The preceding criticism of Chapters 33 and 34 will undoubtedly appear unduly harsh to some. Certainly, both the semantic-differential approach and the repertory grid technique can have a place in the study of environmental meanings and of individual, idiosyncratic aspects of environmental cognition. Used imaginatively, furthermore, and above all programmatically, they can undoubtedly be incorporated into a fruitful approach that integrates the two sides of the environment–behavior equation into a comprehensive whole. If this commentary has focused, perhaps one sidedly, on the perceived shortcomings and limitations of these approaches, it is because this kind of integration has been so studiously avoided by those who have made use of it (and may in fact be philosophically incompatible with the "constructivist

alternativism" underlying personal construct theory). Furthermore, these tools have seen such a mushrooming in popularity in the environment–behavior field, and been put frequently to such mindless use, as to raise grave questions concerning the direction that this whole enterprise is taking.

Fortunately, we are able to conclude this commentary on a happier and more positive note, by turning our attention to a most interesting paper by Zannaras, which in so many ways occupies a healthy and promising middle ground between the somewhat narrow psychophysical focus of the first two chapters and the problematical approach of the last two that we have just reviewed. Indeed, Zannaras's study can, in some ways, stand as a prototype of the kind of research that, in the view of this commentator, the field is most in need of. It starts from a limited set of environments that are not only specifically identified but characterized in terms of differences with respect to an attribute of presumptive relevance to cognitive maps: the type of structural configuration presented by the layout of a city. At the same time, it takes cognizance of the important potential role of individual differences in environmental cognition, and proceeds to obtain information so as to allow the investigator to relate the responses recorded to a variety of dimensions of individual difference chosen, at least in part, for their possible relevance to such responses (e.g., urban experience and navigational experience, although some might quarrel with the way in which these variables were operationalized in this study). Furthermore, Zannaras has chosen an aspect of cognitive mapping that is clearly of central concern in this area, the relative importance of different cues in way-finding behavior, while avoiding the pitfalls of map drawing and similar direct graphic methodologies. And last, but surely not least, the author has been able, because of her judicious selection of environmental and behavioral variables, to formulate a set of hypotheses to put to the test in her individual-differences investigation, an all too rarely encountered feature in this type of research.

The study is, admittedly, not beyond criticism in certain respects, notably as regards the methodology employed to determine the relative importance of these cues. There are undoubtedly more effective approaches to this problem than verbal ratings of importance by a subject; at the very least, that particular method requires cross-validation. Methods that come to mind include having subjects give way-finding instructions to others and recording frequency of mention of the various cues, undertaking multiple-regression analyses to predict success in way-finding for different routes classified in terms of the presence or absence of particular cues on those routes, and, perhaps ideally, manipulating the possible role of such cues experimentally in the context of a way-finding problem, as in the ingenious study by Jones (1972) of clues utilized by motorists in search of an access ramp to a freeway in an unfamiliar simulated environment. Rather unfortunate, too, is the decision to allow the individual to pick a route of his own choosing as the basis for the importance rankings, which renders questionable the pooling of the data for different individuals. Finally, the specification of the sample is needlessly uninformative in major respects: what degree of expertise did the subjects have in interpreting maps or models? Since Columbus was one of the cities selected and the student body sampled in this study is, one presumes, familiar with this city, the familiarity factor clearly confounds the results (one suspects, furthermore, that one or the other of the other two cities may have been somewhat familiar to *some* of these subjects as well, but to an unknown degree).

But these criticisms should not be allowed to detract from the very real merits of this research and the conception that underlies it. It is apparent in what, is, after all, the proof of the pudding: the interest and very real significance of the results obtained, as shown in the discussion of those relating to hypotheses I and II in particular, which bring into relief both the theoretical and practical value of this type of research, i.e., for the study of way-finding behavior and mental mapping as such, and for an understanding of the consequences of different land-use patterns for this type of behavior, which could well be of value in the planning of traffic systems. Note, incidentally, that only the first, more general of Zannaras's two hypotheses concerning the differences related to urban forms was confirmed, but the import of the results obtained is hardly diminished by the failure to confirm the more specific hypothesis concerning the use of "land-use" cues, as the discussion shows convincingly.

We come, finally, to Zannaras' third hypothesis, in which she contrasts the relative contribution to environmental as opposed to individual-experience variables to these responses. In seeming agreement with Carr and Schissler (1969), Zannaras finds (as hypothesized) that the environmental variables constitute more potent determinants of the responses than those relating to the subjects. This outcome might seem to provide this commentator with grist for the mill of the argument developed above, in criticizing the emphasis on individual-based processes and the neglect of environmental determinants in Chapters 33 and 34. Nevertheless, it would be missing the point, I believe, to overstress this particular aspect of Zannaras's data. One might, for instance, easily reverse the relative importance of these variables by selecting subjects of widely different map-reading experience and ability (e.g., children of different ages, or possibly individuals selected from opposite poles of the spatial-ability factor). Indeed, this particular emphasis on the seeming overriding importance of the environmental cues appears unfortunate, since it detracts from the much more impressive aspect of this study in *integrating* the study of environmental factors and those related to the individual cognizer in a conceptually solid fashion, which could, furthermore, bring to light interesting and important forms of *interaction* among these two classes of variables (although Zannaras's analysis is curiously silent on this question). It is in this sense that this commentator sees this study as a bit of "constructive alternativism" (to paraphrase Kelly's term) that permits the organizing processes of the individual cognizer to emerge, not only without ignoring the attributes of the environments to which he or she is responding, but, more important, in such a way as to relate one to the other. It is this feature that makes it, in my view, an example par excellence of behavioral geography.

NOTES

1. This commentary will omit specific consideration of the papers by Golledge and by Wood and Beck.

Chapter 28 is a comprehensive and systematic review of methodology in this field and stands apart from the accounts of specific research efforts (or of a theoretically based program of research, in the case of Chapter 34) that make up the rest of the section; as such it hardly requires extended comment. In Chapter 32, on the other hand, we have a study that stands apart from the rest in a different sense, being a more didactically oriented effort to improve an individual's cognitive map of a foreign city that is not readily relatable to the other studies. It is, in any case, difficult to evaluate, given the lack of detail in regard to the actual nature of the map-learning experience and the results achieved.

2. Hudson chose to change the objective cost and distance values onto 11-point scales (by some unspecified procedure) to make them commensurate with the scales used for the estimates. He then proceeded to compare the objective measures for each subject to the estimates by means of chi square, using the former as "expected" and the latter as observed values—a patently indefensible procedure since the data are not frequency data. The obvious procedure here would have been simply to intercorrelate the two sets of data (using the true objec-

tive measures, rather than the converted ones); admittedly, this would not have yielded a significance value for the discrepancies between the objective and the subjective measures, but statistical significance is not at issue here in any event, particularly as far as the individual data are concerned.

3. Bannister and Mair (1968, pp. 152ff.) argue that it is incorrect to consider Kelly's technique as limited to an idiographic, as opposed to a nomothetic, mode of analysis; yet they do not really indicate by what method individual data are to be aggregated or what problems arise in so doing; at other places in their treatment of personal construct theory (including the chapter on the measurement of personal constructs), these writers clearly identify it themselves with an idiographic (i.e., individual for individual) focus.

4. This commentator is disposed to recommend an intensive grounding in research methodology in the study of perception and problem solving in animals as an antidote to this tendency to reify the results of unbridled, open-ended verbal responses. It may even persuade some workers in this area that to study cognitive maps is something like pulling habits out of a rat!

BIBLIOGRAPHY

Abler, R., Adams, J. S., and Gould, P. (1971). *Spatial Organizations: The Geographer's View of the World.* Englewood Cliffs, N.J.: Prentice-Hall.

Ackoff, R. L., Gupta, S. K., and Minas, J. S. (1962). *Scientific Method: Optimizing Applied Research Decisions.* New York: Wiley.

Acredolo, L. P. (1972). The use of various frames of reference for orientation in an unfamiliar space: a proposed study. Unpublished paper, Institute of Child Development, University of Minnesota.

——. (1974). Frames of reference used by children for orientation in unfamiliar spaces. Unpublished dissertation, Institute of Child Development, University of Minnesota.

——, Barstis, S. W., Genduso, C., and Schulman, D. (1975). "Place" responding verses "response" responding among preschool children as a function of environmental differentiation. Paper presented at the Society for Research in Child Development meeting, Denver.

Adams, J. S. (1969). Directional bias in intra-urban migration. *Economic Geography, 45:* 302-323.

Alarcón, F. R. (1965). A description of the customs of the peoples of Kiangan, Bunhian, and Mayoyao, 1857. (Translated by W. H. Scott.) *Journal of the Folklore Institute, 2*(1): 78-100.

Albin, R. (1975). Current issues in macro-spatial cognition. Unpublished doctoral paper, Department of Psychology, George Washington University.

Albrecht, M. C. (1956). Does literature reflect common values? *American Sociological Review, 21:* 722-729.

Alexander, C. (1965). A city is not a tree. *Architectural Forum, 122* (April): 58-62; (May): 58-61.

——, and Poyner, B. (1970). The atoms of environmental structure. In G. T. Moore (ed.), *Emerging Methods in Environmental Design and Planning.* Cambridge, Mass.: MIT Press, pp. 308-321.

Alexander, R. D., and Tinkle, D. W. (1968). A comparative review: on agression and the territorial imperative. *Bioscience, 18:* 245-248.

Alihan, M. (1938). *Social Ecology: A Critical Analysis.* New York: Columbia University Press.

Allen, J. L. (1971). Geographical knowledge and American images of the Louisiana Territory. *Western Historical Quarterly, 2:* 151-170.

——. (1972). An analysis of the exploratory process: the Lewis and Clark expedition of 1804-1806. *Geographical Review, 62:* 13-39.

Allport, F. H. (1955). *Theories of Perception and the Concept of Structure.* New York: Wiley.

Altman, I. (1970). Territorial behavior in humans;

an analysis of the concept. In L. A. Pastalan and D. H. Carson (eds.), *Spatial Behavior of Older People*. Ann Arbor, Mich.: Wayne State University, Institute of Gerontology, pp. 1-24.

Anderson, J., and Tindal, M. (1972). The concept of home range: new data for study of territorial behavior. In W. J. Mitchell (ed.) *Environmental Design: Research and Practice*, Vol. 1. Los Angeles, School of Architecture and Urban Planning, University of California, 1-1-1 to 1-1-7.

Andrews, H. F. (1973). Home range and urban knowledge of school-age children. *Environment and Behavior, 5:* 73-86.

Angyal, A. (1930). Über die Raumlage vorgestellter Orter. *Archiv für die gesamte psychologie, 78:* 47-94.

Appleyard, D. (1969a). Why buildings are known. *Environment and Behavior, 1:* 131-156.

——. (1969b). City designers and the pluralistic city. In L. Rodwin and Associates (ed.), *Planning Urban Growth and Regional Development: The Experience of the Guyana Program of Venezuela*. Cambridge, Mass.: MIT Press, pp. 422-452.

——. (1970a). Notes on urban perception and knowledge. In J. Archea and C. Eastman (eds.), *EDRA Two: Proceedings of the Second Annual Environmental Design Research Association Conference*. Pittsburgh: Carnegie-Mellon University, pp. 97-101.

——. (1970b). Styles and methods of structuring a city. *Environment and Behavior, 2:* 100-117.

——. (1972). Styles and methods of structuring cities: part two. Paper presented at the Symposium on Conceptual Issues in Environmental Cognition, Environmental Design Research Association meeting, Los Angeles.

——. (In press). *The Hidden City*. Cambridge, Mass.: MIT Press.

——, and Okamoto, R. Y. (1969). *Environmental Criteria for Ideal Transportation Systems*. Berkeley, Calif.: Institute of Urban and Regional Development, University of California, Reprint No. 56.

——, Lynch, K., and Myer, J. R. (1964). *The View from the Road*. Cambridge, Mass.: MIT Press.

Archea, J., and Eastman, C. (eds.) (1970). *EDRA Two, Proceedings of the Second Annual Environmental Design Research Association Conference*. Pittsburgh: Carnegie-Mellon University.

Ardrey, R. (1966). *The Territorial Imperative*. New York: Atheneum.

Asmussen, D. G. (1971). Children's cognition organization of space. Unpublished Ph.D. dissertation, Department of Geography, University of Washington.

Austin, M. (1975). A description of the Maori Marae. In A. Rapoport (ed.), *The Mutual Interaction of People and Their Built Environment: A Cross-Cultural Perspective*. The Hague: Mouton.

Axelrad, S. (1969). Comments on anthropology and the study of complex cultures. In W. Muensterberger (ed.), *Man and His Culture: Psychoanalytic Anthropology after "Totem and Taboo."* London: Rapp & Whiting, pp. 273-293.

Bachelard, G. (1958). *The Poetics of Space*. (Translated by M. Jolas.) New York: Orion Press.

Baird, J. C. (1970). *Psychophysical Analysis of Visual Space*. New York: Pergamon Press.

Baldwin, F., and Page, J. K., Jr. (eds.) (1970) *Law and the Environment*. New York: Walker and Company.

Balzac, H. D. (1912-1940). *La Comedie Humaine*. 40 vols. Paris: Louis Conrad.

Bannister, D. (1970a). *Perspectives in Personal Construct Theory*. London: Academic Press.

——. (1970b). Science through the looking glass. In D. Bannister (ed.), *Perspectives in Personal Construct Theory*. London: Academic Press, 47-61.

——, and Bott, M. (1973). Evaluating the person. In P. Kline (ed.), *New Approaches in Psychological Measurement*. New York: Wiley, pp. 157-178.

——, and Fransella, F. (1971). *Inquiring Man: The Theory of Personal Constructs*. Harmondsworth, England: Penguin.

——, and Mair, J. M. M. (1968). *The Evaluation of Personal Constructs*. London: Academic Press.

Barfield, O. (1957). *Saving the Appearances*. New York: Harcourt Brace.

Barker, M. L. (1974). Information and complexity: the conceptualization of air pollution by specialist groups. *Environment and Behavior, 6:* 346-377.

Barker, R. G. (1968). *Ecological Psychology: Con-*

cepts and Methods for Studying the Environment of Behavior. Stanford, Calif. Stanford University Press.

Barnes, J. A. (1969). Networks and political process. In J. C. Mitchell (ed.), *Social Networks in Urban Situations: Analyses of Personal Relationships in Central African Towns.* Manchester, Manchester University Press, 51-76.

Barnett, P. (1974). The Worcester three-decker: a study in the perception of form. *Monadnock, 48:* 21-33.

Bartlett, F. (1932). *Remembering.* Cambridge: Cambridge University Press.

Barton, R. F. (1919). Ifugao law. *University of California (Berkeley) Publications of American Archaeology and Ethnology, 15:* 1-186.

——. (1922). Ifugao economics. *University of California (Berkeley) Publications of American Archaeology and Ethnology, 15:* 385-446.

Bates, Arlo. (1884). *The Pagans.* Boston: Houghton Mifflin.

——. (1898). *The Puritan.* Boston: Houghton Mifflin.

Beach, J. W. (1936). *Concept of Nature in Nineteenth Century English Poetry.* New York: Macmillan.

Beck, R. J., Cohen, S. B., Craik, K. H., Dwyer, M., McCleary, G. F., and Wapner, S. (1973). Studying moves and relocations. *Environment and Behavior, 5:* 335-349.

Becker, H. S., and Strauss, A. L. (1956). Careers, Personality, and Adult Socialization. *American Journal of Sociology, 62:* 253-263.

Becker, H. S., and Strauss, A. L. (1956). Careers, personality, and adult socialization. *American Journal of Sociology. 62:* 253-263.

Beloff, J., and Beloff, H. (1961). The influence of valence on distance judgments of human faces. *Journal of Abnormal and Social Psychology, 62:* 720-722.

——, and Coupar, S. (1968). Some transactional perceptions of African faces. *British Journal of Social and Clinical Psychology, 7:* 169-175.

Berger, B. M. (1968). *Working Class Suburb: A Study of Auto Workers in Suburbia.* Berkeley, Calif.: University of California Press.

Berger, P. L., and Luckman, T. (1971). *The Social Construction of Reality.* Harmondsworth, England: Penguin.

Bergmann, G. (1958). *Philosophy of Science.* Madison, Wisc.: University of Wisconsin Press.

Bernheimer, R. (1961). *The Nature of Representation: A Phenomenological Inquiry.* New York: New York University Press.

Berry, B. J. L. (1967). *Geography of Market Centers and Retail Distribution.* Englewood Cliffs, N.J.: Prentice-Hall.

Betak, J. F. (1974). Information theory as a basis for studying environmental complexity. *Environment and Planning, 6:* 259-272.

——, Brummell, A. C., and Swingle, P. G. (1974). An approach to elicit attributes of complex visual environments. Unpublished paper, Department of Geography, McMaster University, Hamilton, Ontario.

Beyer, H. O. (1908). *Preliminary Map of Ifugao Country. Scale 1:125,000.* Manila, Philippines: Office of Chief Engineer Officer.

Blank, A. A. (1958). Axiomatics of binocular vision: the foundations of metric geometry in relation to space perception. *Journal of the Optical Society of America, 48:* 328-334.

Blaut, J. M. (1953). The economic geography of a one-acre farm in Singapore Island: a study in applied microgeography. *Malayan Journal of Tropical Geography, 1:* 37-48.

——. (1959). The ecology of tropical farming systems. In Pan American Union (ed.), *Plantation Systems of the New World.* Washington, D.C.: Pan American Union.

——. (1969). *Studies in Developmental Geography.* Worcester, Mass.: Graduate School of Geography, Clark University, Place Perception Report No. 1.

——. (1970). Anthropological approaches to environmental behavior. Unpublished lecture presented at Clark University, March 1970.

——, and Stea, D. (1969). *Place Learning.* Worcester, Mass.: Graduate School of Geography, Clark University, Place Perception Report No. 4.

——, and Stea, D. (1971). Studies of geographic learning. *Annals of the Association of American Geographers, 61:* 387-393.

——, Blaut, A. S., Harman, R. P., and Moerman, M. (1959). A study of cultural determinants of soil erosion and conservation in the Blue Mountains of Jamaica. *Social and Economic Studies, 8:* 403-420.

——, McCleary, G. F., and Blaut, A. S. (1970). Environmental mapping in young children. *Environment and Behavior, 2:* 335-349.

Boal, F. W. (1969). Territoriality on the Shankill-Falls Divide, Belfast. *Irish Geography, 6:* 30-50.

Bochenski, I. M. (1966). *Contemporary European Philosophy.* Berkeley, Calif.: University of California Press.

Bogen, J. E., DeZure, R., Tenhouten, W. D., and Marsh, J. F. (1972). The other side of the brain. IV: the A/P ratio. *Bulletin of the Los Angeles Neurological Societies, 37:* 49-61.

Boorstin, D. (1965). *The Americans: The National Experience.* New York: Random House.

Bott, E. (1971). *Family and Social Networks: Roles, Norms, and External Relationships in Ordinary Urban Families.* New York: Free Press.

Boulding, K. E. (1950). *Reconstruction of Economics.* New York: Wiley.

——. (1956). *The Image: Knowledge in Life and Society.* Ann Arbor, Mich.: University of Michigan Press.

Bowden, M. J. (1969). The perception of the western interior of the United States, 1800-1870: a problem in historical geography. *Proceedings of the Association of American Geographers, 1:* 16-21.

——. (1971). The Great American Desert and the American frontier, 1800-1882: popular images of the plains. In T. K. Hareven (ed.), *Anonymous Americans: Explorations in Nineteenth Century Social History.* Englewood Cliffs, N.J.: Prentice-Hall.

——. (1973). The desert image of the plains: behavioral implications. Paper presented at a conference on Images of the Plains, University of Nebraska.

——. (1975). The Great American Desert in the American mind, 1890-1972: the historiography of a geographical notion. In M. J. Bowden and D. Lowenthal (eds.), *Geographies of the Mind: Essays in Historical Geography in Honor of John K. Wright.* New York: Oxford University Press.

——. (In preparation). Desert wheat belt, plains corn belt: environmental cognition of settlers in the plains margin, 1850-1899. In B. W. Blouet and M. P. Lawson (eds.), *Images of the Plains: The Role of Human Nature in Settlement.*

——, and Lowenthal, D. (eds.) (1975). *Geographies of the Mind: Essays in Historical Geography in Honor of John K. Wright.* New York: Oxford University Press.

Bower, G. R. (1966). The visual world of infants. *Scientific American, 215:* 80-92.

——. (1970). Analysis of a mnemonic device. *American Scientist, 58:* 496-510.

Bowles, P. (1949). *The Sheltering Sky.* New York: Harcourt Brace.

Braithwaite, R. G. (1960). *Scientific Explanation.* New York: Harper & Row.

Bransford, J. D., Barclay, J. R., and Franks, J. J. (1972). Sentence memory: a constructive versus interpretive approach. *Cognitive Psychology, 3:* 193-209.

Bratfisch, O. (1969). A further study of the relation between subjective distance and emotional involvement. *Acta Psychologica, 29:* 244-255.

Bredeson, R. C. (1968). Landscape description in nineteenth century American literature. *American Quarterly, 20:* 86-94.

Breese, G. W. (1949). *The Daytime Population of the Central Business District of Chicago.* Chicago: University of Chicago Press.

Briggs, A. (1963). *Victorian Cities.* London: Odhams Press.

Briggs, R. (1972). *Cognitive distance in urban space.* Unpublished Ph.D. dissertation, Department of Geography, Ohio State University.

——. (1973a). On the relationship between cognitive and objective distance. In W. F. E. Preiser, *Environmental Design Research,* Vol. 2. Stroudsburg, Pa.: Dowden, Hutchinson & Ross, p. 187.

——. (1973b). Urban cognitive distance. In R. M. Downs and D. Stea (eds.), *Image and Environment: Cognitive Mapping and Spatial Behavior.* Chicago: Aldine, pp. 361-388.

Bronte, E. (1971). *Wuthering Heights.* Harmondsworth, England: Penguin.

Brookfield, H. C. (1969). On the environment as perceived. In C. Board, R. J. Chorley, P. Haggett, and

D. R. Stoddart (eds.), *Progress in Geography.* London: Edward Arnold, Vol. 1, pp. 51-80.

Brooks, C. (1966). *William Faulkner: The Yoknapatawphy Country.* New Haven, Conn.: Yale University Press.

Brower, S. (1965). The signs we learn to read. *Landscape, 15(1):* 9-12.

Brown, H. (1972). Perception and meaning. In N. Recher (ed.), *Studies in the Philosophy of Mind, American Philosophical Quarterly Monograph Series,* No. 6. 1-9.

Brown, R. (1963). *Explanation in Social Science.* London: Aldine.

Bruner, J. S. (1957a). On going beyond the information given. In J. S. Bruner (ed.), *Contemporary Approaches to Cognition: A Symposium.* Cambridge, Mass.: Harvard University Press, pp. 41-69.

——. (1957b). On perceptual readiness. *Psychological Review, 64:* 123-152.

——. (1959). Learning and thinking. *Harvard Educational Review, 29:* 184-192.

——, and Postman, L. (1949). On the perception of incongruity. *Journal of Personality, 18:* 206-233.

——, Goodnow, J., and Austin, G. (1956). *A Study of Thinking.* New York: Wiley.

——, Olver, R. R., Greenfield, P.M., et al. (1966). *Studies in Cognitive Growth.* New York: Wiley.

Brunswick, E. (1956). *Perception and the Representative Design of Psychological Experiments,* 2nd ed. Berkeley, Calif.: University of California Press.

Bunge, M. (1967). *Scientific Research I: The Search for System.* New York: Springer-Verlag.

Burch, E. S., Jr. (1971). The non-empirical environment of the Artic Alaskan Eskimo. *Southwestern Journal of Anthropology, 27(2):* 148-165.

Burnham, C. L. (1881). *No Gentlemen.* Chicago: Henry A. Sumner. Published anonymously.

Burton, I., and Kates, R. W. (1964). The perception of natural hazards in resource management. *Natural Resources Journal, 3:* 412-441.

——, Kates, R. W., and White, G. F. (1968). *The Human Ecology of Extreme Geophysical Events.* Toronto: Department of Geography, University of Toronto, Natural Hazard Research Working Paper No. 1.

——, Kates, R., and Snead, R. (1969). *The Human Ecology of Coastal Flood Hazard in Megalopolis.* Chicago: Department of Geography, University of Chicago, Research Paper No. 115.

——, Kates, R. W., and Kirkby, A. (1975). Interdisciplinary environmental approaches theory by discipline: geography (the cognitive reformation). *Natural Resources Journal, 15.*

Busacker, R. G., and Saaty, T. L. (1965). *Finite Graphs and Networks: An Introduction with Applications.* New York: McGraw-Hill.

Butterworth, H. (1883). *Up from the Cape.* Boston: Estes and Lauriat. Published anonymously.

Buttimer, A. (1968). Social geography. *International Encyclopedia of the Social Sciences, 6:* 134-145.

——. (1969). Social space in interdisciplinary perspective. *Geographical Review, 59:* 417-426.

——. (1971). *Society and Milieu in French Geographic Tradition.* Chicago: Rand McNally.

——. (1972). Social space and the planning of residential areas. *Environment and Behavior, 4:* 279-310.

——. (1974). *Values in Geography.* Washington D.C.: Association of American Geographers, Commission on College Geography, Resource Paper No. 24 (includes introduction by E. Soja and commentaries by J. Blaut, T. Hagerstrand, E. Gibson, and Y.-F. Tuan).

Bycroft, P. (1974). Environmental representation and cognitive spatial ability: the case for cognitive mapping as a process. Unpublished M.Sc. thesis, Department of Psychology, University of Surrey.

Cadwallader, M. T. (1973a). An analysis of cognitive distance and its role in consumer spatial behavior. Unpublished Ph.D. dissertation. Department of Geography, University of California.

——. (1973b). A methodological examination of cognitive distance. In W. F. E. Preiser (ed.), *Environmental Design Research,* Vol. 2. Stroudsburg, Pa.: Dowden, Hutchinson & Ross. 193-199.

Calhoun, J. B. (1962). Population density and social pathology. *Scientific American, 206:* 139-148.

Cannitello, N. (1970). Route cognition: a part of environmental cognition. Unpublished seminar paper, Department of Psychology, Clark University.

Canter, D. (ed.) (1970). *Architectural Psychology: Proceedings of the Conference Held at University of Strathclyde.* London: Royal Institute of British Architects Publications.

——. (1972). Royal Hospital for Sick Children, Yorkhill, Glasgow: a psychological analysis. *Architects' Journal, 156:* 525-564.

——. (1975). *Psychology for Architects.* London: Applied Sciences Publishers; New York: Halsted Press.

——, and Lee, T. (1975). *Psychology and the Built Environment.* London: Architectural Press; New York: Halsted Press.

——, and Lee, T. (1975). *Psychology and the Built Environment.* New York: Halsted Press.

Cantril, H., and Bumstead, C. H. (1960). *Reflections on the Human Venture.* New York: New York University Press.

Carmichael, L., Hogan, H. P., and Walter, A. A. (1932). An experimental study of the effect of language on the reproduction of visually perceived form. *Journal of Experimental Psychology, 15:* 73.

Carpenter, E. (1973). *Eskimo Realities.* New York: Holt, Rinehart and Winston.

Carr, S. (1967). The city of the mind. In W. R. Ewald, Jr. (ed.), *Environment and Man: The Next Fifty Years.* Bloomington, Ind.: Indiana University Press, pp. 197-231.

——, and Kurilko, G. (1964). Vision and memory in the view from the road. Unpublished paper, Department of Urban Design, Massachusetts Institute of Technology.

——, and Schissler, D. (1969). The city as a trip: perceptual selection and memory in the view from the road. *Environment and Behavior, 1:* 7-35.

Cassirer, E. (1944). *An Essay on Man: An Introduction to the Philosophy of Human Culture.* New Haven, Conn.: Yale University Press.

——. (1953-1957). *The Philosophy of Symbolic Forms,* Vol. 1, *Language;* Vol. 2, *Mythical Thought;* Vol. 3, *The Phenomenology of Knowledge.* New Haven, Conn.: Yale University Press.

Cather, Willa. (1971; original, 1927). *Death Comes for the Archbishop.* New York: Random House.

Cattell, R. (1965a). Factor analysis: an introduction to essentials: I. The purpose and underlying models. *Biometrics, 21:* 190-225.

——. (1965b). Factor analysis: an introduction to essentials: II. The role of factor analysis in research. *Biometrics, 21:* 405-435.

Chapin, F. S., and Brail, R. K. (1969). Human activity systems in the metropolitan United States. *Environment and Behavior, 1:* 107-130.

Chapin, F. S., and Hightower, H. C. (1966). *Household Activity Systems: A Pilot Investigation.* Chapel Hill, N.C.: Institute for Research in Social Science, University of North Carolina.

Chitty, D. J. (1966). *The Desert a City.* London: Oxford University Press.

Chomsky, N. (1965). *Aspects of the Theory of Syntax.* Cambridge, Mass.: MIT Press.

Chorley, R. J. (1973). *New Directions in Geography.* London: Methuen.

Christaller, W. (1966). *Central Places in Southern Germany.* (Translated by C. W. Baskin.) Englewood Cliffs, N.J.: Prentice-Hall.

Claparède, E. (1903). Le faculté d'orientation lointaine (sens de direction sens de retour). [The ability of distance orientation (sense of direction, sense of return)]. *Archives de Psychologie, Genève, 2:* 133-180.

——. (1943). L'orientation lointaine. (Distance orientation.) (Unpublished translation by J. Wapner.) *Nouveau Traite de Psychologie,* Vol. 8 Paris: Presses Universitaire de France.

Clark, K. (1935). On the painting of the English landscape. *Proceedings of the British Academy, 21:* 185-220.

Clark, L. (1974). Explorations into the nature of environmental codes. *Journal of Architectural Research, 3*(1): 34-38.

Clark, W. A. V., and Cadwallader, M. (1973). Locational stress and residential mobility. *Environment and Behavior, 5:* 29-41.

Clarkson, G. P. E. (1963). *The Theory of Consumer Demand.* Englewood Cliffs, N.J.: Prentice-Hall.

Conklin, H. C. (1957). *Hanunoo Agriculture: A Report on an Integral System of Shifting Cultivation in the Philippines.* Washington, D.C.: United Nations Food and Agriculture Organization, Forestry Development Paper No. 12.

——. (1962). Lexicographical treatment of folk

taxonomies. *International Journal of American Linguistics, 28*(2), Part IV: 119-141.

———. (1967a). Ifugao ethnobotany, 1905-1965: the Beyer–Merrill report in perspective. In M. D. Zamora (ed.), *Studies in Philippine Anthropology: In Honor of H. Otley Beyer.* Quezon City, Philippines: Alemar-Phoenix, pp. 204-262. Reprinted in *Economic Botany,* 1967, *21*(3): 243-272.

———. (1967b). Some aspects of ethnograhic research in Ifugao. *Transactions of the New York Academy of Sciences,* Ser. II, *30:* 99-121.

———. (1972). *Land Use in North Central Ifugao: A Set of Eight Sheet Maps (Scale 1:5000).* New York: American Geographical Society.

———. (1974). Ethnographic research in Ifugao. In E. Z. Vogt (ed), *Aerial Photography in Anthropological Field Research.* Cambridge, Mass.: Harvard University Press, pp. 140-159.

———. (In press). *Ethnographic Atlas of Ifugao.* New York: American Geographical Society.

Conron, J. (ed.) (1973). *The American Landscape: A Critical Anthology of Prose and Poetry.* New York: Oxford University Press.

Corso, J. F. (1967). *The Experimental Psychology of Sensory Behavior.* New York: Holt, Rinehart and Winston.

Cox, K. R., and Golledge, R. G. (eds.) (1969). *Behavioral Problems in Geography: A Symposium,* Evanston, Ill.: Northwestern University Press, Studies in Geography No. 17.

Craik, K. H. (1968). The comprehension of the everyday physical environment. *Journal of the American Institute of Planners, 34:* 27-37.

———. (1970a). Environmental psychology. In K. H. Craik et al., *New Directions in Psychology,* Vol. 4. New York: Holt, Rinehart and Winston, pp. 1-121.

———. (chairman) (1970b). Environmental dispositions and preferences. In J. Archea and C. Eastmen (eds.), *EDRA Two: Proceedings, Second Annual Environmental Design Research Association Conference.* Pittsburgh: Carnegie-Mellon University, pp. 309-339.

———. (1973). Environmental psychology. *Annual Review of Psychology, 24:* 403-422.

Crawford, F. (1885). *An American Politician.* Boston: Houghton Mifflin.

Dasen, P. R. (1972a). Cross-cultural Piagetian research: a summary. *Journal of Cross-Cultural Psychology, 3:* 23-39.

———. (1972b). The influence of ecology, culture, and European contact on cognitive development in Australian aborigines. In J. W. Berry and P. R. Dasen (eds.), *Culture and Cognition: Readings in Cross-Cultural Psychology.*

Davidson, D. A. (1972). Terrain adjustment and prehistoric communities. In P. J. Ucko, R. Tringham, and G. W. Dimblby (eds.), *Man, Settlement, and Urbanism.* London: Duckworth, pp. 17-22.

Davis, J. (1969). Town and country. *Anthropology Quarterly, 42*(3): 171-185.

De Jonge, D. (1962). Images of urban areas: their structure and psychological foundations. *Journal of the American Institute of Planners, 28:* 266-276.

De Lorris, G., and de Meun, J. (1962). *The Romance of the Rose.* (Translated by H. W. Robbins.) New York: Dutton.

Deutsch, K. W., and Isard, W. (1961). A note on a generalized concept of effective distance. *Behavioral Science, 6:* 308-311.

Devlin, A. S. (1973). Some factors in enhancing knowledge of a natural area. In W. F. E. Preiser (ed.), *Environmental Design Research, Vol. 2.* Stroudsburg, Pa.: Dowden, Hutchinson & Ross, pp. 200-207.

Dewey, T., and Bentley, A. F. (1949). *Knowing and the Known.* Boston: Beacon Press.

Dixon, W. J. (ed.) (1967). *BMD Biomedical Computer Programs,* 2nd ed. Berkeley, Calif.: University of California Press.

Dodwell, P. C. (1963). Children's understanding of spatial concepts. *Canadian Journal of Psychology, 17:* 141-161.

Donaldson, O. S. (1971). Geography and the black Americans: the white papers and the invisible man. *Journal of Geography, 70:* 138-149.

Donaldson, W. S. (1969). *The Suburban Myth.* New York: Columbia University Press.

Doob, W. W. (ed.) (1971). *Patterning of Time.* New Haven, Conn.: Yale University Press.

Dotson, F. (1951). Patterns of voluntary association among urban working class families. *American Sociological Review, 16:* 687-693.

Doughty, P. L. (1970). Behind the back of the city: provincial life in Lima, Peru. In W. Mangin (ed), *Peasants in Cities.* Boston: Houghton Mifflin, pp. 30-46.

Downs, R. M. (1970a). The cognitive structure of an urban shopping center. *Environment and Behavior, 2:* 13-39.

——. (1970b). Geographic space perception: past approaches and future prospects. In C. Board, R. J. Chorley, P. Haggett, and D. R. Stoddart (eds.), *Progress in Geography,* Vol. 2. London: Edward Arnold, pp. 65-108.

——, and Horsfall, R. (1971). Methodological approaches to urban cognition. Paper presented at the Association of American Geographers meeting, Boston.

——, and Stea, D. (chairmen) (1970). Environmental cognition and behavior. In J. Archea and C. Eastman (eds.), *EDRA Two: Proceedings of the Second Annual Environmental Design Research Association Conference.* Pittsburgh: Carnegie-Mellon University, pp. 95-142.

——, and Stea, D. (eds.) (1973a). *Image and Environment: Cognitive Mapping and Spatial Behavior.* Chicago: Aldine.

——, and Stea, D. (1973b). Cognitive maps and spatial behavior: process and products. In R. M. Downs and D. Stea (eds.), *Image and Environment: Cognitive Mapping and Spatial Behavior.* Chicago: Aldine, pp. 8-26.

Drayer, C. S. (1957). Psychological factors and problems, emergency and long term. *The Annals, American Academy of Political and Social Science, 309:* 151-159.

Duncan, J. S. (1972). The social order of 200 yards of public street in Hyderabad, India. Paper presented at the Middle States Division meeting of the Association of American Geographers.

——. (1973). Landscape taste as a symbol of group identity: a Westchester County village. *The Geographical Review, 63:* 334-355.

——. (1974). The residential landscape as presentation of self: two elites in Hyderabad, India. Unpublished M.A. thesis, Department of Geography, Syracuse University.

Duncan, O. D. (1964). Social organization and the ecosystem. In R. E. L. Faris (ed.), *Handbook of Modern Sociology.* Chicago: Rand McNally, pp. 37-82.

Duncker, K. (1945). On problem-solving (trans. by Lynne S. Lees). *Psychological Monographs, 58(No. 270):* 356.

Durrell, L. (1962). *Alexandria Quartet.* London: Faber & Faber.

Eibl-Eibesfeld, I. (1970). *Ethology: The Biology of Behavior.* New York: Holt, Rinehart and Winston.

Einstien, A., and Infeld, L. (1938). *The Evolution of Physics: The Growth of Ideas from Early Concepts to Relativity and Quanta.* New York: Simon and Schuster.

Ekman, G., and Bratfisch, O. (1965). Subjective distance and emotional involvement: a psychological mechanism. *Acta Psychologica, 24:* 446-453.

Eliade, M. (1961). *The Sacred and the Profane.* New York: Harper & Row.

Eliot, T. S. (1953a). The love song of J. Alfred Prufrock. In *The Complete Poems and Plays (1909-1950.* New York: Harcourt Brace, pp. 3-7.

——. (1953b). Rhapsody on a windy night. In *The Complete Poems and Plays 1909-1950.* New York: Harcourt Brace, pp. 14-16.

Elkind, D., and Flavell, J. H. (eds.) (1969). *Studies on Cognitive Development: Essays in Honor of Jean Piaget.* New York: Oxford University Press.

Epstein, W. (1967). *Varieties of Perceptual Learning.* New York: McGraw-Hill.

Everett, J., and Cadwallader, M. (1972). The home area concept in urban analysis: the use of cognitive mapping and computer procedures as "methodological tools." In W. J. Mitchell (ed.), *Environmental Design: Research and Practice,* Vol. 1. Los Angeles: School of Architecture and Urban Planning, University of California, pp. 1-2-1 to 1-2-10.

Feinberg, I., and Laycock, F. (1964). Ability of blindfolded children to use landmarks to locate a target. *Child Development, 35:* 547-558.

Fernandez, J. W. (1970). Fang Architectonics. Paper given at Conference on Traditional African Architecture, September.

Feyerabend, P. K. (1970). Against method: outline of an anarchist theory of knowledge. In M. Radney and S. Winokur (eds.), *Analyses of Theories and*

Methods of Physics and Psychology. Minneapolis, Minn.: University of Minnesota Press, Minnesota Studies in the Philosophy of Science, Vol. 4, pp. 1-130.

Firey, W. (1945). Sentiment and symbolism as ecological variables. *American Sociological Review, 10;* 140-148.

———. (1960). *Man, Mind, and Land: A Theory of Resource Use.* New York: Free Press.

Fischer, J. L. (1971). Art styles as cultural cognitive maps. In C. F. Jopling (ed.), *Art and Aesthetics in Primitive Societies.* New York: Dutton, pp. 171-192.

Flannery, K. V. (1955). The ecology of early food production in Mesopotamia. *Science, 147:* 1247-1256.

Flavell, J. H. (1963). *The Developmental Psychology of Jean Piaget.* New York: Van Nostrand Reinhold.

———. (1971). The development of inferences about others. Paper presented at the Interdisciplinary Conference on Our Knowledge of Person Perception and Interpersonal Behavior. State University of New York at Binghamton, N.Y., December. December.

Foerster, N., and Falk, R. (eds.) (1960). *American Prose and Poetry.* Boston: Houghton Mifflin.

Foley, D. (1954). Urban daytime populations: a field for demographic–ecological analysis. *Social Forces, 34:* 323-330.

Follini, M. B. (1966). The construction of behavioral space: a micro-genetic investigation of orientation in an unfamiliar locality. Unpublished M.A. thesis, Department of Psychology, Clark University.

Forbes, J. (1964). Mapping accessibility. *Scottish Geographical Magazine, 80:* 12-21.

Form, W. H. (1954). The place of social structure in the determination of land use. *Social Forces, 32:* 317-323.

Foss, L. (1971). Art as cognitive: beyond scientific realism. *Philosophy of Science, 38:* 234-250.

Frake, C. O. (1962). Cultural ecology and ethnography. *American Anthropologist, 64*(1): 53-59.

Francescato, D., and Mebane, W. (1973). How citizens view two great cities: Milan and Rome. In R. M. Downs and D. Stea (eds.), *Image and Environment: Cognitive Mapping and Spatial Behavior.* Chicago: Aldine, pp. 131-147.

Frank, L. G. (1966). The world as a communication network. In G. Kepes (ed.), *Sign, Image, Symbol.* New York: Braziller, pp. 1-14.

Frankel, D. G. Perceptual implications of reaching, Unpublished manuscript, Special Preliminary Paper, Institute of Child Development, University of Minnesota, 1972.

Fraser, T. M. (1968). Relative habitability of dwellings—a conceptual view. *Ekistics* 27(158): 15-18.

Freeman, F. N. (1916). Geography: extension of experience through imagination. *The Psychology of Common Branches.* Boston: Houghton Mifflin.

Fried, M. (1973). *The World of the Urban Working Class.* Cambridge, Mass.: Harvard University Press.

———, and Gleicher, P. (1961). Some sources of residential satisfaction in an urban slum. *Journal of the American Institute of Planners, 27:* 305-315.

Friedell, M. R. (1967). Organizations as semilattices. *American Sociological Review, 32:* 46-54.

Friedlander, F. (1970). Emerging blackness in a white research world. *Human Organization, 29:* 239-250.

Gans, H. J. (1962). *The Urban Villagers: Group and Class in the Life of Italian-Americans.* New York: Free Press.

Garland, H. (1891). *Jason Edwards: An Average Man.* New York: Appleton-Century-Crofts.

Garling, T. (1969a). Studies in visual perception of architectural spaces and rooms. I. Judgment scales of open and closed space. *Scandinavian Journal of Psychology, 10:* 250-256.

———. (1969b). Studies in visual perception of architectural spaces and rooms. II. Judgments of open and closed space by category ratings and magnitude estimation. *Scandinavian Journal of Psychology, 10:* 257-268.

———. (1970a). Studies in visual perception of architectural spaces and rooms. III. A relation between judged depth and size of space. *Scandinavian Journal of Psychology, 11:* 124-131.

———. (1970b). Studies in visual perception of architectural spaces and rooms. IV. The relation of judged depth to judged size of space under different viewing conditions. *Scandinavian Journal of Psychology, 11:* 133–145.

Garner, B. J. (1966). *The Internal Structure of Retail Nucleations.* Evanston, Ill.: Northwestern University Studies in Geography No. 12.

——. (1967). Some reflections on the notion of threshold in central place studies. Paper presented at the Association of American Geographers meeting, St. Louis.

——. (1968). Models of urban geography and settlement location. In P. Haggett and R. J. Chorley (eds.), *Socio-Economic Models in Geography.* London: Methuen, pp. 303–360.

Gazzaniga, M. S. (1972). One brain—two minds? *American Scientist, 60:* 311–317.

Geertz, C. (1963). *Agricultural Involution: The Process of Ecological Change in Indonesia.* Berkeley, Calif.: University of California Press.

Gerson, E. M. (1971). Notes on locales. Unpublished paper, Department of Sociology, Syracuse University.

Gibson, E. J. (1969). *Principles of Perceptual Learning and Development.* New York: Appleton-Century-Crofts.

——. (1970). The development of perception as an adaptive process. *American Scientist, 58:* 98–107.

——, and Bergman, R. (1954). The effect of training on absolute estimation of distance over ground. *Journal of Experimental Psychology, 48:* 473–482.

Gibson, J. J. (1946). Perception of distance and space in the open air. In *Motion Picture Testing and Research,* AAF program report 7, pp. 181–195. (Reprinted in D. C. Beardslee and M. Wertheimer (eds.), *Readings in Perception.* New York: Van Nostrand Reinhold, 1958, pp. 415–431.)

——. (1950). *The Perception of the Visual World.* Boston: Houghton Mifflin.

——. (1966). *The Senses Considered as Perceptual Systems.* Boston: Houghton Mifflin.

——, and Gibson, E. J. (1955). Perceptual learning: differentiation or enrichment? *Psychological Review, 62:* 32–41.

Gittins, J. S. (1969). Forming impressions of an unfamiliar city: a comparative study of aesthetic and scientific knowing. Unpublished M.A. thesis, Department of Psychology, Clark University.

Glacken, C. (1966). *Traces on the Rhodian Shore.* Berkeley, Calif.: University of California Press.

Gladwin, T. (1964). Culture and logical processes. In W. H. Goodenough (ed.), *Explorations in Cultural Anthropology.* New York: McGraw-Hill, pp. 167–177.

Glaser, B. G., and Strauss, A. L. (1971). *Status Passage: A Formal Theory.* Chicago: Aldine.

Glass, R. (1955). Urban sociology. *Current Sociology, 4*(4): 14.

Gleason, J. J. (1972). Imaginative modes of perceiving the city: the architectural metaphor in twentieth-century American literature. In W. J. Mitchell (ed.), *Environmental Design: Research and Practice,* Vol. 1. Los Angeles: School of Architecture and Urban Planning, University of California, pp. 7-3-1 to 7-3-7.

Goffman, E. (1959). *The Presentation of Self in Everyday Life.* Garden City, N.Y.: Doubleday.

Golant, S. (1969). *Human Behavior Before the Disaster: A Selected Annotated Bibliography.* Toronto: Department of Geography, University of Toronto, Natural Hazard Working Paper No. 9.

Golledge, R. G. (1967). Conceptualizing the market decision process. *Journal of Regional Science* (Supplement), pp. 239–258.

——. (1970). *Process Approaches to the Analysis of Human Spatial Behavior.* Columbus, Ohio: Department of Geography, Ohio State University, Discussion paper No. 17.

——, and Brown, L. A. (1967). Search, learning, and the market decision process. *Geografiska Annaler, B 49:* 116–124.

——, and Moore, G. T. (1973). Symposium on environmental cognition: introductory comments. In W. F. E. Preiser (ed.), *Environmental Design Research, Vol. 2,* Stroudsburg, Pa.: Dowden, Hutchinson & Ross, pp. 183–185.

——, and Zannaras, G. (1973). Cognitive approaches to the analysis of human spatial behavior. In W. H. Ittelson (ed.), *Environmental Cognition.* New York: Seminar Press, pp. 59–94.

——, Briggs, R., and Demko, D. (1969). The configuration of distances in intraurban space. *Proceedings of the Association of American Geographers, 1:* 60-65.

——, Brown, L. A., and Williamson, F. (1972). Behavioral approaches to geography: an overview. *Australian Geographer, 12:* 59-79.

——, Rivizzigno, V. L., and Spector, A. (1975a). Learning about a city: analysis by multidimensional scaling. In R. G. Golledge and G. Rushton (eds.), *Spatial Choice and Spatial Preference.* Columbus, Ohio: Ohio State University Press.

——, Rivizzigno, V. L., and Spector, A. (1975b). Learning about a city: analysis by multidimensional scaling. In R. G. Golledge (ed.), *On Determining Cognitive Configurations of a City,* Vol., 1. Columbus, Ohio: Department of Geography and Ohio State University Research Foundation.

Gombrich, E. H. (1962). *Art and Illusion,* new ed. London: Phaidon Press.

Good, I. J. (1965). Speculations concerning the first ultraintelligent machine. *Advances in Computers, 6:* 31-88.

Goodman, N. (1968). *The Language of Art.* New York: Bobbs-Merrill.

Gould, P. R. (1963). Man against his environment: a game theoretic framework. *Annals of the Association of American Geographers, 53:* 290-297.

——. (1966). *On Mental Maps.* Ann Arbor, Mich.: Michigan Inter-University Community of Mathematical Geographers, Discussion Paper No. 9.

——. (1970a). Is *statistex inferens* the geographical name for wild goose. *Economic Geography, 46:* 439-448.

——. (1970c). The structure of spatial preferences in Tanzania. *Area 4:* 29-35.

——. (1972). Location in information space. Paper presented at the Symposium on Conceptual Issues in Environmental Cognition, Environmental Design Research Association meeting, Los Angeles, January.

——. (1973a). The black boxes of Jönköping: spatial information and process. In R. M. Downs and D. Stea (eds.), *Man and Environment: Cognitive Mapping and Spatial Behavior.* Chicago: Aldine, pp. 235-245.

——. (1973b). On mental maps. In R. M. Downs and D. Stea (eds.), *Image and Environment: Cognitive Mapping and Spatial Behavior.* Chicago: Aldine, pp. 182-220.

——, and Tornquist, G. (1971). Information, innovation and acceptance. In T. Hägerstrand and A. Kulinski (eds.), *Information Systems for Regional Development.* Lund Studies in Geography. Lund, Sweden: C. W. K. Gleerup.

——, and White, R. R. (1968). The mental maps of British school leavers. *Regional Studies, 2:* 161-182.

——, and White, R. R. (1974). *Mental Maps.* Harmondsworth, England: Penguin.

Greeley, A. (1972). *That Most Distressful Nation.* Chicago: Quadrangle.

Greenbie, B. B. (1974). Problems of scale and context in assessing a generalized landscape for particular persons. In E. H. Zube, J. G. Fabos, and R. O. Brush (eds.), *Landscape Assessment.* Stroudsburg, Pa.: Dowden, Hutchinson & Ross.

Gregory, R. L. (1963). Distortion of visual space as inappropriate constancy scaling. *Nature, 199:* 678-680.

——. (1966). *Eye and Brain: The Psychology of Seeing.* New York: McGraw-Hill.

Griffin, D. (1948). Topographical orientation. In E. G. Boring, M. S. Langfeld, and H. P. Wald (eds.), *Foundations of Psychology.* New York: Wiley. (Reprinted, in part, in R. M. Downs and D. Stea (eds.) (1973). *Image and Environment: Cognitive Mapping and Spatial Behavior.* Chicago: Aldine, pp. 296-299.)

Griffin, R. M., Jr. (1969). Ethological concepts for planning. *Journal of the American Institute of Planners, 35:* 54-60.

Gropius, W. (1955). *The Scope of Total Architecture.* New York: Harper & Row.

Gulick, J. (1963). Images of an Arab city. *Journal of the American Institute of Planners, 29:* 179-198.

Gulliver, F. P. (1908). Orientation of maps. *Journal of Geography, 7:* 55-58.

Gutman, R. (ed.) (1972). *People and Buildings.* New York; Basic Books.

Haar, C. M. (ed.) (1964). *Law and the Land: Anglo-American Planning Practice.* Cambridge, Mass.: Harvard University Press.

Haddon, J. (1960). A view of foreign lands. *Geography, 45*(4): 286-289.

Hagerstrand, T. (1970). What about people in regional science? *Papers of the Regional Science Association, 24:* 7-21.

Hall, E. T. (1959). *The Silent Language.* Garden City, N.Y.: Doubleday.

——. (1966). *The Hidden Dimension.* Garden City, N.Y.: Doubleday.

Hallowell, A. I. (1955). *Culture and Experience.* Philadelphia: University of Pennsylvania Press.

Halprin, L. (1963). *Cities.* New York: Van Nostrand Reinhold.

——. (1965). Motations. *Progressive Architecture, 46:* 126-133.

——. (1969). Scores and notation. *The RSVP Cycles: Creative Process in the Environment.* New York: Braziller. pp. 30-43, 92-103.

Ham, L. B., and Parkinson, J. S. (1932). Loudness and intensity relations. *Journal of the Acoustics Society of America, 3:* 511-534.

Handel, S., De Soto, S. B., and London, M. (1968). Reasoning and spatial representation. *Journal of Verbal Learning and Verbal Behavior, 7:* 351-357.

Harman, E. J., and Betak, J. F. (1974). Some preliminary findings on the cognitive meaning of external privacy in housing. In D. H. Carson (ed.), *Man-Environment Interactions,* Part 11. Milwaukee, Wisc.: School of Architecture and Urban Planning, University of Wisconsin, pp. 41-56.

Harris, C. D., and Ullman, E. L. (1945). The nature of cities. *Annals of the American Academy of Political Science and Social Science, 242:* 7-17.

Harrison, E. D. (1971). Studies in the perception of architectural space. I. Judgments of open and closed space. Unpublished paper, Department of Architecture, University of Washington, Seattle.

Harrison, J. (1973). Retailers' mental images of the environment. Unpublished Ph.D. dissertation, Department of Geography, Bristol University.

——, and Sarre, P. (1971). Personal construct theory in the measurement of environmental images: I.

problems and methods. *Environment and Behavior, 3:* 351-374.

——, and Sarre, P. (1974). Personal construct theory and the measurement of environmental images. II: applications *Environment and Behavior, 6:* 3-58.

Harrison, J. D., and Howard, W. A. (1972). The role of meaning in the urban image. *Environment and Behavior, 4:* 389-412.

Hart, R. A. (1971). Aerial geography: an experimental study in elementary education. Unpublished M.A. thesis, Graduate School of Geography, Clark University.

——. (1974). The genesis of landscaping: two years of discovery in a Vermont town. *Landscape Architecture, 65:* 356-363.

——, and Moore, G. T. (1971). *The Development of Spatial Cognition: A Review.* Worcester, Mass.: Graduate School of Geography, Clark University, Place Perception Research Report No. 7. (Translated by A. Pinard and republished as *Le Developpement de la connaissance d'espace: revue critique.* Montreal: Centre de Récherches et d'Innovation Urbaines, Université de Montréal, 1975.)

——, and Moore, G. T. (1973). The development of spatial cognition: a review. In R. M. Downs and D. Stea (eds.), *Image and Environment: Cognitive Mapping and Spatial Behavior.* Chicago: Aldine, pp. 246-288.

Hartman, C. W. (1963). Social values and housing orientations. *Journal of Social Issues, 19:* 113-131.

Hartman, G. (1970). Structuralism: the Anglo-American adventure. In J. Ehrmann (ed.), *Structuralism.* Garden City, N.Y.: Doubleday, pp. 137-158.

Harvey, D. W. (1967). *Behavioural Postulates and the Construction of Theory in Geography.* Bristol: Department of Geography, Bristol University, Seminar Paper Series A, No. 6.

——. (1969a). *Explanation in Geography.* London: Edward Arnold; New York: St. Martin's Press.

——. (1969b). Conceptual and measurement problems in the cognitive-behavioral approach to location theory. In K. R. Cox and R. G. Golledge (eds.), *Behavioral Problems in Geography: A*

Symposium. Evanston, Ill.: Northwestern University Studies in Geography No. 17, pp. 35–68.

———. (1970). Social processes and spatial form: an analysis of conceptual problems in urban planning. *Papers of the Regional Science Association, 25:* 47-69.

———. (1972). Revolutionary and counter revolutionary theory in geography and the problem of ghetto formation. *Antipode, 4*(2): 1-12.

———. (1973). *Social Justice and the City.* London: Arnold.

Haugen, E. (1969). The semantics of Icelandic orientation. In S. A. Tyler (ed.), *Cognitive Anthropology.* New York: Holt, Rinehart and Winston, pp. 330-342.

Hawley, A. H. (1950). *Human Ecology.* New York: Ronald Press.

Hayward, S. C., and Franklin, S. S. (1974). Perceived openness–enclosure of architectural space. *Environment and Behavior, 6:* 37-52.

Heathcote, R. L. (1965). *Back of Bourke.* Melbourne: Melbourne University Press, pp. 5-29, 85-115.

———. (1969). Drought in Australia: a problem of perception. *Geographical Review, 69:* 175-194.

Hebb, D. O. (1949). *The Organization of Behavior.* New York: Wiley.

———. (1963). The semi-autonomous process, its nature and nurture. *American Psychologist, 18:* 16-27.

Heinemeyer, W. F. (1967). The urban core as a center of attraction. *Urban Core and Inner City.* Leiden, Netherlands: Brill, pp. 82-99.

Held, R. (1965). Plasticity in sensory-motor systems. *Scientific American, 213*(5): 84-94.

———, and Hein, A. (1963). Movement-produced stimulation in the development of visually guided behavior. *Journal of Comparative and Physiological Psychology, 56:* 872-876.

———, and Rekosh, J. (1963). Motor-sensory feedback and the geometry of visual space. *Science, 141:* 722-723.

Hemple, C. G. (1965). *Aspects of Scientific Explanation.* New York: Free Press.

Herzog, T. R., Kaplan, S., and Kaplan, R. (1976). The prediction of preference for familiar urban places. *Environment and Behavior* (in press).

Hesselgren, S. (1971). *Experimental Studies on Architectural Perception.* Stockholm: National Swedish Building Research Institute, Document D21.

Hilgard, E. R. (1951). The role of learning in perception. In R. R. Blake and G. V. Ramsey (eds.), *Perception: An Approach to Personality.* New York: Ronald Press, pp. 95-120.

———, and Bower, G. H. (1966). *Theories of Learning,* 3rd ed. New York: Appleton-Century-Crofts.

Hinkle, D. N. (1965). The change of personal constructs from the viewpoint of a theory of implications. Unpublished Ph.D. dissertation, Department of Psychology, Ohio State University.

Hitt, W. D. (1969). Two models of man. *American Psychologist, 24:* 651-658.

Holcomb, H. B. (1972). The influence of culture on the perception of the urban environment. Unpublished Ph. D. dissertation, Department of Geography, University of Colorado.

Holland, J. H. (1974). *Adaptation in Natural and Artificial Systems.* Ann Arbor, Mich.: University of Michigan Press.

Holland, R. (1970). George Kelly: constructive innocent and reluctant existentialist. In D. Bannister (ed.), *Perspectives in Personal Construct Theory.* London: Academic Press, pp. 111-132.

Hollingshead, A. B., and Redic, F. (1958). *Social Class and Mental Illness: Community Study.* New York: Wiley.

Holzner, L. (1970). The role of history and tradition in the urban geography of West Germany. *Annals of the Association of American Geographers, 60:* 315-339.

Honikman, B. (ed.) (1970). *Proceedings of the Architectural Psychology Conference at Kingston-upon-Thames.* Kingston-upon-Thames, England: Kingston Polytechnic Institute.

———. (1972). An investigation of the relationship between construing of the environment and its physical form. In W. J. Mitchell (ed.), *Environmental Design: Research and Practice,* Vol. 1. Los Angeles: School of Architecture and Urban Planning, University of California, pp. 5-6-1 to 5-6-11.

———. (1973). Personal construct theory and environmental evaluation. In W. F. E. Preiser (ed.), *En-*

vironmental Design Research, Vol. 1. Strouds-burg, Pa.: Dowden, Hutchinson & Ross, pp. 242–253.

——. (ed.) (1974). *Cognition and Perception.* In D. H. Carson (general ed.), *Man–Environment Interactions,* Part 11. Milwaukee, Wisc.: School of Architecture and Urban Planning, University of Wisconsin.

Horvath, R. J. (1974). Machine space. *Geographical Review, 64:* 168–188.

Howard, I. P., and Templeton, W. B. (1966). Geographical orientation. In *Human Spatial Orientation.* New York: Wiley, Chapter 10. (Reprinted in R. M. Downs and D. Stea (eds.), *Image and Environment: Cognitive Mapping and Spatial Behavior.* Chicago: Aldine, 1973.

Howell, R. W. (1969). *A Study of Informal Learning.* Washington, D.C.: U.S. Department of Health, Education, and Welfare, Project 8-13-125.

Howells, W. D. (1881). *A Modern Instance.* Boston: Houghton Mifflin.

——. (1884). *The Rise of Silas Lapham.* Cambridge, Mass.: Houghton Mifflin.

Hubel, D. H., and Wiesel, T. N. (1962). Receptive fields, binocular interaction, and functional architecture in the cat's visual cortex. *Journal of Physiology, 160:* 106–154.

Hudson, B. B. (1954). Anxiety in response to the unfamiliar. *Journal of Social Issues, 10:* 53–60.

Hudson, R. (1974a). Consumer spatial behaviour: a conceptual model and empirical investigation in Bristol. Unpublished Ph.D. dissertation, Department of Geography, University of Bristol.

——. (1974b). Images of the retailing environment: an example of the use of the repertory grid methodology. *Environment and Behavior, 6:* 470–494.

Hughes, E. C. (1936). The ecological aspect of institutions. *American Sociological Review, 1:* 180–189.

——. (ed.) (1958). Life cycles, turning points, and careers. *Men and Their Work.* New York: Free Press, pp. 11–22.

Hull, C. (1952). *A Behavior System.* New Haven, Conn.: Yale University Press.

Hunt, E. B. (1962). *Concept of Learning.* New York: Wiley.

Hunt, H. J. (1959). *Balzac's Comedie Humaine.* London: Athlone Press.

Huttenlocher, J. (1968). Constructing spatial images: a strategy in reasoning. *Psychological Review, 75:* 550–560.

Huxtable, A. L. (1973). How we see, or think we see the city. *The New York Times,* Section 2, Nov. 25, 1973, p. 26.

Ittelson, W. H. (1951). The constancies in perceptual theory. *Psychological Review, 58:* 285–294.

——. (1960). *Visual Space Perception.* New York: Springer.

——. (1962). Perception and transactional psychology. In S. Koch (ed.), *Psychology: A Study of a Science,* Vol. 4. New York: McGraw-Hill, pp. 674–697.

——. (1970). Perception of the large-scale environment. *Transactions of the New York Academy of Sciences,* Series II. *32:* 807–815.

——. (1973). Environmental perception and contemporary perceptual theory. In W. H. Ittleson (ed.), *Environment and Cognition.* New York: Seminar Press, pp. 1–19.

——, and Cantril, H. (1960). *Perception: A Transactional Approach.* Garden City, N.Y.: Doubleday.

——, Franck, K. A., and O'Hanlon, T. (1975). The nature of environmental experience. Paper presented at a conference on Experiencing the Environment, Clark University.

Jackson, J. B. (1970). The stranger's path. In E. H. Zube (ed.), *Landscapes.* Amherst, Mass.: University of Massachusetts Press.

Jackson, R. H. (1972). Myth and reality: environmental perception of the Morman pioneers. *Rocky Mountain Social Science Journal, 9:* 33–38.

Jakobson, R. (1957). *Shifters, Verbal Categories, and the Russian Verb.* Cambridge, Mass.: Russian Language Project, Department of Slavic Languages, Harvard University.

James, H. (1886). *The Bostonians.* London: Macmillan.

James, W. (1892). *Psychology: The Briefer Course.* New York: Holt.

——. (1902). *The Varieties of Religious Experience.* New York: Modern Library.

Jonassen, C. T. (1961). Cultural variables in the ecology of an ethnic group. In G. A. Theodorson (ed.), *Studies in Human Ecology.* New York: Harper & Row, pp. 269–273.

Jones, M. (1972). Urban path-choosing behavior: a study in environmental cues. In W. J. Mitchell (ed.), *Environmental Design: Research and Practice,* Vol. 1. Los Angeles: School of Architecture and Urban Planning, University of California. pp. 11-4-1 to 11-4-10.

Jopling, C. F. (ed.) (1971). *Art and Aesthetics in Primitive Societies.* New York: Dutton.

Jung, C. G. (1953). *Two Essays on Analytic Psychology.* London: Routledge & Kegan Paul.

Kahl, J. A. (1967). *The American Class Structure.* New York: Holt, Rinehart and Winston.

Kamau, L. J. (1976). Conceptual patterns in Yoruba culture. In A. Rapoport (ed.), *The Mutual Interaction of People and Their Built Environment: A Cross-Cultural Perspective.* The Hague, Netherlands: Mouton (in press).

Kant, E. (1902). *Critique of Pure Reason,* 2nd ed. New York: Macmillan.

Kaplan, A. (1964). *The Conduct of Inquiry.* San Francisco: Chandler.

Kaplan, B. (1967). Meditations on genesis. *Human Development, 10:* 65-87.

——, Wapner, S., and Cohen, S. B. (1975). Exploratory applications of the organismic-developmental approach to man-in-environment transactions. Paper presented at a conference on Experiencing the Environment, Clark University.

Kaplan, R. (1972). The dimensions of the visual environment: methodological considerations. In W. J. Mitchell (ed.), *Environmental Design: Research and Practice,* Vol. 1. Los Angeles: School of Architecture and Urban Planning, University of California.

——. (1975). Some methods and strategies in the prediction of preference. In E. H. Zube, R. O. Brush, and J. G. Fabos (eds.), *Landscape Assessment.* Stroudsburg, Pa.: Dowden, Hutchinson & Ross, pp. 118-129.

Kaplan, S. (1970). The role of location processing in the perception of the environment. In J. Archea and C. Eastman (eds.), *EDRA Two: Proceedings of the Second Annual Environmental Design Research Association Conference.* Pittsburgh: Carnegie-Mellon University, pp. 131-134.

——. (1972). The challenge of environmental psychology: a proposal for a new functionalism. *American Psychologist, 27:* 140-143.

——. (1973a). Cognitive maps, human needs, and the designed environment. In W. F. E. Preiser (ed.), *Environmental Design Research,* Vol. 1. Stroudsburg, Pa.: Dowden, Hutchinson & Ross, pp. 275-283.

——. (1973b). Cognitive maps in perception and thought. In R. M. Downs and D. Stea (eds.), *Image and Environment: Cognitive Mapping and Spatial Behavior.* Chicago: Aldine, pp. 63-78.

——. (1975). An informal model for the prediction of preference. In E. H. Zube, R. O. Brush, and J. G. Fabos (eds.), *Landscape Assessment.* Stroudsburg, Pa.: Dowden, Hutchinson & Ross, pp. 92-101.

——, and Wendt, J. S. (1972). Preference and the visual environment: complexity and some alternatives. In W. J. Mitchell (ed.), *Environmental Design: Research and Practice,* Vol. 1. Los Angeles: School of Architecture and Urban Planning, University of California, pp. 6-8-1 to 6-8-5.

Kates, R. W. (1962). *Hazard and Choice Perception in Flood Plain Management.* Chicago: Department of Geography, University of Chicago, Research Paper No. 76.

——. (1963). Perceptual regions and regional perception in flood plain management. *Papers and Proceedings of the Regional Science Association, 11:* 217-227.

——. (1967). The perception of storm hazard on the shores of megalopolis. In D. Lowenthal (ed.), *Environmental Perception and Behavior.* Chicago: Department of Geography, University of Chicago, Research Paper No. 109, pp. 60-69.

——. (1970). Human perception of the environment. *International Social Science Journal, 22:* 648-660.

——. (1971). Natural hazard in human ecological perspective: hypotheses and models. *Economic Geography, 47:* 438-451.

——, and Wohlwill, J. F. (eds.) (1966). Man's response to the physical environment. *Journal of Social Issues, 22*(4).

Katz, B. (1961). How cells communicate. *Scientific American, 205*(3):

Kay, P. (1970). Some theoretical implications of ethnographic semantics. *Bulletin of the American Anthropological Association, 3*(2): 19-31.

Keesing, F. M. (1962). *The Ethnohistory of Northern Luzon.* Stanford, Calif.: Stanford University Press.

——. (1972). Pardigms lost: the new ethnography and the new linguistics. *Southwestern Journal of Anthropology, 28*(4): 299-332.

Kelly, G. A. (1955). *The Psychology of Personal Constructs* (2 vols.). New York: Norton.

——. (1970). A brief introduction to personal construct theory. In D. Bannister (ed.), *Perspectives in Personal Construct Theory.* London: Academic Press, pp. 1-29.

Kerlinger, F. N. (1964). *Foundations of Behavioral Research.* Toronto: Holt, Rinehart and Winston.

Kinsbourne, M. (1971). Cognitive deficit: experimental analysis. In J. L. McGaugh (ed.), *Psychobiology.* New York: Academic Press.

Kirk, W. (1951). Historical geography and the concept of the behavioral environment, in G. Kuriyan (ed.), *Indian Geographical Journal, Silver Jubilee Edition.* Madras: Indian Geographical Society, pp. 152-160.

Kirkby, A. (In press). Environmental psychology and social behavior. In H. Taifel and C. Fraser (eds.), *Introduction to Social Psychology.* Hammondsworth, England: Penguin.

Klein, H. J. (1967). The delimitation of the town center in the image of the citizens. *Urban Core and Inner City.* Leiden, Netherlands: Brill, pp. 286-306.

Knight, C. G. (1971). Ethnogeography and change, *70:* 47-51.

Koffka, K. (1922). Perception: an introduction to Gestalt Theorie. *Psychological Bulletin, 19:* 551-585.

Komarofsky, M. (1967). *Blue Collar Marriage.* New York: Random House.

Koroscil, P. M. (1970). The concept of values and cultural value systems in settlement analysis. *Journal of Geography,* pp. 480-484.

Kosslyn, S., Pick, H. L., Jr. and Fariello, G. (1974). Cognitive maps in children and men. *Child Development, 45:* 707-716.

Krech, D., and Crutchfield, R. S. (1948). *Theory and Problems in Social Psychology.* New York: McGraw-Hill.

Kreimer, A. (1973). Building the imagery of San Francisco: an analysis of controversy over high-rise development. In W. F. E. Preiser (ed.), *Environmental Design Research,* Vol. 2. Stroudsburg, Pa.: Dowden, Hutchinson & Ross, pp. 221-231.

Kuhn, T. (1970). *The Structure of Scientific Revolutions,* 2nd ed. Chicago: University of Chicago Press.

Kulik, J. A., Revelle, W. R., and Kulik, C. L. (1970). Scale construction by hierarchical cluster analysis. Unpublished paper, Department of Psychology, University of Michigan.

Künnapas, T. (1960). Scales for subjective distance. *Scandinavian Journal of Psychology, 1:* 187-192.

Ladd, F. (1970). Black youths view their environment: neighborhood maps. *Environment and Behavior, 2:* 74-99.

——. (1972). Black youths view their environment: some views of housing. *Journal of the American Institute of Planners, 38:* 108-116.

Lambrecht, F. (1929). Ifugao villages and houses. *Publications of the Catholic Anthropological Conference* (Washington), *1*(3): 117-141.

——. (1932-1951). The Mayawyaw ritual. *Publications of the Catholic Anthropological Conference* (Washington), *4:* 1-754.

Lamy, B. (1967). The use of the inner city of Paris and social stratification. *Urban Core and Inner City.* Leiden, Netherlands: Brill, pp. 356-367.

Landfield, A. W. (1971). *Personal Construct Systems in Psychotherapy.* Chicago: Rand McNally.

Lang, J., Burnette, C., Moleski, W., and Vachon, D. (eds.) (1974). *Designing for Human Behavior: Architecture and the Behavioral Sciences.* Stroudsburg, Pa.: Dowden, Hutchinson & Ross.

Langer, S. (1953). *Feeling and Form.* New York: Scribner's.

Laurendeau, M., and Pinard, A. (1970). *The Develop-*

ment of the Concept of Space in the Child. New York: International Universities Press.

Lazarus, R. S. (1966). *Psychological Stress and the Coping Process*. New York: McGraw-Hill.

Leach, E. R. (1961). *Pul Eliya, A Village in Ceylon: A Study of Land Tenure and Kinship*. New York: Cambridge University Press.

Leach, E. (1967). Genesis as myth. In J. Middleton (ed.), *Myth and Cosmos*. Garden City, N.Y.: Doubelday, pp. 1-13.

Lee, R. G. (1972). The social definition of outdoor recreational places. In W. R. Burch, Jr., N. H. Cheek, Jr., and L. Taylor (eds.), *Social Behavior, Natural Resources, and the Environment*. New York: Harper & Row, pp. 68-84.

Lee, T. R. (1962). Brennan's law of shopping behavior. *Psychological Reports, 2:* 662.

——. (1964). Psychology and living space. *Transactions of the Bartlett Society, 2:* 11-36.

——. (1967). The psychology of spatial orientation. *Architecture Association Quarterly. 1*(3): 11-15.

——. (1968). Urban neighborhood as a socio-spatial schema. *Human Relations, 21:* 241-268.

——. (1970). Perceived distance as a function of direction in the city. *Environment and Behavior, 2:* 40-51.

Lettvin, J. Y., Maturana, H. R., McCulloch, W. S., and Pitts, W. H. (1959). What the frog's eye tells the frog's brain. *Proceedings of the Institute of Radio Engineers, 47:* 1840-1959.

Levin, H. (1963). *The Gates of Horn: A Study of Five French Realists*. London: Oxford University Press.

Le Vine, R. A. (1973). *Culture, Behavior, and Personality*. Chicago: Aldine.

Lëvi-Strauss, C. (1967). The story of Asdiwal. In E. Leach (ed.), *The Structural Study of Myth and Totemism*. London: Tavistock, pp. 1-47.

Lewin, K. (1936). *Principles of Topological Psychology*. New York: McGraw-Hill.

——. (1938). The conceptual representation and measurement of psychological forces. In D. K. Adams and H. Lundholm (eds.), *Contributions to Psychological Theory*. Durham, N.C.: Duke University Press, pp. 1-247.

Lewis, C. S. (1964). *The Discarded Image*. New York: Cambridge University Press.

Ley, D. (1972). *The Black Inner City as a Frontier Outpost: Images and Behavior of a North Philadelphia Neighborhood*. Unpublished Ph.D. dissertation, Department of Geography, The Pennsylvania State University.

Lindsay, P. H., and Norman, D. A. (1972). *Human Information Processing*. New York: Academic Press.

Littlejohn, J. (1967). The Temne house. In J. Middleton (ed.), *Myth and Cosmos*. Garden City, N.Y.: Doubleday, pp. 331-347.

Litton, R. B. (1972). Aesthetic dimensions of the landscape. In J. R. Krutilla (ed.), *Natural Environment*. Baltimore, Md.: Johns Hopkins University Press, pp. 262-291.

Lofland, L. (1973). *A World of Strangers: Order and Action in Urban Public Space*. New York: Basic Books.

Lopata, H. Z. (1971). *Occupation Housewife*. New York: Oxford University Press.

Lord, F. (1941). A study of spatial orientation in children. *Journal of Educational Research, 34:* 481-505.

Lorenz, K. (1966). *On Aggression*. New York: Harcourt Brace.

——. (1969). Innate bases of learning. In K. Pribram (ed.). *On the Biology of Learning*. New York: Harcourt Brace, pp. 13-88.

Los Angeles Regional Transportation Study (1971). *1971 Travel Time Study: Los Angeles, California*. Washington, D.C.: Department of Transportation, Federal Highway Administration.

Lowenthal, D. (1960). Assumptions behind the public attitudes. In H. Jarrett (ed.), *Environmental Quality in a Growing Economy*. Baltimore, Md.: Johns Hopkins University Press, pp. 128-137.

——. (1961). Geography, experience, and imagination: toward a geographical epistemology. *Annals of the Association of American Geographers, 51:* 241-260.

——. (ed.) (1967). *Environmental Perception and Behavior*. Chicago: University of Chicago, Department of Geography, Research Paper No. 109.

——. (1968). The American scene. *Geographical Review, 58:* 61-88.

——. (1972a). Characteristic qualities of environmental imagery. Paper presented at the Symposium on Conceptual Issues in Environmental Cognition, Environmental Design Research Association meeting, Los Angeles.

——. (1972b). Research in environmental perception and behavior: perspectives on current problems. *Environment and Behavior, 4:* 333–342.

——, and Prince, H. C. (1964). The English landscape. *Geographical Review, 54:* 309–346.

——, and Prince, H. C. (1965). English landscape tastes. *Geographical Review, 55:* 186–222.

Lowrey, R. A. (1970). Distance concepts of urban residents. *Environment and Behavior, 2:* 57–73.

——. (1973). A method for analyzing distance concepts of urban residents. In R. M. Downs and D. Stea (eds.), *Image and Environment: Cognitive Mapping and Spatial Behavior.* Chicago: Aldine, pp. 338–360.

Lucas, R. C. (1963). Wilderness perception and use: the example of the Boundary Waters Canoe area. *Natural Resources Journal, 3:* 394–411.

Lukashok, A. K., and Lynch, K. (1956). Some childhood memories of the city. *Journal of the American Institute of Planners, 22:* 142–152.

Lundberg, U. (1973). Emotional and geographical phenomena in psychophysical research. In R. M. Downs and D. Stea (eds.), *Image and Environment: Cognitive Mapping and Spatial Behavior.* Chicago: Aldine, pp. 332–337.

Luria, A. R. (1968). *The Mind of a Mnemonist.* New York: Basic Books.

Lynch, K. (1960). *The Image of the City.* Cambridge, Mass.: MIT Press.

——. (1973). *What Time Is This Place?* Cambridge, Mass.: MIT Press.

——, and Rivkin, M. (1959). A walk around the block. *Landscape, 8:* 24–34.

Lyublinskaya, A. A. (1948). Learning spatial relations by a child of preschool age. *Anthology Problemy Sikhologii.* Leningrad: Izd-vo LGU Leningrad State University. Cited in F. M. Shemyakin. Orientation in space. In B. G. Anan'yev et al. (eds.), *Psychological Science in the USSR,* Vol. 1. Washington, D.C.: Office of Technical Services, 1962, pp. 186–255.

——. (1956). Peculiarities of the assimilation of space by children of preschool age. *Izvestia Akademii Pedagogicheskikh Nauk RSFSR,* No. 86. Cited in F. M. Shemyakin. Orientation in space.

In B. G. Anan'yev et al. (eds.), *Psychological Science in the USSR,* Vol. 1. Washington, D.C.: Office of Technical Services, 1962, pp. 186–255.

MacCorquodale, K., and Meehl, P. H. (1953). Hypothetical constructs and intervening variables. In H. Feigl and M. Brodbeck (eds.), *Readings in the Philosophy of Science.* New York: Appleton-Century-Crofts, pp. 596–611.

Machlup, F. (1963). Are the social sciences really inferior? In M. Natanson (ed.), *Philosophy of the Social Sciences.* New York: Random House.

Mackay, D. B., Olshavsky, R. W., and Sentell, G. (1975). Cognitive maps and spatial behavior of consumers. *Geographical Analysis, 7*(1): 19–34.

MacKay, D. M. (1966). Cerebral organization and the conscious control of action. In J. C. Eccles (ed.), *Brain and Conscious Experience.* New York: Springer, pp. 422–444.

Mair, J. M. M. (1970). Psychologists are human too. In D. Bannister (ed.), *Perspectives in Personal Construct Theory.* London: Academic Press, pp. 157–183.

Malinowski, B. (1935). *Coral Gardens and Their Magic,* Vol. 2 (*The Language of Magic and Gardening*). London: Allen & Unwin.

Malm, R., Olsson, G., and Warneryd, O. (1966). Approaches to simulation of urban growth. *Geografiska Annaler, 48B:* 9–22.

Marble, D. S. (1967). A theoretical exploration of individual travel behavior. In W. L. Garrison and D. S. Marble (eds.), *Quantitative Geography, Part I* (*Economic and Cultural Topics*). Evanston, Ill.: Northwestern University, Department of Geography, Studies in Geography, No. 13, pp. 33–53.

Mark, L. S. (1972). Modeling through toy play: a methodology for eliciting topographical representations in children. In W. J. Mitchell (ed.), *Environmental Design: Research and Practice,* Vol. 1. Los Angeles: School of Architecture and Urban Planning, University of California, pp. 1-3-1 to 1-3-9.

——, and Silverman, S. (1971). The effect of concrete operations upon the mental maps of children. Unpublished seminar paper, Department of Psychology, Clark University.

Marshack, A. (1971). *The Roots of Civilization.* New York: McGraw-Hill.

Marx, K. (1965). *Capital: A Critique of Political Economy*. Moscow: Progress Publishers.

——. (1971). *Theories of Surplus Value*. Moscow: Progress Publishers.

——. (1973). *Grundnisse: Foundations of the Critique of Political Economy*. (Translated by H. Nicolaus.) Harmondsworth, England: Penguin.

Marx, L. (1964). *The Machine and the Garden: Technology and the Pastoral Ideal in America*. New York: Oxford University Press.

——. (1968). Pastoral ideals and city troubles. In Smithsonian Institution, *The Fitness of Man's Environment*. Washington, D.C.: Smithsonian Institution Press, pp. 121–144.

Maurer, R., and Baxter, J. C. (1972). Images of neighborhood among Black-, Anglo-, and Mexican-American children. *Environment and Behavior, 4:* 351–388.

McCleary, G. F., and Westbrook, N. (1974). *Recreational and Re-creational Mapping*. Sturbridge, Mass.: Old Sturbridge Village.

McCulloch, W. S. (1965). *Embodiments of Mind*. Cambridge, Mass.: MIT Press.

McCully, R. S. (1971). *Rorschach Theory and Symbolism*. Baltimore: Williams & Wilkins.

McLuhan, M., and Parker, H. (1969). *Through the Vanishing Point: Space in Poetry and Painting*. New York: Harper & Row.

Mead, G. H. (1934). *Mind, Self, and Society*. Chicago: University of Chicago Press.

——. (1938). *The Philosophy of the Act*. (Edited by C. W. Morris.) Chicago: University of Chicago Press.

Mehrabian, A., and Russell, J. A. (1973). A measure of arousal seeking tendency. *Environment and Behavior, 5:* 315–333.

Meier, R. L. (1962). *A Communication Theory of Urban Growth*. Cambridge, Mass.: MIT Press.

Meinig, D. W. (1962). *On the Margins of the Good Earth: the South Australian Wheat Frontier 1869–1884*. Chicago: Rand McNally, Association of American Geographers Monograph No. 2.

——. (1971). Environmental appreciation: localities as a humane art. *Western Humanities Review, 25:* 1–11.

Menzel, E. W. (1973). Chimpanzee spatial memory organization. *Science, 182:* 943–945.

Mercer, D. (1972). Beach usage in the Melbourne region. *Australian Geographer, 12:* 123–139.

Merleau-Ponty, M. (1962). *The Phenomenology of Perception*. (Translated by C. Smith.) London: Routledge & Kegan Paul.

——. (1963). *The Structure of Behavior*. (Translated by A. L. Fisher.) Boston: Beacon Press.

Michelson, W. (1966). An empirical analysis of urban environmental preferences. *Journal of the American Institute of Planners, 24:* 355–360.

——. (1970). *Man and His Urban Environment: A Sociological Approach*. Reading, Mass.: Addison-Wesley.

——. (1971). Some like it hot: social participation and environmental use as a function of the season. *American Journal of Sociology, 76:* 1072–1083.

——. (ed.) (1975). *Behavioral Research Methods in Environmenal Design*. Stroudsburg, Pa.: Dowden, Hutchinson & Ross.

Milgram, S. (1970). The experience of living in cities. *Science, 167:* 1461–1468.

Miller, G. A. (1956). The magical number seven, plus or minus two. *Psychological Review, 63:* 81–97.

——. (1969). Psychology as a means of promoting human welfare. *American Psychologist, 24:* 1063–1075.

Miller, H. (1941). *The Colossus of Maroussi*. San Francisco: Colt Press.

Miller, P. (1956). *Errand into the Wilderness*. Cambridge, Mass.: Harvard University Press.

——. (1967). *Nature's Nation*. Cambridge, Mass.: Harvard University Press.

Miller, R. A. (1959). The tricks of architectural space. *Architectural Forum, 6:* 150–153.

Miller, S. M., and Riessman, F. (1961). The working class subculture: a new view. *Social Problems, 9:* 86–97.

Mitchell, J. C. (1969). *Social Networks in Urban Situations: Analyses of Personal Relationships in Central African Towns*. Manchester: Manchester University Press.

Mohr, D., Kuczaj, S., and Pick, H. (1975). The development of cognitive mapping capacities. Paper presented at the Society for Research in Child Development meeting, Denver.

Molano, J. O. P. (1801). Letter to the Provincial (Francisco, Piñero), dated Bayombong, 5 August 1801. APSR (Archivo de la Provincia del Santisimo Rosario), MS, Seccion "Cagayán" (Cartas), 2 pages. Santa Domingo, Quezon City, Philippines.

Moles, A. (1966). *Information Theory and Esthetic Perception.* Urbana, Ill.: University of Illinois Press.

Momaday, N. S. (1967). *House Made of Dawn.* New York: Signet Classics.

——. (1972). *The Way to Rainy Mountain.* New York: Ballantine Books.

Moore, E. G. (1972). *Residential Mobility in the City.* Washington, D.C.: Association of American Geographers, Commission on College Geography. Resource paper No. 13.

Moore, G. T. (ed.) (1970). *Emerging Methods in Environmental Design and Planning.* Cambridge, Mass.: MIT Press.

——. (1971). Review of Jean Piaget, *Science of Education and the Psychology of the Child. Journal of Architectural Education, 25*(4): 113-114.

——. (1972a). Conceptual issues in the study of environmental cognition. In W. J. Mitchell (ed.), *Environmental Design: Research and Practice,* Vol. 2. Los Angeles: School of Architecture and Urban Planning, University of California, pp. 30-1-1 to 30-1-3.

——. (1972b). Elements of a genetic-structural theory of the development of environmental cognition. In W. J. Mitchell (ed.), *Environmental Design: Research and Practice,* Vol. 2. Los Angeles: School of Architecture and Urban Planning, University of California, pp. 30-9-1 to 30-9-13.

——. (1972c). New directions in environmental cognition theory and research. *Man-Environment Systems, 2:* 92-94.

——. (1973a). Developmental variations between and within individuals in the cognitive representation of large-scale spatial environments. Unpubpublished M.A. thesis, Department of Psychology, Clark University.

——. (1973b). Development differences in environmental cognition, In W. F. E. Preiser (ed.). *Environmental Design Research,* Vol. 2. Stroudsburg, Pa.: Dowden, Hutchinson & Ross, pp. 221-231.

——. (1973c). Problems of evaluation: environmental assessment and evaluation models and techniques. Paper presented at the Association of Collegiate Schools of Architecture meeting

at Yosemite National Park, California.

——. (1973d). Structure in environmental cognition. Paper presented at the Third Conference on Psychology and the Built Environment, University of Surrey, Guildford, Surrey, England.

——. (1974a). Developmental variations between and within individuals in the cognitive representation of large-scale spatial environments (summary). *Man-Environment Systems, 4:* 55-57.

——. (1974b). Transactionalism in perception: a critical review. Unpublished doctoral preliminary paper, Department of Psychology, Clark University.

——. (1975a). The development of environmental knowing: an overview of an interactional-constructivist theory and some data on within-individual developmental variations. In D. Canter and T. Lee (eds.), *Psychology and the Built Environment.* London: Architectural Press. New York: Wiley, pp. 184-194.

——. (1975b). Spatial relations ability and developmental levels of urban cognitive mapping. *Man-Environment Systems, 5:* 247-248.

——. (1976). Knowing about environmental knowing: the current state of theory and research on environmental cognition. Paper presented at the Eastern Psychological Association meeting, New York, April.

——. (In press). Environmental cognition: applications for planning, design, and public education. In P. Thiel (ed.), *Environmental Art and Behavioral Science: Bridging the Gap.* Seattle, Wash.: College of Architecture and Urban Planning, University of Washington, College Development Series.

Moran, P. P. (1973). The cognitive structure of spatial knowledge. In Preiser, W. (ed.) *Environmental Design Research, Vol. II.* Stroudsburg, Pa.: Dowden, Hutchinson, and Ross, Inc. 356-365.

Muchow, M., and Muchow, H. (1935). *Der Lebensraum des Grosstadtkindes. (The Life Space of the Child in the Large City.)* Hamburg: Verlag. Cited in H. Werner, *Comparative Psychology of Mental Development,* rev. ed. New York: International Universities Press, 1948.

Muir, M. E., and Blaut, J. M. (1969-70). The use of aerial photographs in teaching mapping to children in the first grade: an experimental study. *Minnesota Geographer, 22*(3): 4-19.

Naipaul, V. S. (1965). *An Area of Darkness.* New

York: Macmillan.

Nash, R. (1967). *Wilderness and the American Mind.* New Haven, Conn.: Yale University Press.

Neisser, U. (1967). *Cognitive Psychology.* New York: Appleton-Century-Crofts.

——. (1968). Cultural and cognitive discontinuity. In R. A. Manners and D. Kaplan (eds.), *Theory in Anthropology.* Chicago: Aldine, pp. 354-364.

Newell, L. E. (1968). *A Batad Ifugao Vocabulary.* New Haven, Conn.: Human Relations Area Files.

Newell, N. D. (1963). Crises in the history of life. *Scientific American, 209:* 76.

Newman, O. (1972). *Defensible Space: Crime Prevention Through Urban Design.* New York: Macmillan.

Nicholson, S., and Schreiner, B. K. (1973). *Community Participation in City Decision Making.* Milton Keynes, England: Open University Press, Open University Social Science Second Level Course, Urban Development Unit 22.

Nicolson, M. H. (1959). *Mountain Gloom and Mountain Glory.* Ithaca, N.Y.: Cornell University Press.

Nigl, A. J., and Fishbein, H. D. (1973). Children's ability to coordinate perspectives: cognitive factors. In W. F. E. Preiser (ed.), *Environmental Design Research,* Vol. 2. Stroudsburg, Pa.: Dowden, Hutchinson & Ross, pp. 240-246.

——, and Fishbein, H. D. (1974). Perception and conception in coordination of perspectives. *Developmental Psychology, 10:* 858-866.

Olver, R., and Hornsby, J. (1970). On equivalence. In P. Adams (ed.), *Language and Thinking.* Harmondsworth, England: Penguin, pp. 306-320.

Orleans, P. (1973). Differential cognition of urban residents: effects of social scale on mapping. In R. M. Downs and D. Stea (eds.), *Image and Environment: Cognitive Mapping and Spatial Behavior.* Chicago: Aldine, pp. 115-130.

——, and Schmidt, S. (1972). Mapping the city: environmental cognition of urban residents. In W. J. Mitchell (ed.), *Environmental Design: Research and Practice,* Vol. 1. Los Angeles: School of Architecture and Urban Planning, University of California, pp. 1-4-1 to 1-4-9.

Ortiz, A. (1972). Ritual drama and the Pueblo world view. In A. Ortiz (ed.), *New Perspectives on the Pueblos.* Albuquerque, N.M.: University of New Mexico Press, pp. 135-161.

Osborne, B. S., and Reimer, D. L. (1973). Content analysis and historical geography: a note on evaluative assertion analysis. *Area, 5:* 96-100.

Osgood, C. E. (1953). *Method and Theory in Experimental Psychology.* New York: Oxford University Press.

——, Suci, G. A., and Tannenbaum, P. H. (1957). *The Measurement of Meaning.* Urbana, Ill.: University of Illinois Press.

Pailhous, J. (1970). *La Representation de l'espace urbain: l'exemple du chauffeur de taxi.* Paris: Presses Universitaires de France.

——. (1971). Elaboration d'images spatiales et de règles de displacements. *Le Travail Humain, 34*(2): 299-324.

——. (1972). Influence de l'order de présentation des sonnees sur la construction de l'image spaciale. *Le Travail Humain, 35*(1): 69-84.

Palm, R., and Caruso, D. (1974). The real estate industry, housing market, and home search. Paper presented at the Association of American Geographers meeting, Seattle.

Panoff, M. (1969). The notion of time among the Maenge people of New Britain. *Ethnology, 8*(2): 153-166.

Papert, S. (1965). Introduction to W. S. McCulloch, *Embodiments of Mind.* Cambridge, Mass.: MIT Press, pp. xii-xx.

Park, R. E. (1926). The urban community as a spatial pattern and moral order. In E. W. Burgess (ed.), *The Urban Community.* Chicago: University of Chicago Press, pp. 3-18.

——. (1927). Human migration and the marginal man. *American Journal of Sociology, 33:* 881-893.

Parr, J. B., and Denike, K. G. (1970). Theoretical problems in central place analysis. *Economic Geography, 46:* 568-586.

Parsons, J. J. (1969). Toward a more humane geography. *Economic Geography, 45.*

Pasternak, B. (1958). *Doctor Zhivago.* New York: Pantheon.

Payatos, F. (1976). Analysis of a culture through its cultureness: theory and method. In A. Rapoport (ed.), *The Mutual Interaction of People and Their Built Environment: A Cross-Cultural Perspective.* The Hague, Netherlands: Mouton (in press).

Pervin, L. A. (1963). The need to predict and control under conditions of threat. *Journal of Personality, 31:* 570-587.

Peters, R. P. (1973). Cognitive maps in wolves and men. In W. F. E. Preiser (ed.), *Environmental Design Research,* Vol. 2. Stroudsburg, Pa.: Dowden, Hutchinson & Ross, pp. 247-253.

——. (1974). Wolf sign: scent and space in a wide ranging predator. Unpublished Ph.D. dissertation, Department of Psychology, University of Michigan.

——, and Meck, L. D. (1975). Behavioral and cultural adaptations to the hunting of large animals in selected mammalian predators. In R. Tuttle (ed.), *Antecedents of Man and After.* Chicago: University of Chicago Press.

Peterson, G. L. (1967). A model of preference: quantitative analysis of the perception of the visual appearance of residential neighborhoods. *Journal of Regional Science, 7:* 19-30.

Pfeiffer, J. E. (1972). *The Emergence of Man,* 2nd ed. New York: Harper & Row.

Piaget, J. (1929). *The Child's Conception of the World.* (Translated by J. and A. Tomlinson.) London: Routledge & Kegan Paul; New York: Harcourt Brace.

——. (1950). *The Psychology of Intelligence.* (Translated by M. Piercy and D. Berlyne.) London: Routledge & Kegan Paul; New York: Harcourt Brace.

——. (1951). *Plays, Dreams, and Imitation in Childhood.* (*La Formation du symbole;* original French ed., 1946). New York: W. W. Norton.

——. (1952). *The Origins of Intelligence in Children.* New York: International Universities Press.

——. (1954). *The Construction of Reality in the Child.* New York: Basic Books.

——. (1967). Review of J. S. Bruner, R. R. Olver, P. M. Greenfield, et al. *Studies in Cognitive Growth. Contemporary Psychology, 12:* 532-533.

——. (1969). *The Mechanisms of Perception.* New York: Basic Books.

——. (1970). Piaget's theory. In P. Mussen (ed.), *Carmichael's Manual of Child Psychology,* Vol. 1. New York: Wiley, pp. 703-732.

——. (1970). *Structuralism.* (Translated by C. Maschler.) New York: Basic Books.

——. (1971). *Biology and Knowledge.* Chicago: University of Chicago Press.

——, and Inhelder, B. (1956). *The Child's Conception of Space.* London: Routledge & Kegan Paul; New York: Humanities Press.

——, and Inhelder, B. (1969). *The Psychology of the Child.* New York: Basic Books.

——, Inhelder, B., and Szeminska, A. (1960). *The Child's Conception of Geometry.* London: Routledge & Kegan Paul; New York: Basic Books.

Pick, H. L., Jr. (1972). Mapping children — mapping space. Paper presented at the American Psychological Association meeting, Honolulu.

——, and Pick, A. D. (1970). Sensory and perceptual development. In P. H. Mussen (ed.), *Carmichael's Manual of Child Psychology,* Vol. 1. New York: Wiley, pp. 773-843.

——, Acredolo, L. P., and Gronseth, M. (1973). Children's knowledge of the spatial layout of their homes. Paper presented at the Society for Research in Child Development meeting, Philadelphia.

Pike, A. (1967; orig. pub. 1834). *Prose Sketches and Poems Written in the Western Country,* D. J. Weber (ed.). Albuquerque, N.M.: Calvin Horn.

Pool, M. L. (1892). *Roweny in Boston.* New York: Harper and Brothers.

Popper, K. (1965). *The Logic of Scientific Discovery.* New York: Harper & Row.

Posner, M. I. (1969). Abstraction and the process of recognition. In G. H. Bower and J. T. Spence (eds.), *The Psychology of Learning and Motivation,* Vol. 3. New York: Academic Press.

——, and Keele, S. W. (1968). On the genesis of abstract ideas. *Journal of Experimental Psychology, 77:* 353-363.

Postman, L. (1955). Association theory and perceptual learning. *Psychological Review, 62:* 438-466.

Potter, M. C. (1966). On perceptual recognition. In J. S. Bruner, R. R. Olver, P. M. Greenfield, et al., *Studies in Cognitive Growth.* New York: Wiley, pp. 103-134.

——, and Levy, E. I. (1969). Recognition memory for a rapid sequence of pictures. *Journal of Experimental Psychology, 81:* 10-15.

Pred, A. R. (1967). *Behavior and Location,* Ser. B, No. 27, Part 1. Lund, Sweden: Lund University Press.

——. (1969). *Behavior and Location,* Ser. B, No. 28, Part 2, Lund Studies in Geography.

——. (1973a). Urbanization, domestic planning problems, and Swedish geographic research. In C. Board, R. J. Chorley, P. Haggett, and D. R. Stoddard (eds.), *Progress in Geography,* Vol. 5. London: Arnold, pp. 1–76.

——. (1973b) *Urban Growth and the Circulation of Information: The United States System of Cities 1790–1840.* Cambridge, Mass.: Harvard University Press.

Pribram, K. H. (1971). The brain. *Psychology Today, 5*(4): 44–48, 89–90.

Prince, H. C. (1971). Real, imagined, and abstract worlds of the past. In C. Board, R. Chorley, P. Haggett, and D. Stoddart (eds.), *Progress in Geography,* Vol. 3. London: Arnold, pp. 1–86.

Pritchett, V. S. (1973). Shadows and substance. *The New Yorker,* November 5, p. 181.

Proshansky, H. M., Ittelson, W. H., and Rivlin, L. G. (eds.) (1970). *Environmental Psychology.* New York: Holt, Rinehart and Winston.

Psathas, G. (1972). Ethnoscience and ethnomethodology. In J. P. Spradley (ed.), *Culture and Cognition: Rules, Maps, and Plans.* San Francisco: Chandler, pp. 206–219.

Pufall, P. B. (1973). Developmental relations between egocentrism and coordinate reference systems. Paper presented at the Society for Research in Child Development meetings, Philadelphia.

——, and Shaw, R. E. (1973). Analysis of the development of children's spatial reference systems. *Cognitive Psychology, 5:* 151–175.

Quinlan, E. (1972). Preliminary experiment on planning behavior manifested in search for object located in large scale environment. Unpublished seminar paper, Department of Psychology, Clark University.

Rainwater, L. (1966). Fear and the house-as-haven in the lower class. *Journal of the American Institute of Planners, 32:* 23–31.

——. (1970). *Behind Ghetto Walls: Black Families in a Federal Slum.* Chicago: Aldine.

Rand, G. (1969). Some Copernican views of the city. *Architectural Forum, 132*(9), 77–81.

——. (1972). Children's images of houses. In W. J. Mitchell (ed.), *Environmental Design: Research and Practice,* Vol. 1. Los Angeles: School of Architecture and Urban Planning, University of California, pp. 6-9-1 to 6-9-10.

W. J. Mitchell (ed.), *Environmental Design: Research and Practice,* Vol. 1 (EDRA 3) Los Angeles: School of Architecture and Urban Planning, University of California, pp. 6-9-1 to 6-9-10.

Rapoport, A. (1969). *House Form and Culture.* Englewood Cliffs, N.J.: Prentice-Hall.

——. (1970a). An approach to the study of environmental quality. In H. Sanoff and S. Cohn (eds.), *EDRA 1: Proceedings of the First Annual Environmental Design Research Association Conference.* Chapel Hill, N.C.: Department of City and Regional Planning, University of North Carolina, pp. 1–13.

——. (1970b). Symbolism and environmental design. *International Journal of Symbology, 1*(3): 1–10.

——. (1970c). The study of spatial quality. *Journal of Aesthetic Education, 4*(4): 81–95.

——. (1972). Australian aborigines and the definition of space. In W. J. Mitchell (ed.), *Environmental Design: Research and Practice,* Vol. 1. Los Angeles: School of Architecture and Urban Planning, University of California, pp. 3-3-1 to 3-3-14.

——. (1973a). Some perspectives on human use and organization of space. *Architectural Association Quarterly, 5*(3): 27–37.

——. (1973b). Images, symbols, and popular design. *International Journal of Symbology, 4*(3): 1–12.

——. (1973c). An approach to the construction of man-environment theory. In W. F. E. Preiser (ed.), *Environmental Design Research,* Vol. 2. Stroudsburg, Pa.: Dowden, Hutchinson & Ross, pp. 124–135.

——. (1973d). Some thoughts on the methodology of man-environment studies. *International Journal of Environmental Studies, 4:* 135–140.

——. (1975). Socio-cultural aspects of man-environment studies. In A. Rapoport (ed.), *The Mutual Interaction of People and Their Built Environment: A Cross-Cultural Perspective.* The Hague, Netherlands: Mouton (in press).

——, and Hawkes, R. (1970). The perception of urban complexity. *Journal of the American Institute of Planners. 36:* 106–111.

——, and Watson, N. (1972). Cultural variability in physical standards. In R. Gutman (ed.), *People and Buildings.* New York: Basic Books, pp. 33–54.

Reif, F. (1974). Educational challenges for the university. *Science, 184:* 537–542.

Reiser, R. (1972). *Urban Spatial Images: An Appraisal of the Choice of Respondents and Measurement Situation.* London: London School of Economics, Discussion Paper No. 42.

Relph, E. C. (1970). An inquiry into the relations between phenomenology and geography. *Canadian Geographer, 14:* 193–201.

Rensch, B. (1959). *Evolution Above the Species Level.* New York: Columbia University Press.

Reps, J. W. (1965). *The Making of Urban America: A History of City Planning in the United States.* Princeton, N.J.: Princeton University Press.

Richardson, L. F., and Ross, J. S. (1930). Loudness and telephone current. *Journal of General Psychology, 3:* 288–306.

Rivizzigno V. L. (1975). Individual differences in the cognitive structuring of an urban area. In R. G. Golledge (ed.), *On Determining Cognitive Configuration of a City,* Vol. 1. Columbus, Ohio: Department of Geography, Ohio State University Research Foundation, pp. 471–482.

——, and Golledge, R. G. (1974). A method for recovering cognitive information about a city. In D. H. Carson (ed.), *Man-Environment Interactions,* Part 11. Milwaukee: School of Architecture and Urban Planning, University of Wisconsin, pp. 9–18.

Roberts, F. S., and Suppes, P. (1967). Some problems in the geometry of visual perception. *Syntheses, 17:* 173–201.

Rølvaag, O. E. (1927). *Giants of the Earth.* New York: Harper and Brothers.

Rooney, J. S., Jr. (1967). The urban snow hazard in the United States. *Geographical Review, 67:* 538–559.

Rosch, E. R. (1973). On the internal structure of perceptual and semantic categories. In T. E. Moore, (ed.), *Cognitive Development and the Acquisition of Language.* New York: Academic Press.

Rose, A. (ed.). (1962). *Human Behavior and Social Processes.* Boston: Houghton Mifflin.

Rose, D. (1968). Culture and cognition: some problems and a suggestion. *Anthropology Quarterly, 41:* 9–28.

Rosenthal, R. (1966). *Experimenter Effects in Behavioral Research.* New York: Appleton-Century-Crofts.

Rowles, G. D. (1972). Choice in geographic space: explaining a phenomenological approach to locational decision-making. Unpublished M.Phil. thesis, Department of Geography, University of Bristol.

Royse, D. (1969). Social references via environmental cues in planning. Unpublished Ph.D. dissertation, Department of Urban Studies and Planning, Massachusetts Institute of Technology.

Rozelle, R. M., and Baxter, J. (1972). Meaning and value in conceptualizing the city. *Journal of the American Institute of Planners. 38:* 116–122.

Rusch, C. H. (1970). On understanding awareness. *Journal of Aesthetic Education, 4:* 57–79.

Rykwert, J. (n.d.) *The Idea of a Town.* Hilversum, Netherlands: F. Van Saane.

Saare, P. (1972). Perception. *New Trends in Geography,* Block Five. Milton Keynes, England: Open University Press, pp. 10–43.

——. (1973). Urban images. In J. Rees and P. Newby (eds.), *Behavioral Perspectives in Geography,* Vol. 1. Middlesex, England: Middlesex Polytechnic Monographs in Geography, pp. 35–43.

——. (1974). Personal construct theory in the measurement of the perceived environment. Unpublished Ph.D dissertation, Department of Geography, Bristol University.

Saarinen, T. F. (1966). *Perception of the Drought Hazard on the Great Plains.* Chicago: Department of Geography, University of Chicago, Research Paper No. 106.

——. (1969). *Perception of Environment.* Washington, D.C.: Association of American Geographers, Commission on College Geography Resource Paper No. 5.

——. (1973a). Student views of the world. In R. M. Downs and D. Stea (eds.), *Image and Environment: Cognitive Mapping and Spatial Behavior.* Chicago: Aldine, pp. 148–161.

——. (1973b). The use of projective techniques in geographic research. In W. H. Ittelson (ed.), *Environment and Cognition.* New York: Seminar Press, pp. 29–52.

Saegert, S. (1973). Crowding: behavioral constraints and cognitive overload. In W. F. E. Preiser (ed.),

Environmental Design Research, Vol. 2. Strouds-burg, Pa.: Dowden, Hutchinson & Ross, pp. 254–260.

Saint Jerome. (1893). *Letters.* xiv, 10. (Translated by W. H. Freemantle.) In *Nicene and Post-Nicene Fathers* (second series, Vol. 6). New York: Christian Literature Company.

Samuel, A. L. (1963). Some studies of machine learning using the game of checkers. In E. A. Feigenbaum and J. Feldman (eds.), *Computers and Thought.* New York: McGraw-Hill, pp. 71-105.

Sanoff, H. (1968). *Techniques of Evaluation for Designers.* Raleigh, N.C.: School of Design, North Carolina State University.

——. (1973). Youth's perception and categorizations of residential areas. In W. F. E. Preiser (ed.), *Environmental Design Research,* Vol. 1. Strouds-burg, Pa.: Dowden, Hutchinson & Ross.

——, and Cohen, S. (eds.) (1969). *EDRA I, Proceedings of the First Annual Environmental Design Research Association Conference.* Chapel Hill, N.C.: Department of City and Regional Planning, University of North Carolina.

Sartre, J. P. (1938). *La Nausée.* Paris: Gallimard.

——. (1966). *Being and Nothingness.* (Translated by H. E. Barnes.) New York: Washington Square Press.

Sauer, C. D. (1971). *Sixteenth Century North America.* Berkeley, Calif.: University of California Press.

Scatterley, D. J. (1966). An investigation into the relationship between 2-D representation of the physical world by primary school children and certain perceptual and conceptual characteristics they exhibit. Unpublished M.A. thesis, Department of Psychology, Bristol University.

——. (1968). Perceptual representation and conceptual characteristics of primary school children. *British Journal of Educational Psychology, 38:* 78-82.

Schak, D. C. (1972). Determinants of children's play patterns in a Chinese city: the interplay of space and values. *Urban Anthropology, 1*(2): 195-204.

Schmitt, P. J. (1969). *Back to Nature: The Arcadian Myth in Urban America.* New York: Oxford University Press.

Schutz, A. (1967). *The Phenomenology of the Social World.* (Translated by G. Walsh and F. Lehnert.) Evanston, Ill.: Northwestern University Press.

——. (1970). *On Phenomenology and Social Relations: Selected Writings.* Chicago: University of Chicago Press.

Seamon, D. (1972). Environmental imagery: an overview and tentative ordering. In W. J. Mitchell (ed.), *Environmental Design: Research and Practice,* Vol. 1. Los Angeles: School of Architecture and Urban Planning, University of California, pp. 7-1-1 to 7-1-7.

Sechrest, L. B. (1963). The psychology of personal constructs: George Kelly. In J. M. Wepman and R. W. Heine (eds.), *Concepts of Personality.* Chicago: Aldine, pp. 206-233.

Seeley, J. R., Sim, R. A., and Loosley, E. W. (1963). *Crestwood Heights: A Study of the Culture of Suburban Life.* New York: Wiley.

Segal, M. H., Campbell, D. T., and Herskovits, M. J. (1963). Cultural differences in the perception of geometric illusions. *Science, 139:* 769-771.

——. (1966). *The Influence of Culture on Visual Perception.* Indianapolis, Ind.: Bobbs-Merrill.

Sewell, W. R. D., and Little, B. R. (1973). Specialists, laymen, and the process of environmental appraisal. *Regional Studies, 7:* 161-171.

Shafer, E. L. (1969). Perception of the natural environment. *Environment and Behavior, 1:* 71-82.

Shelton, F. G. (1967). A note on the world across the street. *Harvard Graduate School Education Association Bulletin, 12:* 47-48.

Shemyakin, F. N. (1940). On the psychology of space representations. *Uchenyye Zapiski Gos. In-ta Psikhologii* (Moscow), *1:* n.p. Cited in F. N. Shemyakin, Orientation in space. In B. G. Anan'yev et al. (eds.), *Psychological Science in the USSR,* Vol. 1. Washington, D.C.: Office of Technical Services, pp. 184-255.

——. (1962). Orientation in space. In B. G. Anan'yev et al. (eds.), *Psychological Science in the USSR,* Vol. 1. Washington, D.C.: Office of Technical Services, pp. 184-255.

Shepard, P. (1967). *Man in the Landscape.* New York: Knopf.

Shepard, R. N., and Chipman, S. (1970). Second-order isomorphism of internal representations: shapes of states. *Cognitive Psychology, 1:* 1-7.

Shibutani, T. (1955). Reference groups as perspectives. *American Journal of Sociology, 60:* 562-569.

———. (1962). Reference groups and social control. In A. Rose (ed.), *Human Behavior and Social Processes.* Boston: Houghton Mifflin, pp. 128-147.

Shostak, A. B. (1969). *Blue Collar Life.* New York: Random House.

Siegel, S. (1955). *Nonparametric Statistics.* New York: McGraw-Hill.

Sieverts, T. (1969). Spontaneous architecture. *Architectural Association Quarterly, 1*(3): 36-43.

Silzer, V. J. (1972). *Personal Construct Elicitation in Space Preference Research.* Toronto: Department of Geography, York University.

Simmel, G. (1971a). The stranger. In D. M. Levine (ed.), *Georg Simmel on Individuality and Social Forms.* Chicago: University of Chicago Press, pp. 143-149.

———. (1971b). The metropolis and mental life. In D. N. Levine (ed.), *Georg Simmel on Individuality and Social Forms.* Chicago: University of Chicago Press, pp. 324-339.

Simon, H. A. (1957). *Models of Man.* New York: Wiley.

———, and Newell, A. (1971). Human problem solving: the state of the theory in 1970. *American Psychologist, 26:* 145-159.

Simoons, F. J. (1961). *Eat Not This Flesh: Food Avoidances in the Old World.* Madison, Wisc.: University of Wisconsin Press.

Slack, R. W. (1956). Familiar size as a cue to size in the presence of conflicting cues. *Journal of Experimental Psychology, 52:* 194-198.

Slater, P. (1967). *Notes on INGRID 67.* London: Biometrics Unit, Institute of Psychiatry, Maudsley Hosptial.

———. (1969a). *The Principal Components of a Repertory Grid.* Privately published under a grant from the Medical Research Council of the United Kingdom.

———. (1969b). Theory and technique of the repertory grid. *British Journal of Psychiatry, 115*(528): 1287-1296.

———. (1972). *Notes on INGRID 72.* London: Biometrics Unit, Institute of Psychiatry, Maudsley Hospital.

Slobin, D. I. (1972). Children and language: they learn the same way all around the world. *Psychology Today, 6*(7): 71-74, 82.

Smith, G. H. (1953). Size-distance judgments of human faces (projected images). *Journal of General Psychology, 49:* 45-64.

Smith, H. C. (1968). Sensitivity to people. In H. Toch and H. C. Smith (eds.), *Social Perception: The Development of Interpersonal Impressions.* New York: Van Nostrand Reinhold, pp. 10-19.

Smith, W. F. (1933). Directional orientation in children. *Journal of Genetic Psychology, 42:* 154-166.

Snider, J. G., and Osgood, C. E. (eds.) (1968). *Semantic Differential Technique: A Source Book.* Chicago: Aldine.

Soja, E. W. (1971). *The Political Organization of Space.* Washington, D.C.: Association of American Geographers, Resource Paper No. 8.

Sommer, R. (1969). *Personal Space: The Behavioral Basis of Design.* Englewood Cliffs, N.J.: Prentice-Hall.

Sonnenfeld, J. (1966). Variable values in space and landscape: an inquiry into the nature of environmental necessity. *Journal of Social Issues, 22:* 71-82.

———. (1967). Environmental perception and adaptation level in the Artic. In D. Lowenthal (ed.), *Environmental Perception and Behavior.* Chicago: Department of Geography, University of Chicago, Research Paper No. 109, pp. 43-59.

———. (1969). Equivalance and distortion of the perceptual environment. *Environment and Behavior, 1:* 83-99.

Spencer, J. E., and Hale, G. A. (1961). The origin, nature, and distribution of agricultural terracing. *Pacific Viewpoint, 2*(1): 1-40.

———, and Horvath, R. J. (1963). How does an agricultural region originate? *Annals of the Association of American Geographers, 53:* 74-92.

Spiegelberg, H. (1965). *The Phenomenological Movement: An Historical Introduction,* Vols. 1 and 2. The Hague, Netherlands: Martinus Nijhoff.

Spoehr, A. (1956). Cultural differences in the interpretation of natural resources. In W. L. Thomas, Jr. (ed.), *Man's Role in Changing the Face of the Earth.* Chicago: University of Chicago Press, pp. 93-102.

Spradley, J. P. (ed.) (1972). *Culture and Cognition: Rules, Maps, and Plans.* San Francisco: Chandler.

Stanislawski, D. (1950). *The Anatomy of Eleven Towns in Michoacan.* Austin, Tex.: Center for Latin American Studies, University of Texas, No. 10.

Stapf, K. H. (1968). *Untersuchunger zur Subjektiven Landkarte.* Unpublished Ph.D. dissertation in natural science, Institute of Technology, Carolo-Wilhelmina zu Braunshweig. Cited in U. Lundberg. Emotional and geographical phenomena in psychophysical research. In R. M. Downs and D. Stea (eds.), *Image and Environment: Cognitive Mapping and Spatial Behavior.* Chicago: Aldine, 1973, pp. 322-337.

Stea, D. (1967). Reasons for our moving. *Landscape, 17*(1): 27-28.

——. (1969a). Environmental perception and cognition: toward a model for "mental maps." In G. J. Coats and K. M. Moffett (eds.), *Response to Environment.* Raleigh, N.C.: Student Publications of the School of Design, North Carolina State University, Vol. 18, pp. 62-75.

——. (1969b). The measurement of mental maps: an experimental model for studying conceptual spaces. In K. R. Cox and R. G. Golledge (eds.), *Behavioral Problems in Geography: A Symposium.* Evanston, Ill.: Northwestern University Studies in Geography No. 17, pp. 228-253.

——. (1969c). On the metrics of conceptual spaces: distance and boundedness in psychological geography. *Proceedings of the Twelfth Congress, Sociedad Interamericana de Psicologia.* Montevideo: Uruguay.

——. (ed.) (1969d). *Working Papers in Place Perception.* Worcester, Mass.: Graduate School of Geography, Clark University, Place Perception Research Report No. 2.

——. (1973). The use of environmental modelling ("toy play") for studying the environmental cognition of children and adults. *Proceedings of the Fourteenth Congress, Sociedad Interameri-*

cana de Psicologia. Sao, Paulo, Brasil.

——. (1974). Architecture in the head: cognitive mapping. In J. Lang, C. H. Burnette, W. Moleski, and D. Vachon (eds.), *Designing for Human Behavior.* Stroudsburg, Pa.: Dowden, Hutchinson & Ross, pp. 157-168.

——, and Blaut, J. M. (1972). From city models to model cities: theory and research on the growth of environmental cognition. Paper presented at the Symposium on Conceptual Issues in Environmental Cognition, Environmental Design Research Association meeting, Los Angeles.

——, and Blaut, J. M. (1973a). Notes toward a developmental theory of spatial learning. In R. M. Downs and D. Stea (eds.), *Image and Environment: Cognitive Mapping and Spatial Behavior.* Chicago: Aldine, pp. 51-62.

——, and Blaut, J. M. (1973b). Some preliminary observations on spatial learning in school children. In R. M. Downs and D. Stea (eds.), *Image and Environment: Cognitive Mapping and Spatial Behavior.* Chicago: Aldine, pp. 226-234.

——, and Downs, R. (eds.) (1970a). Cognitive representations of man's spatial environment. *Environment and Behavior, 2*(1): entire issue.

——, and Downs, R. M. (eds.) (1970b). From the outside looking in at the inside looking out. *Environment and Behavior, 2:* 3-12.

——, and Taphanel, S. A. (1975). Theory and experiment in the relation between environmental modelling ("toy play") and environmental cognition. In D. Canter and T. R. Lee (eds.), *Psychology and the Built Environment.* London: Architectural Press; New York: Wiley, pp. 170-178.

Steiner, G. (1961). *Tolstoy or Dostoevsky.* New York: Vintage Books.

——. (1974). *Fields of Force.* New York: Viking Press.

Steinitz, C. (1968). Meaning and congruence of urban form and activity. *Journal of the American Institute of Planners. 34*(4): 233-248.

Stevens, B. H. (1961). An application of game theory to a problem in location strategy. *Papers and Proceedings of the Regional Science Association, 7:* 143-157.

Stevens, S. S. (1956). The direct estimation of sensory magnitudes—loudness. *American Journal of Psychology, 69:* 1-25.

Stonequist, E. V. (1937). *The Marginal Man.* New York: Scribner's.

Strauss, A. L. (1961). *Images of the American City.* New York: Free Press.

——. (ed.) (1968). *The American City: A Sourcebook of Urban Imagery.* Chicago: Aldine.

——. (1969). *Mirrors and Masks: The Search for Identity.* San Francisco: Sociology Press.

——. (1970). Lifestyles and urban space. In H. M. Proshansky, W. I. Ittleson, and L. G. Rivlin (eds.), *Environmental Psychology: Man and His Physical Setting.* New York: Holt, Rinehart and Winston, pp. 303-312.

——. (1971). *The Contexts of Social Mobility.* Chicago: Aldine.

Stringer, P. (1970). Architecture, psychology, the game's the same. In D. V. Canter (ed.), *Architectural Psychology.* London: Royal Institute of British Architects Publications, pp. 7-11.

——. (1972). Some remarks on people's evaluation of environments. In A. G. Wison (ed.), *Patterns and Processes in Urban and Regional Systems.* London: Pion, pp. 316-324.

——. (1973a). Psychological significance in personal and supplied construct systems: a defining experiment. *European Journal of Social Psychology, 2*(4): 437-447.

——. (1973b). Individuals evaluate alternatives for a shopping centre redevelopment. Paper presented to the Planning and Transport, Research and Computation meeting, University of Sussex.

——. (1974a). A use of repertory grid measures for evaluating map formats. *British Journal of Psychology, 65:* 23-24.

——. (1974b). A rationale for participation. In N. Cross, D. Elliott, and R. Ray (eds.), *Man-Made Features.* London: Hutchinson Educational and the Open University, pp. 183-190.

——. (1974c). Individual differences in the construing of shopping centre redevelopment proposals. In D. Canter and T. R. Lee (eds.), *Psychology and the Built Environment.* London: Architectural Press; New York: Halsted, pp. 96-104.

——. (1975). Repertory grids in the study of environ-

mental perception. In P. Slater (ed.), *The Intra-Personal Space: Measurement of Subjective Variation by Grid Technique.* London: Wiley.

Studer, R. G. (1967). Behavior manipulation in designed environments. *Connection* (Harvard Graduate School of Design), *5*(1): 7-13.

——. (1969). The dynamics of behavior contingent physical systems. In G. Broadbent and A. Ward (eds.), *Design Methods in Architecture.* London: Lund Humphries, pp. 55-70.

Suchman, R. G. (1966). Cultural differences in children's color and form preferences. *Journal of Social Psychology, 70:* 3-10.

Suttles, G. (1968). *The Social Order of the Slum: Territory and Ethnicity in the Inner City.* Chicago: University of Chicago Press.

——. (1972). *The Social Construction of Communities.* Chicago: University of Chicago Press.

Thiel, P. (1961). A sequence-experience notation for architectural and urban spaces. *Town Planning Review, 32:* 33-53.

——. (1971). Notes on the description, scaling, notation, and scoring of some perceptual and cognitive attributes of the environment. In H. M. Proshansky, W. H. Ittelson, and L. G. Rivlin (eds.), *Environmental Psychology.* New York: Holt, Rinehart and Winston, pp. 593-619.

——. (1973). On the discursive notation of human experience and the physical environment. In W. F. E. Preiser (ed.), *Environmental Design Research,* Vol. 2. Stroudsburg, Pa.: Dowden, Hutchinson & Ross, pp. 374-378.

——. (1974). A method for the discursive notation of affect. Paper presented at the 18th International Congress of Applied Psychology, Montreal.

Thomas, W. I. (1966). *On Social Organization and Social Personality* (M. Janowitz, ed.). Chicago: University of Chicago Press.

Thomlinson, R. (1969). *Urban Structure: The Social and Spatial Characteristics of Cities.* New York: Random House.

Thompson, D. L. (1963). New concept: subjective distance—store impressions affect estimates of travel time. *Journal of Retailing, 39:* 1-6.

Thompson, K. (1969). Insalubrious California: perception and reality. *Annals of the Association of American Geographers, 59:* 50-63.

Thompson, M. M. (ed.) (1965). *Manual of Photogrammetry,* 3rd ed. Falls Church, Va.: American Society of Photogrammetry.

Thoreau, H. D. (1963). *A Week on the Concord and Merrimack Rivers.* New York: Holt, Rinehart and Winston.

Thornberg, J. M. (1973). Child's conception of places to live in. In W. F. E. Preiser (ed.), *Environmental Design Research,* Vol. 1. Stroudsburg, Pa.: Dowden, Hutchinson & Ross, pp. 178-190.

Tibbetts, P. (1972). The transactional theory of human knowledge and action: notes toward a "behavioral ecology." *Man-Environment Systems, 2*(1): 37-59.

——, and Esser, A. H. (1973). Transactional structures in man-environment relations. *Man-Environment Systems, 3:* 441-468.

Tilly, C. (1967). Anthropology on the town. *Habitat, 10:* 20-25.

Tillyard, E. M. W. (1962). *Myth and the English Mind.* New York: Collier Books.

——, and Lewis, C. S. (1939). *The Personal Heresy: A Controversy.* London: Oxford University Press.

Tinbergen, N. (1932). Über die Orientierung des bien Enwolfes (Philanthus Triangulum). *Zeitschrift für Vergleichende Physiologie, 16:* 305-334.

Tobler, W. (1961). *Map Transformations of Geographic Space.* Unpublished Ph.D. dissertation, Department of Geography, University of Washington.

——. (1975). The geometry of mental maps. In R. G. Golledge and G. Rushton (eds.), *Spatial Choice and Spatial Behavior: Geographical Essays on Perception and Choice.* Columbus, Ohio: Ohio State University Press.

Tolman, E. C. (1932). *Purposive Behavior in Animals and Men.* New York: Appleton-Century-Crofts.

——. (1948). Cognitive maps in rats and men. *Psychological Review, 55:* 189-208.

——. (1951). A psychological model. In T. Parsons and E. A. Shils (eds.), *Towards a General Theory of Action.* Cambridge, Mass.: Harvard University Press, pp. 279-361.

——. (1958). *Behavior and Psychological Man: Essays in Motivation and Learning.* Berkeley, Calif.: University of California Press.

Torgerson, W. S. (1958). *Theory and Methods of Scaling.* New York: Wiley.

Trevarthen, C. B. (1968). Two mechanisms of vision in primates. *Psychologie Forschang, 31:* 299-337.

Trowbridge, C. C. (1913). On fundamental methods of orientation and "imaginary maps." *Science, 88:* 888-896.

Tuan, Y.-F. (1957). Use of simile and metaphor in geographical description. *Professional Geographer, 9:* 8-11.

——. (1961). Topophilia. *Landscape,* Fall: 29-32.

——. (1968). Discrepancies between environmental attitudes and behavior: some examples from Europe and China. *Canadian Geographer, 12:* 176-191.

——. (1971). Geography, phenomenology, and the study of human nature. *Canadian Geographer, 15:* 181-192.

——. (1973). Environmentalism, environment, and the quality of life. Unpublished ms., Department of Geography, University of Minnesota.

——. (1974). *Topophilia: A Study of Environmental Perception, Attitudes, and Values.* Englewood Cliffs, N.J.: Prentice-Hall.

——, and Everard, C. E. (1964). New Mexico's climate: the appreciation of a resource. *Natural Resources Journal, 4:* 269-276.

Tyler, S. A. (ed.) (1969). *Cognitive Anthropology.* New York: Holt, Rinehart and Winston.

Van Breeman, N. Oldeman, L. R., Plantinga, W. J., and Wielmaker, W. G. (eds.) (1970). The Ifugao rice terraces. *Aspects of Rice Growing in Asia and the Americas.* Wageningen, Netherlands: H. Veenen en Zonen, N.V., pp. 39-73.

Vernon, M. D. (1962). *The Psychology of Perception.* Baltimore: Penguin.

——. (1970). *Perception Through Experience.* New York: Barnes & Noble.

Von Foerester, H. (1974). Logical structure of environment and its internal representation. *Man-Environment Systems, 4:* 161-170.

Von Frisch, K. (1967). *The Dance Language and Orientation of Bees.* Cambridge, Mass.: Harvard University Press.

Von Uexküll, J. (1957). A stroll through the worlds of animals and men: a picture book of invisible worlds. In C. H. Schiller (ed.), *Instinctive Be-*

havior. New York: International Universities Press, pp. 5–80.

Waddington, C. H. (1960). Genetic assimilation. In E. W. Caspari and J. W. Thoday (eds.), *Advances in Genetics.* New York: Academic Press, pp. 257–293.

———. (1962). *New Patterns in Genetics and Development.* New York: Columbia University Press.

———. (1968). The theory of evolution today. In A. Koestler and J. R. Smythies (eds.), *Beyond Reductionism.* New York: Macmillan, pp. 357–395.

Wagner, P. (1960). *The Human Use of the Earth.* New York: Free Press.

Wallace, A. F. C. (1965). Driving to work. In M. E. Spiro (ed.), *Context and Meaning in Cultural Anthropology.* New York: Free Press, pp. 277–292.

Wapner, S. (1969). Organismic-developmental theory: some applications to cognition. In P. H. Mussen, J. Langer, and M. Covington (eds.), *Trends and Issues in Developmental Psychology.* New York: Holt, Rinehart and Winston, pp. 38–67.

———, and Werner, H. (1957) *Perceptual Development.* Worcester, Mass.: Clark University Press.

———, Kaplan, B., and Cohen, S. B. (1973). An organismic-developmental perspective for understanding transactions of men and environments. *Environment and Behavior, 5:* 255–289.

Warfel, H. R. (1941). *American Local-Color Stories.* New York: American Book.

Warnock, M. (1970). *Existentialism.* London: Oxford University Press.

Watson, J. R. (1970). *Picturesque Landscape and English Romantic Poetry.* London: Hutchinson Educational Ltd.

Watson, J. W. (1955). Geography: a discipline in distance. *Scottish Geographical Magazine, 71:* 1–13.

———. (1969). The role of illusion in North American geography. *Canadian Geographer, 13:* 10–27.

Webb, E. J., Campbell, D. T., and Sechrest, L. (1966). *Unobtrusive Measures: Non-reactive Research in the Social Sciences.* Chicago: Rand McNally.

Webb, W. P. (1931). *The Great Plains.* Boston: Ginn.

Webber, M. J. (1964). Culture, territoriality, and the elastic mile. *Papers of the Regional Science Association, 13:* 59–69.

———. (1971). Empirical verifiability of classical central place theory. *Geographical Analysis, 3:* 15–28.

Weber, D. J. (ed.) (1967). *Albert Pike Prose Sketches and Poems Written in the Western Country.* Albuquerque, N.M.: Calvin Horn.

Weber, M. (1947). *Wirtschaft and Gesellschaft,* 3rd ed. Tubingen, West Germany: J. C. Mohr.

Weimer, D. (1966). *City as Metaphor.* New York: Random House.

Werner, H. (1948). *Comparative Psychology of Mental Development,* rev. ed. New York: International Universities Press.

———. (1957). The concept of development from a comparative and organismic point of view. In D. B. Harris (ed.), *The Concept of Development.* Minneapolis: University of Minnesota Press, pp. 125–148.

———, and Kaplan, B. (1963). *Symbol Formation: An Organismic-Developmental Approach to Language and the Expression of Thought.* New York: Wiley.

Wheatley, P. (1971). *The Pivot of the Four Quarters.* Chicago: Aldine.

White, G. (1945). *Human Adjustments to Floods.* Chicago: University of Chicago, Department of Geography Research Paper No. 29.

White, G. F., Kates, R. W., and Burton, I. (1970). *Suggestions for the Comparative Field Observations on Natural Hazards.* Toronto: Department of Geography, University of Toronto, Natural Hazards Research Project Working Paper No. 16.

White, M., and White, L. (1962). *The Intellectual Versus the City.* Cambridge, Mass.: Harvard University Press.

Whorf, B. L. (1956a). The relation of habitual thought and behavior to language. In B. L. Whorf, *Language, Thought, and Reality.* (J. B. Carroll, ed.) Cambridge, Mass.: MIT Press, pp. 134–159.

———. (1956b). *Language, Thought, and Reality.* (J. B. Carroll, ed.) Cambridge, Mass.: MIT Press.

Whyte, W. H. (1968). *The Last Landscape.* Garden City, N.Y.: Doubleday.

Wilcox, P. (1974). Children's Utilization of maps. Unpublished paper, Department of Psychology, University of Cincinnati.

Williams, H. B. (1957). Some functions of communication in crisis behavior. *Human Organization, 16:* 15–19.

Winkel, G. H., Malek, R., and Thiel, P. (1969). The role of personality differences in judgments of roadside quality. *Environment and Behavior, 1:* 199-224.

Wirth, L. (1964). *On Cities and Social Life.* Chicago: University of Chicago Press.

Wish, M. (1972). Notes on the variety, appropriateness, and choice of proximity measures. Unpublished paper, Bell Laboratories Workshop on Multidimensional Scaling, Murray Hill, N.J.

Wober, M. (1966). Sensotypes. *Journal of Social Psychology, 70:* 181-189.

Wohlwill, J. F. (1960). Developmental studies of perception. *Psychological Bulletin, 57:* 249-288.

———. (1962). From perception to inference: a dimension of cognitive development. *Monographs of the Society for Research in Child Development, 27*(2): 87-112.

———. (1966). The physical environment: a problem for a psychology of stimulation. *Journal of Social Issues, 22:* 29-38.

———. (1968). Amount of stimulus exploration and preference as differential functions of stimulus complexity. *Perception and Psychophysics, 4:* 307-312.

———. (1970). The emerging discipline of environmental psychology. *American Psychologist, 25:* 303-312.

———, and Carson, D. H. (eds.) (1972). *Environment and the Social Sciences: Perspectives and Applications.* Washington, D.C.: American Psychological Association.

———, and Kohn, I., (1975). Dimensionalizing the environmental manifold. Paper presented at a conference on Experiencing the Environment, Clark University.

Wolfsy, L. (1973). A preliminary study on the effect of plans involving moving to a new environment on the organization of the present environment. Unpublished seminar paper, Department of Psychology, Clark University.

———, Rierdon, J., and Wapner, S. (1974). Changes in representation of the currently inhabited environment as a function of planning to move to a new environment. Paper presented at the Eastern Psychological Association meeting, Philadelphia.

Wolpert, J. (1964). The decision process in a spatial context. *Annals of the Association of American Geographers, 54:* 536-558.

Wood, D. (1971). Fleeting glimpses, or adolescent and other images of the entity called San Christobal los Cassas, Chiapas, Mexico. Unpublished M.A. thesis, Graduate School of Geography, Clark University.

———. (1973a). The cartography of reality. Unpublished paper, Graduate School of Geography, Clark University.

———. (1973b). *I Don't Want to but I Will. The Genesis of Geographical Knowledge: A Real-Time Developmental Study of Adolescent Images of Novel Environments (London, Paris, and Rome.)* Worcester, Mass.: Cartographic Laboratory, Graduate School of Geography, Clark University.

Woolf, V. (1927). *To the Lighthouse.* New York: Harcourt Brace.

Wright, J. K. (1926). A plea for the history of geography. *Isis, 8:* 477-491.

———. (1947). Terrae incognitae: the place of imagination in geography. *Annals of the Association of American Geographers, 37:* 1-15.

Wynne-Edwards, V. C. (1962). *Animal Dispersion in Relation to Social Behavior.* London: Oliver & Boyd.

Yaker, H., Osmond, H., and Cheek, F. (eds.) (1971). *The Future of Time (Man's Temporal Environment).* Garden City, N.Y.: Doubleday.

Young, M., and Willmott, P. (1962). *Family and Kinship in East London.* Baltimore: Penguin.

Zannaras, G. (1973). An analysis of cognitive and objective characteristics of the city: their influence on movements to the city center. Unpublished Ph.D. dissertation, Department of Geography, Ohio State University.

Zeller, R., and Rivizzigno, V. L. (1974). *Mapping Cognitive Structure of Urban Areas with Multidimensional Scaling: A Preliminary Report.* Columbus, Ohio: Department of Geography, Ohio State University, Discussion Paper No. 42.

Zinn, V. (1969). Piaget: equilibrium and development. Unpublished seminar paper, Department of Psychology, Clark University.

AUTHOR INDEX

PLACE INDEX

SUBJECT INDEX

ABOUT THE EDITORS

Gary T. Moore, a Canadian architect and environmental psychologist, is currently an Assistant Professor in the School of Architecture and Urban Planning at the University of Wisconsin, Milwaukee. He holds a B.Arch. degree from the University of California, Berkeley and an M.A. in psychology from Clark University, where he is a Ph.D. candidate in environmental and developmental psychology. In 1975 he was Visiting Lecturer in architectural psychology at the University of Sydney and in social geography at the University of New South Wales in Australia. In addition to his research on the development of environmental cognition, which is reported herein, he has conducted research, written, and consulted on design and planning methodology, creativity and group problem solving, behavioral evaluation of built environments, and the design of children's environments. He was a co-founder of the Design Methods Group and the Environmental Design Research Association (EDRA), has organized symposia at several national meetings, and has served as an advisory editor for several journals in both psychology and environmental research. His first book was *Emerging Methods in Environmental Design and Planning.*

Reginald G. Golledge is Professor of Geography at Ohio State University. He holds B.A. (Hons.) and M.A. degrees in geography from the University of New England in Australia and a Ph.D. in geography from the University of Iowa. He has taught at universities in Australia, New Zealand, Canada, and the United States. Among his professional writings are a number of monographs and papers dealing with aspects of spatial behavior, both from a theoretical and methodological point of view. He has organized symposia on behavioral problems in geography and on environmental cognition at the national meetings of the Association of American Geographers and at EDRA, and has contributed to several books on these topics. Currently, he is editor of the journal *Geographical Analysis* and is an advisory editor to several other journals. He is a joint author or editor of several other books, including *Traffic in a New Zealand City, Spectral Analysis of Settlement Patterns, Behavioral Problems in Geography, Multidimensional Scaling, An Introduction to Scientific Reasoning in Geography, Spatial Choice and Spatial Preference,* and *Cities, Space, and Behavior.*